Sports Marketing

Sports Marketing

Michael J. Fetchko
ISM USA/Point Park University
Pittsburgh Center for Sports Media and Marketing

Donald P. Roy
Middle Tennessee State University

Kenneth E. Clow
University of Louisiana at Monroe

Routledge
Taylor & Francis Group

LONDON AND NEW YORK

First published 2013 by Pearson Education, Inc.

Published 2016 by Routledge
2 Park Square, Milton Park, Abingdon, Oxon OX14 4RN
711 Third Avenue, New York, NY 10017, USA

Routledge is an imprint of the Taylor & Francis Group, an informa business

Cover Designer: ElectraGraphics, Inc.

ISBN: 9780132135467 (pbk)

Library of Congress Cataloging-in-Publication Data
Fetchko, Michael J.
    Sports marketing / Michael J. Fetchko, Donald P. Roy, Kenneth E. Clow.—1st ed.
        p. cm.
    Includes bibliographical references and index.
    ISBN 978-0-13-213546-7 (alk. paper)
1. Sports—Marketing.   I. Roy, Donald P.   II. Clow, Kenneth E.   III. Title.
    GV716.F48 2013
    796.06'88—dc23

                                                                        2012018581

Dedication

To my beautiful wife and daughters who inspire me every day
and to my dear mom who always encouraged me
to play fair and hard on and off the field.

—Michael J. Fetchko

To my wife, Sara, and my sons Chris, Sidney, and Ethan,
for their support and encouragement to pursue my goals.

—Donald P. Roy

To my sons Dallas, Tim, Wes, and Roy,
who provided encouragement, and especially to my wife, Susan,
whose sacrifice and love made this textbook possible.

—Kenneth E. Clow

Brief Contents

Contents

Foreword

Former PepsiCo CEO Roger Enrico once said that the reason his company spent millions on sports was simple: "Nobody roots for a six pack." Simply put, sports have powerful and enduring equities that can be rented by brands to positively impact sales.

Most date the American sports marketing industry's birth to either IMG's commercial success with golfers Arnold Palmer, Jack Nicklaus, and Gary Player in the 1960s, or to Pete Ueberroth's profitable 1984 L.A. Olympics. As media proliferated since and its ability to deliver sports or any marketing messages grew exponentially, product segmentation also ran rampant.

"In 1970, if you walked into a sneaker store, they asked if you wanted white or black," former MasterCard U.S. president Peter Dimsey told me. "Today, they have sneakers for running, jogging, walking, or whatever—in a thousand colors." That degree of specialization is what makes this book unique; it's a collection of real-life theories and practices from top marketers at America's biggest brands; an unprecedented compilation of industry knowledge from those who built and continue to shape American sports marketing.

—Terry Lefton, Editor
Sports Business Journal
Greenwich, Conn.
June 2012

Preface

Writing a leading textbook on sports marketing is similar to preparing for a major sports competition. Winning coaches spend countless hours reviewing tapes and conducting research to successfully develop the best game plan. They scout for the best players at their respective positions. They intelligently recruit those best players and help direct them through training and practice on how to become a winning team. This dedicated preparation is the same recipe for creating the best sports marketing textbook for today. It requires connections and input from the best practitioners and academicians in the business.

Billions of sports fans worldwide responsible for growing billions in revenues of the sports industry demand those who practice sports marketing to be both highly knowledgeable and extremely prepared for an ever-challenging industry. The glamour surrounding sports today is alluring, but the business is just that—a business.

Too often, young people wishing to enter the field of sports view sports marketing as a profession that just calls for a passion for sports. This belief is a tragic mistake! In addition, too often the textbooks written to teach the subject are done by observers, not practitioners. This trend omits the invaluable perspective of individuals who have been actively involved in sports business.

The goals of this textbook are twofold. First, it fulfills a need to address business and marketing issues pertinent to sports as observed by practitioners and scholars. Most sports marketing texts are crafted using a marketing principles template. The organization and chapter themes of these texts bear a great deal of similarity to principles of marketing texts. *Sports Marketing* strives to depart from that practice by focusing on important conceptual, strategic, and actionable areas of the sports marketing function. Contributions of practitioner thought come not only from within the author team, but a high-caliber roster of successful sports executives from media, marketing, and other areas of sports business.

A second goal of the textbook is to actively involve and engage students in the process of presenting current information in sports entertainment. Critical thinking exercises require students to consider various situations faced by the sports marketers and sports executives. A sports marketing case at the end of each chapter put students in the role of decision maker. Cases enable students to apply knowledge and key concepts to business situations faced by actual sports brands.

The positioning of the textbook reflects the evolution of sports from an emphasis on the competition itself to a broader view of a customer's experience. This customer-centric conceptualization of sports requires an understanding of consumer motives and desire to consume experiences and entertainment. Also, it requires taking a broader view of competition, as all forms of entertainment become obstacles to acquiring customers.

Sports is a global phenomenon that crosses all societal barriers. It is a release from everyday life that appeals to the masses. It draws annually thousands of students just in the United States who wish to make it a career. The demand for competent individuals for sports marketing-related positions is high, but the delivery of graduates who are truly trained and prepared for successful careers in sports marketing is low.

The growing and changing field of sports requires knowledgeable people who understand its dynamic environment. While the business of sports grows, so does the demand for highly educated new young professionals. A need exists for those who understand not only the fundamentals of marketing but the current relevant practices of the industry. This text is a step towards fulfilling this critical need.

Chapter Features

Each chapter has a number of features that are designed to explain concepts and help your students understand the topics being presented. Development of each chapter was guided by a sports business professional to provide content that was relevant and timely for your students. You will find the following features in the book:

- **Lead-in vignettes.** Each chapter begins with a vignette related to sports marketing and the content of the chapter. The vignette describes a practice or occurrence that illustrates a topic appearing in the chapter, setting the stage for more in-depth coverage in the chapter.
- **Industry experts.** Each chapter features an industry expert. Each expert was selected based on his or her knowledge and provided input on chapter content. The "Insider Expert" feature that appears early in each chapter gives biographical information on the chapter's industry contributor.
- **Sports examples.** Throughout the book, concepts are reinforced with examples of practices and events from the sports industry. A variety of sports, properties, and companies are used as examples to bring to life definitions and concepts presented.
- **Expert insights.** The content of each chapter concludes with "Insider Insights," a question-and-answer feature with the chapter's industry contributor. In this feature, experts share examples of best practices from their experiences and opinions about trends in sports marketing.
- **Career planning.** Many students take a sports marketing course because they have a serious interest in pursuing a career in sports business. The final chapter contains information about different career opportunities in sports marketing, steps students can take to position themselves as job candidates, and advice on career planning and management from a panel of the book's industry experts.

End-of-Chapter Features

We have created end-of-chapter materials to help your students learn the materials in this text. Sports marketing is unique but also exciting. These exercises and materials will allow them to share personal experiences as a sports fan and suggest strategies from a marketing perspective.

- **Review questions.** In addition to a summary, each chapter has a series of review questions. These questions highlight the major points of the chapter and content your students should know.
- **New terms.** Understanding new terms is important. Because backgrounds and knowledge of marketing will vary, it is important to provide a comprehensive list of terms that may be new to the majority.
- **Discussion and critical thinking exercises.** To better appreciate the concepts in the text, the discussion and critical thinking exercises are a must. They include a variety of exercises designed to help you comprehend and apply the chapter concepts. They are not simple reviews. Each requires additional thought. These exercises are designed to challenge your students' thinking and encourage them to dig deeper. The best way to know that they have truly learned a sports concept or theory is when you can apply it to a different situation. These critical thinking and discussion exercises require them to apply knowledge to a wide array of marketing situations.
- **You make the call.** At the end of each chapter is a sports-related case. Now it is the students' turn to be the marketing expert or advisor to the marketing manager. Some cases are companies that utilize sports in their marketing efforts while other cases involve sports teams or sports industries. All will test their ability to apply the concepts of the chapter to a marketing situation often faced by sports marketing.

Acknowledgments

We would like to thank the following individuals who assisted in the development of the first edition through their careful and thoughtful reviews:

Reviewers

Charles Barr– Lynn University, Florida

Gregg Bennett– Texas A&M University

Wayne Blann– Ithaca College

Andrew Cannon– Arkansas Tech University

Larry DeGaris– University of Indianapolis

Amanda Fine– Clemson University

Michael Hyman– New Mexico State University

Stephen McDaniel– University of Maryland

Dr. Mark Moore– East Carolina University

Victor Piscitello– University of Arizona

B. David Ridpath– Ohio University

Robert Roundtree– University of North Carolina, Charlotte

Rick Shannon– Western Kentucky University

Although there were many individuals who helped us by supplying ideas and content, we want to thank a few who were especially helpful. We appreciate the guidance of Jeff Gregor, Rob Farinella, Chris Eames, Terry Lefton, Sean Hanrahan, and Tom Hoof in the early stages of this project. Many of the contributions made by the sports industry experts that appear in the book were supported by their capable assistants. We would especially like to thank Julie Diffin, Abraham Ninan, Kimberli Olga, and Lari Was for coordinating communications with the executives in their organizations who contributed to the book. Thank you to Steve Battista (Under Armour), Rob Farinella (Blue Sky Agency), Tom Hoof (Tampa Bay Rays), Brent High (Third Coast Sports), Tom McMillan (Pittsburgh Penguins), Amy Taylor, and Don Wright (Billboard Consultants) for providing advertisements and photographs.

On a personal note, we would like to thank James Heine, who signed us to write this book. Thank you to Laura Fischer, Meeta Pendharkar, and Erin Gardner for helping with this edition as it moved forward and to Jacqueline A. Martin and Judy Leale for guiding the production process. We would also like to thank the entire Prentice Hall production group.

Michael Fetchko is grateful for the hard work of Dr. Don Roy and Dr. Ken Clow and all of the tremendous industry chapter contributors, especially for the vision of Jeff Gregor. He would also like to thank Professor Lee Whiteman and Mary Ellen Adams of La Roche College, Anthony Schluep, Jay Farrell, Michael Dongilli, and Dr. Cokie Fetchko.

Donald Roy would like to thank his colleagues in the Department of Management and Marketing at Middle Tennessee State University for their support. He is grateful to Dr. Colby Jubenville of Middle Tennessee State University and Dr. Ben Goss of Missouri State University for their friendship and being challenged to grow professionally. Also, thanks go out to Dr. Bettina Cornwell of the University of Oregon for her influence in his development as a scholar and sports marketing researcher. A special thank you goes to his family for their patience and support throughout the process of writing the book.

Kenneth Clow would like to thank the University of Louisiana at Monroe for providing a supportive environment to work on this text. He is thankful to his sons Dallas, Wes, Tim, and Roy, who always provided encouragement and support. He would like to especially thank his wife, Susan, for being patient and supportive during those times when the authors were swamped by the work involved in completing this book. She has been enthusiastic and understanding throughout this entire journey.

Sports Marketing

1 Sports Meets Marketing

Learning Objectives

By the end of this chapter you should be able to:

1. Describe the characteristics of sports marketing
2. Discuss the three roles of marketing in sports organizations
3. Summarize the evolution and history of sports marketing
4. Describe contributing factors in the growth of sports and sports marketing
5. Define the components of the framework of sports marketing

© aceshot / Fotolia

Attracting fans to the Georgia Dome was a major priority for Arthur Blank.

Home Improvement: Arthur Blank's Makeover of the Atlanta Falcons

You probably have encountered the influence of Arthur Blank without knowing it. Blank, along with Bernie Marcus, founded home improvement retailer The Home Depot. In the 1970s, the two men were executives for Handy Dan, a chain of home improvement stores. After Blank and Marcus were fired from Handy Dan in 1978, they joined forces to start The Home Depot. The first two stores were opened the following year in Atlanta, which is still the location of the corporation's headquarters. Under the leadership of Blank and Marcus, The Home Depot rose to become the nation's largest home improvement retailer and second largest retailer overall, second only to Wal-Mart. Blank retired from The Home Depot as co-chairman in 2001.

Two of Arthur Blank's passions are the city of Atlanta and sports. Blank found an outlet for putting these two passions together when he purchased the Atlanta Falcons NFL franchise in 2002 for $545 million. The franchise had been owned by the Rankin Smith family since it joined the NFL, and aside from an appearance in Super Bowl XXXIII in 1999 (a loss to the Denver Broncos), the Falcons had been mired in mediocrity for the better part of four decades. When Blank bought the Falcons, he made his top two priorities improving player personnel and persuading more fans to attend games at the Georgia Dome. He would face a major challenge in making the Falcons successful, as the team ranked near the bottom of the NFL in average attendance and revenues.

Arthur Blank brought the marketing magic he worked with The Home Depot to the Falcons franchise. The team conducted surveys and focus groups to find out what fans wanted in their relationship with the Falcons. Some of the responses to fan feedback were relatively minor in impact, such as stocking concessions stands with more ketchup and straws. Other responses were rather bold. In an unusual move, Blank lowered ticket prices for 25,000 seats. He purchased land in downtown Atlanta to improve parking options for fans attending games. And, in response to fans' feedback that they did not want to be exposed to commercial messages during games, the team opted not to sell in-game advertising spots. These changes led to the Falcons enjoying their first sold-out season in more than twenty years.

Under the leadership of Arthur Blank, the Atlanta Falcons have strived to build relationships with the Atlanta community. Blank, long known for his philanthropic efforts in the Atlanta area, brought that focus to the Falcons. The team's charity went from raising a few hundred thousand dollars when Blank bought the team to an annual fundraising figure of about $2 million. All members of the organization are encouraged to be involved in charity and community work. Blank personally donates $2 for every dollar given to charities by anyone in his organization, up to a $10,000 match.

Insider Expert Preview

Marketing of sports has become a big business because of the millions of dollars at stake. As a result, sports properties have searched for the very best people to fill those marketing roles. The authors of this textbook have reached out to those talented people for information about how marketing is really done, in the trenches. While theory and concepts are introduced, they are presented through the input of marketing professionals. For every chapter, a marketing expert has been consulted. A biographical sketch will be presented at the beginning of the chapter followed by the "Insider Insight" section at the end. Each individual has been very influential within his or her company and within the field of sports marketing. Here is the list of experts you will meet in future chapters:

- Chapter 1: Tony Ponturo, Ponturo Management
- Chapter 2: Chris Eames, ESPN
- Chapter 3: Sean Hanrahan, ESPN
- Chapter 4: Rob Farinella, Blue Sky Agency
- Chapter 5: Tom McMillan, Pittsburgh Penguins
- Chapter 6: Steve Battista, Under Armour
- Chapter 7: Tom Fox, Arsenal FC
- Chapter 8: Beatriz Perez, Coca-Cola
- Chapter 9: Kathy Carter, Soccer United Marketing
- Chapter 10: Jeff Hennion, GNC Live Well
- Chapter 11: Terry Lefton, *Sports Business Journal*
- Chapter 12: Tom Hoof, Tampa Bay Rays
- Chapter 13: Jeff Gregor, Turner Broadcasting

Leading off is an executive who was selected by *Sports Business Journal* to be part of its inaugural class of "Champions of Sports Business" in 2010: Tony Ponturo.

For every chapter of this text, a marketing expert has been consulted.

Turner Broadcasting System/ESPN/Soccer United Marketing/Ponturo Management Group/Coca-Cola Company/Pittsburgh Penguins/Blue Sky Agency/*Sports Business Daily and Sports Business Journal*

Despite the successes achieved in transforming the Atlanta Falcons from a mediocre franchise to the talk of the city of Atlanta, Arthur Blank has faced challenges, too. The 2007 season is one Blank would probably rather forget. First, star quarterback Michael Vick was convicted for his role in a dog fighting operation and sentenced to twenty-three months in federal prison. Then, head coach Bobby Petrino quit before finishing his first season. The events created a perception that the Falcons were an organization in disarray. But, that was hardly the case! Following the turmoil of 2007 Blank said, "We've made significant long-term commitments to our fans, and we will deliver on them . . . we will do what it takes to field a highly competitive team and reinforce the standards that define this team." Attendance declined less than 3% in 2007 despite the team's problems, and the number of sponsors and advertisers actually increased. The customer focus that contributed to the phenomenal success of The Home Depot has and will continue to serve Arthur Blank well as he guides the Atlanta Falcons.[1]

Insider Expert Tony Ponturo – Ponturo Management

Sports and marketing executive Tony Ponturo's name and reputation have been synonymous with quality, innovation, and attention to brand detail for over thirty years. First in the advertising world, then in a landmark career at Anheuser-Busch, and now as founder and CEO of the New York–based sports and entertainment consulting firm Ponturo Management Group LLC. He has been responsible for some of the most influential partnerships that have shaped the sports and entertainment landscape as we know it today.

Following a six-year stint in the New York advertising business, Ponturo spent twenty-six years at Anheuser-Busch in St. Louis, Missouri, leading a team that built one of the most iconic sports and event marketing brands in the world. He served as the president and CEO of Busch Media Group and the vice president of Global Media, Sports and Entertainment Marketing of Anheuser-Busch Inc. Ponturo managed over $700 million in media, sports, and entertainment properties per annum and oversaw broadcast exclusives for the Super Bowl and the FIFA World Cup, as well as multifaceted relationships with the United States and International Olympic Committees. He helped vastly expand Anheuser-Busch's leadership stake in the sports business, carving official beer sponsorships with Major League Baseball, the National Basketball Association, the National Hockey League, Major League Soccer, and NASCAR in North

Tony Ponturo, Ponturo Management

America, as well as landmark international deals with Formula One Racing and the English Premier League in soccer. Anheuser-Busch also increased its position in the local and regional areas of sports sponsorship, securing scores of team and event partnerships during this time as well.

His latest venture has him balancing his passions in both sports and entertainment. He is a Tony Award–winning producer of Broadway hits such as the 2009 revival of *Hair* and the original musical *Memphis*, which opened in the fall of 2009. He produced a play entitled *Lombardi*, an original drama of the life of the Hall of Fame football coach and inspirational leader Vince Lombardi. And, he produced the play *Magic Bird* about the rivalry and friendship between Magic Johnson and Larry Bird.

His influence in shaping the sports and entertainment landscape has not gone unnoticed by the media or his peers. Annually recognized as one of the most powerful executives in sports, Ponturo was recently featured by the sport industry's leading publication, Street and Smith's *Sports Business Journal*, as an inaugural member of their "Champions" program, which honors select industry leaders for their career accomplishments. He has been ranked by *BusinessWeek* magazine as the fourteenth most influential sports executive in the world, and as the top sports advertising executive by the *Sports Business Journal*.

Introduction

The customer focus Arthur Blank developed in a home improvement retail store and brought to professional football illustrates how the marketing of sports has both similarities and differences from the marketing of other goods and services. Blank led The Home Depot to its success by emphasizing customer service and creating a positive brand experience for customers. Quality and customer focus are fundamental to marketing. Any brand that excels in these areas can be competitive regardless of the industry in which it competes. However, differences exist between marketing home improvement products and sports such as football. Pricing a ceiling fan or other home improvement merchandise is not comparable to pricing tickets to a football game, since the latter is perishable. When the game is over, any unsold tickets and empty seats are lost revenue. They cannot be sold later.

The marketing methods that influence customers to visit a retail store have some similarities to persuading fans to attend a sporting event. But there are also significant differences. This textbook explores sports marketing with the recognition that the field has its idiosyncrasies, but is rooted in basic marketing concepts.

The Case for Sports Marketing

A natural starting point to begin any study of a topic such as sports marketing is defining the concept and making a case for its relevance. In this case, before defining sports marketing it may be useful to take a step backward and define the term *marketing*. When new marketing students are asked to define marketing, it is common for most definitions to include such words as *advertising*, *selling*, or *persuading*. These words all describe marketing activities in which a firm might engage, but marketing is much more than those activities. A comprehensive definition of marketing offered by the American Marketing Association (AMA) states that "**Marketing** is the activity, set of institutions, and processes for creating, communicating, delivering, and exchanging offerings that have value for customers, clients, partners, and society at large."[2] This definition captures the various activities marketers undertake and acknowledges the strategic nature of marketing. Also, the AMA definition identifies key stakeholder groups to which an organization is accountable. While accountability to customers and clients may be stating the obvious, this definition of marketing calls on marketers to realize a higher level of responsibility to create a positive impact on the communities in which they do business and society at large.

While sports marketing is based on marketing principles, the nature of sports and its customers requires special consideration. **Sports marketing** can be defined as *the use of marketing for creating, communicating, delivering, and exchanging sports experiences that have value for customers, clients, partners, and society*. It is important to note that sports marketing is made up of two distinct elements: 1) marketing *of* sports and 2) marketing *through* sports. It is common for many students to think of the marketing of sports when they think of sports marketing. Marketing efforts of sports leagues, teams, events, venues, or individuals as well as the marketing of sporting goods fall under the marketing of sports. The "product" can be an entire season, a specific event or game, a single player, or a venue. Marketing *through* sports involves the strategic marketing efforts of companies in which they partner with a sports entity for some commercial benefit. A partial list of marketing benefits includes increased brand awareness, an enhanced corporate or brand image, and increased sales.

Sponsorship of a league, team, event, or individual athlete is a prime example of using sports to achieve marketing objectives. Sponsors are partners with the properties being sponsored as well as being their customers, seeking to achieve certain outcomes from their association with the property. For example, consumer brands marketer Pepsico has been an NFL sponsor for nearly thirty years and extended its relationship with the league until 2022. Pepsico links five of its key brands—Pepsi, Frito-Lay, Gatorade, Tropicana, and Quaker—to the NFL as official partners. The sponsorship gives a product presence, such as Gatorade, which is seen on teams' sidelines. It also creates marketing opportunities for the other brands with major NFL events like the Super Bowl. In addition to an estimated $1 billion Pepsico will spend over ten years on sponsorship rights, it is expected that the company will spend $1.3 billion on marketing its NFL sponsorship.[3]

Distinguishing Characteristics of Sports Marketing

The basics of marketing—meeting the needs and wants of customers—are applicable to sports just as they are for any product or service. However, three characteristics distinguish sports marketing from other industries and pose opportunities for sports organizations. These characteristics can be described as: 1) an affinity advantage, 2) a positioning challenge, and 3) experience-based relationships.

Sports brands tend to enjoy an *affinity advantage* compared to brands in other product categories. While loyalty to a sport or team might resemble brand loyalty exhibited for other products, the nature of one's relationship with a sports brand tends to be different than most other brand relationships they have. Connection to sports brands often is based on emotional attachments to a favorite athlete, team, or sport. The source of the attachment may be the result of family influence, desire to be part of a community with shared interests, or feelings of civic pride to support a hometown team. The advantage is that consumers' affinity for sports brands may be immune to threats other brands face such as competition for attention and switching brands when performance does not meet expectations.

In addition, the affinity advantage is demonstrated through consumption of licensed products such as apparel and collectibles. It is an outward sign to other people about one's affinity for a sports brand. Licensed products represent a revenue stream for properties that many brands are unable to realize because of the absence of deep, emotional connections between consumers and brands—it is more likely that people will don a shirt of their favorite college football team, but not their bank! An example of how the affinity advantage translates to a revenue advantage in the sports industry is the official merchandise sales of Minor League Baseball. MiLB had 2010 licensed products sales of $51.1 million for its 160 teams, a 12% increase over the previous year.[4] Consumer behavior issues related to sports are discussed in Chapter 2.

Sports brands often deal with a *positioning challenge* that most brands do not face, particularly properties marketing spectator sports. In many industries, a firm's competitors are other companies whose products, pricing, and distribution strategies are rather similar. Sports leagues, teams, and events may differ from brands in other industries in terms of head-to-head competitors marketing similar offerings, but have competition nonetheless. In order to expand the target market, spectator sports are positioned as providing entertainment as well as sporting competition. The payoff is that the potential market for individuals and business seeking entertainment is greater than that for the sport alone. The challenge is that sports brands that position themselves as entertainment options not only increase the potential audience, but they also will have more competitors from non-sports businesses that seek to meet customers' need for entertainment. Thus, a positioning strategy of sports entertainment may not be distinctive enough to set apart a sports brand from their entertainment competitors.

One sports property that has responded well to the positioning challenge is the Alliance of Action Sports (Alli) and its Dew Tour. The Dew Tour is known as the first ever action sports tour, with events in four major U.S. cities. A narrow positioning strategy on action sports competition would limit interest in the Dew Tour to participants and fans of events like skateboarding and BMX. Instead, the Dew Tour is positioned as an entertainment and lifestyle festival that includes concerts, video gaming areas, interactive exhibits, and athlete autograph sessions.[5] Although such a positioning strategy increases the appeal of the Dew Tour, it must combat other entertainment offerings for the interest of the young, predominantly male target audience. A framework for defining competition and implications for marketing strategy is presented in Chapter 3.

A third distinguishing characteristic of sports marketing is the nature of customers' interactions with sports—it can be described as *experience-based relationships*. While the sports product can be a physical good like golf clubs or a team jersey, more are intangible offerings. Consumption takes place in the form of an experience whether it is attending a golf tournament, playing in a fantasy football league on Yahoo!, or watching streaming video of a college football game on ESPN3. The fantasy football and online streaming of games examples illustrate that consumer experiences with a sports brand are not limited to live events. Experiences have the potential to enhance the value received from a product.

Nike+ is a product that uses a sensor embedded in Nike running shoes and software compatible with Apple iPod or iPhone that collects data and provides feedback to runners. The result is that runners have a greater interaction with Nike that goes beyond wearing running shoes. Nike is a training resource. Experiential marketing is the focus of Chapter 7, and creation of customer-centered experiences is a theme that runs throughout the sports marketing concepts presented in this book.

© Michael Chamberlin / Fotolia

Marketing of sports is unique because of its intangibility and experiential nature.

Marketing's Contribution to the Sports Organization

Marketing's role in sports has grown significantly during the last forty years. Sports are now a multibillion-dollar industry and marketing has been a prominent force in that growth. Figure 1.1 identifies three important roles marketing plays in sports.

> • Catalyst for creating customer value
>
> • Develops and nurtures customer relationships
>
> • Connects organizations with the external environment

FIGURE 1.1
Marketing's Role in Sports

Catalyst for Creating Customer Value

Perhaps more than any other functional area of an organization, marketing has the potential to influence customers' perceptions of value. **Value** can be defined as a customer's judgment of the benefits received from consumption of a product compared to the sacrifices required to acquire that product. It should be noted that benefits and costs are not limited to tangible benefits and monetary costs. Consumers are motivated to buy products for either the functional benefits or psychological benefits provided, or both. In the case of the consumption of sports products, psychological outweigh functional needs.

Sacrifices required by consumers to obtain and use a product extend beyond monetary costs. While pricing is a concern and can influence consumer acceptance (or rejection) of product offerings, other costs should be considered. In the case of a sporting event, nonmonetary costs include the amount of time required to travel to and from an event, time spent going through security checkpoints, and length of lines in concession areas and restrooms. As marketers, the challenge to enhance customer value is not as difficult as it may appear. Two options are available when attempting to add value: 1) increase benefits received or 2) reduce sacrifices required.

Benefits that can be added may be tangible or intangible. At sporting events, the in-game atmosphere is often enhanced with a dazzling display of music, video, and even pyrotechnics. Video replay boards have become common in major league venues and even in many collegiate venues. Promotional activities such as distribution of premiums (i.e., giveaways or freebies) have been a time-honored practice for many sports entities. A marketing tactic used by many teams is to create "bobble-head night" promotions at which bobble-head dolls are given to fans that attend. Fans often respond by lining up hours before gates open to improve their chances of receiving a bobble-head doll. In addition, memorabilia collectors snap up bobble-heads through online auction sites for over $150 for the most popular dolls.[6] Other benefits, such as making players available for autograph sessions, are intangible but can positively influence attendees' perceptions of the value received.

Offering customers alternatives for reducing monetary costs is an effective approach for increasing customer value. One area that sports franchises have begun to offer more flexibility is in their ticket packages. The typical ticket offering for years was to sell tickets either for individual games or for an entire season. However, for some sports the season is so long that many consumers would like to attend games but cannot afford to buy tickets for an entire season (each NBA and NHL season has 41 home games; in Major League Baseball each team has 81 home games). In recognition of this problem, many teams have created "mini plans" that include tickets for multiple games but not for an entire season. Such a package may reduce the "sticker shock" problem that may occur with season-ticket prices. Another tactic sports properties use to add value for customers is to bundle added benefits with the base product of event tickets. The Denver Outlaws of Major League Lacrosse take this approach to increasing value with their "Guy's Night Out" ticket package. A bundle of two tickets, two drinks, and two replica jerseys for $50 is offered for select games.[7] Ticket packages that bundle complementary items like concessions and souvenirs offer customers an incentive to reduce their total outlay (i.e., sacrifices required) to attend a sporting event.

The ability to add value has been enhanced by technological advances. As an added benefit, fans can receive information more often through teams and leagues' websites. Many teams offer e-mail services that enable fans to receive information about players, games, ticket offers, and any other information about the team that may be of interest. Technology can help reduce customers' costs, too. For instance, many teams make available an online service that enables season ticket holders to sell tickets to a secondary market, thus reducing monetary costs by allowing them to recoup part, if not all, of the cost of unused game tickets. Many professional sports franchises have created websites or partner with ticket resale websites to support the secondary ticket market of customers selling tickets they have purchased. For example, MLB's Texas Rangers has designated StubHub as its "official fan-to-fan ticket resale marketplace."[8] Ticket owners can sell tickets through StubHub, taking advantage of StubHub's brand recognition among ticket buyers.

At first glance, it may seem that teams are giving up revenue by creating websites for customer-to-customer ticket transactions that may provide competition for the team. Perhaps a better way to view this service is that it is a value-added feature for season ticket holders that reduces their risk of losing money on tickets to games they cannot attend. The result can be greater customer satisfaction and confidence in doing business with a team.

Develops and Nurtures Customer Relationships

Marketing has more influence on building and maintaining relationships than any other functional area of an organization. This feature of marketing can be attributed to its close proximity to customers. However, it is important to have a broader perspective of marketing relationships, one that includes more than paying customers. A recent emphasis in marketing philosophy has been to advocate relationship marketing instead of transactional marketing. **Relationship marketing** is the process of developing and nurturing long-term relationships with a an organization's customers.

The importance of relationship marketing with a firm's customers is rather obvious. It is understood by most marketers that it costs more to attract new customers than to retain existing customers. A figure cited often is that it costs six times as much to attract new customers through advertising, sales promotions, and selling activities than it does to retain existing customers. The exact amount is not known, nor is it as important as the recognition that it costs less to do business with existing customers, and thus they are more profitable. They have already been "sold" on the product and do not need to be persuaded to the extent that new customers require. The "other stakeholders" term captures many different parties that can benefit a sports property, such as the media and government officials. Both of these groups, while unlikely to be ticket purchasers or to contribute to revenues directly, hold a great deal of influence on how a sports brand is perceived and its treatment by policy makers and elected officials. In many cases, they are important entities in the building of new sports facilities.

Connects Organization with the External Environment

Marketing as a functional activity is often treated as though it operates in a vacuum. Marketers may focus so much attention on the marketing mix issues of pricing, advertising, and inventory levels that they lose sight of the fact that the external environment (i.e., events and trends occurring outside the walls of an organization) influences marketing decisions. In terms of strategic marketing planning, examining the external environment is a crucial starting point. Figure 1.2 identifies external factors and illustrates their influence on marketing decisions and the customer.

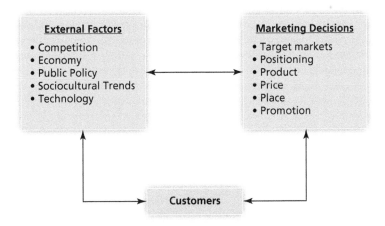

FIGURE 1.2 The Relationship between External Factors, Marketing Decisions, and Customers

The dynamic nature of the external environment necessitates an outside-in approach to marketing. For almost any firm, one or more of the external factors will experience change from one planning period to the next. The entrance of new competition, significant technological innovations, and shifts in consumer confidence (upward or downward) are examples of possible changes in the external environment that would influence subsequent marketing decisions. Failure to adequately assess the external environment or basing marketing decisions on outdated information could result in ill-conceived marketing strategies. Chapter 3 will address assessment of external factors and their implications for marketing decisions.

Evolution of Sports Marketing

The sports industry has become a significant contributor to the global economy and has maintained its status as part of the fabric of American popular culture. The sports environment we live in today is markedly different from what people experienced eighty years ago, thirty years ago, even ten years ago. Like any other industry, sports has experienced an evolution over time, and its development is not fully completed (and likely never will be). The past hundred or so years of sports can be broken down into distinct periods, or eras, identified as monopoly, television, and highlight eras.[9] A fourth period has emerged in recent years and is expected to influence the practice of sports marketing in the coming years. It is the experience era.

Monopoly Era (1900–1950)

The monopoly era marked the infancy of the sports industry in the United States. As the population of the country experienced a shift from a largely rural existence to the growth of urban population centers, opportunities arose to market sports to large audiences. Sports consumption during the monopoly era occurred primarily through newspaper and radio. Live events were not widely accessible because professional sports franchises and major sporting events were limited to major cities. For instance, the National Basketball Association has thirty teams today, but when the NBA was founded in 1946 it had only eleven teams, concentrated in the eastern United States. Smaller markets were served by minor league sports franchises, particularly minor league baseball.

Championship boxing matches broadcast via radio and the Olympics were the only truly global sporting events. It was during the monopoly era that the first "super brands" emerged in the sports industry. High-profile teams like the New York Yankees and University of Notre Dame football rode their success to achieve a nationwide fan base. Also, during this period athletes began to enjoy celebrity status, leading to the practice of marketing through sports. The on-field feats of stars like Babe Ruth and Red Grange led to product endorsement opportunities for athletes. And, venues took on greater importance in the experience of attending a sporting event. Legendary stadiums like Fenway Park and Wrigley Field were built during this period, and large stadiums were built in many urban areas to accommodate hosting professional and collegiate sporting events.

Television Era (1950–1990)

The most significant catalyst for the development of the sports industry has been the television. As TV sets became commonplace in households, sports became valuable entertainment content for TV networks, and major sports were now accessible to the masses. Growth of television as a distribution channel for sports could not have come at a better time; population shifts from urban areas to suburbs could have had a negative impact on sports. However, the reach of television kept people connected with sports regardless of where they lived. Television, along with infrastructure innovations like interstate highways and expanded air travel options, made it more convenient to consume sports directly and indirectly.

Sports programming on television elevated the status of major league U.S. sports. Major League Baseball enjoyed national distribution with its *Game of the Week*, and ABC made *Monday Night Football* a staple of primetime programming. Television was influential in raising the profile of the Super Bowl from the NFL's championship game to an iconic cultural event. Similarly, the pageantry and drama of the Olympics came to life through TV coverage. Perhaps the most symbolic program of the television era was ABC's *Wide World of Sports*. The show ran from 1961 to 1998 and contributed to the fame of the Harlem Globetrotters, daredevil Evel Knievel, and the phrase "the thrill of victory, and the agony of defeat." Sports were transformed from athletic events to entertainment programs filled with drama and stories of triumph and overcoming adversity.

Another major impact on the sports industry during the television era was the development of cable television. The specialized programming of cable TV networks held great appeal, and networks like ESPN (launched in 1979) and CNN (launched in 1980) introduced the 24-hour news cycle. Sports helped to fill programming needs of the around-the-clock TV networks. At about the same time, local television stations WOR in New York, WGN in Chicago, and WTCG in Atlanta gained national distribution on cable TV systems. The sports programming of these stations quickly spread from their home markets to become of national interest. The Atlanta Braves picked up the nickname "America's team" as a result of games being broadcast nationally via cable.

One other noteworthy development in the television era was the emergence of sponsorship as a marketing strategy. The expanded reach of sports created by television was very important for sponsorship's development. The 1984 Olympics in Los Angeles is cited as a groundbreaking event for sponsorship. Organizers bucked the trend of the Olympics being a money-losing proposition and turned a profit of more than $200 million. The key to success was having more than forty corporate partners that used their Olympics sponsorship to market their companies or sell officially licensed Olympics products.[10] The 1984 Olympics not only became the model upon which future Olympic Games organizers have operated, it spread sponsorship as a sports marketing "product" throughout professional, collegiate, and amateur sports.

Highlight Era (1990–2010)

Television solidified the standing of sports in American popular culture by allowing sports brands to reach all corners of the country. But, another technological innovation, the Internet, was the driver of the highlight era. As the World Wide Web became accessible to a mass audience in the late 1990s, sports consumption was no longer constrained by the delivery schedules of traditional media. Instead of waiting to get sports news by watching a segment on a local news broadcast or waiting for the morning newspaper to arrive, the Internet gave instant and constant access to scores, news, and information for one's favorite sports. The immediacy of sports content online threatened traditional media outlets, newspapers in particular.

On-demand access to information changed how people consume sports and led to new formats for presenting sports content. Shows such as *SportsCenter* and *Pardon the Interruption* featured coverage of sports stories in short, quick bursts. Similarly, *SportsCenter* segments such as Top 10 plays of the day and Hot Seat catered to viewers' preferences for short overviews of stories and sports personalities. Also, presentation of scores and news using a ticker across the bottom of TV screens allows viewers a quick look at what is going on in the world of sports with a minimal time commitment.

The appetite for sports content continued to fuel the growth in sports media that began during the TV era. Sports properties have slowly removed the notion of an off-season. The growth in cable television and the Internet led to an increase in creating and distributing content through websites and their own media outlets. The NFL, NBA, NHL, and MLB all have their own cable TV networks that show a variety of content—games (live and classic games), news, reality shows, and other programming related to their sports. The payoff is the ability to create 365-day-a-year interactions with fans.

Another effect of technology on sports consumption during the highlight era was a dramatic rise in fantasy sports participation. Fantasy sports games give players an active role by making decisions similar to those faced by a general manager or owner of a professional sports team. The ease of sports information access along with enhancements in Internet access speeds and user-friendly websites made it easy for people who had never played fantasy games previously to try fantasy sports products. These developments helped spread the distribution of fantasy games on media sites like ESPN and Yahoo! as well as through the websites of sports leagues. An estimated 27 million now participate in some type of fantasy sports activity.[11]

Experience Era (2010–today)

Innovations that sports consumers first enjoyed during the highlight era seemed to create a longing for more. We have constant access to sports information, can watch or listen to sporting events or news from TVs, computers, and smartphones, and are no longer geographically limited to consuming sports in local markets or even our countries, so what's next? That question will likely always exist, and today it is shaping what can be called the experience era. Yes, sports consumers want immediacy and convenience, but they increasingly want meaning, too. All aspects of consuming sports, from engaging with sports as a spectator or participant to interactions with corporate sponsors linked to sports properties, have the potential to be developed into experiences. These points of contact can be designed as experiences in which consumers have a more active role during the time spent in sports consumption. In turn, greater involvement and engagement can strengthen one's relationship with and loyalty to a sports brand. The challenge dealt with throughout this book will be how sports marketers should respond to consumers' desires to engage in meaningful experiences.

A strong influence in the evolution of sports during the experience era is social media. Social networking websites like Facebook and Twitter empower fans to communicate with brands and one another. The concept of fan-initiated communication will shape the way sports experiences are delivered. In the experience era, the TV broadcast of a sporting event is a huge part of the experience, but still only a part. Stadiums and arenas will become TV studios, a production hub for sports experiences. They will be completely interactive social media venues. Fans are already starting to access their own unique camera angles on their smartphones. They are communicating directly with team officials to express complaints about service or security concerns.

Moreover, developments during the experience era are responding to the desires of younger audiences. The younger generation watching sports on TV at home no longer just watch; they are following in-game blogs on their smartphones or tablets—looking up stats, creating their own content, and communicating with each other. The Pittsburgh Penguins have one of the most heavily trafficked websites in the NHL, and the area of the site generating the most hits is the team's in-game blogs. The older generation just watch, but younger audiences want so much more; they *need* their sports consumption to be interactive.

In addition to social media being instrumental in creating fan-initiated communications and experiences, it is also changing how sports journalists, athletes, and agents market themselves. With Twitter and Facebook, they are now going above or around their employers and creating their own news and promotions. Fan access into the lives of those who play the games is greater than ever before because of social media. Leagues, teams, and sponsors have to figure out how to best tap into the interest in sports that social media fuels.

The Sports Industry in the Experience Era

The question may have entered your mind: "Why is there a need for a textbook dedicated to sports marketing?" After all, many of the concepts mentioned in this chapter appear in introductory marketing texts. The answer to this question has been partially revealed already—sports products differ from other goods and services we consume in that sports consumption is often experiential (participation or attendance at a live event) and is often personal (a team's successes and failures are shared by its fans).

Many factors can be cited as reasons for the growth of sports and sports marketing. These factors can be broken down into business-driven factors and consumer-driven factors, as shown in Figure 1.3.

FIGURE 1.3 Sports Marketing Growth Factors

Business-Driven Factors:
- Growth of sports media.
- Increased interest in sports sponsorships.
- Desire to build global brands.
- Inclusion of sports in economic development planning.

Customer-Driven Factors:
- Increase emphasis on leisure activities.
- Introduction of new sports.
- Increased interest in women's sports.
- Increased interest in personal fitness.

Business-Driven Growth Factors

Sports have become a business, a very big business. The sports industry with all of its tentacles, such as sports media, sponsorships, and product merchandise, is a major contributor to the nation's GDP (Gross Domestic Product). Millions of individuals now earn their living either directly or indirectly through sports.

GROWTH OF SPORTS MEDIA. The influence of media on sports cannot be overstated. Major media organizations view sports as a means of building audiences for other network programming. Many experts attribute the development of the Fox network as a legitimate competitor of the "big three" U.S. networks (ABC, CBS, and NBC) to its decision to pursue and ultimately receive NFL broadcast rights in the early 1990s. Professional sports leagues have benefited greatly from networks' desire to broadcast games. The average annual values of the major sports leagues' television broadcast deals skyrocketed in the early 2000s, as shown in Figure 1.4.

The escalation in broadcast rights fees paid to sports properties has made its way into college sports. ESPN negotiated a 15-year deal with the Southeastern Conference beginning in 2009 worth $2 billion for the league that gives ESPN broadcast rights for SEC football and

League	Average Annual Value	Increase over Previous Contract
NFL	$ 2.2 billion	100%
MLB	$ 558.5 million	64%
NBA	$ 935.5 million	385%
NHL	$ 120.0 million	298%

FIGURE 1.4 Value of Television Deals

men's and women's basketball.[12] The ESPN–SEC deal was followed in 2010 by an agreement between the NCAA and broadcast partners CBS and Turner for rights to the NCAA men's basketball tournament for an astounding $10.8 billion over 14 years.[13] Perhaps the most significant development in the sports media landscape of college athletics in recent years was the launch of the Longhorn Network. It is a partnership between the University of Texas and ESPN that created a 24-hour network devoted to Longhorns sports. The payoff for Texas is nationwide exposure . . . and $11 million per year until 2031.[14]

Another media influence on sports is the increased programming devoted to sports news on television. All-sports television programming began with ESPN in the late 1970s. The success of ESPN spawned new networks such as ESPN2, ESPN U, and ESPN News. It led to competitive response by networks that started all-sports networks of their own, such as Fox Sports Net, and the creation of sports channels that concentrate on a particular sport like Speed, Golf Channel, MLB Network, and the Big Ten Network. The influence of broadcast sports media has also spurred growth of some sports. Action sports such as skateboarding and snowboarding have benefited from the exposure received through ESPN's creation of the X Games and Winter X Games.

Media influence is not restricted to television. Radio has fueled an increased interest in sports as hundreds of stations in both large and small markets across the United States have adopted a sports format offering around-the-clock sports programming.[15] Many of these stations are network affiliates of ESPN, Fox Sports, or Yahoo! Sports Radio. Also, satellite radio provider Sirius XM has broadcast deals and related sports programming for MLB, NASCAR, NBA, NFL, NHL, PGA Tour, IndyCar Series, and major NCAA conferences.

The rapid growth moved from the airwaves to the blogosphere, with sports being authored by journalists and everyday fans. ESPN leveraged the popularity of columnist Bill Simmons, a.k.a. "The Sports Guy," by launching the sports and culture blog Grantland.com. Simmons's reach of more than 700,000 monthly visitors to his ESPN.com column and 1.5 million Twitter followers gave Grantland.com a sizeable target market when it launched in 2011.[16] The user-generated media boom includes sports content uploaded and shared on video sites like YouTube and photo-sharing site Flickr. Sports properties, individual athletes, coaches, and sports media are responding to the boom in social media usage to reach sports fans on popular sites like Facebook and Twitter. The effect of these new media is more outlets for consuming sports and opportunities to engage and empower sports consumers.

INCREASED INVESTMENT IN SPORTS SPONSORSHIPS. A second business-driven growth factor for sports marketing is businesses' desire to link their brands with sports. The International Events Group, a leading firm that monitors the sponsorship industry, notes that the growth in sponsorship expenditures in North America in just one year was an estimated $18.2 billion. Sports sponsorships account for 69% of the total sponsorship expenditures.[17]

Two reasons can be cited for the growth in sports sponsorships. First, sponsors recognize the increased interest in sports, both participatory sports and spectator sports, and want to link their brands with consumers' sports experiences. For example, Mountain Dew has effectively developed linkages between an active, on-the-edge lifestyle and the brand through sponsorship of action sports and performer's events as well as featuring action sports in commercials.

Second, sponsors are faced with increasing ad clutter throughout traditional media advertising and view sports sponsorships as a means of breaking through the clutter. Viewers of a televised sporting event can (and often do) tune out commercial messages by changing channels or temporarily stop viewing the program during a commercial break. Sponsorship overcomes audiences' inattention by incorporating brand messages into the event itself. Brand messages may be as simple as the presence of logos on stadium signage, but it can take on a more prominent position at the event by being on participants' uniforms or, in the case of Interstate Batteries, on the car driven in the race. Brand names can be part of the event name

Whether you're refreshing an entire room or making some minor upgrades, get your home on the highlight reel with more project for your money. **That's the power of The Home Depot.®**

Proud sponsor of the
Atlanta Hawks.

More saving. More doing.®

Walter McBride / Contributor.

Pepsi is a proud sponser of the halftime show.

or even part of the venue name. Honda integrates its brand into sports by title sponsorship of a PGA Tour event (the Honda Classic) and naming rights to a sports and entertainment arena in Anaheim, California (the Honda Center). Sponsorship considerations are examined from two perspectives in this textbook: 1) Sports properties' use of sponsorship in their promotional mixes (i.e., promotion of sports) and 2) use of sponsorship as part of their promotional mixes (i.e., promotion through sports).

Interstate Batteries

The sponsorship of Kyle Busch allows Interstate Batteries to place its brand name on his uniform as well as the car he drives.

DESIRE TO BUILD GLOBAL BRANDS. Companies that market their brands outside of their home country often seek to build a global brand identity. That is, they want the brand to have a consistent meaning to all consumers regardless of their geographic location in the world. Events such as the Olympics and FIFA's World Cup are platforms to reach global audiences. The number of such events is rather small, and the cost of association can be high. Top-tier Olympics sponsors, participants in The Olympic Partners (TOP) program, pay up to $60 million for sponsorship rights for a four-year cycle covering one set of Summer and Winter Games. Acer, Coca-Cola, GE, and Visa were among the worldwide eleven TOP partners for the recent London Olympics.[18] Sponsors invest such enormous sums of money into Olympics rights fees because they covet the opportunities to leverage the association with the Olympics through advertising, sales promotions, and other marketing vehicles. Marketing programs can be tailored to appeal to consumers in individual countries or be designed to have global appeal.

SPORTS IMPACT ON LOCAL ECONOMIC DEVELOPMENT. The financial impact of sports goes far beyond valuable television rights deals and sponsorship agreements between corporations and sports properties. Local economies can be positively impacted through sports, too. Local governments realize that professional sports teams and prestigious professional and amateur events not only are ways to build civic pride, but they are ways to fill their coffers. Events that attract large audiences can impact local economies through generation of sales tax revenue at restaurants and retailers as well as additional hotel taxes.

The most prestigious events can have a major impact on a local economy. It is estimated that the city of Phoenix realized an impact of $500 million when it hosted the Super Bowl. The event attracted game attendees as well as an estimated 50,000 people who did not attend the game. It was estimated that more than 120,000 visitors came to Phoenix in the two weeks leading up to the game.[19] Events of this magnitude are few in number, but smaller events are still important to local communities because of the revenues they generate.

Many cities have agencies such as a sports council or a convention and visitors bureau that identify desirable sporting events and make proposals to event properties in an effort to persuade them to hold events in their communities. For example, the mission of the Los Angeles Sports Council is to promote economic development through sports by bidding on rights to host major sporting events like the Super Bowl, NCAA championships, and Olympic Trials.[20] Marketing a city through sports is not limited to major markets. The Greater Savannah (Georgia) Sports Council has a mission similar to the LA Sports Council, with the difference being the size of events it pursues. Savannah has attracted high school, collegiate, and professional events, bringing visitors to the city and generating revenues from lodging, restaurants, and retail sales.[21]

Consumer-Driven Growth Factors

Paralleling the business factors that have spurred the growth of sports are the consumer-driven factors. These include an increased emphasis on leisure activities, the introduction of new sports, a growing interest in women's sports, and an increased involvement in personal fitness.

Growth in sports has been partially fueled by an increased emphasis on leisure activities, such as jogging.

INCREASED EMPHASIS ON LEISURE ACTIVITIES. The consumption of sports, both participation sports and spectator sports, has been fueled in part by an increased emphasis on leisure activities. Note that a distinction should be made between "emphasis on leisure activities" and the amount of time available for leisure activities. According to a study of American workers, 86% of working men and 66% of working women put in more than 40 hours a week at their jobs.[22] Thus, it is important for many individuals to receive maximum utility from the time available for leisure activities. When there is an opportunity to get away from work, people may participate in adventure sports such as mountain biking, mountain climbing, or running in an attempt to "get away from it all." This trend has created opportunities for equipment manufacturers and service providers associated with these sports. Likewise, spectator sporting events provide attendees with a chance to escape from their hectic daily lives and enjoy time with family, friends, or fellow fans.

INTRODUCTION OF NEW SPORTS. In addition to the media influences discussed in the previous section, another influence has been "made for television" sporting events that have led to increased interest among viewers. ESPN started the trend when it held the first X Games in 1995. The X Games are annual competitions in such action or "extreme" sports as skateboarding, inline skating, motocross, skysurfing, and bicycle stunts. The X Games were followed by the Winter X Games beginning in 1997, which include sports as snowboarding, snow mountain bike racing, and ice climbing.[23]

Such sports have broadened the market for sports consumption and have created opportunities for marketers to reach specific target markets by sponsoring events that are meaningful to consumers. Younger consumers are particularly important to marketers and are a core audience of action sports. Action sports events tend to appeal to members of Generation Y, also referred to as Millennials. Members of this demographic group range in age from early teens to early 20s, and many of them became interested in action sports because they were bored with traditional sports competitions.[24]

Another sport that has grown in popularity in recent years among younger audiences is mixed martial arts. The main mixed martial arts organization, Ultimate Fighting Championship (UFC), enjoys cable TV exposure and sells out its events consistently. Three recent events witnessed more than 1 million pay-per-view subscribers each.[25] Like action sports, UFC draws the interest of the 18- to 34-year-old males coveted by traditional sports who may be seeking alternatives to major league sports with which they grew up.

INCREASED INTEREST IN WOMEN'S SPORTS. An increase in interest of women's sports has led to new opportunities in sports marketing. Changes in collegiate sports and the introduction of professional women's sports leagues in the United States have fueled the growth. At the collegiate level, passage of Title IX to the Educational Amendments of 1972 has given women more opportunities to participate in intercollegiate sports. Institutions must provide participation opportunities that are proportional to student enrollments. Also, institutions must provide equivalent practice facilities, equipment, and support services for men and women's athletic programs.[26] The growth in popularity of women's collegiate sports has both benefited from and contributed to the growth of sports media. Niche cable networks like ESPNU and CSTV (CBS College Sports Network) have increased the exposure of women's sports through their programming. Basketball, softball, and volleyball are among the NCAA women's sports that have enjoyed a higher profile in recent years.

At the professional level, the birth and growth of the Women's National Basketball Association (WNBA) helped propel women's sports to high levels of interest. On the international stage, women's events are among the most popular in the Olympics. Women's figure skating, gymnastics, and swimming consistently rank among the events with the largest TV audiences in the United States.

INCREASED INTEREST IN PERSONAL FITNESS. Sports participation has been positively impacted by an increased interest in personal fitness as part of an overall healthy lifestyle. Makers of sporting goods and apparel used in fitness activities have benefited from consumers' desires to improve cardiovascular health and enhance their physical appearance. More than 50 million Americans belong to one of the more than 29,000 health clubs nationwide.[27] Another personal fitness activity experiencing significant growth is running. In 2010 there were more than 13 million road race finishers in the United States, a 73% increase over 2000.[28] Thus, it is reasonable to assume that fitness service providers such as health clubs, marketers of home exercise equipment such as treadmills and stationary bicycles, and athletic apparel and footwear marketers will continue to experience strong demand for their products in the foreseeable future.

A Framework for Creating Customer-Centered Experiences

Marketing contributes to an organization by being a catalyst for creating customer value, building and maintaining relationships with various stakeholders, and linking the firm with the external environment. However, structure is needed to guide marketing efforts in order to achieve dual goals of satisfying customers and meeting organizational needs. The approach to sports marketing taken in this book is based on collaboration between the authors and the industry experts, such as Jeff Gregor, highlighted in each chapter.[29] The "5P" framework shown in Figure 1.5 focuses the marketing function on five activities:

1. Positioning – Understanding customers
2. Platform – Responding to customers
3. Promotion – Engaging customers
4. Profits – Satisfying customers
5. People – Serving customers

FIGURE 1.5 The 5Ps of Sports Entertainment Marketing

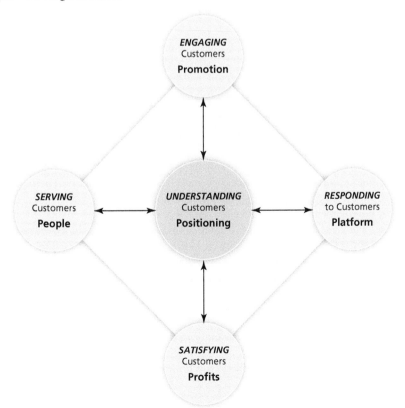

Before discussing the "5P" framework, it is helpful to understand the difference between marketing strategies and marketing tactics. **Strategies** are managerial decisions that affect the organization as a whole, including the marketing of products and services. They tend to be long-term. **Tactics** are decisions made in support of a firm's strategies; they transform plans into actions. They are short-term and relate to the 4Ps of the marketing mix: product, price, place (distribution), and promotion. Sports marketers are charged with putting strategies into action by creating tactics that when executed as planned contribute to successful strategy implementation.

Positioning

The term "customer-centered" is more than business-speak. The marketing function must be coordinated around an understanding of customers. Any marketing efforts that fail to have the interests of the customer at the heart of decisions are risky at best and likely doomed to failure. The positioning element of the customer-centered framework entails organizing the firm to understand and serve customers. Positioning decisions are a mix of developing internal standards and leveraging customer and external environment insights to set marketing strategy. Key marketing tasks related to positioning are: 1) establishing values and mission, 2) conducting market analysis, 3) setting marketing objectives, and 4) selecting target markets.

VALUES AND MISSION. Marketing strategy must be built on a foundation of an organization's reason for being. In short, a manager must be able to answer the question "why do we exist?" An organization's values and mission provide valuable answers to that question. Values are attributes or characteristics held by an organization and often matter to its stakeholders, including employees, customers, and local communities. Values a sports team might hold include excellence on the field of play, family-friendly, educational advocates for youth, and improving quality of life in the community. The **mission** is a statement of what an organization does (line of business or benefits provided), who it serves (target market), and its goals. A well-defined mission is the starting point for formulating marketing strategy. Some mission statements are wordy and contain all of these elements; other statements are more broad and to the point. For example, Reebok's mission simply says "to always challenge and lead through creativity."[30] Values and mission orient a firm to what it should be doing in both the short and long run.

MARKET ANALYSIS. An important strategic activity performed by marketing managers is conducting a **market analysis**, which is a review of occurrences and trends both inside and outside the organization. Components of a market analysis are covered in-depth in Chapter 3. A market analysis is not a strategic decision in itself, but the insight obtained provides valuable information for developing strategies that guide marketing activity.

MARKETING OBJECTIVES. If strategic marketing is like a map, then objectives represent the destination points on the map. **Marketing objectives** are stated outcomes that the marketing function pursues to contribute toward meeting the organization's mission. Once it is determined what needs to be accomplished through marketing (i.e., the objectives), the task of developing tactics becomes easier. If a firm has an organization-wide objective of increasing net profit by 10%, then the marketing area will be expected to orchestrate plans that will help hit the target. The challenge facing marketers is to create tactical plans utilizing product, price, distribution, and marketing communications to achieve the objective.

Marketing objectives are not always restatements of organization objectives such as the net profit, but they should always make at least an indirect contribution toward the firm's overall objectives. A college football bowl game might have a marketing objective of increasing sponsorship revenue by $100,000. Such an outcome is marketing-specific, but if the sponsorship revenue objective is met it would represent a contribution of marketing activity to the bowl's total revenues and, ultimately, its financial health.

TARGET MARKET SELECTION. Not all customers in the population want a particular good or service. Also, marketing resources tend to be limited, so the marketing manager must make the best use of what is available. Thus, the group or groups of customers most likely to use the product must be identified. This group is called the **target market**. Properly identifying a target market or multiple target markets is essential. Errors in determining the size or characteristics of a target market can lead to performance below expectations, or even failure. Creation of a **marketing mix** (the marketing decisions of product, price, place, and promotion) cannot be undertaken until it is understood *who* the customer is. Segmenting customer markets for targeting purposes is the focus of Chapter 4.

Platform

Understanding customers is the starting point for customer-centered sports marketing because it is the foundation for making decisions about how to respond to customers through products, services, or experiences. Platform refers to the bundle of benefits developed for customers and includes: 1) brand relationships, 2) product, and 3) place, or distribution.

BRAND RELATIONSHIPS. Just as we have a tendency to prefer associating with people who we like, trust, and share interests with, consumers form relationships with brands in a similar manner. An important marketing strategy that impacts customers' brand relationships is brand position. A brand position refers to how customers perceive a brand. The position is based on a point of differentiation a brand possesses among competitors—how is the brand different, better, or superior to competitors? Although positioning is customer-based in that it resides in customer minds, marketers can influence brand position by the way a brand creates value (greater benefits offered or fewer sacrifices required). Thus, defining a brand position is important because subsequent marketing decisions (platform, promotion, people, and profits) should be made so that they reinforce the brand's position. Brand management decisions, including options for staking a brand position, are covered in Chapter 5.

PRODUCT. Product decisions entail the bundle of benefits a consumer receives in an exchange with a seller. Product is a broad concept used to describe both tangible goods and intangible services or experiences. Describing products in a sports marketing context requires that we expand the term "product" to include leagues, teams, events, individual athletes, sponsorships, licensed merchandise, support products that are needed to execute a sporting event or activity (e.g., electronic timing equipment and ticket distribution), experiential products (e.g., sports academies and fantasy camps), and sporting goods. Figure 1.6 illustrates different categories of the sports marketing product.

A strategic planning perspective requires that marketers continually look to the future for new product ideas. As is the case with any marketing decision, determining viable product ideas for future development requires examination of the external environment to predict what will occur (e.g., changes in customer needs and preferences and competitors'

FIGURE 1.6 The Sports Product

new product strategy). Issues related to managing products and experiences are discussed in Chapters 6 and 7, respectively.

PLACE (DISTRIBUTION). Decisions about the distribution of a sports product are referred to as place decisions. Distribution considerations include making the product available when the target market wants it, where they want it, and how they want it. It also includes the venue where a sporting event occurs. Examples of sports marketing distribution decisions are choice of geographic markets to locate teams or events, day/time to schedule events, choice of media partners to broadcast events, choice of licensees or retail outlets to market logo merchandise, and the amenities that will be offered inside the sports arena.

The development of the Internet has given sports properties additional options for distributing their products. Many leagues and teams have entered the retail business by opening online stores, either by buying and selling merchandise or by contracting with a retailer. The distribution of media content online is another avenue sports properties have for reaching target audiences. The advent of streaming audio came about in part because two Indiana University alumni (one of whom is Dallas Mavericks owner Mark Cuban) wanted to listen to basketball radio broadcasts but lived in Texas and had no way of receiving such broadcasts.[31] Today, high school, collegiate, and professional sporting events can be heard and watched over the Internet.

Promotion

A customer-centered approach to sports marketing requires a fresh take on the promotion element of the traditional marketing mix. It is no longer sufficient to think of communication tactics only in terms of how many people can be reached or persuaded. A long-term orientation to customer relationships also creates a need to use communication tactics that *engage* customers. Customer engagement is an often used (if not overused) marketing mantra, but what does it mean? Various definitions of engage include "to attract and hold the attention of; engross" and "to draw into; involve."[32] Thus, engaging customers is a vital component of a customer-centered framework for sports marketing because it calls for developing communication strategies that can support building and maintaining customer relationships. For example, social media allows fans of the National Hockey League to post photos and comment on posts on the NHL Facebook page. Providing a gathering place for fans online not only fosters brand–consumer engagement, but fan–fan interactions are another means of engaging people with a sports brand.

Marketing communications are the "voice" of the brand. It is unrealistic to expect a product to sell itself solely on the basis of superior quality or performance; such advantages must be communicated to the target market. Also, a focus on customer experiences requires communications to be more customer-driven, as was highlighted in the discussion of how social media is used for engagement. Marketing communications are influential in supporting a brand's position and creating brand image, because many consumers' perceptions about brands are formed through exposure to marketing messages. Marketing communications planning and implementation are the focus of Chapters 8, 9, and 10.

Sponsorship is an element of promotion that differs in significance for sponsors and sports properties. For sponsors, it is a communications strategy used to market through sports to reach and engage audiences, such as the Pepsi sponsorship of the NFL described earlier in the chapter. For sports properties, sponsorships represent an important revenue stream that impacts the financial position of organizations. The Women's National Basketball Association (WNBA) cited growth in the number of corporate partners and a long-term deal with Boost Mobile for jersey sponsorship of ten of the league's twelve teams as indicators of the WNBA's stability.[33] Sponsorship issues for sponsors and sports properties are the focus of Chapter 11.

Profits

The profits element of the sports marketing mix recognizes the importance of price in creating customer value and positively impacting customer satisfaction. However, price is not the sole focus for profitability—a commitment to measuring results from marketing activities is needed to assess how effective strategies and tactics are for enabling an organization to achieve its financial goals. Pricing and measurement of marketing performance are explained in Chapter 12.

PRICE. Price is the monetary cost incurred by the buyer. Setting the price has many implications for marketing strategy. It determines the revenue a firm will receive per unit sold, it influences profits, it influences consumers' perceptions of the product's quality, it influences the number and types of distribution outlets selected, and it may be a key element in promotion messages. Pricing decisions include not only determining selling prices for products, but also consideration of the other part of the profit equation: costs. Controlling costs is an essential element of creating profits.

MEASUREMENT. Profits are managed not only by setting pricing strategy to maximize revenues and control costs; they are also influenced by a commitment to measure marketing performance. An organization cannot achieve its objectives if it does not know where it stands in meeting those objectives. Measurement of marketing activities is needed to assess past performance as well as set future marketing strategy. For example, it is important for a minor league baseball team to understand the effectiveness of Saturday night fireworks promotions in terms of the number of additional tickets sold and related spending from those customers. Tracking performance in this case would enable a comparison of revenue generated with costs incurred to execute the promotion. Such return on investment analysis should be performed whenever possible to understand the relationship between marketing investment and profits and guide decision making for future marketing activities.

People

The four Ps of positioning, platform, promotion, and profits relate to the traditional marketing mix of product, place, promotion, and price, respectively. However, given that the 4P marketing mix model was introduced more than 50 years ago, when the U.S. economy was driven by manufacturing, the importance of a fifth "P" was not recognized: people. The sports industry is not unique in the role that an organization's employees play in creating customer value. Service businesses in general are heavily dependent on the quality of interactions that employees have with customers.

Front-line service employees and others with creative skills and expertise contribute to serving customers and create experiences. Many of these employees of the organization—ticket salespeople, account services representatives, community relations specialists—either serve a customer directly or provide support to employees with immediate contact. In some situations, customers are better served by outsourcing tasks to an outside firm because of their expertise or resource strengths. A foodservice company may be contracted to operate concessions areas or an advertising agency hired to create a campaign to promote season-ticket sales. Managers must weigh whether outsourcing service tasks will result in a better customer experience along with the impact on profits. Managing service quality and decisions of performing marketing tasks in-house versus outsourcing are the focus of Chapter 13.

Another consideration of the people element is preparation of future sports marketing professionals. The sports industry attracts a great deal of interest from college students and others who wish to connect their love of sports to a job with a company, league, team, or event involved with sports. As the sports industry has evolved, positions have developed into specialized responsibilities like ticket sales, sponsorship, facility management, and marketing operations. Future sports marketers can better position themselves to work in sports marketing if they learn about different career opportunities and the skills and training sought of job candidates. The final chapter (Chapter 14) describes several different career paths and steps one can take to gain experience and develop a professional network that can make one an attractive candidate for entry into the sports industry.

We would like to signal the beginning of your study of sports marketing by borrowing baseball's custom for starting a game . . .

PLAY BALL!

Insider Insights Tony Ponturo – Ponturo Management

Q. What are some of the key differences between marketing sports and other types of products or services?

A. First, a sports team or league is a brand and projects its own image to the consumer. Its image primarily is established and grows based on performance on the playing field. Winners are good; losers are bad. The players have a collective and individual image that contributes to the teams' and leagues' reputations. Second, league brands are made up of many team brands, so how do you get all teams, such as the 32 teams of the NFL, on the same page? Third, sports have a high media profile versus other brands and products. Every move can become a front-page story. Finally, strong emotion is aligned with sports, feelings of passion and local/regional pride.

Q. You have been involved in marketing sports as well as other forms of entertainment. How does sports marketing contrast with entertainment marketing?

A. Sports have more of a local or regional appeal. There is a strong connection between sports and geography: "my team," "my city," "my state." Sports have broad appeal across demographic and ethnic groups, while entertainment is more specific, narrower in its appeal. Sponsorship of entertainment typically entails a single sponsor such as for a film or concert tour. Sponsorships of teams/leagues are driven by multiple sponsorships that are often multiyear deals based on category

Ponturo Management Group

Tony Ponturo of Ponturo Management talks about how the marketing of sports is different.

exclusivities. One similarity between sports and entertainment marketing is that situations that create negative PR arise, whether it is a celebrity problem or athlete problem.

Q. What trends or events have shaped sports marketing practices during the years you have been involved with the industry?

A. Many people believe that the 1984 Summer Olympics began the modern age of sports marketing. Since then, several developments have occurred. One trend is use of the playing field for marketing purposes, which has changed the look of sports. Signs on outfield walls in baseball, in the ice surface and on dasher boards in hockey, and on the scorer's table in basketball are examples. Second, sponsorships have evolved in terms of the size of deals and how brands make use of their investments. Sponsorships have become exclusive deals, reaching tens of millions of dollars a year in some cases. Sponsors have become better at integrating their brands into the action. NASCAR is a good example; drivers are now brand spokespeople and hospitality hosts at races. Third, some sports brands have a global reach. In addition to the Olympics, properties like FIFA World Cup, NBA China, World Baseball Classic, and Manchester United have created a global footprint. Fourth, sports consumption is possible 24/7 because of satellite transmission by ESPN and other networks.

Chapter Summary

Sports are now a multibillion-dollar worldwide industry. Not only the industry's size but its uniqueness warrants a separate textbook and course. Sports differ from other goods and services that are in the marketplace in three ways: sports offer an affinity advantage, possess a positioning challenge, and have experience-based relationships between sports and fans.

Marketing's role in sports has grown tremendously during the last forty years. Marketing has been a catalyst for creating customer value within the sports industry. This value can be created in two ways: 1) by identifying ways to increase the benefits received and 2) by reducing the sacrifices and costs required to attend or participate in sports activities. Marketing is influential in building and maintaining relationships with customers. Marketing connects an organization with the external environment. It requires an examination of external factors such as the competition, economy, public policy, sociocultural trends, and technology. From this information, marketing decisions are made in the areas of target markets, positioning, product, price, place or distribution, and promotion.

The sports industry has seen significant changes and is now a core fabric of American culture. During the monopoly era (1900–1950), consumption of sports was primarily through newspapers and radio. As televisions became commonplace in households, sports moved into the television era (1950–1990). Television sports programming exploded. The invention and widespread use of the Internet moved sports into the highlight era (1990–2010). Sports consumption was now available anytime and anywhere the Internet was available. With the rise of social media, sports have now moved into the experience era (2010–today).

A number of factors can be cited as reason for the growth of sports and sports marketing. Some of the factors are business-driven, others are customer-driven. Business-driven factors include a growth of sports media, increased interest in sports sponsorships, desire to build global brands, and inclusion of sports in economic development planning. Customer-driven factors include an increased emphasis on leisure activities, the introduction of new sports, an increased interest in women's sports, and the increased interest in personal fitness.

Marketing of sports and through sports can be visualized through the "5P" framework. Positioning involves understanding customers. The platform is the way sports properties respond to customers. Promotion provides an opportunity for sports to engage customers. Profits not only involve improving revenue and reducing costs, but also satisfying people through the process. The last "P," people, highlights the critical role employees play in the success of sports marketing, both now and in the future.

Review Questions

1. What is the definition of sports marketing, and what two distinct elements make up sports marketing?
2. Describe the three characteristics that distinguish sports marketing from other industries and pose opportunities for sports organizations.
3. What three important roles does marketing play in sports?
4. What two options are available to create value?
5. In strategic marketing planning, what external environmental factors should a marketer consider?
6. Identify and describe the distinct periods, or eras, of the evolution of sports marketing.
7. What are the business-driven and customer-driven factors that have produced a growth in sports and sports marketing?
8. Explain the "5P" framework for sports marketing.

New Terms

Marketing how value is conceived, implemented, and communicated for the benefit of customers, the organization, and other stakeholders.

Sports marketing use of marketing for creating, communicating, delivering, and exchanging sports experiences that have value for customers, clients, partners, and society.

Value judgment of the benefits received from consumption of a product compared to the sacrifices required to acquire the product.

Relationship marketing creating, maintaining, and enhancing long-term relationships with individual customers as well as other stakeholders for mutual benefit.

Strategies long-term managerial decisions that affect an organization as a whole, including the marketing of products and services.

Tactics short-term decisions made in support of a firm's strategies, transforming plans into actions.

Mission statement of what an organization does, who it serves, and its goals.

Market analysis review of occurrences and trends both inside and outside of an organization.

Marketing objectives stated outcomes that the marketing function pursues to contribute toward meeting the organization's mission.

Target market group or groups of customers most likely to use a product.

Marketing mix marketing decisions involving product, price, place (distribution), and promotion.

Discussion and Critical Thinking Exercises

1. In what ways does marketing of a college football team differ from marketing a(n):
   a. automobile?
   b. soft drink?
   c. restaurant?
   d. professional football team?
2. Consumers purchase products because they create value. What are some examples of marketing decisions that a marketer of running shoes can make to increase customer value?
3. In addition to the growth factors discussed in this chapter, what other factors have contributed to the growth of the sports industry? What factors do you see as having the greatest influence on the sports industry in the next five years?
4. Do a brief analysis of the sporting industry in your area. Where are the closest professional sports teams? What college sports exist in your area? What local sports (such as youth baseball, soccer, etc.) exist in your area? Do any of these sports compete with each other for fan participation? If so, what are some of the factors that determine participation and attendance of the sport?
5. Think about your personal consumption of sports. Create a graph that shows what percent of your personal consumption of sports is through television, radio, newspapers, the Internet, and live events. Discuss how important each medium is for your personal consumption of sports.

References

1. "Arthur Blank," *The New Georgia Encyclopedia*, http://www.newgeorgiaencyclopedia.org/nge/Article.jsp?id=h-1908, accessed October 2, 2008; Daniel Kaplan, "Community Focus Wins Over Atlanta," *Sports Business Journal*, January 23, 2006, p. 1; Marc Pollick, "How Owners, Coaches Can Set the Tone for Charitable Giving," *Sports Business Journal*, July 23, 2007, p. 14; "Sports Ambassadors Look on the Bright Side for Coming Year," *Sports Business Journal*, December 24, 2007, p. 46.
2. American Marketing Association, "AMA Definition of Marketing," accessed October 2, 2008, at http://www.marketingpower.com/AboutAMA/Pages/DefinitionofMarketing.aspx. Courtesy of American Marketing Association.
3. "Pepsico, NFL Renew Sponsorship Deal" (2011), September 6, accessed September 19, 2011, at http://espn.go.com/nfl/story/_/id/6935541/pepsico-nfl-renew-long-term-sponsorship-deal.
4. David Broughton (2011), "Increases at Ballpark Retail Space Help MiLB Teams Boost Merchandise Sales 12 Percent," *Sports Business Journal*, May 16, 2010.
5. "Dew Tour Information" (2011), accessed September 23, 2011, at http://www.allisports.com/dew-tour/tour-info.
6. Chris Kaltenbach, "Dolls Collect Nods of Approval," *Baltimore Sun*, July 31, 2001, p. 1F.
7. "Ticket Specials—Denver Outlaws Lacrosse" (2011), accessed September 25, 2011, at http://www.denveroutlaws.com/ticket-specials/.
8. "StubHub | texasrangers.com: Tickets" (2011), accessed September 25, 2011, at http://texas.rangers.mlb.com/ticketing/stubhub.jsp?c_id=tex.
9. Irving Rein, Philip Kotler, and Ben Shields, *The Elusive Fan* (New York: McGraw-Hill, 2006).
10. "Los Angeles 1984 Summer Olympics" (2009), accessed October 5, 2011, at http://www.olympic.org/los-angeles-1984-summer-olympics.
11. "What Is the FSTA" (2011), accessed October 6, 2011, at http://www.fsta.org/what_is_the_fsta.
12. "ESPN Signs 15-Year Deal with SEC" (2008), August 25, accessed May 10, 2011, at http://sports.espn.go.com/ncaa/news/story?id=3553033.
13. "NCAA Signs New 14-Year TV Deal for D1 Men's Basketball" (2010), April 22, accessed May 10, 2011, at http://www.ncaa.org/wps/portal/ncaahome?WCM_GLOBAL_CONTEXT=/ncaa/NCAA/NCAA+News/NCAA+News+Online/2010/Association-wide/NCAA+signs+new+14year+TV+deal+for+DI+mens+basketball_NCAANews_04_22_10.

14. Michael Hiestand, "Texas Longhorn Network Sparks Debate in College Athletics" (2011), August 12, accessed September 26, 2011, at http://www.usatoday.com/sports/college/football/big12/2011-08-11-texas-longhorn-network-debate_n.htm.

15. Michael C. Keith, *The Radio Station*, 7th edition (Burlington, MA: Focal Press, 2007), 98.

16. Emily Witt, "Bill Simmons Gets Served" (2011), May 11, accessed September 25, 2011, at http://www.observer.com/2011/media/bill-simmons-gets-served.

17. International Events Group (2011), accessed May 9, 2011, at http://sponsorship.com/Resources/Sponsorship-Spending.aspx.

18. "Sponsorship" (2011), accessed September 26, 2011, at http://www.olympic.org/sponsorship.

19. Ashley Loose (2011), "Upcoming Super Bowl Economic Boost Expected for Valley," November 4, accessed March 23, 2012 at http://www.examiner.com/news-in-phoenix/upcoming-super-bowl-economic-boost-expected-for-valley.

20. "The Los Angeles Sports Council" (2011), accessed September 26, 2011, at http://www.lasports.org/.

21. "Annual Sports Council Events" (2011), accessed September 26, 2011, at http://savannah-visit.com/events/sports/annual-sport-council-events.

22. G. E. Miller, "The U.S. Is the Most Overworked Developed Nation in the World—When Do We Draw the Line?" (2010), October 12, accessed September 28, 2011, at http://20somethingfinance.com/american-hours-worked-productivity-vacation/.

23. EXPN.com, http://expn.go.com/, February 25, 2002.

24. Sal Ruibal, "X Games vs. Olympics," *USA Today*, January 17, 2002, p. 1C.

25. Jeff Fox, "UFC Rio Bombs at the Box Office" (2011), September 3, accessed September 28, 2011, at http://mma-manifesto.com/ufc-ppv-data/ppv-main/ufc-rio-bombs-at-the-box-office.html.

26. Mary Curtis and Christine H.B. Grant (2006), "About Title IX," accessed March 23, 2012 at http://bailiwick.lib.uiowa.edu/ge/aboutRE.html.

27. "Industry Research" (2010), accessed September 28, 2011, at http://www.ihrsa.org/industry-research/.

28. Running USA (2011), "2010 Annual Report/Moving Forward," accessed September 28, 2011, at http://www.runningusa.org/sites/default/files/articles/Running%20USA%20Annual%20Report%202010_web.pdf.

29. Jeff Gregor, Chief Marketing Officer at Turner Broadcasting, shared the 5P model with the authors and along with the other industry experts interviewed provided direction for developing the framework further.

30. "Frequently Asked Questions" (n.d.), accessed May 9, 2011, at http://corporate.reebok.com/en/about_reebok/faq_section/general_questions/default.asp.

31. Steve Kaelble, "A Thing for Basketball Bad Boys?" *Indiana Business Magazine*, 44 (March), 2000, 9.

32. *American Heritage Dictionary* (Boston, MA: Houghton-Mifflin, 2009).

33. John Lombardo, "WNBA Metrics 'Pointing in the Right Direction'" (2011), *Sports Business Journal*, September 12, 7.

2 Examining Sports Entertainment Consumption

Learning Objectives

By the end of this chapter you should be able to:

1. Differentiate between utilitarian and hedonic consumption motives
2. Describe the different types of sports consumption motives
3. Discuss the characteristics and implications of low and high involvement sports fan segments
4. Describe the factors and strategies that influence fan relationships with sports brands
5. Contrast the characteristics and benefits of indirect and direct sports consumption
6. Describe the variables that affect an individual's decision to attend a sports event

Connecting individuals to a sport at a young age can create a fan for life.

A Fan for Life . . . and Beyond

Richard Desrosiers of Exeter, New Hampshire, became a Pittsburgh Steelers fan in his youth. He followed his favorite team from a distance, living in northern New England his entire life. Nearly every part of Desrosiers's life reflected his love of the Steelers. His wife estimated that 95% of his wardrobe was made up of Steelers apparel. Even the family dog was part of Desrosiers's identification with the team, aptly named Steeler. Despite his nearly life-long affinity for the Steelers, Richard Desrosiers had never attended a game. That fact changed when Desrosiers went to Pittsburgh's final home game of the 2007 season. Unfortunately, Desrosiers was unable to enjoy the game as he was carried into the stadium in a miniature urn, taken by his grieving widow. Richard Desrosiers had died of brain cancer eight months earlier.

Kathleeen Desrosiers said that her husband had two wishes: to have the Pittsburgh Steelers logo carved into his headstone and to take him to Heinz Field, home of the Steelers. Mrs. Desrosiers's trip to the Steelers game ensured that both of her husband's wishes were fulfilled. Mr. Desrosiers was cremated wearing a Steelers hat, shirt, and pants. At his funeral, floral arrangements with gold, black, and white roses and family members wearing Steelers jerseys were additional reminders of the passion Richard Desrosiers held for the Pittsburgh Steelers. His life may have ended, but Desrosiers would always be remembered for his relationship with the Steelers.

Insider Expert Chris Eames – ESPN

Chris Eames is vice president for ESPN Customer Marketing and Sales. Eames opened the Atlanta-based sales office and oversees one of the multimedia sales teams responsible for national advertising sales across the spectrum of ESPN media assets for Southeast-based clients and agencies.

Eames joined ESPN from Turner Broadcasting, where he was responsible for creating, developing, and executing key client sponsorships, strategic alliances, and marketing partnerships for the sports and entertainment sales divisions during his fifteen years with the company. While at Turner he also handled sports sponsorship and integrated sales, and ran new media sales, where he was responsible for leading a division of digital, wireless, and branded entertainment applications. Prior to that, Eames held positions with a variety of organizations including National Promotion Services, US Communications, and the American Cancer Society. Academically, Eames graduated with honors from Emory University with a bachelor of arts degree in political science and a bachelor of science degree in economics.

Chris Eames, Vice-President ESPN Customer Marketing and Sales

The pain and suffering experienced by Richard Desrosiers in the final months of his life were soothed by his unwavering connection with the Pittsburgh Steelers. In the last days of his life, Desrosiers was so weak he could not speak. When his wife brought a large image of Steelers quarterback Ben Roethlisberger into his hospital room, Desrosiers mustered the energy to open his eyes, smile at his wife, and give her a thumbs-up signal. His love of the Steelers was healthy, even when he was not. Richard Desrosiers's connection with the Pittsburgh Steelers was probably best summarized by Amy Litterini, a hospital counselor and fellow Steelers fan who met Desrosiers while he was being treated for his illness. "Cancer took everything else from this man—he lost the ability to walk, work, concentrate and talk—but he still had the Steelers. In his final days, he had his wife, his family and the Steelers. The lesson he taught me was even in the lowest of lows, in the darkest period of life, you can still have joy through a simple pleasure."[1]

Introduction

A longstanding and passionate connection with a sports team like the one Richard Desrosiers had with the Pittsburgh Steelers is not unusual. He was a sports marketer's dream fan—his identity was heavily influenced by his affinity for the Steelers. Many sports teams and performers have fans that have similarly intense relationships with them. Sports brands evoke emotions and feelings that brands in other industries can only wish they could create among their customers!

Have you ever seen anyone get as excited about the launch of a new soft drink as fans of the New York Jets get on draft day when their team's first draft pick is announced? It is commonplace to see people wearing T-shirts and caps bearing logos of sports brands, but do you see people wearing apparel with logos of their favorite brand of paper towels or socks? Why do more than 3 million people follow the NBA on Twitter, but they do not engage in similar behaviors to connect with their favorite brand of jeans or auto insurance?

Sports entertainment brands possess a unique advantage over brands outside of the category: the ability to stoke emotional responses to create meaningful relationships. The challenge for sports marketers is to understand how these relationships can be cultivated and develop strategies to tap into emotions evoked by sports brands. While emotional bonds between a fan and an athlete or team are powerful connectors, not all consumers will have that type of relationship with a sports brand. Yet, they may be motivated to consume by being attracted to the brand in other ways, such as through the experience delivered at live sporting events or memories created from socializing with family, friends, or other fans through sports.

A main marketing objective for any business is attracting and retaining customers. Sports entertainment properties are not exempt from this challenge. It is essential for profitability and growth. While sports brands often make an emotional connection with their followers that is not found with other types of goods or services, they still must compete for a share of consumers' time and discretionary income. In addition to other sports properties that vie to win over often overlapping target markets, a wide range of entertainment options exist that are obstacles to gaining customers. A family considering attending a minor league baseball game may find itself weighing that option against activities like going to a water park, taking in a movie, or attending an arts festival. The broad positioning of sports as entertainment is a double-edged sword: it expands the potential market for customers, but at the same time increases the number of competitors eager to meet customers' needs.

In order to win over the entertainment-seeking consumer, it is crucial that sports marketers have an understanding of the motives for consuming sports, the factors instrumental in developing an identification with a particular team or athlete, and the variables influencing one's decision to attend a sporting event. Equipped with these insights, marketers can devise marketing strategies that appeal to their target markets.

Unfortunately, the mindset of "If you build it, they will come" is applicable to very few sports properties. Some brands have legions of fans and have little difficulty attracting them to buy event tickets, but most sports properties can only dream of being in that situation. Instead, the challenge is to increase revenues in the face of intense competition from other sports and entertainment options. Even the most successful sports brands must monitor consumer behavior to ensure they understand the reasons for their fans' connection with their brand.

This chapter examines consumer behavior in the context of sports entertainment and how sports marketers respond to consumers' needs. First, a theory-based perspective on consumption motives is presented. Second, the concept of consumption motives is applied to sports—what reasons do people have for becoming sports fans or attending sporting events? Third, a classification of sports fan types, or segments based on consumption behavior, is discussed. Fourth, connection points at which people are influenced to become a fan are identified. Fifth, a framework for explaining sporting event attendance decisions is reviewed.

Understanding Consumption Motives

Before considering strategies and tactics to influence consumers' thoughts, attitudes, or behaviors toward a sports brand, it is necessary to consider *why* people would choose to have a relationship with a brand. Consumption motives can be classified into two categories: utilitarian and hedonic (see Figure 2.1). **Utilitarian consumption motives** are based on a consumer's desire to achieve some functional benefit from using a good or service. Examples of utilitarian consumption motives are purchasing a microwave oven to cook food and taking clothes to a dry cleaner to be cleaned and pressed. In contrast, **hedonic consumption motives** arise from a desire to have a sensory experience that elicits pleasure, fun, or excitement.[2] Of course, sports entertainment falls into the category of purchases influenced by hedonic motives. While a sporting event itself can fulfill consumers' desires to experience excitement or enjoyment, additional experiential elements such as music, contests, and giveaways are often integrated into an event to add to the experiential benefits enjoyed by consuming sports.

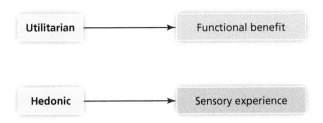

FIGURE 2.1
Consumption Motives

Consumer choice to make discretionary purchases can pit utilitarian and hedonic motives against one another. Purchases influenced by hedonic motives may be considered to be more of an indulgence than utilitarian goods that possess more functional benefits.[3] Thus, if a consumer is forced to decide between buying tickets to a Jacksonville Jaguars game and buying new clothes, one may weigh the experiential benefits derived from attending an NFL game with the benefits of adding new items to his or her wardrobe. In an evaluation of consuming sports entertainment versus a purchase of a utilitarian good providing functional benefits, a rational view would suggest that the utilitarian alternative would win every time. We know that is not the case! Why? The strong feelings or emotions that sports brands elicit in many people influence buying decisions. Choosing to consume hedonic services can be rationalized in many ways. A person debating whether to buy tickets to attend a San Antonio Spurs game might justify the decision with statements such as "I need to escape from the daily grind," "I deserve something special for myself," or "We should support the local team." Hedonic consumption may not be carried out just to satisfy simple desires, but rather they are rationalized by identifying benefits that hold greater value than merely feeling pleasure.

Understanding the distinction between utilitarian and hedonic consumption motives is essential for sports marketers. Choice of market segments to target, brand positioning, elements of event production, creation of advertising and other communications, and facility design all should resonate with the reasons why people would be compelled to consume a particular sports brand.

Sports Consumption Motives

A body of research compiled over the span of five decades suggests different explanations for the motives of sports consumption. A compilation of the research into behaviors of sports fans reveals eight motives.[4] The impact of these eight motives varies among consumers. Some motives may have no relevance while others are particularly salient in the decision to consume sports. As illustrated in Figure 2.2, the eight influences can be grouped into social, psychological, and personal motives.

Social Motives

Sports are a powerful force for bringing people together. *Family* in particular is a social unit that bonds around sporting events, whether it be attending live events or watching on television. Gatherings of extended families that span two or three generations are not uncommon. Traditions develop in which families attend certain events regularly, such as being season ticket holders for the Green Bay Packers or attending annual events like the Indianapolis 500. New fans are introduced to a sport through the role sports have in family traditions.

Sports attract interest through another social mechanism, *group affiliation*. People who desire to connect with others that share a passion for a team or performer can achieve that goal by following the team or performer (i.e., become a fan). Like the influence of family as a social force, a need for group affiliation can attract a person to engage in sports consumption as a means of connecting with other people. Joining friends, coworkers, or other people for an outing at a sporting event could attract interest from people who may not have any other motivations to consume sports.

Psychological Motives

Other motives to consume sports arise from internal desires, in particular self-esteem and escape motives. Becoming a sports consumer is a channel for enhancing one's *self-esteem*. The group affiliation one can attain by identifying himself as a fan of a particular team enhances his personal identity and could influence how he is perceived by other people. Also, the success of a team or individual performer is often celebrated by fans ("we" won; "our" championship). This

FIGURE 2.2 Motives for Influencing Sports Consumption

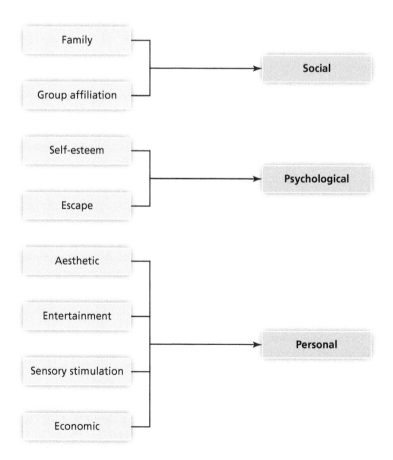

phenomenon, referred to as "basking in reflected glory," enables a person to enjoy the achievements of a team or player as their own.

Escape is another psychological motive that can attract a person to sports. As discussed earlier, hedonic consumption is driven by the desire to experience pleasure. For many people, sports represent a diversion from daily responsibilities and problems. They can attend an event or watch on television and focus on the event instead of other concerns they might face. In a sense, sports are a fantasy experience, allowing a temporary departure from the realities of daily lives.

Personal Motives

A third category of motives for sports consumption corresponds with personal need states. These motives include aesthetic, entertainment, sensory stimulation, and economic. **Aesthetic** motives for sports consumption attract consumers to follow a particular sport, team, or player because of style of play, performance level, or some other observable characteristic. An example would be the interest generated for the game of tennis in general and the ATP Tour specifically by Rafael Nadal. People are attracted to the charisma of Nadal's personality and his intense playing style. Evidence of Rafael Nadal as a trigger for consumers' aesthetic motives can be found in the lower television ratings of tournaments in which Nadal does not play. It is not unusual for those ratings to be 30% lower.[5] Aesthetic motives can pertain to a sport in general, an attraction not inspired by specific teams or individuals. For instance, figure skating and gymnastics are sports that generate a great deal of interest during the Olympics. The grace and precision exhibited by athletes in these sports appeal to audiences even though the sports do not rank high in popularity on an ongoing basis.

Entertainment and sensory stimulation are motives that overlap substantially. Sports can fulfill a general need for *entertainment* much like going to a movie, attending a theatrical performance, or taking in a concert. Marketers create event experiences that appeal to this motive through tactics such as special pregame, in-game, or postgame events, promotions, and giveaways. *Sensory stimulation*, like entertainment motives, is based on hedonic desires for pleasure or arousal. The physical environment in which an event is held and characteristics of a sport such as its pace, intensity, or violent content are all potential triggers for responding to consumers' sensory stimulation motives. Auto racing appeals to the audience's need for sensory stimulation. In NASCAR, drivers race around a track at speeds that approach 200 miles per hour. The high speeds can lead to wrecks or crashes, often involving multiple cars. The prospect of "the big one" is a possibility, if not an expectation, among NASCAR fans watching races at superspeedways such as Daytona International Speedway and Talladega Superspeedway.

Economic consumption motives link sports to gains similar to what an individual might enjoy as a result of gambling. Knowledge about teams and individual players acquired to assist in making sports wagering decisions comes from consuming sport media and sporting events. While the economic motive was initially identified through a link to gambling, another sports consumption context appears to exhibit similar characteristics to the economic motive—fantasy sports. Many fantasy players pay to participate in a league that offers cash or prizes to top performers. Currently, the average amount fantasy football players pay to join leagues is around $75. The stakes of paying to play in a fantasy league and the potential payoff for winning in the form of cash or prizes will usually lead fantasy sports players to consume more of a particular sport. Involvement with a sport can increase if consuming more information or events increase one's knowledge, and thus, their performance abilities in a particular fantasy sport.

Sports Fan Types

A sports fan has been defined as "an enthusiastic devotee" of some particular sports object, whether it be a sport in general, a team, an individual, or an event.[6] The level of fandom a person has with a sports object varies with the involvement he or she has with that object. Involvement is a motivational concept that is comprised of two parts: a cognitive component and an affective component.[7] **Cognitive involvement**, or thinking-based component, pertains to the personal relevance of a sports object's functional performance. **Affective involvement** is the personal relevance a sport object holds based on its ability to allow a person to express his or her ideal self-image to the world.

Based on the definition of a sports fan and the influence of involvement on fan identification with a sports object, it is clear that all fans are not created equal. This recognition is no different than the relationship between customers and a brand for any type of product. Consumers are at different levels of relationship with a sport, team, player, or event. It is useful to understand the various degrees of fan identification based on their level of involvement, as illustrated in Figure 2.3.

FIGURE 2.3
Segmentation of Fans Based on Level of Involvement

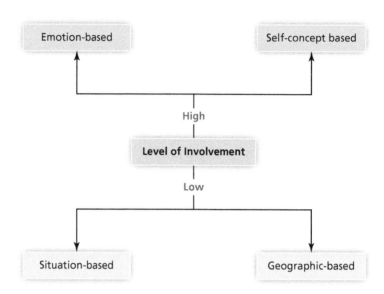

Low-Involvement Fan Segments

Situation-based and geography-based fans have connections with sports that are based on low involvement with that object, team, or sport. They are not avid fans whose lives revolve around that team or sport. The challenge for marketers is how to encourage these individuals to attend sporting events and, more importantly, how to increase that level of involvement.

SITUATION-BASED IDENTIFICATION. Fans with situation-based identification follow a team or individual because of a special event or circumstances that create heightened interest or attention. When a professional sports team advances to postseason competition, it is common for the team's local community to increase their level of interest as the team competes for a championship. The same situation occurs with international competitions such as the FIFA World Cup soccer tournament. People who do not usually follow soccer become interested for a brief period of time as their country competes for the World Cup.

For this segment of fans, sports marketers can benefit from recognizing that some people begin a relationship with their brand because of a special occurrence. The challenge is how to sustain the interest beyond the duration of the event. For example, interest in the U.S. women's soccer team during the 2011 FIFA Women's World Cup tournament led to greater visibility of star players, such as television and endorsement opportunities for goalkeeper Hope Solo. Properties like Women's Professional Soccer (WPS) must figure how to take advantage of the heightened interest in women's soccer before the window of opportunity closes.

GEOGRAPHY-BASED IDENTIFICATION. Geography-based fan identification occurs due to one's proximity to a team, whether it is where they live presently or where they may have lived previously. Supporting a sports team is a way for people to demonstrate their civic pride. Collegiate and professional sports teams tend to bear great significance for the local area in which they are based. Team nicknames often reinforce the idea of geographic identity. Two examples:

- University of Tennessee Volunteers—Tennessee is known as "The Volunteer State"
- Detroit Pistons (NBA)—Recognizes the importance of the automobile industry in Detroit

In addition to being a source of civic pride, the presence of sports teams in a community is considered to add to quality of life by way of offering another entertainment option for local residents. People may become fans of a particular team because of its presence in the community, and that fandom for the team could be parlayed into fandom for a sport in general. When the National Hockey League expanded into Sun Belt markets like Tampa, Miami, and Phoenix, it sought to create new hockey fans in those markets. One route to achieving that aim was to develop local fan followings in each expansion market. Interest in the local team could evolve into interest in the NHL.

A marketing implication of the geography-based fan segment is that community involvement and engagement should be a part of a sport organization's business model. Two ways in which this community interaction is evident are strategic philanthropy and corporate sponsorship. Virtually all professional sports franchises have a community relations department and possibly a charitable foundation, too. The charge of these organizational units is to ensure a team has a visible presence in the community, supporting worthy causes such as education, children's programs, and community nonprofit agencies. For example, the Milwaukee Brewers connect with various groups in their market through initiatives such as an annual blood drive, a front office job shadowing program for middle school girls, and Community Achiever awards.[8] Although the Brewers have been in Milwaukee since 1970, demonstrating commitment to the local community is a priority to develop and strengthen relationships with people who have geography-based identification with the team.

Corporate sponsorship is another avenue for attracting fans with geographic-based identification by forming partnerships with key businesses in the community. Businesses can enjoy image benefits by sponsoring local teams, and having major local businesses as corporate partners can enhance the credibility of the sports organization in the eyes of local residents. The Memphis Grizzlies of the NBA used sponsorship to relate to geographic-based fans. When the franchise was looking to relocate from Vancouver, a new arena was a key piece in the deal to attract the team. The arena received a boost when FedEx Corporation, a global company based in Memphis, obtained the naming rights for the new arena. The FedEx Forum and the Memphis Grizzlies gave the city of Memphis a presence as a professional sports city it had longed to achieve.

High-Involvement Fan Segments

In contrast to situation-based and geographic-based fan segments, fans with high involvement have a more enduring identification with a sports object. Such a relationship is not time or situation dependent, not based on success on the field of play, nor does it require the presence of a geographic connection. High-involvement fans may have situation-based or geographic-based identification initially, but over time their connection can escalate into a more significant relationship. Two segments of highly involved fans are based on: 1) emotion and 2) self-concept.

EMOTION-BASED IDENTIFICATION. The emotion-based segment of fans is those persons that identify with a team, win or lose. They are less likely than situation-based or geography-based fans to stop being a fan of a team or reduce their consumption in terms of attending games or watching games on television if changes occur in performance or personnel. Also, emotion-based fans are distinguished from low-involvement fans in that their identification with a sports object represents a part of their self-concept. While being a fan of a particular team plays a minor role (or no role at all) in defining one's identity for low-involvement fans, it is more important for fans with emotion-based identification to let other people know about their relationship with a team or player. Two ways fans express their relationship are through consumption of officially licensed products bearing brand marks and through social media affiliations. The story at the beginning of the chapter of Richard Desrosiers and his extensive Pittsburgh Steelers wardrobe illustrates how devoted fans communicate their identification with a team through consumption of licensed apparel and products.

Emotion-based fans have a strong identification with their team, which often results in outward expression.

A more recent channel for devoted fans to exhibit and maintain a deeper connection with a sports object is through social media affiliation. Social networking websites allow fans to form communities as well as connect with the object of their identification. Devoted fans of the University of Southern California football team can join the USC Trojans fan page on Facebook as well as follow USC athletics and head football coach Lane Kiffin on Twitter.

The passion and intense interest that are characteristics of the emotion-based fan segment create potential for sustaining and enhancing relationships through marketing. This segment of fans represents potential to become ticket buyers, licensed product purchasers, buyers of premium online content, and patrons of nongame experiences such as team fan conventions, behind-the-scenes tours, and meetings with players, coaches, or other team officials. For example, 24/7 Sports, an online network of sites devoted to in-depth coverage of approximately fifty college athletic programs and recruiting news, offers high-involvement fans in-depth coverage of their favorite teams for a monthly subscription fee ($9.95). This example illustrates the potential to develop a business model around the desire of fans with emotion-based involvement to access information about their favorite teams.

Also, marketers should look to this segment of fans as prospects for spreading positive word-of-mouth communication for the brand. They can invite their friends to join social networks that support the sports brand. Emotion-based fans are a loyal, dedicated segment that represents a potential long-term revenue stream and promote the sports brand in their personal networks.

SELF-CONCEPT-BASED IDENTIFICATION. A second segment of highly involved fans possesses similar characteristics to fans with emotion-based identification, but they differ in the extent to which being a fan of a particular team or individual is part of their self-concept. Two components of self-concept include: 1) how one perceives himself or herself and 2) perceptions about how others view a person.[9] Sports fandom provides an outlet for people to form desired self-perceptions or influence how other people perceive them. Fans in this segment are even more expressive about their identification with a team or athlete than fans with emotion-based identification. They might attend games with their face painted in team colors or dressed in a way that demonstrates their identification.

The impact of self-concept-based identification can be found among fans of the Oakland Raiders NFL team. A group of fans sit together in a section of the Oakland Coliseum known as "The Black Hole." Many fans in this section look more like characters from a horror movie than attendees of a football game! This group of fans lives their identification beyond game days; they have formed a fan club called the Black Hole. The group's website proclaims, "it is not just a name or a section in the Oakland Coliseum, it is an idea and a way of life."[10]

Marketing to this segment of fans should focus on ways a sports property can be supportive of this group of highly passionate fans. A payoff can be that the image of this segment of fans becomes part of the image of the team brand. A person's experience of attending a sporting event can be enhanced if fans like members of the Black Hole exhibit their team identification in a way that is entertaining or enjoyable to other attendees. A fine line seems to exist between fans with self-concept-based identification adding to the entertainment experience and detracting from it with undesirable behaviors. Encouraging this segment of fans to congregate in a particular area of a venue serves the dual purpose of harnessing their collective passions and distancing them from other attendees who may find their behavior unappealing.

Fan Relationship Connection Points

How does a person come to identify with a sports brand (league, team, player, or event)? What are the connection points that prompt someone to enter into a relationship with a brand, one that can last longer than many personal relationships in his or her life? Several different paths can lead to the creation of fan identification with a sports brand (see Figure 2.4). For each of these relationship connection points, sports marketers can devise strategies for appealing to consumers in an effort to engage them in a relationship.

Star Power

A connection point that is largely under the control of marketers is star power. Star power can be leveraged and promoted in the form of players, coaches, team owner, or facility. Players are

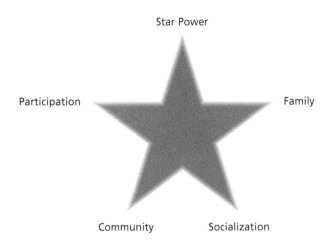

FIGURE 2.4 **Paths to Fan Identification with a Sports Brand**

a frequently leveraged source of star power. Star players are heroes to many fans, are admired by many other people, and at the very least are highly recognized in the community. Players are used in a variety of ways to appeal to prospective fans or strengthen relationships with existing fans. Featuring players in advertising campaigns for teams or events is a long-standing practice that is used to create awareness and interest.

Marketing players' star power is taking on more creative approaches, particularly to appeal to existing fans. Many professional and collegiate teams host "meet the team" events in which fans can get player autographs and have opportunities for one-on-one contact with them. In some cases, such events are perks for season ticket holders. A newer role for players as marketing agents is assisting in ticket sales efforts. Players have made telephone calls to season ticket holders who did not renew tickets, or answered telephones during ticket sales telethons. A more recent trend has been to use players in personal interactions with select customers by personally

This advertisement for the Atlanta Braves features star player Chipper Jones.

delivering tickets prior to the start of a season. The Pittsburgh Penguins of the NHL and the Chicago Bears of the NFL are among many teams that have used star players in this role.

Coaches play a similar role through their inclusion in advertising campaigns and by interacting with fans at team-sponsored events. For example, coaches for teams such as the Washington Redskins (NFL), St. Louis Cardinals (MLB), and Seattle Storm (WNBA) have taken on marketing roles by appearing at fan-oriented gatherings such as draft-day parties and season-ticket holder appreciation events. The impact of a coach's involvement in marketing efforts can be magnified depending on his or her accomplishments and reputation.

Player and coach star power is effective for connecting with fans, but it also presents challenges for team marketers. In professional sports today, player turnover caused by free agency, salary cap restrictions, or player trades means that the possibility of a player remaining with the same team his or her entire career is less than in past generations. In collegiate sports, player star power is even more fleeting, as a player will be part of a team no more than four years, meaning that marketing campaigns featuring players must be updated almost annually to reflect changes in player personnel.

Also, unacceptable player conduct on or off the field of play can put a player in a negative light, and by association, a team that is featuring that player in its marketing efforts. Turnover in coaching staffs can make leveraging coaches' star power a risk. A successful coach could depart for a new opportunity, while a coach whose team does not perform up to expectations could be out of a job suddenly. These concerns do not mean player or coach star power should not be used as a marketing resource, but caution should be exercised in the extent to which they are leveraged given that players and coaches come and go.

Team owners can be a source of star power that attracts fans. Professional sports franchise owners typically are wealthy individuals who have succeeded in other endeavors and are known in the community. In some cases, owners are elevated to star or celebrity status. Perhaps the first owner turned star was George Steinbrenner, who was the face of the New York Yankees from 1973 until 2006. His willingness to give huge contracts to free agents and tendency to meddle in baseball operations made him a polarizing figure in Major League Baseball. Jerry Jones, owner of the Dallas Cowboys, achieved similar status in the NFL. Other owners have cultivated star power in part through embracing technology. Mark Cuban, owner of the Dallas Mavericks NBA team, interacts with fans through his blog (www.blogmaverick.com), e-mail, and Twitter. Similarly, Ted Leonsis, owner of the Washington Capitals of the NHL, communicates via his blog (www.tedstake.com), Twitter, and visiting with fans at games. One reason Cuban and Leonsis have become stars is that their accessibility lets fans know they are customer-focused and are interested in fans' views and, ultimately, their satisfaction.

Facilities are a potential source of star power for sports properties. A venue where a team plays can be promoted for its heritage or importance in the history of the brand, particularly for older facilities. Fenway Park, home of the Boston Red Sox since 1912, and Wrigley Field, home of the Chicago Cubs since 1916, are two examples of facilities that make up part of the star power of those team brands. Alternatively, newer facilities can be touted for modern design and amenities that enhance the fan experience of attending a game. AutoZone Park, opened in 2000 for the Memphis Redbirds Class AAA minor league team, was central in securing the franchise for Memphis. More importantly, AutoZone Park was an important piece in the revitalization of downtown Memphis that included residential and commercial development. Public response to AutoZone Park was so positive that nearly 860,000 people attended Redbird games in the stadium's first season.[11]

Family

A very influential connection point in creating sports fans is the family. This influence should not be surprising given that consumption decisions made by adult members of a household often play a role in shaping brand choices as younger members of a household begin making their own buying decisions. Family influences on which sports teams or athletes a person follows may be even stronger than for other types of consumption decisions because following sports (through live event attendance or indirectly on television) is part of many family gatherings. Parents, especially fathers, impact youths' sports fan behaviors. A study on influences of fan creation for professional sports teams found that fathers were the individuals with the greatest impact on the choice to follow a particular sports team. Other family members trailed only players and coaches as being the next most frequently mentioned person responsible for following a particular team.[12]

Also, the family is an important determinant of sports fan identification because many people develop a relationship with a sports brand at a young age. In the professional sports team identification research mentioned above, more people said they became a fan of a particular sports team between the ages of six and ten than for any other age group. These findings suggest sports marketers should create a dual focus of appealing to families while at the same time reaching children. Special family ticket packages, children's fan clubs, and "kid zone" areas at live events are examples of ways this fan connection point is targeted.

Socialization

The decision to follow a sports team or individual athlete can be inspired by other fans. Sports are a form of social currency. It is a topic of conversation in the workplace, classrooms, and at parties. One way to "get in the game" in these situations is to have interests that are aligned with other people. For example, a salesperson might learn that some of her clients are passionate NASCAR fans. Thus, she starts to follow NASCAR races and drivers in order to have conversation starters when making sales calls. The result can be more engaging visits with customers . . . and a new NASCAR fan! Another consideration about socialization as a fan connection point is that geographic differences exist with regard to the influence of socialization. In the southeast United States, college football and NASCAR are two sports that have a significant socialization influence. In contrast, the northeast United States has a greater concentration of professional sports teams, thus increasing the importance of pro sports leagues as a socialization agent.

Spending time with friends and family is an important factor in the decision to attend sporting events.

Socialization influences on sports fan creation also exist in the form of people desiring to be a part of a group with shared interests. This sense of belonging to a community of fans does not require formal membership and is open to all persons regardless of their demographic characteristics. It enables people to develop a common bond with others, a bond that is based on sharing an affinity for the same sports brand. Social media provides easy access for people to connect with a sports brand via socialization. The San Francisco 49ers has more than 800,000 "Likes" of its Facebook page; people can connect with the team through a single mouse click.

Community

Many people identify with sports teams because they are based in or near their community, including people who would not classify themselves as highly involved with sports. The influence of community as a connection point is based on civic pride as well as sharing in that source of pride with fellow residents. When the city of New Orleans was devastated by Hurricane Katrina in 2005, the New Orleans Saints became a symbol of the city's spirit, something positive for residents to identify with as the city recovered.

The geographic footprint of a sports brand depends on the competition for sports entertainment in a market. When competitors are more numerous or the market is large (New York, for example), the potential of community as a connection point is more concentrated in a smaller geographic area. In contrast, when fewer competitors exist and the market is more dispersed, the geographic distance that a brand can extend to connect with consumers via a community relationship may be greater. For example, the nearest NFL competitor of the New Orleans Saints is nearly 350 miles away, in Houston. Thus, its appeal as the "local" team extends throughout the state of Louisiana and the Gulf Coast region of Mississippi, Alabama, and the Florida panhandle.

Participation

Interest in a sport, and by extension, interest in a particular sports brand, can be cultivated through sport participation. Playing a sport leads to having a greater knowledge of the sport and in many cases, greater interest and appreciation for the sport. Youth sports programs in particular are an important connection point between young people and sports brands. When youth are playing Little League Baseball; their interest in Major League Baseball increases. They may begin to identify with individual MLB players or teams, and youths' team membership could even influence their choice to become fans of a MLB team. Youth players on a team called the Phillies may become fans of the Philadelphia Phillies.

Many professional sports leagues have created or support initiatives that encourage youth participation in their sport. Major League Soccer sponsors various national grassroots soccer programs that encourage youth participation, support development of coaches and referees, and promote formation of competitive soccer clubs.[13] MLS recognizes that creating more interest among youth and their families through playing soccer enables the league to attempt to connect with that audience through the various grassroots programs it supports. Similar efforts to encourage youth sports participation occur at the team level, too.

One way the Nashville Predators seeks to build the market for the NHL and the team is to promote youth participation in ice hockey and inline hockey. The team conducts a program called Get Out and Learn (G.O.A.L.), which allows youth the opportunity to go through several instructional sessions and experience the sport of ice hockey. Equipment is loaned to participants and the program is free. Ideally, G.O.A.L. participants decide to begin playing ice hockey, and their interest in the sport extends to becoming fans of the Predators and the NHL.

The Decision for Sporting Event Consumption

Sports consumption can take the form of direct consumption or indirect consumption. **Direct consumption** of sports is when one makes the decision to attend a live sporting event. It requires expenditure of time and money to acquire tickets, travel to and from the event venue, and watch the event. In contrast, indirect consumption occurs when a sporting event is consumed by someone who is not on-site at the event venue. **Indirect consumption** of sports is done by watching games on television, listening to a broadcast on the radio, viewing it on the Internet, reading stories about it in the newspaper, and connecting with a sports brand through its social networking websites. Indirect consumption is important to a sports property because it means that people who cannot attend or choose not to attend still follow the team and maintain a relationship. Revenues from media companies and advertisers are realized from event broadcasts, adding greater importance to indirect consumption.

Despite the role of indirect sports consumption in attracting and retaining fans as well as creation of revenue streams, direct consumption of sports holds great appeal for attendees and lucrative opportunities for sports marketers. The emotion-laden experience of attending a live sporting event is difficult, if not impossible, to replicate for those persons who are consuming the event indirectly. The intensity of competition on the field of play, interaction with other attendees, pregame and in-game entertainment, and the memories that one can have when special moments occur like a last-second touchdown or walk-off home run are all attractions for individuals to engage in direct sports consumption.

From a business perspective, direct consumption of sports creates avenues to generate revenues beyond ticket sales, such as parking, concessions, and merchandising. Also, attendees of sporting events are often people with whom a deep brand relationship exists. Many people who attend a team's games consume in other ways such as buying licensed apparel and choosing to patronize a team's sponsors because of the sponsors' association with "their team." Event attendees potentially serve as viral marketers, too, telling others in their personal networks about their direct consumption and promoting a team by wearing officially licensed apparel. Another way attendees engage in viral marketing is by identifying themselves as fans on social networking websites, even posting messages about their experiences while at sporting events on sites like Foursquare, a social networking website on which members post information via "check-ins" at places they visit, including sports venues.

Given the potential payoffs from event attendees in the forms of revenues and strengthening the brand, understanding influences on the decision to attend sporting events and devising strategies to respond to those influences is crucial to marketing success for a sports property.

A Framework for Direct Sports Consumption

One explanation for the variables that go into one's decision to attend a sporting event was developed by psychologist Daniel Wann and his colleagues. Consistent with the idea that sporting event attendance requires commitments of time, money, and effort, Wann and colleagues use the Theory of Personal Investment as the basis for a framework to identify the four influences on the decision to attend a sporting event.[14] These factors are identified in Figure 2.5.

- Perceived options
- Team or sport identification
- Personal incentives
- Marketing incentives

FIGURE 2.5 Influences on Direct Sports Consumption

Perceived Options

For any purchase decision, consumers have alternatives to consider in terms of competing choices to fulfill a need as well as an opportunity cost for making a particular choice. The first type of alternative is more obvious—should I buy a Coca-Cola or a Starbucks Java Chip Frappuccino? Buying decisions are often made after considering multiple options that satisfy the same basic need. When the decision is attending a sporting event, the choice might be between two events in direct competition, such as attending a University of Miami football game on a Saturday afternoon or Miami Dolphins game on Sunday afternoon. A consumer may not have enough time or money (or both) to attend both games, even if he or she is a fan of both teams. Or, the decision might be about how to allocate scarce time or money resources when choosing between two sports properties with less overlapping schedules. In this case, the question might be "Should I buy season tickets for the Miami Dolphins or a partial season ticket package for the Miami Marlins?"

A second type of alternative entails the opportunity cost of perceived options in which a consumer evaluates a purchase option against other actions he or she could take instead. For instance, during an economic downturn season ticket holders for a professional sports team might consider not renewing season tickets in order to save money, pay bills, or take a vacation. Variables that represent perceived options for sports consumers include future availability of an option, financial requirements for attendance, and other situational variables that could impact the choice to attend.

FUTURE AVAILABILITY. One consideration a consumer often makes when deciding whether to attend a sporting event is the future availability of that particular event. If an event is one that is held frequently, such as one of the eighty-one regular season home games played by a Major League Baseball team, the decision to attend is easier to postpone than if the event is held less frequently. If a person has the opportunity to attend the Summer Olympic Games, held once every four years in different locations around the world, the influence of future availability might sway his or her decision to attend ("I should go; it's a once in a lifetime opportunity").

The marketing challenges of responding to consumers' evaluation of future availability is greater for sports properties with more events on their schedules. The Tampa Bay Rays strive to attract fans to eighty-one home games during a regular season. One way the Rays deal with this challenge is by offering a variety of events and promotions to appeal to a wide range of audiences. As shown in the advertisement in this section, the Rays offered Joe Maddon (the team's manager) glasses on April 7 to the first 10,000 fans and a Rays alternative jersey T-shirt on April 9. A youth jersey T-shirt was offered on April 10 to the first 10,000 kids 14 and under. On April 8 Tampa Bay offered a super cowbell presented by Chick-fil-A. Properties with a smaller number of events to sell, such as NFL and college football teams, might feel less pressure to sell tickets than their counterparts with more events on their schedules.

FINANCIAL REQUIREMENTS. Sports entertainment is a discretionary expenditure that consumers make, meaning that buying tickets for a sporting event typically occurs after needs such as housing, food, and clothing are met. The nonessential nature of sports entertainment makes those expenditures a prime candidate for reduction or elimination when one's discretionary income decreases. Spending on sports entertainment is more than paying for admission to the event. In some cases, the ability to purchase tickets could be tied to other outlays of money. For example, sales of football season tickets at the University of Alabama require donations to one of seven different levels or clubs in the university's Tide Pride Club Program. Donation levels range from $80 to $1,500 per seat per year, depending on the location of the seat in Bryant-Denny Stadium.[15] A multiple-expenditure commitment such as the one used by the University

The Atlanta Braves offer a variety of promotions to appeal to a wide range of audiences.

of Alabama or a requirement to purchase personal seat licenses (PSLs), a tactic used by many professional sports franchises to raise revenues, adds to the total financial requirements one must make to attend a sporting event. The question is whether the financial outlay required to attend an event is offset by sufficient value to justify making the expenditure.

One effort to quantify the financial requirements of attending certain professional sporting events is the Fan Cost Index developed by Team Marketing Report. The Fan Cost Index (FCI) measures the cost of a typical outing to a sporting event. The result is a dollar amount that is the sum of: [16]

- 2 adult average price tickets
- 2 child average price tickets
- 4 small soft drinks
- 2 small beers
- 4 hot dogs
- 2 programs
- Parking
- 2 adult-size caps

Figure 2.6 shows the highest and lowest FCI figures and the league average for teams in Major League Baseball, the National Basketball Association, the National Football League, and the National Hockey League. A limitation of the FCI is that it is sometimes difficult to compare costs between different markets because of geographic differences in cost of living and the influence of other variables such as quality of team and demand for tickets.

Measuring financial requirements with a method such as the FCI allows team marketers to monitor their pricing relative to the league average. If FCI is below league average, teams can tout that they deliver great value in the form of a total cost. On the other hand, if FCI is above average it could prompt a review of pricing practices across all components of the FCI, or offering special pricing that addresses concerns about the overall cost of attendance. For example, many professional and collegiate teams offer variations of "Family 4 Packs," which bundle a combination of event tickets, concessions, and merchandise for four people at a single price.

FIGURE 2.6 FCI Statistics for Major Sports

Team	Avg. Ticket	Beer	Soft drink	Hot dog	Parking	Program	Cap	FCI
Major League Baseball								
New York Yankees	$72.97	$6.00	$3.00	$3.00	$23.00	$5.00	$25.00	$410.88
League Average	**$26.64**	**$5.92**	**$3.44**	**$3.70**	**$12.40**	**$3.72**	**$15.03**	**$196.09**
Arizona Diamondbacks	$14.31	$4.00	$3.50	$2.75	$10.00	0	$7.00	$114.24
National Football League								
Dallas Cowboys	$159.65	$7.00	$5.00	$5.00	$40.00	$6.00	$7.00	$758.58
League Average	**$74.99**	**$6.80**	**$4.09**	**$4.40**	**$24.13**	**$4.53**	**$15.96**	**$412.64**
Buffalo Bills	$51.24	$7.00	$3.50	$3.50	$25.00	0	$16.00	$303.96
National Basketball Association								
Los Angeles Lakers	$93.25	$7.75	$4.25	$4.75	$15.00	$5.00	$14.99	$479.48
League Average	**$49.47**	**$6.37**	**$3.69**	**$3.97**	**$13.13**	**$3.34**	**$15.45**	**$291.93**
Memphis Grizzlies	$24.11	$7.25	$3.25	$4.75	$10.00	0	$15.00	$182.94
National Hockey League								
Toronto Maple Leafs	$76.15	$5.88	$3.48	$4.14	$17.42	$4.36	$19.16	$411.30
League Average	**$49.66**	**$6.06**	**$3.46**	**$3.64**	**$12.20**	**$2.69**	**$15.75**	**$288.23**
St. Louis Blues	$29.94	$5.25	$3.75	$3.75	$11.00	$1.00	$10.00	$193.26

CONVENIENCE AND COMFORT. Additional variables that must be considered relate to the convenience and comfort of attending a sporting event. These variables are listed in Figure 2.7.

Day and time of events are largely within the control of sports marketers. Event schedules sometimes are dictated by television partners to fit their programming schedules, but in general sports properties have the ability to set a starting time that best meets the needs and preferences of the local market. Event scheduling decisions sometimes allow teams or events to be showcased. For example, some non-Bowl Championship Series (BCS) conferences in the NCAA Bowl Championship Subdivision, such as the Mid-American Conference, Sun Belt Conference, and Western Athletic Conference, will schedule games for a nontraditional day for college football games, such as Tuesdays, Wednesdays, or Fridays. A benefit of this tactic is that these games become prospects for national TV broadcasts, giving the teams involved broader exposure with virtually no competition from other college football games. The opportunity to play on a national stage must be weighed against the fact that the game is not scheduled on a traditional date. Some fans may be unable to attend a weeknight game due to work or family commitments, while other potential attendees could opt to watch the game on TV instead of investing the time to attend the game.

Parking availability may or may not be a variable that a sports property can control. If the venue is owned and operated by a sports property, it has greater ability to determine the number

- Day and time of event
- Parking availability
- Weather
- Driving distance/time to event
- Availability of consumption via indirect means (e.g., TV, radio, or online)

© Robert Crum / Fotolia

**FIGURE 2.7
Convenience and Comfort Factors Affecting Perceived Options**

of parking spaces and location of parking areas near the venue. On the other hand, events or teams that play at a venue that they do not own are largely at the mercy of parking provided by the venue owner and adjacent parking areas. In addition to the convenience aspect of finding parking near a venue, consumers' consideration of parking availability is related to the financial considerations of attending an event, too. Parking fees may be charged, even when the venue is owned and operated by the sports property.

Parking fees could be a flat rate, or parking may be offered as an amenity based on ticket holders' commitment level. Season ticket holders often receive access to free or discounted parking and/or spaces close to venue entrances. In the case of collegiate sports, parking privileges are often extended to persons who make financial contributions to an athletic program. The cost of parking, whether a direct cost in the form of parking fees or an indirect cost in the form of requiring season ticket purchase or financial donations, can deter some potential attendees from taking in a sporting event.

Weather and driving time and distance to an event are two variables beyond the control of sports marketers. Attendance decisions are affected by weather conditions for all types of events, not just outdoor events. A forecast of poor weather conditions could deter potential attendees from traveling to a venue to take in an event, even if it is indoors. Weather, coupled with future availability of an event, could make it easier to postpone attending. Attending a game at Target Field, home of the Minnesota Twins MLB team, could be perceived as a less than desirable entertainment option early in the season. The average high temperature for Minneapolis in the month of April is 58 degrees, with the average low dipping to 37 degrees.[17] Given that one could attend games during the period of May to September each season, games played in the month of April might have less appeal due to the cool temperatures.

Driving time and distance to an event cannot be controlled by sports properties beyond the decision about where to locate a venue. A trend among new stadiums built since the early 1990s has been more venues built in downtown areas of a city. This decision reflects an effort to appeal to working professionals who spend their days in a city's central business district. Also, downtown sports venues appeal to leisure-seeking consumers by creation of commercial developments that include not only a sports venue but dining, shopping, and other entertainment options, too.

If location cannot be managed and a sports property is relegated to making an existing venue as convenient to access as possible, collaboration with public transportation providers can lead to offering affordable, convenient access to sporting events. The Chicago Transit Authority offers a route that runs from downtown Chicago to the United Center for people attending Chicago Bulls or Chicago Blackhawks games.[18] In addition to the convenience public transportation might provide to someone attending a sporting event, the round trip bus fare costs less than $5, compared to the $20–$35 fee to park near the United Center.[19] While driving time and distance might be an uncontrollable variable, it should not be ignored. Transportation-related issues perceived as an inconvenience should be transformed to a benefit in attending a sporting event.

Another consideration for which sports marketers have some control is the availability of consuming the event indirectly. Perhaps the closest substitute for attending a sporting event is watching it on television. The availability to broadcast both the aural and visual channels gives viewers an experience that bears some similarity to watching the game in person. Technological developments now make possible a similar experience via the Internet. ESPN makes available live broadcasts of more than 3,500 collegiate sporting events a year on ESPN3.[20]

The longest-running form of indirect consumption of sports is radio. The history of radio broadcasts of sporting events is traced back to 1921. In that year, radio station KDKA in Pittsburgh broadcast a live account of a heavyweight championship boxing match between Jack Dempsey and Georges Carpentier. Later that same year, KDKA began broadcasting Pittsburgh Pirates baseball games.[21] Today, radio has evolved to not only include live broadcasts of sporting events on AM or FM radio (also called terrestrial radio), but collegiate and professional sports properties have extended their reach through audio streaming of games on the Internet and live event broadcasts and dedicated content channels on satellite radio provider Sirius XM.

© iofoto / Shutterstock

Watching sports on television is a form of indirect consumption.

Indirect consumption creates a dilemma for sports properties. On one hand, broadcasts of games and events on television or online allow people who are interested in following a team but are unable to attend to experience the event through a broadcast. Making games available for consumption via television can create exposure for a team, generate interest in attending games, and be used as a promotional vehicle for encouraging future attendance.

The Nashville Predators National Hockey League franchise broadcasts approximately 70% of its home games each season in addition to airing most of its out-of-town games. Why? In a nontraditional hockey market such as Nashville, the decision to broadcast home games allows the team to give viewers a glimpse of the experience of attending a Predators game. Production of a television broadcast often features information about attending games and opportunities for viewers to place ticket orders for future games during the broadcast. If a franchise is dependent on acquiring new customers (i.e., fans) to build its base of ticket buyers, including many with little familiarity with the sport or team, a game broadcast is a form of product sampling.

On the other hand, the benefits of making sporting events available via indirect consumption must be weighed against opportunity costs. The greatest opportunity cost of enabling consumption of sports through media channels is lost revenues. If a person has the option of attending a game with all of the financial requirements (including ticket, parking, and concessions) or watching the same game on TV without the outlay required to attend, the decision may be to choose the less expensive option and watch on TV. This scenario costs a sports property in terms of reduced revenues in ticket sales and other revenues typically generated when attending sporting events.

One step sports properties have taken to minimize this negative outcome associated with allowing indirect consumption of their events is to impose restrictions on television broadcasts. The most notable example comes from the National Football League. Since 1973, the NFL has had a policy known as the blackout rule. The NFL's policy is that a game cannot be broadcast within a 50-mile radius in a home team's local market if all tickets for a game are not sold within 72 hours of kickoff time for a given game.[22] The intent is to encourage people who want to watch a game to buy a ticket and attend. The NFL has applied the blackout rule consistently over the years, even in the face of occasional criticism that it should be eased during difficult economic conditions.

A middle ground for allowing indirect consumption may be found in an effort to create revenues from televising events or streaming on the Internet. Rather than allow free consumption of events via media broadcasts or denying the opportunity to consume indirectly through policies like a blackout rule, many sports properties offer TV or Internet broadcasts of their events on a fee basis. For example, MLB, NBA, and NHL all offer subscription services on a season or monthly basis that allow fans to watch broadcasts of most games on either a TV or computer. One limitation of these packages is that they usually exclude game broadcasts of the local market team, providing some protection to local franchises from indirect consumption.

Another option for creating revenues through indirect consumption is to package games and other programming as part of a premium content package. Mississippi State University offers such a package called "Maroon to the Max." The package offers audio and video streaming of most sporting events, press conferences, coaches shows, and player interviews.[23] Not only does such an approach potentially generate revenues, it allows fans to strengthen their relationship with a sports property by giving them the ability to consume the brand in multiple ways and at times beyond when games or events occur.

Team Identification

As discussed earlier in the chapter, identification with a sports team or player can be a significant part of a person's identity. Team identification as a factor affecting sporting event attendance is impacted by the extent to which a person views attending games of his or her favorite team is a means of expressing personal identity. A review of several consumer behavior studies found that team identification may be the psychological factor with the greatest impact on sporting event attendance.[24] This conclusion is not surprising; the image of die-hard fans includes persons who regularly attend games regardless of their favorite team's performance.

© Michael Krinke / iStockphoto

A die-hard fan attends even when his team loses.

A prime example of a team whose fans seem to be influenced by sense of self is the Chicago Cubs. The team has not experienced ultimate success in the form of a championship season since 1908, and the cost of an outing to a Cubs game is one of the most expensive in Major League Baseball at more than $300 according to the Fan Cost Index. Also, Wrigley Field is nearly 100 years old and lacks many of the amenities of modern sports venues. Yet, attendance has remained at near-capacity levels as the Cubs draw more than 3,000,000 visitors each season.[25]

Team identification has a strong influence on sporting event attendance. Encouraging a community of highly identified fans to attend games further strengthens their relationship with the team and gives them an outlet for expressing their connection. In some cases, a group of fans exhibiting a high level of team identification become a branded extension of the team. Such is the case at Duke University and with the NFL's Cleveland Browns. Duke's men's basketball games are known for a passionate student section called the "Cameron Crazies," a nickname that plays on the venue name, Cameron Indoor Arena. In Cleveland, the "Dawg Pound" is a section located in one of the end zones that is known for enthusiastic fans, some of whom wear dog noses or other items that let them express their "membership" in the Dawg Pound.

It is important to note that in many cases these sections of highly identified fans congregate in "low rent" areas of a venue such as the bleachers or upper-level seating. While this suggests these fans may not represent a lucrative segment in terms of the dollar amount they spend on tickets, their value as a marketing asset should not be overlooked. They represent loyal customers who will tend to engage in positive word-of-mouth communication to promote the team. Also, their presence can add value to the overall entertainment experience of attending a sporting event. Thus, sports marketers should consider how they can support this segment as long as their behavior does not detract from the experience of other event attendees.

Personal Incentives

Another factor in the decision to attend a sporting event pertains to personal considerations that include one's interest in the sport, the desire to engage in social interaction, and the influence of value-added elements of the event experience. Interest in the sport, referred to by Wann and colleagues as task incentives, can be defined as elements or attributes of a sport that deliver intrinsic benefits to persons attending a sporting event who find the elements or attributes appealing. Such influences would include aggression and collisions in football, speed shown by players in a tennis match, and the strategic moves made by managers in a baseball game. Notice that attracting spectators through task incentives does not require that they be fans of a particular team. Anyone who is attracted to certain characteristics of a sport could be a ticket-buying prospect for a sports property.

Socially based incentives for attending a sporting event are based on one's desire to interact with family, friends, or fellow attendees. These interactions enable attendees to claim membership in a particular group or community. This sense of belongingness gives people a feeling of "fitting in" and sharing a common bond with fellow attendees. This element of live sporting event attendance is one that is difficult, if not impossible, to replicate through indirect consumption of sports via television.

Two areas in which social interaction drives marketing efforts are group ticket sales and event marketing. Group ticket sales programs promote a sporting event as a place to bring together a large group such as a corporate outing or church group. The purpose of the group outing is often to promote socializing between group members in a setting that is different from the group's everyday environment. Thus, group sales efforts do not have to be limited to organizations whose members have an interest in a particular sport (such as a MLS team targeting youth soccer leagues). The potential market expands to any group looking for an outlet to promote interaction between its members.

A second strategy for leveraging social influences on sporting event attendance is to design the event experience to appeal to persons who desire socialization with other attendees. The promotion of tailgating at college and professional football games provides this socialization opportunity. Attending football games can be an all-day event as tailgate gatherings often begin several hours before the start of a game. Visiting with friends, spending time with family members, or sharing the excitement of game-day festivities with other attendees can attract people with little interest in a team.

The downside of social interaction as an attendance influence is that it is a relatively weak connection. If people are attending an event because of the social benefits it delivers, the sporting event itself could become secondary to social events. In the case of tailgating before football games, it is not uncommon for some tailgaters to never make it to the game. While they may have enjoyed social benefits from tailgating, a sports property does not realize their full potential as an attendee. Even if someone leaves without attending a game having bought a ticket, potential concessions and merchandise revenue would be lost.

Marketing Incentives

A final factor that influences sporting event attendance is made up of variables that are under the control of sports marketers. In contrast to personal incentives that reside within individuals, sports marketers have the ability to create incentives that can entice consumers to attend sporting events. These marketing incentives are shown in Figure 2.8.

• Marketing communications

• Promotions

• Physical environment

© Sergey Novikov / Fotolia

FIGURE 2.8 Marketing Influences on Sporting Event Attendance

MARKETING COMMUNICATIONS. Marketing communications are the channels used to deliver messages to prospective attendees. Mass media channels such as newspaper, radio, and television can deliver schedule information (date/time/opponent), shape image for a team or event, give a call to action to attend, or support promotional efforts. Marketers increasingly are using social media such as Facebook and Twitter to deliver similar information. The Bowling Green (Kentucky) Hot Rods, a Class A minor league baseball team, has used Facebook to share information about upcoming promotions such as posting photos of T-shirts to be given away and encouraging fans to vote for a nonprofit organization to be the beneficiary of a ticket sales promotion. A key element of the strategy used by the Hot Rods is including links to online ticket purchase in the promotional messages. The use of social media as a marketing communications channel has the dual benefit of making possible immediate consumer response as well as harnessing the power of fans sharing posts that they like with their friends.

The power of marketing communications to drive attendance is debatable. Attendees that attend most or all of a team's games do not have to be persuaded to purchase tickets, and persons who have little familiarity or interest in attending a sporting event are unlikely to be swayed by a single advertisement. But advertising's effects tend to be cumulative, meaning that repetition of ads or the appearance of ads in multiple channels (for example, an ad campaign that promotes event ticket sales through newspaper, radio, television, and billboards) can move a consumer through the stages of awareness, interest, desire, and ultimately to attendance. Advertising can also build the team's brand and create a stronger image in the minds of consumers. This may lead to a more positive view of the sports team and a greater desire to attend.

PROMOTIONS. Promotions or incentives can enhance the perceived value of event attendance and influence the decision to attend. The extent to which promotions are used to attract customers will depend on the amount of ticket inventory a sports property must sell. A Major League Baseball team has eighty-one regular season home games, with games often scheduled on consecutive days over a period of anywhere from three to ten days. The high frequency of games creates challenges to sell tickets that an NFL team with only eight regular season home games does not face. The role of promotions becomes more important when there is greater future availability of a sporting event.

Incentives to attract attendance can be price-based, benefit-based, or reward-based (see Figure 2.9). Offering a discount to entice buyers is a long-standing marketing practice in many industries, including sports. Offering price-based incentives when demand is low is used frequently to attract customers. For example, during the 2009–2010 season, the Atlanta Hawks of the National Basketball Association had a special price of $15 for upper-level tickets for Wednesday night games.[26] Whether it is a time of year or a particular day of the week when ticket demand is less, price-based incentives can meet the short-term challenge of selling tickets. Ideally, the long-term effect is that attendees who are drawn in by a price promotion will have a satisfactory experience and return for future events, at full ticket price.

FIGURE 2.9 Types of Incentives to Encourage Attendance

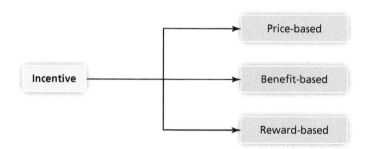

Benefit-based incentives give event attendees added value for the price of admission. Rather than forgoing revenues by offering price-based incentives, use of benefit-based incentives typically involves offering a bundle of benefits for a single price. If consumers perceive the bundled price as a better value than the sum of individual items in the bundle it can be an effective incentive for increasing attendance. Often used bundles include family packs and "all you can eat" seats. In addition to price-based incentives of discounted tickets on Wednesday nights, the Atlanta Hawks target families with a family night package for select weekend games that includes four game tickets and four combo meals for a single price. Another benefit-based incentive used by the Hawks was an all-you-can-eat seats promotion. The promotion gained popularity when the Los Angeles Dodgers created an all-you-can-eat section in the outfield bleachers of Dodger Stadium, which frequently had a high number of empty seats.[27] This promotion has been a popular addition to the marketing strategy of many professional sports teams in the United States.

Sports properties use reward-based incentives to attract customers by offering them something of value in return for their attendance. Giveaways have a long-running tradition in the sports entertainment industry. Minor League and Major League Baseball teams develop a wide variety of promotions with the aim of maintaining customer interest throughout a season that lasts five to six months, with popular giveaways including bobble-head dolls and replica caps. For example, the Reno Aces, a Pacific Coast League AAA minor league baseball team, had eleven different giveaways during the seventy-two home games. In addition to the giveaways, postgame fireworks were held on thirteen dates and special events held on eleven dates.[28] Some of the promotions on the Aces schedule occurred on the same date, giving prospective attendees multiple incentives for taking in an Aces game. Figure 2.10 identifies some of the promotions used by the Reno Aces.

In contrast, NFL teams have far fewer events to sell (usually two preseason and eight regular season games) and thus do not have the challenge of keeping interest over the course of a long season. While challenges to selling ticket inventory exist whether a team has eight games or eighty games, the role of reward-based incentives is relatively minor when there is limited future availability of attending a sporting event. A schedule with fewer events creates scarcity of supply and somewhat of a naturally occurring incentive to make the choice to attend.

PHYSICAL ENVIRONMENT. Consumer evaluation of attending a sporting event can include the physical environment in which the event will be held. The venue or facility hosting a game or event can be designed in a way that it adds value to the consumption experience. A revolution in the role of physical environment in the sports entertainment industry began in the early 1990s.

<u>Giveaways</u>

Fleece blanket presented by Fox Sports Radio 1450AM (April 18–19)
Kids Jerseys presented by Waste Management (June 14)
Collector's Cap (August 1)
Bobblehead (August 15)

<u>Events</u>

Youth baseball weekend (May 2–3)
Spitball gang (May 3)
Breast cancer benefit (May 10)
Family fun fest (July 31)

<u>Fireworks</u>

July 4, Memorial Day, and every Friday night

FIGURE 2.10 Sample of the Promotions Offered by the Reno Aces

As sports stadiums built in the 1960s and 1970s came to the end of their life spans, franchise owners envisioned a new generation of stadiums that were designed with customers in mind. New venues built since the early 1990s have focused on facility design and customer amenities, a departure from the massive steel and concrete multisport stadiums built previously.

Two elements of the physical environment that can influence the attendance decision are aesthetics and spatial layout.[29] Aesthetics are architectural and design considerations such as a venue's external appearance, scoreboard, and overall cleanliness. Architectural features of many new facilities, particularly baseball stadiums, possess characteristics that remind people of baseball stadiums that existed in the earlier days of baseball. Old-style venue architecture creates feelings of nostalgia and thoughts of simpler bygone days. A stadium that exemplifies this trend is PNC Park, home of the Pittsburgh Pirates MLB team. Opened in 2001, PNC Park's external architecture reminds visitors of stadiums from the earlier days of baseball. The stadium's design offers remarkable views of the downtown skyline and the Allegheny River. In addition to the retro architectural design, PNC Park pays homage to two important figures in Pirates history, Roberto Clemente and Willie Stargell, with statues at two of the stadium's entrances.

Alternatively, new facilities can incorporate modern design features that enhance attendees' comfort and convenience. The influence of aesthetics is not limited to venues in large markets or major league teams. The Great Lake Loons, a Class A minor league baseball team located in Midland, Michigan, opened the Dow Diamond in downtown Midland in 2007. The stadium seats 5,500 and features twelve suites, two fireplaces, two outdoor fire pits, a kid's play area, and Wi-Fi Internet access throughout the stadium. It was named best new ballpark of 2007 by *Baseball Digest*.[30]

If architectural features represent the past, scoreboards are an aesthetic feature that brings facilities into the present. Technology advances make today's scoreboards high-definition multimedia entertainment displays, not merely a place to post game information. Replays of game action, music, video, in-game promotions, and audience interaction are additional forms of scoreboard content that add to attendees' multisensory experience.

Spatial layout considerations include ease of entry and exit, spaciousness of concourses and aisles, comfort in the seating area, locations of restrooms, and locations and traffic flow of concessions areas. An advantage newer sports venues possess over older venues is the ability to incorporate desired spatial layout features that were less important or nonexistent when the previous generation of sports venues were built. For example, food service offerings have transformed from rather basic fare to menus with more choices and options for sit-down dining or takeaway to one's seats in the venue.

In addition, venues are positively impacting concessions service through incorporating technology. Increased acceptance of credit cards, both at concessions stands and by vendors serving in the seating areas, has made the process of buying concessions more convenient. Most new venues made allowances for more accessibility and greater convenience in their food service locations when they were built, whereas older venues usually have to adapt to the physical space allocated to food service. Similarly, restroom designs, locations, and facilities in new venues reflect an effort to minimize patron wait times.

Insider Insights Chris Eames – ESPN

ESPN

Chris Eames of ESPN discusses the topic of sports consumption.

Q. What characteristics of sports consumption are unique or different compared with consumption experiences for other products or services?

A. In my experience, sport is advantaged in three significant ways: First, it is almost always consumed live. Second, it has the ability to attract very large audiences in a fragmented world. Third, it engages consumers on a highly passionate level. Immediacy, scale, and engagement are three very powerful marketing attributes that few other properties, if any, can deliver at the same level as sports.

Q. How has the consumption of sports programming and information changed during your career in sports media?

A. Sports used to be a simple proposition, with success measured by attendance and ratings, and to a lesser degree, licensing. Understanding who attended games or watched events on TV was less important than the overall numbers. In today's multimedia 24/7 world, consumption of sports is measured, packaged, and sold across multiple screens around the clock and to highly analyzed and segmented fan bases. Fantasy sports, video games, online video, mobile, and, most recently, the introduction of tablets all fuel the industry by allowing fans access to their favorite sports, teams, and athletes anywhere, at any time. It is exponentially more complicated and more interesting.

Q. Indirect consumption of sporting events is a distribution channel that connects more people with a sport. Or, it may be viewed as a threat to event attendance if watching on TV is seen as an alternative to watching in person. In your opinion, do the benefits of offering fans more opportunities for indirect consumption of sports outweigh the risk of becoming a substitute for attending live events?

A. It's an age-old debate, and although some may argue the jury is still out, I would argue the facts speak for themselves. The reality is that sports fans have an insatiable appetite for sports news and information and will access content whenever and however they can. Interest drives more access and access drives more interest. Sports consumption, therefore, is not a zero-sum game. Indirect consumption and greater access to sports content on multiple screens increases fan bases, which translates into higher attendance. Enhancing the at-game experience and keeping games affordable for families should be the primary focus when addressing attendance challenges.

These elements of the physical environment are important determinants of consumers' evaluations of their experience at a sporting event. The perceived quality of the physical environment, based on perceptions of aesthetics and spatial layout, are related to eliciting an emotional response (excitement) and a cognitive response (satisfaction). In turn, satisfaction with the experience in a sports venue is related to intentions to return for future events.[31] The implications of creating a positive physical environment are significant for sports marketers. Satisfaction judgments in this case have nothing to do with what happens on the field of play. Satisfaction is based on consumers' interaction and experience with the physical environment. A marketing staff cannot control player performance, but they certainly can influence design (or adapt to the design) of the physical space in the venue in which patrons spend their time.

Chapter Summary

Consumption motives can be classified into two categories: utilitarian and hedonic. Utilitarian consumption motives are based on a consumer's desire to achieve some functional benefit from a good or service. Hedonic consumption motives are based on the desire to have a sensory experience that elicits pleasure, fun, or excitement. Sports tend to be consumed from hedonic consumption motives.

Research over the last five decades has identified eight different influences on sports consumption. Social influences include an individual's family and the need for group affiliation. Psychological influences are the desire to enhance one's self-esteem through identifying with a team or sport and the desire to escape from reality or his or her personal situation. Personal motives that influence sports consumption include aesthetics, desire for entertainment, need for sensory stimulation, and economic benefits or enjoyment.

The level of devotion or fandom an individual displays towards a sports object is based on his or her level of involvement. Low-involvement fans tend to have situation-based identification, which is involvement based on a team's or sport's particular situation, or geography-based identification, which is based on a team's or sport's geographic location relative to the sports fan. Fans with high involvement have a more enduring identification with a sports object and are emotion-based or self-concept-based. The emotion-based fan is emotionally tied to a sports object, win or lose. The self-concept-based fan ties his or her self-identity to the sports object.

There are five primary connection points that prompt an individual to enter into a relationship with a sports object. Individuals can be connected through star power, which is a connection through players, coaches, team owner, or the facility. Families, especially fathers, are very influential connection points. Some individuals are connected to a sports object through the opportunity for socialization or because of its geographic location, thus creating a community connection. The last connecting point is through personal participation in playing a sport.

Sports can be consumed directly or indirectly. Direct consumption is the most desirable for a sports property because it involves actually attending a sporting event. Indirect consumption occurs when a sporting event is consumed at a location other than the event's venue, such as on television or the Internet.

A framework for understanding the variables that impact an individual's desire to attend a sports event was developed by Daniel Wann and his colleagues. It is based on the Theory of Personal Investment and involves four primary categories: perceived options, team or sport identification, personal incentives, and marketing incentives. Perceived options include future availability, financial requirements, and convenience and comfort factors. The convenience and comfort factors that consumers consider are day and time of the event, availability of parking, the weather, the distance and time needed to travel to the event, and the availability of consumption through indirect means. Team identification is closely tied with a person's personal identity and self-concept, and thus is an important factor in the decision to attend a sporting event. Personal factors that influence the decision include an individual's interest in the sport itself, the desire to engage in social interaction, and the influence of value-added elements to the event's experience. Marketing can also have an impact on the decision through advertising and marketing communications, promotional offers and incentives, and the physical environment of the sporting venue.

Review Questions

1. What are the two categories of consumption motives? Define each.
2. Identify the eight motives that influence sports consumption.
3. Describe the two types of low-involvement fans.
4. Describe the two types of high-involvement fans.
5. Identify and describe the paths to fans' identification with sports brands.
6. What is the difference between direct and indirect sports consumption?
7. What are the four primary categories of influences on direct sports consumption?
8. Describe the perceived options that influence direct sports consumption.
9. Describe the convenience and comfort variables that affect attendance at sporting events.
10. How can identification influence direct sports consumption?
11. How do personal incentives influence direct sports consumption?
12. What marketing incentives influence direct sports consumption?

New Terms

Utilitarian consumption motives purchases based on a consumer's desire to achieve some functional benefit from a good or service.

Hedonic consumption motives purchases based on the desire to have a sensory experience that elicits pleasure, fun, or excitement.

Aesthetics within sports is an observable behavior such as a particular style of play of a player, team, or sport, a certain level of performance, or other observable traits, behaviors, or characteristics.

Cognitive involvement personal relevance of a sport object's functional performance.

Affective involvement personal relevance a sports object holds based on its ability to allow a person to express his or her ideal self-image to the world.

Direct consumption consumption of a sporting event through actual attendance at the event.

Indirect consumption consumption of a sporting event at a site other than the event's venue.

Discussion and Critical Thinking Exercises

1. Think of all of the purchases you have made over the last week. What percentage of the purchases was based on utilitarian consumption motives? What percentage was based on hedonic consumption motives? Describe your most recent hedonic consumption experience.
2. Look through the eight motives that influence sports consumption listed in Figure 2.1. For the last sporting event you attended, which motives influenced your decision? Explain.
3. The third category of motives for sports consumption is personal motives and consists of aesthetics, entertainment, sensory stimulation, and economics. Think about sports events you attend. Discuss each personal motive as it relates to your sports consumption decisions.
4. Think about sports fans who display low involvement and are either situation-based or geographic-based fans. How does a sports team move that low-involvement fan to a more enduring level of involvement? Do you know of someone who was a low-involvement fan who later became a high-involvement fan? What created the change?
5. Think about a local sports team. Have they used star power to connect consumers to the team? If so, describe how it has been used and evaluate the success of the approach. If not, why not? How could the team use star power to connect consumers to the team?
6. Discuss the influence of your family on your sports consumption behavior. Who had the greatest impact? Why?
7. How important is socialization, in general, to you? Does the fact that you can socialize with others influence your decision to attend a sporting event? Explain.
8. How well does the local community support the college teams where you attend college? Which sports are most supported by the community? Why are some college sports supported more than others by the local community? What suggestions do you have for increasing the community support for your college sports program?
9. Discuss the difference between direct consumption of sports and indirect consumption of sports as it relates to your personal consumption of sports. Discuss when and why you choose direct consumption of certain sporting events and then discuss when and why you choose indirect consumption.
10. In terms of attending sporting events, how much does the financial requirement impact your decision? What was the most expensive sporting event you ever attended, in terms of total costs? Why did you attend? How much does the total cost impact your decision on attending an event?
11. Look through the convenience and comfort factors listed in Figure 2.7. For each, discuss where that factor impacted a recent decision to either attend a sporting event or not attend.
12. Team identification is an important factor in consumption decisions. What teams do you personally identify with? In what way? Describe how you developed the identification.

You Make the Call
Marketing Women's Professional Soccer

It was 1999 and it was a moment that many sports fans, especially fans of soccer, will always remember. It was the women's soccer World Cup and Brandi Chastain had epitomized the euphoria of the United States winning the title when she celebrated the winning goal by baring her Nike sports bra. It catapulted women's soccer from the fringes to the front page of newspapers and magazines.

With excitement running high, a group of investors forged quickly into the development of the Women's United Soccer Association (WUSA) with expensive offices, an almost unlimited marketing budget, and marquee players such as Mia Hamm and Kristine Lilly. Without any marketing research or analysis of the fan base of women's soccer, millions were spent on a national advertising campaign. The WUSA league lost an estimated $50 million the first year and $120 million over its three years of existence before it folded in bankruptcy. The euphoria that existed during the 1999 World Cup did not translate into the fans in the stands, corporate sponsors with deep pockets, or television contracts that the WUSA founders envisioned.

In 2009, a new women's soccer league was formed. The Women's Professional Soccer (WPS) league was founded on a different business model. Instead of league-owned teams, the WPS had seven franchise operations that cost approximately $1.5 million each and could spend a maximum of $565,000 on players' salaries. Players earned an average of $32,000 a year in salary and had to resort to soccer camps, marketing appearances, and other jobs for additional income. Targeted attendance was 4,000 to 6,000 fans per game, but the league struggled to meet that goal, with an average attendance for its first season of 4,684. Encouraging, however, was that attendance during the last four weeks of the season was up for every team in the WPS.

Girls' soccer programs are a primary target for the WPS.

© Stephanie Swartz / Shutterstock

Marketing the WPS has been daunting. There are no television rights, which means no or extremely limited corporate sponsors, because sponsorships are tied closely to television exposure. In 2009, the Nielsen ratings for the twenty-one televised games on the Fox Soccer Channel and the three games on the Fox Sports network was 0.1, which translated to 32,000 households for the Fox Soccer Channel and 100,000 households for the Fox Sports Network. Companies are very reluctant to cough up sponsorships for such small TV audiences.

Without a national advertising budget, WPS teams have resorted to other forms of marketing. To build support, teams and individual players use Twitter and Facebook instead of radio or television. Players make personal appearances at soccer camps, at schools, and in malls. One of the primary marketing approaches has been to talk about it being an affordable family entertainment, with single ticket prices as low as $13. Parking and food are cheaper at the WPS games than with any other professional sporting venue.

Through the pain of losing the WUSA and building the WPS, teams realized that the fan base is local, not national. Not surprisingly, the biggest fans are young girls playing soccer in the summer, in high school, and in college. Coupled with the young girls are their parents. But, as soon as high school or college soccer is over, the girls hold little interest in attending WPS games, and the parents have even less interest. In 2011, WPS had teams in six markets: Atlanta, Boston, New Jersey/New York, Philadelphia, south Florida, and western New York. Disputes between WPS and a team owner led to the decision to suspend operations for the 2012 season. Once team ownership stability is restored, the WPS hopes to resume competition and move forward.

A desire to expand exists, but the WPS must first gain acceptance in its core markets before it can entertain growth opportunities.

Questions:

1. One particularly attractive fan base is the 377,000 girls who play high school soccer. Because many of these will go on to play college soccer, they are an attractive market for the WPS. From the motives listed in Figure 2.2, which ones would be the most prominent for the high school girls in attending WPS games? What about their parents?

2. What level and type of involvement was displayed with the World Cup in 1999 and the ensuing WUSA? How can the WPS build a higher level of involvement with their fan base?

3. Examine the various paths of identification with a sports brand listed in Figure 2.4 and discussed in this chapter. Which means of connection should the WPS pursue in its marketing programs? Suggest strategies for doing so.

4. Figure 2.5 identifies the various factors that influence direct sports consumption. Discuss each factor as it relates to putting fans in the stands of the WPS games.

5. Based on your responses to Questions 1 through 4, develop a plan to increase attendance at WPS games that could be implemented assuming the league resumes operations.

Sources: "From the Ground Up," by Ken Belson, *New York Times*, Section B, Sports Desk, p. 12; "Familiar Faces Back for Women's Kickoff," by Beau Dure, *USA Today*, Sports section, p. 12C; "Down to Earth for New Women's Soccer League, Main Goal Is Not to Be Another WUSA," by Wayne Coffey, *Daily News (New York)*, Sports, End Zone, p. 82; Tripp Mickle, "WPS Teams Commit to Return, Despite Losses," *Street & Smith's Sports Business Journal*, September 14, 2009, p. 6.

References

1. Robert Dvorchak, "Even in Death, Loyal Fan Makes It to Game" (2007), *Pittsburgh Post-Gazette*, December 17. Accessed at http://www.post-gazette.com/pg/07351/842265-66.stm, September 21, 2009.

2. Michael Stahilevitz and J. G. Myers, "Donations to Charity as Purchase Incentives: How Well They Work May Depend on What You Are Trying to Sell" (1998), *Journal of Consumer Research*, 24 (March), 434–446.

3. U. Khan, R. Dhar, and K. Wertenbroch, "A Behavioral Decision Theoretic Perspective on Hedonic and Utilitarian Choice" (2004), INSEAD Working Paper Series.

4. Daniel L. Wann, Merrill J. Melnick, Gordon W. Russell, and Dale G. Pease, *Sports Fans: The Psychology and Social Impact of Spectators* (New York: Routledge, 2001).

5. Richard Sandomir, "How Big is 'Tiger Effect'? Networks Will Soon Learn," *The New York Times*, June 19, 2008. Accessed October 14, 2009, at http://www.nytimes.com/2008/06/19/sports/golf/19sandomir.html.

6. Kenneth A. Hunt, Terry Bristol, and R. Edward Bashaw, "A Conceptual Approach to Classifying Sports Fans" (1999), *Journal of Services Marketing*, 13(6), 439–452.

7. C. Whan Park and Gordon W. McClung, "The Effect of TV Program Involvement on Involvement with Commercials" (1988), *Advances in Consumer Research*, Vol. 13, Richard J. Lutz, ed., Association for Consumer Research, 544–548.

8. "Brewers in the Community" (2011), accessed October 8, 2011, at http://milwaukee.brewers.mlb.com/mil/community/brewers_in_the_community.jsp.

9. *Gale Encyclopedia of Psychology*, Bonnie R. Strickland, ed. (Farmington Hills, MI: Gale Group, 2001).

10. The Black Hole, "Welcome to The Black Hole: BlackHoleFans.com" (2009). Accessed October 15, 2009, at http://www.blackholefans.com/.

11. "Redbirds, AutoZone Setting Record Pace for Attendance," *Memphis Business Journal*, July 10, 2001, accessed October 19, 2009, at http://memphis.bizjournals.com/memphis/stories/2001/07/23/tidbits.html.

12. Richard H. Kolbe and Jeffrey D. James, "An Identification and Examination of Influences That Shape the Creation of a Professional Team Fan" (2000), *International Journal of Sports Marketing & Sponsorship*, 2 (1), 23–37.

13. Major League Soccer, "Grassroot Partners" (2009), accessed March 23, 2012, at http://www.mlssoccer.com/grassroot-partners.

14. Wann, Melnick, Russell, and Pease (2001).

15. University of Alabama (2009), accessed October 1, 2009, at http://www.rolltide.com/auto_pdf/p_hotos/s_chools/alab/genrel/auto_pdf/seatingchart.

16. Team Marketing Report (2010), accessed March 23, 2012, at: https://www.teammarketing.com/btSubscriptions/fancostindex/index.

17. Weather.com (2011), accessed March 23, 2012, at http://www.weather.com/outlook/travel/vacationplanner/wxclimatology/monthly/USMN0503.

18. Chicago Transit Authority, "19 United Center Express" (2009), accessed October 5, 2009, at http://www.transitchicago.com/riding_cta/busroute.aspx?RouteId=325.

19. United Center, "Parking: General" (2009), accessed October 5, 2009, at http://www.unitedcenter.com/unitedcenter/ParkingInformationGeneral.asp.

20. Todd Spangler, "Cox Grabs ESPN360.com" (2009), September 25; accessed October 4, 2009, at http://www.multichannel.com/article/355438-Cox_Grabs_ESPN360_com.php.

21. American Sportscasters Online, "Radio and Its Impact on the Sports World" (2009), accessed October 4, 2009, at http://www.americansportscastersonline.com/radiohistory.html.

22. Sean Gregory, "With Fewer Sellouts, NFL's Blackout Rule Under Fire" (2009), September 10; accessed October 4, 2009, at http://www.time.com/time/business/article/0,8599,1921401,00.html?xid=rss-fullnation-yahoo.

23. Mississippi State University Bulldogs Official Athletics Site (2009), accessed October 4, 2009, at http://www.mstateathletics.com/Login.dbml?DB_OEM_ID=16800.

24. Wann, Melnick, Russell, and Pease (2001).

25. Baseball Almanac, "Chicago Cubs Attendance" (2009), accessed October 6, 2009, at http://www.baseball-almanac.com/teams/cubsatte.shtml.

26. Atlanta Hawks, "Hawks: 2009–10 Promotions" (2009), accessed October 12, 2009, at http://www.nba.com/hawks/promotions/200910_promotions.html.

27. Dave Campbell, "All-You-Can-Eat Seats: Baseball Fans Pig Out" (2009), accessed October 12, 2009, at http://www.komonews.com/economy/bright/50245517.html.

28. The Aces Edge, "2009 Promotions Schedule Announced" (2009), accessed October 12, 2009, at http://www.renoacesedge.com/index.php?option=com_myblog&show=2009-Promotions-Schedule-Announced.html&Itemid=72.

29. Kirk L. Wakefield and Jeffrey G. Blodgett, "The Importance of Servicescapes in Leisure Service Settings" (1994), *Journal of Services Marketing*, 8 (3), 66–76.

30. Great Lake Loons, "Ballpark" (2009), accessed October 13, 2009, at http://greatlakes.loons.milb.com/ballpark/page.jsp?ymd=20090107&content_id=492976&vkey=ballpark_t456&fext=.jsp&sid=t456.

31. Wakefield and Blodgett (1994).

3 Understanding the Marketing Environment

Learning Objectives

By the end of this chapter you should be able to:

1. Identify the five key factors in the external marketing environment and describe the effects of each on sports organizations
2. Explain the process of conducting and utilizing a SWOT analysis
3. Differentiate between goals and objectives
4. Describe the methods used by sports marketers to collect secondary and primary data

Hot dogs are popular at many sports venues.

Sports Venue Foodservice Goes Upscale, Downscale, and Large Scale

When you attend a sporting event today, chances are your experience with foodservice offerings is much different than what was traditionally available at concessions stands. Significant changes in menus and delivery of foodservice make the customary fare of hot dogs, peanuts, and beer seem out of date. Changes made in sports foodservice are efforts to appeal to customers influenced by trends and developments affecting the entire industry. In recent years, the sports foodservice business has at the same time gone upscale, downscale, and large scale, all due to changes observed in the external marketing environment.

Sports foodservice has gone upscale in two different ways. A noticeable trend has been the addition of premium-quality (and premium-priced) menu items. As new sports venues have been built, design considerations allow construction of restaurants and other foodservice areas that offer sit-down dining and greater menu variety. The new Cowboys Stadium, home of the Dallas Cowboys, has made the dining experience a major feature of the new facility.

The trend has created opportunities for foodservice operators. One company, Levy Restaurants, entered the sports foodservice business primarily because of its premium dining expertise and

Insider Expert Sean Hanrahan – ESPN

Sean is a 25-year marketing veteran having worked in positions of increasing responsibility on the agency side until joining ESPN in May, 2000.

Prior to joining ESPN, Sean worked at Tracy Locke. His last position there was as Executive Concept Director of an innovative think tank called the Department of Ideas. Before that he was the head of client services on the Pepsi business where he was responsible for the strategic and creative development of major national promotions such as Pepsi's tie-in with *Star Wars: Episode One*.

During his tenure at ESPN Customer Marketing and Sales, Sean has had a track record of success and increasing responsibility. In 2004, Sean was appointed to the Senior Management team leading the reorganization of the Customer Marketing and Sales division as it assumed the multi-media responsibility of managing the digital and print sales groups as well as television. As a result, Sean was named Senior Vice President, Marketing Solutions and in 2006 assumed responsibility for the entire multi-media marketing department of this division which is comprised of four groups: Marketing Services, Creative Works, Sports Management, and Event Marketing.

Sean is an avid sports fan and a graduate of LaSalle University. He resides in Bucks County, PA with his wife and three children.

ESPN Internet Group

Sean Hanrahan, Senior Vice President of Marketing Solutions, ESPN.

the fact that few foodservice companies were offering premium products.[1] Dessert carts have become part of the landscape at sports venues. In addition, foodservice has gone upscale through the increased use of technology to speed the process of serving customers. Examples of innovations used in recent years include tickets loaded with credits to spend on concessions (eliminating the need for cash transactions), food-ordering capability from seats using wireless devices, and an innovative tap to dispense beer that reduced pour time from 8 seconds to 2½ seconds.[2] Introducing these technologies to foodservice operations makes it more convenient for customers to order, which can lead to a willingness to spend more on food and merchandise.

Economic conditions put pressure on foodservice operators to go downscale in the late 2000s. A number of Major League Baseball teams value-priced concessions, with some items as low as $1. The move was an effort to entice fans to spend money on concessions that they might not spend otherwise. Other teams did not discount as deeply but offered special pricing on certain menu items on weeknights or for early-season games. While the effects of lowering prices on profitability of foodservice operations and the challenges of returning to higher prices in the future can be debated, the short-term impact on consumer behavior was clear. Cincinnati Reds spokesperson Michael Anderson said fan feedback indicated that "our value pricing initiatives are the reasons they are coming to the ballpark."[3] It was the belief of many venue operators that their foodservice offerings could not turn a blind eye to the economic belt-tightening of many of their customers.

A third direction that sports foodservice offerings have taken in recent years is to appeal to consumers on a large scale. "All-you-can-eat seats" came onto the scene in the late 2000s, with sixteen of thirty Major League Baseball clubs offering all-you-can-eat seats. It was a way for clubs to add value to less desirable seating sections.[4] The Los Angeles Dodgers pioneered the concept by offering a section of outfield bleacher seats as its all-you-can-eat area. Similar promotions have been adopted by teams in other major sports leagues, too. It is a way to increase revenues and add convenience for customers as they essentially prepay for concessions.

Introduction

Strategies by sports foodservice companies and their venue/team partners to offer higher-priced, premium-quality dining options, create value menus for price-conscious customers, and offer all-you-can-eat seats occurred as a result of understanding the environment beyond the walls of their organizations. Marketing decisions made without consideration of the external environment are risky at best and likely to end in failure! Likewise, marketing strategy and tactics should follow from the goals and objectives an organization seeks to achieve. Stating the outcomes that should occur from marketing efforts provides direction for deciding on tactics that will be used to reach target markets.

This chapter explores three areas essential to understanding the marketing environment. First, the external marketing environment is discussed and external factors in the marketing environment are identified. Second, managers must translate insight gained from monitoring the external environment by applying strategic planning methods, particularly SWOT analysis, as well as set marketing objectives. Third, gathering information to monitor customers and the external marketing environment focuses on types of data and the role of marketing information systems.

The External Marketing Environment

Any marketing decision should be guided by managerial understanding of occurrences outside the organization. The **external marketing environment** is the term used to describe characteristics, developments, and trends occurring outside an organization that could potentially impact it. An important characteristic of the external environment is that these occurrences are beyond the control of a business. However, it is critical that managers make marketing decisions with these external forces in mind. For example, the economic recession that began in 2008 led many consumers to forgo buying tickets to sporting events in order to save money. Sports properties could not make pricing decisions as if there was no recession. In response, many professional sports teams used tactics to soften the blow of a weak economy. Responses to the change in the economic environment included not increasing ticket prices, offering season-ticket buyers additional benefits such as vouchers for food and beverage to add value to their purchase, and developing value-priced menus in their food concessions.

As shown in Figure 3.1, the external marketing environment consists of five factors, or forces, that should be monitored regularly. These trends should be monitored because they change frequently. The external factors are: 1) competition, 2) economy, 3) technology, 4) political, legal, and regulatory climate, and 5) sociodemographic trends. Examining the external marketing environment is like taking a photograph. It captures what is happening at a given point in time. But, much like a person's personal appearance changes in photographs over time, the "snapshot" of an organization's external marketing environment will look different at various points in time.

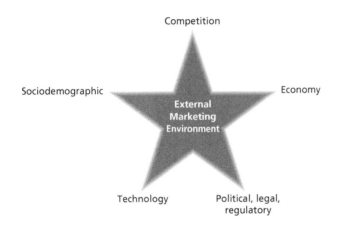

FIGURE 3.1 The Factors of an External Marketing Environment

Competition

Monitoring competition in the external environment involves not only knowing who your competitors are, but it also requires gaining insight into their strengths and weaknesses as well as predictions about future moves they will make. A broad concept of competition is that it is anything that stands between your business and a customer. Why the need for such a broad view of competition? It is because competition often comes from unlikely sources, ones that at first glance are not like your firm in terms of goods or services offered.

In order to define competition, the first task is to identify the customer need or want met by your good or service. In other words, what do customers receive from using your product? For Head tennis rackets, answers to this question might be "high performance," or "greater confidence in one's tennis game." What would the answer be for customers of a minor league baseball team like the Carolina Mudcats? Is it to watch baseball, or is it to be entertained? Some attendees are entertained by the baseball game itself; others are entertained by pregame and in-game promotions, music, food, games, or spending time with friends or family. Failure to ask the question "What benefit does our product provide customers?" would lead to a lack of understanding of why people purchase. More importantly, it would prevent a firm from properly identifying other brands that compete for the same customers.

Competition for sports entertainment properties can be classified as brand competition, category competition, or generic competition. Figure 3.2 provides an illustration of the three levels of competition for a minor league baseball team.

BRAND COMPETITION. **Brand competition** involves brands or firms that target similar customers with comparable products and prices. In the sports industry, it is head-to-head competition such as the NFL's Jacksonville Jaguars vs. top-tier college football teams (University of Florida, Florida State University, and University of Miami), Los Angeles Lakers vs. Los Angeles Clippers (NBA

FIGURE 3.2 Levels of Competition for a Minor League Baseball Team

Customer Need: Entertainment		
Brand Competitors	Category Competitors	Generic Competitors
College baseball team Major League Baseball team	Water park Movie theater Shopping mall Concerts Arts festivals Theatrical performances Movie/video game rental Dining out	Gasoline Groceries Pay Bills Savings

Kenneth E. Clow

teams), and Lakers/Clippers vs. other professional franchises (e.g., NHL's Los Angeles Kings and Anaheim Ducks) and college basketball (UCLA and USC). Focusing on brand competition is logical because they are the alternatives that are most similar to a company's offering. But, if the view of competition is restricted to brand competitors, it is likely that other competitors whose offerings meet the same need will be overlooked.

In the sports entertainment industry, the need to think beyond brand competitors may be even greater. If a minor league hockey team such as the Cincinnati Cyclones of the East Coast Hockey League defined competition as other professional hockey teams, they would have no competition in their local market. Even when the definition of brand competition is expanded to other sports properties, the number of competitors is often relatively small. While the Cyclones would vie for the attention of consumers in the same market as the Cincinnati Reds, Cincinnati Bengals, and University of Cincinnati, it could be argued that because they are different sports and may be in season at different times of the year they are less of a threat than brand competitors in product categories in which competition is ongoing. The temptation to define competition narrowly must be avoided!

CATEGORY COMPETITION. The next level of competition, **category competition**, is the brands or organizations whose offerings meet the same or similar customer needs. An industry-based view of competition is based on what a business does. The reality is that customers do not view products by industry; they view them by what they will do for them. Consider minor league baseball. In many markets, particularly in smaller cities, a minor league baseball team is the only professional sport in the area. However, minor league baseball teams face formidable competition from other summertime entertainment choices like water parks and vacations as well as other entertainment activities such as shopping, movies, and concerts. Consumer focus is on how to meet entertainment needs, and minor league baseball is but one option.

Category competitors cannot be dismissed by sports marketers. A challenge presented by the decision to position sports as entertainment is that the nature of competition expands from other sports brands to all entertainment options available to the target market. For example, college sports face non-sports competition from other entertainment sources. Instead of going to a Temple University men's basketball game, students could opt to attend a concert, go dancing at a club, take in a movie, go to a theatrical performance, or watch a movie or video on their computer at home. These entertainment options are in addition to sports entertainment competitors, both professional and collegiate, that can be found in the Philadelphia market. Category competitors can thwart a sports property's marketing efforts by providing entertainment options that require less expenditure of time, effort, or money.

GENERIC COMPETITION. A third and even broader level of competition is any expenditure that a consumer might consider that could prevent purchase of a ticket to a sporting event. This level is referred to as **generic competition**. Consumers have a limited amount of money available to spend. Decisions must be made about how to allocate that money to meet their various needs. Examples of generic competition include setting aside money for savings, paying bills, spending money on necessities such as food or transportation, or making a major purchase such as an automobile or computer.

Consumers might conclude that spending on sports entertainment is not the best use of available dollars, and thus, decide to spend on something else—or not spend at all, and put money into savings. Generic competitors may not pose as direct of a threat as brand or category competitors, but the possibility of losing customers to a generic competitor must be acknowledged, especially in slow economic times. In response, sports marketers should strive to maximize the value received by consumers purchasing sporting products so that they can better justify discretionary spending on sports entertainment.

Economy

The rapidly changing and potentially volatile nature of the economy, at both the national and local level, is a motivation to conduct external environment analyses regularly. Assessment of trends at the consumer level and for the economy as a whole will yield insight into how economic conditions might affect sports organizations. Economic trends are beyond the control of any one organization. But, if economic trends are ignored or not proactively monitored, poor marketing decisions may be made. A sample of the different economic indicators that can be monitored by sports organizations are shown in Figure 3.3.

Some economic trends focus on the beliefs and behaviors pertaining to economic activity, such as the Consumer Confidence Index, Consumer Sentiment Index, and Institute for Supply

Indicator	Source	Description
Consumer Confidence Index	The Conference Board	Measures consumers' beliefs about future business conditions, job market, and personal income; updated monthly
Consumer Sentiment Index	University of Michigan	National sample of households that gauges opinions about government economic policies, personal job prospects and financial situation, and planned purchases
Consumer Price Index	Bureau of Labor Statistics	Tracks monthly changes in amount consumers spend for a representative basket of goods and services
Personal Income and Outlays	Bureau of Economic Analysis	Aggregate monthly estimate of personal income, disposable income, personal outlays, and personal savings
Buying Power Index	Nielsen Claritas	Annual estimate of local market buying power based on disposable income, retail sales, and population of market area
Reports on Business – PMI	Institute for Supply Management	Monthly survey of 300 business executives concerning expectations of business conditions
Retail Sales Outlook	National Retail Federation	Bimonthly forecast of retail sales nationally based on current environment; includes projection for industry sales for the year
Advance Monthly Sales for Retail and Food Services	Census Bureau	Monthly estimate of sales for different categories of retail industry and food services and drinking places
Gross Domestic Product	Bureau of Economic Analysis	Quarterly estimate of output of goods and services by labor and property in U.S.

FIGURE 3.3 Economic Indicators with Implications for Sports Industry

Management's Purchasing Managers' Index (PMI). These measures reflect views of current economic conditions and expectations of how they will be in the near future. Sports marketers benefit from possessing this knowledge, as it gives insight into the level of optimism consumers and businesses have about the economy now and in the short term. If consumer confidence is declining, it tends to negatively impact sales of tickets and merchandise to individuals. Also, businesses will be more reluctant to spend on corporate hospitality at sporting events or invest in corporate sponsorship programs.

Other economic indicators are aggregate measures of consumer activity. Indicators such as Personal Income and Outlays, Retail Sales Outlook, and Advance Monthly Sales for Retail and Food Services report cumulative expenditures by consumers. The trends revealed by these measures enable businesses to better understand consumer spending in general and spending for discretionary purchases like entertainment in particular. If spending is trending upward, consumers might be more inclined to make entertainment-related purchases. Marketing efforts should appeal to prospective buyers by focusing on the experiential and entertainment benefits offered. On the other hand, if consumer spending is sluggish or even in decline, marketing tactics may need to have more of a value orientation. In this case, added value can be marketed by giving customers more benefits or amenities or by offering incentives or discounts to appeal to price-sensitive customers. Prospective customers need to be shown that buying sports products or event tickets yields sufficient value to justify the expenditure.

The impact of economic variables on consumer behavior was painfully evident in the recession that began in 2008. Changes in spending that were deemed necessary because of the recession were internalized by many consumers, with the result being a change in behavior that lasted past the recession. Practices such as delaying purchases, putting more money in savings, and spending less money on dining out and entertainment continued. As a result, marketers had to face the reality that consumers' attitudes toward spending had changed, which made creating and communicating customer value more important.[5]

At times, a permanent shift in consumer behavior can affect sports properties. This occurred with the way tickets are purchased. Full-season ticket sales are important to team marketers because they represent a rather consistent revenue stream. However, consumers who are reluctant to make an outlay for full-season tickets as a result of modified buying behaviors pose a challenge for ticket sales departments in sports organizations. One response to this change in the economic environment was offering a variety of multiple-game ticket packages to appeal to fans' loyalties and yet not require the outlay of funds necessary for a full-season ticket package. For example, Georgetown University men's basketball offers "mini plan" ticket packages that allow buyers to select either five or eight games to attend of the team's sixteen-game home schedule. Flexibility in offering tickets encourages multiple-game purchases without the commitment required of an "all or nothing" full-season ticket plan.

Technology

Developments in technologies available to firms in the sports entertainment industry, the rate of technological change, and anticipation of future technologies that will potentially impact the industry should all be considered. The term "technology" tends to be associated with high-tech advancements rooted in computer science and information technology. While advances in these areas would be applicable when conducting a situation analysis, technology should be viewed more broadly. Technology should be thought of as ways tasks are accomplished and new methods for conducting business.[6] Technology can impact customer value by adding to the benefits consumers receive from a product or reducing the sacrifices required to obtain and consume the product. In addition to technology influencing the consumer's experience, innovations could potentially increase revenues for a sports organization.

Technology enhancements in recent years have touched several aspects of sports entertainment consumption. The Wichita Wingnuts, a minor league baseball team in the independent American Association, became the first U.S. sports team to go "cashless" at its concessions areas in Lawrence-Dumont Stadium. Fans load money onto cards that are used for payment when purchasing food or merchandise. The team touts that fans spend less time in line and thus spend more time enjoying the game. It has the added benefits to the team of reducing employee theft and potentially increasing per capita spending by fans who are not constrained to spending cash on hand.[7] Added convenience of buying concessions has also come in the form of the use of Wi-Fi technology. The addition of Wi-Fi in stadiums such as University of Phoenix Stadium in Glendale, Arizona, and Jacksonville Municipal Stadium allows fans to place food and beverage orders from their seats. Also, more remote food and merchandise locations can be set up because of the ability to use the Wi-Fi technology to make credit card processing possible.[8]

Another technology enhancement, paperless tickets, adds value for consumers by reducing the time required to buy and consume sports entertainment. In a paperless ticketing system, buyers receive their tickets digitally rather than in the form of the paper tickets customary in the sports industry. Delivering tickets to buyers in this form allows buyers the flexibility of transferring tickets to another person if necessary, potentially reducing the number of unused tickets. Moreover, paperless tickets benefit sports properties by creating significant cost savings. If a sports team were to go completely paperless in its ticket delivery, it could save $30,000 to $60,000 annually on printing and delivery costs.[9] In addition to cost savings, paperless ticketing gives sports properties more information about ticket holders, as recipients of paperless tickets have to create an account to have tickets sent to them digitally. As a result, ticket sales prospects can be identified from persons who use paperless tickets but are not a buyer of multiple-game ticket packages.[10]

Innovations in wireless communications open the door for numerous possibilities for sports properties to integrate technology into the consumption experience and extend connectivity with fans beyond live events. An example of how technological innovation stands to change the live viewing experience is tapping the potential of smartphones to deliver content to fans in the stands. One of the attractions of indirect consumption of sporting events is that fans can watch replays and see action from multiple camera angles. A company called YinzCam has developed a service that overcomes this limitation of watching a game live, enabling fans to use their smartphones to view replays from different vantage points and create a "personal game diary" of replays of their choosing.[11]

Sports media companies are looking for ways to utilize technology to capture audiences in channels besides their traditional strength of television. ESPN has partnered with wireless phone provider Sprint to offer ESPN Pack, a mobile platform that gives users access to some of ESPN's most popular content: the ScoreCenter app for scores and stats, video on demand, fantasy sports team access, and content related to programs such as *SportsCenter* and *Pardon the Interruption*.[12] YinzCam and ESPN Pack are examples of how new technologies can be an opportunity to enhance customers' relationships with a sports brand.

The challenge for sports marketers is to determine which technologies have the greatest potential to affect their business. Just because a technology is available does not mean it will be widely accepted by consumers and be successful for a sports property. For example, several teams experimented with customer loyalty programs that used cards scanned at kiosks when fans attended events. The loyalty programs were designed to offer rewards for frequent attendance, but many of these programs have been discontinued as the technology and promotion costs required to execute the programs did not justify their continued use as a way to grow revenues.

Political, Legal, and Regulatory Climate

Sports properties operate within boundaries imposed on them from two general sources: industry regulation and government regulation. The extent to which an organization is impacted depends on the level of industry and government regulations. A promoter of a tennis tournament could be required to comply with rules of the United States Tennis Association (an industry regulator) but be subject to little oversight from government regulations. In contrast, a sport such as horse racing must comply with governmental regulatory agencies. Pimlico Race Course in Baltimore, whose marquee event is the second race of the Triple Crown Series, the Preakness, is regulated at the state level by the Maryland Racing Commission.

Sports, such as horse racing, must comply with legal and industry regulations.

© Clarence Alford / Fotolia

Furthermore, Pimlico is a member of the National Thoroughbred Racing Association (NTRA), which means the track is subject to NTRA's regulations on such operational aspects as track conditions and treatment of horses.[13] The challenge for sports marketers is to conduct business within established rules of all regulatory bodies. At the same time, they must work to ensure that regulations are as favorable as possible toward the conduct of business and voice the need for regulatory change when conditions are unfavorable.

INDUSTRY REGULATION. Sports properties are often subject to rules set by organizations or sanctioning bodies that oversee a particular sport. For instance, the United States Golf Association has established rules regulating equipment, such as balls and clubs, used in USGA-sanctioned events. It distributes information to USGA courses on caring for courses and promoting environmental stewardship.[14] In this case, these regulations serve to create consistency in terms of equipment used by event participants and quality for courses hosting USGA events. The steps taken are ways to manage the image of the USGA brand, which is the overarching goal. This form of regulation may impose more restrictions than a self-regulated business might establish for itself, but because it is usually a group of organizations with similar aims and agendas, the oversight may be less restrictive than government regulation.

The marketing tactics of an individual team or organization can be subject to approval from a league or conference of which it is a part. The Chicago Blackhawks of the NHL and Chicago Bears of the NFL discussed creating an ad campaign that would promote both teams. The planned ad would feature Bears quarterback Jay Cutler and Blackhawks star Patrick Kane and create exposure for both teams. The planned ad was dropped after the NFL said it was a violation of league policy prohibiting the use of team marks and logos in connection with the promotion of other sports unless approved by twenty-four of the league's thirty-two clubs.[15]

In other cases, the regulatory effects of league policies can be relaxed to create marketing opportunities for individual members. For example, the NBA removed a policy prohibiting distilled spirits brands from being team sponsors. Teams can now feature liquor brands in courtside advertising and on team websites. This decision was influenced in part by a trend in the economic environment (a recession that negatively impacted team sponsorships) and a competitive factor (NASCAR, MLB, and NHL allowed distilled spirit sponsors).[16] Industry regulation must strike a balance between protecting the interests of an industry group and its members and giving individual members leeway to make business decisions as they deem appropriate.

GOVERNMENT REGULATION. In some cases, government oversight of a sport may make expansion into a market difficult, if not impossible. For example, mixed martial arts has enjoyed rapidly growing interest across the United States, but event promoters have had to lobby many states to legalize mixed martial arts events. Currently, more than forty states have passed laws regulating mixed martial arts events, but it required diligent efforts by promoters who were eager to expand the market.[17] Sports that entail high levels of risk to participants typically face greater government regulation in the form of sanctioning bodies that approve events and implement rules intended to protect the sport's participants.

A legal issue that has impacted professional sports in the United States is the antitrust exemption status granted by the federal government. Trusts, also referred to as monopolies, occur when one or a small number of organizations holds vast economic power over an industry or group.[18] The effect of a trust is that it restrains competition and free markets. The Sherman Act was enacted in 1890 to prohibit trusts from exercising excessive influence over markets. However, Major League Baseball was granted an exemption from the Sherman Act in 1922 because it was not considered to be interstate commerce. The exemption has been important to MLB as it has allowed the league to maintain tight control over its franchises and the markets in which they do business. In a 30-year period (1971–2001), only one MLB team was granted permission to relocate to another city (the Washington Senators moved to Arlington, Texas) largely because the league was able to dictate franchise locations as part of its antitrust exemption. In contrast, the same time period saw franchise relocations by seven NFL teams, seven NBA teams, and nine NHL teams.[19] The case of MLB's exemption to the Sherman Act shows that government regulation can be a favorable condition for a sports property. MLB has been able to make decisions regarding markets in which to locate franchises, collective bargaining agreements with players' and umpires' unions, and media broadcasting rights deals in a manner that serves the interests of the league and its team owners.

The ability of Major League Baseball to make market decisions free from restrictions of antitrust laws explains why many organizations and industries favor self-regulation over government regulation. Self-regulation of an industry or group is generally considered preferable to being subject to government regulation. The reasoning is that parties involved in self-regulation have influence over decisions on policies and rules that affect them directly. Self-regulation of an industry can be more than an effort to avoid government influence on the conduct of business. A self-regulated industry that establishes systems and procedures for monitoring itself and encourages innovation among members to better serve customers and other stakeholders has the potential to succeed without government involvement. Unfortunately, research into whether industry self-regulation meets these aims reveals that industry members usually do not improve performance when allowed to set their own direction.[20]

The dilemma between maintaining self-regulation and becoming subject to government regulation in the American sports industry is evident in college football. Major college football is split into two subdivisions: the Football Bowl Subdivision (FBS) and Football Championship Subdivision (FCS). FBS members typically are larger colleges and universities. As the difference in the names of the two subdivisions suggests, FBS members participate in a bowl game system that ultimately determines its champion. Of the 120 members of the FBS, only 65 of them have an opportunity to play for a national championship. The reason is that the champion is determined through a system called the Bowl Championship Series (BCS). The BCS is made up of six of the largest athletic conferences: Atlantic Coast Conference, Big Ten Conference, Big 12 Conference, Big East Conference, Pac-12 Conference, and the Southeastern Conference. Also, Notre Dame, the nation's major independent team, is a BCS member. At the conclusion of the college football season, participants in major bowl games (Fiesta Bowl, Orange Bowl, Rose Bowl, Sugar Bowl) and the BCS championship game are selected from BCS members. This practice excludes members of non-BCS conferences such as Conference USA and the Mountain West Conference to have a chance to play for the national championship.

The dilemma of self-regulation arises from the belief among some people that the Bowl Championship Series is a monopoly that restrains competition because it dictates which institutions have a chance to compete for the FBS championship. Controversy arising from the issue led Congress to conduct hearings as to whether the BCS should be subject to the Sherman Act.[21] The possibility of government becoming involved in how college football champions are determined is frowned upon by people who say it is only a game; let college football take care of itself. On the other hand, the BCS is a very lucrative venture, having signed a contract with ESPN worth $125 million a year for the 2010–2013 seasons.[22] Although non-BCS conferences receive a share of revenues, they miss on the potential for large paychecks that are the rewards for playing in BCS bowl games. The dollar amounts of these payouts suggest that college football and the bowl game system is a business. Some critics argue that the banking industry, health care industry, or oil industry are not allowed to self-regulate; why should the college football "industry" be afforded the privilege to self-regulate? The chance that government could attempt to regulate college football should serve as an incentive for institutions in control to make decisions that protect their interests, but at the same time minimize the desire of legislators to intervene.

Sociodemographic Trends

A final factor in the marketing environment pertains to changes in the characteristics or behaviors of a population of people. These changes are influenced by external variables such as technology and the economy, but also from changes in culture. **Culture** is "a system of shared beliefs, values, customs, behaviors, and artifacts that members of a society use to cope with their world and one another."[23] Patterns or trends that emerge often spread through a population and influence behavior. The trends that shape culture will differ over time, but marketers cannot lose sight of the power of sociodemographic trends to alter consumer behavior. Figure 3.4 identifies six trends that have impacted marketing practice in recent years (and are likely to continue their impact in the foreseeable future).

FIGURE 3.4
Sociodemographic Trends Impacting Marketing Practices

- Aging population
- Greater ethnic diversity
- Increased buying power of women
- Geographic changes in different U.S. regions
- Decreased leisure time
- Demand for social responsibility

© Scott Griessel / Fotolia

AGING POPULATION. The birth rate in the United States has historically experienced periods of large increases and declines. The result is the formation of distinct generations, with each generation having different needs and exhibiting their own consumption behaviors. The generation that will have a significant impact on businesses in the foreseeable future is *baby boomers*. This generation is made up of people born during the years 1946 to 1964. According to data from *The Statistical Abstract of the United States*, 79 million babies were born during this post–World War II period.[24] Today, early baby boomers are at or near retirement age. This life stage change will leave retired baby boomers with more time available for leisure activities, including consuming sports. The size of this group is remarkably large. The number of people age 65 or older was 40 million in 2010; it will increase to an estimated 72 million by 2030. This age group will represent nearly 20% of the population in 2030.[25]

The tremendous growth in the 65+ population creates both opportunities and challenges for sports marketers. While this group has more leisure time available, can a particular sports maintain relevance with older consumers? For example, a Harris Poll found that baseball is the favorite sport among people 65 or older (21%). In contrast, this same age group was most likely to say pro football was their least favorite sport (26%).[26] Information like that in the Harris Poll, coupled with the sheer size of the 65+ market, can be used by sports marketers to determine how their particular sport stands in the eyes of this lucrative marketing segment. Research into this customer segment could reveal their interest in following a particular sport, their willingness to attend sporting events, and the types of experiences they desire from consuming sports. In turn, the insight from analyzing the baby boomer market can be used to help make decisions about product design, pricing, delivery, and communication to appeal to this age group.

GREATER ETHNIC DIVERSITY. The U.S. population has experienced a significant shift in the ethnic mix of the population. Growth rates for the White and Black racial groups slowed during the last decade. At the same time, percentages of the population classified as Asian or of Hispanic origin increased. According to the U.S. Census Bureau, this trend will continue. In the years from 1995 to 2025, the Census Bureau estimates the U.S. population will increase by 72 million people. The majority of the growth will come in the Hispanic (32 million) and Asian (12 million) segments. Population growth for Whites and Blacks will be about 15 million and 12 million, respectively.[27] The growth of the Hispanic segment is particularly substantial. Projections for the years 2000–2050 indicate that the percentage of Hispanics in the U.S. population will nearly double, going from 12.5% in 2000 to 24.4% in 2050.[28]

While it is beneficial for sports marketers to monitor trends in the racial and ethnic makeup of populations in the markets that they serve, the main benefit of these actions is the insight gained that can be used to make marketing decisions. A better understanding of different racial and ethnic groups within a sport property's target market could result in devising sound, customer-focused strategies in terms of product design, experiential elements of live events, pricing, and communications.

Consider Chivas USA, a Major League Soccer team that began play in 2005. The team is located in the greater Los Angeles area, and a key target market is the more than 12 million Hispanics living in the area. One challenge the team faced was attempting to persuade Hispanic fans to commit to purchasing season tickets. According to Don Garber, MLS commissioner, "The Hispanic audience has traditionally not been an advance buyer of tickets. We need to work to provide enough value so that they're making the commitment necessary and we're providing the value necessary for them to want to buy season tickets and buy tickets in advance."[29]

Cultural differences go beyond observable behavior like preferences for buying tickets on game day rather than in advance. The stories that resonate with fans may not be the same across different cultures. For example, Hispanic soccer fans may be more interested in a player's story of overcoming adversity to achieve success rather than his statistical accomplishments on the field.[30] Thus, success in marketing across cultures requires a sports property to go beyond translating messages and experiences to different languages; it requires a deep understanding of the cultures from which they seek to attract customers.

INCREASED BUYING POWER OF WOMEN. It may seem shocking, but until the early 1970s a woman could not get a bank loan without her husband's or father's signature, and as recently as the early 1980s some states would not allow women to be listed on property deeds as joint owners—only the male could be listed.[31] The situation today is drastically different. Women have considerable economic impact and influence on purchases. Consider the facts shown in Figure 3.5.[32]

> - Spend $5 trillion annually on goods and services.
> - 90% hold veto power over family buying decisions.
> - 75% of all mothers are now in the work force.
> - 70% of all new businesses are started by women.
> - 57% of all college degrees are earned by women.
> - 50% of Internet users are women, buying more products online than men.

FIGURE 3.5 The Buying Power of Women

The growth in buying power of women cannot be disputed. The question for sports marketers is the same that any marketer faces when identifying target markets: Is the customer segment interested in the product being offered? The answer to that question is "maybe." A point that would suggest relatively little interest among women to consume sports is that most women do not identify themselves as sports fans. According to a Pew Research study, only 10% of American women said they followed sports very closely. In contrast, 26% of men surveyed reported following sports closely. Even when the 25% of women who said they follow sports somewhat closely is added to the 10% who follow very closely, the result is that approximately two-thirds of adult American women do not identify themselves as sports fans.[33] At first glance, the tendency for sports marketers might be to focus on the 57% of men who reported some interest in sports rather than attempting to appeal to the smaller number of women sports fans. This point is valid . . . if your definition of the product being marketed is "sports." But is that what consumers are buying? In many cases, the purchase is entertainment. Thus, prospects to consume sports are not limited to those persons, male or female, who classify themselves as fans.

The market potential of targeting women has been recognized for many sports properties. Many teams have attempted to help female fans become more informed about rules and information through ladies-only events and seminars, such as the "Football 101 for Women" program held at the University of Georgia. The daylong event, held annually during the summer, is hosted by Georgia's football coaching staff. Participants learn about football strategy and team operations. The event culminates with practicing what they learn on the team's practice field. A recent event attracted 350 participants, and the program has raised more than $60,000 since its inception for women's athletic scholarships at the university.[34]

While events such as the one offered by the University of Georgia can be effective for educating the female audience and increasing their identification with a brand, they often are one-time events that do not encourage continued interaction with a team or with other participants. The Baltimore Ravens of the NFL, however, developed a program that addresses the need to build lasting relationships with the female market. In 2007, the Ravens formed Purple, an official fan club for women only. Purple members can attend club events, receive news updates and other information from the team, and are given special offers for retail purchases. Also, Purple has a page on the team's website. The approach used by the Baltimore Ravens to target women not only acknowledges their buying power, but it also encourages women to become part of the brand community of Ravens fans.

Another area where sports properties are making progress with female fans is in merchandising. Nearly half of the fan base for minor league baseball is female, and as a result clubs are focusing more on meeting the unique needs of females with apparel, souvenirs, and jewelry geared towards female fans. Pam Hastalis is merchandise and events manager for a company that owns two minor league baseball teams, the Lansing Lugnuts and the Montgomery Biscuits. Part of her responsibility is keeping up with fashion trends. In terms of layout design in the retail area of sports properties, Hastalis says, "We want to make sure the women can grab and touch the items. Women like to feel what they are buying. They want good quality."[35] In addition to female items for sale, the minor league teams recognize that females are also behind many of the purchases for male, youth, and child products.

Under Armour, Inc.

This advertisement by Under Armour featuring Olympic skier Lindsey Vonn is targeted to females.

GEOGRAPHIC GROWTH RATES OF U.S. REGIONS. Just as the U.S. population is experiencing changes in its racial and ethnic composition, geographic regions are undergoing changes in population counts that will impact the sports industry. A review of population estimates by the U.S. Census Bureau for the years 2000–2009 reveals that the South and West regions of the country are growing at a greater rate than the Northeast and Midwest. The country's population grew by an estimated 8.2% during the decade of 2000–2009. The South and West regions each experienced a 13% gain in population during that period. At the same time, the Midwest region's population grew by slightly less than 4% and the Northeast region grew by just more than 3%.[36] These estimates reflect what many observers believe is a permanent population migration from the Northeast and Midwest, areas hurt by the eroding manufacturing sector of the U.S. economy, to the South and West, areas that are known for warmer climates and lower cost of living.

These shifts have not been overlooked by the sports industry. For example, expansion and franchise relocations in the National Hockey League in the past twenty years have focused on markets in the South and West (see Figure 3.6). Of the twelve franchises added or relocated during 1991–2000, ten of them went to markets in the South or West. Two of the markets losing franchises were in the low-growth Northeast and Midwest regions (although Minnesota received an expansion franchise in 2000). While the NHL has faced challenges marketing hockey in the warm climate markets to which it expanded, the league's choice of markets reflects the long-term shift in population that has occurred.

Year	Franchise	Relocation or Expansion
1991	San Jose Sharks	Expansion
1992	Tampa Bay Lightning	Expansion
1993	Anaheim Ducks	Expansion
1993	Dallas Stars	Relocation (Minnesota)
1993	Florida Panthers	Expansion
1995	Colorado Avalanche	Relocation (Quebec City)
1996	Phoenix Coyotes	Relocation (Winnipeg)
1997	Carolina Hurricanes	Relocation (Hartford)
1998	Nashville Predators	Expansion
1999	Atlanta Thrashers	Expansion
2000	Columbus Blue Jackets	Expansion
2000	Minnesota Wild	Expansion

FIGURE 3.6 **Franchise Relocation and Expansion in the National Hockey League, 1991–2000**

Regional population shifts, coupled with technology developments, have created marketing opportunities for sports properties. The availability of games and other programming on regional sports networks (RSNs) allows transplanted fans to maintain identification with teams of which they were fans before relocating to another part of the country. A fan of Ohio State University who relocates to Florida can continue to follow her favorite team through the Big Ten Network (television), radio broadcasts on XM Radio, and through the OSU's official website (www.ohiostatebuckeyes.com), and The Buckeye Insider, a paid access area of the website.

DECREASED LEISURE TIME. The ability for one to consume sports, either as a spectator or as a participant, is affected by the amount of leisure time available. Americans typically have fewer hours of leisure time per week than people in other industrialized countries. The amount of time Americans spend each week on leisure activities has declined. Currently, the average number of hours spent on all leisure activities was 4.42 hours for weekdays and 5.88 hours for weekends, down from 4.58 and 6.36 hours, respectively, in 2003.[37] Just as spending money on sports is a discretionary purchase, the decision to allocate time to watch or participate in sports is a choice of how to use limited available time.

Because consumers have less leisure, commitments to multi-game ticket packages for spectator sports is more challenging to attain. This challenge escalates as the number of events held increases. For example, it is less difficult for people to make time to attend one or more of the University of Tennessee's home football games, because the schedule typically consists of six or seven dates. In contrast, the Tennessee Smokies, a minor league baseball team in the Class AA Southern League, is challenged to fill the 6,400 seats at Smokies Park because of the approximately seventy home games each season. Thus, full-season ticket plans may have less appeal than buying single or multi-game tickets. One response to this challenge is to offer a variety of ticket options and incentives. For instance, a multi-game package that is made up of mostly weekend dates can appeal to fans who have more free time on weekends. Also, offering deep price discounts on dates with a history of weak demand can be an incentive to engage in leisure consumption. College students might be targeted on Thursday nights to appeal to their desire to have a "night on the town," and it may help a sports property stimulate demand on a day of the week that is known for less demand than other days of the week.

INTEREST IN SOCIAL RESPONSIBILITY. A trend that reflects changing views about the obligations of businesses to better society will likely impact marketing practice for years to come. For many consumers, it is not enough that marketers offer good value for the products they sell. They must also conduct business in a way that positively impacts the communities in which they operate. Consumers have high expectations of businesses to demonstrate social responsibility by supporting causes or charities. A nationwide survey found that 83% of consumers believe companies have a responsibility to support causes. The payoffs for supporting causes include a more positive image of a sponsoring firm (92%) and consideration to switch to a brand supporting a cause (87%).[38]

The expectations the general public has for businesses to engage in supporting causes and charities carries over to the sports industry. The high profile of athletes and their status as role models to youth and local communities make social responsibility a particularly important strategy for sports properties. While there are possibilities to generate revenue through merchandise sales of cause-themed products and tickets to cause-related promotions at sporting events, sports brands should engage in social responsibility initiatives for the same reasons as other types of firms: it relates closely to the mission of the organization.

Many sports properties support youth-oriented causes given their influence on young people as well as their long-term potential as fans. The National Football League launched a campaign called "Play 60." The program encourages kids to engage in physical activity (not necessarily football) for 60 minutes a day. The idea is to promote health and fitness among a population experiencing alarmingly high obesity rates.

Social responsibility activities can also be found in women's college basketball. Many sports have aligned themselves with cancer-related causes, but the Women's Basketball Coaches Association created an initiative that resonates with the target audience of women's college basketball. In February each year, many women's basketball teams host a "Pink Zone" game to raise awareness and money for the Kay Yow Cancer Fund, named in honor of the North Carolina State women's basketball coach who lost her battle with cancer. Teams wear pink uniforms, and game-worn items are often auctioned to raise money for the cause.[39]

Another aspect of social responsibility for which consumers' expectations are high is how businesses impact the environment. **Green marketing**, the term used to describe practices used in the production, distribution, and promotion of products that promote environmental protection, is not new. However, growth in the world population and debate about the effects of global climate change has prompted more concern about the impact businesses have on the environment. This trend has extended to consumer behavior. A recent study found that 90% of American adults have incorporated some level of green behavior into their daily lives, including 9% of the population indicating they had gone completely green.[40] This level of interest in the environment suggests green marketing is no longer a fad, but a trend that will shape marketing decisions and buyer behavior for years to come.

An advertisement by Interstate All Battery Center highlighting green marketing efforts through recycling.

The sports industry may not face some of the green marketing challenges experienced by product manufacturers such as maximizing use of recycled materials and minimizing waste in packaging, but one area in which concern for environmental impact is evident is energy consumption. Facilities hosting sporting events can consume vast amounts of energy for lighting and temperature control. A nationwide initiative that has made its way to the sports industry is Leadership in Energy and Environmental Design (LEED). It is a designation sponsored by the U.S. Green Building Council (a nonprofit organization, not a government agency) that acknowledges a facility's concern for minimizing environmental impact. Philips Arena in Atlanta, home of the NBA's Atlanta Hawks, was one of the first sports facilities to earn LEED designation. Arena management modified operations resulting in a savings of almost 2 million gallons of water per year and reduction of energy use by 8%.[41]

The benefits of promoting environmental concern include both intrinsic (protecting the environment) and extrinsic (brand image enhancement). A fine line exists between communicating green practices to encourage responsible consumption and promoting green tactics for image benefits. The term "**greenwashing**" refer to companies that make claims about their environmental practices that are deemed questionable or self-serving. While sports entities have to be careful about greenwashing, they have the potential to influence the public's attitudes and behaviors toward environmentalism. Thus, sports businesses should tell their green stories.[42] Sports properties can not only minimize their environmental impact, they can encourage their customers (especially fans) to "go green" by educating them on the property's green efforts and ways that individuals can engage in green behavior at the event and in their daily activities.

Strategic Planning: Process and Methods

The first step in the strategic planning process, establishing the organization's values and mission, was identified in Chapter 1 as a key strategic decision that must be made before any other strategies and tactics can be developed. Discussion of the strategic planning process in this chapter picks up at the second step: conducting a situation analysis. Figure 3.7 lists the steps in the strategic planning process that will be presented.

FIGURE 3.7 **Steps in the Strategic Planning Process**

1. **Determine Values and Mission**

2. **Conduct Situation Analysis**
   • SWOT analysis
   • SWOT actions (MAC)

3. **Set Goals and Objectives**
   • Financial goals and objectives
   • Communication goals and objectives

4. **Gather Information**
   • Secondary data
   • Primary data

5. **Develop Strategic Plans**

Conducting a Situation Analysis

Review of the external marketing environment is an essential step in the strategic planning process. Despite the portrayals of great marketing campaigns being drawn up on napkins at a restaurant during a three-martini lunch, the process of marketing planning is rather structured and systematic. Once the external marketing environment has been assessed, it is possible to conduct a situation analysis of the internal and external issues that could potentially impact an organization's operations. A situation analysis is a snapshot at a particular point in time. In order to gain maximum benefit from a situation analysis, the snapshot must be taken periodically to capture changes in the situation.

SWOT Analysis as an Analytical Tool

A popular analytical tool used at this stage of the strategic planning process is a SWOT analysis. **SWOT** is an acronym that stands for strengths, weaknesses, opportunities, and threats, with strengths and weaknesses being internal characteristics or issues in the firm while opportunities and threats are occurrences or trends taking place beyond the walls of an organization.

STRENGTHS AND WEAKNESSES. Characteristics of an organization that are specific to it can potentially be favorable (strengths) or unfavorable (weaknesses). These characteristics often are the result of previous strategic decisions and actions, good or bad. A starting point for identifying strengths and weaknesses is reviewing performance relative to the marketing mix variables: product, price, place, and promotion. For example, a strength ESPN possesses is its ability to promote its programming across multiple media platforms (television, radio, Internet, mobile, and magazine).

Another important internal area that should be examined is an organization's customer relationships. The Detroit Tigers experienced a significant decline in season ticket sales heading into the 2009 season, with sales down from an average of 27,000 per game the year before to 15,000.[43] Regardless of whether such a decline is due to external factors or missteps within an organization, the trend represents a weakness that must be acknowledged.

Finally, an organization's assets should be evaluated to identify strengths or weaknesses. Assets would include such things as physical structures, technological capabilities, human resources, intellectual property (e.g., trademarks and copyrights), and financial resources. For example, Under Armour has experienced tremendous success in the performance apparel segment of the sporting goods industry. However, it does not have a patent for the fabric that wicks away sweat from the body.[44] The lack of legal protection for this proprietary process could be viewed as a weakness because it leaves Under Armour susceptible to competitors offering similar products. Examples of internal issues that are considered when conducting a SWOT analysis are given in Figure 3.8.

Potential Strengths	Potential Weaknesses
• High brand awareness	• Lack of clear brand position
• Outstanding brand reputation	• Image problems with stakeholders
• Low cost structure	• Inability to charge price premiums
• Extensive distribution network	• High employee turnover
• Product/service design capabilities	• Low customer retention rates
• Facilities	• Unfavorable media rights terms
• Brand licensing agreements	• Late entrant into a market
• Market share strength	• Limited geographic market reach
• Brand loyal customers	• Ineffective promotion campaigns
• Service-oriented culture	• Limited product offering
• Financial reserves	

FIGURE 3.8 **Examples of Strengths and Weaknesses**

OPPORTUNITIES AND THREATS. External trends and developments cannot be controlled by an organization, but they must be recognized. A general rule to apply to an issue to determine if it is internal or external is to ask the question "If our organization went away, would the issue go away, too?" If the answer is "no," the issue is an external matter, which means other organizations in the same industry or category are likely to be affected by it.

Factors in the external marketing environment discussed earlier in this chapter (competition, economy, technology, legal/political/regulatory, and sociodemographic are the areas in which opportunities and threats are located. Given that these external occurrences are beyond the control of an organization, the task of a manager conducting a SWOT analysis is to identify the relevant external issues that could potentially help or harm business. Relevance is important, because some external occurrences may have little bearing on the operations of an organization.

The expansion of mixed martial arts discussed earlier in this chapter was made possible largely by changes in state laws to allow sanctioned events. This development has a tremendous impact on Ultimate Fighting Championship (UFC), a promoter of mixed martial arts events, but it would have no impact on the National Football League. However, regulatory changes benefiting mixed martial arts are very relevant to marketers of boxing and professional wrestling. Expansion of mixed martial arts events would pose a significant competitive threat to both sports. Figure 3.9 contains examples of external factors that a sports organization might identify in a SWOT analysis.

FIGURE 3.9 Examples of Opportunities and Threats

Potential Opportunities	Potential Threats
• Growth of customer markets (current and potential)	• Presence of new competitors
• Economic recovery/boom	• Economic downturn
• New technologies	• Technologies becoming obsolete
• Government deregulation	• Increased government regulation
• New trends/preferences in popular culture	• Changes in customers' tastes/wants
• Expansion into foreign markets	• New products/innovations by competitors
• Higher discretionary spending	• Lower consumer confidence
• Missteps by a competitor	• Cultural differences in foreign markets

Acting on SWOT Analysis Findings

The value of conducting a SWOT analysis is not the creation of a list of internal and external issues an organization faces. A SWOT analysis is useful if findings are translated into strategies an organization will pursue in its quest to carry out its mission. Marketing strategy experts O. C. Ferrell and Michael Hartline state that managers must consider the following in order to make the transition from review of current situation to strategies for the future:

1. Review of strengths and weaknesses must go beyond an organization's resources; consideration of processes that can meet customers' needs is required to provide solutions, not just products.

2. Matching strengths with market opportunities is essential in setting business objectives.

3. Weaknesses can be overcome by committing to invest resources into areas that address limitations (e.g., customer service, marketing communication, and research and development).[45]

An approach for translating SWOT analysis findings into marketing strategies is to follow **MAC: Match, Avoid,** or **Convert** (see Figure 3.10). The ideal starting point is to *match* strengths possessed by an organization with external trends that are viewed as opportunities. A minor league baseball team might identify "affordable family entertainment" as a strength and "consumers seek value in discretionary spending" as an opportunity. The result might be

FIGURE 3.10 Translating SWOT Analysis into Marketing Strategies

Match – strength with external opportunity.

Avoid – exposure to weakness or threat.

Convert – weakness into strength.

creating experiential marketing elements and a promotion campaign that focus on the message that the team delivers family entertainment at an affordable price.

Avoid is a decision to not make strategic choices that expose an organization to its vulnerabilities internally (i.e., weaknesses) or threats in the marketing environment. If a team holds its events in a venue that is not modern in terms of technology or amenities offered, it should avoid marketing strategies that focus on these aspects of attending a sporting event. The team brand, individual performers, or some other relevant source of star power could be emphasized, but the venue would have limited impact as a marketing asset.

Convert is a strategic option in which weaknesses can be addressed so that at a minimum they are no longer limitations, or ideally, they become strengths. The National Football League and its teams have addressed the problem of unruly fan behavior influenced by alcohol consumption that detracts from the experience enjoyed by other spectators, a weakness. A fan code of conduct, "drink responsibly" messages printed on beer cups, security cameras used to monitor crowds, and text message reporting of fan misbehavior are steps that have been taken in an attempt to overcome the weakness, with the ultimate aim being to make security at NFL games a strength.

Setting Goals and Objectives

Decisions about how to use findings from a SWOT analysis lead to establishing performance targets for an organization. Setting goals and objectives is one of the most important strategic planning steps. The terms *goals* and *objectives* are often used interchangeably, and while they are both concerned with performance or results, they are distinct planning activities. **Goals** are general statements about what an organization wants to be, do, or become. They are broad statements that are not necessarily measurable as stated. For example, if the New Orleans Hornets stated a goal of "delivering the best game experience to fans of any team in the NBA," it would provide direction on what the marketing staff and the organization as a whole should do. All marketing strategies and tactics should be developed with the goal of creating a great experience for customers. In that sense, goals orient marketers to what they should be focusing on to improve their business. Goals are valuable because they connect the marketing function to the broader purpose of the organization expressed in its mission statement.

However, goals are lacking in specificity and accountability, which is where objectives come into the strategic planning process to build on stated goals. **Objectives** state the outcomes, or what should be achieved as a result of the investment in marketing activities. An analogy for setting objectives is if you were writing a novel and wrote the concluding chapter first. Once you had established how the story would end, you write chapters that create situations and actions that lead to the conclusion. Marketing planning is no different. Objectives are the "storybook" ending expected from marketing strategy; target market selection, brand positioning, and decisions about how to implement a marketing mix represent the storyline that takes an organization to its desired conclusion. Managers involved in the strategic planning process must always be mindful that objectives set must be consistent with the organization's mission since it guides all actions.

The two general types of marketing objectives are financial objectives and communication objectives. **Financial objectives** are desired outcomes that have direct impact on an organization's revenues or profits. Marketers must include this type of objective in marketing plans. Marketing activities that do not result in more customers, sales, or revenues are questionable at best, and likely wasteful! While financial objectives are a must, it is unrealistic to assume that all marketing tactics have the potential to persuade people to take action. Some consumers will not be close to considering a sports brand; they may not even be aware that it exists. Because a target market can be at different stages of a relationship with a brand, it is necessary to include communication objectives in strategic plans to define the brand in the minds of consumers and pull them toward a decision to buy. **Communication objectives** are desired outcomes from marketing communications. Examples of financial and communication objectives are shown in Figure 3.11. Communication objectives are discussed in-depth in Chapter 8 as an essential strategic decision that must be in place before brand communications tactics can be planned.

FIGURE 3.11 **Examples of Marketing Plan Objectives**

Financial Objectives
• Sell the equivalent of 15,000 full-season tickets (FSEs)
• Increase merchandise sales online by 15%
• Increase per-capita purchases of event attendees by 10%
• Expand operations into 4 new markets
• Convert 500 first-time attendees to multi-game ticket plan buyers

Communication Objectives
• Create brand awareness among 80% of women ages 25–44 in geographic market
• Create brand image of "community oriented" among 50% of target market
• Be considered for purchase as an entertainment option by 35% of target market
• Achieve 10,000 fans on official Facebook fan page
• Add 5,000 persons to database to receive e-mail newsletters and offers

Any objective established, whether it is a financial objective or communication objective, should meet the following five criteria:

- **Specific** – It must be detailed enough to know whether the desired impact was achieved.
- **Measurable** – It must be measurable.
- **Achievable** – Objective must be realistic for the period of time it covers.
- **Challenging** – The purpose of setting objectives is to grow; even if an objective is not achieved, the result should be advancement.
- **Time frame** – A deadline or time frame must be identified.

Taken together, the criteria for developing objectives and a deadline for achieving them create accountability for the actions of marketers in an organization.

Gathering Information to Manage the Marketing Environment

Within the sports industry, leagues, teams, and companies all track developments and trends among customers and the external marketing environment. Tracking trends requires collecting data and turning the data into useful information that can be used to make marketing decisions. Two general types of information are available: secondary data and primary data. It is important to remember that information itself cannot make marketing decisions, but information enables managers to make more informed choices about the marketing strategies and tactics to employ.

Secondary Data Sources

Secondary data represent information that exists already and could be used in the evaluation of the marketing environment. Use of secondary data should be considered the starting point when determining information needs. Secondary data offers advantages of speed of access and low costs compared to collecting data to address a specific information need. The main limitation of secondary data is applicability to specific situations. The information needs of a particular marketing problem or opportunity may not be fully served by using data previously gathered, likely gathered for some other purpose than the situation at hand. Despite this limitation, secondary data provides information in a timely manner that can add to understanding of customers, competition, or some other element of the marketing environment. Figure 3.12 identifies secondary data sources used frequently by sports marketers.

CUSTOMER RELATIONSHIP MANAGEMENT SYSTEM. Information about customers can be collected, analyzed, and used for making decisions on an ongoing basis through implementation of a customer relationship management (CRM) system. While there are many aspects of CRM,

- Customer relationship management systems
- United States Census Bureau
- Professional and industry publications
- Syndicated research
- Social media buzz

FIGURE 3.12 Sources of Secondary Data

the analytical aspect is the "capture, storage, organization, analysis, interpretation and use of data collected from the operational side of the business."[46] A CRM system enables marketers to identify customers based on demographic characteristics, purchase volume, frequency, or profitability. Also, customer transaction data can yield insight into what promotions, events, or other variables influence customer buying behavior. Data are collected through different interactions with customers: website visits, promotion entry forms, and purchase transactions are three examples of data creation points. The result can be a significant accumulation of information about customers. "We know where fans like to sit, which day of the week they bought their tickets, and how to best reach them," says Scott O'Neil, vice president of team marketing and business operations for the NBA.[47] CRM systems can create a rather clear picture of current customers, which sets the stage for devising marketing strategies and tactics to attract new customers as well as strengthen relationships with current customers.

U.S. CENSUS DATA. The U.S. Census Bureau compiles information on the nation's residents. A census of the entire population is undertaken once every ten years, and estimates of population are made during the years in between census years. Typical demographic information collected includes a breakdown by gender, various age groups, and race for the United States, but also by region, state, county, and city. The census data also provide number and types of households, education levels, employment by industry, occupations, and income levels. This type of data is useful for marketing professionals needing general population characteristics of a region or area. It is readily available and easily accessible.

PROFESSIONAL AND INDUSTRY PUBLICATIONS. A useful source of information for characteristics of the sports industry and trends observed is publications from groups and organizations that follow sports. Street & Smith's Sports Group publishes the *Sports Business Research Guide & Fact Book* annually. It contains directory information on more than 8,000 companies representing ten different sectors of sports business. Typical information includes address, phone, website, executive officers, and basic financial information such as revenue, net income, and number of employees. For sports marketers, important information contained in the publication is a list of sponsorships. For instance, 3M's sponsorships include:

- Champions Tour 3M Championships (title sponsor)
- Minnesota Twins (MLB)
- Minnesota Timberwolves (NBA)
- NASCAR Sprint Cup Series 3M Performance 400
- NASCAR Sprint Cup No. 16, Greg Biffle
- Minnesota Lynx (WNBA)

Additional information about sponsorships can be found in *IEG Sponsorship Report*. The publication has news articles about sponsorships regularly. Both publications provide information at a much lower cost than conducting primary research.

SYNDICATED RESEARCH. Market research firms conduct studies and collect data on an ongoing basis and offer reports of their findings to interested firms. This service, known as **syndicated research**, is available for purchase by any member of an industry. Although insight gained from syndicated research reports may not fit information needs perfectly, the speed of acquiring the information at a cost lower than conducting primary research makes this option attractive to many marketers.

A well-known syndicated research firm in the sports industry is Scarborough Research. It conducts consumer research in approximately eighty major markets, measuring consumer demographic characteristics, media usage patterns, shopping behavior, and lifestyles. Suppose NASCAR, or one of its brand sponsors, wanted to locate the cities that had the highest percentage of NASCAR fans. A report by Scarborough ranks the eighty-one DMAs (designated market areas) in the United States by the percentage of fans who are "very, somewhat, or a little" interested in NASCAR. At the top of the list is Charlotte, North Carolina. Figure 3.13 has information on the top ten DMAs for NASCAR.[48]

FIGURE 3.13 Top 10 DMAs of NASCAR Fans as a Percentage of the City's Population

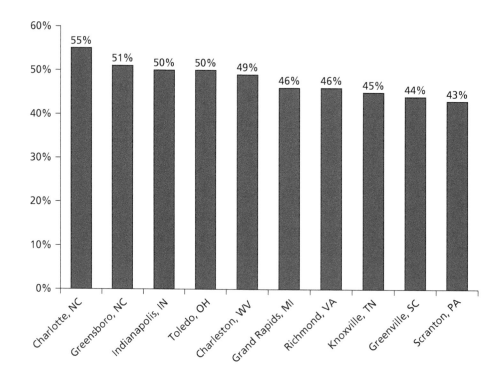

SOCIAL MEDIA BUZZ. One of the newest sources of secondary information is monitoring what is being said about a brand in social media channels. These conversations, often referred to as buzz by marketers, reflect the perceptions and experiences customers and others have for a sports brand or its competitors. Using social media to communicate with customers holds great appeal for marketers, but the ability to listen to what is being said may be an even more important payoff. Listening is crucial because the buzz heard about a brand or its competitors should influence marketing decisions.

An example of a company from outside the sports industry that effectively uses social media as a source of secondary data is Comcast. It uses social media tools like Twitter to monitor what people are saying about the company. If there are complaints or problems with Comcast service discussed in users' tweets, Comcast's official Twitter account, Comcastcares, can respond to the complaint or problem within a matter of minutes. The result is that negative buzz can be stopped or at least minimized, and in this case Comcast's proactive use of Twitter for listening and responding enhances perceptions of service quality.

Sports marketers can follow Comcast's practice and use social media to listen to what fans are saying about their brands. Monitoring social media could be a source for gathering market information that reveals a fan who posts a blog entry about a bad experience at a game or event, tactics that other sports properties are using to reach customers (and what their customers have to say about those tactics), or buzz about current or prospective sponsors. Figure 3.14 provides a partial list of tools for monitoring social media buzz. Social media monitoring will not replace traditional information-gathering approaches, but it adds another means for learning from the marketing environment.

Tool	Source	Description
Google Trends	http://www.google.com/trends	Reports keywords being used in Google search engine
Radian6	http://www.radian6.com	Service offering comprehensive monitoring of various social media channels
Socialmention	http://www.socialmention.com	Real time search for mentions by social media type (e.g., blogs) or platform (e.g., YouTube)
Technorati	http://www.technorati.com	Directory of blogs
Twitter Search	http://search.twitter.com	Current topics being discussed on Twitter
Twackle	http://www.twackle.com	Compiles sports stories and information being shared across the Web

FIGURE 3.14 Tools for Monitoring Social Media

Primary Data Sources

Secondary data collection is often supplemented with primary data. The main benefit of using primary data is that information needs can be tailored to address the marketing problem or opportunity at hand. Information obtained is not limited to what has already been collected by someone else for some other purpose, as is the case with secondary data. The more unique a marketing problem is or the more critical addressing the problem is to an organization, the greater the need to collect primary data. For example, if a team experiences a significant decline in season ticket renewals, it would benefit from conducting a survey of nonrenewal customers to gain an understanding of the reasons for their decision to not renew season tickets. Then, adjustments could be made to ticket-holder benefits, pricing, or other marketing elements that could reduce the number of nonrenewals. Figure 3.15 lists the three most common methods for collecting primary data.

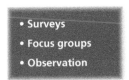

- Surveys
- Focus groups
- Observation

FIGURE 3.15 Methods of Collecting Primary Data

SURVEYS. Survey research has a long tradition in marketing research as a method for interacting with consumers to gather primary data. A key consideration for conducting survey research is deciding what communication channel to use to reach the population you wish to survey. The most common channels for reaching consumers include telephone, mail, online, and face-to-face.

Telephone and mail surveys are more costly and have relatively low response rates. Answering machines, caller id, and cell phones have reduced the attractiveness of telephone research. Online surveys get around the drawback of the high costs since survey invitations can be delivered via e-mail or posted on a sports property's website. Subscribers to e-mail newsletters and records in a CRM system are excellent sources of e-mail addresses. Alternatively, online surveys can be hosted on free web-based platforms such as Survey Monkey, or they can be created and delivered by a service such as Zoomerang. These companies are also able to provide a sample of consumers to participate in a survey. Another advantage of online surveys is that consumers can provide feedback at their convenience, and if they do not respond it is very inexpensive to send a follow-up invitation to participate.

Online surveys can be used to gather a wide range of information about customers. The Detroit Red Wings of the NHL posted an online survey in order to collect information on fan behaviors, such as number of games attended and how tickets were obtained, influences on attendance decision, and attitudes toward different ticket package options. The feedback from this type of research gives the organization a better understanding of its customers and their views on how the team can improve its offerings.

Face-to-face surveys conducted with attendees at a game or event can be a way to capture information quickly and while aspects of the experience are fresh on the minds of attendees. A limitation of face-to-face surveys is that they can be viewed as intrusive to attendees. After all, they came to enjoy an event, not take a survey! Thus, face-to-face surveys should be kept brief. One approach for making face-to-face surveys convenient for attendees is by delivering them on electronic devices. Subjects are given handheld devices and asked to complete survey questions. The added benefit of this approach is data collected can be compiled and analyzed quickly.

FOCUS GROUPS. A method for gathering more in-depth information from a smaller number of subjects is to use focus groups. A focus group consists of six to twelve "typical" customers or prospects who answer questions and give input in a group setting. A moderator guides the conversation, and meetings are recorded and often observed by the organization sponsoring the research. Input from focus group members tends to be more detailed than what can be obtained from survey research. Also, a focus group moderator can guide the conversation to capture information from participants based on points made during the meeting. Surveys lack the flexibility to deviate from the format of the questionnaire.

When Arthur Blank became owner of the Atlanta Falcons of the NFL, he introduced focus group research to the franchise, which was not surprising given that Blank was a cofounder of retail giant the Home Depot. The input from participants may seem minor—more ketchup and straws in concessions areas, more parking, and more convenient entry into the Georgia Dome.[49] However, learning what customers disliked about their experience of attending Falcons games enabled team marketers to make improvements that were within their control. Multiple focus groups can be used to get the perspectives of a variety of customer segments, such as season ticket holders, families with young children, women, and minorities. The main drawback to focus group research is the time and expense involved in recruiting subjects and compensating them for participation.

OBSERVATION. Surveys and focus groups collect data by having researchers taking a prominent role in their interactions with respondents, seeking to obtain answers to specific questions. An alternative approach to collecting primary data is to observe behavior in a natural environment, with the subjects unaware that their behavior is being observed. A frequently used observation method is to employ mystery shoppers who pose as customers but are actually gathering information on their interactions with a firm's employees. In the context of a sporting event, mystery shoppers can be used to assess the process of admission to a venue, courtesy shown by ticket office personnel and ushers, cleanliness of restrooms, and service delivered by foodservice employees. Feedback from mystery shoppers can be used to detect problems in service delivery, identify areas in which greater employee training may be needed, recognize employees for outstanding performance, and counsel employees whose performance does not meet expectations.

The most effective marketing research programs contain a combination of secondary and primary data and also utilize multiple sources of information within each type of data. This approach to gathering information captures data from multiple perspectives and overcomes the fact that there is no one perfect method for collecting data. The NFL's Houston Texans have been proactive in collecting primary data. The team has conducted online surveys of suite holders and season ticket customers, held focus groups made up of customers from the same two segments to assess the quality of fans' game-day experience, and used mystery shoppers to evaluate the customer service performance of game-day personnel.[50]

Developing Strategic Plans

Understanding the marketing environment is the foundation for developing strategic plans for a sports organization. Good strategic plans do not happen accidentally, nor are they devised over a dinner meeting on a napkin; they are developed through hard work and solid analysis.

Insider Insights Sean Hanrahan – ESPN

Q. How do you see marketing research fitting into the process of identifying marketing opportunities? For example, how should a company that uses sponsorship as a marketing platform utilize research in the planning process?

A. After you have done the research and identified the right sport for your brand, you need to determine what mix of media, sponsorship, and activation you need to fulfill your marketing objectives. The critical piece that can often be missing is making sure these things work in concert. Too often, brands do not manage across these disciplines and miss the opportunity to maximize the impact of having the entire marketing mix work together. Oftentimes, the development of sports marketing programs seems more like art than science, but it is much easier to get to the right idea for how a brand can use sports to build equity and drive sales when you have done the proper evaluation.

Q. Can you share some observations on best practices in the use of marketing research in sports media?

A. When it comes to market research, you need to look at three elements of the sports marketing mix separately—media, sponsorship, activation—as each of these has different methods of evaluation and some are more effectively measured than others. Media is the one that has the most discipline around market research, as there are a variety of ways to measure its effectiveness. A very common method is from

ESPN Internet Group

Sean Hanrahan highlights the importance of marketing research in sports marketing.

Nielsen, which provides the ratings and demographic mix of televised events so that brands can see who their message is reaching. There are also media sponsorship evaluation methods like those provided by Image Impact, which measure the exposure a brand receives in televised sporting events. This technology automatically notes when a brand's logo appears on screen and based on its size, duration of time on screen, and whether it is in isolation or appearing with other brands, assigns a media value to that exposure. This gives brands an effective way to measure the added-value components of their media deal.

Q. What are some developments in the use of marketing research that can enhance a marketer's ability to gather information to make decisions?

A. In studying consumers' responses to advertising, sophisticated techniques such as neurofocus testing are being used more often. Neurofocus testing measures the emotional connection a fan makes with a brand in sports content through the use of eye tracking and galvanic skin response. Where media companies are trying to break new ground is measuring the interaction and effectiveness of multimedia campaigns—how each platform (TV, online, mobile, radio, magazine) is used by consumers and how they work together to increase a brand's advertising effectiveness. Sports tends to be the one genre that allows for the greatest integration across platforms, as the content is easily translatable.

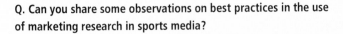

Strategic plans lead to tactical decisions about what the organization is going to offer and to whom it will offer it. This involves developing the brand, defining the product, deciding the pricing structure, choosing the optimal distribution channels, and creating the most effective communications. It involves public relations and sponsorships. It involves delivering an exciting experience to customers. All of these topics are presented in future chapters of this text. Although presented in a sequential manner, marketers must consider the entire realm of activities in totality in order to ensure all of the parts work together and synergy is created to produce a successful sports entertainment property.

Chapter Summary

All sound marketing decisions are made with an "outside-in" approach, examining what is taking place outside an organization before making strategy decisions internally. The importance of monitoring and understanding what is taking place with customers and the external marketing environment cannot be overstated. A quote from the movie *Field of Dreams* that says, "If you build it, they will come" is fantasy, not reality, when it comes to sports marketing. Yes, consumers tend to have more passionate, emotionally based relationships with sports brands that they probably do not have with other types of products that they consume. However, the intensity of competition for entertainment expenditures, uncertain economic conditions, changing preferences and behaviors of consumers, and technology innovations make sports consumption far from a given, even among people who identify themselves as fans of a particular sports league, team, or athlete. Thus, taking a figurative snapshot of the five areas of the external marketing environment on a regular basis is essential in keeping pace with changes outside an organization. The makeup of the snapshot is secondary and primary data that provide insight and answers to what is taking place in the external environment. Then, and only then, are marketers equipped to make decisions on strategy and tactics with the aim of advancing the mission of a sports organization.

Review Questions

1. What is meant by the term "external marketing environment" and what are the five factors or forces within an external environment?
2. Identify the three levels of competition for a sports entertainment property.
3. Identify the various economic indicators that a sports organization might monitor.
4. Explain why it is important to monitor technology changes for a sports entertainment property.
5. What is the difference between industry regulation of a sport and government regulation?
6. Identify the six sociodemographic trends that have impacted sports marketing and are likely to continue to have an impact.
7. Describe how the growth in the age 65+ population will create both opportunities and challenges for sports marketing.
8. Describe the economic impact and influence women have on purchasing of goods and services, including sporting events.
9. How has the shifting of populations in various regions in the United States impacted the sports industry?
10. Discuss the relationship between amount of leisure time and sports marketing.
11. What expectations does society have for sports properties in terms of social responsibility?
12. What is a situation analysis?
13. What is meant by the term SWOT analysis?
14. Explain the concept of MAC (match, avoid, convert).
15. What are the two types of marketing objectives? Define each one.
16. What are the five characteristics of a good objective?
17. What is the difference between secondary data and primary data?
18. Identify the chief sources of secondary data.
19. What is a customer relationship management (CRM) system?
20. Describe the various tools a sports property can use to monitor social media.
21. Identify the chief methods of collecting primary research data.

New Terms

External marketing environment characteristics, developments, or trends happening outside of an organization that could potentially impact it.

Brand competition brands or firms that target similar customers with comparable products and prices.

Category competition brands or organizations whose offerings meet the same or similar customer need.

Generic competition any good or service for which a consumer might make a purchase that would prevent purchasing a ticket to a sporting event.

Sociodemographic trends   changes in characteristics of behaviors and demographic profile of people over time.

Culture   system of beliefs, values, and behaviors that members of a society adopt and pass along from one generation to the next.

Green marketing   practices used in the production, distribution, and promotion of products that promote environmental protection.

Greenwashing   making claims about environmental practices that are deemed questionable or self-serving.

SWOT   acronym that stands for strengths, weaknesses, opportunities, and threats.

MAC (match, avoid, convert)   approach for translating the results of a SWOT analysis into marketing strategies.

Goals   General statements about what an organization wants to be, do, or become.

Objectives   The outcomes to be achieved as a result of the investment in marketing activities.

Financial objectives   desired outcomes that have a direct impact on an organization's revenues or profits.

Communication objectives   desired outcomes from marketing communications.

Syndicated research   research conducted by professional research organizations and available for purchase by any member of an industry.

Discussion and Critical Thinking Exercises

1. Pick a professional sports entertainment property in your area. Using Figure 3.2 as a guide, identify the primary competitors the sports team faces in each of the levels of competition. Be specific with names of teams, products, etc.
2. Pick one of the collegiate sports at your university or a minor league sports team. Using Figure 3.2 as a guide, identify the primary competitors the college sport faces in each of the levels of competition. Be specific with names of products and sports.
3. Suppose one of your responsibilities as an intern for a minor league baseball team in your area is to monitor the economic environment. First, explain why it is important. Second, from the list of potential economic indicators given in Figure 3.3, identify the top three you would monitor. Explain why it would be important and how you could use the information to make marketing decisions.
4. As a sports fan, what do you think of paperless tickets to attend a sporting event? What about e-tickets that you receive and print yourself from the Internet?
5. As you consider technology today, what advances in technology could a sports property use to enhance the fan experience at the event? Explain how it could benefit fans and reduce costs for the sports property.
6. For sports teams, why is self-regulation preferable to government regulations? Justify your answer with examples.
7. Interview three individuals in the baby boomer generation (born between 1946 and 1964) about their attitudes towards sports. Interview five individuals from your generation. Discuss the similarities and differences between the two generation cohorts.
8. Interview three females of various ages and ethnic backgrounds about sports. Ask about their attitudes towards sports, attendance at sporting events, favorite sports, why they attend sporting events or why they don't attend, and what they like and dislike about sporting events. Summarize your findings.
9. Access the websites of three different professional sports teams. For each, identify ways the team is demonstrating its social responsibility.
10. Almost every professional sports property has some type of presence in social media— Facebook, Twitter, and others. Is it important for a professional team to be involved in social media? Why or why not? Describe the benefits of being involved in social media and ways you think a sports property should be involved.

You Make the Call
Marketing Louisiana Downs

Louisiana Downs in Bossier City/Shreveport, Louisiana, has been in existence for thirty-eight years. It is located on a 350-acre plot, and has over 1,500 stables, the horse racing track, a casino operated by Harrah's Entertainment, and a 151-suite hotel operated by Marriott. The season schedule consists of 46 dates for quarter horse races and 84 dates for thoroughbred races. Fans and individuals involved with the horse racing rate Louisiana Downs as one of the finest racing facilities in the nation.

Louisiana Downs, however, faces the same issues most racing tracks in the United States face: declining attendance and declining wagers on the horse races. Horse racing's glory days were in the 1950s, when the only place someone could gamble legally was at the racetrack. The sport was hurt with the rise of state lotteries and then the expansion of riverboats and casinos. Now it is the Internet. Individuals can gamble and even wager on horse races from the convenience of their homes.

The most obvious need facing Louisiana Downs is to attract new fans. The majority of serious fans of horse racing are aging white males. A challenge in drawing new fans to horse racing is the complexity of understanding the sport. Understanding who wins a race is easy; it is the horse and rider that crosses the finish line first. But after that it becomes very complex and difficult to understand horse racing stats. It is a steep learning curve and requires thoughtful and complex analysis, which most potential fans don't want to invest the time or energy to learn. According to Tim Capps, a professor at the University of the Louisville College of Business, horse racing "has been run more for itself than for its fans. One thing racing has to do is make participation in our sport easier for fans, because the fan has not come first in our industry." He further adds, "People don't want to go to school. They want to be entertained."

While all agree that there is a need to attract new fans, there is wide disagreement on what type of fan it should be. Do you market to the individuals who are already going to the track, or do you go after new individuals? Do you go after young people, middle-aged individuals, or market harder to the baby boomers? Which gender, male or female, do you seek?

The most popular horse race in America is the Kentucky Derby, with some 150,000 attending the event and 14 million watching on television. Half of the audience is female. But once the Kentucky Derby is over, the sport reverts back to its core fan, the older male gambler. To counter this falloff, the Kentucky Derby and some of the other more famous racetracks have embarked on a marketing campaign of food, fashion, and celebrities. The two-minute horse race now becomes a two-hour "event" that appeals to the social needs of female attendees.

Realizing horse race betting was swiftly moving online, Louisiana Downs now has a marketing agreement with TwinSpires, making it the official wager provider for Louisiana Downs. TwinSpires is a part of Churchill Downs, which counts the Kentucky Derby among its sports and entertainment properties. Mark Midland, vice president of racing operations, indicates that TwinSpires dominates the online market for people to watch and wager on horse racing. TwinSpires offers Louisiana Downs customers with "a true horse racing experience with handicapping, wagering, live broadcasts, instant replays, and attractive player rewards." To promote Louisiana Downs, TwinSpires features Louisiana Downs content in targeted customer e-mails and mobile phone text messages. Louisiana Downs will use a similar strategy with their database, encouraging their fans to use TwinSpires.com for online wagers.

The future of Louisiana Downs depends on attracting more fans to the racetrack and increasing the level of wagers on the horse races. Doing so will be a difficult challenge.

Questions:

1. Analyze the competitive situation Louisiana Downs faces, using the three types of competitors.
2. Use the Internet and the information provided in this case to conduct a SWOT analysis.
3. Which of the sociodemographic trends should be considered by the marketing staff of Louisiana Downs? Explain why it is important.
4. Identify which sources of secondary data would be good sources of information. Explain how they could be used and the value of the data.
5. What methods of primary data collection could be used with current fans of Louisiana Downs? How could data be collected from individuals who have never been to the racetrack?
6. From your analysis of this case, how can Louisiana Downs attract new fans to the racetrack?

Sources: "2012 Harrah's Louisiana Downs Race Dates, accessed March 30, 2012 at https://www.harrahslouisianadowns.com/images/non_image_assets/2012RaceDateCalendar.pdf, "La. Downs: Plenty of Changes Set for New Meet," *NTRA*, www.ntra.com/content/display/news/MzI0ODE=, May 15, 2008; Burt Helm, "The Race for Kentucky Derby Viewers," *BusinessWeek Online*, April 30, 2009, p. 19; Liz Mullen, "Better Days Ahead for Thoroughbred Racetracks? Horse-racing Industry Faces Long Odds Trying to Attract New Fans, Grow Gambling Business," *Business First*, http://www.bizjournals.com/louisville/stories/2008/05/05/story1.html?page=all, May 2, 2008; "Youbet.com Louisiana Downs Have Marketing Agreement," www.horseracingnews.net/horse-racing-industry/youbetcom-and-harrahs-louisiana-downs, May 16, 2006. http://www.bloodhorse.com/horse-racing/articles/33570/youbetcom-louisiana-downs-have-marketing-agreement

References

1. Don Muret (2005), "Levy Slices into the Pie," *Sports Business Journal*, September 12, 1.
2. Bill King (2006), "Hurry Up and Wait," *Sports Business Journal*, October 30, 19.
3. Don Muret (2009), "Ballpark Value Menus Finding Plenty of Takers," *Sports Business Journal*, June 8, 14.
4. Don Muret (2009), "Dodgers, Bucs Back for More All-You-Can-Eat," *Sports Business Journal*, July 13, 5.
5. Jack Loechner (2009), "Recession's Lasting Effects on Consumers," accessed November 18, 2009, at http://www.mediapost.com/publications/?fa=Articles.showArticle&art_aid=117426.
6. O. C. Ferrell and Michael D. Hartline, *Marketing Strategy*, 4th edition (Mason, OH: Thomson South-Western, 2008).
7. Don Muret (2008), "Club to Take Swing at No-Cash Concessions" *Street & Smith Sports Business Journal*, February 25, 7.
8. Don Muret (2007), "Stadiums Strengthen Their Wireless Coverage," *Street & Smith's Sports Business Journal*, January 22, 5.
9. Don Muret (2008), "Cyrus Tour's Use of Paperless Tickets Gets Clubs' Interest," *Street & Smith's Sports Business Journal*, November 16, 8.
10. Jon Shaw (2009), "Going Paperless," *Street & Smith's Sports Business Journal*, November 9, 23A.
11. "YinzCam" (2010), accessed May 12, 2011, at http://www.yinzcam.com/about.html.
12. Kristie Chong (2011), "ESPN Pack Launches on Sprint ID Devices," January 4, accessed May 12, 2011, at http://www.espnmediazone3.com/us/2011/01/04/espn-pack-launches-on-sprint-id-devices/.
13. National Thoroughbred Racing Association, accessed January 22, 2010, at http://www.ntra.com.

14. United States Golf Association, accessed January 22, 2010, at http://www.usga.org/.
15. Greg Wyshynski, "NFL Ruins Historic Ad Campaign for Chicago Blackhawks, Bears," December 7, 2009, accessed January 22, 2010, at http://sports.yahoo.com/nhl/blog/puck_daddy/post/NFL-ruins-historic-ad-campaign-for-Chicago-Black?urn=nhl,207119.
16. John Lombardo and Terry Lefton, "NBA Cans Ban on Liquor Ads," *Sports Business Journal*, January 19, 2009, accessed January 22, 2010, at http://www.sportsbusinessjournal.com/article/61168.
17. International Kickboxing Federation, "In What States Are Kickboxing and/or MMA Legal?" accessed March 30, 2012, at http://www.ifightsports.com/USAStates.htm.
18. Cornell University Law School, "Antitrust," accessed January 20, 2010, at http://topics.law.cornell.edu/wex/antitrust.
19. Ronald Blum, "Why Is the Antitrust Exemption Important?" *USA Today*, December 6, 2001, accessed January 20, 2010, at http://www.usatoday.com/sports/baseball/stories/2001-12-05-antitrust-explanation.htm.
20. Martha Lagace, "Industry Self-Regulation: What's Working (and What's Not)?" Harvard Business School Working Knowledge, April 9, 2007, accessed January 20, 2010, at http://hbswk.hbs.edu/item/5590.html.
21. Clay Travis, "Is BCS Violating Antitrust Laws? Yes, If It Actually Existed," July 10, 2009, accessed January 20, 2010, at http://ncaafootball.fanhouse.com/2009/07/10/is-bcs-violating-antitrust-laws-yes-if-it-actually-existed/.
22. "Mountain West Conference Signs BCS TV Contract Despite Protest," *Sports Business Daily*, July 9, 2009, accessed January 20, 2010, at http://www.sportsbusinessdaily.com/article/131591.
23. Daniel G. Bates and Fred Plog, *Cultural Anthropology*, 3rd edition (New York: McGraw-Hill, 1976).
24. "Baby Boom," March 6, 2009, accessed January 27, 2010, at http://geography.about.com/od/populationgeography/a/babyboom.htm.
25. "A Profile of Older Americans: 2009," January 15, 2010, accessed January 25, 2010, at http://www.aoa.gov/AoARoot/Aging_Statistics/Profile/2009/4.aspx.
26. "Professional Football Continues Dominance over Baseball as America's Favorite Sport," January 27, 2009, accessed March 30, 2012, at http://www.harrisinteractive.com/vault/Harris-Interactive-Poll-Research-Fave-Sport-2009-01.pdf.
27. "U.S. Population Projections," October 1996, accessed January 25, 2010, at http://www.census.gov/population/www/projections/ppl47.html#tr-race.
28. U.S. Census Bureau, "Hispanics in the United States," accessed January 31, 2010, at http://www.census.gov/population/www/socdemo/hispanic/hispanic_pop_presentation.html.
29. Scott Warfield (2005), "Slow Start on the Field Hinders MLS' Chivas," *Sports Business Journal*, July 25, 6.
30. Tom Cordova (2009), "Success Begins with Understanding the Demo," *Sports Business Journal*, April 27, 17.
31. Lorrie Morgan-Ferrero (2008), "Pulling Back the Curtain on the Buying Power of Women," July, http://www.red-hot-copy.com/Articles_files/Pulling%20Back%20the%20Curtain%20on%20the%20Buying%20Power%20of%20Women.doc, accessed January 25, 2010.
32. Ibid.
33. Pew Research Center (2006), "Americans to the Rest of the World: Soccer Not Really Our Thing," accessed January 25, 2010, at http://www.pewsocialtrends.org/files/2010/10/Sports.pdf.
34. UGA Sports Communications (2009), "Registration for 2010 'Football 101 for Women' Now Open," October 29, accessed March 30, 2012, at http://www.georgiadogs.com/sports/m-footbl/spec-rel/051910aab.html.
35. "Team Shops Cater to the Girls of Summer," *Souvenirs, Gifts & Novelties*, Vol. 48, No. 4, May 2009, pp. 102–106.
36. U.S. Census Bureau, "Population Estimates - 2010," accessed March 30, 2012, at http://www.census.gov/popest/research/eval-estimates/eval-est2010.html.
37. Bureau of Labor Statistics, "American Time Use Survey," accessed January 25, 2010, at http://www.bls.gov/tus/#data.

38. Cone, LLC (2007), "2007 Cone Cause Evolution & Environmental Survey," accessed February 9, 2010, at http://www.coneinc.com/content1091.
39. Michael Smith (2009), "College Sports Shine Spotlight on Causes," *Sports Business Journal*, September 14, 18.
40. Tanya Irwin (2010), "Study: People Willingly Spend More for Green," January 20, accessed January 25, 2010, at http://www.mediapost.com/publications/?fa=Articles. showArticle&art_aid=120962&nid=110234.
41. Don Muret (2009), "Arenas Taking Close Look at LEED Certification," *Sports Business Journal*, September 21, 16–17.
42. Amy J. Hebard and Wendy S. Cobrda (2009), "The Corporate Reality of Consumer Perceptions," accessed January 25, 2010, at http://www.greenbiz.com/files/document/ GreenBizReports-ConsumerPerceptions.pdf.
43. "Tigers Seeing Steep Decline in '09 Season-Ticket Sales," March 26, 2009, accessed February 18, 2010, at http://www.sportsbusinessdaily.com/article/128855.
44. Christopher C. Williams (2007), "Chinks in Under Armour," January 24, accessed February 18, 2010, at http://www.smartmoney.com/investing/economy/Chinks-in-Under-Armour-20690/.
45. O. C. Ferrell and Michael D. Hartline, *Marketing Strategy*, 4th edition (Mason, OH: Thomson South-Western, 2008).
46. Adrian Payne, *The Handbook of CRM* (Oxford, England: Butterworth-Heinemann, 2005).
47. John Lombardo (2008), "Teams Mine Data from Online Ticket Sales," *Sports Business Journal*, July 7, 23.
48. Scarborough Research (2010), "81 Top-Tier Local Market Studies," accessed March 4, 2010, at http://www.scarborough.com/pdf/scarborough-top-tier.pdf.
49. Daniel Kaplan (2006), "Community Focus Wins Over Atlanta," *Sports Business Journal*, January 23, 1, 32.
50. Langton Brockinton (2002), "Texans Bring in J.D. Power to Gauge Service," *Sports Business Journal*, July 29, 8.

4 Segmenting Audiences for Sports

Learning Objectives

By the end of this chapter you should be able to:

1. Define market segmentation
2. Discuss the variables and methods of consumer audience segmentation
3. Discuss the variables and methods for segmenting business audiences
4. Analyze the uses and outcomes of audience segmentation strategies

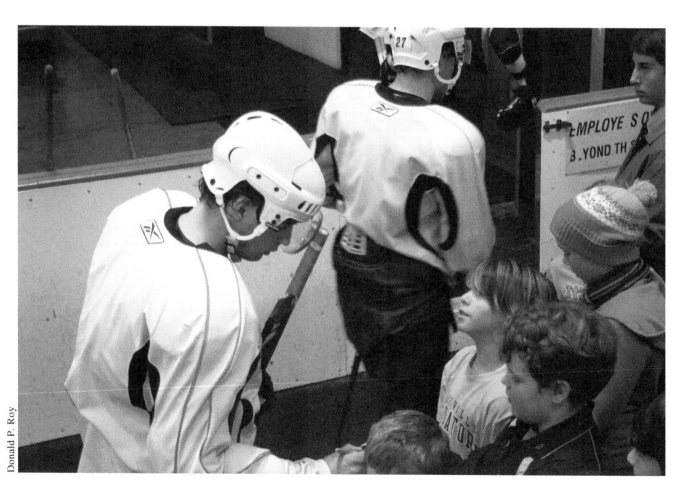

Kids are an important target audience for sports marketing.

Kids' Clubs Go from Child's Play to Serious Business

Sports properties have realized for many years that attracting children to become fans is vital to their success. The benefits are obvious: Children are influential in household buying decisions, and today's youth are future prospects to become paying customers. If kids attend sporting events, they are probably going to go with one or more adults . . . and all will buy tickets! And it is generally accepted that a person who becomes a fan of a team at a young age will likely continue following that team into their adult years. These reasons have compelled many teams to target young audiences by forming kids' clubs. About 75% of teams in the major professional sports leagues in the United States (NFL, MLB, NBA, and NHL) have some type of kids' club.

Recognizing the benefits of reaching the youth market and executing kids' club programs successfully are two very different things. For many kids' clubs, standard practice once was kids join a club, receive a membership card and some small merchandise items like a T-shirt or cap, and that was the extent of the program. Some clubs are free, while others require a fee to join. In either case, the lack of activity and benefits from the kids' club membership did not provide great incentive to join or, for those who joined, to continue their association with a club long term. Not exactly the ideal way to create the next generation of fans.

Insider Expert Rob Farinella – Blue Sky Agency

Rob Farinella is an agency founder and president with over 25 years of experience leading major strategic and creative initiatives. Farinella's company, Atlanta-based Blue Sky Agency, represents a variety of blue chip clients, which includes an extensive resume of sports and media properties, television networks, and destination brands. His shop has created award-winning work and achieved noteworthy results for the Atlanta Braves, the Atlanta Hawks, Bristol Motor Speedway, Wrestlemania, Reader's Digest, and Turner Broadcasting, to name a few.

In addition to his role at Blue Sky Agency, Farinella has served in marketing leadership roles for the Atlanta Super Bowl Bid Committee, Chick-fil-A Peach Bowl selection committee, The Georgia Chamber of Commerce and as an advisor to the Atlanta Sports Council.

Rob Farinella, founder and owner of Blue Sky Agency.

The strategy behind the marketing of kids' clubs has undergone a significant shift. Proactive marketing can boost membership numbers and, more importantly, members' involvement. The New York Islanders grew the size of their kids' club from 400 members to more than 10,000 . . . in six months! The Cincinnati Reds kids' club, the Red Heads, went from 1,000 members in 2007 to 5,000 members by 2010. The key to growth for kids' clubs is interactivity. Becoming a member means getting access to insider events such as autograph sessions, player question-and-answer meetings, and going onto the playing surface. As Corey Hawthorne, the Reds' staffer who launched the Red Heads, puts it, "The events that we offer are the things you can't put a price on; things that will stick with you beyond the longevity of a hat." Similarly, the Philadelphia Eagles, known as having one of the best kids' clubs in professional sports, uses events to attract people who usually do not go to games to visit Lincoln Financial Field.

Interactivity and special access events may attract and keep kids' club members, but the long-term goal is to add customers. Kids' club marketing targets children and their parents. Parents transplanted from another geographic area or who never developed a strong identification with a sports team in their youth can be reached through kids' programs. And, of course, today's kids' club members may become part of the next generation of committed fans. Tracy Marek, senior vice president of marketing for the Cleveland Cavaliers, says merely having a kids' club program is not enough. "Our goal is to . . . make sure these kids grow up Cavs fans." The revenue generated by kids' club membership fees is small short-term gains and is not the point of these programs. Kids' clubs represent a step toward marketing to future customers. Even teams that regularly play to sold-out stadiums today understand that it is never too early to target future customers.[1]

Introduction

Kids represent a potential audience for sports consumers, as do their parents. In fact, instead of a single large audience of potential customers, there are several segments of customers that can be identified by sports brands and properties as targets for marketing efforts. Even among all possible purchasers of a product or service, interest among buyers can be attributed to different reasons or influences. A strategy must be developed that plans how an organization's limited marketing resources should be used on audiences most likely to buy.

Market segmentation is the strategy and process used to analyze a population of consumers or businesses in order to identify groups of potential buyers an organization believes it is best equipped to serve. The result of market segmentation is a **target market**, which is a description of the audience segment (or segments) of buyers that will be the focus of tactical marketing decisions. It is pointless to make any marketing mix decisions (e.g., product features and design, pricing, distribution, and communication campaigns) without establishing which group or groups of buyers would find your brand relevant to them. Market segmentation is like other types of business strategies; many options can be pursued to reach a stated objective. There is no one right way to segment audiences. It is up to managers to gather intelligence to understand characteristics of different audience segments and decide which segments fit well with a sports brand's strengths and value proposition.

Segmenting audiences is a vital step in setting marketing strategy. Imagine taking a spring break trip from Chicago to Fort Lauderdale without a map—you may know the general direction to Florida, but lack details about points along the way and how to get to the final destination. An established route to get where you are going is a must. Market segmentation is a map for guiding marketing strategy in that it gives insight into which groups in a market may be inclined to respond favorably.

Why Segment Audiences for Sports?

Sports have broad appeal, capturing the interest of men, women, and children around the world, in all age groups, and across all social classes. Despite the popularity of sports and their significance in cultures across the globe, the demand for sports and sports entertainment is not universal. A strong case can be made that marketers benefit from not attempting to offer their products to everyone in a population. As accountability demands increase for relating spending on marketing to impact on revenues and profits, marketers are wise to study their markets to decide which groups are their most likely buyers and attempt to meet the needs of those groups.

Also, as businesses mature and revenue growth slows, market segmentation is a strategy for finding new market opportunities. After Reebok experienced tremendous growth in the 1980s, primarily through sales of footwear for aerobics, it needed to find new customer segments to serve when the aerobics craze faded. Reebok segmented the footwear market by introducing sport-specific products for basketball, soccer, and baseball. Market segmentation was instrumental in transforming Reebok from a company focused on exercise and fitness to a performance sports brand.[2]

What Is Market Segmentation?

In answering the question of what market segmentation is, first consider findings from a Pew Research study that 46% of Americans follow sports closely or somewhat closely.[3] While that represents an audience for sports entertainment of approximately 150 million people, the numbers also remind us that a majority of Americans do *not* follow sports. So, should a sports property reach out to nonfans in an effort to stir some interest, or is the focus on strengthening relationships with consumers who already have an interest in sports? To most marketers, the latter option seems a wiser use of marketing resources. Thus, segmentation is seen as a strategy of last resort.[4] Alternatively, a better view of segmentation is that it is a default strategy, meaning that rather than feeling that segmentation is a signal of defeat, it is a process used to identify the most relevant audiences a sports property should serve (see Figure 4.1).

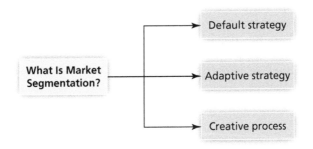

FIGURE 4.1 **What Is Market Segmentation?**

SEGMENTATION IS AN ADAPTIVE STRATEGY. Segmentation is a default strategy not because of a sports brand's flaws or deficiencies. Rather, it reflects an understanding that differences exist among consumers in the marketplace. Even among those persons in a population who have an interest in sports entertainment, not all are going to be interested in the same sports. The motivation for individuals to identify with a sport or specific team, attend sporting events, or consume sports media differs, which means that grouping customers according to their similarities (i.e., segmentation) will allow sports marketers to better serve customers' needs. For example, the benefits that a group would seek from outings at a Major League Baseball game likely differ from benefits sought by families with young children. Marketing efforts to groups might emphasize the social interaction of attending a game. In contrast, the appeal to reach families could focus on experiential elements offered to children such as an interactive game area and running the bases after a game.

Observed differences among groups serve as a call for segmentation as an adaptive strategy. Understanding how different groups can be persuaded to take action (e.g., attend a game, become a fan, or buy tickets or merchandise) is essential to making decisions about product offerings, pricing, distribution, and promotion. Given that all members of an audience are not the same in terms of motives and desires, the challenge for sports marketers is determining how to adapt to their differences in order to create a brand and entertainment experience that appeals to audience segments a sports property is best equipped to serve. Customers' characteristics and preferences tend to evolve over time; recognizing market segmentation as an adaptive strategy means that organizations are capable of modifying their targeting strategy as changes in the market are observed.

SEGMENTATION IS A CREATIVE PROCESS. When it comes to market segmentation, it can be said there is good news and bad news about accomplishing this important strategic task. The good news about market segmentation is that there is no single recipe or formula for segmenting audiences. This fact means marketers have a great deal of flexibility to decide how to identify subgroups of a population that will be the target of marketing campaigns. The bad news about market segmentation is . . . well, it is the same as the good news; there is no uniform set of steps for segmenting audiences. It requires use of a creative process to understand buyers and uncover similarities within population groups. Identifying characteristics or motivations by which audience members differ is perhaps the most creative part of the segmentation process. Segmentation often goes beyond a simple separation of groups based on obvious demographic characteristics such as males/females or businesses with less than 50 employees versus businesses with more than 50 employees.

Segmenting a market into distinct groups should result in a more complete, vivid picture of distinct customer segments. The Atlanta Braves recognized that not all game attendees have the same reasons for buying tickets and, therefore, different types of customers had been reached through different strategies. Audience research conducted by the Braves revealed five strategic segments:

1) Avid fans
2) Families
3) Entertainment seekers
4) Casual sports fans
5) Businesses

Although all of these segments are drawn to attend baseball games, the influence that the game itself has on the attendance decision will vary greatly among the segments. Families may place a greater emphasis on ticket price than avid fans; or business customers may be more concerned with foodservice options than casual fans. The challenge for a sports property like the Atlanta Braves is to not only identify differences between different groups in its audience, but to determine how to use that insight to tailor its offerings to appeal to each segment.[5]

Segmenting Consumer Audiences

Buyers of licensed merchandise, memorabilia, sporting goods, event tickets, and other products represent a tremendous selling opportunity for sports marketers. At the same time, they pose a major challenge, as consumers have many sports and entertainment options from which to choose. Also, consumers' attention is difficult to gain because of competition for share of mind from brands in other product categories and an unprecedented amount of choices in media channels available for information and entertainment purposes. This challenge is described perfectly by the title of a book by Irving Rein, Phil Kotler, and Ben Shields, *The Elusive Fan*. They call attention to the threat facing sports properties:

> "In a marketplace so crowded, the search for fans has become essential to the very survival of sports."[6]

The daunting task of breaking through in an environment of intense competition for attention and a consumer's discretionary income increases the importance of identifying relevant customer segments that become the focus of marketing efforts. Segmenting consumer audiences can be accomplished by answering the questions listed in Figure 4.2.

Descriptive Characteristics of Customers

A good starting point for understanding typical customers is to be able to describe them in terms of who they are: gender, age, geographic location, and other characteristics that describe their state of being. The descriptors used to answer this question can be found in sociodemographic characteristics of an audience. Sociodemographic characteristics describe people in terms of demographics

© sjlocke / Shutterstock

FIGURE 4.2
Segmenting Consumer Audiences

- What are the descriptive characteristics of our customers?

- What benefits do our customers seek?

- What behaviors do our customers exhibit?

- How can we reach and engage our customers?

(gender, age, ethnicity, and family life cycle stage), geography (region, state, county, city, or zip code where they reside), and socioeconomic groups (social class, annual household income, education level attained, and occupation). These variables are used frequently to examine audience characteristics because: 1) they are easy to understand for managers and other personnel not directly involved in the marketing function, 2) they are relatively easy to measure, and 3) adequate information may be available in the form of secondary data such as U.S. Census Bureau reports or syndicated marketing research studies.

When groups are examined along demographic variables, significant differences can be large enough to justify targeting specific audiences with unique marketing messages and product offerings. The San Antonio Spurs offered an interactive area designed for kids in the upper level of its arena, the AT&T Center, for several years. The team's marketing staff noticed that as ticket prices increased fewer families and more adults were buying tickets in that area of the venue. The space was converted to more of an adult-targeted fan zone featuring an open-air bar, while keeping features that would appeal to families such as a basketball arcade and video games.[7] For the San Antonio Spurs, the decision to convert a kids' area to a space targeting adults does not mean the team is abandoning families and youth as a target market. Instead, the Spurs observed a change in the demographic characteristics of patrons in the upper level of AT&T Center and adapted its experiential marketing strategy to better serve that particular group of patrons.

Under Armour, Inc.

Children and their parents are an important segment for Under Armour.

Benefits Sought from Purchase

Consumer behavior is not accidental. It is driven by motivations to receive certain benefits or outcomes from product use. While some decisions are made impulsively, most sports consumption is the outcome of a planned purchase. Consider a salesperson who determines he needs to purchase a set of golf clubs in order to take clients on golf outings. The buying decision may be influenced by motives that extend beyond the basic need of having the necessary equipment to play golf. For example, he may be conscious that the brand of clubs he plays with can affect clients' perceptions of him as well as impact his self-image . . . not to mention self-confidence in his golf game. Thus, he may be motivated to buy a highly recognized brand like Callaway.

An often used theory that explains the pursuit of obtaining benefits through consumption is Maslow's hierarchy of needs. Psychologist Abraham Maslow first proposed his theory in 1943, stating that individuals are motivated to fulfill five different levels of needs: physiological needs (nourishment, rest, and other basic needs), safety needs (comfort and security), social needs (relationships with family, friends, and others), esteem needs (confidence, achievement, and respect of others), and self-actualization needs (morality, creativity, and lack of prejudice).[8] The implication of Maslow's hierarchy for marketers is that goods and services can be positioned as solutions to meeting unmet needs that motivate buying behavior. Spectator sports and

FIGURE 4.3 Maslow's Hierarchy of Needs and Sports Consumption

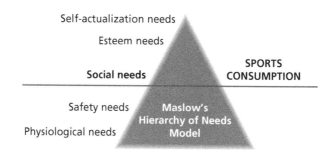

experiential events are typically marketed to meet the target market's social needs, but can also fulfill esteem needs (see Figure 4.3). Certain experiential activities such as fantasy camps and performance sports products may meet a consumer's esteem or self-actualization needs.

In terms of segmentation, answering the question of benefits sought from a purchase means understanding what buyers expect a product or sports purchase to do for them. Then, marketing tactics can be structured to create offerings that are relevant for different customer segments. D.C. United of Major League Soccer might segment their audience base for ticket purchases into hard-core soccer fans, casual sports fans, entertainment seekers, price conscious buyers, and groups planning a social event. Each segment would have a distinguishing set of benefits sought from attending the team's matches. The type of ticket plan, price each segment is willing to pay, and amenities expected would vary for each customer segment. To be successful, D.C. United needs to understand the benefits each segment seeks and what motivates each segment to make a ticket purchase.

Understanding benefits sought through sports consumption is useful not only for identifying audience segments that are potential customers; it also provides insights into the triggers of consumer action that can then be used to develop marketing messages to reach the different target audiences. If the trigger is social needs, then print and television advertisements for a college football team can show images of tailgating areas, interactive games, pregame concerts, or fans enjoying themselves in the company of others at a game. Similarly, a YouTube channel for the same team can provide videos with information about upcoming events and highlights from past events. In both cases the focus is on the benefit the consumer seeks (meeting social needs) rather than selling the product itself (the football program). This fundamental approach to marketing, meeting the needs and wants of customers, will be more effective if consumers' motivations for entering into a relationship with a brand are understood.

Customer Behaviors

Another aspect of market segmentation that probes into the makeup of different audience segments is identifying patterns of behavior exhibited by customers. In contrast to descriptive characteristics that categorize customers in terms of readily observable variables such as age, geography, and family life cycle stage, behavioral characteristics relate to the meaning, priorities, and choices that represent how they lead their lives. A class of segmentation variables marketers employ for this purpose is **psychographic variables**. These variables classify individuals on the basis of the personal values they hold, hobbies and interests (such as being a participant or follower of a particular sport), and lifestyle.

Psychographic segmentation is useful because it enables marketers to go beyond static characteristics of an audience to define them in terms of what they do with their lives. This fits especially well with sports brands. The passion that can be elicited from identifying with a team, player, or coach is an observable trait, so a sports property can target individuals with a high level of interest to strengthen brand relationships as well as reach out to other segments with less interest but similar demographic characteristics. Sports products have also used psychographic segmentation. Under Armour went from a startup brand to a formidable competitor in the sports apparel category in a span of a few years by segmenting the market. Its focus was on consumers who were more serious athletes and valued the performance of Under Armour's moisture absorption technology.

Another approach to segmenting consumer audiences based on behavior is to categorize customers according to the frequency, volume, or dollar amount of purchases made. This approach is known as **usage rate segmentation** and is used by marketers in many industries. Usage rate segmentation is a prevalent practice for a simple reason: it enables marketers to identify their best customers and develop marketing strategies to maintain customer loyalty and even increase their financial value to the firm by generating more revenues from current users. It is a very practical strategy. A sports property such as the NBA's Portland Trail Blazers can target individuals who have purchased a half-season ticket for the past three seasons or multi-game tickets as being more likely to purchase season tickets than someone who has just attended one or two games.

Usage rate segmentation is rooted in the concept of the 80/20 rule, which suggests that a vast majority of an organization's revenue and profit (80%) is realized from a relatively small percentage of the customer base (20%). While the ratio of revenue to customers may not literally be 80–20 for every organization, the rule tends to hold true overall. The mix may be 74% of revenue coming from 24% of customers, or, in an even more extreme case, 85% of revenue coming from 13% of customers. The latter case points out a risk in focusing marketing efforts only on heavy users. If too many resources are being directed at heavy users then it is highly likely that opportunities are being missed to attract new buyers or up-sell existing customers who may be moderate users. While heavy users in a firm's customer base are vital to their profitability and continued financial success, the reality is that some customers will be lost each year. Thus, marketers must continually mine their customer databases for opportunities to escalate the relationship of moderate users and light users of their brand.

The non-user segment of the audience should be identified and a determination made of whether marketing efforts can be used to attract buyers from this segment. The Florida Panthers of the NHL went after this market segment when the team introduced a "First Timer" program that offered anyone with a valid Florida driver's license two free tickets to a game. The promotion allowed up to 250 people who had never attended a Panthers game to sample the product.[9] This tactic can be particularly effective when the seller has excess capacity available and can potentially generate some revenue from the first-time visitor in the form of food and merchandise sales. More importantly, the new customers' data are entered into the customer database and future marketing efforts can then be made to entice them to make purchases.

Reaching and Engaging Customers

A final question that must be addressed when determining the audience segments to be marketed to is how each audience segment can be reached in terms of messages and communication channels. An audience segment that is potentially lucrative in terms of generating interest and revenue may not be a viable segment if they are difficult to reach. In this case, relationship building is difficult, and the likelihood of customer acquisition is uncertain. In order to deal with this challenge, sports marketers must answer the questions identified in Figure 4.4.

WHERE ARE THE AUDIENCE SEGMENTS FOUND? The process of identifying relevant segments should uncover characteristics about consumers that aid in selecting the best marketing channels

Questions to be answered

- Where are the audience segments found?
- What are the communication touch points for interaction?
- What media vehicles are most appropriate and cost effective?

© MShep2 / iStockphoto

FIGURE 4.4 How Can We Reach and Engage Our Customers?

to reach them. Communication with audience segments can be more effective when it is linked to their interests or lifestyles. When the Carolina Hurricanes of the NHL relocated to Raleigh, North Carolina, from Hartford, Connecticut, it dealt with reaching consumers who had little or no familiarity with hockey. One tactic the Hurricanes used to reach fans was to connect hockey with a sport brand that has enormous popularity in the region, NASCAR. The decision to cross-promote with NASCAR was made because the demographic characteristics of the audiences for the two sports matched well. Also, the fast-paced, intense action of auto racing is similar to the sensations experienced by attendees of an NHL game.[10]

In order to develop insight into ways to access consumers, some considerations that should be made include:

- What types of magazines do segment members read?
- How much time do they spend online and what types of sites do they access?
- What types of leisure activities do they enjoy?
- How important is spending time with family or friends?
- What sources do they use to obtain sports information?
- How important is receiving information from others through word of mouth?

Coca-Cola Company

Understanding the touch points of NASCAR fans is important to a sponsor such as Coca-Cola to ensure its message is being heard.

Answers to these questions provide guidance for decisions on where a target audience can be found. If it is determined that word-of-mouth communication is important to consumers for product purchases, a sport brand might try accessing the audience through participation in social media channels such as Facebook or Twitter. Such an approach would be beneficial because it would provide a way to communicate with the audience as well as provide a channel to learn from consumers through their interactions with others.

WHAT ARE THE COMMUNICATION TOUCH POINTS FOR INTERACTION? The question of how an audience segment can be accessed cannot be answered completely without an understanding of the communication channels that segment members use to obtain information and entertainment, participate in communities, and manage their personal networks. An organization's marketing strategy can result in creating products or services with exceptional value, priced fairly, and with an availability that is convenient to acquire and use. But, if the communication efforts are unsuccessful at reaching the target market because of improper use of media channels, then marketing effectiveness is diminished. An audience segment's media consumption is studied by sports marketers and, if they outsource promotion functions, by their advertising agencies, to learn the communication touch points that are most effective for reaching the segment.

A review of trends in spending for marketing communications reveals an overall shift in what marketers believe are the channels that work best for promotion campaigns. Internet advertising (which includes display advertising on websites, search engines, online video, and social networking websites) is projected to increase from 17% of total media advertising spending to 26% between 2010 and 2015. In contrast, the share of advertising expenditures for traditional mass mediums (newspapers, magazines, television, and radio) are expected to remain flat or decrease over the same time period. Newspapers will experience the greatest decline, dropping from 15% to around 11%.[11]

The shift in promotion expenditures from mass mediums that have long been the focal point for reaching audiences to new mediums is based on observing how consumers use media. A Harris Poll study found that only about two in five adults read a newspaper almost every day, either in print or online. The percentage of 18- to 34-year-olds is even smaller, with 23% reading papers almost every day, and 17% of the members of this age group do not read newspapers at all.[12] Thus, newspapers have become a less than ideal communication channel for marketers to connect with young adults. Instead, interactive media channels have taken on more importance. The trend toward new media channels appears to include the sports entertainment industry, too. An ESPN Sports Poll found that a team website is a preferred information source (42% prefer) compared to a newspaper (30%) or a newspaper's website (21%).[13]

Consumers' changing patterns of media consumption have led to greater use of digital media as communication touch points. Social media in particular has become a cost-effective option for connecting with consumers online and on wireless devices. Use of social media should be dictated more by the target audience's use of the medium than cost compared to traditional media. For example, lacrosse is a sport that is growing in popularity across the country. In particular, it is enjoying growth among youth who are picking up the sport. A significant audience segment made up of younger consumers is an ideal situation for using digital media to reach and engage fans. Major League Lacrosse uses social media extensively through the MLL Facebook page and Twitter feed. Also, each team has a branded presence on Facebook and Twitter. Smartphone and tablet users can connect with the league with the MLL mobile app to get scores, highlights, and news.[14]

Another way digital media can be used to reach consumers is opt-in text messaging services. People with differing levels of involvement with a team may take advantage of being able to receive updates sent to their wireless phones. Score updates, news, ticket offers, and other information are a few ways text messaging is used to communicate with fans. Text messaging services can be encouraged using signage and promotional announcements at events as well as offered online. For example, the University of Missouri has a sign-up page on its website that allows fans to select the sports for which they wish to receive news or scores via text messaging, customizing the opt-in experience.

WHAT MEDIA VEHICLES ARE MOST APPROPRIATE AND COST-EFFECTIVE? Gaining consumer insight into their usage of different mediums is necessary for developing marketing strategy that targets a specific audience segment, but it is not sufficient for gaining access to a segment. Knowledge of general media usage should be complemented with information about specific media venues typically used by a market segment. A **media vehicle** is a specific platform that can be used to deliver a message to an audience. While cable television is a medium, ESPN and MLB Network are media vehicles. Definition of a media vehicle can be refined even further, identifying a specific program (i.e., subbrand) associated with the media vehicle. In the case of ESPN, *SportsCenter* is a media vehicle in itself distinct from the core ESPN brand. The tremendous growth in the number of media vehicles in mediums such as television, magazines, the Internet, and social networking websites makes it rather clear to sports marketers that a broad understanding of mediums individuals use to access information and entertainment is not detailed enough to make decisions about where to place messages to reach them.

Selection of media vehicles to access an audience segment is often based on the targeted reach a media vehicle delivers. **Targeted reach** is a measure of the number of persons that are exposed by a media vehicle that are also part of the target market. It is a more refined audience measure than total reach, which includes all persons who might be in a media vehicle's audience regardless of whether they are in the marketer's target market. For example, the Super Bowl is a great media vehicle for achieving a high total reach through advertising, with more than 100 million people watching the game on television each year. However, it is not the ideal media vehicle for delivering targeted reach, because a broad range of demographic characteristics is represented in the Super Bowl audience. Thus, marketers are often better served to use media vehicles with less total reach but more effective targeted reach for their specific market segment.

Another key consideration when answering the question of what media vehicles should be used is the cost-effectiveness of different options. Cost-effectiveness considers two factors: 1) dollar cost to place messages in a media vehicle, and 2) audience size exposed to the media vehicle in which a marketing message is placed. The cost of message placement in a media vehicle usually reflects the audience size it delivers. If the Syracuse Crunch of the American Hockey League is considering using radio to access consumers it is targeting, it would expect to pay more to place messages on WBBS, a country music station that is consistently one of the top stations for audience ratings (i.e., reach) in the Syracuse market, than it would to advertise on WHEN, an all-sports station with about one-seventh of the audience size of WBBS.[15] In this case, the Syracuse Crunch would consider the audience size of WBBS and whether the level of targeted reach it offers justifies the higher cost compared to the all-sports station with a comparatively small audience (high targeted reach, low total reach). If an audience segment cannot be reached cost-effectively, it is questionable as to whether that segment is a viable market for a sports organization.

Segmenting Business Audiences

Discussion of audience segmentation in the preceding section focused on how to identify groups of individual consumers within an audience. Other audience segments can be identified among businesses or organizational markets in which the buyers are motivated to consume sports offerings to meet needs of a business or an organization. Business-to-business (B2B) customers for sports properties include corporate sponsors, advertising partners, businesses that are not sponsors or advertisers, institutions, and nonprofit organizations. The overarching goal for marketing to business audiences is the same as it is for consumers: meet customer needs and wants while at the same time meeting the needs of the organization (i.e., carrying out the marketing concept).

Although the end goal of satisfying the customer is the same for marketing to both consumers and businesses, distinguishing characteristics of each market dictate different marketing mix approaches to serving a given segment effectively. Figure 4.5 summarizes five of the most notable differences between B2C and B2B marketing.

FIGURE 4.5
Differences between B2C and B2B Markets

- Different types of buyers
- Different motivations for purchasing
- Length of time to make a purchase decision
- Different promotional tactics
- Differences in how buying decisions are evaluated

First, the two types of audience segments have different target buyers. For B2C segments, the buyer is usually individual consumers or a closely networked group of individuals, family or friends. For B2B segments, the buyer is one or more individuals who represent the interests of the organization with which they are associated. An LPGA Tour event host that is attempting to sell a title sponsorship to a large corporation may need to persuade several individuals within the company, such as a brand manager, marketing director, and even the CEO in order to successfully establish the partnership.

Second, purchase motivations are likely to differ between consumers and businesses. Consumers are prompted to consume sports to satisfy a blend of emotional and social needs such as feeling like they belong to a community with other fans. Businesses see sports as a vehicle to advance their interests through creating more brand awareness, gaining new customers, or even enhancing employee morale.

Third, the length of time required for buyers to make decisions varies greatly between consumers and businesses. Individuals make decisions relatively quickly; businesses may make

Coca-Cola's sponsorship of NASCAR and its drivers involves a long-term commitment of multiple years.

decisions on an annual planning cycle and are obligated to follow established timetables. Also, the length of commitment business customers are asked to make could be longer than that asked of individual consumers. A sponsorship deal may have a three-year or five-year length, while individuals rarely go beyond an annual commitment to make ticket purchases from sports properties.

A fourth difference between B2C and B2B audiences is the promotion tactics that are most effective for reaching audience segments. Communication mediums with extensive audience reach such as advertising and social networking websites are ideal for marketing to B2C segments because they allow sports properties to reach consumers for a relatively low cost per person, and in the case of social media, it provides a cost-effective channel for engaging individuals with a sports brand. Also, these media have the capability to deliver messages that appeal to their rational, emotional, and social motivations.

For B2B segments, personal selling is a preferred promotional tactic because there are fewer customers to contact and multiple stakeholders are often involved in the buying process, a long sales cycle, and typically a high selling price. Relationship building can be accomplished through a sales force's connections, which can be key to a business customer deciding to invest in corporate tickets, sponsorships, event marketing, or media advertising.

Finally, consumers and business buyers differ in how they evaluate buying decisions. Consumers will base their post-purchase evaluation largely on their personal level of satisfaction with the experience. Did they enjoy their experience? Did it meet or exceed expectations? Future buying decisions and brand loyalty will be impacted by these criteria. In contrast, B2B buyers are likely to evaluate their buying decision on criteria related to their business objectives. Did Coca-Cola's investment in sponsorship and involvement in NASCAR increase brand equity among the sponsor's target market? Have relationships with key accounts been strengthened as a result of investing in corporate hospitality at races?

Recognition of the difference in how sports consumption is evaluated by B2B customers is very important. Sports properties must work with their partners to assist in pursuing their business objectives. Unmet objectives could prompt businesses to reconsider their future relationship with a property. NASCAR has been relatively successful in reinforcing B2B partners' decisions to invest in the sport. In 2009, NASCAR formed a "B2B council," a group of official NASCAR sponsors representing different industries and product categories. The group was formed to help sponsors build new business opportunities from their association with NASCAR through learning from best practices of other NASCAR sponsors and teaming up on joint promotions linked to their NASCAR sponsorships. The B2B council was formed because many official NASCAR sponsors needed direction on how to market their association with NASCAR beyond logo usage and standard business-to-business opportunities such as client entertainment.[16] Sports properties that become a resource to their B2B partners by collaborating with them to explore opportunities to activate a sponsorship add value to a sponsor's investment and possibly reduce the likelihood that a sponsor will walk away from the partnership.

The role of audience segmentation in defining the target market for business audiences is no different than that for consumer audiences discussed earlier in the chapter. The same four questions that reveal customer segments to target that are a good fit with an organization's strengths should be asked when analyzing segments of the business audience.

Descriptive Characteristics

Descriptive characteristics used to segment business audiences include industry or category membership, organization size, and geographic location (see Figure 4.6). Industry or category membership refers to the line of business in which a firm operates. Segmenting according to category membership can be broad or narrow. Major League Baseball, for instance, may offer sponsorship opportunities in the financial services industry by having an official bank sponsor (Bank of America) and an official credit card sponsor (MasterCard International).[17] Industry membership segmentation can be useful to identify prospective customers within a certain business sector, and it is possible to determine whether firms are B2B customers for other sports properties. Sponsorship consultancy agency IEG publishes the *IEG Sponsorship Sourcebook* annually that segments a list of more than 2,000 corporate sponsors into more than 100 industry categories. Sports properties seeking sponsors whose product offering and target market would be a good match can use such a resource to narrow their focus on prospecting for corporate partners.

FIGURE 4.6 Methods of Segmenting B2B Markets

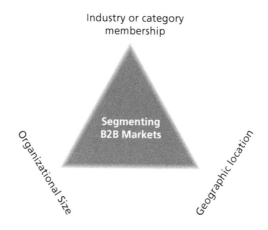

Organization size is a descriptive characteristic that can establish a prospective business customer's potential from a financial perspective. If a business is publicly owned, it is required to release financial data including annual sales. Such information can be used to make judgments on a firm's ability to make expenditures on sports marketing platforms such as sponsorships, media advertising rights, or corporate hospitality.

When a NASCAR racing team seeks support in the top-level Sprint Cup Series, it is likely to segment the B2B audience for prospective sponsors on the basis of organization size. A primary sponsorship for a Sprint Cup team can cost more than $15 million per year. Only companies whose marketing budgets can support an investment in the sponsorship rights fee and additional spending on supporting marketing campaigns would be considered viable prospects. A company with $100 million in annual sales would not be a prospect for a primary sponsorship for a NASCAR team, but it is possible that it may be a prospect for a lower-tier sponsorship requiring a lower investment.

Geographic location of prospective B2B customers is used to establish boundaries on where sports marketers should focus their marketing efforts. Given that most business customers invest in sports marketing to gain access to a sports property's customers, geographic segmentation for B2B audiences should mirror the geographic market area from which consumers are drawn. Information about ticket buyers' locations can be obtained from a customer database or fan surveys. Geographic areas such as counties, cities, or zip codes with large concentrations of customers become the same areas that sports properties prospect for B2B customers. Examining consumer behavior should not be limited to ticket purchasers, however.

A sports brand can have appeal across a wide geographic area, far beyond where most ticket buyers live. The St. Louis Cardinals have one of the most extensive radio networks of any Major League Baseball team. The network includes more than thirty radio stations that cover all corners of Missouri as well as affiliates in Arkansas, Illinois, Indiana, Iowa, Kentucky, Mississippi, Oklahoma, and Tennessee.[18] The wide reach of the Cardinals radio network means that the area in which prospective sponsors and advertisers are located can be beyond the greater St. Louis area. Companies that wish to target consumers who are Cardinals fans throughout the Midwest and into the Southeast could efficiently reach them by partnering with the Cardinals radio network.

Benefits Sought

Business buying decisions are considered to be influenced by pursuit of benefits that will serve the best interests of the organization. In the case of consuming sports entertainment, the assumption among B2B buyers is that they will buy based on an evaluation of whether the purchase will help advance a firm's goals and objectives. Contrasting business buyers' benefits sought from consuming sports with individuals' benefits can be explained by the distinction between utilitarian and hedonic consumption discussed in Chapter 2. The explanation for individual consumption of sports entertainment is that it is influenced primarily by hedonic consumption motives, a desire to achieve an internal state of pleasure or sensory gratification. A season ticket holder for Auburn University football is likely motivated to purchase because of a desire to maintain a connection to the individual's alma mater, spend time with friends at pregame tailgating festivities, or exhibit an identification with Auburn football. In contrast, utilitarian motives would most likely be the rationale for business buyers.

As shown in Figure 4.7, benefits sought from sports consumption by business buyers can be classified as meeting marketing objectives, internal objectives, or personal objectives. Marketing objectives are usually the primary motivation for the decision to invest in sports, especially for sponsorships. Two marketing objectives frequently identified by sponsors are increasing brand awareness and creating a desired brand image. Both of these outcomes are measurable, meaning that a sponsor could evaluate its involvement in a sponsorship to determine if brand awareness increased following the sponsorship or if the target market's image of the brand had been influenced by the sponsorship.

FIGURE 4.7 **Sports Consumption Benefits Sought by Motivations for Business Buyers**

Strengthening client relations is another possible marketing goal. Client hospitality, often executed through the purchase of event tickets in a suite or club area, could be a tactic used to add new clients or increase sales from current clients. For example, businesses that purchase premium hospitality suites at Crew Stadium, home of the Columbus Crew of Major League Soccer, receive benefits such as tickets to all events held at the venue, access to a club area on a non-event date, indoor and outdoor seating, and a climate-controlled environment to entertain guests and clients.[19] These amenities are offered to persuade B2B buyers to use the Columbus Crew as a connection point with customers and prospects.

Benefits sought through sports consumption among business audiences can be based on meeting internal objectives. Employees are considered by many firms to be a stakeholder group,

An advertisement by the Atlanta Braves highlighting the importance of employees to business organizations.

just like customers. Sports can be used as a channel for building employee morale within an organization and providing employees incentives or rewards for performance. Companies will purchase naming rights to sporting venues in areas in which they have significant local operations or corporate headquarters. The FedEx Forum in Memphis, Gillette Stadium in Foxboro, Massachusetts, and Heinz Field in Pittsburgh are three examples of venue-naming rights purchased in the sponsor's headquarters city. These sports investments usually target customers, but a dual audience is the sponsor's employees, whose commitment to their employer could be positively influenced by a sponsorship.

Sports can be used as employee incentives or rewards, too, using event tickets or other forms of employee hospitality. NAPA Auto Parts created an employee contest around Major League Soccer's MLS Cup championship. NAPA held an employee contest resulting in ten winners traveling to the event in Seattle.[20] The Atlanta Braves recognized the importance of employees to business organizations and ran the advertisement shown in this section using the headline "Is there anything better than treating your employees like family?"

Businesses that use sports to meet internal objectives must exercise caution to select sports properties that have appeal among their internal audience. Otherwise, the investment in sports will not have the desired effect on employee morale and performance, and it could even be perceived negatively by employees who question the wisdom of the company spending money on sports. . . . "Why not give us raises with that money?" might be the view of skeptical employees.

A third benefit that can influence sports consumption by B2B buyers is to meet personal objectives. This objective may seem out of place given the view that business buyers are supposed to act rationally on behalf of the organizations they represent, and thus, would not be acting to achieve personal objectives. In theory, that is correct. However, not only are business buyers agents for their organizations, but they also represent *their own* interests. Occasionally, buying decisions are influenced by the personal preferences of the decision maker. This phenomenon has been referred to as managerial whim, and it occurs when a decision maker for a business decides to make an investment in sports that is not the best use of the firm's resources. A CEO of a department store may decide that his company should sponsor an event on the PGA's Champions Tour, a property whose participants are older golfers. The underlying motivation for the sponsorship is that the CEO is an avid golfer and PGA fan, and he relishes the opportunity to meet tournament participants that the sponsorship would afford.

This personal bias in making B2B sports investments has become less prevalent as costs required to sponsor sports have increased coupled with greater accountability placed on marketing expenditures. It is simply too expensive and too risky for a manager to make sports-buying decisions today based solely on personal objectives.

Behaviors Exhibited

Business audiences can be segmented according to behavior, and the primary behavioral variable that is of interest to B2B marketers is purchase activity. An organization's customer base can be grouped into segments based on the dollar value of revenue or profit customers generate. Segmenting customers in this way enables a sports property to identify its most important customers and devise strategies to maintain their loyalty and reward their behavior. Also, behavioral segmentation of B2B customers can identify prospects that could possibly be persuaded to increase commitment or purchase volume. This method of segmentation is essentially the same as segmenting consumer audiences on the basis of usage rate, applying the 80/20 rule to identify key customers.

An application of behavioral segmentation for B2B customers is called an **ABC analysis**. Customer segments are grouped based on the revenue or profit they are responsible for creating for an organization. The best customers are classified as "A" customers. This segment is small in number (15% to 20%), but they account for a significant percentage of revenue or profit from business customers. The next group, "B" customers, is the largest segment in the B2B customer base (60% to 70%), and their buying activity can be described as moderate . . . an average customer, in other words. The third segment, "C" customers (15% to 20%), is made up of occasional and low-dollar buyers that represent a small percentage of revenue or profit from B2B customers.

Using an approach like ABC analysis to segment business customers is rooted in the idea that all customers are not equal in their importance to an organization's success. Key customers should be treated differently (i.e., better) than customers whose relationship to the organization only contributes marginally to profitability. The "A" customers are usually the easiest segment to persuade to take action; they are already sold on the value the seller delivers and on the benefits of having a relationship. Businesses in the A category could be afforded amenities that recognize their value to an organization, such as assigning high-level marketing personnel to be liaison between the organization and the customer and offering inside access to customers such as meet-and-greet sessions with coaches and players. Identifying B and C customers is important for uncovering opportunities to escalate a customer's relationship with the organization. This approach could be used by the Huntsville Stars, a class AA minor league baseball team, to review its roster of customers that have purchased tickets and hospitality for a corporate outing during the last three seasons, but have no other purchase history with the team. These infrequent buyers could be analyzed to determine their potential as purchasers of season tickets, official team sponsors, or venue and broadcast media advertisers.

Implementation of Segmentation Strategies

The case for segmenting consumer and business audiences is very compelling. The question regarding audience segmentation is not whether it should be done, but rather how audiences should be segmented. Once that question is answered then it is time to identify segments that will become the focus of marketing efforts. These segments should meet the following criteria:

1. They can be reached through communication channels
2. The organization has the capabilities and resources to serve their needs
3. Relationships with customers in the target segments will be profitable

The following sections describe applications of audience segmentation approaches discussed in this chapter. Figure 4.8 identifies product offering decisions that are impacted by the segmentation approach decision.

FIGURE 4.8 Product Offering Decisions Impacted by Segmentation

Ticket Sales

Ticket sales for games and events are an important revenue stream for sports properties, and both the consumer and business markets are tapped to locate and acquire customers. Options for segmenting audiences for ticket sales are limited only by the creativity of marketers. Three applications of segmentation shown in Figure 4.9 illustrate innovative methods sports properties have used to define the audience for tickets.

FIGURE 4.9 Application of Segmentation to Ticket Sales

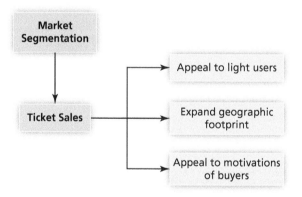

APPEAL TO LIGHT USERS. Season ticket sales are important for team sports properties because they represent guaranteed revenue, and a large percentage of season ticket holders are potential repeat customers if they can be persuaded to purchase additional tickets. How can a sports property go about identifying customers that would be classified as light users or occasional purchasers and encourage the segment to spend more money on tickets? The Minnesota Timberwolves of the NBA dealt with this dilemma as it segmented its audience for season tickets. The team's attendance ranked twenty-fifth out of thirty teams and new season ticket sales were low the previous year. The response by the Timberwolves was to entice new buyers to become season ticket holders. The tactic: a 50% discount on the price for season tickets if purchased during a promotion period. This bold move gave loyal fans a price break for their loyalty to the team, and it had the potential to entice prospects who had been to a few or even no games to consider investing in season tickets. The result was that the team sold an estimated 1,000 new season tickets.[21] Although price discounts can be an effective promotion tactic for marketing to new customers, discounting must be done sparingly and with regard to its effect on overall brand image and profit margins. Frequent discounting could suggest to consumers that a product is overpriced or otherwise not worth the asking price.

EXPAND GEOGRAPHIC FOOTPRINT. The geographic market area served by a sports property should be evaluated periodically to determine if underserved areas exist. It is possible that both consumers and businesses can be persuaded to become customers in locations that have not been targeted previously. At an extreme, a sports property can expand its geographic reach by setting up a subsidiary operation in another market. That approach is how the NBA expanded globally, specifically into Asia. The league opened an office in Hong Kong in 1992, and it launched NBA China in 2008, a separate entity charged with building fan interest and promoting fitness and teamwork to communities throughout the country.[22]

Expanding a sports property's geographic footprint does not require venturing across the globe. It can be an extension of marketing efforts adjacent to the current geographic footprint. The Detroit Red Wings have been the most successful team in the NHL in recent years, winning the Stanley Cup four times since 1997. However, the decline of the American auto industry hit the Detroit market particularly hard, creating a situation in which the Red Wings were no longer selling out every game. One response to address the decrease in ticket sales was to redefine the market area the team targets to generate fan interest. The economic woes of Detroit prompted the team to expand its marketing efforts into southwest Ontario, targeting a region passionate about hockey that was a shorter distance to Detroit than to Toronto.[23]

APPEAL TO BUYERS' MOTIVATIONS. For all of the options for segmenting audiences to identify a target market, the most fundamental question a marketer can ask might be "What do customers want from using our product?" In other words, are their motivations for making a decision to consume sports known? What's in it for them? Understanding why consumers or businesses would engage in a relationship with a sports property can set the stage for marketing efforts designed to attract other buyers with similar motivations. Once the answer to "What's in it for the buyer?" is known, enhancements or improvements to products or services offered can strengthen the appeal a sports brand has for buyers to meet their needs.

As discussed earlier in the chapter, both individual consumers and B2B customers have motivations for consuming sports, although the motives may differ between the two types of customers. A sports property that has segmented business audiences on the basis of buyer motivation for ticket sales is the Denver Nuggets of the NBA. Like most sports properties, the Nuggets already targeted corporate ticket buyers. However, the team introduced a program that added benefits for their business buyers and attempted to enhance the impact of being a Nuggets season ticket holder. The Nuggets Business Alliance program gives businesses that are full-season ticket holders opportunities to target other alliance members (B2B marketing) and gain exposure among Nuggets fans via the team's website.[24] A value-added program like the Nuggets Business Alliance is a means of helping B2B customers achieve business objectives through an association with team. Expenditures on sports tickets may be more justifiable for a business if managers can point to sales increases or customer acquisitions that occur as a result of an association with a sports property.

Experiential Events

Events and other forms of experiential marketing provide customer engagement that can be more enduring and impactful than mere brand exposure. Awareness-oriented marketing tactics like venue signage and advertising can blend into the landscape and even suffer from clutter created by competing messages. Experiential events are a way to involve customers and create memorable associations with a brand. Segmenting audiences to market experiential events is based on a realization that their engagement capabilities can strengthen commitment of existing customers and escalate commitment of new customers.

Experiential events can be used as a differentiator for a business to demonstrate commitment to customer care. American Express took this approach in its sponsorship of the U.S. Open golf and tennis tournaments. American

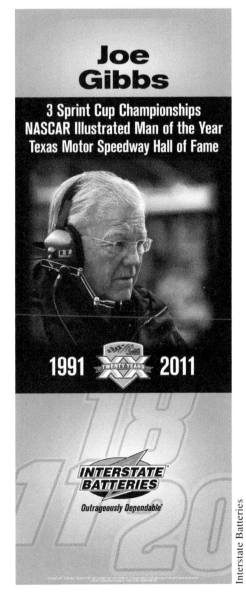

This banner featuring the racing accomplishments of coach Joe Gibbs hung in Interstate Batteries' NASCAR hospitality tents.

Express card members could purchase tickets before they were available to the general public, and special hospitality areas were available to view the events. This "insider" treatment can be given to B2B customers, too, as a means of creating brand interaction. IBM leverages its role as official information technology partner for the Masters and U.S. Open golf tournaments to give clients behind-the-scenes tours of how IBM services are used to support event operations.[25] Interstate Batteries used a similar strategy, allowing its best business customers to experience NASCAR and Joe Gibbs Racing at its hospitality suite.

The tactics used by American Express and IBM illustrate how segmenting consumer or business audiences can be accomplished by identifying customers who value the benefits of a relationship with a company via sports-related experience and rewarding their patronage by offering access to special events.

Experiential events can also be used as a tactic to implement audience segmentation that is based on the participation level of a customer, or usage rate, with a sports property. Full-season ticket holders are a key stakeholder group in terms of their long-term financial value to a sports property. Their loyalty can be rewarded by adding benefits to their commitment through offering access to experiential events. Locker room tours, visits with coaches, retired star players, or broadcasters, and player autograph sessions are events that can be held to strengthen fan relationships. More importantly, customer value is impacted positively by offering more benefits without having to discount price. If anything, drawing fans closer using these types of events could potentially justify price increases if buyers believe they are receiving fair value in return.

The Chicago White Sox targeted two segments of its season ticket customer base the season after winning the World Series. The team recognized the importance of demonstrating value to new season ticket holders to increase the likelihood of ticket renewal in subsequent seasons. A "Rookie Party" was held for new season ticket customers so that they could meet White Sox staff and learn about the services available to them as season ticket holders. Another initiative that targeted all season ticket customers was parties giving fans access to the playing surface of U.S. Cellular Field and photo opportunities to pose with the World Series trophy.[26] Not all fans would desire these types of interactive experiences. More importantly, not all customers are of sufficient value to an organization to justify offering experiential events to the entire customer base. But, experiential marketing can be an effective strategy to appeal to certain segments that place importance on having a relationship with a sports brand, and where it is meaningful and will build bonds between them and the brand.

Licensed Merchandise

Identifying prospective customers using audience segmentation approaches could be more important to growing revenue from officially licensed merchandise than for most other revenue streams, because licensed products represent an extension of the core sports brand. Buying an Indianapolis Colts jersey or license plate is not a requirement for someone to be a Colts fan or even be a purchaser of Colts game tickets. Conspicuous consumption in the form of wearing or displaying products with a team's logo does not motivate all members of a sports property's customer base. The question is who among a sport property's target market would be prospects for licensed merchandise? Segmenting audiences for licensed merchandise would focus primarily, if not exclusively, on consumer audiences using one of the approaches shown in Figure 4.10.

An obvious starting point to identify markets for licensed products is to appeal to fans whose identification with a sports brand is important in terms of defining their self-identity. Buying products with a team's logo or other brand marks is a way for highly involved fans to show their loyalty to their favorite team or player. For this segment of fans, showing others their connection with a team or player is important. Also, consumption of licensed products, particularly apparel, is a way for fans to identify with fellow fans and not only show support for their team, but also help build community with each other.[27] This approach to audience segmentation would focus on consumers' motivations for purchasing. Given the high involvement of this audience segment with the sports brand and its importance in their self-identity, they become an attractive target for new licensed products. Whether it is a new style of cap or a relatively new licensed product item like a Snuggie, marketers of officially licensed products recognize the importance of appealing to the affiliation and sense of community motives of highly involved fans.

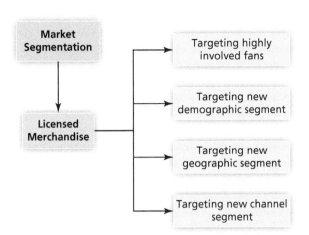

FIGURE 4.10
**Application of
Segmentation to
Licensed Merchandise**

Evaluating audience segmentation opportunities in the licensed merchandise market should include the viability of targeting new demographic segments. As sales growth slows or matures among existing customer segments, expanding the target market to include segments not served currently may be a feasible growth strategy rather than attempting to stimulate sales in core market segments. Sociocultural trends are a prime source for uncovering potential new market segments. Consumer preferences and interests shift with time. Marketers that observe these shifts can respond with offerings that appeal to the needs of segments that may have been underserved previously.

A sociocultural trend noticed by National Football League was more females attending and becoming fans of football. The NFL has made licensed merchandise sales to women a business priority. Sales attributable to women doubled during the last five years. The league aims to increase the percentage of women's licensed apparel in its overall business from 15% to 25%.[28] The strategy of adding women as a target audience for licensed merchandise is possible because of changes in the external environment, such as the increased buying power of women.

A similar approach to identifying segments for licensed merchandise sales is based on assessing potential geographic markets to target for expansion. The National Basketball Association found a solution to low growth rates in licensed product sales in the United States by expanding to Europe and Asia. In just one year the NBA reported sales increases of 50% in Europe and 60% in Asia over the previous year, and sales outside of the United States now make up 30% of total sales.[29] Two external factors that spurred these sales were a weak U.S. economy and greater interest globally for the NBA.

Reaching consumers with licensed merchandise requires going beyond the sports properties. It involves distribution strategies with various retail outlets and other channel members. Segmenting by the type of retail store enables a seller to identify consumer niche markets that are not being served fully. For example, the National Football League Players Association (NFLPA) launched a venture in which it marketed officially licensed apparel and products bearing the names and images of high-profile NFL players such as Peyton Manning and Chad Ochocinco. Merchandise licensed by the NFL features team names and logos. In contrast, NFLPA-licensed products could not use any of these brand marks, only the name and likeness of individual players.

The retailer segments chosen to sell these items were chain supermarkets and drugstores. These segments were appealing for two reasons. First, supermarkets and drugstores are typically not known for selling officially licensed sports products, particularly apparel. Although licensed products were in these stores already, a greater variety of NFL-licensed products is more likely to be found in a specialty store, department store, or mass merchandise discount store. The move to not sell through retailers frequently used to market licensed sports products means the NFLPA may face less direct competition from NFL products by not selling through the same channels. Second, the price point of NFLPA-licensed products is lower than what consumers might expect to pay for a comparable product with NFL brand marks. The price point for NFLPA products fit well with the price points and image of the chain supermarkets and drugstores chosen as channel partners, such as Kroger, Walgreens, and CVS.[30] The strategy used by the NFLPA is similar to the approach made famous by Baseball Hall of Famer "Wee" Willie Keeler, who credited his hitting success to the philosophy "hit 'em where they ain't." In some cases, marketing success can be found by finding channel partners that others have either ignored or chosen not to pursue.

Sponsorships

Target audience selection is one of the most important determinants of a sponsorship's success. A company that associates its brand with a sports property is counting on a match between the characteristics of a sports property's audience or fan base and the characteristics of the company or sponsoring brand's target market. The extent to which consumers accept a sponsor and sports property as a good fit has a significant impact on whether the target audience perceives the brand in a positive manner, develops a liking or preference for the brand, and, ultimately, buys the sponsor's brand. Three different uses of audience segmentation in sponsorships are identified in Figure 4.11.

FIGURE 4.11
Application of Segmentation to Sponsorships

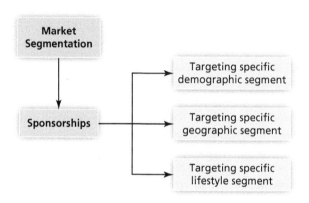

TARGETING A DEMOGRAPHIC SEGMENT. A characteristic of many sports properties is that their audiences can be defined rather clearly in terms of their demographic characteristics. For example, the average age of NASCAR fans is about 43 years old, with the 45–54 and 65 and older segments showing growth and the 18–24, 25–34, and 35–44 segments shrinking.[31] In contrast, the audience demographic characteristics of fans of the Association of Tennis Professionals (ATP) World Tour are more diverse (with a high percentage of women as part of the ATP fan base), are scattered across more than thirty countries, and have above-average household income and education level.[32]

Distinctive customer profiles like those of NASCAR and ATP World Tour add appeal to sponsorship as a channel for businesses to reach customers. Stanley Tools is a company that historically has had little presence in sports marketing beyond NASCAR sponsorships. The company identified Major League Baseball as a property that would deliver a large audience of 18- to 34-year-old males. Stanley went from sponsorship of one MLB team in 2008 to twelve teams two years later.[33] The strategy of sponsoring individual MLB teams rather than being a league sponsor is a segmentation decision in itself, as Stanley controls which geographic markets it wishes to reach through its association with MLB.

TARGETING A GEOGRAPHIC SEGMENT. Selecting specific geographic markets as target audiences for marketing campaigns can be achieved using sports sponsorship. In some cases, the geographic market is not necessarily segmented at all, and an entire market area is targeted with a sponsorship. A national sponsorship such as Sprint's title sponsorship of NASCAR's top-tier league, the Sprint Cup Series, is beneficial to Sprint because of the nationwide reach of NASCAR. Even though Sprint Cup races are not held in all fifty states, NASCAR still enjoys national media coverage and has fans across the entire country.

In other cases, a sponsorship that delivers an audience that is in a smaller geographic area is the proper segmentation decision. C Spire Wireless, a regional wireless communications provider serving customers in Mississippi and parts of Alabama and Tennessee, partners with sports properties located in its market area such as Mississippi State University, University of Mississippi, and University of Memphis.

Geographic segmentation can be used to target specific areas within a broad market footprint. Candy marketer Hershey is based in the United States and sells products around the world. Hershey identified a sponsorship platform to strengthen its brand in Canada when it became the official chocolate and candy of the National Hockey League. Instead of seeking a sponsorship that covered all NHL markets (more than 75% of NHL teams are in the U.S.), Hershey's deal covers Canadian markets only.[34] The sponsorship gives Hershey access to fans of the country's most popular sport. In contrast, a sponsorship of the NHL in the United States would compete for the attention of sports fans who are also targeted by sponsors of properties that draw greater interest among American sports fans such as NFL, MLB, NBA, NASCAR, and NCAA.

TARGETING A LIFESTYLE SEGMENT. Consumer audiences can be segmented according to lifestyle, interests, or activities that are important to a group of people. Sports are a natural lifestyle segmentation vehicle. The affinity people have for their favorite sports, teams, and players take sports consumption beyond merely being a leisure activity; it becomes a key part of how people define themselves. Brands that aspire to reach audiences based on their lifestyle characteristics can use sports sponsorship by associating with properties that fit a desired lifestyle profile. For example, vitaminwater, a Coca-Cola brand, became an official sponsor of the NCAA. The brand is seen on bottles, cups, and coolers at all eighty-eight NCAA championships. The passion that college sports fans exhibit for their favorite team or watching games was recognized by vitaminwater's vice president of sports marketing, Bob Cramer. He said "We're a lifestyle beverage, and we think we can take the insight of seeing NCAA championships as a lifestyle occasion."[35] If being a fan of a particular sport or attending certain sporting events gives consumers social currency or status enhancement, segmenting audiences on the basis of lifestyle is a viable strategy.

Media Content

An initial reaction to the thought of segmenting audiences to market sports media content would be "target sports fans." It stands to reason that individuals with an interest in a particular sports team or event would be good prospects for consuming programming or information delivered through communication channels. However, a closer look at the benefits delivered by sports media suggests that it would be beneficial to engage in more extensive audience segmentation to identify people who could be persuaded to become customers. Three types of sports media products that offer examples of different segmentation strategies are shown in Figure 4.12.

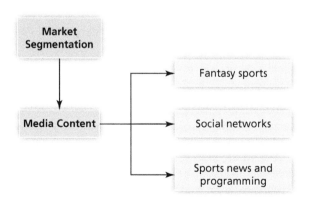

FIGURE 4.12
Application of Segmentation to Media Content

FANTASY SPORTS. The overall market size of fantasy sports has grown rapidly, with an estimated 30 million people in the United States and Canada now playing some type of fantasy sports game. During the 2000s, the average annual growth rate in participation was more than 20%.[36] The growth in the fantasy sports market is due largely to more free games being offered and attracting casual players (i.e., light users). However, a market for highly involved players willing to spend money to play games and obtain related research and information also exists. Thus, marketers of fantasy sports products have created offerings designed to appeal to each of these usage segments. Bloomberg, a company known for its research and analysis of financial markets, created a package of statistical analyses, charts, and other information for fantasy baseball players called Bloomberg Sports Fantasy Tools. The product is aimed at hard-core fantasy baseball players who seek to gain a competitive edge and are willing to pay $24.95.[37]

At the same time, casual gamers continue to be an attractive audience segment to game publishers and Internet portals that value the ability of fantasy games to attract visitors to their websites, making the websites more valuable in terms of advertising rates. Attractive to casual gamers are sites that offer free games and games with short durations, which mean players do not have to be involved throughout the course of an entire season. One reason for the popularity of NCAA men's basketball tournament bracket contests is that the competition has a short duration (about three weeks) and requires less daily maintenance by players than season-long fantasy sports games. It is expected that casual players will continue to be drawn to fantasy sports through short-form games delivered by wireless phone applications and social networking websites such as Facebook.[38]

SOCIAL NETWORKING WEBSITES. The decision on which audience characteristics or behaviors to use to segment audiences is one issue; effectively communicating and engaging a segment being targeted is a different matter. Reaching target segments has become more difficult because of the enormous number of media options and changing media preferences of consumers. Young audiences (teens and young adults) are a challenging demographic group to reach due to their decreased usage of traditional media such as television and newspapers. They spend more time engaged with digital media by texting, watching videos online, and frequenting the Internet in general and social networking websites in particular. In response to this trend, sports properties are stepping up their efforts to communicate with online audiences using social networking sites such as Facebook and Twitter. Seattle Sounders FC of Major League Soccer is typical of sports properties that use Facebook to proactively reach fans. The club has more than 225,000 fans on its official Facebook page. Photos and videos posted by the Sounders and fans as well as information about upcoming games and events are at the fingertips of a community of Sounders fans.

A key source of power for a social networking website is its viral message capabilities. People who become fans of the Seattle Sounders will at the same time spread the message about the Sounders to people in their networks. While the core audience for social networking sites might be persons who would classify themselves as fans, other individuals whose identification with the team is not as great may be influenced to become part of the fan community because of the membership of their peers.

SPORTS NEWS AND PROGRAMMING. Sports are a global phenomenon, but many sports fans are most passionate about teams and athletes in their local areas. Thus, segmenting the market for sports news and programming by geographic area allows sports media to be tailored to the local tastes of an audience. The trend toward geographic segmentation of sports media began with the formation of regional sports networks (RSNs). The leader in RSN programming is Fox Sports Net. The network has sixteen RSNs covering regions across the country, with each featuring broadcasts of professional, collegiate, and even high school sporting events. Other RSNs are operated by media companies such as Comcast and Cablevision, and some sports properties have ventured into media broadcasting, including the New York Yankees (Yankees Entertainment and Sports—YES) and Boston Red Sox (New England Sports Network—NESN).[39] RSNs provide a channel for sports properties to strengthen connections with fans in their local markets by offering more coverage of their team or event while at the same time giving fans a means for satisfying their appetite for following local sports teams.

The emergence of digital media channels has given media companies and sports properties additional options for geographic segmentation of consumer audiences. Television and newspapers, two media that have traditionally been important sources of sports information for fans, have struggled as audiences spend more time online. This trend creates opportunity for offering sports content tailored to geographic markets, as sports fans' tendency to follow local teams has not changed.

Insider Insights Rob Farinella – Blue Sky Agency

Q. Why is market segmentation an important decision for sports properties to manage?

A. One of the cornerstones of any sports property is understanding your customer base. Having a clear profile of current customers and potential new ones helps you market to them more effectively. Audience segmentation acknowledges that all consumer and business constituents are not motivated by the same aspects of a sports and entertainment experience or association. Ultimately, successful audience segmentation will drive more fans in seats and eyeballs to television sets as well as driving brand affinity and audience loyalty.

Q. How is the role of audience segmentation different when the target market is businesses instead of consumers?

A. As it pertains to business constituents, audience segmentation helps direct what television network, radio station, and media outlets align best with their audience. As it pertains to increasing sponsorship relationships, it creates a demographic and psychographic profile to match

Blue Sky Agency

Rob Farinella discusses the role of segmentation in sports marketing.

that of other companies. A more comprehensive definition of your audience through an audience segmentation approach helps validate associations with your property. In selecting a sports property, audience segmentation can often direct a company to which sport, entertainment entity, franchise, or property best aligns with their audience segments.

Q. How important is gathering and analyzing data for making sound segmentation decisions?

A. Ongoing measurement research to verify and refine segmentation hypothesis is a critical tracking component. Understanding product usage and actual behavior such as buying patterns, channel preferences, media consumption, image, brand loyalty, and attitudes towards the entities are components that should be carefully analyzed to uncover marketing insights. Insights are valuable only if they are actionable. Actionable insights affect critical factors such as prospecting, messaging, tactical approaches, timing and frequency of message, and budget allocation, to name a few.

ESPN recognized that the quantity and quality of local sports news coverage was decreasing and responded by launching ESPN Local in 2009. ESPN Local is a network of websites with sports news and coverage within a specific geographic market. The first year of the venture included content for two markets (ESPNChicago.com and ESPNBoston.com), and the second year ESPN added Dallas, Los Angeles, and New York.[40] In addition to targeting sports fans in these cities with dedicated websites, ESPN appeals to fans' need to consume local sports news by offering team-specific sections on ESPNLocal.com. The result is that the entire United States is segmented geographically by giving sports fans the ability to choose specific content for a professional or collegiate team. The benefit of geographic segmentation for ESPN is that it becomes a one-stop destination for news and information on professional and college sports. Sports fans can meet their needs to follow sports at a broad level through content offered by the core ESPN brand, and can do the same for local sports by interacting with ESPN's local content rather than being limited to local media outlets such as television news and newspapers.

Chapter Summary

Market segmentation is the process of analyzing a population in order to discover groups or segments of consumers that would be the most interested in a product, such as a sports property. While it may seem that everyone is a sports fan, reality is that only about 46% of Americans closely or somewhat closely follows sports. Therefore, a sports property must look at segmentation to understand the best way to market itself and decide which group or groups of consumers are the most viable target markets to pursue.

Segmenting consumer audiences requires an understanding of the consumer audience in terms of demographic characteristics such as age, gender, and income. Geography and socioeconomic groupings are also important. In addition to these characteristics, an understanding of consumer motivations for purchasing sports is a factor. It is more than just entertainment. Motivations often include meeting social needs and self-esteem needs, as proposed by Maslow.

Segmenting consumer markets requires studying customer behaviors. This can be done through psychographics, which involves a person's interests, values, hobbies, and lifestyle. It allows marketers to go beyond the demographic variables and better understand why consumers get involved with sports. From psychographics, marketers can study usage rate to determine which segments are the most viable for pursuing and how they can be marketed.

The last element of the consumer audience to consider is to understand how a sports property can reach its customers and how it can engage them with the sport or team. It involves discovering where the audience can be found, what types of communication touch points can be used for interaction, and the most appropriate media vehicles to use.

Sports are not limited to just consumers. Businesses are an important component of sports marketing. However, there are major differences in who makes the purchase decision, motivations for making purchases, the length of time it takes to make a decision, the promotional tactics that are used, and how the purchase decision is evaluated. Same as with consumers, businesses can be segmented using demographic variables such as company size and industry. More important, however, is the motive for making a purchase. The most common motive is to meet marketing objectives, such as increased brand awareness or to create a desired image. Internal objectives and even personal objectives can also be factors in the decision.

Marketing segmentation is beneficial because it can be used to create actionable strategies for ticket sales, experiential events, sponsorships, licensed merchandise, and media content. In each area, a sports property can look at feasible market segments that can be pursued. For instance, in ticket sales a sports property may decide to expand its geographic footprint or appeal to light users. For sponsorships, a sports property may decide to target a specific demographic group, geographic segment, or lifestyle segment. Similar strategies can be used for licensed merchandise and experiential events. The key is deciding which market to pursue and how to pursue it.

Media is an important element in sports. In addition to news programming, fantasy sports and social networks have grown in popularity. Segmentation is an important marketing tool for each of these since there are considerable differences in how individuals view news programming and what they want from the news. The same is true for fantasy sports and social networks.

Review Questions

1. What is market segmentation, and why should audiences for sports be segmented?
2. Explain the difference in the three views of segmentation as default strategy, adaptive strategy, and creative process.
3. In segmenting consumer audiences, what four questions should marketers ask?
4. Why are descriptive characteristics, such as demographics, used to examine audience characteristics?
5. What is the relationship between sports consumption and Maslow's hierarchy of needs model?
6. How can psychographic variables and usage rate be used to segment consumer audiences for sports?
7. In reaching and engaging consumers, what three questions should be addressed? Describe why each is important.
8. Explain the differences between segmenting consumer audiences and business audiences.
9. What descriptive characteristics are used to segment business audiences?
10. Describe the consumption motives for business buyers.
11. What is ABC analysis and how is it used for business segmentation?
12. Discuss the options marketers can use to segment audiences for ticket sales.

13. Explain how segmentation can be used based on experiential events and engagement.
14. What segmentation options do sports entities have in terms of licensed merchandise?
15. Identify the segmentation approaches that can be used for obtaining sponsorships.
16. What are the ways segmentation can be applied to media content?

New Terms

Market segmentation   strategy and process used to analyze a population of buyers in order to identify groups of buyers an organization believes it is best equipped to serve.

Target market   the audience group (or segments) of buyers that will be the focus of marketing strategy decisions.

Psychographic variables   variables used to classify individuals on the basis of personal values, hobbies and interests, and lifestyle.

Usage rate segmentation   segmentation based on the behavior of individuals (or businesses) such as frequency, volume, or dollar amount of purchases.

Media vehicle   specific platform that can be used to deliver a message to an audience.

Targeted reach   measure of the number of persons that are exposed by a media vehicle that are also a part of the target market.

ABC analysis   grouping or segmenting customers into three categories based on the revenue or profit they generate for an organization.

Discussion and Critical Thinking Exercises

1. How important are kids to the future of sports? Should professional sports actively pursue kids? Why or why not?
2. The Atlanta Braves have identified five unique market segments: avid fans, families, entertainment seekers, casual sports fans, and businesses. Describe a marketing strategy that the Atlanta Braves could use to reach each market segment in terms of ticket sales, experiential events, and licensed merchandise.
3. Pick your favorite professional or college team. Answer each of the questions in Figure 4.2 in terms of segmenting consumer audiences.
4. Motivations are an important determinant of customer purchase behavior. Discuss your personal motivations as they relate to attending sporting events, purchasing licensed merchandise, and viewing sports on one of the media outlets (such as television or the Internet).
5. How important are social media websites such as Facebook in marketing a professional sports team? What about college sports? How can Facebook be used by professional sports and by college sports?
6. Pick a sports team located near you. Identify all of the ways businesses participate with the team. How important are businesses to the sports team?
7. Use the Internet to locate a minor league baseball team close to where you live or attend college. Examine the three applications to increasing ticket sales suggested in Figure 4.9. Which strategy would you recommend? Why? Discuss how you would implement the strategy.
8. Have you ever participated in an experiential event or engagement activity? If so, describe the experience and your reaction to the event. If you have not, describe an experiential event you would consider and how much you would be willing to pay for the experience.
9. Many sports teams have increased their efforts toward female fans in terms of licensed merchandise. What do you think of this strategy? What tactics would you suggest for increasing female interest in licensed merchandise?
10. Do you participate in fantasy sports? If so, how much? What motivates you to participate? If you do not participate in fantasy sports, why not?

You Make the Call
IndyCar

The origins of IndyCar can be traced back to the formation of Championship Auto Racing Teams (CART) in 1978. For the first seventeen years of its existence, CART dominated auto racing in the United States, and open-wheel racing enjoyed greater notoriety than other forms of racing. However, Tony George, president of the Indianapolis Motor Speedway, was concerned that CART was beginning to lose sight of the interests of American open-wheel racing by holding events in foreign countries, putting too much emphasis on racing at road courses instead of oval tracks, and focusing too much on promoting top foreign drivers as CART stars. So in 1996, George created a new open-wheel league that would compete with CART, the Indy Racing League (IRL). Team owners were forced to decide whether to remain with CART or move to the new IRL. The IRL–CART feud distracted both leagues and as a result thrust stock car racing into prominence, making stock car racing the favorite motorsport in the United States. By 2001 an ESPN Sports Poll survey found that 56% of American auto racing fans said stock car racing was their favorite type of racing, with open-wheel racing third at 9% (drag racing was second at 12%). The diminished appeal of open-wheel racing contributed to additional problems with sponsor relationships. Three major partners left CART—Honda, Toyota, and FedEx.

Open-wheel racing is popular globally, but struggles in the United States.

© John J. Klaiber Jr. / Shutterstock

In response to declining interest in the IRL, marketing initiatives were taken to reverse the trend. In 2005, the IRL launched a new ad campaign that targeted 18- to 34-year-old males. Instead of focusing on the cutting-edge technology found in IRL cars, the campaign shifted to drivers and the drama created on the track. The campaign was part of a broader strategy to expand the association of IRL beyond a sport for middle-aged Midwestern males. The idea was to position the brand as hip and young.

The IRL then followed a trend observed in NASCAR, which was to get celebrities involved in the sport through team ownership. David Letterman, NBA star Carmelo Anthony, former NFL quarterback Jim Harbaugh, and actor Patrick Dempsey all became involved. Next, driver personalities began to give the IRL some visibility. The emergence of Danica Patrick as a star in the IRL broadened appeal of the league and assisted the efforts to reach young males. Patrick was a 23-year-old IRL rookie who finished fourth in the 2005 Indianapolis 500. The combination of the novelty of a female driver and her captivating looks and personality made her the darling of American sports. Patrick's effect on the IRL was very noticeable—the IRL reported gains in event attendance, merchandise sales, website traffic, and television ratings.

The auto racing leader in the U.S. motorsports market is NASCAR (National Association for Stock Car Auto Racing). NASCAR fields three racing circuits in the United States: the Sprint Cup Series, the Nationwide Series, and the Camping World Truck Series. The league has become popular as it has focused on marketing drivers, especially young drivers often referred to as NASCAR's "Young Guns" such as Dale Earnhardt Jr., Jimmie Johnson, and Kyle Busch.

Today, NASCAR towers over IndyCar in the United States in terms of sponsor support and audiences. The average television audience for NASCAR races averages approximately 5% of U.S. households, compared to less than 2% for IndyCar. As a result of NASCAR's popularity and growth, it was able to negotiate a lucrative, multibillion-dollar contract with Fox and ESPN, while IndyCar has struggled to secure a favorable television deal.

Many racing observers believe that open-wheel racing could have been as popular as NASCAR is today if it were not for the split which destroyed attendance, sponsors, and television interest. Finally, in 2008 the IRL and CART reunited, with the new corporate entity now known as IndyCar. Rather than focus on on-track action, the unified IndyCar Series marketed the race as a "Festival of Speed." In addition to the race, fans had access to such activities as kids' zones, beach volleyball, wine tasting, or live concerts. One description of this approach is "We throw a party and a race breaks out. We don't want people to come out and sit in metal grandstands for three hours and get sweaty and get sunburned and go home. We want stuff going on everywhere." The festival concept appeared to be a success. For instance, the street race at Long Beach, California, attracted an estimated 200,000 people during the three-day event, including more than 80,000 people on race day.

Both optimism and uncertainty exist as IndyCar moves beyond reunification. Long-time leader Tony George was replaced before the 2010 season by Randy Bernard, who had developed a reputation as an innovative marketer as head of Professional Bull Riders (PBR). Optimism exists in growing business opportunities with Coca-Cola, Orbitz, and the National Guard. A partnership with Mattel will bring Hot Wheels–branded IndyCars to retail stores and IndyCar Series events. A new media broadcast partner, NBC Sports Network (formerly Versus), gives the IndyCar Series much more coverage each week than offered by ESPN, although NBCSN has a smaller audience reach. IZOD became the series title sponsor. Michael Andretti believes the cost advantage of attending IndyCar races compared to NASCAR gives the league an upper hand in reaching fans.

The momentum IndyCar gained was dashed late in the 2011 season. First, fan favorite Danica Patrick announced that she would be leaving IndyCar to compete in NASCAR beginning in 2012. Then, tragedy struck IndyCar at its season finale in Las Vegas. Dan Wheldon, another fan favorite, was killed in a horrific crash that led to safety concerns that threaten IndyCar's growth. Auto racing is the fastest-growing spectator sport in the United States. Unfortunately, open-wheel racing experienced a period of decline while other forms of auto racing grew. IndyCar is a distant second to NASCAR in terms of popularity. And, IndyCar's worst fears were realized when Patrick announced that she would be leaving to compete in NASCAR. The new IndyCar must strengthen its standing in the American motorsports market if it hopes to survive.[41]

Questions:

1. What is your evaluation of the strategy of marketing the IndyCar Series as a "Festival of Speed" rather than an auto race? What are the pros and cons of such an approach?
2. What type of segmentation strategy would you recommend for the IndyCar Series for consumers? What about for businesses?
3. Design a segmentation strategy to increase ticket sales at auto races.
4. Which segmentation questions would you recommend be asked to develop a strategy for targeting potential corporate sponsors of IndyCar?
5. How could experiential events be used to develop audience loyalty among consumers as well as obtain corporate partners?

References

1. Bill King (2009), "Members Only" *Sports Business Journal*, November 23, 17.
2. Reebok History," accessed March 14, 2010, at http://corporate.reebok.com/en/reebok_history/default.asp.
3. Pew Research Center (2006), "Americans to the Rest of the World: Soccer Not Really Our Thing," accessed January 25, 2010, at http://www.pewsocialtrends.org/files/2010/10/Sports.pdf.
4. Brian Sternthal and Alice Tybout, "Segmentation and Targeting," in *Kellogg on Marketing*, ed. Dawn Iacobucci (New York: John Wiley & Sons, Inc., 2001), 3–30.
5. Interview with Rob Farinella, Atlanta Braves, February 2011.
6. Irving Rein, Philip Kotler, and Ben Shields, *The Elusive Fan* (New York: McGraw-Hill, 2006).
7. Don Muret (2009), "Spurs Re-Do Kids Area after Shift in Upper-Deck Demographics," *Sports Business Journal*, October 26, 12.
8. Janet A. Simons, Donald B. Irwin, and Beverly A. Drinnien, *Psychology: The Search for Understanding* (New York: West Publishing Company, 1987).
9. Tripp Mickle (2008), "Panthers Hope Free Tickets Create New Buyers," *Sports Business Journal*, October 20, 3.
10. Scott W. Kelley, K. Douglas Hoffman, and Sheila Carter (1999), "Franchise Relocation and Sport Introduction: A Sports Marketing Case Study of the Carolina Hurricanes' Fan Adoption Plan," *Journal of Services Marketing*, 13 (6), 469–480.

11. "Television Ad Spending Bounces Back, Virtually Unaffected by Online Growth," accessed March 30, 2012, at http://www.emarketer.com/PressRelease.aspx?R=1008308.

12. Alyssa Hall (2010), "Just Two in Five Americans Read a Newspaper Almost Every Day," accessed March 28, 2010, at http://www.b2i.us/profiles/investor/NewsPDF.asp?b=1963&ID=35425&m=rl.

13. Bill King (2009), "No News Is Bad News," *Sports Business Journal*, July 20, 1.

14. "MLL Launches Mobile App" (2011), March 30, accessed May 13, 2011, at http://www.longislandlizards.com/press-release/2278/mll-launches-mobile-app.

15. "Radio Stations: Arbitron Ratings Data for Syracuse," accessed March 29, 2010, at http://www.arbitron.com/radio_stations/home.htm.

16. Michael Smith (2009), "NASCAR Launches New Programs to Bolster B2B," *Sports Business Journal*, November 9, 3.

17. MLB.com (2010), "Official Sponsors," accessed April 2, 2010, at http://mlb.mlb.com/mlb/official_info/official_sponsors.jsp.

18. MLB.com (2010), "Cardinals Radio," accessed April 2, 2010, at http://mlb.mlb.com/stl/schedule/tv_radio_affiliates.jsp.

19. "Hospitality," accessed March 30, 2012, at http://www.thecrew.com/content/hospitality.

20. Tripp Mickle (2009), "Activation Hits 100 Percent for MLS Cup," *Sports Business Journal*, November 16, 7.

21. John Lombardo (2010), "Half-Price Season-Ticket Offer Produces Results for Wolves," *Sports Business Journal*, March 29, 6.

22. NBA.com (2008), "NBA Announces Formation of NBA China," January 14, accessed April 7, 2010, at http://www.nba.com/news/nba_china_080114.html.

23. Tripp Mickle (2009), "First to See Fallout, Red Wings Were First to Change Game Plan," *Sports Business Journal*, October 5, 30.

24. John Lombardo (2009), "League Expects Lower Revenue as Renewals Dip *Sports Business Journal*, October 26, accessed March 30, 2012 at http://www.sportsbusinessdaily.com/Journal/Issues/2009/10/20091026/SBJ-In-Depth/League-Expects-Lower-Revenue-As-Renewals-Dip.aspx?hl=denver%20nuggets%20business%20alliance&sc=0.

25. Jon Show (2009), "Making the Connection," *Sports Business Journal*, June 29, 15.

26. John Lombardo (2006), "Franchises Upgrade Team Services, Create Events to Cure Their Retention Headaches," *Sports Business Journal*, August 28, 44.

27. Donald P. Roy (2010), "Motivations for Consuming Licensed Sports Products," working paper.

28. Terry Lefton (2010), "NFL Licensing Targets: 'Back to Football' and Women's Markets," *Sports Business Journal*, March 8, 9.

29. Terry Lefton (2008), "NBA Sees Growth in Merchandise Sales in Europe and Asia," *Sports Business Journal*, October 13, 10.

30. Liz Mullen (2009), "NFLPA Encouraged by Early Sales of Player Merchandise," *Sports Business Journal*, November 30, 43.

31. Michael Smith (2010), "I'm Not Going to Be Someone Else," *Sports Business Journal*, February 8, 1.

32. ATPWorldTour.com (2010), "ATP World Tour Sales Brochure," accessed April 14, 2010, at http://www.atpworldtour.com/~/media/F79026FEBAC34527A783E590DDFCFC31.ashx.

33. Terry Lefton (2010), "SportsNet Sees Ad Sales Uptick; Stanley Tools around in Sports," *Sports Business Journal*, April 12, 8.

34. NHL.com (2010), "NHL, Hershey Canada Sign Three-Year Partnership Deal," March 10, accessed April 14, 2010, at http://www.nhl.com/ice/news.htm?id=520839.

35. Terry Lefton (2008), "Vitaminwater Flows onto NCAA Sidelines," *Sports Business Journal*, October 20, 5.

36. FantasySportsBusiness.com (2008), "Fantasy's Growth Rate Is Strong," accessed April 16, 2010, at http://www.fantasysportsbusiness.com/wordpress/tag/ipsos/.

37. BloombergSports.com (2010), "Bloomberg Sports Fantasy Tools on MLB.com," accessed April 16, 2010, at http://www.bloombergsports.com/.

38. Eric Fisher (2010), "A More Casual Approach," *Sports Business Journal,* March 1, 15.

39. AllExperts.com (2010), "Fox Sports Net: Encyclopedia," accessed April 17, 2010, at http://en.allexperts.com/e/f/fo/fox_sports_net.htm.

40. Meg James (2009), "ESPN Plans Websites for L.A., New York, and Dallas," *Los Angeles Times*, July 21, accessed April 17, 2010, at http://articles.latimes.com/2009/jul/21/business/fi-ct-espn21.

41. Robin Miller (2008), "Miller: A Brief History of CART," April 16, accessed March 30, 2012 at http://auto-racing.speedtv.com/article/miller-a-brief-history-of-cart/; "Andretti Has Eye on Regaining Market Share," *Street & Smith's Sports Business Journal*, May 18, 2009, 19; Tony Fabrizio, "Racer Danica Patrick Embraces Celebrity Exposure," *Tampa Tribune*, February 27, 2009; Reggie Hayes, "What's Next for IndyCar?" *Fort Wayne News-Sentinel*, July 1, 2009; Terry Lefton, "Ad Sales Encouraging as IRL Launches Season," *Street & Smith's Sports Business Journal*, March 30, 2009, 8.

5 Building a Relevant Brand

Learning Objectives

By the end of this chapter you should be able to:

1. Summarize the four roles of brands
2. Describe the characteristics and components of brand names and marks
3. Discuss rebranding and ethics issues that are unique to the sports industry
4. Explain the components, strategies, and effects of brand equity development and brand positioning
5. Discuss the benefits of brand extension and brand licensing
6. Discuss the role of corporate social responsibility in brand strategy

Pittsburgh Penguins

The Pittsburgh Penguins conducted extensive research to understand and define the team's brand.

Pittsburgh Penguins Ask Questions to Define Brand

In 2007, the new president of the Pittsburgh Penguins, David Morehouse, posed a question to the team's staff: "What is our brand?" It was a fair question. The Penguins, two-time Stanley Cup champions in the early 1990s, had been mired in Chapter 11 bankruptcy as recently as 1998-99, had fallen to the bottom of the NHL standings (in both record and attendance) by 2004, and weathered an unprecedented season-long league lockout in 2004-05. Their image and brand had been fluid and generally undefined. But, the lockout produced a favorable labor agreement with the players, and the 2005 draft yielded the best prospect in a generation, Sidney Crosby. The Penguins were assembling a cast of exciting young players, selling lots of tickets, and making inroads into the community. Morehouse demanded "We have to identify our brand."

Morehouse, a Pittsburgh native who used to sneak into Penguins games as a kid, had come to the team out of the political world – he had worked in the Clinton White House and had been a senior advisor to Vice President Al Gore. He brought a perspective unique to professional sports. He engaged Minneapolis-based Stellus Consulting to help find the answer to that burning question. Stellus was not a sports-centric operation. It had done brand research and

Insider Expert Tom McMillan—Pittsburgh Penguins

Tom McMillan has served as VP of communications for the Pittsburgh Penguins since 1996, following a seventeen-year career in the Pittsburgh sports media as a writer, columnist, editor, and broadcaster. McMillan oversees corporate communications strategy, media relations, broadcasting, and website content. He also serves as team spokesman on a variety of hockey and business matters. He was a charter member of the National Hockey League's Communications Advisory Board and helped author the NHL's new media and communications regulations as the league re-launched following the 2004–2005 work stoppage. He filled the joint role of VP of communications/marketing for the Penguins from 1999–2004.

McMillan worked ten years as a sports writer for the *Pittsburgh Post-Gazette* and covered the Penguins exclusively for five seasons—including their Stanley Cup campaigns in 1991 and 1992. During his career he also covered the Olympics, the Super Bowl, the World Series, the NBA Finals, the Stanley Cup Finals, the NCAA Final Four, the Orange Bowl, the Fiesta Bowl, and the MLB, NBA, and NHL All-Star Games.

McMillan hosted sports radio talk shows for three years on WTAE and KDKA in Pittsburgh, and made regular appearances on FSN

Pittsburgh's Hockey Hotline. He authored a history of the team, *The Penguins: Cellar to Summit* in 1994 and edited a book about Hall of Famer Mario Lemieux.

Tom is a graduate of Point Park University with a degree in journalism and communications.

Tom McMillan, VP of Communications, Pittsburgh Penguins

development dozens of companies including Nestle's Ice Cream and Northern Tools and Equipment. Also, Stellus had been a driving force behind the Minnesota Wild's phenomenally successful "State of Hockey" branding initiative.

The Penguins' preconceived notion was that the end result would be something similar to the Pittsburgh Steelers' proud and successful blue-collar brand. The Steelers personified Pittsburgh history with their steel industry logo and hard-nosed work ethic. It was one of the dominant brands in all of professional sports. Stellus knew it faced a unique challenge: Pittsburgh was a football town, and that was not about to change. Nonetheless, Stellus set out to learn if there also might be an underlying emotional connection between fans and the Penguins – perhaps, even, among a new segment of fans. They interviewed Penguins employees, players and former players, season ticket holders, corporate sponsors, local political leaders and significant non-stakeholders. In addition, they met with a series of segmented focus groups – regular folks, average fans – not only Penguins fans but also local sports fans who had yet to warm to hockey.

The compilation of all this information – more than a year in the making – produced a Brand Essence and a Brand Promise and set the course for the team's marketing future. The findings of Stellus Consulting were summarized by CEO Corky Hall's statement to Penguins management: "This is a football town, and the Steelers are one of the iconic brands in sports," he said. "But what we learned was that the young people in this town also have developed an extraordinary affection for the Penguins. They love the Steelers AND the Penguins. You've got a chance to really establish yourselves with the next generation. It's always going to be a dominant football town, but if you work hard and do things the right way, it can be a hockey town, too."

Of all the words fans and stakeholders had used during Hall's exercises to describe what they thought of the Penguins, three words emerged as the Brand Essence: Drive, Energy and Innovation. Those words matched perfectly with what the Penguins wanted to be: A young dynamic, tech-savvy organization with a new arena on the way, one devoted to championships and fan outreach. The new Brand Promise exemplified this feeling for a new generation of fans – The Pittsburgh Penguins Fuel Your Desire to Break Away. Young people of the region liked the speed of Penguins hockey, the game's frenetic pace, and they were already energized by the team's growing commitment to technology and social media.

Morehouse had his answer. Now, the work began.

Introduction

The information gathering approach taken by the Pittsburgh Penguins to managing its brand serves as a reminder about brand ownership. While an organization owns tangible pieces of its brand such as trademarks for brand name and logo, a brand is ultimately owned by customers. What does that mean? A brand matters to customers and others because of the meaning the brand holds for them, the benefits or value the brand delivers, and the feelings of trust that develop when a brand delivers a consistent experience. Marketers are caretakers of brands, not their owners. Because professional sports teams and leagues are constantly evolving—much more than most other products—it is important to re-examine a brand and perhaps even re-energize it every few years, as the Pittsburgh Penguins did. This chapter examines the role of brands in developing and maintaining customer relationships.

What Is a Brand?

Brands are central to the practice of marketing. If someone unfamiliar with marketing were to ask, "What is it that is marketed?" the best answer may be "brands." While it could be argued that people buy products, services, and experiences, the buyer-seller exchange that is at the heart of marketing occurs between a consumer and a brand that is the representation of what the seller has to offer. A brand has four different purposes or roles: 1) an identity, 2) an image, 3) a promise, and 4) a relationship (see Figure 5.1). Brands add value for both buyers and marketers through each of these roles.

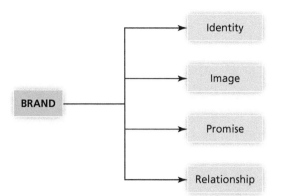

FIGURE 5.1 **Roles of Brands**

An Identity

The American Marketing Association's definition of a brand fits the notion of a brand serving as a form of identification: "A name, term, design, symbol, or any other feature that identifies a seller's good or service as distinct from those of other sellers."[4] This functional role of a brand adds value for consumers by informing them who to contact in case of questions, complaints, or other needs. Also, brand elements such as the name, logo, and colors serve as mental shortcuts that associate a product with its owner. In the sports industry, the name "Cubs" is instantly connected to Chicago's MLB National League team, a blue star is recognized as being part of the identity of the Dallas Cowboys, and pinstripes are synonymous with the New York Yankees baseball team.

Identity elements are important because they can play a role in creating brand awareness among consumers. In the case of a sports franchise, choice of team name, logo, and colors are important because they not only create an identity for that team, but the identity serves to set the brand apart from other sports entertainment brands in the same geographic market as well as other teams in the conference or league in which the team competes. For example, a unique name like the Montgomery Biscuits, a Class AA minor league baseball team in Montgomery, Alabama, creates a distinct identity for the team that differentiates it from other professional and collegiate sports brands in Alabama and the other nine teams in the Southern League. An effective brand name aids in building awareness because consumers can relate the brand's identity to the product or service it represents.

An Image

Another purpose a brand serves is as a representation of thoughts or mental associations that people hold for a product or service, which is **brand image**. A definition of brand that acknowledges the role of a brand for projecting an image is that a brand is a "customer or user experience represented by images and ideas. . . . Brand recognition and other reactions are created by the accumulation of experiences with the specific product or service, both from its use, and as influenced by advertising, design and media commentary."[5] The thoughts and perceptions that one has for a person or object, known as **brand associations**, influence the image developed. Formation of brand associations that comprise image does not require product ownership or usage. For example, you likely have perceptions for brands such as Lexus, Taco Bell, and American Eagle regardless of whether you have ever bought or used them . . . including associations created by these brands' involvement in sports sponsorship.

Similarly, people have images of sports brands regardless of whether they are fans of a particular sport or team. For example, NASCAR has faced challenges with its brand image, being perceived by many nonfans as a sport for blue-collar white males in the southern United States. While NASCAR's roots fit those perceptions, the appeal of NASCAR has grown to a nationwide following as well as having gained a greater appeal among women and ethnic groups. NASCAR's dilemma illustrates the difference between brand image and brand identity. Brand image resides in the minds of consumers. Image is thoughts about a brand based on past experiences, existing knowledge, and knowledge obtained from other sources, including marketing communications. **Brand identity** is made up of associations that a marketer aspires to project or communicate to the target market. Identity represents how the marketer wants a brand to be perceived.

For virtually every brand, a gap exists between brand identity and brand image. A team that has desired associations of "excellence," "success," and "quality" may find it difficult to succeed in building brand identity if people's perceptions of the team are based on a history

Coca-Cola's involvement with NASCAR impacts the brand identity it wants to project.

of mediocre performance, managerial missteps, or other negative associations with the team. The identity–image gap is a situation of bad news, good news. The bad news is that public perceptions that influence brand image may be inconsistent with associations the brand aspires to maintain, or worse, are simply inaccurate or untrue perceptions. So what is the good news? The seemingly never-ending quest to align image and identity means that there will always be a need for marketing . . . and marketers like you! Even the most admired and successful brands must proactively manage brand identity to maintain their standing among consumers.

A Promise

Brands represent a promise of action that will benefit a customer. People value brands because they stand for intent to deliver value. Promises made by brands can be explicit or implicit. Explicit promises are statements of action such as a warranty or service guarantee. Performance standards are spelled out and it is up to the brand to meet those standards.

Perhaps a more important role brands play is the implied promises they make to the customer. Think of an implied promise as reducing all of a brand's attributes, benefits, ad slogans, and brand associations to a single claim that sets it apart from other brands. Some of the most successful global brands have risen to their status in part because they deliver effectively on an implied promise. For Coca-Cola, the promise is "refreshment"; for McDonald's it is "consistency"; and for Apple it is "simplicity." These brands are great because their promises matter to consumers, and they are exceptional at fulfilling their promises through product innovation, designing great customer experiences, and connecting their brands with their customers' lifestyles.

The importance of brand promises must not be overlooked by sports marketers. In some cases, brand promises are explicit, such as a refund or tickets to a future game if a person has a bad experience at a game. However, explicit promises about brand performance in sports are generally avoided given that on-field performance is out of the control of managers responsible for the brand. Thus, implied brand promises take on great significance through developing brand associations that give meaning to a brand for consumers. Many sports properties place an emphasis on community relations in an effort to create implied brand promises. Support for schools, donations to nonprofit organizations, and promoting youth sports are examples of ways

Interstate Batteries

Interstate Batteries promotes NASCAR drivers, Joey Logano, Kyle Busch and Denny Hamlin on point-of-purchase (POP) banners.

sports brands create and deliver against an implied promise of "community partner." This strategy can be important for gaining acceptance among casual fans and nonfans of a sport as well as obtaining support from local government and the community at large.

A Relationship

Exchanges between buyers and sellers may be business relationships, but one's decision to buy from a business is often guided by the same criteria applied to personal relationships. An individual may choose friends or associates based on whether he or she believes a person can be trusted. Also, the likeability of that person can influence a decision to forge a friendship. Similarly, consumers tend to enter into business relationships with companies and brands that they trust, like, or perceive to be similar to them.

Most relationships with the brands are discretionary. People have a choice whether to drive a Chevrolet or Ford, eat at Burger King or Wendy's, and so forth. For many individuals, a brand is more than a name or an image; it is a trusted friend that can be relied upon to deliver consistent quality or enjoyable experiences. Whether people realize it or not, brands are often thought of in terms of personality traits (e.g., dependable, caring, friendly) that attract individuals to engage personal relationships.

The prevailing thought in marketing with regard to a brand as a symbol of a relationship between buyers and sellers is a shift from a focus on customer transactions to long-term relationships. An approach that advocates a long-term orientation toward managing customer interactions is called **relationship marketing**. It has been defined as "marketing with the conscious aim to develop and manage long-term and/or trusting relationships with customers, distributors, suppliers, or other parties in the marketing environment."[6]

For sports brands, two motivations exist for practicing relationship marketing. First, it is generally accepted that the expense to retain existing customers through marketing activities is much lower than the investments needed to attract and acquire new customers. This principle tends to hold true regardless of the product category or industry in which a brand competes. Thus, viewing a customer's interaction with a brand as an ongoing relationship rather than a one-time purchase will influence how a marketer engages customers.

This shift toward focusing on customer retention leads to the second motivation for sports brands to practice relationship marketing. As established in previous chapters, consumers' motivations for consuming sports are often based on emotional connections—affinity for a sport, team, or athlete—that are not felt for other brands that one uses. For example, a subscriber to DirecTV might use the company's satellite TV service and even like the company, but the relationship likely will lack the excitement and feelings of identification that one often has when consuming sports. Sports brands have the luxury of tapping the passion felt by fans to deepen relationships with them.

A trend in relationship marketing observed in the sports industry is attracting customers that desire a more intimate connection with their favorite team or player by offering more insider access. Whether it is locker room tours, private meetings with team executives, or other behind-the-scenes experiences, relationships can be forged that move a brand from an identity and image to a trusted friend. Dennis Moore, vice president of sales and marketing for the Denver Broncos, predicts that the future will bring greater convergence of team brand and its fans, and inside access will become the norm as a relationship-building strategy to connect with premium customer segments.[7]

Brand Building

As shown in Figure 5.2, responsibilities for marketing a brand fall under two broad areas: brand building and brand leveraging. Brand building entails decisions such as selecting a brand name and designing marks associated with the brand such as a logo and color scheme. While these branding decisions are obviously needed when a new brand is launched, they are decisions that should be evaluated on a regular basis. Brand leveraging is strategies devised to capitalize on aspects of a brand (identity, image, promises, and relationships) to develop product offerings that add value for customers and drive business growth for an organization.

FIGURE 5.2 Marketing a Brand

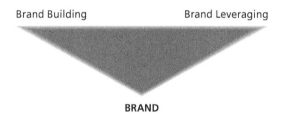

Brand Building   Brand Leveraging

BRAND

Brand Name

The first step in building a brand is selecting a name. A brand's name is the branding element most closely identified with a company or product. It may be one of the few things (if not the only) that is recognized and remembered when a person encounters a brand. The significance of selecting an effective name is great because a brand name is considered to be the cornerstone of building customer relationships.[8] For sports brands, a name ideally possesses three characteristics: 1) recognizability, 2) fit, and 3) contrast (see Figure 5.3).[9]

FIGURE 5.3 Characteristics of a Good Brand Name

- Recognizability
- Fit
- Contrast

RECOGNIZABILITY. In a crowded market for consumers' entertainment dollars, creating a brand that is easily remembered and associated with a sports property is important. Some names are recognized from years of existence, history, tradition, or uniqueness. For example, names like the Detroit Lions and St. Louis Cardinals have no particular connection or relationship to their local geographic markets like many sports brands, but they are good brand names because sports fans are familiar with their names after decades of existence and associating them with the cities in which they play. In contrast to relatively generic names like Cardinals and Lions, some sports properties create a brand name that is a unique spelling of a common word or a made-up word. Interesting brand names that meet the criterion of recognizability are plentiful in Minor League Baseball. The Batavia (New York) Muckdogs, Everett (Washington) AquaSox, and Richmond (Virginia) Flying Squirrels are brand names that do not have wide-scale recognition but are unique names that can establish prominence in their local markets.

FIT. A name should not only be recognizable, but it should fit, or have some sort of match or connection with the brand's target market. A "catchy" brand name may gain the attention of consumers, but if the name does not resonate with an audience the impact of being recognizable may be lessened. For example, media and communications company Comcast rebranded itself by changing its name to Xfinity. The company abandoned years of name recognition and brand building when it switched to a name that means . . . well, that was the question asked by many marketing experts who criticized the rebranding. It is possible to place emphasis on a name being distinctive to the point of it not having meaning to the target market.

Fit can be achieved in many ways. A name can fit the local market through a geographical reference, historical connection, or a match with an area's personality. Minor League Baseball provides unique names that are designed to achieve fit:

- The Asheville (North Carolina) Tourists acknowledges the importance of tourism to the western North Carolina region.
- The Kannapolis (North Carolina) Intimidators shares the same nickname as the city's most famous resident: NASCAR legend Dale Earnhardt Sr.
- The Louisville Bats recognizes one of that city's most famous businesses, Louisville Slugger, manufacturer of baseball bats.
- The Las Vegas 51s connects to the lore of Area 51, a region in western Nevada famous for sightings of unidentified flying objects.
- The Stockton (California) Ports is named in recognition of Stockton having California's only inland port.[10]

Examples of sports brands that have a strong fit for their target market can also be found throughout professional and collegiate sports. Achieving fit in a brand name can be done only if market and product characteristics are defined before a name is given to a product. It is not a good idea to establish a brand name before clearly defining the target market as well as a product's features and benefits. A more complete definition of market and product makes it easier to create a brand name that the target market will accept as being a good fit with the product.

CONTRAST. The third criterion of an effective sports brand name is that it differentiates an offering from other sports entertainment brands. In the team sports sector of the sports industry, a franchise does more than compete on the field against other teams in their same league; it also competes with teams in other sports leagues to create a distinct image. Thus, it is important that a brand name separate a brand from others vying for consumers' attention.

Examples of instances in which contrast is sometimes not achieved can be found in college athletics. Athletic programs that select brand names that are not unique hinder efforts to develop a strong brand identity. Although a brand name might be unique to an institution's conference or geographic region, the national reach of college athletics through cable television and the Internet means that brands that do not meet the contrast criterion could have the same name as other institutions. Two examples:

- Auburn Tigers (Southeastern Conference), Clemson Tigers (Atlantic Coast Conference), and Memphis Tigers (Conference USA)
- Arizona Wildcats (Pac-12 Conference), Northwestern Wildcats (Big Ten Conference), and Kentucky Wildcats (Southeastern Conference)

Similarly, a brand name that is ineffective in contrasting an offering from competition may be shared by more than one organization, potentially diminishing the strength of the brand name for all affected parties. For example, the Orlando Predators brand (Arena Football League) has existed since the early 1990s, but it was joined in the late 1990s by the Nashville Predators

(NHL). Although this situation appears to have not negatively affected either brand, a preferable situation would be to not share any elements of brand identity with another professional sports team.

The preceding discussion makes a strong case for selecting a brand name that contrasts with other sports entertainment offerings, but there are circumstances in which choosing brand names that are similar to existing brands has been a strategy that paid dividends. This scenario took place when the Women's National Basketball Association (WNBA) debuted in the late 1990s. The WNBA sought to leverage the name recognition of NBA teams by giving teams names that bore similarity to their NBA counterparts in the same market. Examples of this practice included:

- Minnesota: Lynx (WNBA) and Timberwolves (NBA)
- Phoenix: Mercury (WNBA) and Suns (NBA)
- Utah: Starzz (WNBA) and Jazz (NBA)

When marketing synergies can be enjoyed by departing from a strategy of selecting a name that contrasts or separates a sports property, it is appropriate to forgo a contrasting brand name. For example, some minor league baseball teams have brand names that associate the team with its MLB affiliate, such as the Mississippi Braves, Memphis Redbirds, and Pawtucket Red Sox. In each of the cases, the MLB team has a strong fan base in the market where the minor league affiliate is located. While a unique name that contrasts the minor league team from other professional baseball teams would be a viable option, these teams capitalize on the popularity of their MLB parent clubs.

Brand Marks

A second element of brand building is creation of brand marks that project an identity and influence image development. **Brand marks** are forms of communication other than words that are used to communicate brand identity. Examples of brand marks are logos, colors, and characters (see Figure 5.4). Logos and colors are branding elements common across all industries, while utilization of brand characters is a branding tactic used more extensively in sports than in other product categories.

FIGURE 5.4 Examples of Brand Marks

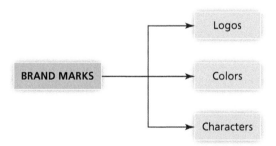

LOGO. A **logo** is a symbol or other visual element that is associated with a brand. The purpose of a logo is to develop a visual form of brand identification. An effective logo is one for which consumers recognize the brand or company it represents even if the brand name is not present. For example, iconic figures like the burnt orange Texas Longhorns silhouette, the five interlocked rings representing the continents that compete in the Olympics, and the Nike swoosh are so deeply ingrained in consumers' minds as part of those brands' identities that they can stand on their own. Logo development is a creative process that does not come with "one right way" to effective design. However, there are some considerations that should be made when a logo is being designed or evaluated for possible redesign:

- *Is it distinctive?* A logo should be unique and stand out and differentiate a brand.
- *Is it relevant?* The imagery used should relate to the good, service, or experience it represents.

- *Is it versatile?* A logo must look attractive across a variety of media—on billboards, letterhead, and websites as well as on uniforms and licensed products.

- *Is it enduring?* Logos are unlike ad slogans or campaigns that are changed or updated frequently. The expense to develop and communicate a logo necessitates a long-term orientation to logo use.[11]

In addition to these four questions that should be asked when designing a logo for a sports brand, another consideration related to the versatility question is: Can a brand character such as a mascot be developed from the logo concept? Mascots are brand marks in their own right, and a mascot that embodies the visual image of a logo or relates to the logo in a meaningful way reinforces a brand's identity. While it is not essential that a character be based on a brand's logo, examples of popular mascots whose characters relate to their team's logo include Wild Wing (Anaheim Ducks), Miles (Denver Broncos), and Oriole Bird (Baltimore Orioles). Adding the element of a brand character can be simplified if the logo design can be brought to life.

COLORS. Like a logo, colors can be associated with a brand as a branding element that aids in recalling a brand from memory and influences brand image. Consider the role of color for the University of Nebraska brand. Many people think of "red" when encountering the Nebraska name. The color red is a prominent feature of Nebraska's branding strategy as evidenced by a second nickname often used in addition to its Cornhuskers nickname: Big Red. Selection of

Color	Meanings
Blue	Trustworthy; dependable; secure
Red	Aggressive; energetic; provocative
Green	Health; freshness; prestige
Orange	Exuberance; fun; vitality
Purple	Sophistication; royalty; mystery
Black	Bold; powerful; classic
White	Simplicity; cleanliness; purity

FIGURE 5.5 Meanings Associated with Various Colors

colors is important because color is more than a visual branding element; consumers construct meanings of colors that are part of a brand's identity. Figure 5.5 gives examples of connotations people have for colors used in branding.

When making decisions about logo design and brand colors, choice of colors to incorporate into these branding elements should be guided by how consumers interpret colors and not what colors are popular at that time or managers' personal preferences. In the 1990s, teal gained popularity as a brand color. Expansion franchises in professional sports such as the San Jose Sharks, Florida Marlins, and Jacksonville Jaguars adopted teal as part of their team colors. However, the popularity was driven more by fashion trends than the meaning conveyed by the colors. In recent years, these teams have refined the appearance of their brand colors to downplay teal because of changing consumer tastes. In contrast, a sports brand with traditional colors such as the black and gold of the Pittsburgh Steelers is a constant that withstands fashion trends. The meanings attached to those colors resonate with the values and associations many people hold for Pittsburgh such as "strong work ethic" and "solid."

In addition to colors being central to the design of a logo, they also can become part of the brand identity. A sports brand's colors can become shorthand for the brand itself. Can you identify each of the "color" brands shown in Figure 5.6 with its correct team? Colors do more than distinguish a sports brand from competition; they contribute to the brand's meaning and personality.

CHARACTERS. For more than a century, brand characters have been used to add another dimension to brand identity and to shape brand personality. Some brand characters have reached iconic status in popular culture, like Ronald McDonald and the Michelin Man. Brand characters

FIGURE 5.6 Can You Identify the Sports Teams Connected with These Colors?

1. Maize and Blue

2. Silver and Black

3. Big Red

4. Purple and Gold

Answers

1) University of Michigan
2) Oakland Raiders
3) University of Nebraska
4) Minnesota Vikings and
   Los Angeles Lakers

serve a key role beyond being part of a brand's identity. Consumers' feelings of trust toward brand characters can influence attitudes and behaviors toward the brand.[12] The prevalence of brand characters as a branding strategy in the sports industry is much greater than for other types of goods and services. The nicknames of many sports brands are easily transferable to developing brand characters (e.g., Tigers, Huskies, and Panthers).

Even when a brand character does not arise naturally from the brand name, a brand character can still be created to reinforce a brand's identity and shape its personality. Western Kentucky University illustrates how a brand character can energize a brand and heighten its profile in the marketplace. WKU's nickname, Hilltoppers, does not exactly lend itself to a brand character that is closely related to the brand name. However, WKU's mascot, Big Red, is the best-known element of the WKU brand. The red, furry creature has been associated with the Hilltoppers since 1979. It has nothing to do with a Hilltopper, but it is recognized by many sports fans as belonging to WKU. And its playful personality creates favorable associations of the WKU brand in consumers' minds.

Special Cases in Sports Branding

The branding issues discussed so far (name, logo, colors, character) are generally faced by a marketer regardless of product category. For sports brands, there are two other situations that may arise for which changes in branding strategy may be needed: 1) brand makeovers and 2) franchise relocation.

BRAND MAKEOVER. A brand is a dynamic asset owned by a business. It should be adapted and updated as customer tastes and marketing environment conditions change. This concept applies to any brand. However, there are certain cases in which a change or makeover to a brand can serve as a signal of positive change to stakeholders. For sports brands, a brand makeover may be in order when perceptions of poor performance or quality exist. Updating one or more branding elements can revitalize a brand and position it more competitively in the marketplace. Three sports properties that used a brand makeover to adjust to changes in their business model are the National Hockey League, Tampa Bay Rays, and NBC Sports Network.

The National Hockey League hit a low point in 2004 when a labor dispute between owners and players completely wiped out the 2004–2005 season. The NHL used the one-season layoff to make rule changes and other enhancements to the game. The NHL's branding received a makeover, too. The traditional NHL shield was updated with color and design changes. The orange letters and trim on the existing logo was replaced by silver. The arrangement of the letters "NHL" changed from sloping downward to the right to sloping upward to the right, and the new logo took on a more dimensional, stronger look. The timing of the new logo coincided with the launch of the "new" NHL in 2005.

The Tampa Bay Devil Rays were considered one of the worst franchises in Major League Baseball—on the field, in the front office, and in ownership—before Stu Sternberg purchased the team in 2005. Previous ownership had alienated fans. Sternberg realized a fresh start would be beneficial to energizing the brand. The team made changes throughout the organization, including shortening the team nickname to Rays, updating the logo to reflect the new name, and modifying the colors used in the logo and uniforms. The branding changes were symbolic of the culture of change that was instilled throughout the Rays organization. The result? In 2008, the first season with the new brand marks, the Rays won the American League championship. Of course, the Rays' AL pennant was not due to the brand makeover, but the franchise's unprecedented success coinciding with fresh branding could not have happened at a better time.

In certain situations, new directions in marketing strategy may necessitate a more drastic rebranding than tweaking the logo or name. Media giant Comcast found itself in this situation as it repositioned OLN, originally known as the Outdoor Life Network. Comcast aspired to compete with ESPN, but its OLN brand was too limiting, as it positioned the network as a brand associated with outdoor sports and recreation activities. In 2006, OLN was rebranded as Versus. The new brand identity held a broader meaning of "shorthand for competition."[13] The rebranded Versus expanded its programming to include spectator sports properties including the NHL, NCAA football, and IndyCar Series. A characteristic of an effective brand name is that it conveys brand meaning (i.e., a brand's point of difference), but if a business expands into new products or markets it is possible to outgrow a brand name, as Comcast experienced with OLN.

Versus became a candidate for rebranding again when Comcast and NBC Universal merged in 2011. The rebranded network, called the NBC Sports Network, prominently features the NBC brand. Including the NBC brand in the network's name leverages the brand equity NBC has built over decades in television, radio, and the Internet.

FRANCHISE RELOCATION. Sports brands sometimes face a dilemma concerning their brand identity typically not faced by companies in other industries. If a sports franchise decides to relocate to another market, it is faced with the decision of whether to change name, logo, or colors. If Starbucks expands into a new market, it is a foregone conclusion that the store name will be Starbucks. Brand names in non-sports product categories usually fit wherever the brand is offered. In contrast, the meaning contained in the name of a sports brand may be market specific and would not transfer if the brand relocated operations to another market. When the Houston Oilers relocated to Nashville in the late 1990s it was evident that rebranding would be necessary because the Oilers name did not fit with the new home of the franchise. In some cases, it may be possible and preferable to maintain the existing brand identity, while in cases like that of the Houston Oilers a new identity is in order.

This issue is not trivial, as franchise relocation in professional sports has occurred with some regularity since the mid-1990s as market saturation has slowed expansion of teams. Thus, the best option a market may have for securing a professional sports franchise is to convince an existing franchise to relocate. Since 1995, relocations have occurred for three NBA franchises (Vancouver to Memphis, Charlotte to New Orleans, and Seattle to Oklahoma City), four NFL franchises (Los Angeles Raiders to Oakland . . . again, Los Angeles Rams to St. Louis, Cleveland to Baltimore, and Houston to Nashville), four NHL franchises (Quebec to Denver, Winnipeg to Phoenix, Hartford to Raleigh, and Atlanta to Winnipeg), and one MLB franchise (Montreal to Washington). Similarly, franchise movement has been experienced in other professional leagues (MLS, WNBA, and Minor League Baseball).

Some general rules can be applied to the decision to keep or change brand identity when relocating to a new market. From the standpoint of cost required to create and grow a brand, retaining an existing brand would be preferred if the right conditions exist. A brand with high familiarity or strength among consumers should be considered for retention. When the Oakland Raiders moved to Los Angeles in 1982 it kept the nickname because of its immense popularity, not just in California but nationwide. The Raiders brand was accepted by fans, and it posed no problems in terms of fit with the local market. Another situation in which retaining the current brand name is appropriate is when it is broad or general enough to be relevant in the new market. The Charlotte Hornets relocated its NBA franchise to New Orleans in 2002, choosing to keep the Hornets name. The name did not have specific meaning or significance in either market, so it transferred easily to the New Orleans market.

While retaining a brand name when relocating a sports brand may be preferable and in line with branding practice in other industries, rebranding a franchise when it moves to a new market is often necessary. The primary reason the decision to rebrand is made is because the brand name does not fit the new market as well as it did the former market. In the Houston Oilers situation, the team name was a great fit for Houston given the significance of the oil industry to the area. However, when the franchise moved to Nashville, a new name was needed because Oilers was not a general name, nor did it have meaning or significance in its new home. Similarly, when the Montreal Expos MLB franchise moved to Washington, D.C., in 2005, the need to rebrand was a given, since the Expos brand was a reference to a World's Fair held in Montreal in 1967. The problem was solved when the franchise took the name Nationals; that acknowledged two previous professional teams by that name and was a good fit with the city's patriotic significance.

Another situation in which rebranding is the right strategy to follow is when a brand needs a fresh start. If a franchise would benefit from distancing itself from its former home, past problems, or poor performance, a makeover in the form of a new name, logo, and colors can essentially provide a fresh start for the business. When Cleveland Browns owner Art Modell moved the team to Baltimore in 1996, it was the conclusion of a bitter battle with the city of Cleveland. The former Cleveland team moved management, coaches, and players to Baltimore, and along with them was the negative baggage of the move that hurt Browns fans and the local community. Although the franchise had to give up a great deal of brand equity it had accrued over the years, the renamed Baltimore Ravens gave the franchise a new start in its new city.

Ethical Considerations

The criteria for guiding decisions on brand name, marks, and characters have an underlying benchmark that should be met when setting brand strategy—do brand elements fit with the values and norms of stakeholders? A name, logo, or character may fit or have relevance with the target market in some way, but if a brand offends or creates negative associations among some people, rebranding could be necessary.

This ethical dilemma occurred in the sports industry with the use of brand elements with Native American references. Some Native American groups have expressed strong opposition to sports teams carrying nicknames like Indians or Braves and are also against sports properties using brand characters that they believe portray negative images of Native Americans. Among those brand elements singled out for criticism were Chief Knockahoma, a brand character that appeared at Atlanta Braves games, and the logos of the Cleveland Indians and Washington Redskins that depicted Indians with red faces. The feelings of many people opposed to the use of Native American branding elements in sports can be summed up by the position "Native Americans are people, not mascots. Using our names, likeness and religious symbols to excite the crowd does not feel like honor or respect, it is hurtful and confusing to our young people."[14]

The response taken by sports properties concerning Native American names and symbols in sports brands has varied. Professional sports properties have given the appearance of listening to opponents' concerns but have made virtually no changes. Not even a lawsuit that made its way to the U.S. Supreme Court (but was not heard) concerning the Washington Redskins name and logo caused pro sports teams to back down from this practice. In contrast, the NCAA was proactive in giving direction to its member institutions about the use of Native American brand elements. In 2005, the NCAA adopted a policy against the use of names, imagery, and mascots that it characterized as "abusive" and "hostile" toward Native Americans.

The NCAA's leverage to gain member institutions' cooperation was that it would prohibit teams that did not drop Native American brand elements from participating in NCAA championship events. Exceptions were granted for institutions whose Native American brand elements had historical significance. But more than a dozen institutions that had brand names such as Indians or Redskins that did not have a historical connection to the institution or its

ULM Mohawks / ULM Athletics

The new logo of the University of Louisiana at Monroe (ULM) after changing from "Indians" to "Warhawks."

geographic area were required to rebrand. The stance taken by the NCAA was based on the desire of the organization's leadership to promote diversity and inclusiveness among its member institutions.

Brand Leveraging

The roles of a brand (identity, image, promise, and relationship) are crucial—they are the answer to the question of what a company "markets" in marketing. Another question to ask, for which there is no simple answer, is "How does a company go about building a great brand?" Part of the answer relates to the previous section, through effective use of names, brand marks, and characters. In addition, there are certain strategies that can be implemented to take advantage of brand strengths and acceptance in the marketplace to take a brand from a great idea to a financially successful asset. The overarching strategy that manages a brand for growth is the development of brand equity. More specific strategies tied to a brand's equity are identified in Figure 5.7.

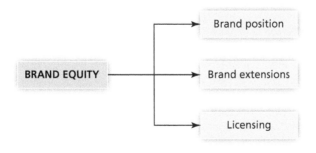

FIGURE 5.7 **Brand Leveraging**

Developing Brand Equity

Brand management and leveraging are based on the view that a brand is an asset owned by a business. As such, brands have financial value for an organization because they are involved in the exchange of value with customers, just as equipment, real estate, and patents are assets that are used by a business to earn a profit. Thus, the goal of a marketer should be to maximize the value of brand assets. The concept of brand equity recognizes brands as assets. Investments should be made in the asset to grow its value, and if managed effectively, dividends or payoffs to the investments are realized. **Brand equity** is "a set of assets linked to a brand's name and symbol that adds to the value provided by a product or service to a firm and/or to that firm's customers."[15] Specifically, the assets that comprise brand equity shown in Figure 5.8 are: 1) brand awareness, 2) brand associations, and 3) brand loyalty.

FIGURE 5.8 Assets of Brand Equity

Brand awareness is an asset developed from recognition and familiarity among consumers and sponsors. For sports properties, exposure received through media coverage can be instrumental in building brand awareness. On one hand, some sports brands are recognized globally, such as the New York Yankees and Manchester United; but for lesser-known brands, media coverage adds value to a brand in consumers' minds. Development of this component of brand equity can be observed in men's college basketball when a team that is a lesser-known brand advances in the NCAA tournament. Although George Mason University (GMU) has more than 30,000 students, it was relatively unknown throughout most of the United States until it advanced to the Final Four in the NCAA tournament. GMU's success in the tournament and the exposure it brought the university paid off as the university experienced a 10% increase in new student applications and a 20% increase in donations.[16]

Brand associations are thoughts and perceptions people hold for a brand. While marketing communications are instrumental in shaping brand associations, it is important to remember that any "touch point" where a person is exposed to or interacts with a brand is an opportunity to develop brand associations. Brand associations are developed at the product level and organization level. At the product level, marketing mix elements such as product attributes, price, distribution channels, and communication determine how a brand is perceived.

One type of product association that is particularly influential on consumer behavior is perceived quality. Quality associations are influential because they can shape perceptions about other aspects of a brand (e.g., trustworthiness, competence, and value). For sports brands, perceived quality associations can be developed through perceptions about sports performance such as wins and championships or the enjoyment and excitement of the experience of attending sporting events. At the organization level, social responsibility is an organization-wide strategy for developing desirable brand associations. The emergence of social responsibility as an expectation consumers have for businesses was covered in Chapter 3, and managerial considerations for building corporate associations through brand reputation management will be discussed later in this chapter.

Brand loyalty differs from awareness and associations in that it is an asset that is a customer-driven facet of brand management. Marketers can make investments in branding and communications that lead to greater awareness and desired brand associations, but loyalty is determined by a customer's willingness to have an ongoing relationship with a business. For example, a person who buys tickets to the Indianapolis 500 each year may be loyal because of affinity for a particular driver, enjoyment of taking in the race with family or friends, or the pageantry of this major sporting event.

Loyalty is an output of branding and marketing, enjoyed by brands that stand out in terms of creating awareness and associations that resonate with their target market. However, the fact that loyalty is dictated by consumer behavior does not mean that marketers are passive spectators who can do little to influence loyalty. The same associations that arise from perceptions of brands at the product and organization levels lead to decisions about loyalty toward a company. Sports properties can cultivate loyalty through strategies such as frequency or reward programs, identifying customers with high purchase frequency and monetary value through database marketing, and providing special access to fans and sponsors that intensify their connection with the brand.

Staking a Brand Position

One of the most important decisions made with regard to activating a brand is how the brand should be positioned. **Brand position** is "the part of the brand identity and value proposition that is to be actively communicated to the target audience and that demonstrates an advantage over competing brands."[17] Determining a brand position is important because a well-defined and articulated brand position clarifies the meaning of a brand to a single idea or association. It is unrealistic to expect consumers to remember *everything* about a brand—so what is the *one thing* that should come to mind when encountering the brand? Brand positioning is a strategy to hone in on an attribute, benefit, or characteristic of a brand that sets it apart from competitors. Without a clear brand position, a brand is doomed! That declaration may seem an exaggeration, but for brands without a clearly communicated point of difference, consumers will likely have difficulty understanding why they should buy that brand versus one of the other options that exists.

A brand risks being viewed as a commodity when it lacks uniqueness or superiority to competitors. One of the primary reasons products fail in the market is lack of a distinct brand position. For evidence, consider brands that have competed for the attention of American football fans. In 2009, the United Football League debuted with a fall league that focused on markets in which there are no NFL teams such as Las Vegas, Orlando, and Omaha, Nebraska. In terms of positioning, the UFL did little to set itself apart from the NFL other than putting teams in non-NFL markets and playing games on days other than Sundays. It remains to be seen whether the UFL will be a viable competitor to the NFL.

Ian Dagnall/Alamy Stock Photo

In 2001, the XFL, a joint venture between World Wrestling Entertainment and NBC, launched a spring league that lasted only one season. The positioning flaw of the XFL was that its difference may have lacked relevance to the target market. One of the criticisms of the XFL was that its position as a rebellious departure from the status quo was not well received by pro football fans. It came across to many fans as different simply for the sake of being different.

A brand position may be one of the most important strategic decisions a marketing manager will make, but its final form can be reduced to a single sentence. A well-defined brand position contains three elements: 1) it specifies the target market, 2) it clarifies the business or category in which a brand competes, and 3) it states the advantage or point of difference that will resonate with the target market.[18] The first element pertains to relevance. It is understood that everyone in the market will not value what a brand has to offer, so the brand position narrows the focus to the group or groups who will be most interested in the brand.

The second element, business definition, may seem like a given, but it may be less obvious than one might think. For example, an appropriate business definition for marketing a college basketball team is "sports entertainment" rather than basketball. Why? A broader view of what the brand offers expands the potential market for customers—more people want to be entertained than want to watch basketball. Inclusion of a business definition in the brand position forces reflection on the benefit provided to customers.

The third element, point of difference, should state not only uniqueness or superiority but also identify the payoff or benefit of that advantage to customers. This element of positioning offers marketers latitude in decision making as there is no single method or approach to identifying a point of difference. Managers must determine what point of difference possessed by the brand will resonate with customers and prospects. Four approaches to brand positioning with applicability to sports are identified in Figure 5.9.

FIGURE 5.9 Brand Positioning Strategies in Sports

• Product attribute   • Quality   • User imagery   • Value

© Jacek Kozyra / Fotolia

ATTRIBUTE POSITIONING. When a brand possesses a product feature or characteristic that provides superiority over competitors, attribute positioning can be used to communicate the advantage. In sports marketing, use of attribute positioning is a strategy that leverages a unique aspect a sports property possesses to appeal to the target market. The Professional Bull Riders (PBR) deals with misperceptions of nonfans that a PBR event is a rodeo (it is not a rodeo; bull-riding events only). PBR can expand its potential market by defining its product as "eight seconds of action," which refers to the length of time a rider hopes to stay on a bull. The audience PBR strives to meet is action or thrill seekers, a market that is much larger than if it focused on bull-riding fans only. Any relevant attribute of a sport can be the basis for brand position, such as speed or physical play. Any attribute that can be tapped as a point of difference to the current or a new target market can be used as a positioning approach.

QUALITY POSITIONING. An advantage of developing perceptions of perceived quality is that those associations can be leveraged to be the basis of brand position. A brand that develops a reputation or image for delivering high-quality performance to customers can use that strength to its advantage by touting it. A quality position can be very convincing to consumers as it can convey dependability and trust. One way non-sports brands can reinforce a quality position is through their involvement in sports sponsorship. For example, IBM has partnered with prestigious golf events (the Masters) and tennis tournaments (Wimbledon and U.S. Open), providing its information technology services and expertise in support functions. IBM's sponsorships enhance quality perceptions for the company and the elite sports properties with which it partners.

Sports brands are not manufactured products, so a quality position does not take the same form as a product brand that touts superiority in design or engineering. Yet quality can be the basis of brand position for a sports property. Quality associations can be based on success, tradition, star players, level of competition, or the customer experience. All of these aspects of a sports product, with the exception of the customer consumption experience, are largely out of a marketer's control. However, the existence of current or past success, tradition, well-known players, or high level of competition are assets that can be used to position a brand.

The Montreal Canadiens have won the Stanley Cup as NHL champions a record twenty-four times. However, the team's last championship was in 1993. Despite the lengthy drought, the Canadiens are positioned on their storied tradition. The team dominated the NHL in the 1950s through 1970s, and some of its top players achieved legendary status among Canadiens fans and throughout the world. Not every sports brand has the luxury of leaning on a storied history as its brand position. Yet quality can be the basis for brand position if aspects of delivering sports entertainment that can be controlled by marketers are managed in a way that consumers positively value their experience regardless of performance on the field of play.

USER IMAGERY POSITIONING. While attribute and quality positioning differentiate a brand on the basis of a functional benefit, user imagery positioning seeks to use an emotional or social connection to set a brand apart. User imagery seeks to appeal to a target market by suggesting the type of person who would have a relationship with the brand. The emotionally grounded relationships many people have with sports makes user imagery an attractive positioning option. People who desire to become part of a community with a shared affinity for a brand are a prime target through user imagery. Under Armour has used this approach, positioning the brand as a resource for performance athletes, leaving no doubt as to the type of person or user that should consider using Under Armour products. Similarly, user imagery can be used by team sports brands to make a connection between consumers and the geographic market. Some people may follow a team because it is local, and being a supporter is a form of demonstrating civic pride.

VALUE POSITIONING. The positioning strategy that has been practiced so long that it predates the concept of brand position is to differentiate on the basis of value received for price paid. Customer value is a comparison of benefits received to sacrifices made. While other positioning strategies

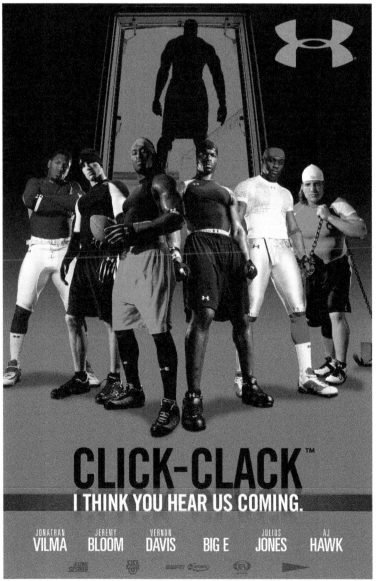

Under Armour positions its brand for high-performance athletes.

focus on differentiation in terms of a benefit received, a value position emphasizes a brand's capabilities in terms of low price or favorable benefits-to-cost ratio. Use of a value positioning strategy by sports brands may be dictated by external environment factors that shift consumers' attention toward purchases that save money or stretch the entertainment dollar. The recession that impacted the U.S. economy from 2008–2010 forced marketers of discretionary products like sports to reconsider their brand proposition, placing more emphasis on customer value to appeal to cautious consumers.

For a professional sports franchise, positioning of the team brand may have not changed because of the recession—attribute, quality, or user imagery positioning still had relevance. However, positioning for marketing games or events may have shifted to focus on customer value. Chapter 3's opening vignette describes how foodservice operations responded to the recession by creating more value-priced options. Similarly, ticket prices, all-inclusive packages of tickets and concessions, and flexible payment plans are examples of tactics that were implemented to reinforce a value position.

Another situation in the external environment that can lead to implementing a value position is the intensity of competition faced by a sports property. When many entertainment options exist for consumers, some properties may face difficulties competing for attention and gaining interest. A solution to this challenge is to offer attractive pricing or enhance benefits offered. This situation is faced by some minor league baseball teams, particularly in markets where significant competition exists from major league or collegiate sports brands on top of non-sports entertainment options. The relatively lower cost of the minor league sports experience, coupled with promotions that enhance entertainment value such as concerts and fireworks, sets the stage for leveraging customer value as a brand differentiator.

RELATIONSHIP BETWEEN BRAND POSITION AND PRICING. Like other marketing decisions, brand position is not an isolated strategy. Rather, it is interrelated with other aspects of marketing strategy. One of the most important connections is the relationship between brand position and a product's price. Consumers process price information, resulting in brand associations being formed and stored in memory. For example, people often have connotations with high price of "high quality," "prestige," or "exclusivity." Connotations with low price can be positive (e.g., "good value for the money") or negative (e.g., "questionable quality").

Pricing decisions should be made after brand position is defined so that price reinforces the brand differentiation that is the focal point of the positioning strategy. In the case of a quality position, price should be consistent with what people expect to pay for high quality. For example, a single-game ticket for a University of Oklahoma football game can exceed $100.[19] While some people may perceive the price as excessive for a college football game, the consistency of the on-field product and team popularity influence the decision to charge one of the highest single-game prices in the country.

When attribute or user imagery positioning is used, price should be appropriate for the point of difference emphasized. For example, if attribute positioning is used to promote the Nashville Sounds minor league baseball team as affordable entertainment, ticket prices should be set so that customers' perceptions are that attending a Sounds game is indeed an affordable purchase. On the other hand, the North Face, a brand of outdoor apparel and equipment, uses imagery positioning to differentiate itself as a brand for persons who like to "push their limits" outdoors. When brands are able to stake a position as a lifestyle brand like the North Face has done, they have leeway in setting higher prices for their products because consumers perceive value in the intangible benefits contained in brand image.

Extending Brands to New Products

One of the payoffs of building brand equity is growth opportunities in the form of adding new products that share a connection with the core brand. New products are crucial to driving growth in a business. A strong brand is an asset that provides an advantage when bringing new products to market. A brand extension of a successful brand is not guaranteed success, but the credibility and trust an established brand possesses removes barriers to market entry and consumer acceptance. Brand extensions fall into two general categories: 1) within a brand's core product category and 2) outside the core product category. Several different product development opportunities exist under these two categories and will be discussed in-depth in Chapter 6.

Extensions within the core product category typically pose lower risk of failure because the new product taps into the brand's strengths such as popularity or high perceived quality. For example, some NFL team owners purchased ownership in Arena Football League (AFL) teams in their markets in the late 2000s. The idea was to take advantage of the NFL team's popularity and marketing resources to build their new AFL brands. The AFL ran into financial troubles that led to the league suspending operations for one year in 2009, and the failed extension into the AFL demonstrates that even strong brands have failed extensions.

In contrast, extensions outside the core product category carry greater risks but can give a company access to new markets. A company that has embarked on an extension outside of its core category is Legends Hospitality Management. The company, owned jointly by the Dallas Cowboys and New York Yankees, extended beyond its core services of concessions and premium dining at sports venues when it created a unit called Legends Premium Services. The new venture provides sales training and customer relationship management implementation for clients in the sports entertainment industry.[20] Although the services provided by Legends Premium Services are outside of the foodservice category, the expertise and client relationships it has built within the core category make the leap to sales training and customer relationship management (CRM) consulting a viable strategy.

As indicated in Figure 5.10, brand extensions serve several purposes beyond the obvious of potential business growth. First, new offerings can expand the customer base. Brand extensions may attract persons who previously had not been interested in the brand. The National Hockey League has experienced this phenomenon with its Winter Classic brand. The New Year's Day outdoor game quickly became the highest-rated NHL TV broadcast each season. People who may not watch another NHL game all season are drawn to the Winter Classic.

- Business growth
    —Within core product category
    —Outside core product category
- Expand customer base
- Energize a brand
- Prevent market share erosion

FIGURE 5.10 **Benefits of Brand Extensions**

Second, extensions can energize a brand. New products valued by consumers can kindle interest in the core brand. This occurred with brand extensions by HBO Sports. Addition of behind-the-scenes shows *Hard Knocks* and *24/7* have attracted viewers to the network. These programs have had the dual effect of bringing viewers to HBO and creating interest in the subjects of these programs such as the New York Jets and the NHL.

Third, expanding into new products can prevent market share erosion. A brand extension may be a needed strategic weapon to retain customers or prevent competitors from exploiting weakness in the product portfolio. This was the case with a brand extension by Horizon Media. The company's expertise in media buying and planning was leveraged to create a sports marketing unit. The move to develop a dedicated sports practice was motivated in part by the prospect of clients dropping Horizon for a firm that specialized in sports media or sponsorship.[21] To use sports terminology, brand extensions can be used to play offense (expand customer base and energize the brand) or to play defense (discourage competition).

Leveraging Brands through Licensing

Another growth opportunity arising from owning a strong brand is licensing the brand to other firms. **Licensing** is a legal agreement in which a brand owner (i.e., the licensor) grants use of its brand name or marks to another company (i.e., a licensee). The licensing agreement specifies how the licensee may use the brand, on what products it can be placed, and the compensation that must be paid to the licensor for use of the brand assets. Sports brands are in an enviable position of great interest among licensees and consumers for licensed products. Many sports fans want to show their identification with their favorite teams or player by wearing or using products bearing brand marks. Licensed product consumption gives fans an outlet for expressing their support for a team, and some fans even view wearing apparel with a team name or logo as the best way they can help the team short of stepping onto the field.[22]

OVERVIEW OF LICENSING. Brand licensing in the sports industry represents significant revenues for leagues, events, teams, universities, and individuals. Figure 5.11 provides a glimpse of the size of the market for officially licensed products for top sports properties. According to the International Licensing Industry Merchandisers' Association, sports licensing royalties for professional properties were $660 million, and collegiate licensing royalties totaled $200 million.[23] Royalties are payments that a licensee makes to the licensor that is a percentage of a licensed product's selling price. Royalty percentages vary depending on the type of product and the brand. In addition to royalties, an up-front fee may be charged for a company to secure a license to use a sports brand. A licensee for the University of Texas, consistently among the top collegiate brands in terms of licensed product sales, may pay an advance fee as high as $2,500 for some non-apparel products, with all licensed products subject to 10% royalties on sales. In contrast, Saint Louis University, a brand that does not have national clout (i.e., brand equity) like the Texas Longhorns, charges no advance fees to licensees and an 8% royalty rate.[24]

FIGURE 5.11 Revenues of Licensed Products by Sports League

League	2009 Licensed Product Revenues
Major League Baseball	$2.82 Billion
National Football League	$2.74 Billion
NASCAR	$2.0 Billion
National Basketball Association	$1.80 Billion
National Hockey league	$750 Million

Marketing managers responsible for branding decisions should view licensing as a type of brand extension. The licensee's capabilities to produce quality products, meet the design, distribution, and pricing specifications of the licensor, and willingness to collaborate to create innovative products are considerations of a prospective licensee. Licensed products may not be manufactured by the sports property whose name and logo appear on products, but its brand becomes associated with the product. Thus, any judgments about product quality and value could impact the sports brand because the source or manufacturer of a licensed product is often unknown to the consumer.

Brand licensing offers a number of benefits to both the licensor and the licensee. These benefits are identified in Figure 5.12. For licensing to work, it must benefit both parties.

FIGURE 5.12 Benefits of Brand Licensing

For the Licensor
- Creation of a revenue stream
- Form of brand advertising
- Protects a sports property's assets

For the Licensee
- Capitalize on affinity fans have for sports
- Grow product line
- Provides legitimacy

LICENSOR BENEFITS. The primary benefit is creation of a revenue stream without expenses incurred. A licensee takes on the responsibility and risk for product manufacturing, securing distribution outlets, and promoting the products. The licensor enjoys the fruits of building a successful brand by receiving royalties from licensees that make investments to produce and market licensed goods.

The sale of licensed sports products is a form of brand advertising. People who wear caps bearing the logo of the San Diego Padres, T-shirts with the word "Duke" emblazoned across the front, or use a Visa credit card with a Cincinnati Bengals theme are giving exposure to the featured brand among other consumers.

Licensing also protects a sports property's brand assets. Companies that obtain licenses to sell products not only have the permission of the licensor to use its brand marks, but the licensee and licensor have collaborated on product design and marketing considerations. This benefit of licensing insures a licensee meets quality standards set by the licensor, and gives a licensor legal protection against unauthorized use of brand marks by companies that have not gone through the license approval process.

LICENSEE BENEFITS. Brand licensing is advantageous to companies that pay for the rights to use a brand's name or logo, too. First, a licensee can capitalize on the affinity sports fans have for their favorite teams and players to sell products. Demand exists for apparel and other products as a symbol of one's identification with a team or player. Licensees meet that need; sports properties are in the business of sports entertainment, not manufacturing products. Licensing their brands to product makers is a form of outsourcing that benefits both licensor and licensee.

Second, licensing sports brands allows a manufacturer to grow its product line by offering sports-themed products. A recent product that expanded its product line by offering sports-branded items was Snuggie, described as a "blanket with sleeves." Snuggie was an immediate success, generating $40 million in retail sales in less than six months.[25] Yet, Snuggie enhanced its product line beyond basic colors by adding officially licensed Snuggies for NFL teams and more than one hundred universities. Price points for licensed products typically are higher than for comparable products that do not have a logo. Sports Snuggies initially sold for $19.95, a $5 premium over the basic Snuggie. Even when royalty payments are taken into account, a successful licensed product can deliver a licensee greater profits than the same product without a logo.

Third, a licensee's products are given legitimacy through designation of "officially licensed product." This benefit is important because it sends a signal to consumers concerning product quality. Counterfeit versions of name-brand products are a problem that plagues reputable brands across many different categories of consumer goods, and unauthorized production of products bearing sports brand marks is no exception. One tactic licensors and licensees can use to respond to unauthorized products in the market is to prominently label products that are officially licensed by a sports property. Collegiate Licensing Corporation—the largest licensing agency for colleges and universities in the United States, representing nearly two hundred clients—uses an Officially Licensed Product hologram label on all products sold by licensees. The purpose of the label is to show evidence to consumers that a product is licensed by the sports property and meets its quality standards.

Brand Alignment

The strategy behind brand management and leveraging must be grounded in guiding principles that an organization should apply to developing strategy, decision making, and long-term plans for growth. A key concept that aligns a brand with marketing decisions is its mission. Introduced in Chapter 1, an organization's mission is its reason for existence, its purpose. Consider two examples from the sports industry:

Fuse:
"Fuse is a youth culture agency that connects brands with teens and young adults through sports, music, fashion, gaming, and other interests. We help brands reach a mass audience while maintaining credibility with key influencers."[26]

PGA Tour:
"The mission of the PGA TOUR is to expand domestically and internationally to substantially increase player financial benefits while maintaining its commitment to the integrity of the game. The PGA TOUR events are also committed to generating revenue for charitable causes in their communities."[27]

The missions for Fuse and the PGA Tour are clear. Fuse's mission statement is well written in that it defines its business and how it delivers value. Ideally, any marketing decision (target market, marketing mix) will be evaluated against its contribution to an organization's mission. For example, if the PGA Tour seeks to expand its presence by holding tournaments in Asia and the Middle East, it is fulfilling part of its mission—international expansion. Mission statements must figure prominently in setting strategy or they become little more than a decoration hanging on an office wall or appearing on a website.

The Role of Corporate Social Responsibility

Statements about values and mission are commendable steps for an organization to take, but statements without actions have little impact. One way that mission and brand values can be demonstrated is through an organization's commitment to corporate social responsibility (CSR). CSR is more than a strategy; it is a blueprint that guides business decisions and affects relationships with customers, suppliers, and all other stakeholders. **Corporate social responsibility** is "a commitment to improve community well being through discretionary business practices and contributions of corporate resources."[28]

The implications of CSR on brand strategy are that decisions about how a company should give back to stakeholders is shifting from an obligation to engage in philanthropy to a strategy that differentiates a brand from competitors and reinforces positioning. Sports properties are likely to feel responsibilities to give money and resources to certain groups or communities where they do business out of a sense of obligation as role models and beneficiaries of government subsidies for stadiums. However, corporate philanthropy based on this mindset overlooks how giving back or supporting social issues should be approached strategically so that a brand aligns its values with issues that are important to customers and the local community.

"Giving back" should not be viewed from the standpoint of a donation but instead a strategy for achieving business objectives. In Chapter 3, social responsibility was identified as a sociodemographic trend in which consumers have greater expectations of companies to "do good" in their business operations. A sports property should consider how it can make a positive impact on customers or other people while at the same time creating a positive impact on its own business. The NHL's Dallas Stars used philanthropy strategically to support youth of the Dallas metro area while simultaneously expanding its fan base. The franchise moved to Dallas in 1993 from Minnesota, but it faced a challenge of being in a nontraditional hockey market.

One of the keys to success for building interest in ice hockey and the Stars was the team's commitment to youth hockey. When the Stars moved to Dallas, there were three ice hockey rinks and four high schools with ice hockey teams. In 2012 there were more than twenty rinks. The addition of rinks contributed to the growth of high school hockey as there are now

Involvement with youth is an important CSR initiative.

© Galina Barskaya / Fotolia

44 high school teams in the Dallas area.[29] The Stars were involved in expanding youth hockey, recognizing that participation is a way that many people connect with a sport, and building interest in hockey among youth would attract parents, too. Not only did the Dallas Stars build positive brand associations through its concern for area youth, but it attracted new fans for now and years to come.

Aligning with a social issue is the heart of CSR, but it is an oversimplification to say that is CSR. The questions that must be answered to implement CSR include the following:

• *What social issue(s) should be supported?* Selecting an issue or cause that matters to the target market is a key consideration.

Program	Description
Basketball without Borders	Global program that uses basketball to promote social change and connect with youth through basketball
NBA/WNBA FIT	Focuses on wellness, nutrition, and exercise education for children and parents
Read to Achieve	Promotes interest in reading among children and adults reading to kids
NBA Green	Environmental stewardship program that raises money and awareness for environmentally friendly consumption

FIGURE 5.13
Corporate Social Responsibility: NBA Cares

- *What initiative should be selected to support the issue?* What will be used to connect the brand to the issue? The NFL's "Play 60" program mentioned in Chapter 3 is an example of how a brand should relate its mission and values to an issue that affects its stakeholders.

- *How will the initiative be activated?* CSR programs are similar to any other strategy that needs to be carried out; activation programs are needed that go beyond promoting the brand. CSR initiatives must be supported with tactics that show a brand's genuine concern for a social issue or cause while at the same time delivering a positive business impact (e.g., enhanced brand image, increased sales, and new customers).[30]

A good example of strategic planning and activation of a CSR program is the initiatives of the National Basketball Association through its NBA Cares platform. NBA Cares is a CSR strategy that is integrated across the league and team brands as well as tapping the star power of players, coaches, and alumni. Like the use of strategic philanthropy by the Dallas Stars, NBA Cares has a self-interest component, building basketball as a global sport. But, as is the case with any CSR initiative, business benefits are secondary to the impact that can be made on stakeholder groups. Figure 5.13 gives examples of philanthropic programs under the NBA Cares umbrella. A common thread running through most NBA Cares programs is promoting the physical and mental well-being of youth and their families. NBA Cares exemplifies how a sports brand can go about answering the three CSR implementation questions of what issues to support, what programs to implement, and how to activate programs.

Chapter Summary

Brands are central to the practice of marketing. Brands have four different purposes or roles: an identity, an image, a promise, and a relationship. Brands add value for both buyers and sellers through each of these roles. Brands serve as a form of identification allowing a seller to set its brand apart from competitors. Brands have an image that consists of thoughts and mental associations that people have for a product or service. The image is influenced by brand associations, which are thoughts and perceptions people have for a person or object. Brands represent a promise of action that will benefit customers. That promise can be explicit or implicit. Lastly, brands offer the opportunity of relationships between customers and the brand.

Marketing a brand requires two broad areas: brand building and brand exploitation. Brand building entails selecting a brand name and designing marks associated with the brand, such as a logo and color scheme. Brand exploitation focuses on how to leverage the aspects of a brand (identity, image, promises, and relationships) to develop offerings that add value for customers and drive business growth for the organization.

The first step in building a brand is selecting the name. It should possess the characteristics of recognizability, fit, and contrast. The second element of branding is creation of brand marks that project an identity and influence brand image development. Brand marks include logos,

Insider Insights Tom McMillan – Pittsburgh Penguins

Q. Brands have evolved to be much more than the name and logo of a product or service. What role do brands have in a sports property's marketing strategy?

A. Your brand has the most important "role." Your brand is—or should be—the essence of your marketing strategy across all platforms. For a professional sports team, it may be implemented in different ways, from advertising to broadcasting to community outreach to social media, but that brand is the driving force behind the message you send—and the way you send it. In our situation, the extensive brand research showed that we'd developed an exceptionally strong connection to the younger demographic. As a result, everything we do now is geared younger, in an effort to deepen and broaden the brand and build loyalty that will last years and, hopefully, decades.

Q. How important is having a well-defined brand position?

A. It is essential to a focused, coherent, and effective marketing strategy. You don't want to be "guessing." You don't want to be "hoping." A well-defined brand position, based on research, analysis, and planning, gives you the confidence to move forward with a strong message and a clear voice. Many people on your staff will be involved in delivering that message over many platforms, and understanding the brand position enables them to essentially speak as one. There have been times when an outside agency has come in with its own ideas of how we should execute our brand. It's tempting to be swayed

Tom McMillan discusses branding issues in sports marketing

by a clever slogan or a funny TV spot. However, that doesn't always mean it aligns with your own understanding of your own brand. If you do it correctly, define it correctly, you know your brand better than anyone else.

Q. The Pittsburgh Penguins transformed from a weak franchise that almost left town to one of the strongest organizations in the NHL. How did branding strategy figure into the turnaround?

A. There's no question that having a superstar face-of-the-franchise (Sidney Crosby) and having a winning team (2009 Stanley Cup) are huge parts of that turnaround. But effective brand strategy is what ensures that you maximize that success. For instance, the Penguins of the early 1990s had a superstar cast, led by Mario Lemieux, and won back-to-back Stanley Cups in 1991 and 1992, yet never sold out every game in a season and didn't maximize revenue. The Penguins didn't sell out a season for the first time until 2007–2008, and the streak has surpassed two hundred straight games. In 2010–2011, the team led all the U.S.-based NHL teams in local TV ratings, website hits, and merchandise sales—and it had a season ticket waiting list for the first time since the club's inception in 1967. Brand strategy and implementation played a big part in that. More importantly, it was geared to build loyalty for the future—to (hopefully) handle the inevitable up-and-down cycle of professional sports. The best time to market aggressively is when you're at or near the top—when so many eyeballs are watching you.

colors, and characters. Sports face two very unique branding situations. First, brands may need to be modified or updated, which requires a brand makeover to make it relevant to the current target market or to reflect environmental changes. Second, franchise operations sometimes must relocate, requiring decisions about the brand name, brand marks, and other aspects of brand identity.

Brand exploitation and brand management are based on the view that a brand is an asset that is owned by the sports property. It has financial value. Therefore, the goal should be to maximize the value of the brand's assets, i.e., build a strong equity in the brand, through brand awareness, brand associations, and brand loyalty. Strategies marketers can use to increase the value of the brand assets or brand equity include brand position, brand extensions, and licensing. The brand position is the one thing that a brand stands for and involves positioning the brand through the strategies of attributes, quality, user imagery, or value. Payoffs of building brand equity include the opportunity for growth through offering extensions of the brand and through licensing agreements.

The strategy behind brand management and exploitation must be grounded in guiding principles of the organization—that is, its mission statement. It is also important to make a commitment to corporate social responsibility (CSR) to ensure a brand's value is accepted by society.

Review Questions

1. What are the four purposes or roles of a brand?
2. How can a sports property develop an identity?
3. Explain the differences between brand image, brand associations, and brand identity.
4. What is relationship marketing?
5. Responsibilities for marketing a brand fall under what two broad areas?
6. What characteristics should a sports brand name possess?
7. What is a brand mark? Identify examples of brand marks.
8. In designing or evaluating a logo, what considerations should be considered?
9. Why is color important in designing a logo, brand name, or team uniforms?
10. Why would a sports brand consider a brand makeover?
11. Identify some general rules that can be applied to the decision to keep or change brand identity when relocating a sports property to a new market.
12. What three strategies are associated with brand leveraging and tied to building brand equity?
13. What assets comprise brand equity?
14. Why is creating a brand position important?
15. A well-defined brand position contains what three elements?
16. What strategies can be used by sports properties in brand positioning?
17. Brand extensions fall into what two categories?
18. Beyond the potential for growth, brand extensions serve what other purposes?
19. Identify the primary benefits of licensing for the licensor.
20. Identify the primary benefits of licensing for the licensee.
21. What is meant by brand alignment?
22. What is the role of corporate social responsibility (CSR) in branding?

New Terms

Brand image consumer thoughts or mental associations about a good or service.

Brand associations thoughts and perceptions that an individual has for another person or object.

Brand identity associations that a marketer aspires to project or communicate to a target market.

Relationship marketing An approach to marketing that focuses on building and maintaining long-term relationships with customers and other important stakeholders.

Brand mark form of communication other than words used to communicate brand identity.

Logo symbol or other visual element that is associated with a brand.

Brand equity The added value a brand possesses that can be attributed to the brand (name, logo, and image).

Brand awareness asset developed from recognition and familiarity among consumers and sponsors.

Brand loyalty customer-driven asset demonstrated by a willingness of customers to have an ongoing relationship with a business.

Brand position A strategy used to communicate a point of difference that a brand possesses in its marketing communications to set it apart from competition.

Licensing legal agreement in which a brand owner grants use of its brand name or marks to another company.

Corporate social responsibility A managerial philosophy that guides an organization's business decisions to have an overall positive impact on society.

Discussion and Critical Thinking Exercises

1. Identify three sports teams in any sport that you think have developed strong brand identities. For each team explain why you think the team has been successful in developing such a strong brand identity.

2. For each of the following brand names, discuss the three characteristics of recognizability, fit, and contrast.
   a. Durham Bulls (minor league baseball, North Carolina)
   b. Toledo Mud Hens (minor league baseball, Ohio)
   c. Portland Sea Dogs (minor league baseball, Maine)
   d. University of Richmond Spiders (college team, Virginia)
   e. Nebraska Cornhuskers (college team, Nebraska)
   f. Toronto Maple Leafs (NHL team)

3. Pick two professional sports teams, two minor league teams, and two college teams. Go to each team or university website and copy their logo into a word processing document. For each logo, discuss the following elements of design.
   a. Is it distinctive?
   b. Is it relevant?
   c. Is it versatile?
   d. Is it enduring?

4. Identify two teams (professional or college) that you believe have a nice logo, nice use of colors, and a great mascot. Explain why it all fits well together. Identify two teams for which you think these elements do not fit well together and that are a mismatch in some way. Explain why you believe the colors, logo design, and mascot do not fit well together.

5. Suppose a coed summer volleyball league was formed in your region. Your town has put a team together. Identify a team name that you believe fits well with your town and the sport. What colors would you use? Design a logo. Explain your choices.

6. Identify a sports team that has recently moved to a new market. Discuss the team's strategy in terms of changing its name, logo, and colors, or not changing anything. Do you think the team made a good a decision? Why or why not?

7. What do you think about using Native American names for teams, such as the Braves and Indians? Should professional sports teams be allowed to use these names? Why or why not? Do you agree or disagree with the NCAA decision to ban all Native American nicknames from collegiate teams? Why or why not?

8. How successful has your college been in building brand equity? Is it well known in your region? What about in the United States? Discuss its level of brand equity in terms of brand awareness, brand associations, and brand loyalty.

9. The WNBA continues to struggle for identity, recognition, and fan support. Review the section in this chapter on "Staking a Brand Position." Do you believe the WNBA has done a good job of identifying a brand position in sports entertainment? Why or why not? What would you suggest for the WNBA in terms of brand position?

10. What professional league or team has done a great job of licensing? Explain why. What professional league or team has done a poor job with licensing? Explain why.

11. Evaluate your college in terms of license agreements. What other products could your university license, or in what other ways could it develop license agreements to generate additional revenue?

12. Do you think it is important for sports teams to make a commitment to corporate social responsibility (CSR)? Pick a professional sports team that is close to you and discuss its involvement with CSR.

You Make the Call
Professional Bowlers Association

The Professional Bowlers Association (PBA) was founded in 1958 in Akron, Ohio, by Eddie Elias. There were thirty-three founding members, although the first hundred members were considered charter members. The PBA Tour started off with a bang in 1959 with three tournaments worth $49,500 and its first televised tournament, Jackpot Bowling. During the 1960s, 1970s, and 1980s bowling was a major feature on television with ABC, CBS, and later with ESPN. In 1979, at its height, thirty-three of the thirty-four national bowling tournaments were televised on either ABC, CBS, or ESPN. In 1980, True Value Hardware became a major sponsor and Willie Willis became the first African-American bowler to qualify for the Firestone Tournament of Champions. Bowling had become a popular sport followed and played by consumers of all ages, genders, and ethnicities.

In the 1990s bowling began its decline. Not only was the decline seen in television viewers, but bowling alleys struggled to turn a profit as consumers sought other sports. The popularity of bowling had faded. In 1997 the Pro Bowler Tour series with ABC came to an end after thirty-six years. Few bowling events were seen on television, and as a result sponsors quickly fled to other more lucrative sports.

In April 2000, former Microsoft executives Chris Peters, Mike Slade, and Rob Glaser purchased the PBA, turning it into a for-profit business. The new owners had a number of challenges to overcome, from attracting new sponsors to changing the image of the sport. The image of pudgy, cigarette-smoking bowlers was revamped to look more like a first-class sports league, with slick bowling alleys, live music, and cheering fans.

To obtain sponsors, Peters knew they had to obtain television interest. New television contracts were negotiated with ESPN. Then new sponsors, such as Lumber Liquidators, were solicited. What is unique about Lumber Liquidators is that they do not sell the specialized maple, pine, and synthetic boards used in bowling alleys. But, they do sell hardwood flooring, and association with bowling created a clever way to tout the flooring business.

During the 2000s the television audience for professional bowling averaged 1% of United States cable households, or approximately 1 million viewers. It wasn't the 2% to 3% the PBA had sought, but it was large enough to keep afloat and attract more new sponsors such as Budweiser, GEICO, Go RVing, Golden Corral, and Brunswick.

The PBA gained a huge break in terms of fan interest in 2010 when Kelly Kulick became the first female to win the PBA Tournament of Champions. She defeated Chris Barnes, one of the world's best bowlers, 265 to 195. With new fan interest, the owners of the PBA shifted eyes to Las Vegas. Instead of the $40,000 purse Kelly Kulick won in 2010, the top prize was now $250,000, with a total purse of $1 million. It was a huge gamble, but it was time for the PBA to gain national attention, and the owners felt it was worth the risk.

Bowling has struggled to maintain an audience base.

© Peter Atkins / Fotolia

Questions:

1. Evaluate the Professional Bowlers Association (PBA) brand. Discuss the PBA in terms of brand roles, such as identity, image, promise, and relationship.
2. Discuss the PBA's level of brand equity in terms of brand awareness, brand associations, and brand loyalty.
3. How has the PBA brand been positioned? How should it be positioned? Which of the four strategies suggested in Figure 5.9 is being used currently? Is that the best strategy? Why or why not?
4. What brand extensions should the PBA pursue? Why?

5. What could the PBA do to create revenues through brand licensing?
6. How important is a CSR strategy for the PBA? Discuss feasible CSR strategies for the PBA.
7. What do you see as the future of the PBA?

Sources: "Bowling Tour a Natural Fit for Flooring Company," (2009), *Sports Business Journal*, June 22, accessed January 21, 2011, at http://www.sportsbusinessdaily.com/Journal/Issues/2009/06/20090622/SBJ-In-Depth/Bowling-Tour-A-Natural-Fit-For-Flooring-Company.aspx; "PBA History," (2011), accessed January 21, 2011, at http://www.pba.com/Resources/PbaHistory/; Kent Lowe, (2011), "Important Few Weeks Coming Up for PBA Tour," January 4, accessed January 21, 2011, at http://www.2theadvocate.com/sports/112844009.html; Bob Velin, (2011), "Bowling Goes for Broke with Million-Dollar Purse in Vegas," *USA TODAY*, January 19, accessed January 21, 2011, at http://www.usatoday.com/sports/bowling/2011-01-18-vegas-bowling-tourneys-big-purse_N.htm.

References

1. "About the Alliance," (n.d.), accessed October 1, 2010, at http://www.soundersfc.com/Alliance/About.aspx.
2. ""Who is Gorilla FC?" (2010), accessed April 6, 2012 at http://www.gorillafc.com/about/.
3. "Turnstile Tracker," (2010), *Sports Business Journal*, August 30, 13.
4. "Dictionary," (2010), accessed December 29, 2010, at http://www.marketingpower.com/_layouts/Dictionary.aspx?dLetter=B. Courtesy of American Marketing Association.
5. "Search Engine Marketing Glossary of Terms," (2010), accessed December 30, 2010, at http://www.sempo.org/learning_center/sem_glossary#b.
6. "Dictionary," (2010), accessed January 4, 2011, at http://www.marketingpower.com/_layouts/Dictionary.aspx?dLetter=R. Courtesy of American Marketing Association.
7. "Trends and Challenges," (2010), *Sports Business Journal*, November 1, 26–27.
8. Paul McNamara, (1998), "The Name Game," *Network World*, April 20, 77–78.
9. Irving Rein, Philip Kotler, and Ben Shields, *The Elusive Fan* (New York: McGraw-Hill, 2006).
10. "Ports Team History," (2011), accessed January 4, 2011, at http://web.minorleaguebaseball.com/team4/page.jsp?ymd=20090116&content_id=496687&vkey=team4_t524&fext=.jsp&sid=t524.
11. Jack Gernsheimer, *Designing Logos: The Process of Creating Symbols that Endure* (New York: Allworth Press, 2008).
12. Judith A. Garretson and Ronald W. Neidrich, (2004), "Creating Character Trust and Positive Brand Attitudes," *Journal of Advertising*, 33, 2, 25–36.
13. "OLN Network Getting New Name," (2006), April 24, accessed January 7, 2011, at http://www.bizjournals.com/philadelphia/stories/2006/04/24/daily9.html.
14. Charlene Teters, (n.d.), "American Indians Are People, Not Mascots," accessed January 8, 2011, at http://aimovement.org/ncrsm/.
15. David A. Aaker, *Building Strong Brands* (New York: The Free Press, 1996).
16. "George Mason University Continues to Benefit from Final Four Run," (2007), accessed January 10, 2011, at http://eagle.gmu.edu/newsroom/591/.
17. Aaker (1996).
18. Scott M. Davs, *Brand Asset Management* (San Francisco: Jossey-Bass, 2002).
19. Rachel Bachman, (2010), "College Football Tickets: Despite Recession, Tickets to Nation's Top Games Cost Fans More than Ever," August 14, accessed October 11, 2011, at http://blog.oregonlive.com/pac10/2010/08/college_football_tickets_despi.html.
20. Don Muret, (2011), "Legends Adds Premium Sales Training," *Sports Business Journal*, January 10, 1.
21. Terry Lefton, (2010), "Horizon's Big Play," *Sports Business Journal*, November 22, 1, 8.
22. Donald P. Roy, (2010), "Fan Identification and Licensed Products Consumption: An Exploratory Study," presented at Sport Marketing Association Conference, New Orleans, LA.

23. "Licensing Royalty Revenues Decline; Industry Develops Avenues for Future Growth," (2010), June 12, accessed January 14, 2011, at http://www.lvtsg.com/imho/2010/06/licensing-royalty-revenues-decline-industry-develops-avenues-for-future-growth/.

24. "Clients," (2005), accessed January 14, 2011, at http://www.clc.com/clcweb/publishing.nsf/Content/institutions.html.

25. Jack Neff, (2009), "Marketing's New Red-Hot Seller: Humble Snuggie," *Advertising Age*, January 26, 1, 36.

26. "Fuse Youth Marketing Agency Company Overview," (n.d.), accessed January 17, 2011, at http://www.fusemarketing.com/Company_Overview.

27. "About PGA Tour," (2011), accessed January 17, 2011, at http://www.pgatour.com/company/about_us.html.

28. Philip Kotler and Nancy Lee, *Corporate Social Responsibility* (Hoboken, NJ: John Wiley & Sons, 2005).

29. Riba, George (2012), "Stars' Mission to Build Youth Hockey in Dallas No Passing Fad," March 19, accessed April 6, 2012 at http://www.wfaa.com/sports/hockey/Stars-defenseman-Daley--143432386.html.

30. Kotler and Lee (2005).

6 Defining the Product Offering

Learning Objectives

By the end of this chapter you should be able to:

1. Identify the different categories of sports products
2. Describe the characteristics and implications of the three product levels
3. Explain three types of marketing innovations
4. Describe four factors that influence the adoption of innovations
5. Analyze three strategies for connecting target market characteristics with products

An advertisement by Under Armour.

Product Growth No Sweat at Under Armour

Kevin Plank was a senior captain on the University of Maryland football team in 1995 when he came to two conclusions. The first was made abundantly clear by his play on the field—or perhaps the play of others on the field. The fullback was good enough to succeed on the collegiate gridiron, but had no future playing professional football in the National Football League. The second conclusion was that playing in a sweat-soaked cotton T-shirt was doing him no favors in regards to his performance on field.

It was this second thought that inspired the question that led to the invention of Under Armour performance apparel. What if there was a synthetic compression T-shirt that would not retain moisture or its weight? Plank went through rounds and rounds of working with different prototype "tight muscle shirts." By using special fibers that "wicked" the sweat from an athlete's skin, much like the Spandex biking shorts many players had adopted for underneath their pads, Plank eventually invented a shirt that enabled an athlete to compete without the heavy, perspiration-soaked cotton T-shirt that could weigh four or five pounds.

Plank's shirts were loved by his teammates, and especially by those who had graduated from the collegiate ranks and were now "playing on Sundays." Those NFLers were not alone.

Insider Expert Steve Battista – Under Armour

Steve Battista, Senior Vice President of Brand, was the number 19 employee at Under Armour in 2000 and worked with Founder Kevin Plank to build the brand's voice, imagery and iconic stature. He built the teams that now run domestic and international communications, including advertising, public relations, marketing communications, product integration, events, and sponsorships. He is responsible for penning some of the company's most memorable taglines and slogans, such as "The Advantage is Undeniable™," "Click-Clack™ (I think you hear us coming) "and "WE MUST PROTECT THIS HOUSE™."

Battista was named to the *Sports Business Journal* "40 Under 40" in 2009 and 2010, is a 2007 Webby Award Interactive Advertising Official Honoree, and has been awarded a 2006 Gold ADDY for the "Big Logo" print campaign, a Silver ADDY for "Protect this House" campaign, a Silver ADDY for Web design, and other awards. Under his leadership, the company's internal creative team has earned a number of prestigious awards, including a 2004 ADDY Award for their first-ever advertising campaign.

Prior to joining Under Armour, Battista was a market analyst with responsibility for writing, designing, and editing advertisements as well as reports and proposals for several Fortune 500 companies. Battista's writing has appeared nationwide via the *Washington Post*, *USA TODAY*, and the Associated Press. Previously, Battista worked on fellowship in the heralded Writing Seminars at Johns Hopkins University, where he earned his masters of arts in 2000 and was awarded the Most Promising Young Artist endowment from the National Society of Arts and Letters.

Steve Battista, Domestic and International Communications, Under Armour

Baseball players, soccer players, basketball players, not to mention runners, track and field enthusiasts, even members of military and tactical police forces were ordering Under Armour to wear beneath their uniforms.

They began calling Plank directly—who was operating his business at all hours in a Washington, D.C., row house owned by his grandmother. He had absolutely no money for marketing at the time, and had only a P.O. Box at the local post office, but word was spreading organically, and his cell phone number was passed along from athlete to athlete, school to school, locker room to locker room. How well the product performed on the field, coupled with the fact that a player "had to know somebody" to get some product, gave Under Armour a strong sense of authenticity among the best athletes in the world. When the first primitive Under Armour logo appeared during a nationally tele-vised college football game, Plank thought he would be filling in the orders while sitting on a tropical beach, smoking a cigar without a worry in the world.

More calls came in, as he expected, but along with the orders came the requests for more products. Athletes and equipment managers were looking for long sleeve shirts, sleeve-less shirts, compression shorts, long leggings—base layers for cold weather, base layers to protect from artificial turf, loose shirts to wear over top their base layer . . . even women's Under Armour! Fourteen years later, Under Armour has men's, women's, and youth per-formance apparel; cleats, running shoes, and basketball shoes; sports bras, tanks, and underwear; hats, bags, and sunglasses.

The thought of resting on a tropical island is far from Plank's imagination now as the need for outfitting athletes for all parts of their lives drives the expansion of product lines. Still there is more opportunity. Now, for Under Armour, the primary responsibility for managing the brand is assessing the opportunities and aligning the product develop-ment, the line and brand extensions, and the next opportunities.[1]

Introduction

Under Armour is a shining example of how developing a brand that delivers value to custom-ers and building an image with which consumers aspire to associate opens doors for business growth. Like many companies, Under Armour began with a single product, the microfiber T-shirt inspired by Kevin Plank's experiences while playing football at the University of Mary-land. As brand development efforts expanded Under Armour's presence and recognition as a performance apparel leader, it created opportunities to leverage the brand by moving into related categories that connect with the core benefit of supporting high performance.

This chapter builds on the importance of developing a reputable brand that was introduced in Chapter 5. When a brand is accepted in the marketplace either for its functional benefits (e.g., performance, quality, or cost) or psychological benefits (e.g., self-image enhancement or social acceptance), consumers are receptive to evaluating new product offerings associated with that brand because of the potential to deliver similar benefits. This characteristic of brands does not ensure all extensions or new products will succeed, but it provides an advantage over introduc-ing brands with which consumers have less familiarity.

Product strategy is the starting point in marketing management decisions. It is no coinci-dence that virtually every marketing management textbook first covers the product element of the marketing mix. There is a simple explanation for the priority placed on product strategy. If there is no product, there is no need to make decisions about pricing, distribution, and communi-cation! Among the decisions that must be made for any product are:

- What features should be included to enhance the product appeal for a chosen target market?
- How to achieve a balance between value-added features and not "over-engineer" a product with features that add to a product's price but do not necessarily add to a consumer's enjoyment of the product.

- In the case of an intangible service, how to design a blueprint or process for efficiently and conveniently providing consumers a quality experience.
- What new products could be developed to meet underserved customer needs or markets?

These decisions and other issues involved in product strategy and management will be examined in this chapter.

The Sports Product

New product development should be an ongoing concern because new products are a key driver of business growth. Firms have two options: 1) find new customer markets to serve or 2) develop new products to offer in current markets. As sales growth slows due to market saturation, a business must look for new sources of revenue. Even thriving businesses continuously look to new products as a way to sustain growth. The National Football League, which enjoys a reputation as the most successful professional sports property in the United States, is not interested in resting on its past performance. The NFL has an ambitious revenue growth strategy set by Commissioner Roger Goodell. The goal is to reach $25 billion in annual revenue by 2027, a jump from annual sales of $8.5 billion in 2009[2]. For the NFL to reach its goal, it will require a combination of appealing to new customer markets and introducing new products. The two strategies are interrelated in that new customer markets may be persuaded to consume NFL products because of new products that attract their interest. For example, digital experiences such as fantasy sport games or video games may fulfill that role by attracting gaming enthusiasts who may follow NFL less than other types of fans but can be lured by NFL-themed gaming entertainment.

In developing a product strategy for sports entities, it is helpful to step back and define the term. The most common definition of **product** is that it is the value received by a buyer in an exchange with a seller. This broad view of a product encompasses different types of offerings a sports property can develop for its target market. Within sports marketing, the term product is used interchangeably to describe:

- A tangible *product*
- An intangible *service*
- A *live event or experience*
- A *digital experience*
- A *personal identification*

In short, a product is anything of value a buyer receives from a sports property. This broad definition of product expands options for creating new offerings to reach customers (and new revenue streams for a sports property). Figure 6.1 illustrates this broad definition of a sports product.

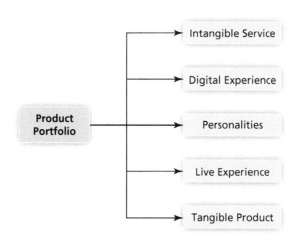

FIGURE 6.1 The Sports Product

Products

When discussing the marketing of products, it is natural that goods that can be experienced with one's senses immediately come to mind. The product portfolios of many sports properties differ from non-sports businesses in the number of product types offered. Many firms sell only one type of product. CCM, a brand owned by the Adidas Group, markets hockey equipment but nothing else. In contrast, for many sports brands tangible products are an extension of their core product. League and team properties' primary product is live events and games. For sports brands in these categories, tangible products like officially licensed apparel and souvenirs are extensions arising from the popularity of the on-field product. Licensed products add value for consumers by enabling them to exhibit their identification with a team or athlete.

Another tangible sports product that may not come to mind immediately is sports venues. The stadiums and arenas where sporting events are held are branded and are a marketable asset. A major argument made by proponents of new stadium development is that a new venue can be designed to provide the layout and amenities desired by today's sports consumer. The high quality of a venue can entice people to attend games, which in turn will lead to higher expenditures on tickets, concessions, and other purchases related to sporting event attendance. Thus, the observable features of a venue (i.e., the tangible product) have the potential to influence sales of other products in a sports property's portfolio. The impact of venues on the customer experience is discussed further in Chapter 7.

Services

Unlike products whose features can be experienced with our senses, services are intangible offerings that consumers cannot evaluate fully until after or during consumption. Sports leagues, conferences, organizations, and teams are best classified as services. The performance delivered *is* the product. In the case of a sports team, the service that is delivered is sports entertainment. A broad view of consuming team sports is that it is both a transactional relationship (buying tickets to a game) and an emotional relationship (identification with a team being part of one's self-concept). Neither of these aspects of sports team consumption can be evaluated until one actually attends games or becomes a fan.

The challenge for marketers is to make the service more tangible. For the Philadelphia Phillies, it means using tangible cues to create associations with the brand. Elements such as the team's logo, color scheme, uniforms, and mascot (the Phillie Fanatic) are observable characteristics consumers can use to help form judgments about the value offered by the Philadelphia Phillies. In addition, other types of sports elements such as facilities, live event experiences, and digital experiences contribute to the tangibility of the service offering.

Sponsorships are another intangible service marketed by sports properties. When a company signs a sponsorship agreement, it can be said that they receive nothing in return! At least nothing tangible is received. What sponsors receive are rights to associate their brands with a sports property. It is the association of the two brands and marketing opportunities that arise from the partnership that provide value to sponsors. Just as teams use tangible cues to bring their service to life in consumers' eyes, sponsorships contain tangible elements that communicate the sponsor's connection with the property. The most common tangible cue of sponsorship is signage in venues. Signage placement is a standard feature of most sponsorship agreements, in part because it provides a valuable visual cue for visitors to associate the sponsor with a team or event.

The tangibility of sponsorships can be enhanced through utilization of other sports products. For example, Amigo Energy, a corporate sponsor of the Houston Dynamo MLS team, presented a team replica jersey giveaway at the final home game of the 2010 season.[3] Communicating an association with the Dynamo by placing the Amigo Energy logo on replica jerseys is a way to create a long-lasting visual cue of the association between sponsor and team.

Similarly, sponsors can be integrated into the live experience, such as in-game contests or games involving the sponsored brand that are designed to entertain attendees during breaks in game play. The Portland Pirates, an American Hockey League team and affiliate of the Buffalo Sabres, used this approach. Among its in-game production elements are contests to be the Subway Stick Kid, seat upgrade promotions to sit in the Dunkin' Donuts Corner or Country Kitchen Breadbox, and free pizza coupons for an entire row from Portland Pie.[4] These promotions allow sponsors to go beyond mere exposure on venue signage and become an element in the event itself.

As a sponsor of Bobby Labonte, Coca-Cola has visual cues prominently placed that will be easy to see as he gives the starting command at the Coca-Cola Zero 400 race.

Another category of services in the sports industry can be classified as *support services*. Many tasks that must be performed in the execution of service or experience delivery to customers are not performed by sports properties. Instead, they are outsourced to firms that can perform the services more effectively and typically at a lower cost than a sports property could do on its own. The foodservice operations profiled at the beginning of Chapter 3 were conducted by non-sports firms. They were foodservice companies contracted by teams to handle all aspects of food and beverage operations. Support services are a B2B category as they target sports firms as their customer, and the end consumer does not usually make a distinction that security staff at a sports venue work for a security firm hired by the venue or team. Extensive coverage of support services that can be performed in-house or outsourced is presented in Chapter 13.

Live Event/Experience

At the heart of service delivery for team or event properties is the live experience. Sports are like other services in that they are produced and delivered in the presence of people. Interested individuals pay for the privilege of watching the service experience take place. The live event as a sports product has a history that can be traced back to the 1860s and is an important revenue source for sports properties today.[5]

Live events include those that are part of a regular season schedule, preseason and postseason events, and branded events. The National Hockey League branded its season-opening week (NHL Face-Off), tour of European cities by six NHL teams (NHL Premiere), a New Year's Day outdoor game (Winter Classic), All-Star Game, and Stanley Cup Playoffs. The emphasis on special events to complement the regular season schedule has been cited as contributing to the revenue growth of the NHL.[6]

Sponsors also have the capability of impacting their target audiences through live events and experiences. The use of client hospitality at sporting events to entertain customers or prospects is one way sponsors activate their association with a property. Another way sponsors can engage customers at live events is to create interactive exhibits with displays, games, or face-to-face conversations. American Express used this approach to achieve audience interaction with attendees at the PGA Tour's U.S. Open through the "American Express Championship

Experience." The experience-based initiative included access to TV and radio coverage of the tournament, kiosks that connect visitors with their favorite social networking websites, and personalized ten-minute golf lessons.[7]

Digital Experience

A fast-growing product category is consumption of sports through digital experiences. Indirect consumption of sports has a rich tradition, dominated first by radio in the first half of the 20th century, then by television during the second half.[8] Today, technology advancements have opened new channels for sports fans to connect with and follow their passion (see Figure 6.2).

FIGURE 6.2 **Digital Experience Products**

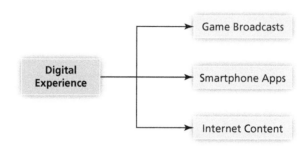

Development of digital products benefits consumers by giving them greater connectivity with their favorite sports, teams, and players. Sports properties benefit from digital products indirectly through their power to keep brands relevant with consumers, and they benefit directly from digital sports products through creation of a revenue stream from fans who are willing to pay in order to access live events, news, and other content.

Two particular digital products that are in the early stages of existence that offer great potential for the future are streaming of live events and smartphone applications. Live streaming of games over the Internet is being offered in both free and for-pay business models. The Arena Football League offers fans the ability to watch games on their computers. The league's AFL Live Network lets fans download a video player, send reminders about upcoming games via text message or e-mail, invite friends to watch, and access video on demand from previous games.[9] Offering live streaming of AFL games is important to the league's success for two reasons. First, the AFL seeks to rebuild its fan base that was hurt by the league's suspension of operations for the 2009 season. Free access to games makes it easier for consumers to become acquainted with the AFL. Second, the market reach of the AFL's television partner, the NFL Network, is not as extensive as previous TV partners such as ESPN and NBC. Offering games on the Internet for free reduces lack of TV availability as a barrier to the AFL's potential to build a strong fan base.

Digital products like the AFL Live Network are more than a new medium to reach sports fans. They can become a key component in a firm's business model. Delivering sports entertainment digitally allows consumers to stay connected with their favorite sports without being "tethered" to their home electronic devices, particularly television. Sports media giant ESPN has made delivery of live sporting events via digital devices a priority through its ESPN3 platform. Launched initially in 2005 as ESPN360, ESPN3 has evolved from a service limited to cable TV subscribers to a free service that allows site visitors to watch up to six live sporting events at the same time at ESPN3.com.[10] The impact of digital access to sports programming on computers and smartphones is strengthening loyalty to the ESPN brand and as a result is being noticed by top executives. ESPN3 has been tapped as one of the top priorities for the company.[11]

The next frontier of digital sports products has arrived. It is the application, or "app" for smartphone and tablet platforms supported by Apple (iPhone), Google (Android), and Research in Motion (Blackberry). Apps provide direct connectivity to website content, or it can be customized software that provides unique content to app users. Many apps are free to download, while most of the paid apps can be purchased at a modest price. Sports-related apps are products that deliver new value to users because they are a means to consume sports through what is referred to as the "third screen." Handheld digital devices join television and computers as visual channels for accessing digital content.

Fantasy sports play can be supported directly via apps that allow players to connect with fantasy games using their wireless devices. The major fantasy sports service providers ESPN and Yahoo! offer apps for playing their fantasy baseball games. Some apps cater to fantasy players' appetite for statistics and scores such as Sportacular, a free app developed by Citizen Sports that covers most professional U.S. sports leagues as well as college football and basketball.[12]

Another role for sports apps includes creating an additional channel for content delivery for sports media properties. For example, apps are offered by Fox Sports and ESPN Radio. Apps have been developed to deliver content for specific properties such as the Ultimate Fighting Championship and the U.S. Open golf tournament. Apps have even been created for individual athletes, such as MLB player Nick Swisher and NBA player Chris Bosh.

Apps are an important addition to the product portfolio of many sports properties, but not because of the direct revenue they will generate. In fact, free apps will only generate revenue if advertising or sponsorships are offered for sale. Instead, the payoff is fan engagement. In an environment in which competition for consumers' attention from other marketers as well as other providers of digital content such as media organizations and music is intense, maintaining relevance through convenient access will be a key to sports properties' efforts to develop a competitive advantage over other entertainment options.

One exception to the potential for apps to be a revenue source is in the area of event ticketing. Apps that connect fans looking for game tickets at the last minute with a ticketing service is one scenario that suggests ticket-related apps will become more important in the future. Whether free or paid, apps will get a serious look from many sports organizations as a potential product addition. An executive with an app developer that has developed an app for Las Vegas Motor Speedway remarked that "this feels like the early 1990s when everybody was just starting to get a website."[13]

Personalities

Perhaps the most marketable product a sports property can leverage is the personalities associated with the organization. In Chapter 2, star power was identified as a connection point between consumers and a sports brand, making images and personalities marketing assets. Whether it is star players, former players, coaches, broadcasters, or team executives, individuals represent the face of a franchise (see Figure 6.3). Whether individuals in these positions are role models has been the subject of considerable debate, but regardless of where one stands on the issue it is clear that people in these positions are highly visible and often admired. A star player is a particularly strong brand asset that frequently is the focal point of promotion campaigns for teams or events.

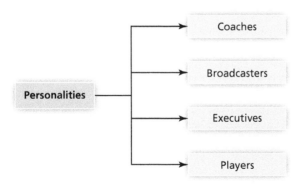

FIGURE 6.3
Personalities Associated with a Sports Organization

However, creating marketing programs around individual players entails risk. If a player is injured and does not play with his or her team or if traded to another team, marketing materials developed in advance of a season become obsolete. Worse, an individual that is featured prominently in a marketing campaign that is arrested or accused of engaging in behavior that is embarrassing to the player or team can hurt the effectiveness of the campaign. Even when players do not engage in conduct detrimental to their organization, their effectiveness as marketing assets may be diminished if there is a possibility that they would eventually leave their team via free agency. The Cleveland Cavaliers are a good example of this phenomenon. The Cavs rode the star power of LeBron James for seven seasons, but when he decided to sign with the Miami Heat as a free agent, the team's strongest marketing asset was gone.

The tenuous relationship individual players and coaches have with their employers makes it important to build a team or organization brand that endures while players and coaches come and go. A tactic that leverages the star power of individuals while avoiding issues such as free agent departures and trades is utilizing former players as a product. Alumni or retired players can make appearances for their former teams through autograph signings, participation in special events such as Old Timers games, and effectively maintain connections with fans who followed the accomplishments of the former players. The power of former players as marketers has been captured by organizations such as the Major League Baseball Alumni Association. The MLBAA has a "product" known as the Legends Entertainment Group. Retired players, including Hall of Fame members, are hired to give keynote speeches, make appearances at sporting events, and participate in autograph signings.[14] The hero status of these retired players lends star power to organizations that hire them.

Broadcasters inject their own personalities into fans' experience of listening or watching sporting events. The goodwill created by broadcasters adds to the total product offered by a sports property. In their day, legendary broadcasters such as the Chicago Cubs' Harry Caray and Los Angeles Lakers' Chick Hearn were closely associated with their teams and were woven into the experience of consuming games via radio. Broadcasters are marketers that are used to promote the team at special events and in advertising campaigns.

Broadcasters can have a similar impact on sports media brands as well. An element of ESPN's story of going from start-up sports network to global sports media powerhouse is the role that broadcasters have in ESPN programs, notably *SportsCenter*. On-air personalities such as Chris Berman, Dan Patrick, and Stuart Scott elevated the sports anchorperson from one who reported news to a creative type who injected their own works into news delivery. The notoriety of broadcasters can be instrumental in bringing credibility to upstart sports media brands. For example, Major League Baseball launched the MLB Network in 2009 as a niche cable channel that promotes the MLB product. Bob Costas and Peter Gammons, accomplished sports journalists and broadcasters, were hired as on-air talent. The name recognition and expertise of Costas and Gammons sent a signal that MLB intended to deliver high-quality programming on its new network.

Another off-field personality that can become part of the organizational product is top executives. Team owners, league commissioners, and other high-level figures have become brands in their own right and are effective marketing agents for their properties. The modern-day phenomenon of executives becoming an extension of a team brand is former New York Yankees owner George Steinbrenner. His association with the Yankees spanned from his 1973 purchase of the team to his death in 2010. During that time, Steinbrenner was highly involved with the team (as evidenced by the frequent manager changes he made) and was influential in the rising importance of using free agents to build a winning team and in the emergence of team-based regional sports networks. Similarly, prominent executives at a league or sanctioning body level can become part of the total product. Influential leaders such as Pete Rozelle (NFL commissioner, 1960–1989), Bill France (NASCAR president, 1972–2000), and David Stern (NBA commissioner, 1984–present) are examples of league executives who played key roles in leading their leagues to becoming global brands during their long tenures.

Defining the Product Offering

Proactive development and management of products can enable a sports property to serve customers better and bring more revenue to an organization. A major challenge for effective product management is pinpointing which elements of a product are pivotal in delivering value to customers. One approach to analyzing the relationship between product characteristics and customer value is to think of a product as having multiple levels or layers, with each level having a role in the delivery of value: 1) core product, 2) actual product, and 3) augmented product. These levels are illustrated in Figure 6.4.[15]

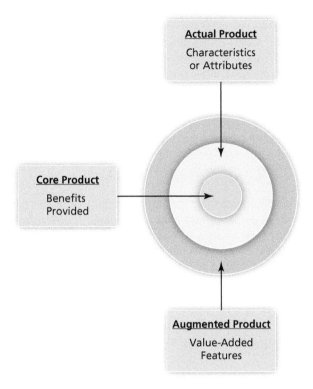

FIGURE 6.4 **Levels of a Product**

Core Product

A customer-focused view of a product rightfully considers the benefits received from consumption as the essence of a product. It is these benefits that make up the **core product**. Definition of a product's core provides a basic answer to the question "Why do consumers use the product?" A long-used example of understanding the core product has been used by many a sales manager to train salespeople on the importance of understanding buyers' needs. The point made in this classic training moment is "people do not buy drills, they buy holes." In other words, people have little desire to own a drill. Its true benefit is in what the drill does—create holes that help in completing projects that add value for drill buyers. In the case of sports consumption, answers to the question "Why do consumers use the product?" might include entertainment, escape from daily life, vicarious experience (eliciting emotional responses through the accomplishments of others), or appreciation of a high level of athletic competition.

Understanding customers' expectations of the core product is essential, because it affects design of a product's features, decisions on features to include or emphasize, and how brand communications should be developed (e.g., advertising messages or social media communications). For example, TV commercials for a NASCAR Sprint Cup race should communicate information and images consistent with what race attendees value from the race experience. Motivation to attend may be based on a desire to watch the fast-paced, suspenseful racing between drivers traveling at speeds of more than 200 miles per hour. For other attendees, race attendance may be a social event, an opportunity to spend time with friends. Yet others may be motivated to attend because a day at the racetrack is a chance to get away from the rigors of the workweek. Given that Sprint Cup race fans will have different reasons to attend, the design of the race experience and the approach to promotion should be tailored to appeal to these diverse desires that the core product can fulfill.

Engineering and design features can impact the quality of the core level for sports products. Innovations that improve product performance can have a noticeable impact on player performance and influence the quality of the on-field product. An example of how product development has the potential to impact game play is college baseball's bat dilemma. Aluminum bats have been used in NCAA baseball for almost forty years. As the manufacturing technology for aluminum bats has improved, so have the general trends for batting averages, runs scored per game, and home runs per game.

In addition to the offensive outburst associated with aluminum bats, concerns have been raised about the safety of fielders hit by powerful drives off aluminum bats. In response, the NCAA implemented new rules that replaced traditional aluminum bats with technology that makes aluminum bats behave more like wooden bats. The predicted result is fewer runs scored and home runs, with many coaches believing it will negatively affect the quality of the sport.[16] In this case, the NCAA's decision to use bats with technology that will have the effect of lowering runs and home runs could create an experience for fans that is vastly different from what they are accustomed to enjoying. Thus, an unintended consequence of adopting the new technology for bats could be a loss of some fans who are turned off by the change in the core product.

Actual Product

A product's identifiable features make up the **actual product**. In terms of the example of drills and holes, a drill's attributes would comprise the actual product. A drill's weight, design, color, speed, and other tangible characteristics represent what a buyer receives when purchasing that product. The actual product is the basic framework by which the core product (i.e., the consumer benefit) is marketed to buyers. For a sports product like a baseball game, the actual product would include some of the following features:

- Two teams
- A baseball field
- Nine innings of competition
- Umpires
- Unique features of the sport (e.g., home runs, strategy decisions by managers, warm-up period between innings)

Sponsorship is another type of sports product, but the product's identifiable features are significantly different than for a baseball game. Among the attributes offered to buyers in a sponsorship are:

- Signage at events
- Advertising in game programs, media broadcasts, or sports property's website
- Event tickets
- Client or employee hospitality opportunities
- Shared brand associations with the sports property

In these illustrations for a sporting event and a sponsorship, it is evident that buyers probably do not consume these products strictly to experience the actual product. Rather, the actual product is the means by which the core product benefit is delivered. Sponsors do not partner with sports teams merely to place their logos on signs or to receive game tickets (actual product), they seek to strengthen their relationships with a sports property's audience and build a stronger brand through their association with the property (core product).

Augmented Product

The final level of product, the **augmented product**, is made up of features that enhance the value that buyers receive from consuming the product. Augmented product attributes are not required for a product to function properly, and the core product benefit could still be delivered even if the augmented product did not exist. But the presence of the augmented product usually improves quality. In addition to the effect on quality, the augmented product also serves to differentiate a brand from similar offerings from which buyers choose. It is at this level of the product that marketers have leeway to create elements that transform an ordinary product or service to an extraordinary experience.

Sports marketing can demonstrate how the augmented product contributes to customer value. A college football game, for instance, could be held without augmented product elements being added to the total product. The core product of entertainment, escape, or vicarious experience could be delivered to customers. Actual product elements such as two teams, a football field, game officials, and four 15-minute quarters of competition would be present (or else there would be no game). The limitation of the total product at this point is that its appeal would be primarily to an audience that has rather high involvement with football. Casual fans or people who attend football games for reasons other than a great interest in football would likely not be attracted by core and actual product elements alone. Even among highly involved football fans, the product would not have the capability to engage attendees in a way that adds an experiential element to the game itself.

Figure 6.5 contrasts how the actual product can be enhanced by the addition of augmented product elements. In each case, an actual product feature that meets a basic customer need is supplemented with value-added features that make the total product more powerful by creating stronger brand touch points (contact points) between customer and sports property. Chapter 7 will focus on how sports products can be transformed into experiences that engage consumers and strengthen relationships.

Actual Product Element	Augmented Product Element	Value Added
Parking Lot	Reserved lots, trolley service, tailgating areas	Convenience, socialization
Seating Area	Suites, club seats, chair-back seats	Exclusivity, comfort
Concessions	Restaurants	Quality, variety
Scoreboard	HD video scoreboards	Entertainment, aesthetics
Halftime	Halftime contests	Entertainment, involvement
Home Team	Pregame team "walk"	Excitement, access

FIGURE 6.5 How the Augmented Product Adds Value for College Football Game Attendees.

A trend that has been observed by properties across a wide variety of sports is the blending of sports with music to appeal to a broad audience and add a new dimension to the augmented product. Prior to the sports–music cross-marketing trend, music artists' involvement with sports properties consisted primarily of singing the national anthem at events. Today, sports properties view music as an additional channel to attract new consumers, while music artists view sports as a platform for promoting their works.

The Tampa Bay Rays incorporated postgame concerts as a key strategy to stimulate attendance to Saturday games. During the season, the Rays held eight postgame concerts in its Summer Concert Series by nationally known recording artists such as John Fogerty, ZZ Top, Nelly, and Barenaked Ladies.[17] In addition to creating a strong augmented product, the Rays strategically selected dates for concerts to coincide with opponents that may draw fewer fans without the postgame concert as a value-added feature. Other teams have engaged in similar cross-marketing with entertainment brands to create opportunities to reach sports and music fans within a single audience. Coca-Cola was involved with the Food Lion Speed Street Festival in uptown Charlotte, North Carolina, during a NASCAR racing weekend in an effort to draw music fans to the NASCAR racing events.

© Crystal A Macleod/Cal Sport Medi/AP/Press Association Images

An aerial view of the Coca-Cola Stage at the Food Lion Speed Street Festival in Charlotte, North Carolina.

While a strong augmented product can make a sports offering more appealing to some customers, marketers must bear in mind that there could be a risk of alienating other customers who are attracted to the core or actual product. The NHL's Edmonton Oilers became the first Canadian team to have cheerleaders. Some Oilers fans who are followers because of their interest in the sport, team, or players may be turned off by the "intrusion" of cheerleaders. These fans may perceive that the presence of cheerleaders detracts from the core and actual product rather than enhancing them.

Managerial Implications

The concept of levels of a product breaks down a product's makeup to identify sources of customer value. One source of value is the presence of product capabilities that influence satisfaction of customer need states (core product); another source of value resides in product attributes or characteristics that are involved in its delivery (actual product); the third source of value can be found in the "extras" that sports marketers add to products to increase engagement and excitement (augmented product). The concept is logical and is a reasonable explanation for how product decisions can impact customer value, but the question that arises is how does it translate into managerial decision making? An often used approach is shown in Figure 6.6.

FIGURE 6.6
Translating Product Levels into Managerial Decisions

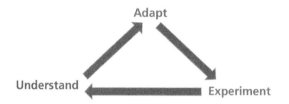

Understand refers to having an awareness of why customers buy and use a product. The discussion on consumer motivations in Chapter 2 identified several different reasons why people consume sports products. The fact that not all customers buy for the same reasons cannot be overlooked or overstated. Different customer motivations can be the foundation for market segmentation strategies as discussed in Chapter 4. The goal of managing the core product should be to develop insight into the outcomes customers wish to attain from buying and consuming a product.

Market research into motivations is invaluable at this stage, whether it be a random survey of fans at a PGA Tour event or a focus group of season ticket holders for a minor league hockey team. A tactic being used by more sports properties that blends customer service with market research is the use of sales representatives and customer service specialists charged with maintaining dialogue with customers. Sports marketers are turning to the hospitality industry for best practices and training methods to equip their employees to better understand customers' needs. Customer-contact personnel with the Philadelphia Eagles have received training from hospitality brands such as Walt Disney World, Ritz-Carlton, and Marriott in an effort to help front-line employees develop a better grasp on the core product benefits sought by customers.[18]

Adapt is a managerial response to the actual product. In some respects, a sports marketer is constrained in managing the actual product because many of its elements are associated with the sport or game itself and are beyond the marketer's control. In the case of sporting events, the rules of a game or sport are uniform and are managed by a league or sanctioning body and cannot be modified by individual teams or properties. Thus, adapting to the rules or framework of the sport is a must.

An NFL game is going to have four 15-minute quarters, and there will be several official timeouts for commercial breaks when games are televised. Managers responsible for game production recognize that the numerous "TV timeouts" will create several periods of downtime at the live event. Their response might be to fill the commercial breaks with contests or games with randomly selected fans, video presentations on the scoreboard, or sponsor messages.

It is even possible that marketing considerations can alter the actual product. Major League Baseball, the National Football League, and the National Collegiate Athletic Association experienced problems with the length of time required to complete games. For MLB, slow-paced games could result in TV viewers becoming disinterested or even deter fans from attending games. In the case of the NFL and NCAA, the average length of time to play a game increased to the point that long-running games could overlap with the broadcast of other games. MLB, NFL, and NCAA enacted rules designed to reduce the amount of time required to complete a game to make the product more fan-friendly and media-friendly. For example, MLB began more stringent enforcement of rules concerning length of time a pitcher has to throw to a batter, length of time a relief pitcher has to arrive at the pitcher's mound, and length of time a coach can visit with a pitcher during an on-field meeting.[19]

If marketers follow the steps of understanding consumers' motivations to pursue benefits offered by the core product and adapting the elements of the actual product to more effectively deliver core product benefits, it would seem that developing the augmented product would flow from the first two steps rather easily. Unfortunately, successful implementation of augmented product elements is not assured. A willingness to *experiment* with value-added enhancements is needed to determine what will be accepted by consumers. It requires an investment in returning to the first step, understanding consumers, through use of market research to gather their reactions to the augmented product.

An illustration of how the augmented product is an evolving level of the total product is provided by *Monday Night Football*. The long-running NFL broadcast brand now aired by ESPN would seem to have little need to experiment with the augmented product given its storied history and having no other competition for professional football viewers on Monday nights. However, experimentation with some of the content elements in a *Monday Night Football* broadcast injected more discussion and coverage of popular culture by having entertainers, actors, and musicians appearing as guests in the broadcast booth during games. This strategy sought to expand the appeal of the product to a broader audience beyond avid NFL fans. Viewer focus groups were overwhelmingly opposed to the non-football elements of *MNF* broadcasts. ESPN responded by returning the production focus to football.[20]

Marketing Innovations

Innovation is a buzzword that grabs the attention of managers because of its importance in developing new products and ultimately impacting an organization's growth. Dozens of definitions have been offered for the concept of innovation, so it is not surprising to find differences of opinion about what innovation is. An issue that is often misunderstood when discussing innovation is the perspective from which innovation should be viewed. An innovation is relevant only if it is relevant to customers. Thus, the definition of **innovation** applied to sports products throughout this chapter is simply "the ability to deliver new value to a customer."[21] The key point is that innovation resides in the eye of the customer. If a good or service is perceived as new by customers, then it is new . . . even if it is not new! When Major League Soccer expanded into Salt Lake City in 2005 with the Real Salt Lake franchise, MLS represented an innovation to that market even though the league has been in operation since 1996.

Types of Innovation

Just as a product is an offering made up of different levels or layers instead of a singular concept of "the product," innovation is not a simple managerial process. Instead, innovation can be viewed as a continuum in terms of the degree of newness a product offers. Three types of innovation along the continuum are: 1) continuous innovation, 2) dynamically continuous innovation, and 3) discontinuous innovation. Continuous and dynamically continuous innovations are considered *evolutionary* because they entail relatively minor changes or adaptations of existing products. Discontinuous innovations are *revolutionary* due to the potential "game changing" effect they have on consumer behavior and an industry (see Figure 6.7).

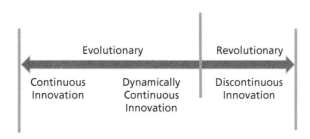

FIGURE 6.7 Types of Innovation

Continuous Innovation

The innovation type that has the least amount of "new value" is **continuous innovation**. New products that are relatively minor adaptations of existing products would be classified as continuous innovations. Rules changes made by MLB, NFL, and NCAA to quicken the pace of games are continuous innovations. Continuous innovations do not require significant changes in consumer behavior in order to receive benefits from the innovation.

Other continuous innovations would be the addition of a twelfth regular season game for Football Bowl Subdivision (FBS) institutions in NCAA football and the advent of conference championship games for the Atlantic Coast Conference, Big East Conference, Conference USA, and the Southeastern Conference. For licensed products such as New Era caps, a licensee of many major U.S. sports properties, a continuous innovation would be introduction of new styles or colors of team caps.

Most new products are continuous innovations because minor changes or adaptations are less risky to bring to market than innovations that require substantial learning and behavior change by consumers. Managing risk in new product development is important, because statistics frequently cited for the failure rate of new products suggest that 80 to 90 percent of all new products do not survive in the marketplace. New products that bear some relation to existing products that already have acceptance in the market are considered to have a better chance to overcome the failure rate odds. At the same time, continuous innovation represents the least amount of creativity or departure from the status quo. The result is consumers may not be introduced to some ideas for creating new value because marketers deem them too risky given the amount of change they would represent.

Dynamically Continuous Innovation

A dynamically continuous innovation presents more challenges to penetrate the market successfully because more learning is required by consumers in order for the innovation to be adopted. **Dynamically continuous innovations** for sports products are often variations of a core product that contain too many unique product attributes to be considered a continuous innovation. For example, when the sport of arena football expands into a new market, the target audience is familiar with football already through exposure to professional or collegiate products (NFL and NCAA). However, the sport of arena football differs from the football that people have known. Differences in field size, number of players, leagues, teams, and many other actual product attributes mean that football fans must invest effort to learn about the arena football product. There is no assurance that learning about an innovation like arena football will lead consumers to accept it by following local teams, attending games, and watching game broadcasts.

Marketing efforts for dynamically continuous innovations are helped by the fact that consumers may have a basic understanding of the new product. Football is the most popular sport in America, so introducing a football-related product means that the target market will have less to learn about it than if the product was completely new to the market. Thus, the challenge for sports marketers is to inform the target audience about an innovation's unique attributes and how they provide value. In the case of arena football, the new value brought by the product may be reasonably priced entertainment, football action during the NFL and NCAA off-season, or excitement in a climate-controlled environment. The benefits offered that are valued by consumers must be understood and become the focal point of a strategy to market the innovation.

Discontinuous Innovation

Relatively few innovations can be considered truly new to the world or revolutionary. Throughout the history of industrialized countries, the introduction of automobiles, televisions, and personal computers can be cited as examples of discontinuous innovations. **Discontinuous innovations** are fewer in number than continuous and dynamically continuous innovations, but if they are accepted by consumers they can influence changes in buyer behavior and industry competition. Consumers have relatively little experience or understanding of discontinuous innovations because they are so unlike existing products. These products represent a departure from the status quo, and the value contained in discontinuous innovations gives consumers benefits that existing products or even evolutionary innovations cannot match.

Of course, technological developments often play a role in creating discontinuous innovations. The experience of watching a football game on television has been significantly impacted by a discontinuous innovation developed by Sportvision. Its 1st and Ten video technology provides the yellow line that appears on the screen showing where the first down marker is located on the field. Today, the 1st and Ten line has become a staple for televised football because Sportvision applied technological capabilities to improving fans' experience.

Sports properties are no different than their counterparts in other industries when it comes to the role of discontinuous innovation in new product development. Few innovations in the sports industry would be classified as new to the world. Under Armour founder Kevin Plank's quest for a performance T-shirt that would absorb moisture led to a discontinuous innovation, a microfiber material that would wick away moisture to the outside of the shirt.[22] Adoption of Under Armour's innovation not only launched the company on a path to success, but it spurred development of a new product category that was soon entered by other athletic apparel marketers.

Discontinuous innovation in the sports industry is not limited to tangible products like apparel. The Ultimate Fighting Championship (UFC) debuted in 1993, inspired by mixed martial arts competitions that can be traced back many decades. However, the UFC built its brand by developing a total product that included championships, pay-per-view events, and a television contract.[23] This form of mixed martial arts entertainment represented a new product sports consumers had not experienced previously. As is the case with many discontinuous innovations, the UFC has attracted interest from consumers of products that have not been innovative such as boxing as well as spawned new properties seeking to gain a piece of the mixed martial arts audience and sponsorship market. Approximately twenty mixed martial arts leagues operate in the United States, many of which seek to build on the success of UFC's discontinuous innovation.[24]

Under Armour was the first to develop a moisture-absorbing shirt for performance athletes.

Managing Influences on Adoption of Innovations

The high percentage of new products that fail serve as a reminder that success cannot be guaranteed, even when innovations are based on learning from consumers and competitors through market research and design that is inspired by the marketing concept of meeting customers' needs. The risk of product failure is not limited to radically new products (discontinuous innovations); brand extensions that are slight modifications of the core product are frequently rejected in the market as well. The odds against a new product succeeding seem daunting, but there are certain variables that impact consumer acceptance of innovations that managers can observe and manage to improve chances of successful adoption. As shown in Figure 6.8, four influences on the adoption of innovations are: relative advantage, compatibility, complexity, and trialability. These influences are based on consumers' perceptions, but managers can develop the product offering and related marketing mix decisions to minimize these obstacles and improve odds of successful adoption.

- Relative advantage
- Compatibility
- Complexity
- Trialability

FIGURE 6.8 Influences on Innovation Adoption

Relative Advantage

Defining and communicating relative advantage is a high priority when marketing an innovation. Relative advantage is the benefit or point of difference the innovation offers compared to existing alternatives available to consumers. If the relative advantage is not understood by the target market, buyers may not be compelled to change their current behavior to try, and eventually adopt, the innovation. If an innovation does not offer a relative advantage, its likelihood of successful adoption is diminished. Three characteristics a relative advantage needs to possess are shown in Figure 6.9.

FIGURE 6.9
Characteristics of Relative Advantage

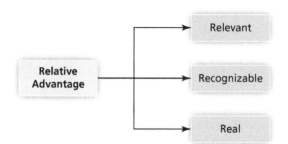

First, an advantage must be real. Marketing slogans or claims such as "unique," "exciting," or "high caliber" that are not experienced when consumers interact with the product will ring hollow with the target market. Second, a relevant advantage is a point of difference that actually matters to the product user. Different for the sake of being different is not a viable competitive advantage! A Major League Baseball team could modify the appearance of its logo or uniform colors, but if there is no strategy behind the change or communication with the target market to position the change as new added value, then the innovation does not add any meaning to the brand.

The third and possibly the most important element of relative advantage is that an innovation must be recognized by the target market in order for consumers to judge that it is differentiated from existing product offerings. It is this characteristic of relative advantage that heightens the importance of brand communication to tell the story of a new product. A strategy that coordinates mass media, social media, and interpersonal communication tools is essential to create awareness, shape brand image and personality, and ultimately influence product adoption decisions.

One sports property that exemplifies the dilemma of recognizing relative advantage is the Women's National Basketball Association (WNBA). This brand extension of the National Basketball Association began play in 1997, and despite increased interest in women's college basketball it has faced challenges gaining acceptance among basketball fans. WNBA teams have not always succeeded, even in markets in which the presence of NBA teams offered potential consumers for women's basketball. Franchises in Charlotte, Cleveland, Detroit, Houston, Miami, Orlando, Portland, and Sacramento folded or relocated despite having established NBA teams in their markets.[25] The WNBA experience in these markets illustrates that even when an innovation has points of difference that are real and are relevant to sports fans, there is no assurance that it will be recognized by sufficient numbers of consumers needed to achieve market sustainability.

Compatibility

A crucial factor affecting consumer adoption of innovations is acceptance by consumers in terms of a new product being perceived as compatible with their values, beliefs, and practices. Consumers may reject a new product if it is perceived as incongruent with their morals, lifestyle, or behaviors even if an innovation possesses relative advantage characteristics (real, relevant, and recognized). For example, challengers to the NFL have come and gone since the 1970s, including the World Football League, United States Football League, and XFL. The latest entrant into the pro football market is the United Football League. The UFL began play in 2009 as a four-team league, and added a fifth team for 2010.[26] Unlike other leagues that have challenged the NFL, UFL's season is played during the fall, with many games on Fridays and Saturdays.

Some differences possessed by the UFL product include market location (teams are not located in NFL cities), TV camera access to locker rooms during halftime, and audio transmissions of coach-quarterback communications. However, the value proposition offered by UFL may clash with consumers' existing beliefs, attitudes, and behaviors toward football. For instance, Fridays are the primary night for high school football in many states, and Saturdays have a long-standing tradition in college football, making acceptance of another football property challenging because it conflicts with how many football fans view these days. Also, an upstart professional football league may be perceived as being of lesser quality than the NFL. This perceived difference between NFL and UFL, coupled with playing an overlapping schedule, may prompt football fans to opt to focus their attention and interest on the established NFL instead of an unknown entity.

Complexity

The likelihood of an innovation being adopted can be aided by managing the learning and behavior modification required to receive benefits from the product. Marketers of innovations that possess

© modestil / Fotolia

In moving into nontraditional markets, NHL teams provided "Hockey 101" seminars to educate consumers.

only slight changes from existing product offerings must inform their target customers about the new product, but learning can occur quickly and in many cases does not require extensive education efforts. Such was the case with Ticketmaster, the official ticket resale partner of the NBA, NFL, and NHL. Season ticket holders can create an account and sell individual game tickets to other fans. The service provides easy-to-follow instructions on the Ticketmaster TicketExchange website, thus adding value to customers by giving them a convenient outlet to sell unwanted tickets.

For dynamically continuous and discontinuous innovations, complexity is a larger issue that can threaten successful product adoption. Managing complexity was important when the National Hockey League located franchises in nontraditional markets in the 1990s. Cities with warm climates such as Dallas, Phoenix, Raleigh, and Nashville had fewer residents that grew up playing ice hockey or were familiar with the NHL than in traditional hockey markets. This characteristic of Sun Belt markets required marketing efforts to include educating prospective fans about the rules of the game. "Hockey 101" seminars before games, publishing basic rules and explanations of game situations in game programs, and promoting youth hockey programs were tactics used in these markets to increase consumers' familiarity with the sport. Regardless of the innovation type and the degree of newness a product possesses, failure to account for complexity by marketers can result in consumers being unwilling to adopt a new product because of perceived inconvenience in its acquisition or use.

Trialability

An innovation can clear the hurdles of possessing a relative advantage, have compatibility with consumers' values and beliefs, and reduce the level of complexity in product use, but unless consumers are able to experience a new product firsthand in order to judge the value it delivers, adoption of the innovation may not occur. Stimulating product trial, or first-time use, is a major task facing marketers of consumer packaged goods. If consumers do not try a new flavor of potato chips or a new formula of toothpaste in large numbers, those new products may fail because sales do not meet expectations. Similarly, sports properties need to encourage trial of an innovation. Consumers will ultimately decide if the value possessed by an innovation merits purchase and ultimately adoption. But if they do not try a new innovation at least once, it is likely to become part of the high failure rate statistic for new products.

Sampling is an effective promotion tactic that enables consumers to try a product with little or no financial risk. Financial information services company Bloomberg understood the importance of sampling when it developed research products geared toward fantasy sports players. Its MLB Front Office mobile application provides statistics for all batters and pitchers. A free trial version containing data on the top ten batters and pitchers can be downloaded. Fantasy players can assess the benefits offered by the service by using it on a small scale at no cost. If the application is judged to deliver "new value," then fantasy players may decide to purchase the full version of the application for $4.99.[27]

In addition to sampling, price discounts can be used to encourage trial usage. Reducing the costs of an innovation reduces the financial risk in making a trial purchase. A ticket sales representative responsible for selling groups may invite a group leader or influencer to attend a game in order to demonstrate the benefits a group can enjoy if they attend a game, or offer a group to attend at a reduced price level. Experiencing a product for the first time can persuade consumers about its value proposition more forcefully than a salesperson, advertisement, or website, especially when they have little or no prior knowledge of the product.

Brand Leveraging Strategies

New products play an important role in helping a sports property achieve its growth goals. However, products will be ineffective at driving growth unless they are developed in concert with a strategy for targeting customer segments. Thus, new product development should begin with identifying market segments to target, understanding consumers' needs, and determining how a new product can add value over existing product options. Figure 6.10 identifies three approaches for connecting target market characteristics with products.

FIGURE 6.10
Approaches for Connecting Target Market Characteristics with Products

Target Market Characteristics ⟷ Products

1. Expand existing customer relationships
2. Attract new customers in existing markets
3. Break into new markets

Expand Existing Customer Relationships

A logical starting point for a sports property to consider is how it can leverage new products to increase revenues by targeting existing customers. This approach is a logical starting point because current customers already have a relationship with the company. They are convinced that they receive value from the relationship . . . otherwise they probably would not be customers! New offerings have an advantage in terms of familiarity. If customers have an affinity for a brand, those positive feelings normally transfer to a new product offered by the same organization.

Major League Baseball fans often have favorite teams and players that they follow and support. They are involved with the sport and are good prospects for new products that enable them to maintain their connections with teams or players. Digital products introduced by Major League Baseball Advanced Media (MLBAM) appeal to fans' needs to be connected to MLB wherever they are. One of the digital products is MLB.TV, a service that delivers MLB games, statistics, and fantasy baseball information to customers' personal computers with a monthly or annual subscription. Another digital offering, MLB At Bat, is an application for mobile devices that gives buyers access to a live game video broadcasts, home and away team audio broadcasts for all radio season games, breaking news, and video archives.[28] These products add value by making it more convenient for MLB fans to follow the sport.

Brand licensing is a strategy that can fuel growth through offering new products to existing customers. For sports properties, licensing is a revenue stream that shifts much of the financial risk associated with producing and selling products to licensees, the entities that pay for the rights to use a sports property's brand marks. When licensing is mentioned, products like caps, T-shirts, and jerseys usually come to mind. However, the possibilities for brand licensing are seemingly limited only by one's imagination. Many opportunities can be found to license a sports property's name and logo. NASCAR took advantage of its growth in popularity by establishing a NASCAR Hall of Fame in Charlotte, North Carolina. It is an entertainment complex that consists of interactive exhibits, a theater, restaurant, retail shops, and NASCAR broadcast studio. Instead of taking on responsibility for facility construction and operation, NASCAR licensed its name to the city of Charlotte, which owns the facility.[29]

Attract New Customers in Existing Markets

A second strategy for using products to drive business growth focuses on using products to attract customers in existing markets who currently do not buy the marketer's brand. Two considerations should be made with regard to this strategy. First, unlike marketing tactics for many consumer products that are based on attracting new customers by inducing brand-switching behavior, sports properties do not necessarily need to assume that someone who is a fan of one sport cannot follow other sports or teams. The seasonal nature of sports makes it possible for a Cleveland resident to be a fan of the Indians, Browns, and Cavaliers. New customers may be acquired by appealing to fans of other sports.

Cross-marketing between two different sports properties that target similar customers but whose seasons have little overlap provides a fertile opportunity to grow business via attracting customers in existing markets. Collaboration between two properties in the same geographic market occurred when the St. Louis Cardinals and St. Louis Blues provided radio commercial time and advertising space on scoreboards to promote the other team's ticket packages for their upcoming seasons.[30] The timing of MLB and NHL seasons (April to October for MLB; October to April for NHL) creates an ideal situation for joint marketing efforts to appeal to customers of another sport.

A second consideration for driving growth by targeting new customers in existing markets is exploring how a product's value proposition can be refined to better suit the needs of a customer segment that has previously shown little interest or desire for the product. Acquisition of new customers can occur if new products are introduced that appeal to noncustomers. The NFL seeks to increase the number of female fans, and in turn, revenues from women. The connection point the NFL is using to grow its female customer base is licensed products. Licensed product sales targeted to females are currently about 15 percent of the NFL's licensed sales total. The goal is to increase that percentage to 25 percent in the future.[31] Stating a goal to increase sales in a customer segment is a starting point for marketing planning, but arriving at that destination can be a more challenging task. In the case of the NFL, one strategy to reach their goal with the female market is the offering of licensed products in nontraditional categories such as wicker baskets, scented candles, and garden accessories.

The NFL has set a goal of attracting more females, especially for licensed products.

© Brian McEntire / iStockphoto

Sports products can be used by non-sports entities to attract customers, and at the same time give sports properties a channel for reaching customers of the non-sports entities with which they partner. This type of marketing partnership can be found in the different fantasy games offered by Yahoo! The popular Internet portal has partnered with MLB, NHL, and the PGA Tour to be the official online fantasy games of those leagues. The online games give fantasy sports players draft preparation materials, game highlights, and statistics.[32] Perhaps more important than the $9.95 in revenue Yahoo! receives from each customer for a product such as Yahoo! Fantasy Baseball are the visits fantasy players make to the Yahoo! website. Yahoo! Sports has more unique visitors per month than any sports website, which has a positive effect on advertising rates Yahoo! can charge on the site. Fantasy sports games serve to steer traffic to Yahoo! instead of other websites.

Break into New Markets

An alternative to growth in existing markets is to seek markets that provide access to new customers. The new customer markets can be a geographic area, demographic group, or value segment. New products can be introduced for the purpose of targeting a new market, existing products may be viable with some modifications, or a mix of new and old products can be utilized to appeal to a new market segment.

Hispanics are a large demographic group that has not been fully tapped by sports marketers.

© Monkey Business / Fotolia

The NBA used this approach when it launched NBA China, a business unit responsible for growing the NBA brand in that country. The NBA is targeting this lucrative global market through different products beyond league competition. The NBA has partnered with sports entertainment company AEG to manage arenas in key Chinese cities that will host sports and other entertainment events. Sponsorship revenues have been realized from Chinese companies marketing their association as official sponsors of the NBA. Entertainment products have been created in the form of an NBA-themed movie and a cheerleader reality TV show. Licensed product sales are driven by an NBA store that opened in Shanghai and sales of NBA-licensed products by official partner Adidas in its more than 6,000 Chinese outlets.[33] The NBA's presence in China is not new in that games have been televised in the country for more than twenty years. What is new is a strategic focus based on a product portfolio that will enable Chinese NBA fans to experience the league through a variety of channels, transforming eyeballs watching games on TV to customers who buy products to exhibit their affinity for the NBA.

Accessing a demographic group that previously has not been part of the target market is another means of achieving growth. A key question that must be asked when considering this strategy is whether existing products are capable of meeting the needs of this demographic group, or if adaptations will be needed for a product to interest customers in that segment. Or will new products be required that offer customer benefits that existing products cannot provide? In the United States, a demographic group that has drawn great interest from companies in many different industries is Hispanics. Approximately 45 million Hispanics live in the U.S., making it the country's largest minority group.[34] Yet their impact as sports consumers has gone largely untapped.

The fast-growing Hispanic population offers a major opportunity for sports properties. A survey of Hispanic adults found that the two U.S.-based sports properties that were among their favorite sports were MLB and NBA, each being a favorite sport for 49% of persons surveyed. Major League Soccer also had a solid fan base among Hispanics, with 44% indicating it was among their favorite sports.[35] The interest level that exists already for MLB, NBA, and MLS is beneficial to these properties, as their growth initiatives can focus more on strengthening relationships and attracting more Hispanic fans (i.e., the strategies of expand customer relationships in existing markets and attract new customers in existing markets). In contrast, a property such as NASCAR has not penetrated the Hispanic market to the same extent as MLB, NBA, and MLS. A potentially lucrative market exists given research that shows that 38% of Hispanic adults report having some interest in NASCAR, which is only slightly less than the percentage of the general population with some interest (42%).[36]

Culture and other distinguishing characteristics of a demographic group influence consumer behavior in such a way that sports marketers cannot simply adapt marketing campaigns by translating into another language or using different visual imagery. In the case of sports consumption, certain cultural characteristics of Hispanics differ substantially and create a need for audience-specific marketing strategies. One difference is the central role of family in consumption experiences. An image of American sports consumption often involves a group of males watching sports together. Hispanics' sports consumption would likely begin within families then extend to other males. Another characteristic of Hispanic consumers with implications for sports is an interest in athletes' stories of struggle and success, over athletic achievements as measured by statistics.[37] The premium Hispanics place on the role of family and connecting with athletes through their personal stories are two reasons why a sports product may need to be adapted or new products introduced to meet the needs of a new market. Observing and understanding consumers within a demographic audience is essential when pursuing growth through entering new markets so that mistakes are not made in product development, brand communication, or other marketing tactics.

Similar approaches can be applied to grow revenues in business markets. Sports properties can leverage the expertise possessed in their business operations to create professional services brands that serve clients in the sports industry and other industries. Examples of marketing strengths that have been parlayed into business units include sponsorship sales, licensing, event marketing, and digital media services. In each case, sports properties have extended their competencies associated with serving their customers and fans to adding value to other companies and their ability to serve their customers. A strategy of attracting new customers in business markets can be advantageous because properties already have relationships with sponsors, suppliers, and advertisers. It is possible that business opportunities exist with these current partners or within their network of customers. And, even though marketing operations are a year-round endeavor, the seasonal nature of most sports means that periods of less activity (and revenue inflow) that may occur can be reduced if engaged in providing marketing services.

Major League Baseball has been successful in applying expertise from sports operations to serve business clients. One of the first organizations to pursue growth through this strategy was the Boston Red Sox. Its Fenway Sports Group formed a partnership with a top NASCAR team, Roush Racing. Roush Fenway is a venture that includes marketing of Roush's racing teams in NASCAR's top three leagues (Sprint Cup, Nationwide Series, and Truck Series), managing sponsorship sales for the racing teams, and overseeing licensing agreements for Roush's racing teams.[38] Roush Fenway operates separately from the baseball organization, but the business knowledge and relationships developed by Fenway Sports Group have been leveraged to build

Insider Insights Steve Battista – Under Armour

Q. How do brands serve to guide or inspire product development at Under Armour?

A. To help lay guardrails for the brand's growth, the new thought for Under Armour is best described as this: A brand is like a great novel. It has many chapters in the arc of the storyline. Each chapter must take the storyline from the previous and set up the next chapters. For a brand that's known by tight long sleeves and apparel that wicks sweat, founder and CEO Kevin Plank is constantly pushing the product creation teams to come up with the new signature product of his brand. And this time, he's expecting his team—not his own thoughts or experience—to deliver the inspiration and design of what Under Armour will look like in its next chapter.

Q. What has been Under Armour's strategy for using product development as a driver of business growth?

A. Under Armour's early outlook was keeping a narrow focus. The mantra in marketing and product development became "Finish Team Sports." This meant making great football and baseball cleats before entering non-cleated footwear; making cross-training shoes before running shoes; testing basketball shoes on court with collegiate and NBA players for years before releasing them to the public for purchase. Entering smaller

Steve Battista talks about branding and product development.

Under Armour, Inc.

categories—or holding off entry for longer periods of research and development—allowed for Under Armour to fill in the blanks for their teams on field and during training while maintaining its disciplined focus on designing and building the greatest apparel and footwear in the world.

Q. Now that Under Armour has established itself as one of the premier sports apparel and footwear brands, how does innovation figure into the company's future growth plans?

A. The driving force that spurs innovation at Under Armour is the answer to this question: What problem can Under Armour solve for the athletes of today? The performance nature of Under Armour is the only "definite" for product designers and marketers. Creativity is nurtured, not discouraged, but designers know they must create an advantage with a shirt, shoe, or accessory that helps improve performance. And now that Team Sports are finished, there's a new mantra at Under Armour. This inspirational thought, the idea that keeps designers and marketers flocking to the Under Armour headquarters, is the notion that Plank has written on the walls of the design house and, quite often, ends his speeches with: "Under Armour has not yet made its defining product."

the business of Roush Fenway. The payoff for Fenway Sports comes from having a 50 percent ownership stake in the venture.

Two other MLB teams, the Chicago White Sox and Tampa Bay Rays, launched business units that market services in the sports industry and beyond. Silver Chalice Ventures, which was started by the White Sox, includes a digital media business that designs online and mobile media content for clients in the sports and entertainment industries. White Sox Chief Marketing Officer Brooks Boyer sums up the rationale for pursuing this strategy by saying "Ballparks can only be so big and so full, and sponsorship can only be so abundant, so it's incumbent upon us to also look to other avenues to generate additional revenue."[39]

The Tampa Bay Rays started Sunburst Entertainment Group as a consulting company in the areas of brand management, sponsorship sales, and event marketing. Also, a focus for increasing revenue through the new unit is to attract more entertainment events when Tropicana Field is not in use.[40] The strengths possessed in marketing the Rays and the team's familiarity in the market are advantages Sunburst Entertainment can use to attract clients and grow revenue for the Rays' organization.

Chapter Summary

Within sports, the term *product* can refer to a tangible product, an intangible service, a live event or experience, a digital experience, or a personal identification. The tangible product includes apparel, souvenirs, and the sports venue. The intangible service aspect refers to the fact that sports deliver entertainment, and it is through a live event or experience that individuals can watch. It also has a digital component through television, radio, and the Internet. Streaming of live events and smartphone applications are recent innovations in the digital arena. The last component of the product is the people and their personalities. These can be utilized to market a sports property as well as define the property.

A product consists of three levels: the core product, the actual product, and the augmented product. The core product is the set of benefits that customers receive from the consumption of the product, or sports entertainment. The actual product is the identifiable features of the product, or sports offering. The augmented product is the features that enhance the value of the product that consumers purchase. Translating these different product levels into managerial decisions involves understanding, adapting, and experimenting.

Developing new products and growing revenue often requires innovation, which is the ability to deliver new value to customers. Innovation can be viewed as continuum, but with three distinctive levels: continuous innovation, dynamically continuous innovation, and discontinuous innovation. The continuous and the dynamically continuous innovations are considered to be evolutionary in nature while the discontinuous innovation is considered to be revolutionary.

While consumers decide the rate of adoption of new innovations, marketing managers can influence the rate of adoption through attention to four influences: relative advantage, compatibility, complexity, and trialability. Relative advantage is the benefit or point of difference the innovation offers over existing alternatives and should possess the characteristics of being real, relevant, and recognizable. Compatibility refers to the acceptance of a new product in terms of it being compatible with consumers' values, beliefs, and current practices. Complexity involves the amount of learning and behavior change necessary to adopt a new innovation. The more complex an innovation, the greater the challenge of adoption due to the amount of learning and behavior change necessary. Trialability refers to the ability of consumers to try an innovation before making a purchase.

In marketing innovations, sports properties have three alternatives in connecting target market characteristics with new products. These strategies are to: 1) expand existing customer relationships, 2) attract new customers in existing markets, and 3) break into new markets.

Review Questions

1. When it comes to growth, what two options do firms have?
2. What other terms in sports are used interchangeably for the word "product?"
3. Describe the difference between a tangible product and an intangible service.

4. Discuss the growth of sports consumption through digital experiences.
5. Perhaps the most marketable product a sports property can leverage is the personalities associated with the organization. Explain how this can be done.
6. Identify and define the three levels of a product.
7. What are the three steps in translating product levels into managerial decisions?
8. Define the word "innovation" as it relates to sports products and describe the three major types of innovations.
9. Describe the four influences that affect the adoption of innovations.
10. What are the three characteristics a relative advantage of an innovation needs to possess to be adopted?
11. What three approaches can be used to connect target market characteristics with new products?

New Terms

Product value received by a buyer in an exchange with a seller.

Core product first level of a product, which specifies benefits customers receive from product consumption.

Actual product second level of a product, which is the identifiable features.

Augmented product third level of a product, made up of features that enhance the value buyers receive from product consumption.

Innovation delivering new value to customers through products, services, or ideas.

Continuous innovation relatively minor adaptations of existing products.

Dynamically continuous innovation variation of a core product that contains unique attributes beyond minor adaptations of continuous innovation.

Discontinuous innovations radical departures from status quo products.

Discussion and Critical Thinking Exercises

1. Figure 6.1 identifies five terms that are used interchangeably with the word *product.* Select one of your college's sports and go through the five terms, describing how each applies to the college sport you chose.
2. Pick one of the following major pro sports (football, baseball, basketball, soccer, hockey, golf, or auto racing) and discuss the importance of offering a digital experience to fans. Describe the various digital offerings now available in that sport.
3. What sports-related apps have you used or purchased? What is your evaluation of the apps? If you have not used or purchased any apps, then locate at least two apps you would like to purchase or download. Describe the benefits of the apps.
4. Identify three sports personalities who you believe have a positive impact on their team or sport. Discuss what type of benefit each generates. Identify three sports personalities who you believe have been detrimental to their team or sport. Why have they been detrimental? What can the team or sport do about their negative impact?
5. Review the three levels of a product that are described in the chapter and shown in Figure 6.4. Apply this concept to some type of entertainment that is not sports related, such as music concerts, movies, or a circus presentation.
6. Review the three levels of a product that are described in the chapter and shown in Figure 6.4. Discuss each level in terms of your college's football team or one of the other sports offered by your school.
7. Review the three types of innovation presented in the chapter. Present a sports example of each type of innovation that is not highlighted in the chapter. Explain why you think your example illustrates that particular type of innovation.
8. Review the four influences on the rate of adoption of a new innovation. Pick a recent sports innovation not discussed in the chapter and go through each of the influences and what the team or sport did to manage the innovation adoption process.

9. One reason horse racing has a difficult time attracting new fans is the complexity of the sport, especially in terms of statistics. Using the Internet, examine some statistics from horse racing. How complex are they to understand? What approaches can horse racing use to make them simpler and attract new fans to the sport?

10. Pick a pro sports team located near your home or college. Which of the brand leveraging strategies discussed in the chapter could the team use to grow revenue? Justify your answer.

You Make the Call
World Baseball Classic

The World Baseball Classic (WBC) is a creation of Major League Baseball aimed at being a world championship event for the sport. The WBC is sanctioned by the International Baseball Federation and has the support of professional baseball leagues around the world. The inaugural WBC was held in March 2006. The second WBC was held in March 2009, with future WBC tournaments planned every four years.

WBC features a sixteen-team field representing countries from across the globe. The event begins with four pools of four teams each that play a round-robin schedule within a pool. The top two teams from each pool advance to round two. Teams in round two are divided into two pools and play a double-elimination round. The winner and runner-up from each of the two pools make it to the semifinals round. The semifinals winners meet in the championship game.[41]

In 2006, the WBC held thirty-nine games at seven international venues over eighteen days. The tournament generated sales of 737,112 tickets, was broadcast in nine languages, and was covered by 5,354 credentialed media members. Japan defeated Cuba 10–6 to claim the WBC title. The United States finished a disappointing eighth place in the 2006 WBC despite having a roster made up entirely of major league players. Financially, the WBC was deemed successful, with Major League Baseball earning an estimated $10–15 million above costs of $45–50 million, including $5 million in television rights fees paid by ESPN only three months before the tournament. Television ratings for the first tournament were solid in the U.S. and soared in Asian and Latin American nations, including a 36 share in Japan for that country's semifinal game with Korea.

The second WBC was held in March 2009. The sixteen-team field was comprised of the following countries:

Pool A	Pool B	Pool C	Pool D
China	Australia	Canada	Dominican Republic
Chinese Taipei	Cuba	Italy	Netherlands
Japan	Mexico	United States	Panama
Korea	South Africa	Venezuela	Puerto Rico

First-round games were held in Japan, Mexico, Canada, and Puerto Rico. Round two and the semifinals/finals were held in the United States. Uncertainty as to whether a baseball tournament held in March would attract interest had been erased by the success of the 2006 WBC. Television broadcasts of WBC games reached more than 200 countries. Japan repeated as WBC champion, defeating Korea 5–3 in the final game. The United States finished in fourth place. Fan interest in the 2009 WBC exceeded the 2006 tournament in terms of ticket sales and TV ratings. Ticket sales increased 8.5% to 801,408. ESPN telecasts of the first two rounds of WBC games saw a ratings gain of 30% (1.3 in 2009 vs. 1.0 in 2006). Increased interest in WBC games is a win for ESPN, which, along with the MLB Network, televised the 2009 WBC games.[42] "We're looking for this to become our own version of March Madness," said Len DeLuca, ESPN senior vice president of programming and acquisitions.[43]

Sponsor interest in the 2009 WBC was greater, too. Although 2006 global sponsors Anheuser-Busch and MasterCard did not renew their deals for 2009, sponsorship revenue increased by over 50%. This growth occurred because more regional sponsorships were sold. For example, rather than having a single beer sponsor for the WBC, five beer companies were involved on a regional basis, such as Asahi in Japan and Presidente in the Dominican Republic. The greatest challenge for signing WBC sponsors in 2009 was in the United States. The weak economy, no first-round games in the U.S., and uncertainty as to whether Team USA would advance past the first round were cited as reasons sponsorship sales were difficult in the U.S.[44]

Despite successes enjoyed by WBC after holding its first two tournaments, there are challenges that remain. One concern is the lack of widespread participation among elite Major League Baseball players. The WBC is held during MLB teams' spring training periods. Some players are reluctant to be away from their MLB teams for two to three weeks at a critical time of preparation for the upcoming season. Also, some players and team owners are worried that participating in WBC games creates an injury risk that is too great to take. If a pitcher hurts his arm while participating in the WBC, he could be lost to his team for an extended period of time and hurt his future earnings potential. MLB players who would have likely been welcomed additions to their country's team but elected not to play included stars such as Albert Pujols, Johan Santana, Ryan Howard, Grady Sizemore, and Josh Hamilton.

While attractive, the World Baseball Classic faces significant challenges.

Another concern is the timing of WBC. It occurs before baseball season, so fan interest may be less in March than if the event were held in summer or in fall after the World Series. One idea for scheduling WBC is to have MLB take an extended all-star break on WBC years and not play an all-star game. Another issue with scheduling WBC in March is the competition for attention it has with college basketball's postseason tournaments. NCAA "March Madness" dominates sports coverage and fan interest for three weeks in March every year. In 2009, the 1.3 rating for ESPN telecasts of WBC games paled in comparison to the 5.4 rating for CBS telecasts of the first two rounds of the NCAA men's basketball tournament. In addition, NBA and NHL are nearing the climax of their regular seasons in March, with teams battling to earn playoff positions. The drama of the NCAA basketball, coupled with that of NBA and NHL seasons winding down, make for a crowded sports landscape at that time of the year. MLB commissioner Bud Selig insists that the March time frame is the only option for WBC: "I know people have said it's the wrong time, but . . . it's really the only time we can do it."[45]

The WBC gives the sport of baseball a high-profile world championship event. It comes at an important time, as baseball has been eliminated as a sport in the Olympic Games. The success of other sport-specific championships like FIFA World Cup soccer and the World Ice Hockey Championships offers the promise that WBC could be elevated to a top-tier global event. However, MLB must generate more interest among baseball fans and corporate sponsors, particularly in the key U.S. market, to transform the WBC from a niche event to a global marquee event.

Questions:

1. Can the World Baseball Classic (WBC) obtain the popularity of other world championship competitions, such as is seen with soccer and hockey? Why or why not?
2. The timing of the WBC seems to be a major issue. Evaluate the pros and cons of the current March time frame as well as having it in July at the All-Star Game break or at the end of the current season. In your opinion, when should the WBC be held? Justify your choice.
3. The WBC is having difficulty gaining popularity in the United States. Why? What can Major League Baseball do to increase the WBC popularity in the U.S.?
4. The WBC has difficulty attracting some of the stars of Major League Baseball. Why? What can be done to encourage a higher level of participation?
5. What concerns do team owners have about players participating in the WBC? Are the concerns legitimate? Why or why not? What can be done to win greater support of the MLB team owners?
6. Evaluate the current format of the WBC games with the pools and selection of venues. What suggestions do you have for improving the format?

References

1. Steve Battista, (2010), Personal correspondence, August 9, 2010.
2. Daniel Kaplan, (2010), "Goodell Sets Revenue Goal of $25B by 2027 for NFL," *Sports Business Journal*, April 5, 1.
3. ""2010 Dynamo Promotional Schedule" (2010), March 31, accessed April 6, 2012 at http://www.bigsoccer.com/forum/showthread.php?t=1380289
4. "Portland Pirates – Promotions," accessed July 20, 2010, at http://www.portlandpirates.com/promotions.asp.
5. Elliott J. Gorn, "Spectator Sport," accessed July 21, 2010, at http://www.answers.com/topic/spectator-sport.
6. Tripp Mickle, (2010), "NHL Expects Total Revenue to Top $2.7 Billion," *Sports Business Journal*, June 28, 1.
7. "American Express to Enhance Fan Experience with Interactive Technology at the 2010 U.S. Open at Pebble Beach," (2010), June 8, accessed July 21, 2010, at http://home3.americanexpress.com/corp/pc/2010/opb.asp.
8. Irving Rein, Philip Kotler, and Ben Shields, *The Elusive Fan* (New York: McGraw-Hill, 2006).
9. "Arena Football League," accessed July 23, 2010, at http://www.niftytv.com/AFL.
10. "ESPN3," accessed July 25, 2010, at http://www.fewpb.com/CableTelecom/ESPN3/tabid/304/Default.aspx.
11. John Ourand, (2010), "Can World Cup Boost ESPN3?" *Sports Business Journal*, May 31, 1.
12. "Sportacular 2010," accessed July 26, 2010, at http://iphone-apps.toptenreviews.com/sports/sportacular-review.html.
13. Michael Smith, (2010), "Speedway's App More Than a Map," *Sports Business Journal,* July 19, 8.
14. BaseballAlumni.com, (2010), accessed July 27, 2010, at http://mlbpaa.mlb.com/mlbpaa/marketing/appearances.jsp.
15. Gary Armstrong and Philip Kotler, *Marketing: An Introduction*, 10th edition (Upper Saddle River, NJ: Prentice Hall, 2011).
16. Michael Phillips, (2011), "New Bat Regulations Change College Baseball," February 16, accessed May 15, 2011, at http://www2.timesdispatch.com/sports/2011/feb/17/tdsport01-new-bat-regulations-change-college-baseb-ar-849101/.
17. "Rays Summer Concert Series," (2010), accessed June 14, 2010, at http://mlb.mlb.com/tb/ticketing/summer_concerts.jsp.
18. Adam Thompson, (2010), "Teams Give Upper-Deck Fans Courtside Service to Keep Season-Ticket Holders Happy," accessed June 18, 2010, at http://www.nba.com/nets/news/All_Access_Online_WSJ_3_19.html.
19. "Discipline Potential Speeds Pace of Game," (2009), June 12, accessed June 18, 2010, at http://mlb.mlb.com/news/article.jsp?ymd=20090609&content_id=5222578&vkey=news_mlb&fext=.jsp.
20. John Ourand, (2008), "Favre's Move Stirs Interest among Ad Buyers," *Sports Business Journal*, August 25, 10.
21. John W. Hawks, (1999), "An Exchange on the Definition of Innovation," accessed June 23, 2010, at http://www.innovation.cc/discussion-papers/definition.htm.
22. "History of Under Armour," accessed June 24, 2010, at http://www.gobros.com/under-armour/under-armour-history.php.
23. "History of the Ultimate Fighting Championship," accessed June 24, 2010, at http://www.ufc.com/index.cfm?fa=learnufc.history.
24. "MMA Leagues: Mixed Martial Arts," accessed June 24, 2010, at http://www.sportspool.com/MMA/mma_leagues.php.
25. "WNBA: Former Teams," accessed July 7, 2010, at http://hoopedia.nba.com/index.php?title=Category:WNBA_Former_Teams.
26. "About Us," accessed July 7, 2010, at http://www.ufl-football.com/about-us.
27. "Bloomberg Fantasy Sports Tools," accessed July 8, 2010, at http://www.bloombergsports.com/mobile/.

28. "MLB.com for iPhone and iPod Touch," accessed July 12, 2010, at http://mlb.mlb.com/mobile/iphone/.
29. "The NASCAR Hall of Fame – Learn About the Hall," accessed July 12, 2010, at http://www.nascarhall.com/about.
30. Christopher Tritto, (2009), "Cardinals, Blues Team up on Promotions," *Sports Business Journal*, March 30, 10.
31. Terry Lefton, (2010), "NFL Licensing Targets: 'Back to Football' and Women's Market," *Sports Business Journal*, March 8, 9.
32. "Yahoo! Sports Fantasy Baseball '10 Named Official Online Fantasy Game for Major League Baseball," *Entertainment & Travel*, March 27, 2010, 20.
33. John Lombardo, (2010), "After Two Years, NBA China on Steady Course," *Sports Business Journal*, May 24, 1, 24–25.
34. Bill King, (2007), "Learning the Culture," *Sports Business Journal*, January 22, 15.
35. Bill King, (2009), "Tapping the Passion," *Sports Business Journal*, April 27, 12.
36. Darren Marshall and David C. Tice, (2009), "Engage Hispanic Race Fans through Speed, Success, Community," *Sports Business Journal*, February 9, 14.
37. Tom Cordova, (2009), "Success Begins with Understanding the Demo," *Sports Business Journal*, April 27, 17.
38. David Caraviello, (2007), "Roush Fenway Makes Its Pitch to Red Sox Nation," June 28, accessed July 17, 2010, at http://www.nascar.com/2007/news/headlines/cup/06/28/cedwards.red.sox.car/index.html.
39. Eric Fischer, (2009), "White Sox Form Silver Chalice Ventures for Revenue Lift," *Sports Business Journal*, October 26, 3.
40. Alexis Muellner, (2009), "Rays Start Marketing Operation," *Sports Business Journal*, September 7, 6.
41. "2009 Tournament Schedule by Venue," http://mlb.mlb.com/wbc/2009/schedule/.
42. "Brown, Maury (2009), "Attendance and Television Ratings Shine for '09 World Baseball Classic," March 15, accessed April 6, 2012 at http://www.bizofbaseball.com/index.php?option=com_content&view=article&id=3080:attendance-and-television-ratings-shine-for-09-world-baseball-classic&catid=76:world-baseball-classic&Itemid=168.
43. Eric Fischer, (2009), "WBC Finds More Support Second Time Around," *Sports Business Journal*, February 23, 4.
44. Terry Lefton, (2009), "Sponsor Revenue Up, But U.S. Remains a Challenge for WBC," *Sports Business Journal*, January 12, 9.
45. Barry N. Bloom, (2009), "Selig: Classic to Get Bigger and Bigger," March 21, accessed April 2, 2009, at http://mlb.mlb.com/wbc/2009/news/article.jsp?ymd=20090322&content_id=4045676&vkey=wbc&team=.

7

Tapping into Passion through Experiential Marketing

Learning Objectives

By the end of this chapter you should be able to:

1. Describe experiential marketing and discuss the reasons for its growth
2. Compare and contrast four experiential marketing strategies
3. Discuss the fundamental considerations of experiential marketing design and implementation
4. Differentiate between three types of sponsorship activation experiences
5. Summarize the strategic issues to consider when designing an experiential marketing program
6. Describe experiential marketing tactics that increase organizational revenue

O_2 uses experiential marketing to connect with customers.

O$_2$ Connects with Experiential Marketing

O$_2$ is the leading mobile communications provider in the United Kingdom, with more than 22 million customers. A unit of Telefónica Europe, O$_2$ has gone from its launch in 2002 to being the number one mobile network in the UK in terms of market share. A key to O$_2$'s success has been its efforts to develop and maintain customer relationships. O$_2$'s customer **churn rate**, a measure of the percentage of the subscriber base that exits their relationship with a company in a given time period, is the lowest among mobile brands in the UK. Also, O$_2$ has received accolades for the quality of its services, being named "Best Network Operator" in the UK two years straight.[1] In a competitive industry in which new technologies and intense marketing continually are used to woo customers, O$_2$ continues to expand its customer base.

Like many brands that target a broad audience, O$_2$ has used sponsorships as a vehicle for marketing to current and prospective customers across the UK. It is the naming rights sponsor of the O$_2$ Arena, a 23,000-seat entertainment venue in London, and O$_2$ Academies, a collection of smaller music venues across the UK. O$_2$ appeals to the passions of sports fans by its sponsorship of the English Rugby Team and Arsenal FC of the Premier League, the UK's top soccer league.[2] When one thinks of a brand sponsoring sports or entertainment, the image conjured is often creating exposure by placing signage at venues and events. Yes, O$_2$ has

Insider Expert Tom Fox – Arsenal FC

Tom Fox is a twenty-five-year marketing veteran and the second-highest-ranking executive with Arsenal of the English Premier League. His current role at Arsenal is the second sports property on Fox's résumé. He worked at the NBA as director of sponsor programs for NBA Properties in 1993, and then went to Hong Kong in 1995 as vice president and managing director of NBA Asia. Following his NBA stint, Fox in February 1997 was hired by Nike to run its Asian sports marketing business. He moved to the company's U.S. operations as sports marketing director in September 1997.

Fox joined former Gatorade parent Quaker Oats in 1985 in its brand management program and moved to Gatorade's sports marketing department in 1988. He returned to Gatorade in 1999 as senior vice president, sports marketing. Fox left Gatorade in 2007 for a consulting position at Wasserman Media Group. He joined Arsenal in 2009.

The objective of this chapter is to stress the importance of experiential marketing in connecting with fans and leveraging their emotional bonds with a sports property. Experiential marketing is an aspect of sports marketing that seems to be better presented through applications and best practices rather than concepts and theories. Tom Fox draws on his work at Gatorade and, more recently, Arsenal to give examples of how experiences can be used to connect sports properties or sponsors with consumers.

Arsenal F.C.

Tom Fox, second-highest-ranking executive, Arsenal of the English Premier League.

signage and other standard benefits of sponsorship, but it is the ways in which it uses experiential marketing that makes O_2's sponsorships relevant and memorable to the target audience.

O_2 has built a customer engagement theme of "priority" into its sports and entertainment sponsorships. Priority is a focus on O_2 customers, giving them special treatment at events sponsored by O_2. While the brand exposure O_2 creates by sponsoring the English national rugby team and Arsenal casts a wide net to the entire audience, its experiential marketing programs serve as a form of reward exclusively for O_2's customers. At English rugby matches played at Twickenham, O_2 customers can send a text message to a designated number and receive a code to scan at the entrance to the O_2 blueroom, a branded area outside the stadium for O_2 customers and their friends. Once inside, guests can have a free meat pie or pint of beer, meet players, and take part in postgame question-and-answer sessions.[3] O_2 provides similar experiences at Arsenal's venue, Emirates Stadium. In addition to O_2 blueroom access, O_2 customers receive priority seating for screenings of away matches and the chance to win exclusive experiences such as watching the team train, meeting players, and coaching at the team's training ground. O_2's engagement with Arsenal fans does not end at the gates to Emirates Stadium; O_2 offers Arsenal text alerts, video, wallpaper, and ringtones.[4]

O_2 successfully leverages the passion of sports through its experiential marketing programs. Like most marketers, O_2 strives to build and strengthen relationships. Adding pleasure and enjoyment to customers' lives by offering them exclusive benefits related to a rugby team or soccer team for which they have great affinity can deepen the bonds between O_2 and its customers. Providing quality mobile communication services is a way to stand out in the market. But, providing unique experiences that are virtually impossible for competitors to duplicate creates a connection between O_2 and its customers that can last far longer than the technology of the latest gadgets.

Introduction

The practice of experiential marketing is increasing in usage across all types of businesses desiring more meaningful, extensive engagement with customers. The idea that consumers have an experience when consuming goods or services is hardly new. Everyday situations such as having a meal at a restaurant, buying fuel for your automobile, and paying bills online are consumption experiences. Consumers interact with a seller, either physically or virtually, and have a multisensory experience while going through the process of acquiring or using the seller's product or service. Unfortunately, many of the consumption experiences in which individuals routinely participate are just that—routine.

Evaluations of the value received can be positively influenced if the process or ritual of consumption is made more enjoyable or exciting. It is here that experiential marketing enters the picture. A distinction can be made between "consumption experiences" and "consumer experiences." Consumption experiences are unremarkable, ordinary steps taken to receive value from a seller. On the other hand, consumer experiences are created by exposure to extraordinary events or stimuli that lead to changes in learning, attitude, or behavior.[5]

Experiential marketing is relatively new as a distinct marketing practice, and because of its brief existence there is a lack of consensus on its definition. A broad definition of experiential marketing from a marketing management standpoint is that it is planned "occurrences designed to communicate particular messages to target audiences."[6] From a consumer's perspective, experiential marketing is a personal response resulting from exposure to or interaction with stimuli that are embedded in events. It is event participation or attendance that leads to consumers' relationship with an object such as a brand.[7] While experiential marketing may be a newcomer in terms of a strategy used to build or strengthen brand relationships with target markets, the roots of consumers' longing for experiences are traced back to the European Romantic period of the 18th century. This period is characterized by individuals seeking states of pleasure or arousal as escapes from the mediocrity of everyday life.[8]

The evolution of experiential marketing has created a need to establish a definition that clarifies its objectives and impact. For the purposes of applying experiential marketing to the sports industry, **experiential marketing** is defined as the creation of a multisensory, interactive environment by a sports property or sponsor designed to add value to a consumer's experience in the short-term and strengthen relationships in the long-term. The effect of a consumer's experiential interaction goes beyond the moment in which the experience occurs. An attendee of an IndyCar Series race can enhance her experience of watching the race itself by going to a drivers' autograph session the day before the race or by purchasing a pit pass that gives access to the garage area. These experiences add to the pleasure experienced while at the race, but more importantly, they create vivid memories that will be relished for years into the future and shared with friends and others.

Why Experiential Marketing?

If experiential consumption is not new to marketing, then why is experiential marketing being treated as an innovative practice? The answer is that conceiving and designing experiences for consumers has become viewed as a strategy for building customer relationships and defining a brand's meaning in the minds of customers. This view is echoed by marketing executive Rebecca Brock, who says, "A brand is no longer what a company wants to proclaim; it's fast becoming the sum of customers' opinions and experiences."[9] If brands are based on customers' experiences, then marketers can benefit by strategically developing experiential contact points with brands to influence brand perceptions. All products contain some level of symbolic meaning for consumers, setting the stage for using experiential marketing to connect the symbolic meaning brands possess to the opinions and feelings of customers. Sports brands are a category that is very rich with symbolic meaning[10] Given this characteristic of sports, experiential marketing can be an effective platform for sports properties desiring to deepen bonds with their fans as well as corporate sponsors that seek to leverage fans' affinity for sports to associations held for the sponsored brands.

Experiential Marketing's Distinguishing Characteristics

Experiential marketing has evolved from a tactic of one-time events to a strategy of managing all contact points customers have with a brand. As this evolution has taken place, three key characteristics have emerged that are central to the success of experiential marketing: sensory experience, interaction, and relationship (see Figure 7.1).[11] The design of experiential marketing programs should incorporate these characteristics to maximize audience impact.

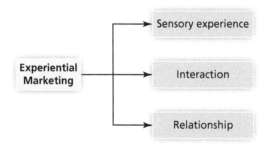

FIGURE 7.1 Key Characteristics of Experiential Marketing

SENSORY EXPERIENCE. One way to engage customers is to appeal to one or more of the five senses (sight, sound, touch, smell, and taste). Even in environments in which customers have a rather passive role such as sitting in their seats during a game, senses are engaged through music, video, signage, fireworks, mascots, and cheerleaders or some other stimulus that will gain interest, appeal to emotions, and intensify feelings of pleasure or arousal. The timing of sensory exposure strengthens the intensity of the experience. For example, a flyover by military aircraft at football games or auto races just before the event begins adds to the anticipation of what is about to take place.

This advertisement by the Atlanta Braves highlights the sensory experience of seeing yourself on the big screen at the baseball game.

INTERACTION. Experiential marketing has changed the role of consumers from recipients to participants in the delivery process. The significance of having customers become more involved is marketers that wish to impact an audience's thoughts, feelings, or actions can use interactive experiences as a means of connection. In the sports industry, this implication extends to sponsors using sports to reach their target markets. A company that has complemented traditional sports marketing with interactive experiences is FedEx. The global logistics company became the venue naming rights partner of the Memphis Grizzlies' home, the FedEx Forum, when it opened in 2004. One way FedEx activated its naming rights sponsorship was to create an interactive area in FedEx Forum known as the FedEx TimeCenter. In this space, visitors can select a destination served by FedEx, listen to musical rhythms and melodies of that area, and learn about historic events, all delivered in a FedEx-branded environment. Rather than a mere passive presence in the form of having its name on the building, FedEx becomes part of the experience of attending events at the FedEx Forum.

RELATIONSHIP. A third characteristic that makes experiential marketing a distinct strategy is its impact on customer relationships. While consumers may be intrigued to engage in experiential marketing offerings at sporting events or via digital media channels because of their novelty or entertainment value, marketers should have a strategic focus that goes beyond the moment. If consumers are willing to invest time and attention to partake of an event or experience, a positive interaction can have a lasting impact on how they feel and act toward the brand or brands involved. For sports properties, these outcomes include creation of favorable brand attitudes (i.e., liking) and desire to stay longer in the service environment and return in the future (i.e., repeat purchases). Similarly, sponsors can reap benefits in terms of creating favorable brand associations via the sponsor's connection to the experience, favorable brand attitudes, brand preference, and brand purchase/repurchase.

Interactivity is highly correlated with relationship building using experiential marketing. Experiences go beyond mere brand exposure offered by traditional media advertising. They create two-way communication between sellers and buyers. IBM has been a sponsor of the U.S.

Open tennis tournament since 1992. Although sponsorship of a major event like the U.S. Open has obvious potential branding impact such as reinforcing brand awareness and shaping brand image, an important part of IBM's sponsorship is the use of client hospitality to show off its technology-based services in action. IBM entertains dozens of clients at the U.S. Open each year, enabling the company to spend extensive time with customers while demonstrating the capabilities of its services.[12]

Other interactive experiences may be less involved and shorter in duration, but they can have a positive impact on customers' relationships with brands, nonetheless. The X Games and Winter X Games add value to attendees' overall experience (and add value to their sponsors' involvement) through an area called X Fest. Visitors to this experiential space enjoy exhibits by partners such as Sony PlayStation and Olympus cameras where they can try new products in an environment in which the sponsor does not have to compete with other brands for consumers' attention.[13]

Reasons for Growth of Experiential Marketing

A combination of factors has contributed to experiential marketing gaining greater interest and utilization among marketers, including sports properties and sponsors. At the heart of experiential marketing's growth has been a desire to better engage customers and other brand stakeholders as well as successfully set apart brands from competition. The specific drivers of this growth are listed in Figure 7.2.[14]

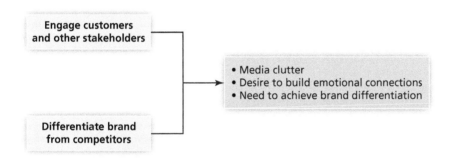

FIGURE 7.2 Drivers in the Growth of Experiential Marketing

Media clutter refers to the large number of marketing messages directed toward consumers in a given communication channel. Mass mediums in particular are plagued by clutter. Consumers can choose from hundreds of magazine titles, television stations, newspapers, and radio options. Even media considered more innovative such as social networking websites and sponsorship are beginning to suffer from media clutter. As a result, competition for consumers' attention is intense, and marketers find it more difficult to capture attention and interest. The immersion and interactivity of events and experiences require active participation by the audience, and as such are much more difficult to ignore.

Sports brands have the fortunate advantage of being admired, liked, and even loved by scores of people. The special bond that sports can create with persons who have an affinity for a particular sport, team, event, or athlete serves as leverage for connecting with customers on an emotional level. This characteristic of sports holds true not only for sports properties; corporate sponsors that associate with sports also stand to benefit from the emotionally charged environment created by sports. And, it should be noted that connecting with an audience through experiential marketing does not necessarily require a physical presence. While on-site experiences at a sporting event often come to mind, all points of interaction are experiential marketing opportunities.

Digital media are a good illustration of using a brand touch point outside of an on-site experience. A larger audience can be reached, and the duration of the connection can be much longer than physically interacting with an event audience. In Canada, food marketer Kraft masterfully linked its brand to the nation's obsession for ice hockey. An experiential program known as Kraft Hockeyville engages millions of Canadians during the NHL season. Communities across Canada can be nominated for the designation "Hockeyville." Finalist communities are selected, and videos from finalists are posted online in which they make a case why they should be named Hockeyville. Voting for the community to be named Hockeyville has attracted nearly ten million participants, and the winner receives funding for upgrades to local hockey facilities and is the host to an NHL exhibition game the following season.[15] Kraft Hockeyville reaches Canadians through their love of hockey, with a focus on the meaning hockey has for youth and adults at the grassroots level.

The need to differentiate brands in the marketplace is related closely to the media clutter problem. More messages competing for an audience's attention and consumers' increasing resistance to pay attention are factors in experiential marketing's appeal because of its capability to have brands noticed and, more importantly, be remembered. A key to achieving brand differentiation is establishing and strengthening customer relationships. Experiential marketing is viewed as a strategy that supports relationship-building objectives. One survey of marketing managers found that 89% agreed that experiential marketing succeeds in building customer relationships for the long term.[16] The high value placed on experiential marketing as a means of achieving brand differentiation is not surprising given its distinguishing characteristics of offering a multisensory environment that encourages interaction and fosters relationships.

Experiential Marketing Strategies

Although experiential marketing is a strategy to engage customers, it is also a tactic to achieve broader marketing goals and objectives. In other words, when managers ask questions like "How will we achieve our objective of a 5% sales increase?" or "What programs are needed to reach our goal of greater top-of-mind brand awareness?" one possible answer might be experiential marketing. The allure of creating exciting interactive experiences that consumers enjoy must be guided by an understanding of the organization's marketing needs. Experiences are not created for the sake of entertaining or dazzling customers. They should be created to support strategies intended to advance a brand or organization. It is conceivable that experiential marketing could be a strategy to achieve many different objectives. But in terms of sports properties and corporate sponsors, the four experiential marketing strategies shown in Figure 7.3 tend to stand out.

FIGURE 7.3 **Strategies of Sports Properties and Sponsors for Experiential Marketing**

- Achieve brand differentiation
- Provide benefits through exclusivity
- Offer rewards to key customers
- Motivate product evaluation and trial

Differentiate a Brand

The need to differentiate brands because of intense competition within product categories was discussed earlier as a factor in the growth of experiential marketing. In addition to challenges posed by the number of competitors or intensity of competitive battles, a marketer's task is often made more difficult by the fact that competitors often have offerings with few, if any, discernable differences. This situation is known as **brand parity**.

If a brand cannot tell a compelling story that it is different, unique, or better in some way, then consumers may not be convinced that they should buy the brand. This issue is particularly relevant for new products. However, the challenge is not limited to new products. Virtually all brands have to figure out how to break through extensive media clutter and brand parity beliefs to engage their target market. The solution to this challenge is not more messages, but developing innovative ways to deliver messages so that: a) the audience can be reached, b) the audience will pay attention, and c) the audience can be engaged with the brand. Marketers agree with this outlook. In a survey of more than four hundred marketing managers, 91% agreed that audience impact *and* cost savings could be realized if media innovation occurs.[17]

One may think of brand differentiation as a challenge faced primarily by brands that fight intense battles for attention and market share with one or more competitors (think Coca-Cola vs. Pepsi or the athletic shoe wars fought by Nike, Reebok, Adidas, and others). Effective communications that result in being viewed as different, unique, or superior by the target market is a lofty goal for any company or brand, regardless of market share.

Gatorade is a brand that uses experiential marketing to achieve brand differentiation while building customer relationships. At first glance, the clutter-busting differentiation benefits of experiential marketing do not appear to be needed by Gatorade as much as other brands in the sports drink category. After all, Gatorade holds a commanding 74% share of the sport drink market.[18] But all is not well, as its share declined 10 percentage points in just two years and is down from a high of 93% two decades ago.[19] Another challenge facing Gatorade is that the core benefit it provides, hydration, can be met by an alternative that was available long before Gatorade and can be accessed easily: water! How does a brand differentiate itself in the face of competition from other sports drinks, other beverages, and consumers who may not be convinced to purchase Gatorade instead of drinking water despite its scientifically proven superiority?

Gatorade uses a variety of experiential marketing programs to move out of a brand parity situation, setting itself apart as the sport drink of choice and making a case for being a better hydration alternative than water. One initiative targeted high school athletes to educate them on the benefits of proper hydration. Gatorade used a mobile locker room that included large-size lockers, white boards, video games, and hydration stations. Athletes received information about Gatorade's G-Series product, consumed it before and during a workout, and took a fluid loss test following the workout. Also, professional athletes visited with event attendees to discuss the importance of hydration. Gatorade's objective was educating athletes and coaches, not selling products.[20] An experience like Gatorade's mobile locker room enables a brand to tell its brand story in an engaging message that successfully differentiates it from other sport drinks and reinforces its value proposition as the pioneer in hydration research for athletes of all ages and levels of competition.

Provide Benefits through Exclusivity

The concept of customer value presented in Chapter 1 focuses on a consumer's evaluation of benefits offered by a product compared with the sacrifices required to acquire and use it. Thus, two basic approaches marketers have for adding value to their offerings are increasing benefits received or reducing sacrifices. From a financial standpoint, it can be argued that the ideal route for marketers to pursue is increasing benefits. Higher selling prices can be justified if consumers deem benefits received from their consumption experience are worth the higher price paid and provided the additional benefits can be offered without adding significantly to costs to deliver the experience. The multisensory environment characteristic of experiential marketing can be used to create engaging, memorable events for consumers that enhance benefits one expects from a sports consumption experience.

Enhancing benefits received in consuming a sports brand can be accomplished by incorporating exclusivity into an offering. "Exclusivity" has two different meanings that can be woven into experiential marketing programs. First, exclusivity can be a theme to communicate existence of a special group that is limited in size or is high in importance. Second, the limited size of a group receiving exclusive benefits may be related to the cost associated with delivering the benefits. In other words, it may be too expensive to offer a benefit to all customers, so it is offered to only a select group.

Exclusivity is used by many National Hockey League teams at the last home game of the regular season—a "shirt off their backs" promotion in which randomly selected game attendees go on the ice after the game and receive the game-worn jersey of a player from the home team. It gives a few lucky fans the chance to meet a player and receive his jersey. The experience is limited to approximately twenty fans (small number), and is well suited to be an experience for a limited group given the cost of the benefit. It would not be feasible to give away jerseys to all attendees at the season finale.

The ways that sports properties can offer exclusivity by enhancing tangible or intangible benefits received is seemingly limited only by their creativity . . . and of course the cost to deliver benefits. Sponsors can reach patrons of sports properties using experiences tied to their partnerships. It is a way to strengthen customer relationships with the sponsor's brand and at the same time create a more satisfactory experience with the sports brand. Lexus has partnered with the Atlanta Braves to offer Lexus owners access to a special parking lot near Turner Field. It is one of the closest parking areas to the stadium, and it creates a "club" for Lexus owners, a way

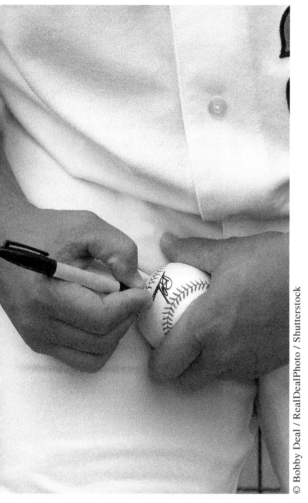

Autograph sessions by baseball stars can be used as an exclusivity benefit.

© Bobby Deal / RealDealPhoto / Shutterstock

of reinforcing their decision to drive a Lexus. In addition to customer impact of the experience realized by Lexus, the Atlanta Braves benefit, too, because fans receiving the benefit of parking in the Lexus Lot may associate the special treatment with the Braves as well. The convenience of parking near the stadium will likely influence their evaluation of the value received from attending Braves games.

Offer Rewards to Key Customers

Utilization of experiential marketing as a reward for key customers allows sports properties and sponsors to leverage its relationship-building and differentiation capabilities. All customers are not equal in terms of their loyalty, revenue impact, and profit contribution. It is a difficult point to accept for marketers who have an ingrained mindset that all customers are important. And, those marketers are correct. All customers are important . . . but some customers are *more* important than others. The fact that some customers spend more on tickets, corporate hospitality, or advertising cannot be overlooked. Given that all customers are not equal in their significance, marketers should deliver value to customers at a level that is commensurate with their importance. Experiences are one way to show appreciation to certain customers and further build emotional bonds.

Rewards delivered through experiences can be extrinsic or intrinsic, with the purpose of both types of rewards being a goodwill gesture that acknowledges a customer's value to the organization. **Extrinsic rewards** are typically tangible objects or items received by customers. The Lexus Lot at Turner Field in Atlanta discussed earlier is an extrinsic reward for Braves ticket holders who are also Lexus owners. They receive the privilege of parking closer to the venue than most fans. Similarly, many sports properties offer season ticket holders extrinsic rewards that add value to their purchase as a form of reciprocation for their commitment to buy multiple-game ticket packages. In addition to preferred parking locations, these may include food vouchers or merchandise (e.g., jersey, T-shirt, or memorabilia item).

Intrinsic rewards add value to recipients by offering intangible benefits that extend beyond value received for the product or service purchased. Intrinsic rewards appeal to consumers' psychological motivations for wanting to enter into a relationship with a sports brand. They may not give recipients a tangible benefit like special parking or premium gifts, but the rewards are memorable interactions that typically have longer and more powerful impact than most extrinsic rewards. For example, the Joliet Slammers, a member of the Frontier League (an independent minor baseball league), offers season ticket holders both intrinsic and extrinsic rewards. Extrinsic rewards such as free tickets to pre-season and post-season games may lack the "wow factor," even though they are tokens of the team's appreciation of these customers. Intrinsic rewards complement extrinsic rewards by providing more personal benefits such as an invitation to an exclusive season ticket holders' pre-season party with team players and staff.[21]

Offering extrinsic and intrinsic rewards through incentives to certain customer segments is a way to differentiate a sports property's most valuable customers and focus on strengthening relationships with them. However, a simple stratification of customers that identifies the top 20% of customers as "key accounts" (applying the 80/20 rule discussed in Chapter 4) may be an oversimplification of identifying a firm's most valuable customers. For example, grouping all season ticket holders as key customers would be an inappropriate strategy. Just as it has been established that not all customers are equal, it can also be said that not all key customers are equal! An illustration of this idea is made using the Houston Rockets of the NBA. Three price points in its twenty-three different 2010–2011 season ticket prices included an upper-bowl end-zone seat for $572 ($13 per game), a lower corner seat for $2,860 ($65 per game), and a mid-range club level seat for $7,920 ($180 per game).[22] The revenue contribution of each of these customers is markedly different, and for that reason the rewards offered to each group should differ to reflect their value to the organization.

The Houston Rockets illustration shows why there is a need for using a tiered approach to offering customer rewards. Grouping key customers into tiers that reflect their importance to the organization is a strategy for managing relationships, and experiential marketing is often used as a strategy to create additional connection points between a sports property and its valuable customers. The number and types of rewards offered increase as the financial value of a particular customer tier increases.

This tiered approach was used by the Tampa Bay Lightning of the NHL. For the Lightning, the most loyal customers would be buyers of half-season plans, full-season plans, and two different premium seating areas. All four tiers of customers received rewards such as an invitation to attend select team practices, locker room tours, and a skate party on the Lightning's home ice. Certain rewards are available to the top three tiers only, such as premium gifts throughout the season, a holiday party, and chalk talk with a member of the coaching staff. The top two tiers have even more intimate interaction with the Lightning by having private autograph sessions with players, concierge service at games, and VIP parking.[23] Many customers that are valuable to an organization in terms of annual spending or lifetime customer value realize their worth and appreciate, if not expect, special treatment. Experiences packaged as customer rewards are a way to meet customers' expectations.

© Don Bayley / iStockphoto

The number and types of rewards offered to customers varies based on their financial value to the sports property.

Similarly, sponsorships are another sports product in which all buyers are not equal. Sponsors represent varying levels of financial value to a sports property in terms of fees, durations, and commitments. Sponsors receive different, typically tangible benefits such as venue signage, advertising exposure, and event tickets depending on their investment in a property. The value of a sponsorship can be enhanced by rewarding key sponsors with experience-based intangible benefits similar to the examples shared for individual consumers. Inside access to events and opportunities for sponsors to demonstrate product capabilities or interact with customers and prospects are tactics sports properties can use to go beyond usual sponsor benefits to offer experiences that serve as rewards for sponsors. Using experiences as rewards for major sponsors is not only a way to acknowledge the value of key partners, but it is also a means of differentiating a sports property that can give it an upper hand in the competition for sponsorship dollars.

Motivate Product Evaluation/Trial

The strategies for experiential marketing programs discussed to this point can lead to achieving vital marketing outcomes that advance a brand in terms of its standing in customers' minds. A fourth strategy for experiential marketing focuses on drawing consumers closer to committing to a relationship by creating experiences in which product evaluation and trial can occur. Interactive environments can be designed to attract people to spend time with a brand, not just be exposed to a brand name, logo, or ad message. Product sampling has long been a staple of sales promotion tactics used to encourage product trial, or first-time use of a product. Product trial is important for marketers because without initial use and evaluation of the value offered, even the best-designed, best-manufactured, and best-priced products will not be purchased or adopted by consumers. Getting products into the hands of prospective customers is a key marketing achievement that must occur. This task is particularly important for new products or brands with little recognition among a target market.

Customer experiences can be designed to create memorable interactions with a brand. Despite the widespread use of sampling as a tactic for gaining product trial, most sampling programs do not exhibit much creativity or imagination. They are usually executed at the point of purchase, such as sampling of a new variety of breakfast cereal in a supermarket. Delivering samples through customer experiences, on the other hand, could result in the brand standing out in consumers' minds due to the absence of message clutter that is often present at point of purchase.

Beverage marketer SoBe has effectively used action sports to reach its target market of primarily young males through sponsorships and experiential marketing. At the U.S. Open of Snowboarding Championships, SoBe had a strong presence that included a branded limousine, fireworks, and a light show. The brand used the experiential event to distribute more than 57,000 samples of its products, making the event SoBe's best activation of a sponsorship.[24] It is one thing for a brand to make claims about product benefits and capabilities in advertising messages; it is quite another thing for consumers to be able to experience a product in action firsthand to make their own evaluations. Experiential marketing can serve as a platform to bring brands and consumers together in a way that allows brands to tell their stories about the benefits provided by their products.

Experiential Marketing Design

Establishing objectives for experiential marketing programs is a necessary first step in putting strategy in place. This section addresses the issue of moving experiential marketing programs from planning to implementation. The three areas shown in Figure 7.4 must be considered when designing experiential marketing programs.

**FIGURE 7.4
Experiential
Marketing Design**

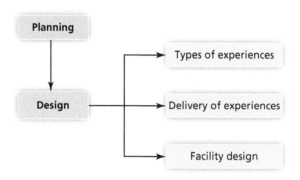

Types of Experiences

The starting point for designing customer experiences is to determine what type of experience should be created to achieve the desired audience impact. Experiential marketing has been discussed so far as a singular concept, but there are different types of experiences that can be created to engage an audience with a brand. Bernd Schmitt, an experiential marketing expert, identifies five types of experiences that are listed in Figure 7.5: 1) sense, 2) think, 3) feel, 4) act, and 5) relate.[25]

**FIGURE 7.5 Types
of Experiences
in Experiential
Marketing Design**

- **Sense experiences** – target sight, sound, touch, taste, or smell.
- **Think experiences** – appeal through surprise, intrigue, and provocation.
- **Feel experiences** – appeal to emotions connected to attitude toward an object.
- **Act experiences** – target bodily experiences, lifestyles, and interactions.
- **Relate experiences** – appeal to the desire to be perceived positively by others.

This framework of marketing experiences goes beyond the strategic decision of "let's do an experiential marketing program" to pinpoint the nature of the interaction desired with the target audience. While it is useful to think in terms of offering specific experiences, a program or event need not be limited to a single experience type. Callaway Golf engages golfers across the United States with its Demo Day events. Participants try out the latest products from Callaway, have their swing analyzed electronically, and learn more about Callaway products from company representatives.[26] Although the event name is Demo Day, the impact extends beyond participants hitting golf balls with Callaway clubs. It is an experience that targets Schmitt's experience types of sense, think, and act, and, depending on participants' involvement with golf, perhaps feel and relate experiences, too.

Delivery of Experiences

Another approach to managing the design of an experience or event focuses on two dimensions of the target audience's relationship to the proposed experience:

1. Participation in the event
2. Connection with the physical environment in which the experience occurs[27]

The first dimension considers one's involvement and level of activity while taking part in an experience. The two levels of delivery are passive and active. Most spectator sporting events would be categorized as passive participation experiences. The audience has little or no active role in the process of delivering the experience. This description does not suggest that sports marketers are powerless to create memorable experiences for audiences whose participation is passive. But in-game experiences must be created with the recognition that it may not be feasible for attendees to take on an active role while in their seats. In contrast, active participation entails the audience being a "doer" rather than a spectator. Active participation experiences may be offered as stand-alone events, such as Callaway Golf's Demo Days, or they can be in-game experiences such as the between-innings contests that are a staple of entertainment at minor league baseball games.

The second dimension of experience design, audience connection to the physical environment in which experience occurs, deals with the physical interaction between consumers and the experience or event. Two levels of physical interaction are absorption and immersion. Experiences delivered in an absorption environment place a barrier of sorts between the event and audience; consumption occurs from a distance. The same event or experience can possess different levels of physical interaction for different attendees. In their book *The Experience Economy*, Joseph Pine and James Gilmore use the Kentucky Derby to illustrate the concept. Fans seated in the grandstands will partake of the race through absorption, while fans watching the race from

Maksim Shmeljov/Shutterstock

Fans along the railing of monster truck will be immersed in the sights and sounds of the monster vehicles.

the rail at track level will be immersed in more vivid sights and sounds of the Derby.[28] Given that different levels of experiences can be delivered at the same event or time (passive vs. active, absorption vs. immersion), opportunities exist for sports marketers to segment their audiences to offer certain types of experiences to specific groups.

The Four Es of Experiential Marketing

Four different kinds of experiences emerge from the combination of the participation and physical interaction dimensions: 1) entertainment, 2) education, 3) escape, and 4) esthetic—the four Es of experiential marketing. Figure 7.6 shows the four types and the dimensions of experience on which they are based.

FIGURE 7.6 The Four Es of Experiential Marketing

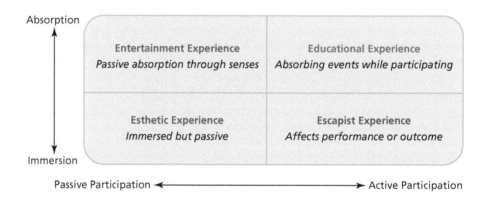

Entertainment experiences are events that are absorbed through the senses, such as watching a sporting event or listening to a concert performance. An entertainment experience for a sports property would be a "caravan" style event in which personalities from an organization speak to groups of fans in different cities. The University of Tennessee's Big Orange Caravan has conducted events across Tennessee and other cities in the Southeast annually for more than twenty years, with head coaches and broadcasters serving as featured speakers.[29] Essentially, all experiences are entertainment, but audience engagement can be strengthened by incorporating additional design elements.

Educational experiences allow an audience to absorb the event through active participation. The FedEx TimeCenter described earlier in this chapter is an example of an experience that has an educational focus. **Escapist experiences** encourage participants to take charge (active participation), requiring immersion in the environment. Fantasy sports games create an experience in which participants assume the role of a team general manager to select rosters, make trades, and perform other personnel decisions made by an actual general manager.

Esthetic experiences limit participants in terms of involvement but thrust them into the event's physical environment. Texas Motor Speedway offers season ticket holders access to a garage party on race days that includes entertainment, food, and driver appearances, as well as the opportunity to purchase discounted pit passes that give them access to pit road during practices and race qualifying runs.[30] This experience puts fans close to the action on the track, albeit in a passive role. Each of these experience types has potential to add value to customers. The challenge for sports marketers is to assess their options to decide which type (or types) would have the greatest appeal to their target market.

Facility Design or Sportscape

The importance of environment in experiential marketing is a major reason that sports properties have put greater emphasis on the quality of their facilities where customers interact with the brand. A boom in the construction of major league and minor league sports venues began in the 1990s and continued into the first decade of the 21st century. Many reasons can be cited for the trend, among them an understanding that a pleasant, exciting environment can enhance customer satisfaction and influence repeat purchase behavior (i.e., attendance of more events in the future).[31] The physical environment in which a service is delivered is referred to as **servicescape**. Known as **sportscape** in the context of sports marketing, the physical environment has an even greater effect on a consumer's evaluation of the service received, the more time spent in the servicescape, and when the service delivers leisure benefits as opposed to functional benefits.[32] The quality of the physical environment for an LPGA tour event would be more influential in attendees' satisfaction judgments of their experience than for a dry cleaner store. Consumers might spend several hours and perhaps multiple days at an LPGA event while spending only a few minutes in a dry cleaner location.

Research into service delivery makes it clear that the servicescape influences customer satisfaction. But how should sports marketers approach managing a sportscape? What factors should be included in designing a high-quality sportscape that can add value to customers' experience with a sports property? As shown in Figure 7.7, five sportscape factors enter into the satisfaction judgments of fans: 1) aesthetics, 2) layout accessibility, 3) seating comfort, 4) electronic equipment and displays, and 5) cleanliness.[33] Even the best efforts to attract customers through advertising, sales force, or even success on the field of play can be negatively affected by failure to manage one or more of these sportscape elements.

FIGURE 7.7
Sportscape Factors Impacting Fan Satisfaction

AESTHETICS. The visual aspects of the physical environment are vital to creating a quality sportscape. As discussed in Chapter 2, aesthetics are a dimension of the physical environment that can influence one's decision to attend sporting events. Aesthetics include a facility's architectural design, colors, and visual attractiveness. Aesthetics have been found to be the sportscape design factor with the greatest impact on perceived quality of a sportscape.[34] Before jumping to a conclusion that the only solution to improving the aesthetics of a venue is to invest in new construction, it must be noted that there are faster, less costly alternatives to strengthening this sportscape dimension. Enhancements such as painting concourse walls and restrooms, hanging banners or murals on exterior or interior walls, or erecting statues that honor a team's heritage or memorialize a legendary player can change the visual appearance of a sportscape. In a challenging economic environment for securing funding for new stadiums, sports properties must be creative in developing short-term actions to enhance the experience offered by their facilities.

LAYOUT ACCESSIBILITY. The convenience and comfort of getting in, moving around, and exiting a sportscape are issues related to layout accessibility. How convenient is entry to the venue from parking or public transportation areas? Once inside the venue, how spacious are walkways and hallways that lead to seating areas? Do the number and location of restrooms meet the needs of event attendees? Do locations of foodservice vendors offer convenience to customers? Is the traffic flow entering and exiting foodservice locations spacious, with minimal intrusion into walkways? These questions fall under the management of layout accessibility. This factor is perhaps more important for sporting events than for many other types of services. If patrons have to wait in long lines for concessions or restrooms, it takes away from time spent enjoying the event. And if layout design does not create smooth flow of traffic through the venue, frustration and perceived crowding may negatively affect the decision to attend future events.

In addition to meeting customers' desires for convenience through a well-designed layout, venue operators have a legal obligation to provide equal access for all persons. The **Americans with Disabilities Act (ADA)** was passed in 1990, and gives mandates about construction, design, and renovation of public accommodations that allow access to people with disabilities.[35]

Convenience and access to a sports venue are important layout issues for fans.

For sports venues, ADA compliance requires a focus on layout accessibility. Wide hallways, elevators, and an adequate number of wheelchair and companion seats are some of the considerations that must be made. New stadium construction, whether it is a new stadium or an addition to an existing stadium, is required to allocate at least 1% of seats for wheelchairs.[36] Renovation projects at existing stadiums are not required to comply with the 1% set aside rule, but it is in a sports property's interests to use the renovation as an opportunity to insure accommodations for disabled patrons.

SEATING COMFORT. The amount of time attendees are seated at a sporting event can range from two to four hours, or longer. This extended period of time spent in a seat makes comfort an important sportscape design issue. Evaluation of seating comfort takes into account arm room, leg room, width of seat, and space between seats. Another aspect of seating comfort is the actual comfort of a seat. For most people, the experience of sitting on an aluminum bleacher may be less enjoyable than sitting in a chair with a back. Also, the presence (or absence) of a cup holder for drinks could affect the evaluation of seating comfort. Sports properties face a delicate balance when managing the layout of a seating area. On one hand, it is clear that providing a comfortable environment for patrons can influence their decision to stay longer (possibly spending more money on concessions) and return for future events. On the other hand, can potential payoffs that come from maximizing space for guests be justified if some seats are removed (and revenue forgone) to provide more space?

As is the case with aesthetics and layout accessibility, many new stadium construction projects are including more spacious designs with the aim of creating a more satisfactory experience. Another reality that is confronting venue managers in the United States is that Americans are getting larger, on average. The percentage of American adults classified as obese more than doubled from 1980 to 2004. By 2006, more than one-third of all adults were obese.[37] This trend means that future stadium construction must take into account that seating comfort needs have changed since the last generation of stadiums were built.

ELECTRONIC EQUIPMENT AND DISPLAYS. The role of marketing incentives in sporting event attendance discussed in Chapter 2 included scoreboards and other electronic displays. These traditional fixtures of sports venues increasingly feature the latest technologies that enhance the multisensory event experience. This element of the sportscape serves functional purposes such as reporting game information (e.g., score and time remaining), venue information such as upcoming events and location of services within the facility, and advertisers' information.

Electronic scoreboards provide information and entertainment in a sportscape.

But it is obvious that electronic equipment and displays provide entertainment benefits, too. Replays of game highlights, playing popular music, and showing movie scenes or recorded skits are ways electronic displays can be used to entertain event attendees. The presence of a modern scoreboard or use of LED signs throughout a venue can positively impact perceptions of sportscape quality. In addition to providing information and entertainment during an event, this sportscape dimension is important because video or audio can occupy time during breaks or intermissions, helping to maintain fans' engagement with the event.

CLEANLINESS. The level of cleanliness maintained in a servicescape has been found to impact consumers' evaluations of retail and service environments.[38] For sportscapes, the appearance of seating areas, floors, restrooms, foodservice areas, and maintenance of trash cans and restrooms have a similar influence on evaluations of the quality of the physical environment. Unclean conditions may go unnoticed when customers spend a short period of time in a servicescape, but when event attendees spend several hours in a venue they may be more likely to observe shortcomings in maintaining a clean environment. The importance of cleanliness must be understood and advocated by facility managers.

Cleanliness and social responsibility can be promoted through on-site recycling programs. Encouraging patrons to recycle used packaging can communicate a message that a sports property cares about minimizing its negative environmental impact. At the same time, it is enlisting the help of event attendees to maintain facility cleanliness. Sioux Falls Arena, home to ice hockey, basketball, and arena football teams, is one of many facilities that have established a recycling program. A "single stream" recycling program lets visitors put all recyclable items in the same container, making the recycling process easy to complete.[39]

Sponsorship Activation

It is obvious that sponsors add value to sports properties by paying rights fees or making in-kind payments of products or services, but they also can add value to a sports property's customers' experience at games and events. Sponsors that include experiential marketing as part of their activation programs not only create interaction opportunities with customers, but they can engage people in ways that leave memorable brand associations with a sponsor long after the experience itself occurs. The message is not that the more outlandish a sponsor's experiential marketing program, the better, but rather that effective experiential marketing is about creating relevant

FIGURE 7.8 Types of Sponsorship Activation Experiences

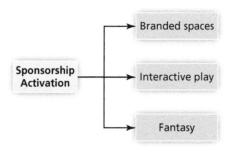

interactions with an audience. The three types of sponsorship activation experiences that can be created are shown in Figure 7.8.

A **branded space** is an area at a venue or event that bears a sponsor's name and is often designed and maintained by the sponsor. Possible marketing objectives for branded spaces include increasing brand exposure, engaging fans, and creating a desired brand personality. A trend toward branded spaces can be found in premium seating areas and club areas at sports stadiums. Branding these locations enhances the physical environment by transforming an area of a venue into a themed space.

Quicken Loans Arena, home of the Cleveland Cavaliers of the NBA, formed a partnership with Patrón tequila. Instead of a nondescript area that contains suites and a bar, the space has been branded the Patrón Platinum Lounge & Suites.[40] Such a partnership adds value to patrons by offering distilled spirits through a recognizable brand in an enjoyable environment. Another branded space is the JetBlue Tarmac at the Bank Atlantic Center, home of the NHL's Florida Panthers. A space outside the arena has been branded with a replica JetBlue tailfin that measures 22.5 feet high and 26 feet wide. The size and location of the JetBlue Tarmac make it a gathering place for fans before and after games.[41] And the unique nature of the life-size jet tailfin will capture attendees' attention and interest in ways that typical signage cannot.

Sponsor activation executed through interactive play is an effective means of engaging a sports property's audience to connect them with a sponsor's brand. **Interactive play activation** goes beyond the exposure benefits of branded spaces. Audiences participate in games or exhibits instead of spending time in the space passively. A higher level of involvement by an audience with interactive experiences has the potential to create more memorable, longer-lasting impact.

Similarly, **fantasy activation** experiences put an audience in a unique, dream-like environment in which they are engaged with a sponsor's brand. One of the most powerful fantasy experiences is having access to the field of play. Sports properties have realized the playing area is a valuable marketing asset, and granting access to a very limited number of people creates exclusive benefits for recipients. Arsenal FC has one of the best pitches (fields) in the Premier League. At the conclusion of a season and before the pitch is replaced for the following season, Arsenal rents the Emirates Stadium pitch to sponsors to entertain clients or host company events. The chance to play soccer in one of the best-known venues in England can strengthen relationships between Arsenal's sponsors and their clients. Participants can take away tangible evidence of their experience such as photos and video. The intangible feelings arising from playing the role of a professional soccer player will last longer than almost any standard type of corporate hospitality event could offer.

An experiential event designed to activate a sponsorship can incorporate more than one activation experience type. Having multiple types of activation experiences is a proper design decision when the audience a sponsor seeks to reach has diverse characteristics. Dr Pepper uses interactive play and fantasy to activate its association with the Southeastern Conference. Dr Pepper SEC Fanfare is held in conjunction with the SEC football championship game each December and men's basketball tournament each March. The events include interactive games such as kicking field goals and shooting baskets, autograph sessions with former star players from SEC teams, music entertainment, and giveaways from SEC sponsors. Dr Pepper uses the "borrowed interest" of SEC sports to connect the brand with fans through SEC Fanfare. It is a single experience in name, but many different experiential opportunities are offered to attendees at one time. Kids and young adults may be attracted to the interactive games; attendees that have followed SEC sports for many years may be excited at the prospect of meeting a star player they remember from the past. Less involved fans may find the festive atmosphere or the music entertainment the most stimulating aspect of the event.

Design Considerations

Experiences and events should serve a strategic purpose. In other words, there are marketing outcomes that should be achieved as a result of investing resources into an experiential marketing program. This statement may seem obvious, but it is important that decisions about the design of experiences and events be consistent with a sports property or sponsor's marketing strategy. The five questions appearing in Figure 7.9 should be asked during the design phase to guide development and maximize the potential of successfully differentiating the brand.[42]

> • Who is the target audience?
>
> • What are the objectives of the experience?
>
> • What does the target audience appreciate most about the brand?
>
> • What approaches have competitors used?
>
> • What practices of noncompetitors can serve as a model for creating experiences?

FIGURE 7.9 Design Considerations

Who Is the Target Audience?

The first question is needed to determine who should be pursued to engage with the brand through an experience or event. Is the intention to narrow the target to a specific group? For example, an invitation-only party for prospective high-dollar season ticket buyers at which guests meet and spend time with coaches and players has a very small target audience. Or, in contrast, is the experience designed to appeal to a wider audience? When the NHL's Nashville Predators invite the public for a skating session on its home ice at Bridgestone Arena, it casts a wide net to attract current and prospective fans with varying levels of involvement with the team. If multiple audience segments are targeted, experience design may need to incorporate multiple experience types (sense, feel, think, act, or relate), as illustrated with the Dr Pepper SEC Fanfare example.

What Are the Objectives of the Experience?

If audience impact desired from exposure to an experience or event cannot be clearly stated, the benefit of investing in the initiative is questionable. Objectives should focus on what happens to the target audience as a result of interaction with the experience. For example, if Full Throttle energy drink had an audience reach outcome objective of "500,000 fans at National Hot Rod Association (NHRA) races will be exposed to our branded space areas," the outcome is measurable, but its effect on creating customer relationships between NHRA fans and Full Throttle is debatable. In fact, brand exposure objectives are not ideal for experiential marketing given the power of experiences and events to capture attention and engage an audience. That is not to say brand awareness and brand exposure objectives should not be part of an experiential marketing program, but these types of objectives should not be the only outcome anticipated from the program. Educating the target audience about brand features and benefits, creating or changing associations that make up brand image, changing attitudes toward a brand, and encouraging product trial are marketing objectives that if achieved can build a brand's standing among its target market.

What Does the Target Audience Appreciate Most about Your Brand?

The creative approach to the design of a customer experience is really no different than the creative execution of advertising messages. Marketers must understand their target audience so that they can determine which types of marketing experiences will resonate with them. In advertising, message appeal is the strategy used to gain an audience's attention in order to present a persuasive message. Some messages focus on delivering information related to the brand such as product features, unique brand benefits, or a comparison to competing brands. Other messages tap into an audience's emotions to communicate how a brand fits with a consumer's lifestyle. There is no single formula for advertising design. Likewise, there is no one strategy for creating customer experiences.

© Denise Kappa / Fotolia

A golf club manufacturer can create unique experiential marketing programs that will differentiate it from competitors.

In experiential marketing, knowing what an audience appreciates most about a brand can lead to decisions on which type (or types) of experiences should be targeted—sense, think, feel, act, or relate. The Gatorade mobile locker room described earlier in the chapter communicates the differential advantage of the brand's hydration technology through multiple experiences—senses (tasting the product), thinking (learning about hydration), feeling (the simulated environment of a professional team locker room), acting (drinking the G2 product before and after a workout), and relating (interaction with guest speaker in small group setting). A well-designed marketing experience need not include all five types of customer experiences, but multiple touch points with a brand increase the potential for an experiential marketing program having the desired impact on the target audience.

What Approaches Have Competitors Used?

Marketing strategy places a premium on being able to differentiate or set apart a brand from competitors. Brand differentiation was cited as an objective that experiential marketing can be used to pursue. Thus, creating customer experiences that are similar to efforts made by competitors to reach the same audience should be avoided. Achieving brand differentiation through experiential marketing is unlikely to be achieved if the design of an experience or event resembled a competitor's experiential marketing campaign. This consideration does not mean that an experience type similar to one created by a competitor should be avoided when designing a customer experience. Competitors of Callaway Golf would not have to limit the design of experiences or events to types not used by Callaway. Experiences that involve sensing (holding golf clubs), thinking (analysis of swing), acting (hitting shots with clubs), and relating (receiving feedback on swing) like Callaway's Demo Days can be created. The challenge is designing an experience in a way that these experiences are delivered uniquely, so that the competitor is not perceived as mimicking Callaway's experiential program.

What Practices of Noncompetitors Can Serve as a Model?

Competitors' experiential marketing tactics can be studied to determine what not to do or what can be duplicated. Likewise, learning from best practices of brands in noncompeting industries can stretch the creative boundaries of a brand's experiential efforts. Brands across many different industries have mastered the delivery of exceptional customer experiences. Why not draw from their experiences to take away strategies or ideas that worked for other brands and apply to one's own experiences or events? Certain brands have developed a reputation for delivering customer experiences that are among the best in their class. A few examples are:

- Entertainment: Blue Man Group, Bonnaroo, Disney
- Retail: Hollister, Nordstrom, Zappos
- Restaurants: Chipotle, Rainforest Café, Starbucks
- Products: Apple, Dyson, Timberland
- Services: Google, IBM, Zipcar

While these brands' core product or service may not be related to sports, they all have the same overarching mission of meeting customers' needs and wants. The approaches used by these brands to create marketing experiences that engage their customers can be a source of inspiration for designing experiences that enable a sports property to reach its experiential marketing objectives.

Revenue Creation Opportunities in Experiential Marketing

Objectives for using experiential marketing discussed earlier in the chapter identified key audience impacts recipients experience such as differentiating a brand from other brands with similar offerings, offering rewards to key customers, and motivating product trial. Another objective of experiential marketing is creating experiences or events that will increase revenues. In some cases, revenue generation may be directly connected to the experience if the audience must pay to participate in the experience. In other cases, revenue growth occurs indirectly, as engagement with a brand through an experience or event may lead participants to engage in behaviors that result in sales for the brand with which they interacted. Visitors to the Patrón Platinum Lounge & Suites at Quicken Loans Arena in Cleveland may be motivated to purchase Patrón in other settings because of their exposure to the brand via the branded space experience. Experiential marketing tactics that can be used to create additional revenue streams for consumer and business markets are shown in Figure 7.10.

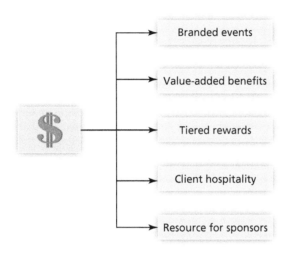

**FIGURE 7.10
Experiential
Marketing Tactics
That Can Create
Additional Revenue
Streams**

Branded Events

A potential marketing asset may exist in an organization, waiting to be tapped. It is in the form of events that a sports property holds to attract fans to generate interest and even sell tickets and merchandise. The untapped potential is in events that could be branded to develop a distinctive identity, in effect marketing the event as a brand extension of the core sports property brand. An event that has evolved into a branded event is Cardinals Care, an off-season three-day "convention" for all things St. Louis Cardinals. The annual Cardinals Care event takes place in January and features autograph sessions with current and former players and coaches, talks by front office staff, exhibits, and auctions. Fans pay up to $40 for event tickets as well as buy tickets for autograph sessions with the most sought after stars. The event serves as a type of cause marketing, too, as Cardinals Care is a fundraiser for the team's charitable foundation.[43]

In addition to direct revenue generation from ticket sales, events like Cardinals Care should be leveraged as an opportunity to promote game or event tickets, officially licensed merchandise, fan clubs, or other products that fans may wish to purchase. Branded events can not only reach thousands of interested people with a single message, but they also present opportunities for corporate partners. Access to a sports property's audience through a branded event gives sponsors an additional channel to reach fans beyond games. Properties benefit from sponsor involvement because rights fees can be used to help offset costs to hold an event. For example, the Washington Capitals are one of several NHL teams that hold preseason fan conventions. The team offsets an estimated $300,000 in costs to hold the convention by signing sponsors.[44]

Value-Added Benefits

Adding value to customers' experience with a brand requires a delicate balance of adding more benefits received for the price paid or reducing sacrifices required to acquire and consume. A temptation that befalls many marketers, including sports marketers, is to attempt to add value by discounting prices (i.e., reducing sacrifices). Two significant risks are attached to this strategy. First, discounting price is a direct hit on profits. The line of reasoning often used to justify lowering price is based on a hope that lower prices will result in a higher sales volume that will more than offset the discount effect. Unfortunately, any gains in sales volume rarely make up for the forgone revenue from the price drop. Second, an issue about which team marketers are particularly sensitive is that price breaks to occasional customers may be perceived as a slap in the face to loyal customers that have purchased multi-game ticket plans. For these reasons, adding value through greater product benefits is a preferable tactic.

Experiences and events are an attractive means of enhancing customer value. In many cases, properties are only leveraging existing assets in a way that provides customers with additional benefits as part of their consumption experience. Locker room tours, player autograph sessions, access to the playing area, and a dedicated customer service representative are tactics that can be used to give customers more benefits for the money paid. In fact, perceptions that a sports property goes all out to provide experiences that make customers feel special and appreciated may justify *raising* prices. The key is whether perceived value from benefits offered is worth the sacrifices required in customers' minds.

Tiered Rewards

The use of tiered rewards is an indirect way to increase revenues from ticket sales and sponsorships. The experience-based assets owned by a sports property can be leveraged to provide rewards for customers as their commitment escalates in terms of dollars spent or number of years as a customer. A theme presented previously is that all customers are not equal. While it is noteworthy to maximize the number of fans or supporters for a team or event, not all of them have the same financial worth to an organization. Rewarding customers for their level of spending not only acknowledges the value of a customer relationship; experiential rewards can be an incentive used in efforts to up-sell customers. A tiered rewards system provides benefits or perks to customers based on establishing tiers, or levels of customer spending. Simply put, the more a customer spends, the more rewards received and the more exclusive the rewards will be (i.e., limited to a smaller number of recipients).

A frequently used approach to offering tiered rewards is to enhance reward packages in the top tiers through experiences or events. A tiered system of ticket buyers for an NBA team might include four tiers: partial-season ticket, season ticket, season ticket club level, and season ticket premium level. As depicted in Figure 7.11, the number of customers in each tier varies, as does the financial value of customers in each tier. As customer commitment required escalates, fewer customers move to a higher tier. Also, "membership" in the top tiers may be exclusive due to a limited number of club- or premium-level seats. The relatively small number of customers as a proportion of a sports property's customer base in the highest tiers should receive more experience-based benefits.

The exclusivity of certain experiences coupled with cost considerations of delivering those experiences makes offering unique experiences to an organization's best customers an appropriate strategy. Several NFL teams have surprised a small, select number of customers by having

FIGURE 7.11 Example of Ticket Consumer Tiers for an NBA Team

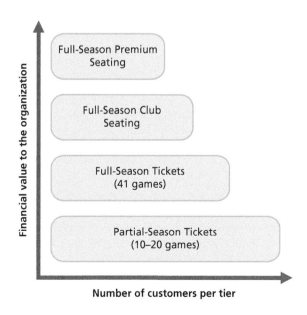

players deliver season tickets to their homes or businesses. This experience would be impractical to deliver beyond ten to twenty customers each season because of the limited availability of players to perform marketing tasks. But, for the lucky few customers who had their tickets delivered by an NFL player, it is an experience that acknowledges their value to the organization.

Client Hospitality

For businesses that use sports as a marketing vehicle to reach their customers, entertaining clients or prospects at a game or event is an extended sales call. They can engage clients in a more casual, exciting environment that is usually not offered in typical business meeting settings. Client hospitality at sporting events is used to get to know new customers or prospects, renew acquaintances with existing customers, and reward key customers with unique experiences. These strengths of client hospitality, along with the interest in sports in popular culture, create lucrative revenue opportunities for sports properties to market events and experiences for business customers. The actual product that sports properties sell is a game or event, but the actual product is augmented with amenities and experiences that create greater impact on a business customer's guests than attending just the event itself. It is the augmented features packaged for business customers that make client hospitality an important revenue stream.

So what exactly do sports properties offer in client hospitality packages that make them popular among business customers? Typical packages for sports that generate significant revenues from hospitality marketing such as PGA Tour and NASCAR include event tickets for guests, an area to entertain guests such as a tent or chalet, catering services, parking passes, and cobranded merchandise featuring logos of the sports property and the business customer. Premier hospitality packages at top-tier events such as the Super Bowl and Kentucky Derby include hotel accommodations and celebrity guest speakers, enabling these properties to command a price premium for these marquee events.[45]

Two different approaches can be used when selling hospitality packages. One, a sports property handles the sales and marketing of hospitality itself. Two, hospitality packages are sold

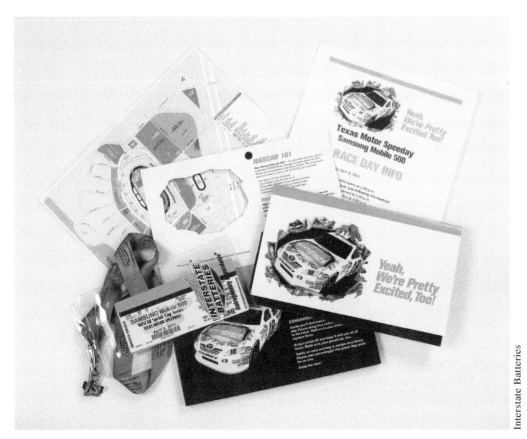

Example hospitality materials from Interstate Batteries for the NASCAR Sprint Cup Series at the Texas Motor Speedway.

to an agency or firm that markets them to businesses on behalf of the property. Client hospitality customers not only create revenue for sports properties by tapping the business market for new customers, but a business's guests also add to revenues indirectly by purchasing concessions and licensed merchandise while at an event.[46]

Resource for Sponsors

A corporate sponsor partners with a sports brand to gain access to an audience whose characteristics match the sponsor's target market. Ultimately, the sponsor desires the access in order to engage the audience in a business relationship. Achieving brand awareness and shaping brand image are important foundations that sponsorship can deliver, but if the impact on audience behavior does not result in sales increases or new customers, the partnership will have not realized the desired end result. So, sports properties should evaluate how they can be a resource for sponsors to achieve their business objectives. Creating experiences or events that co-brand property and sponsor can allow sponsors to create revenues from their association with a sports property. In turn, this approach to using experiential marketing adds value to sponsorships and can be built into the value of rights fees charged.

The design of marketing experiences can be done in a way to appeal to a sponsor's customers or prospects. A branded space can transform a generic space at a venue such as a concessions stand or parking lot into a branded experience that creates interaction between customers and a sponsor's brand. More intimate contact between audience and sponsor delivers greater impact on the customer's relationship with the sponsor than passive contact points such as signage and advertisements.

Branded events can be developed that connect a property's sponsors with potential customers and give sponsors tools to market more effectively through sports. It is understood that sponsorship enables a brand to connect with a sports property's customers, but why not call on sports properties to bring together their corporate partners to learn from each other? More importantly, why not call on properties to bring together their partners to explore opportunities for how the partners can do business *with each other*? Sponsorship management and implementation tactics are including more education and networking events that put a property's partners in front of one another to discuss their businesses.

Sponsors are increasingly looking for this resource from sports properties. An example of a response to sponsors' desires for a property being a resource for business development is the MSG Presidents Club. MSG Sports, which includes the New York Knicks, New York Rangers, New York Liberty, and Hartford Wolf Pack, created the group to provide a forum for the exchange of ideas between its corporate sponsors, suite holders, and season ticket holders. The group was put together at the request of some corporate partners that saw cross-selling opportunities between the companies that market through MSG Sports properties.[47]

Insider Insights Tom Fox – Arsenal FC

Q. During your tenure at Gatorade, you oversaw the company's sports and events marketing. Can you give an example of how an understanding of the consumer is essential in creating experiential marketing programs?

A. In the 1970s, '80s, and early '90s, Gatorade played in a category that it created called Sports Drinks. Throughout most of these three decades its share was either in the 90s or mid 80s. But in the early '90s the brand leadership began to realize that this category was potentially too narrow and limiting and really did not define the more aspirational opportunity that would lead to greater growth.

Tom Fox relates his thoughts on creating experiential marketing programs.

This realization came on the back of a strong piece of consumer segmentation research which began to categorize users by their activity levels, frequency, and mindset about the role that physical activity played in their lives. It ranged from a group called "contented inactives," people who were not active and didn't care to be, all the way to competitors, people who played sports to win. The latter were a small group but per capita had the most occasions (frequency). As importantly, they were the leaders, the ones even more casual athletes looked to for information about products and what worked. This is where Gatorade began focusing its efforts because even though they were not the largest group, there was a belief that you could be inclusive by being exclusive, a belief which proved to be true in later research.

Gatorade began to create a new category frame of reference called "Active Thirst" on the back of this and other research they were doing at the time, and this category definition went a long way to more accurately define their true category, and it suddenly opened up a huge opportunity. Within this new category, Gatorade's share was now only around 12%, and among their heaviest users, people who believed in Gatorade's efficacy and loved the brand, Gatorade was only consumed once every four occasions. Their best, most loyal customers were drinking something they did not believe to be as effective, as good, or as satisfying in the moment a staggering three out of four occasions. A look at the other beverages that people were consuming when hot, sweaty, and physically active (what should have been only Gatorade's domain) showed that water dominated, but juices and soft drinks were also in use.

Water usage was driven by free availability, water fountains mainly, as well as the unassailability of water's goodness. Hard to poke holes in water's story and tell people not to drink it when Gatorade's whole reason for being was hydration. Soft drinks were driven by vending machine availability. If you were at a park and were thirsty, you bought what was close, and Gatorade being part of Quaker at the time had very little cold availability at the "point of sweat." Convenience stores were Gatorade's answer to vending machines but that required the consumer to think ahead and plan; to buy a Gatorade, bring it with them, and find a way to hopefully keep it cold. So in order to make this happen, the consumer had to see fairly a compelling reason to choose Gatorade, an expensive and not broadly available option in cold form, over free and easy water. And this was where experiential came into being.

In 2000, Gatorade took a look at its seventy-plus sponsorship agreements with top colleges and universities and spotted an opportunity. On many of these campuses the coaches ran lucrative summer camps where kids paid good money to learn basketball from Coach K, football from Urban Meyer, and over a dozen other sports from the finest coaching brands in the country. Putting Gatorade into these camps, and asking the coaching and athletic training teams to explain why Gatorade was there, why they used Gatorade for their athletes, and then reinforcing usage through frequent hydration breaks—it was amazing it had not been thought of sooner. So, these athletes would no more leave the house without a Gatorade in their backpack as they would forget their cup or their shoes. In their minds it became fundamental sports equipment and they had to have it with them. Gatorade's business from 2000–2005 had a double-digit compound annual growth rate (CAGR) in what was thought to be a mature market.

Chapter Summary

The concept of experiential marketing is gaining in popularity and is being used by all types of businesses. Experiential marketing is the creation of multisensory, interactive environments by a business designed to add value to a consumer's experiences in the short run and strengthen relationships in the long run. Because experiential marketing can build strong bonds with fans, it is now being used by sports marketers.

Experiential marketing is distinguished by three characteristics: sensory experience, interaction, and relationships. Sensory experience is when the marketing experience involves one or more of the five senses. Experiential marketing changes the role of consumers from passive recipients to active participants. The goal of such experiences is to develop lasting, bonding relationships with customers.

Experiential marketing has grown out of the need to differentiate brands due to increased media clutter and brand parity. While experiential marketing can be used to fulfill a number of marketing objectives, the best match occurs when experiential marketing is used to meet the objectives of 1) achieving brand differentiation, 2) providing benefits through exclusivity, 3) offering rewards to key customers, and 4) motivating product evaluation and trial. In designing an experiential marketing event, marketers need to consider 1) the types of experiences, 2) how those experiences will be delivered, and 3) facility design. Five types of experiences can be designed. These include sense experiences, think experiences, feel experiences, act experiences, and relate experiences.

By examining the level of a fan's involvement and the level of interaction with the physical environment, a 2 × 2 matrix can be developed identifying the four Es of experiential marketing. An entertainment experience involves a high level of absorption and passive participation. An educational experience has a high level of absorption and a high level of participation. Esthetic experiences involve immersion and passive participation while escapist experiences involve immersion and active participation.

When it comes to the physical facility, or sportscape, five factors should be considered: aesthetics, layout accessibility, seating comfort, electronic equipment and displays, and cleanliness. Each is important to ensure fan satisfaction with the physical facility and experience with the brand.

Sponsors should also be involved in experiential marketing. Three types of sponsorship activation experiences can be created. These are branded spaces, interactive play, and fantasy. Partnering with sponsors in developing experiential marketing programs can be a win-win situation for both parties.

In designing an experiential marketing program, it is important that it meet a strategic purpose. Some questions that should be answered include:

- Who is the target audience?
- What are the objectives of the experience?
- What does the target audience appreciate most about the brand?
- What approaches have competitors used?
- What practices of noncompetitors can serve as a model for creating experiences?

Experiential marketing programs can create additional revenue streams for a firm. Some income will be related directly to the experiential campaign while other revenue will be seen indirectly. Experiential marketing tactics that can be used include branded events, value-added benefits, tiered rewards, client hospitality, and being a resource for sponsors.

Review Questions

1. Why is experiential marketing an effective strategy for sports properties?
2. What are the three key characteristics of experiential marketing?
3. What factors have contributed to greater interest in and utilization of experiential marketing?
4. What are four objectives for which experiential marketing is an appropriate strategy?
5. What is the difference between intrinsic and extrinsic rewards?
6. What three areas must be considered when designing experiential marketing programs?
7. Identify the different types of experiences in experiential marketing design and define each one.
8. Explain the four Es of experiential marketing.
9. Identify the five factors of physical design that impact fan satisfaction.
10. Why is the physical environment of a sports property called a servicescape, or sportscape?
11. Describe the various types of activation experiences available for sponsorships.
12. Experiences and events in experiential marketing should serve a strategic purpose. Describe the experiential design considerations that should be considered.
13. Discuss experiential marketing tactics that a sports property can use to create additional revenue streams.

New Terms

Churn rate measure of the percentage of customers that exit their relationship with a company in a given time period.

Experiential marketing creation of a multisensory, interactive environment by a company or brand designed to add value to a customer's experience.

Brand parity market situation where competing firms (or brands) are viewed as having offerings with few, if any, discernable differences.

Extrinsic reward reward that has tangible value to a consumer.

Intrinsic reward reward that has intangible, internal meaning to a consumer.

Entertainment experiences events that are absorbed through a consumer's five senses.

Educational experiences events that are absorbed through active participation.

Escapist experiences events that encourage participants to become actively involved with immersion in the environment.

Esthetic experiences events that limit participants in terms of involvement, but immerse them in the environment.

Servicescape physical environment in which a service is delivered.

Sportscape physical environment in which a sport is delivered.

Americans with Disabilities Act (ADA) federal law that establishes guidelines for construction, design, and renovation of public accommodations (including facilities such as sports venues) to provide access to people with disabilities.

Branded space area at a venue or event that bears a sponsor's name.

Interactive play activation audiences are participants in games or exhibits within a branded space or sponsor's brand.

Fantasy activation audience is put in a unique, dream-like environment where they are engaged with a sponsor's brand.

Discussion and Critical Thinking Exercises

1. After reading this chapter, can you think of an experiential marketing program in which you participated? Describe the experience. Evaluate the experience from the viewpoint of the brand or company. What could have been done differently to improve the experience?
2. Pick one of the sports at your college. Describe an experiential marketing program that could be used by the sport. Before you decide on the experiential marketing program, which of the objectives listed in Figure 7.3 will it fulfill?
3. In developing experiential marketing programs, which do you consider to be more important, extrinsic or intrinsic rewards? Why? Describe the types of extrinsic and intrinsic rewards that would be important to you in an experiential marketing program.
4. Suppose the local golf course would like to use experiential marketing to attract new golfers. Design an experiential marketing program that could be used. Discuss the various types of experiential marketing programs in terms of the types of experiences listed in Figure 7.5.
5. Pick a major professional sports team that is located near you. Describe how the professional team could use the four Es of experiential marketing to design experiential marketing programs. Describe an event for each of the four Es.
6. Examine the four Es of experiential marketing in Figure 7.6. Discuss each one in terms of your personal experiences. Which ones are most effective at getting you to participate? Why?
7. How important is the physical facility, or sportscape, in your attendance at sporting events? Describe a sportscape that you like and is well designed. Why do you like it?

Describe a sportscape that you believe is poorly designed. Why? What does the sports property need to do to attract more fans, in terms of the sportscape?

8. Examine the sportscape factors listed in Figure 7.7. List them in the order of importance to you, in terms of fan satisfaction. Discuss why you listed them in that particular order.

9. Using the design considerations listed in Figure 7.9, design an experiential marketing event for a sports property by answering each of the questions listed. Pick either a sports team that is your favorite or one that is close to you. It can be either a professional or collegiate team.

You Make the Call
C Spire Wireless

C Spire Wireless is a privately held wireless communications carrier. The company was founded as Cellular South on the Mississippi Gulf Coast in 1988 and is headquartered today in Ridgeland, Mississippi. For the first twelve years, the company's network area consisted only of the state of Mississippi. In 2000, coastal Alabama and the Florida Panhandle were added to Cellular South's service area. The next year, the company expanded its network into southwest Tennessee, including the Memphis market. The company rebranded itself as C Spire Wireless in 2011.

Cellular South places an emphasis on sponsoring high school sports.

C Spire Wireless is competitive with national carriers in terms of calling plans offered. Similarly, C Spire Wireless's text messaging plans allow customers to enjoy more use from the service than its competitors through its Unlimited Nationwide Text Messaging Plan. Despite the appeal of C Spire Wireless service plans, the company's size is only a fraction of that of the major wireless companies. Verizon Wireless has about 33% of the U.S. wireless subscriber market, AT&T has 31% market share, and Sprint Nextel has 16%. In contrast, C Spire Wireless has less than 1% market share. Although C Spire Wireless's market area is small compared to the major national wireless carriers, it is challenged to get noticed in a competitive market that includes companies with enormous marketing budgets. AT&T and Verizon Wireless each spend more than $2 billion annually on advertising and both Sprint and T-Mobile spend more than $1 billion.

C Spire Wireless's history of using sports as a marketing vehicle goes back to the very first call placed over the company's network. On February 4, 1988, Ole Miss football legend and former NFL quarterback Archie Manning called then U.S. representative Trent Lott at his Washington office. Since then, sports have been an important part of the company's marketing strategy. Today, C Spire Wireless partners with a variety of high schools, colleges, and professional sports properties through sponsorship. The sponsorships give the company a connection point with audiences in most major C Spire Wireless geographic markets. Also, the sponsors enable the company to reach consumers through their emotion-filled relationships with their high school and college sports teams. A summary of C Spire Wireless sponsorships appears in Figure 7.12.

C Spire Wireless is heavily involved in sports sponsorships throughout the geographic markets it serves. For most of its sponsorships, C Spire Wireless has focused on brand exposure objectives such as creating brand awareness and getting media exposure for the company through its association with sporting events. Now, C Spire Wireless desires to elevate its sponsorship program to a higher level. Brand exposure is nice, but it is an outcome focused on the brand, not customers' relationship with the brand. So the challenge facing C Spire Wireless is how to use its relationships with sports properties in a way that enables the company to take advantage of people's passion for sports. Ultimately, C Spire Wireless wants to grow revenues and subscribers, and it views sports as a means for pulling customers through the "think" and "feel" stages of experiential marketing.[48]

Sponsorship	Description
C Spire Outstanding Player Awards	Recognize top collegiate players in Mississippi • Conerly Trophy (football) • Howell Trophy (basketball) • Ferriss (baseball)
Mississippi State University University of Mississippi (Ole Miss) University of Southern Mississippi University of Memphis	• Sponsorship of football, basketball, baseball, and Olympic sports teams • Designated "official wireless provider" • Football coaches' headsets bear CS logo
Mississippi High School Basketball Championship Tournament	Boys' and girls' tournaments held in Jackson, MS

FIGURE 7.12 C Spire Wireless Sports Sponsorships

Questions:

1. Review Exhibit 7.12. Evaluate the current list of sponsorships in terms of effectiveness for C Spire Wireless. Which sponsorships do you think are a good match, and which are not a good match? Why?
2. Do you believe C Spire Wireless is wise to invest money into sponsoring so many different sports properties, or should they concentrate on just a few? Justify your answer.
3. Do you think C Spire Wireless should invest more money in traditional advertising and less on sports sponsorships? Why or why not? What potential customers are they not reaching with their sports involvement? How important are these potential customers, and should they modify their marketing approach to reach this group also? Why or why not?
4. Figure 7.8 identifies three types of sponsorship activation experiences. Discuss each one in terms of C Spire Wireless's current sports sponsorships.
5. Based on information in this chapter, design a comprehensive experiential marketing program that C Spire Wireless could participate in with one of the sports entities identified in Figure 7.12.
6. Pick two other sports properties from Figure 7.12. Describe ways experiential marketing can be used to enhance the C Spire Wireless brand and engage fans with the brand as well as the sports property.

References

1. "O$_2$ News Center," accessed April 13, 2012 at http://news.o2.co.uk/About-O2/Awards-Recognition-219.aspx .
2. "O$_2$ Sponsorship," accessed May 31, 2010, at http://www.o2.co.uk/abouto2/o2sponsorship.
3. "Twickenham Stadium Blueroom," accessed May 31, 2010, at http://www.o2blueroom.co.uk/microsites/twickenham/.
4. "O$_2$ & Arsenal," accessed May 31, 2010, at http://www.o2.co.uk/abouto2/o2sponsorship/o2arsenal.
5. Emma H. Wood, (2009), "Evaluating Event Marketing: Experience or Outcome?" *Journal of Promotion Management*, 15, 247–268.
6. Philip Kotler, *Marketing Management*, 11th edition (Upper Saddle River, NJ: Prentice Hall, 2003).
7. Bernd H. Schmitt, *Experience Marketing* (New York: The Free Press, 1999).

8. Antonella Carù and Bernard Cova, (2003), "Revisiting Consumption Experience: A More Humble but Complete View of the Concept,"*Marketing Theory*, 3(2), 267–286.

9. "Experiential Marketing: Q&A Homebase," (2010), *Marketing Week*, April 15, 21.

10. Morris B. Holbrook and Elizabeth C. Hirschman, (1982), "The Experiential Aspects of Consumption: Consumer Fantasies, Feelings, and Fun," *Journal of Consumer Research*, 9 (September), 132–140.

11. Gavin Finn, (2009), "A Dimensional View of Experiential Marketing," January 19, accessed April 28, 2010, at http://www.brandchannel.com/brand_speak.asp?bs_id=210.

12. Daniel Kaplan, (2009), "IBM Renews Deals with U.S. Open Tennis," *Sports Business Journal*, July 20, 1.

13. "Winter X Games 13 Sponsors," (2009), January 13, Accessed May 5, 2010, at http://espn.go.com/action/news/story?id=3810984.

14. Wood (2009).

15. Jeromy Lloyd, (2010), "Kraft's Scores with Hockeyville at Sponsorship Marketing Awards," *Marketing*, April 10, accessed May 10, 2010, at http://www.marketingmag.ca/news/marketer-news/krafts-scores-with-hockeyville-at-sponsorship-marketing-awards-2326?.

16. "Is Experiential the Future of Marketing?" (2012), March 29, accessed April 13, 2012 at http://www.bizcommunity.com/PressOffice/PressRelease.aspx?i=121735&ai=73066.

17. "Is Experiential the Future of Marketing?" (2012).

18. Burt Helm, (2009), "Gatorade Sales Plummet," *Business Week*, April 24, accessed May 12, 2010, at http://www.businessweek.com/the_thread/brandnewday/archives/2009/04/gatorade_sales.html.

19. Natalie Zmuda, (2008), "Why Gatorade Is Losing Its Zip," *Advertising Age*, April 21, accessed May 12, 2010, at http://adage.com/article?article_id=126538.

20. Patricia Odell, (2010), "Gatorade Takes High School Athletes Through G-Series Paces," *Promo*, May 6, accessed May 12, 2010, at http://chiefmarketer.com/news/gatorade-takes-high-school-athletes-through-g-series-paces? .

21. "Season Tickets," accessed April 13, 2012, at http://jolietslammers.com/tickets/season-tickets.

22. "Seat Map – 2010–11 Prices," accessed May 19, 2010, at http://www.nba.com/media/rockets/seatmap_201011SeasonwPrices.pdf.

23. "2010–2011 Lightning Season Ticket Holder Benefits," accessed May 20, 2010, at http://lightning.nhl.com/club/page.htm?id=50453.

24. "SoBe Activation Case Study," accessed May 21, 2010, at http://www.fusemarketing.com/modules.php?name=Content&pa=showpage&pid=96&cs=2&nav=2&subnav=8&c_cs=2.

25. Schmitt (1999).

26. "Callaway Golf Demo Days," accessed May 23, 2010, at http://www.callawaygolf.com/global/en-us/customfitting/demodays.html.

27. B. Joseph Pine and James H. Gilmore, *The Experience Economy* (Boston: Harvard Business School Press, 1999).

28. Pine and Gilmore (1999).

29. "Big Orange Caravan," accessed May 23, 2010, at http://alumni.tennessee.edu/chapters/caravan.shtml.

30. "2012 Season Ticket Holder Benefits," accessed April 13, 2012 at http://www.texasmotor-speedway.com/Tickets/Season-Tickets/Season-Tickets.aspx.

31. Mary Jo Bitner, (1992), "Servicescapes: The Impact of Physical Environment on Customers and Employees," *Journal of Marketing*, 56(April), 57–71.

32. Kirk L. Wakefield and Jeffrey Blodgett, (1994), "The Importance of Servicescapes in Leisure Service Settings," *Journal of Services Marketing*, 8(3) 66–76.

33. Kirk L. Wakefield and Jeffrey Blodgett, (1996), "The Effect of the Servicescape on Customers' Behavioral Intentions in Leisure Service Settings," *Journal of Services Marketing*, 10(6), 45–61.

34. Wakefield and Blodgett (1996).

35. "ADA Accessibility Guidelines," accessed May 24, 2010, at http://www.access-board.gov/adaag/html/adaag.htm#purpose.

36. Bill King, (2007), "Renovations Highlight Need for Clearer Rules," *Sports Business Journal*, July 16, 18.

37. "Obesity among Adults in the United States—No Significant Change Since 2003–2004," accessed May 24, 2010, at http://jama.ama-assn.org/cgi/content/full/303/3/235?ijkey=ijKH q6YbJn3Oo&keytype=ref&siteid=amajnls.

38. Wakefield and Blodgett (1996).

39. "Going Green," accessed May 25, 2010, at http://www.sfarena.com/contact_info/ going_green.

40. "Coast to Coast," (2010), *Sports Business Journal*, March 22, 44.

41. Florida Panthers (2010), "Bank Atlantic Center Unveils JetBlue Tailfin," accessed May 26, 2010, at http://panthers.nhl.com/club/news.htm?id=521624.

42. Emma H. Wood, (2009), "Evaluating Event Marketing: Experience or Outcome?" *Journal of Promotion Management*, 15, 247–268; Bernd H. Schmitt, *Experience Marketing* (New York: The Free Press, 1999); Jon Show, (2009), "A Host of Issues for Hospitality," *Sports Business Journal*, August 17, 1.

43. Matthew Leach, (2010), "Cardinals Winter Warm-Up Set to Kick Off," January 15, accessed May 29, 2010, at http://stlouis.cardinals.mlb.com/news/article.jsp?ymd=20100115&content_ id=7925628&vkey=news_stl&fext=.jsp&c_id=stl.

44. Tripp Mickle, (2009), "NHL Teams Flock to Conventions," *Sports Business Journal*, August 31, 8.

45. Jon Show, (2009), "A Host of Issues for Hospitality," *Sports Business Journal*, August 17, 1.

46. Show (2009).

47. Terry Lefton, (2009), "New MSG Team Touts Spirit of Cooperation," *Sports Business Journal*, June 22, 3.

48. "About C Spire Wireless" accessed April 13, 2012 at http://www.cspire.com/ company_info/about/?_requestid=23751?.

8 Planning the Brand Story – Communications Strategy

Learning Objectives

By the end of this chapter you should be able to:

1. Describe the features and benefits of integrated marketing communications (IMC)
2. Differentiate between pull and push marketing strategies
3. Discuss the fundamentals and implications of IMC objectives
4. Explain the principles and steps of the hierarchy of effects model for sports brands

The Coca-Cola Racing Family.

NASCAR: A Family Tradition for Coca-Cola

Coca-Cola is an iconic global brand. Despite the tremendous amount of familiarity and good-will it has built over the years, Coca-Cola faces marketing challenges to its standing as the market leader in carbonated beverages. An obvious challenge comes from its chief beverage

Insider Expert Beatriz Perez – Coca-Cola

Beatriz R. Perez is the chief sustainability officer for the Coca-Cola Company. She is responsible for creating and overseeing Coca-Cola's integrated global sustainability strategy; setting high-level goals and commitments; assessing and driving scaled investments; and stewarding and tracking all global partnerships and key sustainability projects through the company's Office of Sustainability.

Perez most recent role has been chief marketing officer for the North America Division of the Coca-Cola Company. She was responsible for knowledge and insights, consumer communication, brand programming, media, sports/entertainment, interactive marketing, African-American consumer marketing, Hispanic-American consumer marketing, marketing capability, and the university marketing recruitment program. Bea's role was critical in this continuously changing landscape, where content and contacts are integrally linked to bring all of Coke's North American brands to life.

Previously, Perez has been senior vice president of Integrated Marketing for Coca-Cola North America, where she and her team have made significant contributions in bringing Coca-Cola brands to life with consumers in a continuously changing landscape. Bea has been responsible for negotiating and leading efforts with media, interactive entertainment, and sports partnerships, including NASCAR, PGA, U.S. Olympic Committee, NBA, LeBron James, *American Idol*, Dick Clark Productions, the Oscars, Ryan Seacrest, and many others across film, music, television, and sports.

Perez's accomplishments include recently launching the Coke Digital Network (CDN), an innovative media communication tool, and developing the company's award-winning Motorsports marketing platform, which launched Coca-Cola as the official soft drink of NASCAR, created the Coca-Cola Racing Family, and secured a partnership with International Speedway Corporation, which includes the prestigious Daytona 500. Bea served as a member of the Women's Leadership Council from 2007–2009, advising Muhtar Kent and the senior leadership team on ways to increase the number of women in senior leadership positions, specifically focusing on general management positions.

Perez continues to be recognized externally for her achievements. In 2009, she was inducted into the American Advertising Hall of Achievement and led her team in winning the Sports Business Awards by *Sports Business Journal*. In 2007, she was named the Industry

Beatriz Perez, Chief Marketing Officer of the North America Division, Coca-Cola Company.

Career Achiever by the American Advertising Federation's Mosaic Center. In 2006, she was recognized for her leadership in the media industry as an "Ad Age Media Maven." In 2000 and 2005, she was named one of *Sports Business Journal's* "Top 25 Women in Business." She was named one of *Sports Business Journal's* "Forty Under 40" for three consecutive years (2001–2003) and was inducted into their Hall of Fame in 2003. In 1997, Bea was named the "Most Promising Manager of the Year" by the National Hispanic Employees Association.

Perez is chair of the Grammy Foundation and sits on the boards of Children's Healthcare of Atlanta Foundation, the Victory Junction Gang Camps founded by Kyle and Pattie Petty, and HSBC North America Holdings Inc. Bea holds a bachelor of science degree in marketing from the University of Maryland and resides with her family in Atlanta.

rival, Pepsi. Coke and Pepsi have been engaged in intense competition for decades. Competition has emerged in other forms, too. Coca-Cola's share of overall beverage sales has been threatened by the growth in popularity of bottled water, teas, coffee, and energy drinks. Given these forces that aim to cut into Coca-Cola's sales and take customers away from the brand, creating and strengthening customer relationships takes on greater importance. A strategy that Coca-Cola has used for many years to connect with its target market is to use sports as a communication channel. International mega-events like the Olympics and FIFA World Cup are an excellent fit given the global footprint of Coca-Cola. In the U.S. market, Coca-Cola markets through a variety of sports, but its most ambitious sports marketing partnership is with NASCAR.

Coca-Cola has been associated with NASCAR for more than forty years, engaged in various sponsorships with NASCAR, individual racetracks, as title sponsor of races, and individual drivers. In 1998, the relationship extended into new territory as Coke created the Coca-Cola Racing Family. This program associated the Coca-Cola brand with NASCAR by partnering with a collection of many of the sport's top drivers. This approach to reaching consumers through NASCAR was a way to appeal to fans' affinity for their favorite drivers. Coca-Cola connects with a much broader audience by sponsoring twelve current and four retired drivers under the Coca-Cola Racing Family brand. The program includes top drivers such as Greg Biffle, Jeff Burton, and Tony Stewart as well as retired drivers Kyle Petty and Dale Jarrett.[1] The drivers not only lend their name and likeness to the Coca-Cola brand, but they also appear in TV commercials and at special events and are part of experiential events that give fans a chance to meet the drivers.

The Coca-Cola Racing Family is more than a promotion tactic. It is a program that brings Coca-Cola and NASCAR fans together in several channels, many of which are away from the racetrack. Fans are exposed to the Coca-Cola Racing Family on product packaging, at point-of-purchase displays in stores, in media advertising, on vending machines, and online.[2] Multiple marketing objectives are supported through the Racing Family program. Exposure across multiple communications channels aids top-of-mind brand awareness. The affinity fans have for NASCAR and their favorite drivers can transfer to affinity for Coca-Cola with product sales driven by promotions linked to the Racing Family. A relationship with driver Tony Stewart led to the opportunity to place Coca-Cola vending machines featuring Stewart's image at 2,000 Home Depot stores.

NASCAR fans are passionate about the sport, and their interest does not subside when a race or season is over. Coca-Cola effectively tapped into fans' feelings toward NASCAR by creating a program whose family theme fits well with how many NASCAR fans perceive themselves—as part of a large family of racing fans. The uniqueness of the Coca-Cola Racing Family coupled with Coca-Cola's sponsorship of NASCAR running through 2017 suggests that more family time is to come!

Introduction

Challenges posed by changing consumer tastes and other external marketing environment forces lead to a situation that it is the best of times and worst of times in sports. More sports choice for the consumer is fueled by greater interest in sports entertainment, but the growth and other pressures on consumers' time and money create more competition than ever before. A future trend predicted for the sports industry is that fans will be easier to reach, but harder to engage.[3] The good news is that there are more communication channels available to send messages to a target audience. The bad news is that the heightened competition for their attention as well as the numerous options for consuming information and entertainment makes it more difficult to have meaningful impact that strengthens consumers' relationships with a brand.

Marketing communications are the "voice" of the brand. In Chapter 5, brands were described as being an identity, an image, a promise, and a relationship. How are these different

Coca-Cola Racing Family members Greg Biffle and Bobby Labonte with Papa John's founder John Schnatter at a prerace event before the Coke Zero 400 NASCAR event.

characteristics of a brand brought to life? They are transformed from ideas into the interactions and experiences people have with brands through marketing communications. The Coca-Cola Racing Family is an excellent example of a strategic program that takes the easier-to-reach, harder-to-engage challenge head on. Coca-Cola has effectively linked its brand identity and image to NASCAR, a brand for which many fans have a strong, emotion-based connection with the sport and its drivers, just as many of those same people have a long-time connection with Coca-Cola.

The Coca-Cola Racing Family program is neither a public relations campaign nor a gimmick to boost sales. It is a brand extension of Coca-Cola that connects with NASCAR fans through coordinated placement of messages using sponsorship, advertising, sales promotions, public relations, event marketing, and social media. The days have passed of reaching consumers easily through mass mediums (like the pre-1980 era when TV advertising options consisted primarily of three national networks) and one-way communications that promote a seller's products.

This chapter explores the role of marketing communications in building a great sports brand by nurturing relationships with customers and other target audiences. First, a framework used by many brands to strategically plan creative design of messages and channels used to deliver messages is presented. Second, strategies are presented for using the promotion element of the marketing mix to get the sports product into the hands of customers. Third, objectives for integrated campaigns are outlined and connected with different relationship stages customers have with a sports brand. Also, a framework is presented that aids in understanding how marketing communications influence consumer behavior and guides how objectives are set.

Integrated Marketing Communications

The promotion element of the marketing mix may be the voice of the brand, but that voice needs guidance on what to say, how to say it, when to say it, and where to say it. In other words, a strategy that manages communication exchanges between a marketer and its target customer segments is needed to insure that the overarching objective of building and maintaining a brand's identity is realized. An approach to managing brand communications used widely today is **integrated marketing communications (IMC)**. IMC is defined as "the coordination and integration of all marketing communication tools, avenues, and sources within a company into a seamless program that maximizes the impact on customers and other stakeholders at a minimal cost."[4] A combination of external forces (intense competition and declining customer brand loyalties) and internal needs (aligning brands with promotion mix and more accountability for a return on investment from marketing expenditures) led to the emergence of IMC as a business practice in the mid-1990s. It continues today to be a prevailing philosophy marketers practice to guide brand communications with their stakeholders.

Many channels exist for a marketer to communicate with a target audience. The traditional promotion mix of advertising, direct marketing, personal selling, public relations, and sales promotion has mushroomed to include digital channels such as e-mail, search engines, social media, and video. The challenge faced in using the wide range of tools for communicating with audiences is not only to select the ones that are used by the target market, but to use them in a way that the values and meaning of the brand are delivered consistently across all channels. Figure 8.1 illustrates the concept of IMC. While it does not depict a complete list of all communication channels, it captures its essence of coordinating communications to support the different forms a brand takes on (identity, image, promise, and relationship). Characteristics of different communications channels are discussed in greater depth in Chapter 10.

FIGURE 8.1 Concept of Integrated Marketing Communications

Why IMC?

As one considers the definition of integrated marketing communications, the benefits of having a "seamless program that maximizes the impact on customers" would appear to be so obvious that it is hard to believe that IMC was heralded as a breakthrough concept when it emerged in the 1990s. However, external challenges in the form of greater competition for consumers' attention and audience fragmentation led to a need for greater coordination among different brand communication tools used to promote a brand. In addition to an obvious need to maintain consistency in the identity projected through the use of the brand's name and marks, brand communications should work in concert to create associations that form brand image and clearly articulate brand promises. A brand is an important element in a customer's relationship with a business—it is what consumers are aware of and loyal to. It is also what customers can switch from or leave. Just as communication quality can make or break personal relationships, marketing communications can attract and retain customers or turn them away from engaging in a brand relationship.

It is vital that brand consistency be maintained when sending messages across many types of media channels. If a minor league baseball team like the Class AA Akron Aeros positions itself as a brand offering affordable, relaxing entertainment, then messages sent by the team should reinforce that position regardless of the medium used. Newspaper ads, radio commercials, the team's website, its Facebook page, and the sales force should be sending messages that articulate the brand's position. How messages are crafted (creative execution) and when they are communicated (media planning) may vary by channel used, but the goal for sending the messages of communicating the brand's position and meaning (the brand story) is the same for all channels used.

The primary benefit to organizations of using IMC as the framework for brand communications is the synergy created among the different platforms. The term **synergy** suggests that brand communications are working together toward a shared objective, making brand communications more effective. Research by Millward Brown and AC Nielsen found that when messages are delivered using two or more media, brand awareness is higher than if only one medium was used, such as only television or only newspapers.[5] By strategically coordinating messages across various platforms, communication messages can work together and reinforce what is being communicated. Again, this benefit of IMC may seem so obvious that one might question why managers would use communications any other way. The answer is that a disjointed brand communications program is not the goal that managers pursue, but contradictory messages can arise from lack of coordination.

This situation can occur quite easily, especially when sports properties are using advertising agencies to do some work and their own marketing department to do other communications, or using multiple agencies. It is not unusual for a sports entity such as a "mid major" conference college football team to use TV, newspaper, and radio advertising to tout its brand as "big-time college football," which carries along with it associations of "high quality" and "premium priced." At the same time, another marketing campaign may make heavy use of price-based sales promotions that offer sharp reductions in ticket prices. This tactic is at odds with the message of the advertising campaign. IMC reduces the likelihood this scenario would occur. Messaging for all communication tools is coordinated to strive for a complementary, not contradictory, effect of using different media to reach the target market.

IMC in Action

The University of Kentucky used an integrated approach in developing a campaign for its 2009 football season. The seasonal nature of most sports means that to an extent, a new season should be treated like a new product, including placing an emphasis on creating awareness. In this case, UK football has been played for decades, but since several months had passed since the last game of the previous season, creating awareness of the upcoming season is the starting point in the process of persuading fans to buy game tickets. The IMC campaign used by UK featured a blend of traditional media advertising and social media. Billboards placed in key markets of Lexington and Louisville were used to get attention and featured phrases from UK's fight song. Some of the billboards featured technology that enabled drivers to tune into an AM radio frequency as they drove past the billboard and hear the fight song sung by cheerleaders.

The billboards were complemented by a photo contest carried out on Flickr, a photo-sharing social networking website. The first three fans to upload pictures of three different billboards with different phrases from the UK fight song won season tickets. Additionally, a website was set up to promote the photo contest and allow fans to watch a video of former UK players singing the fight song. The campaign successfully promoted the upcoming University of Kentucky's football season.[6]

In addition to recurring situations like the need to promote a football season, unique situations can arise that benefit from planning and executing an IMC campaign. Integrated brand communications was crucial to preparing fans for the move of the New York Jets into the New Meadowlands Stadium. The larger capacity of the new facility meant that for the first time in decades, season tickets were available for new customers. Two years prior to the move, the Jets launched its "Opportunity Knocks" campaign to market the new ticket inventory created by the larger stadium. The campaign consisted of three parts: 1) a branding effort designed to create awareness, 2) a call-to-action component using TV and print advertising, Internet ads, and direct mail, and 3) follow-up messages with interested buyers using personal selling, e-mail, and direct mail.

The campaign helped the New York Jets fill its new home stadium, and the IMC campaign was cited as a key to making it happen. As one team executive said, "We learned that there were plenty of people out there who wanted Jets season tickets—but they had to be notified and marketed to. You can never take for granted that people will know about the availability of your product, no matter what it might be."[7] Regardless of a brand's standing in the market, it is beneficial when communications with customers and other stakeholders are strategically coordinated to support the brand's marketing objectives.

Pull versus Push Marketing

An initial consideration when planning brand communications is to determine the role brand messages will play in getting products into the hands of the end user. Two strategies that can be employed to influence buyer behavior are to *pull* the product through the channels of distribution or *push* the products toward the end user. While these are separate concepts, it is beneficial to think of them as a continuum, as shown in Figure 8.2, since seldom is just one or the other strategy used. Most IMC programs will utilize a combination of pull and push strategies.

FIGURE 8.2 Push versus Pull Strategies

Pull Strategy

A **pull strategy** is based on the ability of brand communications to appeal to the end user to respond positively to the brand. In turn, the end user will "pull" the product to him or her by seeking it out through channels where it is available. While the ultimate response is taking action in the form of purchase, other responses that are short of making a sale may occur and, in fact, may be a more realistic outcome. For example, advertising to consumers is a long-used pull strategy. In some cases, a sports property might run ads with the expectation that the ultimate action will occur (e.g., ads with a core message of "Game on Tuesday night at 7:00 P.M."). This type of message is planned with the aim of attracting ticket buyers for the game.

Other advertising messages might be planned with the objective of increasing the target audience's knowledge of the brand, but without an expectation of immediate action. A billboard ad campaign used by Texas Motor Speedway (TMS) to promote an IndyCar Series race featured star drivers Danica Patrick and Helio Castroneves along with date, race name, and the TMS website.[8] Ads such as the billboards placed by TMS realistically are not expected to result directly in ticket sales for the race, but they can aid in meeting important audience objectives such as awareness of race date, favorable associations with the IndyCar Series, and even visits to the TMS website.

Advertising, digital and social media, public relations, and some sales promotion tactics (e.g., coupons and premium giveaways) can be used as part of a pull strategy. Advertising and public relations are particularly well suited for achieving necessary responses from an audience such as awareness of a brand, knowledge that leads to formation of brand associations, or a desired brand image/personality. Digital media can be used to communicate information that can engage consumers with a brand and potentially lead to desired actions.

The Philadelphia Phillies placed quick response (QR) codes on drinking cups at Citizens Bank Park foodservice locations. A QR code is a two-dimensional bar code that can be read by software available for most smartphones. For marketing purposes, QR codes often are embedded with code that links to a website. The Philadelphia Phillies used the QR code to direct people to a website that contained information such as the Phillies' schedule and upcoming events at the ballpark.[9] IMC tactics that are more action-oriented are direct marketing (either by mail or e-mail) and targeted sales promotions that provide incentives to take action (e.g., buy a product or ticket). Figure 8.3 summarizes pull strategies that can be used.

FIGURE 8.3 Pull Strategy Communication Approaches

Push Strategy

A different approach for selecting the communications tools of an IMC program is to use tactics that effectively move products through distribution channels from seller to buyer. Known as a **push strategy**, this approach relies heavily on persuasion to convince channel members to take action. Channel members refer to organizations and people involved in distribution steps between the origin or manufacture of a product and the end user. Wholesalers, retailers, and salespeople are examples of channel members that could be targeted by promotions using a push strategy. Whereas a pull strategy might include using messages designed to move consumers closer to taking action such as providing information about a product's features and benefits, tactics associated with a push strategy aim to obtain channel commitment or action. A key element in an IMC program that is used to execute a push strategy is an organization's sales force. Salespeople are responsible for building and maintaining customer relationships, but in most organizations the important metrics of job performance are related to sales (e.g., dollar sales, number of new accounts opened, or number of sales interviews). Most sports organizations, particularly those that market teams and events, rely heavily on ticket sales as a revenue source.

Many organizations have expanded their ticket sales staffs, realizing that using a push tactic in which salespeople prospect for and contact potential buyers can add ticket revenues and, ultimately, loyal customers. Major League Soccer recognized the importance of personal selling in its brand communication efforts and responded by starting the MLS National Sales Center in Blaine, Minnesota. MLS is the first major professional sports league to operate a centralized sales training program. The motivation for MLS to undertake the initiative was that internal research revealed that sales reps with three or four years of sales experience generate four to five times more revenue than first-year reps. Given that MLS teams had rather inexperienced sales staffs (85% of teams' sales reps had less than three years of sales experience), the league saw a potential benefit in sending qualified candidates through a forty-five-day training program.[10]

In addition to training, salespeople can be involved in using another push tactic: sales promotions that target salespeople. Sales contests in which cash or other prizes are awarded can provide short-term incentives for salespeople to increase sales calls and work more diligently to close sales with customers and prospects. Incentives can be used to offer rewards to salespeople responsible for ticket sales, sponsorships, concessions, or merchandise—any product category in which an organization desires to increase revenues.

Dual Strategy

The roles played by pull and push communications tactics in motivating and influencing buyers make it rather clear that decisions regarding use of pull and push tactics are not either/or situations. Both approaches are needed to advance an organization's brand and achieve business objectives. A marketing manager would be naïve to believe that a reliance on push tactics exclusively would be a sound brand communications strategy. Yes, push tactics are effective for eliciting consumer actions such as trial (first-time use) and purchase, but not everyone in the target market is at a point in their relationship with the brand that they are considering purchase. Some people are at that stage, and push elements such as a salesperson's presentation is the nudge needed to persuade them to buy. Other people may know little about a brand or otherwise not have a relationship with it. For this segment of the target market, communications that motivate consumers to pull products through to them are needed. Relationship progression can result from using both pull and push strategies and lead people closer to taking actions that have business impact such as buying tickets or licensed merchandise.

Brand Communications Objectives

Just as the steps in creating a marketing plan call for establishing objectives or outcomes before outlining the marketing strategies and tactics that should be used, planning a sports property's brand story should begin with that end in mind. What should be achieved as a result of the communications plan that tells this story? How can an IMC campaign support the organization's marketing and financial objectives? If the answers to these questions are known, decisions regarding the types of brand communications tools selected to reach the target market and timing of their implementation are clearer than if IMC objectives are not clearly established.

Having objectives in place is an important step in IMC planning, but their usefulness as a strategic planning tool depends on meeting the four criteria illustrated in Figure 8.4. First, the IMC objective must have sufficient detail so it can be determined if it is met. For example, if "increase sales" was an IMC objective, it would be a nice outcome if it happened, but it lacks a specific target for growth. Is it higher dollar sales? Is it more customers? Or is it some other measure of sales? In contrast, if an IMC objective is "increase season ticket holders by 15%," then it is specific.

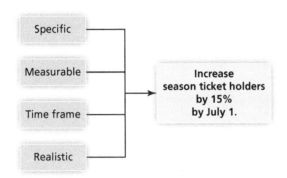

FIGURE 8.4 **Criteria for IMC Objectives**

A second criterion of an effective IMC objective is that the outcome can be measured in some way. Certain outcomes of a brand communications campaign can be measured directly, such as the number of new fans added to a Facebook page. Other measurable outcomes could be the number of coupons redeemed from a direct response campaign or the number of sales presentations scheduled as a result of a direct mail campaign targeting small businesses for suite rental. Other tactics that do not lend themselves to direct measurement can be measured using surveys or other market research methods. For example, if an IMC campaign had objectives to increase brand awareness or create a specific brand image, these outcomes could be measured provided there is a willingness to invest in a market research study of the target market.

The third criterion is the objective need to have a time frame. It can be stated as specific date, such as July 1, or within six months. Measurements can be taken along the way also to ensure the target will be met by the target date. This also allows for modifying the marketing approach if sufficient progress is not being made towards the target goal.

Lastly, the IMC objective must be realistic. A benefit of setting objectives is that they encourage an organization to stretch to improve. But if the outcomes desired have a low probability of being realized, an unintended consequence is that employees become demoralized because they realize their best efforts may still not be enough to meet an objective. For instance, weak economic conditions such as those experienced during a recession diminish sponsorship revenues of many sports properties. An objective to add fifteen new sponsorship partners may be plausible during good economic periods but could be an unreachable objective in a period when businesses are making conservative decisions about spending their marketing dollars.

Objectives that meet the criteria of specific, realistic, within a time frame, and measurable may or may not be achieved as the result of executing an IMC campaign. But not meeting these four criteria ensures that a campaign will not have the audience impact that it is capable of delivering. Also, it is important to note that strategies and tactics should *not* be considered as IMC objectives. Stating an objective of "spend $500,000 on advertising" is marketing activity, not a measure of audience impact. Similarly, stating "create an official page for our event on Facebook and Twitter" is not an outcome but rather a tactic that would be used to achieve an outcome such as increasing brand awareness or developing greater brand knowledge among an audience segment. Figure 8.5 identifies some objectives that could be used by a sports property that meet the four criteria.

FIGURE 8.5 **Sample Objectives**

- Add 7 new sponsors by April 1.

- Increase sales of weekend ticket packs by 10% by May 15.

- Increase brand awareness of home football games by 20% by the first home game (September 2).

- Increase image of the sports brand by 18% by December 31.

- Increase average home game attendance by 2,000 by August 1.

- Increase paid attendance at home games by 4% by the end of the season (October 4).

Types of IMC Objectives

Setting objectives for an IMC campaign prompts managers to consider on the front end what a target market should think, feel, or do as a result of the brand communications directed toward them. Different brand communications tools have strengths or advantages that can contribute to the overall effectiveness of an IMC campaign. This characteristic is important because audience impact is not a single-factor concept. The term *audience impact* refers to moving customers or prospects through different stages of relationship with a brand. Some people need very little persuasion to make a purchase, while others may hardly know the brand exists! Thus the need for both pull and push marketing approaches. In addition, this variation in relationship states that people in a target market have with a brand makes it necessary to consider two types of objectives: communication objectives and behavioral objectives (See Figure 8.6).

FIGURE 8.6 **Types of IMC Objectives**

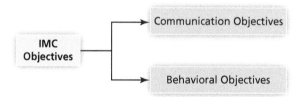

COMMUNICATION OBJECTIVES. **Communication objectives** lay the foundation for integrated marketing communications to build customer relationships. Setting communication objectives recognizes that not everyone in a target market is at a relationship stage in which they are buyers . . . or even are considering buying. For this segment of the market, the role of brand communications is to begin building a relationship by using exposure tactics that create awareness and some knowledge of the brand. At the same time, engagement tactics connect consumers with a sports brand on a deeper, more intimate level and complement exposure tactics. If communication objectives are set and tactics executed that succeed in moving consumers through early relationship stages such as awareness and favorable perceptions of the brand, the stage is set for escalating the relationship to the point that ultimate outcomes such as purchase and loyalty occur.

For achieving communication objectives, the longtime tactic of choice has been media advertising. A variety of channels exist: television, radio, newspaper, billboards. The short exposure periods people have with TV, radio, and billboard ads make those mediums ideal for focusing on achieving outcomes such as creating awareness or delivering small amounts of brand knowledge. Billboard ads for the University of Miami (Florida) football team consisted only of the picture of a player, the team's logo, and the message "Storming Back," and a toll-free number to order tickets. Will such a message be persuasive enough to get people to buy

Interstate Batteries

Brand exposure is an important communication goal for Interstate Batteries at NASCAR events.

tickets? Probably not, but exposure to the billboard serves as a reminder that football season is approaching and it puts the University of Miami brand in front of people in the Miami area.

Sponsorship is another tactic used in support of communication objectives. Signage exposure and brand mentions that sponsors receive have the potential to reach an audience over an extended time period while attending an event or watching on television. As a result, brand awareness is the most frequently cited objective in sponsor surveys.

Social media holds great potential for reaching an audience to engage fans in ways that build interest in a brand and create favorable brand associations on which brand image is based. Social media channels are important not only because they deliver the voice of the brand, but because the voice of the audience plays a prominent role in the flow of communication. Online communities give interested people a place to gather around a shared interest, and take the form of a site within popular social networking platforms like Facebook and Twitter or a brand-specific website. For example, the NHL's New York Rangers has a dedicated website for its online fan community, BlueShirtsUnited.com. Members can upload pictures and video, make blog posts, and participate in discussions about their favorite team. Sports brands can use social media in this way to solidify relationships with committed fans as well as capture the attention and interests of people who are not as highly involved with the brand.

BEHAVIORAL OBJECTIVES. While communication objectives are based on achieving important advances in customer relationships, an IMC campaign that focuses exclusively on communication objectives would miss the mark in terms of linking brand communications tactics to ultimate measures of marketing success. After all, what is gained if more brand awareness or a desirable brand personality is created but there is little impact on financial measures such as revenue and profit? **Behavioral objectives** seek to connect brand communications to customer responses that can directly or indirectly affect an organization's revenue.

Direct impacts on revenue realized through brand communications tactics include sales promotions such as coupons or a premium giveaway such as caps or bobble-head dolls. The success of these tactics is measured in terms of the incremental sales they create such as tickets and concessions. In other cases, a behavior that is desired might not result directly in a sale, but it may pull consumers closer to making a purchase. An open house event in which fans are given behind-the-scenes tours and shown available seats to purchase may have as its ultimate objective to increase season ticket sales, but the event's effectiveness can also be measured by number of people attending or the number of leads gathered for follow-up by the sales staff. Both outcomes are actions that may or may not result in someone buying season tickets, but they move them closer to the point of considering such action.

Behavioral objectives should be included when sports properties set their IMC strategy. The connection of communications tactics with consumer responses that can impact a business's growth make marketers accountable for their decisions and link the communications function with an organization's overall marketing goals and objectives. However, there are limitations to behavioral objectives. The main limitation is that an "X causes Y" assumption that brand communications tactics are related to sales and other actions oversimplifies how consumers make buying decisions. Many other variables influence consumer choice, including price, quality, alternative choices, and economic conditions, to name a few.

In the case of sports marketing, quality has more than one dimension. Marketers have control of most aspects of the quality of a fan's experience at a game or event, but they have virtually no control over the quality of the on-field product. The Pittsburgh Pirates have one of the best venues for delivering an exceptional fan experience, PNC Park, but the team has not had a winning season since 1992. In such a case, it may be unrealistic to believe that investment in brand communications alone will lead to increased ticket sales. In fact, season attendance is now down by more than one-third from the Pirates' first season attendance total of 2.4 million when the new PNC Park opened in 2001.[11]

Strategic Implications

IMC planning does not require that setting objectives become a situation of pitting communication objectives versus behavioral objectives. Both types of objectives have a role in a brand's IMC strategy; each type of objective complements the other. An IMC strategy that consisted of communication objectives only would, in effect, be stating that no impact or benefit on consumer action is expected from the investment in brand communications—not the ideal way to grow a business! Similarly, an IMC campaign planned exclusively with behavioral objectives unrealistically assumes that the target market is at or near a buying state and that tactics such as advertising or sales promotion can give the nudge needed to persuade consumers to take action. In his book *Marketing Outrageously*, veteran sports marketer Jon Spoelstra advocates making advertising decisions largely on the basis of return on investment: How much revenue is generated or how many tickets are sold when an ad runs, and what is the ratio of revenue per ad dollar spent?[12]

The accountability that comes with measuring ROI for brand communications is needed, but this view assumes a marketing message alone like a newspaper ad is responsible for generating a response from someone who sees the advertisement. However, multiple research studies on the motivations of sporting event attendees have found that advertising is one of the least influential factors in their decision to attend.

Does the apparently minor effect of advertising on attendance decisions mean sports marketers should decrease their advertising budgets? Absolutely not! Advertising and other communications serve roles other than to persuade people to buy tickets. Awareness, knowledge, and liking can all be influenced by advertising, setting the stage for later purchases. Remember, certain communications tactics pull customers toward a purchase decision, and other tactics push the product toward buyers. Setting communication and behavioral objectives is done with the understanding that neither a pull nor push strategy alone can succeed in advancing customer relationships.

Linking Consumer Behavior to IMC Objectives

IMC objectives are customer-focused. That is, objectives are developed in terms of how customers' relationships with a brand should be affected as a result of exposure to brand communications. Pinpointing the outcomes that should be realized among the target market is important, because if the desired end results are set, the task of selecting tactics and creating specific messages is clearer. Obtaining that insight can be aided by linking different stages consumers go through in their relationship with a brand and IMC objectives. An explanation of the process that consumers move through when making buying decisions is known as a **hierarchy of effects**. The six steps in the model are illustrated in Figure 8.7. The premise of this model is that consumers move through a sequence of thinking, feeling, and doing. Hierarchy of effects explains individual customer relationships with a brand, although the amount of time a person spends in a stage varies.

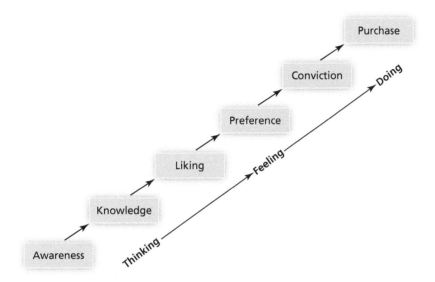

FIGURE 8.7 **The Hierarchy of Effects Model**

The good news for marketers is that they are not bystanders, passively watching consumers as they interact with the world around them. Brand communications can be used at each stage and can help move a consumer into the next stage. Before someone can like Adidas ("feeling"), he or she must possess awareness of the Adidas brand, have information about Adidas stored in memory that can form positive associations with the brand, and have favorable beliefs about Adidas's products, athlete endorsers, or any other aspect of the brand, all outcomes associated with the "thinking" stage. Adidas and other brands can influence how consumers feel about their brands by developing a coordinated strategy of messages that shape their thinking.

An adaptation of the think → feel → do model for sports brands is illustrated in Figure 8.8. It features three stages: knowledge, affinity, and action. Knowledge (thinking) is comprised of awareness and associations. Affinity (feeling) stages are attitude and preference. Action (doing) consists of trial, purchase, and loyalty.

Awareness

The first relational accomplishment a brand must achieve with a consumer is creating awareness. It is no different than a personal relationship. The freshman who spots a female in his biology class will not have to worry about making date plans until he first gets his classmate's attention and she learns that he exists. The challenge to create awareness for new products or brands is great, and failure to build awareness among sufficient numbers in the target market can lead to product failure. Many sports brands face an additional obstacle not experienced by brands in other product categories in that the seasonal nature of sports means that other brands and thoughts may occupy consumers' minds during off-seasons. This characteristic leads to the need to build awareness for specific events, whether it is a campaign to promote an entire season or a focus on creating awareness for a single game. It is likely that a sports property would use a combination of the two approaches for creating awareness.

FIGURE 8.8 Hierarchy Model for Sports Brands

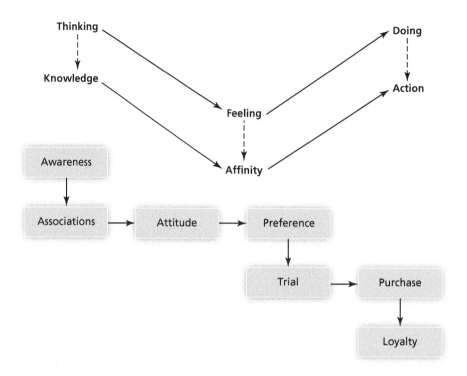

The NHL's Carolina Hurricanes use exposure-oriented tools like advertising and the team's website in advance of a new season to promote season ticket sales and deliver information that the team fans will hopefully store in memory for future access. Once the season begins, brand communication tactics are used to create awareness for specific games, such as a focus on weekend home games when the Hurricanes have a greater chance to sell more tickets. Similarly, awareness might be the objective of advertising messages that promote the opposing team or star players. Several NBA teams have used this tactic to create awareness for specific games by touting superstar opponents such as Kobe Bryant and LeBron James.

Associations

The first step in a consumer's relationship with a brand is awareness, but the extent of the relationship may be extremely limited to "I have heard of you." That level of connection would hardly be classified as even a casual relationship with a customer. Awareness can be created virtually against someone's will simply through repeated brand exposure (think about a brand that you remember because of a jingle or slogan you have seen or heard so many times that you cannot get it out of your head).

The second level of a consumer's relationship with a brand is the set of associations that is held about the brand. In other words, what does the consumer know about a brand? The thoughts and beliefs held in memory are the basis of **brand image**, which is the perception of a brand created by the various associations held about the brand. Marketers use brand communications to send their target market information about their brands that if processed will result in learning about the brand and influence brand image.

Various IMC tactics are used to accomplish development of brand associations. Community involvement by sports properties is one way to create associations that a team or individual athletes care about the local community where they play. Whether it is visiting a children's hospital, reading to elementary school students, or delivering Thanksgiving meals to needy families, a benefit of the community outreach efforts of sports properties is that the general public's perceptions of the brand can be positively impacted by adding associations such as "our local NFL team cares about the community." A side benefit of supporting causes through community service is that the high profile of sports teams and athletes often draws media coverage, providing further exposure of the good works, and results in even greater audience reach.

When areas of Nashville sustained heavy flood damage in 2010, Tennessee Titans players and coaches took a day off from workouts to go into a neighborhood and assist homeowners with debris removal. Local TV stations and newspapers documented the Titans' involvement and helped deliver brand associations of "concerned about the community."

Sponsorship is another IMC tool considered to be effective for forming brand associations. Mountain Dew has been very successful in using sponsorship to shape people's associations with the brand. Action sports have long been associated with Mountain Dew via sponsorship, and associations with action sports such as "young," "energetic," and "extreme" have become part of many consumers' associations with Mountain Dew. For Mountain Dew, sponsorship has been instrumental in supporting the brand's positioning as a youthful, high-energy carbonated beverage.

Interstate Batteries has been successful in using sponsorship of NASCAR races and drivers to build strong brand associations.

Attitude

As consumers move from knowledge to affinity, their relationship with a brand focuses more on feelings and emotions about the brand. The knowledge stage forms a vital foundation, but consumers generally are not moved to take action based on awareness and associations alone. Sports brands possess an advantage that brands in other product categories envy. The emotion-based relationships many sports fans have with their favorite sport, team, player, or product differs from their other brand relationships in terms of the intensity of passion. From a marketing communications standpoint it is important to tap into the affinity of fans through messages and tactics that reinforce the emotional benefits of being a fan and then of consuming goods and services.

Experiential marketing is one way to make emotional appeals to a target audience.

Team fan conventions, described in Chapter 7, illustrate how experiences can be created to fuel the passion felt for a fan's favorite team. Using experiences and events to influence attitude is not limited to reaching highly involved fans. Casual fans and even nonfans can be impacted on an emotional level by experiential marketing. Such is the case with the Faith and Family Night events held by baseball teams such as the Houston Astros, Colorado Rockies, and Arizona Diamondbacks. Faith and Family Night is an event that targets church groups and Christian fans by holding a postgame concert by a Christian music artist and a talk by a member of the baseball organization about his spiritual journey. Events such as Faith and Family Night can draw people into a relationship with a team by linking the team with individuals' spiritual journey.

Other brand communication tactics have the potential to impact brand attitude, most notably advertising. The challenge that marketers face is determining which IMC tools are best suited to have a positive effect on consumers' liking of a brand.

Preference

A major accomplishment in moving a consumer toward a decision to buy a specific brand is the consumer developing a preference for one brand over alternatives. This affinity state still falls short of making a sale, but it sets the stage for an action such as trial or purchase to occur later. Consumption of sports is different from other types of products in that sports fans may feel a preference for multiple sports brands. A Denver sports fan is not forced to choose between the Broncos (NFL), Nuggets (NBA), Avalanche (NHL), Rockies (MLB), and Rapids (MLS). He or she can be a fan of all five major league sports teams.

At the same time, a realistic view of the sports consumer leads to the conclusion that the individual probably does not have enough time or discretionary income to be a loyal customer of all five teams in terms of buying tickets and merchandise, watching media broadcasts, and

Interstate Batteries

Faith and Family Night at Chase Field, home of the Arizona Diamondbacks.

participating in fan communities on social networking websites. Not only do sports properties compete among themselves for the limited resources of consumers, but their positioning as entertainment means that movies, concerts, festivals, shopping, and any other form of entertainment vie for consumers' hearts and wallets, too.

A key to achieving preference is creating brand relevance. Brands that matter to consumers have an advantage over brands that fail to make a meaningful connection. Engagement tools that promote immersion and interaction are well suited for increasing brand relevance among consumers. One of the greatest assets sports properties possess that can impact relevance is access to players, coaches, broadcasters, facilities, or any other brand element with which fans have an affinity.

Experiences and events are brand communication tools that can create access points that allow fans to look "behind the curtain," beyond what can be observed by usual forms of consumption. This tactic is not limited to sports properties alone; sponsors can partner with properties to impact their brands in a similar way. For example, Best Buy held launch parties for the debut of Windows 7 that appealed to sports fans through a connection with retired NBA greats. In select markets, the parties included appearances by NBA legends such as Dominique Wilkins and Kareem Abdul-Jabbar.[13] The excitement surrounding events such as the Best Buy parties can strengthen brand preference by appealing to an audience's feelings about a team or player.

Engagement that influences preference can be achieved through other brand communication tools, also. Social media can be particularly effective for this purpose. Creating a channel that encourages interested people to gather together to share their affinity for a brand (e.g., league, event, team, or player) not only enables meeting others with a similar interest, but it lets fans express their feelings through message posts and picture uploads. When consumers are connected with a brand and given a voice in this way, the likelihood that they will discontinue the relationship in favor of a competitor is reduced.

Trial

Before a person can become a buyer and loyal customer of a brand, he or she must make the decision to consume it for the first time. This first-time use is referred to as **product trial**. For purchase decisions that consumers make often, such as for entertainment, trial is crucial in determining whether a brand will be considered as an option when the same need arises in the future. Trial is important in escalating customer relationships because it enables users to make judgments about the value offered by a product or service. No amount of exposure to advertising, salesperson presentations, and word-of-mouth communications can take the place of the actual consumption experience. In the case of an experiential purchase like sports entertainment, enticing consumers to try the brand can be a powerful means of getting them "hooked" and intensifying their relationship with the brand.

A tactic used frequently to encourage product trial is to reduce the commitment required for consumers to use the good or service. Coupons and other price-based incentives have long been

Church groups are targeted by the Colorado Rockies for group ticket sales.

used by marketers to attract new or former customers, whether the product is ice cream or ice hockey. In theory, consumers who are attracted to try a brand because of a coupon or sample will have the opportunity to evaluate the benefits delivered by the brand and deem it worthy of purchase in the future . . . at full price.

A different tactic that can have the effect of bringing in first-time buyers is group ticket sales. For properties that rely on ticket sales as a revenue stream, targeting groups is a way to boost revenues and possibly attract new customers who will return in the future, either with their group or as individual ticket buyers. The social aspect of group affiliation compels some members to go along with the group's activities in order to be affiliated with the group. Businesses, church groups, school organizations, scouting groups, and youth sports organizations are just a few of the possible targets for sports properties. The incentive offered to many groups is a quantity discount based on number of tickets sold. This feature serves as a risk reducer that enables trial.

Purchase

The ultimate "moment of truth" occurs when a consumer decides to buy a specific brand. At this point, the marketer has succeeded in converting a prospect to a customer. But, as the discussion of the different stages in the hierarchy of effects illustrates, a great deal of effort is expended by a sports marketer to bring a person to the point of making a buying decision.

Even at this stage, IMC tactics can be employed to assist in moving consumers from purchase intent to actually making a purchase. The sales force is a valuable tool for "closing the deal" with prospective buyers, persuading them to commit to buy. Certain promotions or offers can also be influential in tipping the consumer's decision. Season ticket prospects may be converted into buyers with incentives such as extended payment plans with no interest or special benefits offered exclusively to season ticket holders such as special parking areas or special pricing for other events at the team's venue like concerts. Marketers must never forget that an intense competition exists for consumers' discretionary dollars. The battle to make a sale is not over until a customer commits! Tactics that either persuade or reassure prospects that they are making the right choice by buying a particular sports brand are a way to effectively fend off competitors for their entertainment dollars.

Loyalty

One of the major contributions the marketing function makes to an organization is managing and growing customer loyalty. Repeat buyers are valuable buyers because they are less expensive to reach than prospective buyers. Moreover, loyal customers represent significant financial benefits to an organization long term. A measure of a customer's financial worth to the firm is **customer lifetime value (CLV)**, which is the present value of future profits that are projected to be realized from a customer.[14] The rationale behind maximizing CLV is that the longer a customer relationship exists, the greater the likelihood that their expenditures with the firm will increase, either through trading up to bigger ticket purchases or by purchasing other products offered by the firm.

A customer that begins as a single-game ticket buyer may escalate his relationship with a team to a partial-season ticket and perhaps even to a full-season ticket. A business that initially buys advertising space could increase its spending with a sports property to include corporate hospitality or higher sponsorship levels. Realizing the long-term financial payoff of a customer for a sports property provides motivation to influence repeat purchases.

Certain IMC tools are more effective at rewarding existing customers and cementing their relationship with a brand than others. Customer relations and personal selling are two tools that are effective for servicing needs of customers post-purchase. A personal touch shown to ticket holders or sponsors through assigning specific service employees as a liaison between the organization and customer can effectively build trust and demonstrate concern for customers. These steps can aid in detecting and addressing sources of dissatisfaction before they can damage a relationship.

Database-driven marketing tactics that are part of a more comprehensive customer relationship management (CRM) system are effective for up-selling certain customers as well as rewarding the loyalty of customers with high financial profit value to an organization. Special offers or incentives can be used to target buyers to increase their purchases or spending level, such as targeting partial-season ticket customers with an offer to upgrade to full-season tickets. In contrast, the segment of customers that are among the highest dollar spenders should be treated with exclusivity and rewarded for their business with special perks and access. One marketing expert distinguishes between the focal points of loyalty management by recommending top-level customers be targeted with service programs while other customers that are prospects to escalate their relationship be targeted with marketing programs.[15]

MARKETING OBJECTIVES. Our objectives were to grow volume in the months leading up to and during the tournament, attract youth and retain existing drinkers, and build love for our brands.

We saw the tournament as an opportunity for Coca-Cola to offer people a global invitation to release themselves from the pressures of modern-day life. This program was Coca-Cola's biggest ever global marketing program, with 160 markets executing elements of the program. The program was also Powerade's first ever global marketing program.

COMMUNICATION OBJECTIVES. Objectives for the campaign were to:

1. Leverage and drive global scale – implemented in more than 100 countries
2. Deliver mass engagement – one billion minutes of user engagement
3. Expand the duration of the activation – more than one-third of the year

MULTIDIMENSIONAL CONSUMER CONNECTION PLAN. Coca-Cola and Powerade's programs reflected a multidimensional connection plan:

1. Packaging, Point-of-Sale (POS) Displays, and Premiums
2. Music
3. Cinema, Out-of-Home (OOH), TV, and Radio
4. Digital
5. Events
6. Live Positively

RESULTS. Through this integrated global approach, Coca-Cola saw global growth in volume and brand equity throughout the activation period, creating an indelible association between our brands and the world's biggest sporting event. We worked as one team around the world to leverage a core creative idea and execute programs on a scale that delivered efficient and impactful return on our marketing investment. In the U.S., the program successfully transitioned from being historically a multicultural activation to becoming a mainstream marketing program. Finally, we ensured that agreed upon metrics and research methodologies were in place to track, measure, and evaluate each of our marketing initiatives. This process allowed us to gather learnings and help prepare for the next FIFA World Cup tournament.

LEARNINGS FOR THE FUTURE. While adhering to an integrated marketing communication development process required perseverance, it provided significant productivity and savings in the use of our global marketing investment. We made important strides by activating two major brands at a global event, but we also recognized that doing so requires significant time and resources to successfully execute.

Insider Insights Beatriz Perez – Coca-Cola

Q. Can you share an example of how Coca-Cola uses sports as a platform to develop an integrated marketing communications campaign?

A. The Coca-Cola Company has been an uninterrupted sponsor of the FIFA World Cup Tournament since 1970. Our company used an integrated approach for its activation of the FIFA World Cup marketing program. The journey to this program began after the end of the FIFA World Cup 2006 Tournament itself.

Coca-Cola Company

Bea triz Perez shares an example of how Coca-Cola used sports to develop an integrated marketing campaign.

Chapter Summary

Telling the brand story involves the use of integrated marketing communications (IMC), which is the coordination and integration of all marketing communication tools, avenues, and sources within a company into a seamless program that maximizes the impact on customers and other stakeholders. The primary benefit of using the IMC framework for brand communication is the synergy created among the different marketing programs.

Selection of the appropriate brand communication tools should be guided by the desired impact on the chosen target market. This selection process involves deciding on the level of product access determined by the degree of push strategies versus pull strategies. Pull strategies involve the ability of the brand to appeal to the end user, who then requests the product from channel members, thus pulling the product through the distribution channel. The push strategy involves providing incentives to the channel members to sell the product to consumers. Extremely rare would be the use of one or the other exclusively. Most firms use both a pull and push approach.

Before choosing the marketing approach, it is important to set the communication objectives the sports entity wants to accomplish. Good objectives meet four criteria. It is specific, measurable, has a stated time frame, and is realistic. Because of the variation in relationship states of people in a target market, it is necessary to consider two types of objectives: communication objectives and behavioral objectives. Communication objectives lay the foundation for the IMC program and are designed to build customer relationships. This is accomplished primarily through various forms of advertising and sponsorships. Behavioral objectives are based on achieving important advances in customer relationships, resulting in purchases or some type of action.

IMC objectives are customer-focused and should move consumers through the six steps in the hierarchy of effects model. The premise of the model is that consumers move through the steps of thinking, feeling, and then doing. In sports marketing, this can be translated into knowledge, affinity, and then action. Knowledge involves awareness and associations, affinity involves attitude and preference, and action involves trial, purchase, and then loyalty.

Review Questions

1. What is integrated marketing communications?
2. Why is integrated marketing communications important for sports brands?
3. What is the difference between a pull and a push strategy?
4. Describe the four criteria of good objectives.
5. What is the difference between communication objectives and behavioral objectives?
6. Identify tactics that can be used to support communication objectives.
7. Identify tactics that can be used to support behavioral objectives.
8. Why is it important to have both communication and behavioral objectives in an IMC plan?
9. What are the six stages in the hierarchy of effects model?
10. Which stages of the hierarchy of effects model match the process of consumers moving through the three stages of thinking, feeling, and doing?
11. Describe the hierarchy model for sports brands.
12. What is customer lifetime value (CLV) and why is it important?

New Terms

Integrated marketing communications (IMC) coordination and integration of all marketing communication tools to achieve synergy in brand communications with the goals of building brand equity and strengthening stakeholder relationships.

Synergy effect of brand communications working together toward a shared objective, making brand communications more effective because of strategic use of multiple communication channels.

Pull strategy ability of brand communications to appeal to end users, who then seek the brand out through channels where it is available.

Push strategy marketing approach that relies heavily on persuading channel members to take action.

Communication objectives objectives that lay the foundation for integrated marketing communications to build customer relationships.

Behavioral objectives objectives that connect brand communications to customer responses that can be directly or indirectly measured.

Hierarchy of effects steps consumers move through when making a buying decision.

Brand image perception of a brand created by the various associations held about the brand.

Product trial first-time use of a product.

Customer lifetime value (CLV) present value of future profits that are projected to be realized from a customer.

Discussion and Critical Thinking Exercises

1. Assume you have been asked to market your college's golf team or the golf team of a nearby university. Write two communication objectives and two behavioral objectives. Be sure each meets the criteria identified for a good objective. For each objective, describe how you would go about ensuring the objective is met. What type of marketing tactics would you use?

2. Think about a recent sports-related purchase. Go through each of the stages in the hierarchy of effects model. Describe the type of communication that brought you to that next stage. How long was it from the awareness stage to the purchase stage?

3. Consider the thinking → feeling → doing stages that consumers go through before making a purchase. Locate three advertisements or marketing promotions for sports. Which of the three stages is being advertised?

4. Suppose you have been asked by your university to help promote the women's basketball program. Go through each of the seven stages outlined in Figure 8.8 for the hierarchy model for sports and outline an IMC program that would lead university students to become loyal fans of women's basketball.

5. Because of limited time and financial resources, sports fans must make choices on the level of involvement with various sports and teams. Review the hierarchy model for sports brands in Figure 8.8. Identify sports or teams for yourself that you would place in the *action component*, i.e., trial, purchase, and loyalty. What moved you from trial to loyalty, and how long did it take? What marketing incentives or tactics, if any, were factors?

6. Because of limited time and financial resources, sports fans must make choices on the level of involvement with various sports and teams. Review the hierarchy model for sports brands in Figure 8.8. Identify sports or teams for yourself that you would place in the *affinity component*, i.e., attitude and preference. What marketing factors, or other factors, moved you from just knowledge to affinity? What incentives would it take to move you to the action component and make a trial purchase?

7. Because of limited time and financial resources, sports fans must make choices on the level of involvement with various sports and teams. Review the hierarchy model for sports brands in Figure 8.8. Identify sports or teams for yourself that you would place in the *knowledge component*, i.e., awareness and associations. In what way has marketing created that knowledge for you? From your list, which ones do you think might move to the affinity stage in the future? Why? What about those you do not see moving beyond the knowledge stage? Why do you not see them moving to the affinity stage?

You Make the Call
NASCAR Hall of Fame

With NASCAR having some of the most brand-loyal fans of any major sport, obtaining the rights to the NASCAR Hall of Fame was a prize a number of cities sought. In addition to the jobs and income generated from the $100 million construction, the Hall would be a tourist attraction that would be an attractive boost to the local economy. Preconstruction estimates indicated as many as 800,000 people would visit the Hall the first year and 400,000 a year afterwards.

With a pledge of $154 million, the city of Charlotte, North Carolina, won the rights to build the NASCAR Hall of Fame. Groundbreaking ceremonies were held in January of 2007. Grand opening was in May 2010. The NASCAR Hall of Fame is a 150,000-square-foot interactive entertainment attraction that honors the history and heritage of NASCAR. The facility is located in uptown Charlotte and is a high-tech venue designed to educate and entertain race fans as well as nonfans. Located on five acres, the Hall facility includes interactive exhibits, a state-of-the-art theater, the Hall of Honor, a Buffalo Wild Wings restaurant, Sports Avenue retail outlets, and a NASCAR Media Group–operated broadcast studio. Also on the site is a privately developed nineteen-story office tower and 102,000-square-foot expansion to the Charlotte Convention Center with a 40,000-square-foot ballroom.

A major challenge faced by the Hall of Fame is the relationship between NASCAR and its sponsors. While Charlotte owned the facility and operated the Hall, all decisions had to be approved by NASCAR. This included soliciting sponsors for the Hall. Since many of the sponsors had exclusive contracts with drivers and race teams, it was difficult to negotiate sponsorships for the Hall. When it opened, only four sponsors had been signed: Lowe's, Mars (M&Ms), Food Lion, and NASCAR Performance Group. Additional sponsors were showcased inside the Hall, but were tied to specific exhibits, such as 3M, Goodyear, Mobil 1, and O'Reilly Auto Parts.

Obtaining sponsorships was not the only problem faced by the NASCAR Hall of Fame. Attendance during the first year was less than half of what was predicted. To balance the budget, the advertising budget was slashed for the year from the budgeted $500,000 to less than $50,000. Making it more difficult to earn a profit is the agreement with NASCAR that the NASCAR association receives

Attracting visitors to the NASCAR Hall of Fame is a marketing priority.

10 percent on all sponsorship sales and between 7.5 and 10 percent of all revenue generated from ticket sales, retail sales, and tours.

Charlotte, North Carolina, was chosen because it is a major hotspot for NASCAR, with two races per year held in the city, and because of its long-time support for NASCAR. Supporters believed that many attending the races would take the short trip uptown to visit the Hall of Fame while in Charlotte. During its early operation, the Hall found that approximately 70 percent of the visitors lived more than 100 miles away and 25 percent came from 500 or more miles away. The average distance traveled was 368 miles.

Although the future of the NASCAR Hall of Fame is bright, challenges are mounting. Obtaining sponsorships remains a key issue. Negotiating with each individual driver, team, and company has become a challenge. Then obtaining permission from NASCAR on every decision, even down to what vendor is used for paper cups, has further taxed the staff. Lastly, attendance has to be increased. Marketing has to reach beyond the local area to NASCAR fans scattered throughout the United States. One opportunity for increasing attendance appears to be in the region surrounding Charlotte. Data collected from visitors show that only 45 percent of attendees live within 200 miles of Charlotte, suggesting that many more people who reside within a day's drive could be targeted.[16]

Questions:

1. Research and describe the current state of the NASCAR Hall of Fame.
2. In terms of marketing the NASCAR Hall of Fame, what combination of pull strategies and push strategies should be used? Explain.
3. Examine the list of communication tactics in Figure 8.3 that can be used with pull strategies. Which components would be most effective? Describe an IMC program that would build awareness of the Hall.
4. Write two communication objectives and two behavioral objectives that the NASCAR Hall of Fame could establish for an IMC campaign.
5. Consider the hierarchy model for sports brands in relation to the NASCAR Hall of Fame. For each of the seven stages, discuss what types of marketing communications tactics should be used.

Sources: Don Muret (2010), "NASCAR Hall of Fame 'Looks Fast Sitting Still'," May 17, accessed April 13, 2012 at http://www.sportsbusinessdaily.com/Journal/Issues/2010/05/20100517/This-Weeks-News/NASCAR-Hall-Of-Fame-Looks-Fast-Sitting-Still.aspx; *NASCAR Hall of Fame*, www.nascarhall.com, September 16, 2010; Brooke A. Beyer, Jr., "Homegrown in N.C.: Contract Drafting in the Fast Lane," http://sportsandentertainmentlaw.ncbar.org/newsletters/sportsentertainmentjune2009, June 7, 2010; "NASCAR Hall of Fame," www.jayski.com/pages/hallsfame-nascar.htm, accessed September 16, 2010.

References

1. "Coca-Cola Family Track Walk, Quarter-Mile Cookout Returns to CMS," (2010), May 4, accessed September 2, 2010, at http://www.thehotlap.com/2010/05/04/coca-cola-family-track-walk-quarter-mile-cookout-returns-to-cms/.
2. "Coca-Cola and Speedway Motorsports Toast Partnership Extension," (2010), March 5, accessed September 2, 2010, at http://www.thecoca-colacompany.com/dynamic/press_center/2010/03/coca-cola-and-speedway-motorsports-toast-partnership-extension.html.
3. Irving Rein, Philip Kotler, and Ben Shields, *The Elusive Fan* (New York: McGraw-Hill, 2006).
4. Kenneth E. Clow and Donald Baack, *Integrated Advertising, Promotion, and Marketing Communications*, 4th ed. (Upper Saddle River, NJ: Prentice Hall, 2010).
5. Lindsay Morris, (1999), "Studies Give Thumbs Up to Mags for Ad Awareness," *Advertising Age*, 70(32), 16–17.

6. "Benefits of Outdoor Advertising: How to Make your Billboards 'Sing' ", (2009), September 10, accessed August 30, 2010, at http://www.reachocala.com/ benefits-of-outdoor-advertising/how-to-make-your-outdoor-advertising-sing.

7. Thomas Haire, (2010), "Jets Audible into Direct Response," *Response Magazine*, January 14, accessed August 30, 2010, at http://www.responsemagazine.com/editorial/ sports-fitness/jets-audible-direct-response-2292.

8. "TMS Unveils Danica, Helio Billboards to Promote June IRL Race," (2008), April 25, accessed August 4, 2010, at http://www.sportsbusinessdaily.com/article/120349.

9. "Phillies, Acme Add Codes to Cups," (2011), *Sports Business Journal*, April 25, 23.

10. Tripp Mickle, (2010), "MLS Will Be First League to Run Extensive Ticket Sales Training," *Sports Business Journal*, May 24, 5.

11. "Pittsburgh Pirates Attendance Data," accessed August 21, 2010, at http://www. baseball-almanac.com/teams/pitatte.shtml.

12. Jon Spoelstra, *Marketing Outrageously* (Atlanta: Bard Press, 2001).

13. Justin McTeer, (2009), "Your Chance to Meet an NBA Legend," November 6, accessed August 24, 2010, at http://bleacherreport.com/ articles/285335-your-chance-to-meet-an-nba-legend.

14. Phillip E. Pfeifer, Mark E. Haskins, and Robert M. Conroy, (2005), "Customer Lifetime Value, Customer Profitability, and the Treatment of Acquisition Spending," *Journal of Managerial Issues*, 17(Spring), 11–25.

15. Arthur Middleton Hughes, (n.d.), "Customer Retention: Integrating Lifetime Value into Marketing Strategies," accessed August 26, 2010, at http://www.dbmarketing.com/articles/ Art112.htm.

16. "NASCAR Hall Launching Summer Campaign," (2011), *Sports Business Journal*, April 25, 22.

9 Creating the Brand Story – Communications Campaigns

Learning Objectives

By the end of this chapter you should be able to:

1. Describe the five steps of the brand communication campaign planning process
2. Discuss the features of three sports brand message strategies
3. Explain the risks and benefits of four presentation strategies used in the sports industry
4. Discuss the use and effectiveness of different types of execution strategies

© Todd Taulman / Shutterstock

Should the LPGA promote good play or good looks of its female golfers?

LPGA's Dilemma: Good Play vs. Good Looks

The Ladies Professional Golf Association (LPGA) has a history that dates back to 1950, but as it enters its seventh decade of existence, marketing challenges exist to bring the LPGA out of the shadows of the PGA Tour. The LPGA has weathered difficult economic times before, but the recession that began in 2008 seemed to hurt more than past recessions. A combination of public relations blunders and controversial leadership along with the loss of seven tournaments between 2007 and 2009 called into question the future of the LPGA.[1] In 2008, the LPGA had to deal with backlash from an English-only policy for players that appeared to target the sizeable contingent of Asian golfers competing on the LPGA tour. Less than a year later, a group of LPGA players banded together to call for the ouster of commissioner Carolyn Bivens. The players faulted Bivens for alienating tournament organizers and hurting the LPGA in the process. Bivens resigned and was replaced by Michael Whan, a former executive at TaylorMade Adidas Golf and newcomer to managing a sports league.[2]

Insider Expert Kathy Carter – Soccer United Marketing

Kathy Carter is president of Soccer United Marketing, a position which oversees the commercial and marketing aspects of the business for Major League Soccer's commercial subsidiary. Carter and her group are responsible for all sales and servicing for some of the premier soccer properties in the United States, including Major League Soccer, the Mexican National Team and famed Mexican club team Chivas de Guadalajara's rights in the U.S., multiple CONCACAF properties, and U.S. Soccer and all of its National Teams.

Carter serves as the U.S. representative on FIFA's Committee for Women's Football and the FIFA Women's World Cup. She also served as vice president, sales and marketing, for Anschutz Entertainment Group (AEG) prior to her position with SUM. At AEG, Carter worked to sign major partnership deals with the Home Depot Center, as well as oversaw the sponsorship sales division for AEG, which included the then six AEG-operated MLS teams; the NHL's Los Angeles Kings; the Women's Tennis Association (WTA) Tour Championships; and the Home Depot Track & Field Invitational.

Prior to her work with AEG, Carter was a vice president for Envision, where she opened and managed the firm's New York office, with a primary focus on facility representation. Carter joined Envision from ISL United States in 2001. As vice president, sales and marketing, for ISL U.S., Carter was responsible for partnership and advertising sales for the Tennis Masters Series, the Association of Tennis Professional's (ATP) premier series of men's professional tennis tournaments.

Carter served as Major League Soccer's vice president of corporate marketing from the league's inception until late 1999. Carter's five years with the league office came on the heels of two years with the World Cup USA 1994 organizing committee. Kathy is a recipient of *Sports Business Journal* and *Crain's New York Business* Forty Under 40 awards, as well as the 2009 Women in Sports and Events (WISE) award. She is a graduate of the College of William and Mary and was a starter on the nationally ranked women's soccer team.

Kathy Carter, President of Soccer United Marketing

Marketing of the LPGA is at a crossroads because of the upheaval experienced in recent years, and a recurring question is being asked: should the LPGA leverage the physical attractiveness of some of its players in its appeal to golf fans and perhaps attract a broader audience intrigued by the beauty of some LPGA stars? The question is delicate on two fronts. First, if the LPGA uses sex appeal in its message to attract fans, does it affect perceptions of the LPGA as a top-tier sports league? Sex is not used to sell the NBA, NHL, or any other major professional property, nor is it used to promote the PGA Tour. A comparable property, the Women's Tennis Association (WTA), focused its latest marketing campaign on characteristics exhibited by WTA players such as determination and grit, not their beauty or femininity.

Second, the LPGA's longing for star power after the retirement of the tour's most recognizable player, Annika Sörenstam, may be met in Michelle Wie. While Wie was a rookie on the LPGA Tour in 2009 at the age of 19, she had already captured interest in the golf world by being invited to compete in women's and men's tournaments as an amateur. Wie's sponsors, Omega (watches) and Kia (automobiles), have stepped up their use of Wie as an endorser. Tournament organizers and the Golf Channel are featuring Wie more prominently in promotional messages. Even the LPGA is considering how to utilize Wie in its advertising efforts.[3]

The divide over whether to celebrate the beauty of LPGA players at the expense of promoting competition on the course will likely continue. The famed agency Wilhelmina Models recently branched out into sports and signed seven LPGA players to contracts.[4] The players represented by Wilhelmina will undoubtedly receive publicity and enjoy media exposure, which could lead to greater familiarity of the players among golf fans. But, is the basis for this familiarity what the LPGA wants its players to be known for? On the other hand, if the sex appeal of a few LPGA players brings the entire tour greater notoriety, is it not worth positioning on the glamour of players such as Natalie Gulbis and Anna Rawson rather than the performance of players such as Wie and Jiyai Shin, the LPGA's leading money winners? These are questions the LPGA must answer as it looks to rebound.

Introduction

The LPGA faces a brand communications dilemma encountered by all marketers: What are the most effective ways to create messages that will lead to the desired responses among the target audience? Decisions concerning content and presentation of brand messages are enhanced, yet at the same time complicated by the wide range of possibilities for developing creative communications. Selection of creative approaches benefits from there being no "one right way" or single method for developing brand messages. Marketers have tremendous leeway concerning how they structure communications with their target market. Unfortunately, this characteristic of brand communications complicates the creative process. If there is no single formula or method for creating brand messages, what method should be used to have the best chance of having the desired effect among the target audience? What should be said, and how should it be presented?

This chapter covers two major areas of brand communications management. First, five steps that comprise a brand communications campaign plan are presented. The five steps cover planning and implementation needed to execute a campaign. Second, creative strategy considerations for brand messages address how the key idea of a message will be delivered, situational factors that influence message content, and how the message itself will be presented to the audience.

Communications Campaign Planning

The strategic nature of integrated marketing communications means that building a great brand is difficult to achieve without a coordinated plan. Ad campaigns and ticket sales drives, staples of sports properties promotion programs, have a role in a marketing plan, but should not be stand-alone efforts. Instead, a broad view of communication tactics is needed so that IMC tools work together to advance customer relationships and ultimately aid in achieving business objectives such as meeting revenue and profit targets. Five steps required in the execution of a brand communications campaign are shown in Figure 9.1. Following the five steps enables marketers to work toward delivering consistent brand messages while pursuing a course that will result in a stronger brand by linking communications tactics to objectives.

1. Define the target market

2. Set objectives

3. Establish the budget

4. Determine IMC strategy and tactics

5. Implement the campaign

FIGURE 9.1 **Steps in Brand Communications Campaign Planning**

© Abdolhamid Ebrahimi / iStockphoto

Step One: Define Target Market

The starting point for a strategic communications plan should be specifying which segments of the target market should be impacted. Defining the target market for an IMC campaign is necessary for three reasons. First, budgets for communications tactics are usually limited, so it is beneficial to prioritize which group or groups of customers will be the target audience. In the case of sports, one consideration at a broad level is whether to target nonfans. After all, the percentage of the population that is classified as nonfans is much greater than the percentage that are sports fans, but there would also be risk assumed in investing precious marketing dollars to appeal to people who have little or no interest in what is offered. Thus, the decision may be to focus brand communications on segments for which conversion to customers is a realistic possibility.

Chrysler Group LLC

Ram Trucks placed this ad during the Kentucky Derby because the audience for the Kentucky Derby is a good match with Ram's target market.

Second, a clear picture of the characteristics of the intended recipients of brand messages will influence decisions on the channels used to reach the audience as well as design of messages to reach them. If the St. Louis Blues of the NHL chooses to target college students, the team may decide to offer discounted tickets on Thursday and Friday home games as part of a Student Night ticket promotion.[5] Communicating Student Night to area college students would be best accomplished through niche media like campus newspapers and radio stations and social media used extensively by college students such as Facebook. Appropriate media channel choices are difficult to make unless the target audience is clearly defined and the message channels most likely to reach and impact them are known.

Third, segments to be targeted in a communications campaign must be identified, because the focus may be only a subset of a firm's overall target market. For example, in the Chapter 8 "You Make the Call" case, it is noted that the NASCAR Hall of Fame determined that only 45% of its visitors live within 200 miles of the museum. If a communications campaign is planned to target people in the greater Charlotte area, that customer segment represents only one audience that the NASCAR Hall of Fame seeks to engage. The target market identified in the marketing plan is not necessarily the same groups that should be targeted in a particular campaign.

The criteria used to segment audiences discussed in Chapter 4 in the context of identifying target markets for an organization's overall marketing strategy apply for brand communications strategy as well. Audiences can be identified on the basis of certain characteristics (e.g., women, college students, or families), benefits sought from consuming sports (e.g., socializing needs), or behavioral characteristics (e.g., up-sell an occasional buyer to a partial-season ticket plan). While a certain tactic may be used to reach a specific audience segment like targeting college students with special offers on designated nights, it is likely that an IMC campaign will target multiple audience segments. The clearer the profile of audience segments to be targeted in terms of their characteristics or needs, the more effective managers responsible for planning and executing the plan can be in devising strategies that will appeal to members of the different segments.

The St. Louis Blues may define college students as the target market for an IMC campaign.

© Andres Rodriguez / Fotolia

Step Two: Set Objectives

Another significant decision that must be made prior to embarking on the creative process to develop an IMC campaign is to set objectives, or outcomes that the campaign will achieve. Two types of IMC objectives were introduced in Chapter 8: communication objectives and behavioral objectives. Communication objectives seek to use IMC tactics to develop and strengthen consumers' cognitive (thinking) and affective (feeling) relationship states with a brand. An outcome such as creating awareness among an audience of an upcoming event, game, season, or new product is an example of a communication objective. Awareness alone will not lead to customer action, but absence of it ensures no sale!

In contrast, behavioral objectives link communication tactics to action by the target market. Product purchase, visits to a website, becoming a follower of a brand's Twitter feed, and calling a sales representative are examples of actions that can be influenced by marketers' communications with a target audience. Use of behavioral objectives implies a direct relationship between brand communications and action. Such an assumption may be too great of an expectation of the capability of most communications tactics, but behavioral objectives serve as a reminder of the ultimate purpose of brand communications.

The strategic implications of setting IMC objectives discussed in Chapter 8 pointed out that an IMC plan should include both communication and behavioral objectives. A singular emphasis on either type of objective would not meet the full scope of a sports property's brand-building needs. The number of objectives and mix of communication and behavioral outcomes to be pursued depends on: 1) the customers' relationship state (e.g., unaware, low brand knowledge, loyal customer) and 2) the resources available to invest in IMC tactics.

Step Three: Establish Budget

Strategic planning can lead to identifying outcomes that an IMC campaign should achieve, but the vision and ideas that could result in building a great brand are often constrained by dollars available to spend on brand communications. For that reason, establishing a budget serves as a bridge between objectives and strategy, used to prioritize communication tactics, so that the most pressing marketing communications needs are addressed before tactics that may be less crucial to achieving objectives. Managers have some latitude in selecting a budget method for brand communications, with each one having strengths and limitations. Four common methods are: 1) affordability, 2) percentage of sales, 3) return on investment, and 4) objective and task (see Figure 9.2).

1. Affordability

2. Percentage of sales

3. Return on investment

4. Objective and task

FIGURE 9.2 **Methods of Setting Communication Budgets**

AFFORDABILITY. For many organizations, marketing is viewed as an expense category just like payroll, insurance, and office supplies. It is viewed as a cost of doing business. This mindset treats expenditures on brand communications as an income statement item that must be controlled. The sole criterion for establishing a budget for a communications campaign using this method is the answer to the question "How much can we afford to spend?" The brand communications budget is based on managers' discretion.

With this approach, the budget is vulnerable to external events impacting judgment of the various managers within the organization and their perceptions of what is affordable. When the recession gripped the U.S. economy in 2008, many corporate sponsors scaled back on dollars spent on their sponsorships. Budget sensitivity to the external environment is felt by organizations of all sizes. DuPont, a Fortune 100 company with more than $30 billion in annual revenues, scaled back its spending on client hospitality that is part of its NASCAR association with driver Jeff Gordon. At one time, DuPont entertained as many as 20,000 guests at NASCAR races in a season. In 2009, the number of guests was reduced to 2,000 as the company decided to curb expenses in a weak economy. As the economy improved, DuPont expanded the number of races and customers in its hospitality marketing program, but the expenditures were far from their prerecession peak.[6]

The affordability method is perhaps the most realistic view of budgeting from a cost standpoint. The main limitation of this method is that it does not treat marketing as an investment that can grow a business. Instead it is an expense that must be managed and, at times, reduced. However, when challenging business conditions exert pressure to reduce spending, it could be the very time that brand communications are needed to reach customers and prospects in order to stimulate sales.

PERCENTAGE OF SALES. Another expense-oriented approach to managing brand communications is to set a budget as a percentage of sales or revenue taken in by an organization. This IMC budget–revenue link can have a historical basis, using the previous year or period as the revenue basis, or it can be based on projected revenue for the upcoming year or period. This method is favored by many marketing managers for two reasons. First, the process of setting a dollar amount for communications is rather simple. No complex quantitative models or other forms of analysis are needed to set a budget. Second, limiting the brand communications budget to a percentage of sales has a more objective basis than the affordability method while maintaining the fiscal control characteristic of treating it as an expense.

Although setting a communications budget in proportion to past or future revenues seems more logical than an arbitrary figure based on what is deemed affordable, two significant limitations must be acknowledged. First, brand communications are still treated as an expense that must be contained instead of an investment that can contribute to advancing a brand or organization. The basis of the budget is not how to build a brand or become a stronger, more relevant firm, but rather it is how to keep costs of IMC spending in line with revenues flowing into the organization.

Second, budgeting in this way creates a situation in which communications follow revenues, when ideally the sequence is the other way around. Investment in a brand communications program will *lead* to revenue generation. If percentage of sales budgeting is used, declines in revenues would result in a call for a lower brand communications budget. If an objective of an IMC campaign is to influence revenue growth, the task will be made more difficult if IMC budgets shrink when revenue drops. If an MLB team experiences an 8% decrease in revenues because of fewer season ticket renewals and wants to target new and former customers to rebuild its season ticket base, a percentage of sales approach to budgeting would call for a lower brand communications budget the following year because of the revenue decline. If anything, a larger budget may be needed to attract new customers and appeal to lost customers.

RETURN ON INVESTMENT. In contrast to the affordability and percentage of sales methods that are driven by viewing brand communications as an expense to control, return on investment (ROI) budgeting pegs IMC expenditures to the revenues they are projected to create. It is important to understand how ROI is calculated. The "return" of ROI is contribution profit, or margin (revenue minus cost of goods sold), divided by the investment in brand communications. Investment dollars that should be included in ROI calculations include media time or space, agency fees if communication tasks are outsourced, printing and postage costs for direct mail campaigns, and any other cost incurred in executing a campaign's tactics. And it is important to note that *contribution profit* after costs of a sale is the measure of interest. This value represents the incremental dollars that IMC contributes to the operation of the sports property.

ROI can be calculated for the entire IMC program as well as calculated for specific tactics. Certain communication tactics lend themselves to easy measurement, while for others it is more difficult to establish a direct link between tactic and revenue. A direct mail campaign that offers a partial-season ticket package sent to customers who bought single-game tickets can be structured in a way that the response can be traced. Codes can be printed on the mail piece, a specific URL can be used to take advantage of the offer online, or a code can be given to a telephone sales representative if the respondent orders using that channel. Even some media advertising efforts can be structured in a similar manner so that response to a specific ad can be traced. In contrast, public relations efforts usually lack the ability to connect their impact on revenue generation, as does brand image and brand awareness advertising that does not call for a specific action.

Managers who value the accountability that ROI budgeting offers must resist the temptation to rely solely on communication tactics for which ROI is relatively easy to measure. The need to measure ROI is influenced by increasing demands for accountability of marketing expenditures. Even when economic times are good, top managers in an organization look for indicators that money spent on marketing activities yield measurable results that positively affect an organization's financial picture. However, the need remains for a blend of tactics that meet the communication and behavioral objectives that move customers through the hierarchy of effects to the point where they engage in buying behavior. A commitment to ROI-driven communications such as the philosophy of Jon Spoelstra discussed in Chapter 8 is commendable because of its pursuit of meaningful impact from communication tactics. However, the drive to measure every tactic undertaken must be tempered with an understanding that direct measurement is not possible every time.

OBJECTIVE AND TASK. The budgeting methods described so far require that a budget for brand communications be set before decisions can be made concerning tactics to reach the target market. This sequence of events potentially constrains the effectiveness of a planned IMC program. The constraint is that communication strategy is influenced disproportionately by available funds instead of the communication messages and channels needed to create awareness, shape image, influence purchase, and other possible objectives an IMC plan might have.

Objective and task budgeting overcomes this limitation of what is known as "top down" budgeting, which refers to the sequence of setting budget first, then building out an IMC program to fit within the budget amount. Instead, objective and task budgeting begins with defining outcomes the IMC program should achieve, then coming up with specific tactics that will be used in pursuit of the objectives. For example, suppose one objective of a communications campaign for a season at the Miami Homestead Speedway, a motorsports facility that hosts

NASCAR and Grand-Am Series races, is to create awareness of the season's race weekends among 75% of its target market. Once this objective is established, marketing managers would develop tactics that are intended to create awareness of the schedule. Decisions might include a billboard ad buy, radio advertising, search engine advertising, and a postcard mailing to people who have bought tickets during the last three years. The costs to create and place messages via the various communication channels used in pursuit of achieving the awareness objective are added together. The same sequence of actions would be repeated for each objective. The sum of all costs that would be incurred if the tactics were executed would be the total IMC budget.

In concept, objective and task is the ideal budgeting method for marketing communications. It follows a strategic sequence of setting objectives followed by devising strategies and tactics that provide the best chance to reach objectives. The centerpiece of IMC budgeting in this approach is the brand, and the communications needed to build the brand and customer relationships. In practice, objective and task is probably the least feasible budgeting method. An underlying assumption of the objective and task method is that whatever communication needs exist, resources will be available to make them happen. Budget constraints make this best-case scenario impractical in many cases. A variation of the objective and task method would be to set objectives and develop the various communication tools that are planned to pursue the objectives. Then, communication and brand-building needs are prioritized so that the tactics deemed most critical to an IMC program receive funding. Other tactics remain in the IMC plan as the budget allows.

With the objective and task method of budgeting, decisions by the Pittsburgh Penguins on media, such as this kiosk, are made after the marketing objectives are established.

Step Four: Determine IMC Strategy and Tactics

Once objectives for an IMC campaign are in place and a budget is determined (or decided that it will be set once all communication tactics are developed), then the focus of brand communications planning turns to the messages and channels to be used to reach the target market. It is fruitless, if not dangerous, to engage in the creative process without first having established parameters in the form of intended outcomes of the IMC program and a budget. Managers' attention now turns to devising the strategies and tactics that will guide and ultimately determine the effectiveness of an IMC program.

The terms *strategy* and *tactics* are sometimes used interchangeably, which is incorrect. Instead, they are complementary decisions, with tactical moves flowing from strategies set to achieve a desired outcome. As shown in Figure 9.3, strategy is the general game plan or direction that an organization plans to follow in pursuit of objectives. Tactics are the actual decisions made and implemented to enact the strategies. Both are needed for strategic planning to be effective. The importance of a dual focus on setting strategy and tactics is made clear by Sun Tzu, the legendary general from ancient China, who said that "Strategy without tactics is the slowest route to victory. Tactics without strategy is the noise before defeat."[7]

Strategy and tactics should flow from objectives set in the second step of the brand communications planning process. Once an objective is set, the question becomes "How do we go about achieving the objective?" The answer is found in strategy, a statement of what communications

FIGURE 9.3
Relationship between Strategy and Tactics

needs should be pursued. Then, tactical decisions are made that specify the communication tools that are to be used to carry out the strategy.

Figure 9.4 provides examples illustrating the relationship between objectives, strategy, and tactics. The plan elements are hypothetical, but they demonstrate the sequential relationship of the strategic planning steps. First, objectives must be established to outline the results that an IMC

FIGURE 9.4 Examples of Objectives, Strategies, and Tactics

Objective	Strategy	Tactics
Create awareness of the upcoming season among 80% of the target market by the start of the season.	Use media advertising and public relations to maximize audience reach	• Billboard ad placement • Radio advertising • Banner ads on local websites • Player appearances on sports TV and radio shows • Media Day event
Have image of "affordable entertainment" among 60% of the target market within 6 months of launch of campaign.	Use media advertising and social media to communicate fans' experiences	• TV and radio commercials featuring fan testimonials • YouTube channel featuring fan testimonial videos • Communicate entertainment value on Facebook and Twitter
Increase average attendance at weeknight games by 500 fans by the end of the season.	Target groups and develop incentives to attract weeknight attendees	• Sales contest among ticket sales staff • Themed events to attract large groups • Sales promotions to influence weeknight ticket purchases
Increase ticket revenue by 10% over last year by the end of the season.	• Increase purchase frequency of occasional buyers • Up-sell partial season-ticket holders • Expand geographic footprint of attendees	• Target specific customers in database with offers to increase purchase level • Sales force make calls to targeted buyers • Ads in specific media vehicles that reach targeted outlying areas • Theme nights for cities or countries in outlying areas

campaign should realize. A sports property has communication needs such as "create awareness for an upcoming season" and "build a desired image such as offering affordable entertainment." If these communication objectives are met, it sets the stage for consumers possibly moving on to the action stage of the buying decision process and purchasing tickets and attending events. The strategic planning shown in Figure 9.4 has two communication objectives (awareness and image) as well as two behavioral objectives (weeknight attendance and ticket revenue).

Strategies are derived from the objectives that guide decisions on the communication tactics needed to achieve the desired results. In Figure 9.4, the objective of increasing "ticket revenue by 10% over last year by the end of the season" will be nothing more than a hope or wish unless managers specify how the organization will go about making the increase happen. The three strategies shown (increase purchase frequency of occasional buyers, up-sell partial-season ticket holders, and expand geographic footprint of attendees) provide general direction of what brand communications need to accomplish. At this point, the challenge moves to the third step: creating ideas for specific communication tactics that bring the strategies to life. In this case, up-selling partial-season ticket customers is made actionable by specifying criteria that will be used to identify buyers in the customer database who are the best prospects. Also, a tactic in support of this strategy would be to create a sales promotion that contains a special offer or incentive for a customer to trade up to a higher-priced plan. Examples of incentives could be free merchandise, access to special team events, or special discounts.

The progression from objectives to strategies to tactics can be thought of as moving from broad statements about desired results, to more general plans about how to get those results, to specific ideas for impacting the target market. Returning to Sun Tzu's quote about strategy and tactics, it is evident that these two planning elements are complementary; one cannot be discarded in favor of the other. If there is a tendency to not fully consider one of these planning stages, it is more likely that strategy will not receive adequate attention. Sometimes there is a tendency to think tactically in terms of placing ads, running promotions, or developing ideas for social media content. When this occurs, then the ultimate question of "What should this tactic accomplish?" is not answered adequately ahead of a communications campaign being executed.

Step Five: Implement Campaign

A final planning step required to execute a brand communications campaign is to specify the actions needed to put plans into effect. Two types of decisions that are made at this stage are: 1) assigning responsibilities for carrying out tasks (person or department), and 2) establishing a timetable for communications to occur (scheduling). The best-conceived plans will be unsuccessful if managers do not follow through to this stage of communications planning. Responsibilities for implementation of communication tactics may fall to a single staff person such as a fan relations manager, collaboration by personnel from different departments such as community relations and marketing, or an alliance with an outside firm or services provider such as a Web designer or advertising agency. Regardless of who is assigned responsibility for executing tasks, the benefit of including this step in the communications planning process is that accountability is created for carrying out IMC plans.

The other consideration at the implementation stage of the communications planning process is to set a timetable that specifies when each planned tactic should be carried out. As shown in Figure 9.5, media planners use three approaches to planning timetables for communicating with target audiences: 1) continuous, 2) flighting, and 3) pulsating.

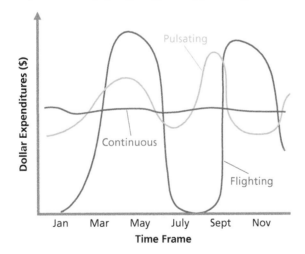

FIGURE 9.5 **Timing of Communications with Target Audiences**

Continuous scheduling calls for a steady flow of communication between the marketer and its audience over the course of a campaign. Products for which there is year-round demand with relatively little fluctuation in demand are ideal candidates for continuous scheduling.

Flighting is a communications scheduling method characterized by periods of communication with a target audience and other periods with no communication activity. This approach is best suited for products with seasonal demand. Sports properties have generally been viewed as a product that fits the mold of marketers that should use flighting scheduling. After all, college football tickets are not in high demand in March because it is at nearly six months ahead of the season. However, many sports have extended fan interest in the off-season with events such as free agency, league meetings, and player drafts. As a result, the downtime that a seasonal sports brand has today is much less than before the information explosion created by forces such as the Internet, cable TV channels dedicated to sports, and sports talk radio. The reduction of distinct season/off-season periods for sports brands in terms of fan interest leads to a need to use a communications scheduling method that calls for more regular contact. Also, the availability of low-cost communication channels like social media and e-mail make it more affordable for sports properties to remain in contact with their target markets continuously.

The third communications scheduling method, **pulsating**, may be the most appropriate choice for a sports property that seeks to maintain year-round contact with consumers but capitalize on opportunities to maximize sales and customer impact at certain times of the year. A pulsating plan employs the continuous scheduling approach of regular contact with target segments and complements it with periods of more frequent, intensive communications that coincide with marketing opportunities on the calendar. For example, many sports properties that sell season tickets launch renewal campaigns with their customers for the following season prior to the end of the current season. Similarly, sales efforts to attract groups to commit to buy tickets for outings to games will occur months in advance of a season beginning. On the other hand, media advertising to stimulate ticket sales for specific games or events throughout a season may be scheduled to run just a matter of days before each game. Also, the pulsating method recognizes that certain sales opportunities arise that can be maximized by investing more in communications with prospective customers. Marketing efforts to promote rivalry games, the appearance of a superstar player on an opposing team, or special events like opening day or season finale are examples of how the added significance of a game or event can become the theme of messages aimed at eliciting purchases.

Creative Strategy

The heart of planning a communications campaign is determining creative strategy. Other key decisions have been made: the target segment or segments for the campaign, objectives that should be achieved, how much money to budget for communications, and the strategies and tactics that will be used. Now, the task is deciding what needs to be communicated to the target market and how to communicate it. When it comes to creative strategy and the creative process, one could view making creative decisions with optimism or pessimism.

Optimism can be found in the fact that marketers are not limited in options for structuring or encoding messages they send. There is no one formula or step-by-step process that must always be followed when creating messages. The approach used is limited only by the creativity of persons responsible for communications design. On the other hand, the seemingly limitless possibilities for managing the creative process may contribute to a pessimistic view toward setting creative strategy. Because there is no single "right way" to create brand messages, marketers take on risk every time they launch a campaign. Will the target market respond to messages in the desired manner? Will they respond at all? Sound strategic planning can still fail if creative strategy decisions do not make a meaningful impact with the target audience.

Creative strategy involves three important creative decisions: 1) the message strategy, 2) the presentation approach, and 3) the message execution (see Figure 9.6). These decisions focus

FIGURE 9.6 Creative Strategy Decisions

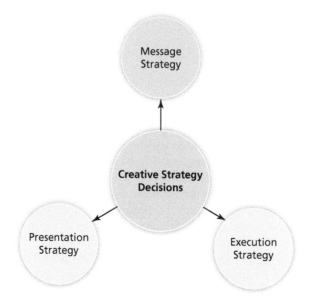

on the approach to be used to gain an audience's attention and how to structure messages to carry out the attention-getting strategy. Although discussed separately, these three decisions are made simultaneously in order to ensure a powerful message. It is at this stage of communications planning that a brand is given a "voice" through decisions about messages to be sent to the target market.

Message Strategy

A **message strategy** is the primary tactic or approach used to deliver the key ideas in a message.[8] Choice of message strategy is important because it will have an influence on whether messages gain the attention of the target audience. Choice of message strategy should be guided by the stage in the hierarchy of effects sports model at which marketers believe they can have the greatest impact with an audience. As shown in Figure 9.7, the three message strategy options that correspond with the three general stages of the hierarchy sports model discussed in Chapter 8 are: informational (knowledge) strategies, emotional (affinity) strategies, and behavioral (action) strategies.

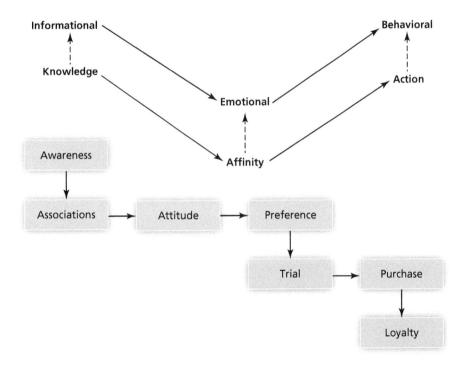

FIGURE 9.7 Message Strategies and Hierarchy Sports Model

INFORMATIONAL STRATEGY. The use of an informational strategy in brand messages is based on a manager's judgment that buyers and prospects are most likely to be persuaded by messages that contain features, attributes, product benefits, or other information. The goal is to create awareness and associations. Most informational messages are not designed to encourage action, but simply to provide the target market with information. The information can be upcoming games or it can be special events that are scheduled such as fireworks after a July 4 game.

Information processing can influence the buying decision if needed information is presented in a way that gets the attention of a consumer and affinity for the brand has already developed. A radio commercial for Indiana Pacers season tickets that contains the number of games in a ticket package, opponents and star players, price, and ordering information would be an example of a message using an informational strategy. In this case, it is expected that buyers for NBA game tickets would be persuaded by the facts contained in the commercial. For purchases requiring a substantial investment like Indiana Pacers season tickets, which range from $400 to $28,000, it is assumed that buyers do not act on impulse.[9] They seek to make decisions based on information such as product features and benefits. Brand messages like those delivered in a radio

FIGURE 9.8 **Examples of Informational Messages**

- Season starts at home this year with a game against the Buffalo Bills on September 3.

- The St. Louis Cardinals will be here for a huge weekend at Wrigley Field. Tickets are still available.

- Pittsburgh Penguins score one for life: Blood drive, February 27 at the CONSOL Energy Center. Jersey-style T-shirts for donors and an opportunity to meet Penguin stars. (American Red Cross)

commercial can provide the needed input to influence decision making. See Figure 9.8 for some examples of informational messages.

EMOTIONAL STRATEGY. Another approach to gaining the attention of an audience is to appeal to them through an emotion that connects the brand to the consumer in some way. The goal is to change attitude or develop preference. An informational message strategy may be effective for reaching a certain percentage of the target market, but it is likely that not all consumers will be persuaded by a rather straightforward presentation of product information. Motives for sports consumption were discussed in Chapter 2, and some of the underlying reasons people follow or consume sports can be used as the means of persuasion. Emotional message strategies can be effective for communication of sports offerings given the emotionally charged relationships many sports fans have with their favorite teams or players.

Marketing managers must decide which emotions and corresponding brand messages will have the greatest impact with the target market. The options are plentiful. One emotion that can be used to appeal to consumers is excitement, whether it is the action on the field of play or the overall experience of attending a sporting event. Belongingness is another emotion that can be particularly powerful in a consumer's relationship with a sports brand in terms of being a fan of a team or a community of fellow fans with a shared passion. Happiness can be an emotional

This advertisement by the Atlanta Braves uses an emotional appeal to attract couples to a game.

appeal to reach sports fans by connecting the joy felt when attending a sporting event with family or friends and getting away from one's daily routine for a few hours. Figure 9.9 provides some examples of emotional messages. The communications strategy of the LPGA discussed at the beginning of the chapter is an example of a campaign using an emotional strategy. The beauty of certain golfers and the connection of beauty to lifestyle are emotional elements that the LPGA uses to appeal to its target market.

FIGURE 9.9 **Examples of Emotional Messages**

- Fun-packed excitement this weekend as the No. 1 ranked LSU Tigers clash with our Crimson Tide. The stadium will be rocking!

- Bored, nothing to do? Come out to the ballpark and watch the Salt Lake Bees take on the Colorado Sky Sox. Special $1 hot dogs and music by the local band, RiverBoys, during and after the game.

- Be part of Christian Night at Minute Maid. After the game with the Pittsburgh Pirates listen to Christian music and inspirational messages by Houston Astros players and staff.

BEHAVIORAL STRATEGY. A third message strategy seeks to persuade consumers by making a call to action. The goals include generating trial purchase, encouraging additional purchases, or developing loyalty. As shown in the examples in Figure 9.10, the intent of the messages that use a behavioral strategy is to have members of the target audience do something: make a telephone call to a ticket sales representative, visit a website to enter a ticket giveaway promotion designed to add contacts to a database, buy tickets, or any other desired response from customers or prospects. In some cases, the call to action is "sweetened" with an incentive, such as giveaways like team caps, bobble-head dolls, or other items that add value beyond the experience of attending a game or event. Another form of behavioral strategy can be the use of scarcity to appeal to fans. Scarcity takes the form of a limited supply of tickets or product, with the implication being that failure to act promptly could result in missing out on the opportunity to buy.

FIGURE 9.10 **Examples of Behavioral Messages**

- Get a David Ortiz bobble-head. Be among the first 20,000 fans 12 and older at this Saturday's game in Fenway Park.

- Portland Sea Dogs Welcome Back Dinner to Benefit Youth Alternatives - April 6, 2011, 5:30 p.m. at the Portland Expo. Meet and greet the 2011 team. Help yourself to a delicious ballpark-style meal, including Sea Dogs Biscuits. Enjoy the raffles, balloons, games, and more. Purchasers of the first 50 tickets have dinner with a Sea Dogs team member.

- Buffalo Sabres Fan Pack for Feb. 23 vs. Winnipeg now on sale. Package includes two 300 level II tickets, New Era Sabres hat, 40th anniversary program. Only $69 ($95 value). Go to www.ticketmaster.com.

CONSIDERATIONS FOR SELECTING MESSAGE STRATEGY. As one considers the three different message strategies that can be used to guide creative development of brand messages, a logical question that might be asked in the course of planning an IMC campaign is: Which strategy should be used in message development? The answer very likely is "all of them." If different customer segments are being targeted, different messages will be needed to appeal to each segment's interest in the brand. A ticket sales campaign that targets businesses will use a different message strategy from a campaign targeting individuals. An informational strategy could be used to outline the features and benefits of a corporate ticket-buying program to reward employees and entertain customers. For the consumer segment, an emotional strategy might be utilized to appeal to the person's civic pride and need to support the community.

Customers are at different relationship stages with a sports brand, ranging from unaware to loyal fan. Thus, using a single message strategy would be ineffective for reaching all persons in the target market. Using multiple messages with various message strategies will allow a sports property to reach individuals at each of the stages of the relationship.

Presentation Strategy

Options for message presentations for sports brands are perhaps more numerous than for other types of products. The reason is that there are some situations unique to the sports industry that give sports marketers additional options for developing brand messages. The **presentation strategy** is the situational foundation for the message and execution of the brand story. Four unique presentation situations found in sports are listed in Figure 9.11.

FIGURE 9.11 Unique Presentation Situations in Sports

© karaboux / Fotolia

- Marketing a team brand versus individual star players
- Marketing the home team versus opponents
- Marketing a team with a poor on-field performance
- Marketing a team with little history or tradition

TEAM BRAND VERSUS INDIVIDUAL STARS. Perhaps one of the most difficult decisions sports marketers face when developing execution of brand messages is whether to focus on the team brand or the star power of individual players. It is a difficult choice because the popularity of a star player can attract attention and create interest for the team—two communication outcomes that form part of the foundation for customer relationships with a sports brand. Top-tier players can have a noticeable effect on ticket and merchandise sales.

One of the greatest individual influencers on fan interest and purchases in recent years has been NBA star LeBron James. His free agent status in 2010 was cited as an influence on an increase in season ticket sales for the New York Knicks even though the Knicks did not sign James.[10] The absence of LeBron James has been observed to have the opposite effect. When James's Cleveland Cavaliers were eliminated from the playoffs, prices for NBA playoff tickets in the secondary market on websites such as StubHub dropped immediately.[11] Individual players can become the face of a franchise, and their personality traits are often admired by fans, making them valuable marketing assets.

The benefits of tapping the goodwill that can be attributed to star players must be balanced with risks that come along with focusing on one or a few individual players. If a player receives negative publicity for problems off the field (or on the field), the negative perceptions created could have a damaging effect on perceptions of the team or sponsor associated with the individual. When Tiger Woods became embroiled in controversy over behavior in his personal life, consulting firm Accenture quickly ended its association, saying that Woods was no longer the "right representative" for the company. Given that Accenture's ad campaign featuring Tiger Woods sought to personify brand attributes such as integrity and high performance through its association with Woods, the company had little choice but to distance itself from an individual who personal integrity was being scrutinized.[12]

The risks of building message execution around stars are not limited to players behaving badly off the field. In professional sports, player free agency has created challenges to using individuals as marketing spokespersons long term. If a player leaves a team because of free agency, in most cases fan allegiances do not change to the player's new team, they stay with the old team, an indication that fans' connections are often to the team and not a player. A financial cost exists, too, when players featured in marketing campaigns leave via free agency or trade. Promotional material, banners, advertisements, and other creative work produced in support of a campaign built around a departed player become obsolete.

Other issues that can arise beyond the control of sports marketers are subpar player performance and injuries, unexpected developments that take individual players off of center stage. This happened to the Dallas Stars of the NHL when they created an ad campaign featuring two of the team's best players, Marty Turco and Brendan Morrow. Turco had one of the worst seasons of his career and Morrow suffered a season-ending injury after less than one-fourth of the season.[13] The uncertainties concerning individual players in terms of their behavior, performance, and health should not eliminate them from utilization in brand messages. However, the team brand is more enduring and stable, two characteristics that could influence creative direction to emphasize the team brand.

HOME TEAM OR OPPONENT. Message execution decisions for a brand communications campaign for a sports team may involve whether to feature opposing teams that will be visiting to play games or to focus exclusively on the home team brand. A sporting event differs from other types of products in that the two teams involved in a contest are also two brands. Each brand possesses equity, or value that can be leveraged in brand communications. The consideration that must be made is to what extent, if at all, the visiting team brand will be used to persuade the target market to make the decision to attend.

In some cases, the visiting team brand has very high equity and can be an attribute to be included in the description of features and benefits. When Major League Baseball teams take part in interleague play during a season, it creates matchups that occur very infrequently. When marquee teams such as the New York Yankees, Chicago Cubs, and Boston Red Sox pay a rare visit to a city during interleague play, the series is often highlighted in the home team's ticket sales campaign for that season. Not only can the high level of interest fans hold for some opposing teams lead to increased sales for those games, but fans may be motivated to buy a multiple-game ticket package in order to assure that they will have tickets for the best opponents on the schedule.

Another creative execution involving opponents is to focus on rivalry games to maximize interest and ticket sales for those special games. Some rivalries have evolved into their own brands that add to the storyline of the games being played. The Los Angeles Kings and Anaheim Ducks are nearby neighbors competing in the NHL's Pacific Division. The teams created a rivalry brand known as the "Freeway Face-Off" intended to generate greater interest in the teams' six regular season games against each other. In addition to adding to the significance of the six games for fans of both teams that can translate into more ticket revenues, the teams realized a benefit by attracting Subway as a title sponsor for the Freeway Face-Off.[14] Many rivalries garner such a high level of attention and interest from fans that advertisements or other communication tactics designed to promote the events are not a high priority. However, in the case of a six-game series over the course of a season there may be games for which ticket sales opportunities remain or revenues can be realized in other ways, such as sponsorships or licensed merchandise sales.

Featuring opposing teams or their star players in brand communications poses a dilemma for sports marketers. A motive for using this strategy is to maximize revenues in the short term. A high-profile opposing team or player could spark interest among people who rarely attend or who are fans of the opposing team. The result could be higher ticket and concessions revenues attributable to the fans attracted by featuring the opposition. This strategy can be beneficial when a property has difficulties selling its ticket inventory to a base of fans committed to their team. Marketing unsold tickets to fans of opposing teams or casual fans attracted to high-quality opponents is a revenue-generating opportunity that cannot be ignored.

In the long term, this strategy does little to build the home team brand. The ideal is forming relationships between customers and *your* brand, and if the reason people are attending is because of the other team, the motivation to consume is not sustained. Drawing attention to opponents can elicit action from consumers, but at a potential price of detracting from growth of the home team brand.

POOR PERFORMANCE OF ON-FIELD PRODUCT. A creative execution issue that is uniquely experienced in the sports industry is developing creative ideas for marketing messages for a brand whose performance on the field is mediocre, or in rare cases extremely poor. In most industries, marketing is the link between customers and production of the product or service. Any shortcomings or weaknesses customers have experienced with a brand can be observed by marketers and steps taken to improve quality. In contrast, sports marketers have no control

over the on-field product. They are tasked with developing customer experiences around the core and actual product. Conventional wisdom holds that winning solves many marketing problems a sports property might experience. Success can lead to more talk about the team in offices and pubs, larger audiences for TV and radio broadcasts, and higher attendance at games. But if a team is mired in mediocrity, what should properties communicate to their target markets?

One strategy for message execution in this situation is to focus on the entertainment value or experience delivered by sports consumption. If the product offering is based on meeting people's need for entertainment, then it is possible to deliver a quality experience to customers regardless of a game or event's outcome. The value proposition may be based on family fun, affordable entertainment, watching star players of the future, or some other attribute that is independent of wins and losses.

Another strategy that can be employed when on-field performance is poor is to acknowledge and embrace poor performance. This unusual approach was adopted by the Minnesota Timberwolves in 2010. First, the team placed billboard ads that acknowledged its poor performance and the need to rebuild the franchise following the loss of star player Kevin Garnett. Messages such as "A message for our harshest critics: you're right" and "An honest assessment of the past. A plan for the future" communicated to fans and the community that the Timberwolves organization accepted responsibility for its lack of success and suggested a long-term commitment to returning to its winning ways.[15] Those messages were followed by a season with a record of 15 wins and 67 losses.

For teams mired in mediocrity or poor performance, campaigns emphasizing fun, excitement, or affordability may be a good presentation strategy.

Timberwolves management placed a newspaper ad in the *Minneapolis Star Tribune*, thanking fans for their support and providing a blunt assessment of the organization. The following excerpt from the letter to fans sums up how the organization positioned the team for the next season:

> "We are now a deep team, with quality backups at nearly every position. But we remain young, perhaps even the youngest team in the league. It's highly unlikely we will challenge for the NBA championship this season, but I believe we now have a collection of talent that could form most of a core nucleus that has its best days ahead."[16]

An approach like that taken by the Minnesota Timberwolves does not make promises that the team cannot deliver. In fact, it does the opposite, "underpromising" or setting low expectations for fans. However, the honesty and transparency shown by Timberwolves management in its billboards and letter to fans is a message execution that may win over some fans disheartened by the team's poor performance.

LITTLE HISTORY OR TRADITION. In contrast to situations in which a sports property's performance has been subpar or below expectations, there are times when there is little in the way of past accomplishments on which to base presentation strategy. If there are no championships or other notable successes in a sports property's past, what can be done to fill the void? Two options exist: avoid the lack of tradition or embrace it.

Avoidance means simply that one of the other situations discussed earlier (focus on team brand, promote individuals, or feature opponents) is looked to for a presentation strategy. Similarly, other aspects of customer experience could be emphasized in brand messages. Images of people enjoying themselves at a game, groups appearing in social settings such as tailgating before a football game or in a suite at a baseball game, or other messages that communicate the idea that people have fun at a sporting event are ways to skirt limited history or tradition.

An alternative to avoiding dealing with a lack of a storied past is to develop connection points that can serve as a link to the past. One approach to making this happen is to relate an unfamiliar brand with something that does have traditions. When the Carolina Hurricanes of the NHL relocated to Raleigh, the franchise had an unimpressive background in terms of winning and playoff appearances. Moreover, the team was now located in a nontraditional hockey market, meaning that traditions associated with the sport of hockey would not resonate with many sports fans in the market. As discussed in Chapter 4, a segmentation strategy employed to attract area sports fans to the Hurricanes was to link the team with NASCAR, a sport rich in tradition in the North Carolina region. In addition to NASCAR being popular locally, the two sports share similar target market characteristics and fans experience similar sensations at NHL games and NASCAR races such as speed, aggression, and contact. And, the Hurricanes enlisted popular driver Jeff Burton to help promote the team and the experiential similarities between NASCAR and NHL.[17]

Execution Strategy

The **execution strategy** is how the message will be presented to the target audience. In general, execution strategies align with the three types of message strategies as illustrated in Figure 9.12. In addition, the presentation strategy will have an impact on which approach is used.

FIGURE 9.12 **Message Strategies and Executions**

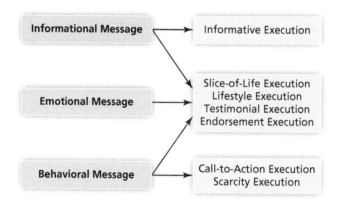

INFORMATIVE EXECUTION. With the **informative execution**, information is presented to the audience in a straightforward, matter-of-fact way with no drama or emotion, so it fits well with the informational message strategy. The goal of informative executions is to provide the audience with some type of information to create awareness and associations with the brand. It may be the home dates for a college football team or the announcement of players appearing at an event to sign autographs. It could be a starting time for a baseball or football game that has been changed due to ESPN televising the game. Informative executions are common for radio, but can also be seen with print media and online. For short messages, billboards are an excellent medium.

SLICE-OF-LIFE AND LIFESTYLE EXECUTIONS. These executions have the most flexibility and can be used with all three message strategy approaches. The slice-of-life execution was made famous by Procter & Gamble in the 1950s, advertising products such as Tide. The typical **slice-of-life execution** has four stages: encounter, problem, interaction, and solution. With Tide, the encounter was a child playing soccer and her uniform becoming dirty or stained. The problem occurs when the child states it will never become clean for the championship game. A voice-over, the mother, or a neighbor then highlights the power of Tide, the interaction. Then the final scene shows the daughter playing in the championship game in her clean uniform, the solution.

The **lifestyle execution** approach shows how the product or brand fits into the lifestyle of the consumer or audience. For the consumer who loves excitement, an ad could highlight an upcoming football game with Florida State or the number one ranked team in the nation. Visuals of students having a good time, fast-paced action on the football field, and tailgating could be used to show how the game would fit into the person's lifestyle.

TESTIMONIAL AND ENDORSEMENT EXECUTIONS. The effectiveness of these execution strategies resides in the source, or sender of the message. **Testimonial executions** involve an individual or individuals espousing a particular sports team or event. The individual could be a member of the sports team, the media covering the team, announcers, team personnel, or even other fans. For example, a season ticket sales campaign could use testimonials from existing customers to communicate the benefits of being a season ticket holder to prospective buyers. Testimonials are perceived as highly credible messages because the source of the message is an actual customer or user, often a person with whom target audience members share common characteristics.

A strategy with great relevance in the sports industry is **endorsement execution**. An endorsement is a variation of a testimonial that associates a prominent or well-known person with a brand. The familiarity and likeability of a star athlete, coach, or broadcaster can capture an audience's attention and influence liking of the brand via consumers' liking of the endorser. An endorsement differs from a testimonial in that the relationship of the endorser to the brand may be more limited. Testimonials feature actual users, customers, employees—people who have an established connection with the brand. In contrast, an endorser may have no connection with a brand beyond his or her paid association. The extent of the endorsement may be lending one's name and likeness to a brand. The endorser may not even use the product being endorsed.

This characteristic of endorsements is typically viewed as a limitation of its effectiveness as an advertising execution, but brands can benefit from association with an athlete. An often cited example is Tiger Woods's endorsement of Buick. From 1999–2008, Woods was associated with Buick. On one hand, many consumers were skeptical that a wealthy athlete like Woods would drive a non-luxury brand like Buick. The perception was that he simply was endorsing Buick for the money. On the other hand, the impact of Woods's relationship with Buick was measurable. Global sales for Buick increased 17% during Woods's endorsement contract, and the average age of Buick owners decreased by about ten years.[18] Other evidence of the effectiveness of athlete endorsement is found in a study of consumers' response to print advertisements. Presence of an athlete endorser increased ad readership 7.5% over ads without an endorser.[19] Figure 9.13 lists the highest-earning athlete endorsers in the United States. These high-profile athletes bring notoriety to the products and services they endorse through their associations with the brands.

Rank	Athlete	Sport	Annual Endorsement Income
1.	Tiger Woods	PGA	$70,000,000
2.	Phil Mickelson	PGA	$52,000,000
3.	LeBron James	NBA	$30,000,000
4.	Dale Earnhardt, Jr.	NASCAR	$22,000,000
5.	Jeff Gordon	NASCAR	$15,000,000
6.	Peyton Manning	NFL	$15,000,000
7.	Shaquille O'Neal	NBA	$15,000,000

FIGURE 9.13 Top American Athlete Endorsers

Selection of an endorser includes consideration of two criteria: 1) perceived fit between endorser and brand and 2) likeability. Consumer response to an endorser's connection with a brand can be more favorable if it is perceived that the two "go together." Tiger Woods's endorsement of Buick did not necessarily rate strong on this criterion. However, Buick was able to address the issue through marketing campaigns that communicated Woods's relationship with Buick. Activating a marketing partnership like an athlete endorsement is a strategy for persuading the target market that a fit exists between endorser and brand. The likeability or popularity of an athlete can also impact perceived fit. Athletes like LeBron James, Dale Earnhardt Jr., and Peyton Manning are highly paid endorsers because many of their deals are with brands that are outside their expertise area (i.e., their particular sport). Personality traits of certain endorsers make them attractive to a wide range of companies, while other athletes find that their endorsement opportunities may be limited to products related to their sport.

These three categories of executions offer marketers considerable flexibility, because they can be used with any of the message strategies. They can be used to provide information, creating awareness and associations. They can be used to instill affinity, creating emotional reactions that result in stronger attitudes and preferences for the sports product. Lastly, they can be used to change behavior and spur action to try a sports product for the first time, to return, or to become a loyal customer.

CALL-TO-ACTION AND SCARCITY EXECUTIONS. While providing knowledge is important and creating emotional bonds is beneficial, it is the change of behavior or the spurring of action that is vital to an organization's viability. **Call-to-action executions** urge individuals to do something. It may be to join a brand's Facebook page, it may be to access the website for more information, or it may be to purchase tickets. With the **scarcity execution** the caveat is added that there is limited time or availability. It may be that only two hundred tickets are left, or it may be that the special promotional price will last for only one week or until the end of the month. With both

Insider Insights Kathy Carter – Soccer United Marketing

Q. What are the steps in the promotion campaign planning process for Soccer United Marketing?

A. Three major steps are:

1. Setting objectives – What is the goal? For a team it is ticket sales. What is the manifest (i.e., how many of each do you need to sell to achieve revenue targets)?
2. Establish promotion mix – What is the best way to create a reason to purchase?

   - Access – Use experiences and insider access to strengthen relationships
   - Gifts – Reward loyal customers
   - Incentives – Appeal to casual or occasional ticket buyer

3. Implementation – How do you reach your target audience?

   - Premium seat inventory (luxury suites, boxes, premium dining and seating areas)
   - Season tickets
   - Renewals – work begins before the end of the season
   - New seasons – ongoing
   - Group tickets
   - Youth soccer groups
   - Other groups
   - Individual ticket sales

Soccer United Marketing

Kathy Carter shares her thoughts on promotions and creative strategies

Q. What advice can you give for making creative strategy decisions when developing a brand communications campaign?

A. The key is to stay true to the brand. For an MLS team, this means focus on the product, even though each team is different. While the MLS brand is made up in part by our clubs, each club has a unique image and personality in its local market. Creative strategy for a club's marketing campaign should communicate the distinctiveness of the brand.

Q. How does the target market for MLS clubs affect creative strategy?

A. It is possible and beneficial to tailor the message to specific audiences. Key fan groups for MLS and directions for creative strategy to reach them are:

- Core fans – These are key supporters of the club; stay true to the core, focus on the product
- Casual fans – With this group you may focus on the experience, the opponent, and star players; ways that MLS clubs have appealed to casual fans include:

  - Star players – David Beckham and Landon Donovan with the Los Angeles Galaxy, Thierry Henry and Rafa Márquez with the New York Red Bulls
  - Rivalries (New York vs. Philadelphia, Toronto vs. Montreal)

- Non-MLS soccer fans – With this group of fans a focus might be on the similarity of the experience between MLS and soccer with which this audience is familiar.

approaches, the goal is to change behavior and get the audience to act. Similarly, promotions or special events may use a scarcity execution to encourage immediate action. Examples include limiting a cap giveaway to ten thousand people or holding an autograph session with a retired player before a game. These tactics may motivate attendees to arrive early—staying longer and possibly spending more money while at the venue.

Chapter Summary

The strategic nature of integrated marketing communications requires a coordinated plan. While planning does not ensure success, lack of planning almost always assures failure. The five steps in communication campaign planning are: 1) define the target market, 2) set objectives, 3) establish the budget, 4) determine the IMC strategy and tactics, and 5) implement the campaign.

The four common methods of determining communication budgets are affordability, percentage of sales, return on investment, and objective and task. With the affordability method, the communications campaign is seen as an expense item and the budget is based on what management feels they can afford to spend. With the percentage of sales method the budget is set based on a certain percent of either last year's revenues or anticipated revenues for the next year. With return on investment, the budget is based on the revenues the communication plan is expected to create. The best and most difficult method to use is the objective and task, because objectives are set and then the costs of achieving each objective is calculated. The problem with this method is firms do not have unlimited dollars to spend on marketing and therefore not all objectives can be achieved, and certainly not with optimal tactics for each one.

In developing strategies and tactics, it is important to first determine the objectives to be achieved. Then for each objective a strategy is developed. The tactics then follow the strategies. Too often communication plans are developed by immediately thinking of tactics rather than the sequential steps from objective to strategies to tactics.

In implementing the communications plan, three approaches can be used in terms of timing of the expenditures. Continuous scheduling calls for a steady flow of communication expenditures during the campaign. Flighting schedules call for periods of expenditures, with no expenditures at other times. Pulsating schedules have communications during the entire campaign, but with spikes of extra spending during certain times.

Creative strategy involves three decisions: message strategy, presentation strategy, and execution strategy. The message strategy is the tactic or approach used to deliver the message and corresponds to the three components of the hierarchy sports model. Informational message strategy is used to relay knowledge, the emotional strategy is used to develop affinity, and the behavioral message strategy is used to spur action.

The presentation strategy involves the unique opportunities present in sports. Unique presentations include marketing the team brand versus individual star players, marketing the home team versus an opposing team, marketing a team with a poor on-field performance, and marketing a team with little history or tradition.

The last creative strategy decision is the selection of the execution approach. Informative execution is used with the informational message strategy. Slice-of-life, lifestyle, testimonial, and endorsement executions can be used with any of the three message strategies. Call-to-action and scarcity executions are used with the behavioral message strategy.

Review Questions

1. Identify the five steps in brand communications campaign planning.
2. What are the four methods of setting budgets? Describe each method.
3. Describe the relationship between objectives, strategies, and tactics.
4. Identify and describe the three approaches to planning the timing of marketing communications.
5. What are the three creative strategy decisions that must be made?
6. What is a message strategy?
7. What are the three types of message strategies?
8. Explain the relationship between message strategy options and the hierarchy sports model's primary components of knowledge, affinity, and action.
9. What is meant by the term presentation strategy, and what are the unique presentation situations found in sports?
10. What is an execution strategy? Identify the various execution strategies.
11. Describe the relationship between execution strategies and message strategies.

New Terms

Continuous scheduling   steady flow of communication spending over the course of a campaign or year.

Flighting   communications at select times during a campaign or year, with no communications at other times.

Pulsating   steady flow of communication expenditure over the course of a campaign or year, with bursts of additional communications at select times.

Message strategy   primary tactic or approach used to deliver the key ideas in a message.

Presentation strategy   situational foundation for the message and execution of the brand story.

Execution strategy   defines how the message will be presented to the target audience.

Informative execution   straight-forward, matter-of-fact method with no emotion or drama.

Slice-of-life execution   presentation of a message through the four stages of encounter, problem, interaction, and solution.

Lifestyle execution   describes how the product will fit into the lifestyle of the consumer.

Testimonial execution   involves individuals espousing a particular sports team or event.

Endorsement execution   associating a celebrity or well-known person with a brand to influence liking of brand through liking of the endorser.

Call-to-action execution   urging of individuals to act or do something.

Scarcity execution   conveying a message that there is limited time or availability of a product.

Discussion and Critical Thinking Exercises

1. Review the opening vignette about the LPGA. Should the LPGA use sex appeal to attract a larger audience, or does this approach destroy the professionalism of the sport? What other approaches could the LPGA use to rebuild its audience and image?

2. Why is it important to identify the target market before setting objectives? Identify the different target markets for developing a communication plan for marketing sports at your college. What types of objective might be used with each target market?

3. Timing of communications involves three different schedules: continuous, flighting, and pulsating. For each, describe a sports product that would use that type of scheduling.

4. Pick a professional sports league or team. Describe an informational message strategy that could be used to build awareness and another one that could be used for associations. Describe an emotional message strategy that could be used to change attitudes and another one to build preference. Describe a behavioral strategy that could be used to encourage initial trial purchase, another one for a repeat purchase, and a third for building loyalty.

5. Sports offers unique situations not typically found with products. Pick your favorite sports team. Does the team focus on marketing the team brand or individual players, or both? What are the pros and cons of marketing the team brand versus the individual star players?

6. What is the closest professional baseball team to you (major league or minor league)? Discuss the team's marketing approach in terms of marketing the team versus individual star players. Describe instances where they have marketed an opponent versus the home team.

7. Think of a sports team, either college or pro, that has performed poorly the last few years. What type of marketing approach has the team used? What type of marketing approach should the team use?

8. Suppose the LPGA has asked you to assist with the execution of a communications plan. The decision has been made to use an informational message strategy. Recommend an execution strategy that can be used with an informational message strategy. Describe an advertisement or marketing idea using the recommended execution.

9. Suppose the LPGA has asked you to assist with the execution of a communications plan. The decision has been made to use an emotional message strategy. Recommend an execution strategy that can be used with an emotional message strategy. Describe an advertisement or marketing idea using the recommended execution.

10. Suppose the LPGA has asked you to assist with the execution of a communications plan. The decision has been made to use a behavioral message strategy to increase attendance at LPGA golf tournaments. Recommend an execution strategy that can be used with a behavioral message strategy. Describe an advertisement or marketing idea using the recommended execution.

You Make the Call

K-Swiss

K-Swiss was founded in 1966 in California by brothers Art and Ernest Brunner. The pair enjoyed skiing and tennis, and it was their desire to design a shoe specifically for the demands of tennis players. The result was the first all-leather tennis shoe, and it caught on quickly among tennis players and upscale consumers. K-Swiss was different from most athletic footwear companies in that it did not bring new styles to market frequently, nor did it branch out to other sports as companies like Nike and Reebok did during the 1980s. And, unlike other footwear brands, K-Swiss spent little money on advertising. The focus continued on offering high-quality shoes for tennis until the early 1990s. At that time, K-Swiss extended its product line to include shoes for aerobics, basketball, and hiking. In the mid-1990s, K-Swiss sought to appeal to a young, active market in addition to its core upscale market.[20]

The move to expand the target market worked for K-Swiss, as sales grew by positioning K-Swiss as a lifestyle brand. K-Swiss targeted 14- to 24-year-olds, a lucrative segment that buys 50% of all athletic footwear.[21] But, the fact remained that K-Swiss is a tiny company compared to Nike and Reebok. Also, other brands known for athletic footwear were positioned against lifestyle, most notably Puma and Converse. Competition from brands such as Vans, SKECHERS, and Under Armour made competition in the footwear market even fiercer. The K-Swiss classic tennis shoe continued to perform decently in the tennis market, but styles aimed at the lifestyle segment did not always meet expectations.

In the late 2000s, a shift in marketing strategy began. The performance category that was the inspiration for the K-Swiss brand would become the focus again. A shift in sales occurred rather quickly; sales in the performance category increased from 16% of total footwear sales in 2008 to 23% in 2009.[22] As part of the new focus on performance footwear, K-Swiss entered the training shoe category. The K-Swiss Tubes training shoe is competitively priced at $75. Targeting customers for training shoes is supported by sponsorship of the Ford Ironman Triathlon and champion triathlete Chris Lieto. K-Swiss continues to keep a sharp focus on its product line, focusing on tennis, training, and running. It has stayed away from developing cleats and has not re-entered the basketball category. The quest to design shoes for performance is a priority again at K-Swiss.

Tennis professionals and amateurs are attractive markets for K-Swiss.

© Freefly / Fotolia

Being a small player in the large athletic footwear market creates challenges for K-Swiss. Its marketing budget pales in comparison to Nike, and a 26% decline in sales in 2009 created a sense of urgency to build the K-Swiss brand through brand communications. K-Swiss has taken different approaches to communication strategy for the tennis and training categories. K-Swiss actively sought to sign a top-ranked tennis player to an endorsement deal. In 2009, K-Swiss signed 22-year-old Sam Querrey, the third-ranked American male and expected to ascend to the top rank within a year or two.[23] The expectation is that sponsorship of a top pro player will spark interest in the K-Swiss brand. "We are looking for a brand changer, one that will move the needle," said Erik Vervloet, K-Swiss director of sports marketing.[24]

A different approach has been taken with communication strategy for the training category. The teen market is a focal point, as evidenced by a partnership between K-Swiss and one thousand high schools across the United States. K-Swiss will invest $1 million into this campaign that includes advertising and donations to the high schools. Advertising messages with a tagline of "Train for summer, train for life" appeared when the campaign launched in the spring of 2010. Another tactic used to promote the Tubes training shoe line was an unusual association with a fictional TV character. K-Swiss signed actor Danny McBride of the HBO series *Eastbound & Down*. McBride's character, a former big-league pitcher turned physical education teacher named Kenny Powers, appears with product endorsers Patrick Willis (NFL) and Urijah Faber (mixed martial artist) in K-Swiss commercials that associate the Tubes brand with top athletes. The humorous, irreverent tone of the Tubes commercials may capture the attention of the young males K-Swiss is targeting, but whether the messages can persuade them that Tubes are high-performance training shoes remains to be seen.

Questions:

1. What is your opinion of the K-Swiss brand? Which brands would you identify as its primary competitors? Compare and contrast the K-Swiss brand to the competitors you highlight.
2. Review Figure 9.4, the relationship between objectives, strategies, and tactics. Develop a similar table for K-Swiss in marketing their Tubes training shoe to the teen market. Develop another table to market its tennis shoes to tennis amateur and professional athletes.
3. Which type of communications scheduling timetable (continuous, flighting, pulsating) should be used for marketing Tubes to the teen market? Why? Which type should be used for the tennis market? Why?
4. Pick either the teen market or the tennis market. Identify an informational message strategy, emotional message strategy, and behavioral message strategy for creating a message about K-Swiss targeting the market you picked.
5. Refer back to Question 4. For each message strategy, choose an appropriate execution format. Describe an advertisement or marketing idea that could be used with each execution.

References

1. Leonard Shapiro, (2009), "Only a Matter of Time until Bivens' LPGA Tenure Expires," July 7, accessed October 11, 2010, at http://www.cbssports.com/golf/story/11931612.
2. Randall Mell, (2009), "Michael Whan Named LPGA Commissioner," October 28, accessed April 20, 2012 at http://www.golfchannel.com/news/randall-mell/michael-whan-named-lpga-commissioner/.
3. Jon Show, (2010), "LPGA, Golf Channel Put Trust in Power of Wie," *Sports Business Journal*, February 15, 6.
4. Alan Shipnuck, (2009), "Is Marketing the Sex Appeal of LPGA Golfers Good for the Game?" July 28, accessed October 11, 2010, at http://www.golf.com/golf/tours_news/article/0,28136,1912980-1,00.html.
5. "2010-2011 Student Nights," accessed September 7, 2010, at http://blues.nhl.com/club/page.htm?id=34471.
6. Michael Smith, (2010), "DuPont Races Back to Offer More NASCAR Hospitality," *Sports Business Journal*, March 29, 3.
7. James McCarthy, (n.d.), "The Difference between Strategy and Tactics," accessed September 11, 2010, at http://ezinearticles.com/?The-Difference-Between-Strategy-and-Tactics&id=1558273.
8. Kenneth E. Clow and Donald Baack, *Integrated Advertising, Promotion, and Marketing Communications*, 4th ed. (Upper Saddle River, NJ: Prentice Hall, 2010).
9. "Indiana Pacers Full Season (44 Events)," (2010), accessed April 20, 2012, at http://www.pacersmvp.com/wp-content/uploads/2011/12/BLFseating_revised.pdf.
10. Matt Ehalt, (2010), "As LeBron James Mania Mounts, Season Ticket Sales for New York Knicks, New Jersey Nets Climb," *New York Daily News*, July 1, accessed September 16, 2010, at http://www.nydailynews.com/sports/basketball/knicks/2010/07/01/2010-07-01_as_lebron_james_mania_mounts_season_ticket_sales_for_new_york_knicks_new_jersey_.html.
11. Michael McCarthy, (2010), "LeBron James' Playoff Exit Creates Ripple Effect in Ticket Sales," *USA Today*, May 20, accessed September 16, 2010, at http://www.usatoday.com/sports/basketball/nba/2010-05-19-lebron-affects-ticket-sales_N.htm.

12. "Accenture Cuts Tiger Woods as Sponsor," (2009), December 14, accessed September 16, 2010, at http://sports.espn.go.com/golf/news/story?id=4739219.

13. Prentice Howe, (2010), "When Teams Market upon One Star, Not All Dreams Come True," *Sports Business Journal*, August 30, 20.

14. "Subway Freeway Face-Off Kicks Off Tuesday," (2009), November 30, accessed September 16, 2010, at http://kings.nhl.com/club/news.htm?id=508029.

15. Bob Geiger, (2010), "New Minnesota Timberwolves Ads Admit Losing Ways to Woo Fans," January 30, accessed April 20, 2012 at http://www.dolanmedia.com/view.cfm?recID=562496.

16. Jerry Zgoda, (2010), "To You, from David Kahn," September 14, accessed September 16, 2010, at http://www.startribune.com/sports/wolves/blogs/102873004.html?elr=KArksi8cyaiUo8cyaiUiD3aPc:_Yyc:aULPQL7PQLanchO7DiUr.

17. Scott W. Kelley, K. Douglas Hoffman, and Sheila Carter, (1999), "Franchise Relocation and Sport Introduction: A Sports Marketing Case Study of the Carolina Hurricanes' Fan Adoption Plan," *Journal of Services Marketing*, 13, 6, 469–480.

18. "GM to Halt Nine-Year Endorsement Deal with Woods," (2008), November 24, accessed May 18, 2011, at http://sports.espn.go.com/golf/news/story?id=3722964.

19. Jack Loechner, (2011), "Celebs in Ads Bump Awareness; Entertainers Top Jocks," March 8, accessed May 18, 2011, at http://www.mediapost.com/publications/index.cfm?fa=Articles.showArticle&art_aid=146181.

20. K-Swiss, Inc., (n.d.), accessed October 12, 2010, at http://www.fundinguniverse.com/company-histories/KSwiss-Inc-Company-History.html.

21. "Keeping K-Swiss on its Toes," (2004), June 7, accessed October 12, 2010, at http://www.businessweek.com/magazine/content/04_23/b3886103.htm.

22. K-Swiss, Inc. 2009 Annual Report

23. Daniel Kaplan, (2009), "K-Swiss Signs Third-Ranked U.S. Men's Player," *Sports Business Journal*, November 2, 7.

24. Daniel Kaplan, (2009), "K-Swiss Eyes Key Endorser to Drive Business," *Sports Business Journal*, September 21, 6.

10

Telling the Brand Story – Communications Channels

Learning Objectives

By the end of this chapter you should be able to:

1. Compare and contrast exposure and engagement strategies
2. Discuss the strengths and limitations of marketer-controlled communications channels
3. Describe the steps of the personal selling process
4. Discuss direct response marketing benefits and methods
5. Discuss the role of consumer-controlled communications channels in marketing

"Bring Your Pet Day" is a popular promotion for minor league baseball teams.

Minor League Baseball Brings Out Best, Worst in Creativity

Giveaways, promotions, and themed events are staples of marketing plans for minor league baseball teams. Competition from other leisure and entertainment options as well as the large number of home games (about thirty for Class A teams, as many as seventy for Class AAA teams) offers challenges to teams' efforts to maximize attendance. A tactic used for many years to spark fan interest and increase attendance is to utilize promotions. Some tactics add value by giving an additional benefit for attending, such as bobble-head dolls, team caps, and posters. Other promotions add value by making a night at the ballpark more affordable. Specials such as $1 hot dogs and two-for-one drinks are favorites with fans. A third way promotions influence consumer behavior is to add excitement to the normal routine of a baseball game. A postgame "diamond dig" in which contestants look for a diamond ring buried in the infield or "bring your pet" day that invites attendees to bring their four-legged friends are examples.

Insider Expert Jeff Hennion – GNC Live Well

Jeffrey R. Hennion became executive vice president, chief marketing officer & e-commerce in 2011, responsible for all of the company's marketing and e-commerce activities. Prior to joining GNC, Mr. Hennion spent eleven years at Dick's Sporting Goods. From January 2005 to September 2010, Mr. Hennion served as executive vice president and chief marketing officer at Dick's Sporting Goods, responsible for the company's marketing and, from 2008 to 2010, e-commerce activities. From 2004 to 2005, Mr. Hennion held the position of senior vice president of strategic planning at Dick's Sporting Goods, responsible for the company's growth and M&A strategies. From 2002 to 2004, Mr. Hennion was vice president of finance at Dick's Sporting Goods, during the time of the company's initial public offering, and from 2000 to 2002 he was vice president and treasurer.

Prior to his tenure at Dick's Sporting Goods, Mr. Hennion spent eleven years at Alcoa Inc., a global metals and manufacturing company, in Pittsburgh, Pennsylvania, and in Lausanne, Switzerland, serving a variety of finance roles, including assistant treasurer and director of investor relations. Mr. Hennion currently serves on the Board of Advisors of Branding Brand, LLC, a privately held mobile and social commerce company, as a Senior Advisor of Consigliere Brand Capital, LLC, a venture capital fund and brand consultancy hybrid, and as an Advisor to Metamorphic Ventures, a seed stage venture capital fund. Previously, he was on the Board of Directors of the Pittsburgh Marathon, the Pittsburgh Penguins Foundation, and the Carnegie Museum of Natural History. Jeff has a BA in economics from Northwestern University and an MBA in finance, graduating with highest honors, from Duquesne University, where he also was an adjunct professor.

Jeff Hennion

Jeff Hennion, Executive Vice President, Chief Marketing Officer & E-commerce of GNC Live Well

The boundaries for possible promotions are almost unlimited, set only by the creativity of managers responsible for developing a promotions schedule. The large number of home games on a team's schedule leads to a need for creative, cost-effective promotions that will appeal to fans. Here are some of the best promotions from Minor League Baseball according to the website the Biz of Baseball:

- Bowie Baysox – "CSI: Bowie" – Solve a crime at Prince George's Stadium
- Carolina Mudcats – "Christmas in July" – Discounted tickets if wearing Christmas attire; Christmas music played and presents given away
- Modesto Nuts – "Stitch 'N Pitch" – A special night for fans who enjoy knitting, crocheting, or needlepoint

Then, there are promotions that are risky, but the possibility of something going wrong may just be the appeal to bring fans out to the ballgame:

- Fort Myers Miracle – "Public Apology Night" – What will happen when dark secrets are revealed in front of thousands of strangers?
- Savannah Sand Gnats – "Man on Fire Running the Bases" – No doubt the hottest promotion of the summer, but how will young children react when seeing a man on fire?
- Arkansas Travelers – "Midget Wrestling Farewell Appearance" – A championship wrestling match of which the blog Biz of Baseball notes wryly "only in Arkansas."[1]

Finally, there are promotions that fall under the category "just because they can be done does not mean they should be done." Witness the following promotions held in recent years:

- Charleston RiverDogs – "Nobody Night" – Rather than striving to maximize attendance, the RiverDogs wanted to set an attendance record for fewest fans. No one was allowed in until the end of the fifth inning, making it an official game and an official attendance of 0.
- Altoona Curve – "Awful Night" – For fans looking for the least enjoyable experience at a sporting event, "Awful Night" is the answer. Spam and cheese sandwiches at concession stands, giveaways that included bubble wrap and pictures of a gall bladder, and clips from bad movies playing on the video board were designed to give fans a truly miserable experience.
- Hudson Valley Renegades – "Toilet Seat Night" – Stadium cushions shaped like toilet seats were given to fans.[2]

Introduction

Promotions and other special events in Minor League Baseball show that it is okay to associate your brand with fun and lightheartedness. But at the same time, managers responsible for decisions about brand communications must not lose sight of the different needs a sports brand has in order to tell its story to customers, prospects, the community, and other stakeholders. Promotions are but one channel used to influence consumer behavior. A **channel** is the means used to transmit or deliver a message to a target audience. An organization's marketing objectives will dictate what brand communications should accomplish and which channels should be used to reach those outcomes. The overarching purpose of integrated marketing communications (IMC) introduced in Chapter 8 and continued in Chapter 9 is to strategically tell and deliver a brand's story—what is relevant to customers and why they and other stakeholders should care.

This chapter covers two aspects of strategic decisions for brand communications campaigns. First, understanding the difference between exposure and engagement is presented, with accompanying tactics for each. Second, an overview is presented of communications channels that can be used to implement a brand communications strategy. It is divided into those channels that are under the control of marketing managers and those channels that are not under the marketer's control.

Exposure versus Engagement

Consumers buy the benefits and experiences that products and services provide. This characteristic of consumer behavior increases the importance of using integrated marketing to connect a brand with a customer and build long-term relationships. When determining the communications needs of a sports brand, managers should evaluate the state of customer relationships in terms of exposure to the brand and extent to which customers and prospects are engaged or have interaction with the brand (see Figure 10.1).

Exposure ➡ Engagement

FIGURE 10.1 Exposure versus Engagement Strategies

Exposure

Exposure is a low-level outcome that can be achieved through communication channels with mass distribution such as advertising, public relations, and sponsorship. In terms of the hierarchy of effects that was discussed in Chapter 8, exposure is a low-level outcome, because the impact of these tactics may go no further than creating brand awareness and brand associations. It is the knowledge component of the hierarchy sports model. Figure 10.2 identifies the various types of marketing tools that can be used to gain exposure for a sports brand.

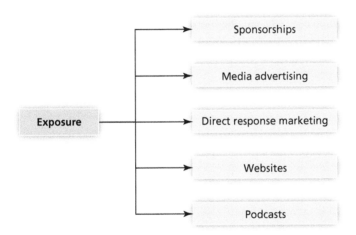

FIGURE 10.2 Marketing Tools That Can Be Used to Build Exposure

Sponsorship can be effective for creating awareness through the presence of sponsors' names and logos on signage at events as well as mentions in media coverage of an event. NASCAR fans who have never heard of Lenox Industrial Tools have at least encountered the brand name if they attended the Lenox Industrial Tools 301 Sprint Cup race at Loudon, New Hampshire, or consumed the race indirectly such as by watching it on TV or reading news stories about the race.

Media advertising is ideal for creating brand awareness and delivering information that will add to recipients' brand knowledge, but it is not the only IMC tool capable of achieving this impact. Direct response marketing is another communications tool that can reach a sports property's audience. Major forms of direct response marketing include direct mail, direct e-mail, and direct response advertising in media outlets such as magazines, newspapers, television, and the Internet.

An organization's website is a digital medium that provides opportunity for building awareness. If you consider the layout of a website for most minor league and major league sports teams in the United States, some categories of information are rather predictable: news about the team, player roster, coach biographies, community relations, and kids' area. Communicating this information on a website gives the message global reach at a very low cost, and it is a channel in which the marketer has total control over the presentation and delivery of information.

Another digital communications tool effective for impacting brand exposure is podcasts. A **podcast** is an audio or video program available for streaming over the Internet or for download to digital music players. Podcasts give the producer access to a broad geographic audience that is reached without having to purchase advertising airtime. Moreover, instead of the promotional message taking the form of advertising, a podcast's content is the message. Podcasts give sports properties opportunities to give exposure to players, coaches, team executives, and items of interest. For example, the Big Ten Men's Basketball Podcast posts audio and video content including game highlights, coaches' interviews, and in-depth player profiles from all Big Ten member schools. A brand for which coverage in traditional media is geographically concentrated like the Big Ten Conference can benefit from a podcast's ability to reach fans that are scattered geographically outside the core market.

Engagement

In contrast to exposure's focus on message penetration among a target market (e.g., number of people reached or frequency that an audience is exposed to a message), **engagement** is concerned with the quality of brand communications in terms of the target audience processing brand stimuli. Exposure is necessary to create impact with an audience, but exposure alone will likely not be persuasive enough to lead to the most desired responses, such as purchase and brand loyalty.

A primary goal of brand communications is to strengthen relationships with target audiences. Sports consumption is influenced heavily by an emotional connection to a player or team. Engagement creates a link between a consumer's experience with a sport and his or her self-concept. The role of events and experiences in creating meaningful engagement with consumers was discussed in Chapter 7, but as shown in Figure 10.3 there are additional brand communications tools that can be used to create high-quality communication interaction with an audience. In terms of the hierarchy sports model, these brand communication tools should develop affinity towards the sports brand that then leads to some type of action.

FIGURE 10.3
Marketing Tools That Can Be Used to Build Engagement

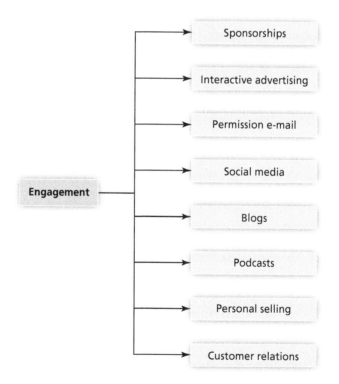

One communication tool that can be used in support of a brand's engagement objectives as well as creating exposure is sponsorships. Engaging customers and prospects in more extensive contact has gained importance in recent years. Increasingly, sponsors want more than signage or name mentions at sporting events where they have a presence. A trend in sponsorship has been for sponsors to become more integrated into the physical environment of a venue so that patrons are exposed to a sponsor's products.

When electronics retailer Best Buy partnered with the Minnesota Twins, more than six hundred of its private-label high-definition Insignia televisions were placed throughout the team's new stadium, Target Field. Attendees at Target Field events are able to see Insignia products in action, which could influence purchase decisions for consumers shopping for high-definition televisions. Sponsor integration of products and services into sports facilities will likely continue to grow. A recent study found that 85% of sports business executives surveyed believed that sponsor development of customer engagement areas in new venues will be a benefit of top-tier sponsorships in the coming years.[3]

Traditional media advertising, one of the best IMC tools for creating brand exposure, is not as effective for engaging consumers to spend more time interacting with a brand. However, **interactive advertising** is a form of online advertising that can be used to achieve audience engagement. Interactive ads are designed to elicit an audience response in the form of "clicking" on the advertisement. The most popular form of interactive advertising is placing messages on search engines such as Google or Bing. Clicking on the text ad takes the visitor to a page where the marketer has the opportunity to engage the visitor more deeply. Currently, search engine ads account for about 45% of all Internet advertising expenditures.[4]

E-mail is an excellent customer engagement tool. One of the greatest strengths of e-mail is that an e-mail marketing program can be structured so that only persons who wish to participate will receive messages. This approach to e-mail communication is known as **permission marketing**. Many permission-based e-mail programs allow consumers to specify the types of information they want to receive. A permission e-mail program run by Talladega Superspeedway lets participants choose to receive the track's newsletter, information on special ticket offers, or information for current ticket holders.[5]

Perhaps the greatest change in how marketers engage customers and others is the emergence of a category of communication tools referred to as **social media**, which has been defined as "a set of technologies and channels targeted at forming and enabling a potentially massive community of participants to productively collaborate."[6] This definition contains three keywords that distinguish social media from mass media communications:

1. Community – Social media enables people with shared interests or passions to gather in a single location such as a Facebook group, blog, or YouTube channel. The emotional connection people have with sports make social media an ideal channel for engaging fans.

2. Participants – Instead of marketers talking *at* an audience as they do in mass media communication channels, social media focuses on conversations that lead to talking *with* the audience. Social media users are cocreators of communication, not merely recipients.

3. Collaborate – Highly correlated with participation is a community's involvement to collaborate on creating content and dialogue. The two-way flow of communication in social networks means that marketers should invite community members to give opinions, ask questions, or make suggestions.

© Avid Creative, Inc. / iStockphoto

Racetracks utilize permission marketing e-mail campaigns to increase attendance at racing events.

Social media channels should be managed with the same strategic considerations as more established channels. Merely setting up a Facebook page or uploading photos to Flickr does not make for a strategic use of social media to achieve the overall brand communications objective of engagement. Ultimate Fighting Championship (UFC) has effectively integrated social media into its IMC strategy. The mixed martial arts organization engages fans through its presence on Facebook, YouTube, and Twitter. UFC's Facebook page gives information about upcoming events, allows for fans' comments and photo uploads, and promotes related UFC products such as live events and *UFC* magazine. The Ultimate Fighting Championship channel on YouTube has more than 250,000 subscribers. Content that UFC fans can access includes previews of upcoming events, highlights from past events, fighter interviews, and UFC press conferences. UFC promotes its use of Twitter to offer its followers (almost 400,000) access to behind-the-scenes information and breaking news. Even more impressive is the following UFC CEO Dana White has cultivated; more than 1.7 million people follow White's personal Twitter account. White enjoys communicating with fans via Twitter, and he encourages UFC fighters to tweet.[7]

Another engagement tool closely related to social media is the blog. **Blogs**, shorthand for Weblogs, are Web pages containing information, commentary, photos, videos, or links to other information sources on the Web. The emergence of blogs as a communication tool gives a voice to the audience that was limited previously to a role as recipient of information. More than 145 million blogs now exist, strong evidence that the public wants to engage and be engaged.[8] Blogging has impacted sports by giving fans, sports executives, and media properties a platform to share opinions, and it gives others with shared interests a channel for giving feedback by posting comments to blog entries. As mentioned in Chapter 2, tech-savvy team owners Ted Leonsis (Washington Capitals – NHL and Washington Mystics – WNBA) and Mark Cuban (Dallas Mavericks – NBA) maintain blogs to discuss their teams and other issues important to them.

Although it is a one-way communication tool, podcasts are another engagement tool. Free access to podcasts makes wide distribution possible, and the low cost of producing podcasts allows episodes to be created frequently. Audiences can interact with a podcast's creators by sending questions and comments via e-mail or interacting via other communication channels such as the podcast creator's website or in social media. An example of using podcasts for engagement is the video podcast produced by the NHL's Vancouver Canucks. The team uses its weekly podcasts to give fans a glimpse of players' personalities with episodes such as "Best and Worst Vacations," "Favorite Movie Quotes," and "Holiday Memories."[9]

Personal selling has great engagement capabilities. The human interaction between a sports property's sales representative and a customer or prospect allows for a rich, two-way exchange of communication that cannot be matched by any other brand communications tool. The New Orleans Saints utilizes a sales force as a customer engagement tactic, beginning at the top of the organization. Mike Stanfield, vice president of ticket and suite sales, requires each of member of his sales staff to send twenty handwritten notes to ticket and suite customers daily. Stanfield sends twenty notes, too, and all 18,000 customers receive a note over the course of a year regardless of the dollar amount they spend with the Saints.[10] The cost of engagement through personal selling should be viewed as an investment in building relationships that can increase customer retention rates.

The customer engagement role that is performed by many sales departments can also be carried out by employees who are assigned to perform customer relations. A customer relations department within a sports organization might be called Fan Relations (for ticket holders) or Client Services (for sponsors), but regardless of the unit's name, the responsibility is to maintain relationships with customers that will positively impact satisfaction and loyalty. The NBA's Phoenix Suns assign an account experience specialist to each season ticket holder to assist with account issues, ticket needs, and service needs. This level of service can reinforce a customer's decision to be a ticket buyer, an important impact in terms of positively influencing ticket renewal decisions.

Brand Communications Mix

A major decision in planning brand communications is to decide on the communication channels that will be used to deliver brand messages. Sports marketers have an array of channels available to deliver the messages once decisions are made concerning the message strategy and the level of awareness versus engagement that is desired. Selection of the appropriate channels depends on the three criteria listed in Figure 10.4:

1) Communications channels used by the target audience
2) IMC objectives being pursued (communication or behavioral)
3) Message strategy used to create the message

Two general types of channels can be used: marketer-controlled channels and consumer-controlled channels. Unfortunately, there is no such thing as the perfect channel for impacting an audience. Each channel has strengths and limitations, meaning that managers must accept tradeoffs of a channel's limitations given the benefits the channel offers. In addition, the choice of channel is impacted by the need to build awareness versus the desire to engage the consumer in the affinity and action steps of the hierarchy sports model.

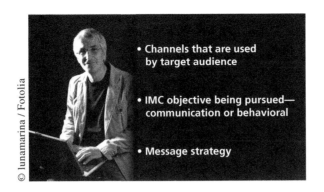

FIGURE 10.4 **Criteria for Selecting Appropriate Channels**

- Channels that are used by target audience

- IMC objective being pursued— communication or behavioral

- Message strategy

© lunamarina / Fotolia

Marketer-Controlled Channels

When planning delivery of brand messages, use of channels initiated and controlled by marketers is usually what comes to mind. After all, marketing communication campaigns have relied on traditional media for decades. These channels are known for enabling marketers to exert a high level of control over message delivery in terms of time and place as well as creative content. Marketer-controlled communication channels that are highly relevant to sports marketers are shown in Figure 10.5.

- Media advertising

- Sales promotions

- Public relations

- Sales force

- Direct response marketing

© Jenner / Fotolia

FIGURE 10.5 **Marketer-Controlled Communication Channels**

Media Advertising

Mass media channels are perhaps the most efficient way to reach consumers. Although total advertising expenditures on certain mass media channels have slowed, they remain an important part of the media mix of IMC campaigns for sports properties. Four channels that are useful for reaching sports consumers are television, radio, newspapers, and outdoor advertising (see Figure 10.6). A fifth channel, magazines, has less relevance for marketing sports entertainment to consumers, but is part of the brand communications mix for apparel and equipment brands as well as for some B2B marketers.

TELEVISION. Advertising opportunities for television are available on networks, cable channels, and local cable systems. TV networks are a nationwide system of affiliate stations that broadcast

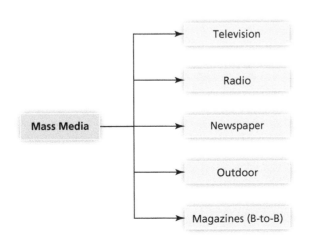

FIGURE 10.6 **Mass Media Channels**

Mass Media → Television

→ Radio

→ Newspaper

→ Outdoor

→ Magazines (B-to-B)

the signal of their parent, such as ABC, CBS, NBC, and Fox. Advertising can be placed at either a national level or by buying commercial time on a network affiliate station in a specific geographic market. The national distribution of network programming makes it an ideal medium to reach a large audience. Similarly, if a sports property seeks to reach a wide geographic market in its home area, local network affiliates are beneficial because they often have a signal that reaches for many miles in all directions.

If the Memphis Grizzlies of the NBA want to send ad messages to a wide geographic area, advertising on local TV stations will send the signal into southeast Arkansas, north Mississippi, parts of Missouri, as well as west Tennessee. This strength of network TV advertising can be a limitation if a property is targeting a more concentrated geographic area. If the Memphis Grizzlies narrowed the focus of its marketing efforts to a 50-mile radius around the city of Memphis, the wide reach of local network TV affiliates would mean that part of the Grizzlies' ad expenditures would be going to reach consumers who are not in its target market. Also, the cost of airtime for network TV advertising is usually high, which can cut into IMC budgets rather quickly.

An alternative to advertising on networks is cable TV. Advertising on cable can be done in two ways: 1) buying airtime on a cable network to run nationally or 2) buying airtime from a local cable system in a specific geographic area. Cable TV networks are distributed through local cable systems and satellite TV providers. One of the primary strengths of using cable to place ad messages is the ability to select specific audiences. Most cable TV networks are content-specific, such as news, movies, special interest, or sports. The narrow focus of cable programming tends to draw an audience with relatively similar characteristics, whether it is demographics such as a particular age group or gender, or psychographics such as interest in travel or history. In contrast, network TV tends to draw more diverse audiences.

Advertising on local cable provides an opportunity to take advantage of the narrow audience characteristics of a cable channel like Bravo or the Golf Channel and at the same time reach an audience in a local market only. This form of cable advertising makes it possible for marketers that wish to reach consumers in a specific city or county to place ads on local cable. If Western Kentucky University (WKU) buys commercials on cable systems in areas around the university to promote football and basketball, it would avoid placing messages in the nearby Nashville market that has a great deal of competition from other sports teams and entertainment options. Advertising on network TV would not give WKU the geographic flexibility that buying time on local cable affords.

RADIO. Another mass medium that offers a high level of audience selectivity is radio. Figure 10.7 provides a general view of demographic groups attracted by different radio formats. In addition to the ability to target certain demographic groups with radio advertising, the rather narrow geographic reach of most station signals make radio an attractive ad medium when targeting specific cities or areas. Another frequently cited advantage of radio advertising is its relatively low cost, particularly compared to TV. This feature gives advertisers leeway to run more

FIGURE 10.7
Demographic Groups Attracted by Radio Formats

Format	Primary Demographic Group
News/Talk/Sports	Men ages 30 and up
Country	Men and women ages 25 and up
Contemporary Hits	Youth and adults ages 15–30
Adult Contemporary	Men and women ages 30 and up
Modern Rock	Young adults ages 16–25
Classic Rock	Men ages 30 and up
Oldies	Men ages 40 and up
Urban Contemporary	Youth and adults ages 15–30; primarily African-American

commercials. The repetition of greater message frequency can be helpful in achieving objectives such as building awareness and developing brand knowledge among the target audience.

The advantages of radio as an advertising medium are offset by some limitations. The narrowly focused audiences that most radio stations draw mean that the audience of any given station represents a relatively small percentage of the total market in a geographic area. For example, the radio station in San Francisco with the highest rating, or percentage of total audience listening, has only about 6% of the total radio audience in the market. Many stations have ratings below 3.0, meaning fewer than 3% of persons ages 12 and older in San Francisco listen to a given station. There are more than fifty stations that have ratings below 1.0.[11] Thus, a sports property that includes radio in its IMC plan will find it necessary to advertise on multiple stations given the low reach and homogeneous audience characteristics of each station.

NEWSPAPER. An effective channel for reaching local audiences is newspapers. The distribution of most newspapers is limited to a single city or its immediate surrounding area. This allows for geographic targeting, making for an efficient use of IMC budget. Also, the frequency of publication for newspapers creates opportunities for high frequency of messages sent to the target audience. Newspapers in large markets that publish daily offer 365 different chances to reach consumers. Audience segmentation is possible using newspapers, as the different sections of a newspaper (news, sports, business, lifestyles, etc.) attract readers with shared interests. For sports properties, the sports section of a newspaper is an obvious location for placing messages to reach persons interested in sports. Newspapers are advantageous in terms of flexibility in scheduling ads to run. The lead time, or number of days, is typically just three to four days in advance of the scheduled run date. On occasion, ads can go from idea to appearing in print in just one day.

Advertising in newspapers has come under increased scrutiny by marketing managers concerned about readership rates. Total circulation for newspapers in the United States peaked in 1973 at approximately 63 million copies; by 2009 that figure was less than 47 million.[12] Fewer people are reading print versions of newspapers because of the availability of news 24/7 on cable TV and the Internet. In addition, the audience characteristics of newspaper readers are very narrow. Typical readers:

- Are more likely to be middle-aged; young adults prefer getting news from TV and online
- Have higher household incomes and are in higher socioeconomic classes than nonreaders
- Are more likely to be college educated
- Have a professional or executive occupation
- Own a home worth more than $100,000[13]

If the target audience does not fit these characteristics, newspaper may not be the best channel for reaching them.

OUTDOOR ADVERTISING. Outdoor ads consist of billboards, kiosks, and mobile signs on buses and other vehicles. They are a channel to reach mobile consumers, and they enable messages to be placed in strategic geographic locations. Outdoor ads are effective for creating awareness. Consumers have limited time to process messages (as little as three to four seconds), so advertisers must develop creative messages that are short and get attention. Placing billboard ads in high-traffic areas is a way to reach a large audience very efficiently, and motorists that travel the same road frequently will be exposed multiple times to the same ad message, strengthening recall ability for the brand and ad message. The same is true for placing messages on buses and other vehicles. Moreover, consumers value billboards, as evidenced by a study in which 83% of persons surveyed said billboards were informative.[14]

However, outdoor advertising is limited in the ability to deliver engaging messages due to the short time exposure. Copy included in a billboard must be brief and conducive to getting attention. Also, billboards can become part of the landscape that motorists over time will tune out and not observe. Billboards may be effective for connecting with the target market in terms of creating awareness, but for many types of products, brief exposure to an ad on a billboard is not persuasive enough to move people to take an action such as buying game tickets.

MAGAZINES. A mass medium ideal for reaching large yet highly targeted audiences is magazines. The reason that magazines are effective for attracting audiences with rather homogeneous

An effective way to reach runners is through advertising in the magazine *Runner's World*.

characteristics is the editorial focus or content of magazines attracts readers with specific demographic or psychographic characteristics. More than 7,000 titles are published that target consumers, according to the Association of Magazine Media.[15] Magazines are a viable channel for sports marketers in two ways. Consumer brands that seek to reach audiences of sports fans can use popular publications such as *Sports Illustrated* and *ESPN The Magazine*, magazines with circulations of 3.1 million and 2.1 million, respectively.[16] Such sports publications have readers with demographic similarities (primarily males; readership for each magazine has heavy concentrations within a certain age range, such as 18- to 30-year-olds) and psychographic similarities (interest in sports and lifestyles of sports personalities). Another way magazines have applicability to sports marketers is that makers of sports apparel or equipment can use a general sports magazine or sport-specific publication to reach the audience they desire. For example, *Runner's World* reaches approximately 600,000 people. Although this number is small compared to the total U.S. population, it is a coveted audience for companies marketing running shoes, apparel, or accessories.

For B2B marketers serving the sports industry, advertising in trade magazines can be an effective channel for reaching decision makers. A **trade magazine** is a specialized periodical published with content targeted toward members of a particular occupation or industry.[17] Hundreds of trade magazine titles pertain to the sports industry in some way, whether they are sport-specific (e.g., golf, tennis, or basketball), focus on a certain segment of sports (e.g., collegiate athletics), or target certain functional areas (e.g., facility management or marketing). For example, *Volleyball* magazine is a publication read by volleyball players, coaches, officials, and event organizers that reaches some 250,000 people.[18] Companies that market products of interest to volleyball participants and administrators can use this outlet to place ad messages knowing that the magazine's audience would likely have an interest in the product being advertised.

The primary drawback to advertising in trade magazines is usually cost. Small companies in particular may find that buying a half-page or full-page ad in a trade magazine is cost prohibitive. Ads that are less expensive, such as purchasing space in a directory or classified ads section in the back of a trade magazine, make it more likely that a message will get lost among other ads competing for the reader's attention. Also, small ads do not communicate brand prestige like larger ad placements.

Sales Promotions

Sales promotions are excellent for achieving IMC objectives designed to engage consumers, urging them to take some type of action. Objectives such as sales increases, new customers or accounts, or event attendance can be pursued through use of sales promotion. A **sales promotion** is the use of an incentive or something of value to influence the target audience to respond in a desired way. Consumers can be exposed to a brand, learn about its features and benefits, and have an image and attitude for the brand, but may lack sufficient motivation to extend their relationship with the brand any further. Sales promotions serve as a "nudge" or persuasive effort to elicit action by the target audience. As illustrated in Figure 10.8, two approaches to using sales promotions are available to sports marketers: 1) offering incentives that reduce consumers' risk to take action and 2) offering incentives that add value to a product or service, thus enhancing the consumption experience.

FIGURE 10.8 Sales Promotion Incentives

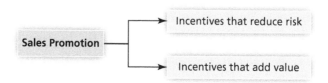

RISK-REDUCING INCENTIVES. An effective tactic for eliciting a response from consumers is to offer an incentive that lessens the risk required to buy or use a product. Two sales promotion tactics that are used by marketers in many types of industries are sampling and coupons. **Sampling** is a sales promotion tactic that enables a consumer to try a product with no cost or obligation. Often, a sample is not a full unit of the product offering. Instead it is a smaller unit of the product that allows the user to evaluate the benefits provided by the product.

Sampling is used to promote professional league TV game subscriptions to allow sports fans to try the service for free for a few days. MLB Extra Innings, NBA League Pass, NHL Center Ice, and MLS Direct Kick all offer sampling promotions early in their seasons. The aim of this promotion is to let fans enjoy the service and experience it for a short time. Then the marketing challenge is to convert the fan into a paying customer who buys the TV package for the remainder of the season.

Sampling is the most effective way to put a product in the hands of consumers with little or no risk to them. The limitation of sampling is that not all products and services may lend themselves to sampling. A pro league TV package can be marketed through a sampling program with relative ease and is not limited by supply capacity. In contrast, a sports property that has high demand for tickets may find sampling an impractical approach to attract new fans. Sampling can work if there are occasions when ticket demand is significantly lower than usual.

An example of using sampling as a risk-reducing incentive is when the Nashville Predators of the NHL engaged in a sampling program by giving away tickets to its preseason games. Giving away tickets may not be practical (or profitable) during the regular season, but giving away tickets for games for which there is usually a high number of unsold seats is a way to bring new and former customers to games. If fans enjoy their experience when sampling a game, ideally they will purchase tickets for future games. And when people accept sampling offers like free tickets, a sports property should use the promotion to build its database of prospective customers. People who are interested enough to request free game tickets are prospects for a ticket sales staff and should be targeted following their sampling experience.

Another sales promotion tactic that influences action by reducing consumers' risk is coupons. **Coupons** offer a price discount or other cost reduction as an incentive for a consumer to take an action. The benefit of coupons is that a marketer has some control over who receives the offer by deciding what channels to use to distribute coupons. If the NBA's Milwaukee Bucks wants to attract more families to attend its games, it may decide to distribute coupons for specially priced family packs through elementary schools or youth basketball programs. In addition to controlling how coupons are distributed, coupons are a favored sales promotion tactic by marketers because of the ability to measure the effectiveness of a coupon offer. Coupon redemption rate, which is the number of coupons used by customers divided by the total number of coupons distributed, can be calculated to determine how effective a coupon promotion was at generating the desired result. Even if the answer is the offer did not perform well, that outcome can be determined and future offers can be modified in an effort to improve their effectiveness.

The main concern with using coupons is that excessive coupon offers can damage brand equity. If price-based incentives are offered frequently via coupons, customers may perceive that the experience of attending a game or event is not worth the full ticket price. Also, excessive couponing may inadvertently "train" customers to wait on special offers before buying, which hurts profitability. A related concern is the effect frequent price discounts have on relationships with a sports property's most loyal customers, season ticket holders. These loyal customers may receive a discount for buying multiple games, but the per-game investment is often higher than a customer who receives a price break with a coupon for a single game. Figure 10.9 summarizes these concerns.

Managers responsible for customer retention and fan relations must be mindful of the potential negative effects coupons can have on relationships with season ticket customers. Among

- Can damage brand equity
- Perception that tickets are over-priced
- Train customers to wait for coupon specials
- Negative impact on season ticket holders

FIGURE 10.9 Concerns with Excessive Use of Coupons

the remedies for this situation are restricting coupon offers to games with a high percentage of unsold ticket inventory and adding value to the benefits of being a season ticket holder by offering such amenities as food and beverage vouchers, special parking privileges, or access to events or team members or facilities.

VALUE-ADDED INCENTIVES. While some sales promotion tactics entice consumers to take action by reducing financial risk to try or use a product, other tactics are effective for prompting action by adding value to a product or consumption experience. Rather than give away samples or reduce price using coupons, consumers are rewarded for buying at regular price. In the sports industry, value-added incentives have a long tradition going by the name of giveaways, freebies, or premiums. The marketing term is **premium**, which is a tangible item given to consumers when they attend a sporting event. In some cases, a premium item may be given away to every attendee at a game or event. In other cases, a limited number of premiums items may be distributed (e.g., free T-shirt to the first 10,000 fans entering the venue) or items may be distributed to a designated target audience (e.g., free mascot doll to first 5,000 children ages 14 and under).

Premiums can be effective incentives for driving attendance at sporting events. One situation in which premiums meet a strategic need is when a sports property has a large number of games or events to sell. Typically, this makes achieving sellouts more difficult when consumers have more opportunities to buy. NFL teams do not experience this challenge as they have only eight regular season games, and their home games are a week or longer apart. In contrast, Major League Baseball has eighty-one home games to sell, including home stands that include games on several consecutive days. MLB teams can benefit from sweetening the offer of attending a game when a giveaway is included. Figure 10.10 shows the three most effective and least effective premiums and promotions during a recent MLB season. Webkinz toys and team blankets were very persuasive in generating attendance gains compared to games without giveaways.

FIGURE 10.10 Most Effective and Least Effective Premiums in MLB

Incentive		% Change in Attendance
Giveaways:		
	Webkinz Toy	31.6%
Most Effective	Blanket	21.2%
	Banner/Pennant	15.6%
	Helmet/Gloves	−8.5%
Least Effective	Shirt	−11.6%
	Baseball Cards	−33.5%

Promotions can have a similar effect on motivating a target audience. A **promotion** is an event held in conjunction with a sporting event that does not involve giving away a tangible item but adds value to the consumption experience in some other way. In Figure 10.11, the best-performing promotions in MLB involved experiences that connected fans with former or current

FIGURE 10.11 Most Effective and Least Effective Promotions in MLB

Incentive		% Change in Attendance
Promotions:		
	Team History Tribute	13.8%
Most Effective	Autographs	9.9%
	Fan Appreciation Day	9.2%
	Pet Day	−13.5%
Least Effective	Little League Day	−13.9%
	College Night	−20.2%

players. This intangible value-added experience is quite different from receiving a calendar or cap, but it enhances the benefits received from sporting event attendance, nonetheless. Promotions can be used to attract attendees who may not be necessarily motivated to attend because of the sport alone. Concerts, fireworks, and group recognitions are promotions that are effective because they may appeal to people who have relatively little interest in a sport but have an interest in the promotion tied to the game or event.

Value-added promotions are advantageous primarily because of their potential to motivate consumers to engage with the brand and take action. A highly valued giveaway or a promotion that resonates with consumers' interests can result in an observable short-term impact on attendance and revenues. Another advantage of promotions is that the cost to execute a promotion is often underwritten by corporate sponsors. Sponsors recognize the impact giveaways can have, and that in many cases a giveaway item is kept by the consumer for an extended period of time. Thus, a sponsor often can be found that is willing to pay for part or all of the cost of the giveaway item in return for the right to put its name and logo on the item.

While sponsors' willingness to absorb costs can be a strength of value-added incentives, the cost of the giveaway item can be a drawback if a sponsor does not cover all of the costs. Some items have relatively high costs, such as a blanket, and if a property has to cover the cost itself, the return on investment in terms of revenue per fan divided by cost of the item will be lower. Also, a premium may be ineffective if the item is perceived to be of low quality or is otherwise not valued highly by recipients. If consumers' evaluation of an item received is that it does not add value to their overall experience, then perceptions of giveaway promotions they encounter in the future may be negatively affected.

Public Relations

Brand communication objectives that have the aim of increasing awareness, building brand knowledge, or developing a desired brand image potentially benefit from the use of public relations to reach target audience segments. According to the Public Relations Society of America, "**public relations** help an organization and its publics adapt mutually to each other."[19] The term "publics" acknowledges the different stakeholder groups with which an organization engages in relationships. An obvious stakeholder group is customers, but local communities, news media, government agencies, and public policy makers are all publics that sports properties benefit from engaging with strategically planned communications.

An examination of the organization structure of a typical sports organization will likely find managers with responsibilities to manage public relations in the form of an in-house PR department. Other departments that sports properties use to execute PR activities focus on community relations and media relations. Outreach efforts to these two publics are vital to influencing consumer awareness and knowledge of a sports brand even though the focus of these departments is not to "sell" to individual customers.

Public relations is an effective communications tool for shaping a favorable brand image. Sports properties that create or provide financial support to programs that help residents of the cities in which they play can influence creation of brand associations among consumers that the property "cares about the local community" and "are good corporate citizens." The Oklahoma City Thunder of the NBA utilizes its Community Relations department to connect the team to the local community through support of programs that benefit young people, such as youth basketball camps, fitness programs, teacher recognition, and reading initiatives.[20] These programs send messages that the Oklahoma City Thunder care about the physical and intellectual development of children. The impact of PR tactics like those used by the Oklahoma City Thunder serve as a reminder that not all IMC tactics need to be action-oriented (i.e., linked directly to sales).

In addition to image enhancement capabilities, public relations is a valuable IMC tool because of its perceived credibility. The reason for the higher level of credibility is that the source of a PR message delivered via the news media is perceived by consumers as the media outlet distributing the story, not the sports property. Thus, information delivered in this manner is typically viewed as being delivered by an unbiased source. Although much of the publicity generated for brands can be attributed to PR efforts to interest media outlets in carrying a story, consumers do not see those tactics, only the results in the form of media coverage. Also, PR is favored by marketing managers because of its low cost compared to advertising, since there is no ad space or time to buy.

This advertisement for the Atlanta Braves offers both risk-reducing incentives as well as value-added incentives.

The chief limitation of public relations is the inability to control message placement and content. This characteristic is the flip side of PR's strength of being unpaid media. A marketer has little control over whether information it has distributed to media outlets (e.g., a news release) will even be covered. And, if it is covered, a media outlet will control what is said and when it is said, not the sports property.

Media relations is another function of an organization's PR activities that targets a different but influential stakeholder group: media professionals that cover sports, business, or the local community. While a community relations staff focuses on strengthening relationships between a sports brand and various publics in the local market such as schools, nonprofit organizations, and civic leaders, media relations is tasked with promoting brand communications by working with media professionals to provide information and content. Many intercollegiate athletics departments have a staff position called sports information director (SID). This individual's primary responsibility is to garner exposure through multiple channels using tools such as media guides, press releases that preview upcoming events or summarize past events, coaches' media conferences, player media interviews, and the athletic program's website.

Sales Force

The brand communication tools discussed to this point share a common characteristic of messages being produced and delivered to a mass audience. Advertising, sales promotions, and public relations are very efficient communication tools because of their capability to reach large numbers of people with a single message. However, efficiency does not equate to effectiveness. Messages sent via a mass media channel may not have the desired impact due to the target audience never receiving the message, choosing not to pay attention to the message, or failing to process information in the manner the marketer planned.

Personal selling can be used to build and maintain customer relationships.

An alternative to these shortcomings of mass-delivered messages is to use personal selling to communicate with consumers and businesses individually. **Personal selling** is personal communication between a representative of a business and customers or prospects for the purpose of making sales and building customer relationships.[21] The rich dialogue that can occur between buyer and seller enables a salesperson to capture the attention of a prospect, make a case for the value offered, and encourage the buyer to take action. Messages delivered via mass media channels simply cannot engage consumers in the ways that personal selling can. Also, the high-quality communications offered using personal selling are effective for building and maintaining customer relationships. Customers may buy from a company, but their buying decision can be affirmed and brand loyalty can be strengthened through their interactions with salespeople. The sales force literally is the face of the company to customers, and assigning a salesperson to service individual customers is a way to nurture customer relationships using a personal touch.

The primary limitations of personal selling are cost and inefficiency. Costs to recruit, train, and compensate a sales force make personal selling expensive in terms of absolute dollar cost and cost per customer reached. In contrast, mass media advertising tends to be very cost-effective when the cost of an ad is divided by the number of people who may be exposed to an ad's message. Personal selling is also inefficient in that a salesperson usually can only interact with one buyer at a time. Thus, over the course of a day a salesperson can only make a relatively small number of contacts with buyers or prospects. If their duties include servicing existing customers as well as selling to new ones, their ability to produce new business is reduced by the time required to service existing accounts. This limitation can be addressed by using a dedicated fan relations department to manage the customer care function, freeing salespeople to focus on customer acquisition. The image of personal selling is another drawback. Many people view salespeople as trying to persuade them to buy something that they may not need, that the salespeople are more interested in their own goals such as meeting a sales quota rather than meeting the customer's needs.

THE PERSONAL SELLING PROCESS. The steps involved in persuading a person to buy are essentially no different for sports entertainment and products than for other types of products. Figure 10.12 summarizes five steps that occur. The first two steps are preparatory tactics salespeople make before actually engaging in selling. First, salespeople seek out potential buyers, a process known as **prospecting**. The prospecting process entails two tasks—generating leads and qualifying leads. Leads are possible buyers, with their level of interest or likelihood of buying unknown. For example, attendees at a player autograph event could complete registration forms for an autographed ball giveaway. The registrations collected can be turned over to the ticket sales department to follow up with these persons to determine their interest. Some people may be ticket customers already, others may not be customers but their interest as shown by attending the event can be taken as evidence of interest and may be prospects for salespeople to contact.

The second task of prospecting is qualifying leads, or determining the quality of a lead in terms of potential to buy. Some people who registered for the autograph ball giveaway may have limited income and not be serious prospects. Other people may have entered the drawing not because of their personal interest, but rather they were trying to win the ball for someone else. Their potential as a serious prospect to buy tickets may be low. Similarly, sponsorship salespeople must engage in prospecting, generating leads for potential corporate partners and assessing the commitment level (i.e., sponsorship rights fees) a lead might be able to pay.

The second step is pre-call planning, which involves collecting information about the background and needs of a prospect prior to making a sales presentation. Salespeople equipped with information about a customer's likes and dislikes, needs and wants, and personal background such as family, hobbies, or college alma mater allow tailoring the sales presentation to meet the prospect's situation, which assists in relationship building. For sponsorship sales, pre-call planning is a critical step in the selling process. It can shed light on a prospective sponsor's current marketing tactics and how a corporate partnership with the salesperson's organization can be developed to be a useful marketing vehicle for the firm.

Once pre-call planning is done, a salesperson is ready to make the sales presentation. At this step, a salesperson's focus should be to communicate how the sports property meets the prospect's needs. Sales presentations can be scripted or adapted. A scripted sales presentation is based on predetermined talking points, with little or no deviation from the script. Ticket sales presentations made by telemarketers follow scripts to the point that scripted responses are prepared based on common questions or concerns raised by prospects. In contrast, an adaptive sales

FIGURE 10.12 The Personal Selling Process

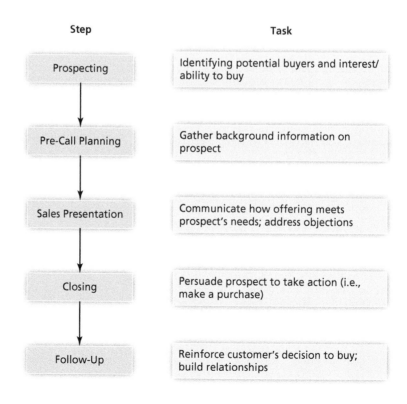

Step	Task
Prospecting	Identifying potential buyers and interest/ability to buy
Pre-Call Planning	Gather background information on prospect
Sales Presentation	Communicate how offering meets prospect's needs; address objections
Closing	Persuade prospect to take action (i.e., make a purchase)
Follow-Up	Reinforce customer's decision to buy; build relationships

presentation is more of a blank canvas, with the content and direction of a sales presentation guided by a prospect's situation and the rapport developed between salesperson and prospect.

A sales presentation is not a one-way broadcast of a product's features and benefits. It is a conversation between salesperson and prospect, including the salesperson acknowledging and addressing a prospect's concerns, questions, or complaints, which is known as responding to objections. In a broad sense, an objection is any obstacle a prospect presents to closing a sale. In a scripted presentation, common objections are known and responses prepared in advance so that salespeople are prepared to address them. Objections raised during an adaptive sales presentation require a salesperson to think fast to satisfactorily address the objection while moving the prospect closer toward agreeing to buy.

The fourth step in the selling process is the closing, which occurs when a salesperson asks a prospect to make a commitment to buy. Strong closing skills are often possessed by top-performing salespeople. They are unafraid to ask for the order. Many sales presentations end without a firm request for the buyer to take action, which represents a significant missed opportunity to persuade a prospect to make a purchase. Two tactics that a salesperson can employ to nudge a prospect to make a commitment if he or she is hesitant are: 1) incentive close or 2) scarcity close. An incentive close "sweetens the pot" for the prospect by offering additional value for immediate action. A salesperson could offer an incentive for a prospective customer interested in a suite rental agreement by mentioning an invitation-only event for new suite holders to meet coaches or players. A scarcity close can be an effective tactic when the product or service offered is in limited supply. Instead of allowing a prospect to "think it over," a scarcity close seeks to persuade action now or risk missing out on the opportunity to buy.

Effectively handling customer objections is an important part of successful ticket sales for sports properties.

The final step is post-sale interaction with the customer. One of the strengths of personal selling is its relationship-building capabilities. Failing to follow up with new customers to thank them for their commitment and advance the relationship with the customer is a missed opportunity. Follow-up is so important to building long-term customer relationships that many sports properties dedicate personnel to perform this step. As discussed earlier in this chapter in the section on engagement, customers acquired by ticket salespeople are often assigned a customer service representative to handle their needs. The advantage of this practice is two-fold. First, the organization sends a signal to customers that they are important by assigning a staff member to serve them. Second, freeing salespeople from follow-up responsibilities allows them to focus on performing the first four steps of the selling process, acquiring new customers for the organization.

Despite the drawbacks of personal selling, the benefits of relationship building and revenue generation are too great to ignore. The MLS Sales Center mentioned in Chapter 8 illustrates sports properties' recognition of the importance of personal selling. In the first year of operation, MLS Sales Center graduates hired by MLS teams generated more than $1 million in ticket sales. The sales program is expanding its training to offer workshops for veteran MLS team ticket sales personnel for professional development.[22]

Direct Response Marketing

Direct response marketing can be defined as "the interactive use of advertising media to stimulate an immediate behavior modification in such a way that this behavior can be tracked, recorded, analyzed, and stored on a database for future retrieval and use."[23] Three keywords in the definition of direct response marketing distinguish it from other communication tools. First, direct response marketing is *interactive*. Marketers use direct response marketing when they desire some sort of feedback from the message recipient. Unlike advertising messages that could have objectives of creating awareness or developing brand associations among consumers or engaging fans with the sports property, direct response marketing messages are designed to encourage feedback.

Second, direct response marketing seeks *immediate* response. Direct response messages are not sent in order to impact the target recipient's behavior six months or two years from now or to strengthen their attitude towards the brand; the objective is to motivate the audience to engage in particular behavior now.

Third, behavioral responses to direct response marketing can be *tracked*. This characteristic of direct marketing describes the accountability offered by direct response communication channels. Metrics such as number of messages delivered, number of responses received, number of sales, cost per response, and return on investment are all relatively easy to measure through use of direct response channels. These characteristics of direct response marketing have contributed to its increased usage by marketers as demands have increased for accountability on the effectiveness of marketing spending. Approximately 54% of all advertising expenditures in the U.S. are spent in direct response channels, and that figure is expected to remain at or above that level in the coming years.[24]

Figure 10.13 highlights the four direct response communication tools that can be used by sports marketers in their IMC programs. Each has its own set of strengths and weaknesses.

FIGURE 10.13 Direct Response Communication Tools

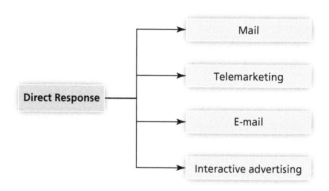

MAIL. This channel can be used to send messages to consumers who are judged to be viable prospects with greater efficiency than mass media such as radio and newspapers. The key to effective use of direct mail is the quality of the customer list used to specify the target audience. A list can come from two sources: in-house or external. An in-house list is generated from a firm's marketing database. The customer records used to compile the list can be specified by a marketing manager so that the customer characteristics of the audience targeted for a mailing match well with the offer contained in the mailing. The Kansas City Royals may want to target prospects for purchasing special weekend ticket packages to its MLB games. It could compile a list of all buyers of single-game tickets who live within 150 miles and who have purchased in the past three years. Anyone meeting these criteria could be sent a direct mail piece containing the offer for weekend ticket packages.

If a high-quality in-house list does not exist or a manager wishes to cast a wider net to target prospective buyers, then an external list can be acquired that provides a target audience based on desired characteristics. Again, the Kansas City Royals could contract with a mailing list broker to rent or buy a list of names that meet desired criteria such as live within 100 miles, are Major League Baseball fans, like to attend live sporting events, and subscribe to sports publications. The difference between list rental and purchase is that use of names is limited to one time when renting a list, and the task of sending the mail pieces is usually done by the broker. A purchased list, although more expensive than a rented list, gives the buyer unlimited access and use of the list.

Another strength of using direct mail is the creative leeway marketers have in crafting messages to attract attention and motivate prospects to take action. A message can be placed on a postcard, in a brochure, or in a letter. The size, color, and stock (stiffness and rigidity) of paper used can be selected in a manner that increases the chances it stands out when it lands in a recipient's mailbox. Calls to action can be structured in a way that measurement of responses to a direct mail piece is easy to perform through a dedicated telephone number or website address (a.k.a. URL) specific to that direct mail piece, or a special code can be provided that the consumer uses when responding.

The main limitation of direct mail is its high cost for printing, postage, and the creative work. It also suffers from a low response rate. Typical estimates put the percent of responses at less than 3 percent.[25] Even campaigns that have high-quality lists tend to have low response rates. Figure 10.14 summarizes the advantages and disadvantages of direct mail.

Advantages:
- Audience selectivity
- Creative flexibility
- Measurability

Disadvantages:
- High costs
- Low response rate

© GWImages / Shutterstock

FIGURE 10.14
Advantages and Disadvantages of Direct Mail

TELEMARKETING. Telemarketing provides efficiency for a sports property's sales efforts by creating a channel that can be used to communicate with prospects and customers from a central location. The "list" used for targeting consumers for a telemarketing campaign can be internal or external, like direct mail, with the same set of advantages and disadvantages.

Telemarketing offers a number of benefits to sports properties. Telemarketing is less expensive than using outside salespeople. Another advantage of telemarketing is its capability to "close the deal," persuading prospects to take action and buy. Although many telemarketing calls require follow-up calls to get a decision from the prospect, the ease with which contact can be made makes multiple calls on a prospect practical. For properties with an urgent need to sell ticket inventory, reaching prospects that have been qualified (identified as meeting criteria of a prospect) quickly in an effort to persuade them to take action immediately may be done best through telemarketing.

The drawbacks of telemarketing are tied to its image and cost. Telemarketing is viewed as highly intrusive and perceived by many people as a salesperson pushing something that a person does not need or want. The intrusiveness of telemarketing calls has been deflected by consumers by using caller ID on phones and signing up for "Do Not Call" lists. The federal government and forty states offer consumers an opt-out program that telemarketers are required to honor. An exception to Do Not Call programs is that if a business has had a prior relationship with a person within a specified time period, then it is permissible to contact by telephone. This exception benefits sports marketers that wish to make telemarketing calls to someone who has purchased tickets in the past. The upfront costs to implement a telemarketing program are significant for equipment, customer lists, recruiting, and training, although telemarketing is less expensive than fielding an outside sales force once it is implemented. Figure 10.15 summarizes the advantages and disadvantages of telemarketing.

E-MAIL. An alternative to direct mail that gets around much of the expense incurred for postage and direct mailers is to use e-mail as a communication channel. E-mail provides marketers great

Advantages:
- Less expensive
- Ability to persuade action
- Quick responses

Disadvantages:
- High setup costs
- Poor image of telemarketers
- High employee turnover

© IKO / Shutterstock

FIGURE 10.15
Advantages and Disadvantages of Telemarketing

flexibility in terms of the frequency that messages are sent and the creative content of messages. Since there is no postage or printing costs, e-mails can be sent more frequently and as situations arise that require rapid communication with the target audience.

If the NHL's Phoenix Coyotes has a large number of unsold tickets for a Saturday night home game, it can send an e-mail in the days preceding the game to selected addresses in its customer database with an offer (e.g., buy one ticket, get one 50% off; or buy a ticket and get a $5 food voucher). E-mail can be very effective in these situations because of the perishable nature of services. When an event is held and there are unsold seats, that selling opportunity is gone forever.

The use of e-mail is not limited to making a call for action such as buying tickets. Newsletters or other content can be sent periodically to keep a sports team's fans informed about what is going on with the team, upcoming events, community involvement, and any other news that would be of interest. Maintaining contact with customers via e-mail is an effective way to keep a fan engaged with the brand throughout the year, even in the off-season.

The main disadvantage of using e-mail to reach an audience is message clutter, specifically spam (unsolicited e-mail). One estimate on the extent of the problem puts the amount of spam messages at about 70% of all e-mail sent daily.[26] A tactic for navigating the spam problem is to use a permission-based e-mail marketing program. Implementation of permission marketing does not mean customers will open and read all e-mail messages, but it limits delivery to persons who have an interest in receiving and reduces the likelihood that messages will end up in a recipient's junk mail folder. Despite the benefits of reaching interested persons through permission-based e-mail marketing, the percentage of people who follow through and click a link in an e-mail message is rather low. One estimate puts the click rate at less than 6% of commercial e-mail messages sent.[27] The keys to success for e-mail marketing are similar to those for direct mail: 1) have a quality list of e-mail addresses for viable prospects and customers, 2) include a call to action that gives people a reason to open and click through e-mail messages, and 3) use creative design in terms of copy (text) and visual presentation that attracts and maintains consumer interest. The pros and cons of using e-mail are summarized in Figure 10.16.

FIGURE 10.16
Advantages and Disadvantages of E-mail

© Blend Images / Shutterstock

Advantages:
- Low cost
- Flexibility in frequency and creative content
- Provide avenue for communication and information

Disadvantages:
- Clutter (spam)
- Unopened e-mails

INTERACTIVE ADVERTISING. Interactive advertising is a hybrid of traditional media advertising and direct response marketing. It is like media advertising in that copy and visuals are used to communicate a message. It is a form of direct response marketing in that its design seeks an immediate response from the recipient. The emergence of interactive advertising is related directly to the development of the Internet and wireless technologies that keep consumers connected wherever they go.

Two primary channels for placing interactive advertisements are the World Wide Web and search engines. Placement of ads on the Web can be based on the content of particular websites or the surfing behavior of Internet users. Ad placement based on website content is similar to decisions made with selecting traditional media, like magazines or radio. For example, a secondary ticketing service like FanSnap places ads in the sports section of online newspapers to attract sports fans to search for tickets to sports and entertainment events.

The other approach to placing Web ads is to place messages using an approach known as **behavioral targeting**. Rather than making ad placement decisions based on the content of a particular website, behavioral targeting serves ads to Web surfers based on the types of websites

Interstate Batteries

Interstate Batteries took over Fox Sports' website during Super Bowl XLV with a sales promotion interactive advertising campaign.

visited. For instance, a consumer who is browsing websites for motocross accessories may later receive an ad selling tickets to a motocross event.[28] This tactic is very efficient for marketers as it minimizes money spent to advertise to people who have no interest in the product. For privacy advocates and some consumers, behavioral targeting is very intrusive because of the use of technology to monitor a consumer's Web surfing behavior and serve ads accordingly.

Search engine ads are advantageous because they reach consumers who are already in a buying decision mode, usually at the information search stage. Thus, the advertiser can target users based on particular needs they seek to meet and design the message to appeal to those needs. Moreover, costs for placing search engine ads typically are not incurred unless a Web surfer clicks on an ad. In contrast, the cost of traditional media advertising is fee-based, meaning that an advertiser pays the same rate if 2 responses are received or 272 people respond.

Another advantage of search engine advertising is the accountability built into the channel. Marketers have a wide range of metrics, or results, available that can be reviewed to assess a search engine ad campaign's effectiveness. Number of ad clicks, cost per sale, and effectiveness of different search keywords for generating responses are three examples of performance measures that can be easily determined. While there are drawbacks to using search engine advertising, namely the expertise needed to plan and manage search engine ad campaigns, search engines provide an additional channel to target consumers and generate an immediate response.

The next frontier in interactive advertising is in your pocket or purse: the mobile phone. Consumers are now connected to what is being called "the third screen," as mobile phones are being used to receive information and entertainment in the same ways that we use televisions and personal computers. The development of smartphones that are multimedia devices used for telephoning, texting, photos, videos, and Internet access makes it possible for people to remain connected to their interests (including sports) everywhere they go. Mobile marketing is in its infancy. In early 2010 about 20% of the U.S. population had a smartphone. Greater choice of smartphone models and more attractive pricing is projected to grow the percentage of smartphone users to about 50% of the population within a very short time.[29]

As smartphone penetration increases, sports marketers will expand their use of mobile advertising to reach customers and prospects. One way that mobile advertising is currently being used is to engage fans via text messaging, also known as Short Message Service (SMS). Several professional teams have implemented SMS systems that invite fans to sign up to receive messages from the team. The SMS platform can be used to send messages about upcoming games, special events, offers and promotions, or news of interest to fans. The opt-in nature of SMS advertising means that consumers will receive messages from a sports property only if they have chosen to participate. And the geo-locating features of smartphones mean that advertisers can target consumers based on where they are located in relation to the advertiser's business. For example, a team with ample supply of unsold tickets one or two days before a scheduled game could place ads on mobile Internet websites to reach customers in a specific geographic area with a coupon offer for discounted tickets for the upcoming game.

The main limitation of mobile advertising is its reach. Even as the proportion of the population using smartphones approaches 50%, that figure means half of the population cannot be reached via mobile marketing. In the above example, sending geo-targeted ads on mobile Internet websites would probably need to be supplemented by sending messages using channels such as e-mail and social media. This weakness of mobile marketing will likely fade over time as more consumers adopt smartphones. Figure 10.17 summarizes the pros and cons of using interactive advertising.

FIGURE 10.17
Advantages and Disadvantages of Interactive Advertising

Advantages:
- Reaches consumers online
- Behavioral targeting
- Availability of various online metrics
- Growing use of smartphones
- Ability to use SMS

Disadvantages:
- Invasion of privacy
- Reach

© Andre Blais / Shutterstock

Consumer-Controlled Channels

The telling of a brand story has traditionally been accomplished by use of marketer-controlled communication tools. In order to tell the brand story, the brand owner made decisions about what should be said about a brand, what channels to use for message delivery, and when messages should be delivered. This approach is based on the marketer initiating communication and having influence over communication flow. The tight grip held on the power in the interactions between buyers and sellers has loosened. Consumers increasingly have a stronger voice and more channels to initiate conversations. Marketing experts Charlene Li and Josh Bernoff have described this trend as a "groundswell" defining it as "a social trend in which people use technologies to get the things they need from each other, rather than from traditional institutions like corporations."[30] The rise of two communication technologies has contributed to the emergence of consumer-controlled channels as part of a brand's IMC strategy: social networking platforms and online communities.

Social Networking Platforms

Individuals can connect with sports brands and individuals that they like as well as communicate with other people with shared interests through social networking platforms. Thousands of social networking websites exist, from the ubiquitous Facebook to niche networks like Athlinks, a social network for endurance athletes. Opportunities for sports properties to reach target audiences exist by creating an official branded page on sites like Facebook and Twitter. The use of social networking websites as a communication channel offers many advantages, but communicating through these channels requires a departure from the mindset that sports properties must control communication content and timing.

A prime advantage of using social networking websites is their low cost compared to buying ad space or time in traditional mass media. A branded page on a social networking website can be set up at no cost, and messages can be posted whenever a desire to communicate arises. A related advantage is that members of a sports brand's page can be tapped to provide input in a cost-effective manner that can be used to help deliver a better customer experience. A minor league baseball team could use its Facebook page to solicit comments from fans about promotions and giveaways they like most or would like to see added. Rather than planning a promotion schedule based entirely on past experience and managerial intuition, inviting fans to share their views can add a depth of knowledge about the customer that would be missed otherwise. Also, it gives fans a feeling of empowerment and that their opinions matter.

Another benefit of open communication channels is that consumers have the ability to spread the word on a sports brand's behalf. Whether it is direct recommendations such as suggesting to one's friends that they "like" the Rochester Americans (American Hockey League team) on Facebook or noticing that a friend follows the Americans, the reach of social networking websites depends heavily on person-to-person communication to promote a sports brand. This viral distribution of brand messages may be perceived as more credible, as friends' recommendations and influence are more instrumental than anything the sports brand says or does.

Social networks are an important medium to interact with fans.

The decision to give fans a voice by creating a branded presence on social networking websites means a decision is made to give up some control over the communication content and distribution. The spirit of social media contains an element of inviting frank expression of views and opinions from customers and the general public, even if they are negative toward a company or brand. If fans of the St. Louis Rams post negative comments about players, coaches, or the organization on the team's official Facebook page, those comments should remain as long as they are not offensive to any persons or groups. Squashing criticism is a characteristic of one-way mass media communications and is contrary to the invitation for dialogue with stakeholders.

Online Communities

Social networking websites are convenient, inexpensive channels to use for engaging fans and building a community of followers, but they are not the only option for using social media. Online communities hosted by a sports property are another channel for harnessing the passion

Insider Insights Jeff Hennion – GNC Live Well

Q. How do choices of message channels to reach a target market relate to broader strategic considerations such as brand positioning?

A. Positioning the brand and associating it with the correct partners is a critical decision. Just like the decision to use sports as a marketing vehicle in the first place is critical, picking the right sport is just as important. For example, a power tool company could be a great marketer, but if they choose to advertise on Lifetime vs. on ESPN, it could potentially not matter at all how well it markets its products. The audience is not ready for it. Carrying that one step further, if that power tool company opted to sponsor a women's tennis event on ESPN vs. a NASCAR race, the message could be diluted substantially as well.

Jeff Hennion discusses the various facets of selling the sports story.

Q. What is the relationship between creative strategy (the message) and message channel (the medium)?

A. As in any area of marketing, messaging is crucial. There are key guidelines to make sure your messaging across the brand platform holds. Key guidelines for brand messages to be effective across all channels are: 1) consistency, 2) authenticity, 3), originality, and 4) simplicity. The difference with messaging in sports is that it needs to be relevant. The closer an attachment you can make between your brand product/message and the sports with which you associate your brand, the more effective the message will be. An example is that Dick's Sporting Goods almost

exclusively advertises its golf business and products on the Golf Channel.

Q. Can you share an example of a promotion tactic with which you had involvement that had no direct impact on revenue generation yet was successful?

A. Sometimes, promotions cannot involve direct sales. Part of Dick's Sporting Goods' strategy with ESPN involved sponsorship of "ESPN the Weekend" at Disney World. This event linked perfectly with the message, the target market, and the relevance. "ESPN the Weekend" was an event drawing huge crowds of primarily families (perfect for Dick's), great sports association (the weekend is all about athletes, leagues, and sports), national coverage (many of the events are broadcast by ESPN), and singular sponsorship (Dick's was the only sponsor, which helps solidify the brand association with the event).

Disney's restrictions prohibited selling product. Instead, Dick's brought in its Sports Caravan, a 53-foot mobile trailer/store on wheels that was converted to an interactive demonstration trailer. Set up inside the park, people could throw footballs at targets, test out new golf clubs with launch monitors, try out the newest lacrosse equipment, etc. Not only did it attract huge numbers of people, many athletes stopped by as well, which drove even bigger crowds and created some great associations with Dick's and these athletes.

of fans. The advantages of hosted online communities are similar to the benefits of social networking websites, with two exceptions. First, the cost of online community infrastructure and maintenance is much higher than cost incurred for a presence on social networking websites. Second, the reach of online communities is not as great as that of social networking websites. People are added to the community more easily on networks like Facebook and Twitter because they are using those platforms already. In contrast, an online community hosted by a sports property grows only if efforts succeed to drive traffic to the community to sign up and participate.

Many sports properties had their own online communities before social networking websites became popular. NASCAR has had a Community section on NASCAR.com for many years. The NASCAR.com Community began as a collection of discussion forums where fans could gather to talk about drivers, races, tracks, and other issues. Today, the NASCAR.com Community has more tools for connecting fans with each other, such as a "Crews" feature that allows fans with shared interests to form a group. Also, members can write blog entries, comment on blogs, and upload photos and videos to the NASCAR.com Community.

The Phoenix Suns of the NBA takes the concept of a hosted online community a step further by branding its channel "Planet Orange." This area of the Suns' website is an all-inclusive social media space, containing links to discussion boards, blogs, photos, videos, member profiles, and the team's pages on social networking websites such as MySpace and YouTube.[31] The investment in and upkeep of hosted online communities are tradeoffs that must be accepted in order to create a space exclusively for fans and followers of a sports brand. For some properties, a destination online community may be preferred over the increasing clutter of pages set up by businesses on social networking websites.

Chapter Summary

When determining the appropriate communication channels, it is important to begin with an evaluation of customers' relationships with the brand and to what extent they are engaged with the brand. At the lowest level of the relationship is an awareness of the brand. For these individuals, exposure through channels such as sponsorships, media advertising, direct response marketing, websites, and podcasts are desirable. However, for purchases to occur customers must become engaged with the brand. Vehicles that can be used include sponsorships, interactive advertising, permission e-mail, social media, blogs, podcasts, personal selling, and customer relations.

The next step involves deciding on the appropriate brand communication mix. Multiple channels are available. The best choice depends on the target market being addressed, the objective being pursued, and the message to be communicated. Two general types of channels are available: marketer-controlled communication channels and consumer-controlled channels.

Marketer-controlled channels to build awareness and engagement include media advertising, sales promotions, public relations, sales force, and direct response marketing. Mass media advertising may be the most efficient way to reach consumers in terms of cost per contact. Television offers wide reach through network channels, cable channels, and local cable channels. In addition to reaching national audiences, local and regional audiences can be reached through spot TV ads and cable productions.

Radio allows for greater selectivity in audiences based on station formats. Unfortunately, radio is also highly segmented in terms of overall audience for a given region, with most stations garnering less than 3% of the population. Thus, using radio often requires running ads on multiple stations. Newspapers also offer selectivity, but are hampered by declining readership, especially among younger consumers. Outdoor advertisements provide regional coverage for sports brands but are limited to only awareness-type messages.

Sales promotions are excellent for achieving engagement-type objectives, especially calls to action. Two types of sales promotions can be used. Risk-reducing sales promotions offer incentives to consumers to make a purchase or to act in a specific manner by reducing financial risk. Sampling and coupons are the two major types of risk-reducing incentives. Value-added incentives provide something of value, a premium or promotion to encourage consumers to make a purchase or take an action.

Public relations is an effective means of building brand awareness and brand image. Although sports entities provide information for public relations, the public sees the messages as more credible since the marketer has no control over what the media publishes or broadcasts. PR can be used to promote the positive causes and good community activities in which a sports brand is involved.

The sales force is an excellent means of building engagement with consumers because of the one-on-one interactions. It is also an effective means of maintaining relationships. However, once the sale is made the relationship may be handled by customer relations personnel.

Direct response marketing is especially attractive to sports marketers because of the ability to track results and build a database for future use. Common forms of direct response marketing include direct mail, telemarketing, e-mail, and interactive advertising. Two features of interactive marketing that are especially attractive are behavioral targeting and the increased usage of smartphones.

Not all marketing channels are controlled by marketers. Two recent channels have emerged that are in the control of consumers—social network platforms and online communities. Both allow consumers to interact with one another and communicate both positive and negative things about a brand. While marketers cannot control these channels, they must utilize them to build awareness and engage consumers with the brand.

Review Questions

1. Explain the difference between exposure and engagement. What marketing tools are best suited for each?
2. Selection of the appropriate communications channels depends on what three criteria?
3. What is the difference between marketer-controlled channels and consumer-controlled channels?
4. What communications channels are classified as being marketer-controlled?
5. What are the advantages and disadvantages of using television as an advertising medium?
6. What are the advantages and disadvantages of using radio as an advertising medium?
7. What are the advantages and disadvantages of using newspapers as an advertising medium?
8. How can outdoor advertising be used by a sports brand?
9. What are the two types of sales promotions? Explain how each can be used.
10. What is public relations? How can it be used by marketers to promote a sports brand?
11. How can a sales force be an effective tool for building engagement and encouraging action?
12. What are the various forms of direct response marketing that can be used by a sports property? What are the advantages and disadvantages of each?
13. How can a sports property use social networking platforms and online communities to build a sports brand?

New Terms

Channel the means used to transmit or deliver a message to a target audience.

Exposure low-level outcome that can be achieved through communication channels with mass distribution, such as adverting, public relations, and sponsorships.

Podcast audio or video program available for streaming over the Internet or for download to digital music players.

Engagement higher-quality communications with a target audience involving deeper processing of brand stimuli.

Interactive advertising form of online advertising that is designed to elicit a response from viewers in the form of clicking on an advertisement.

Permission marketing marketing program in which participants have given permission to an entity to send promotional materials.

Social media online communications channels or websites that allow users to create, post, and comment on content.

Blog short for "weblog;" Web pages that contain information, commentary, photos, videos, or links to other information sources on the Web

Trade magazine specialized publication with content targeted toward members of a particular occupation or industry.

Sales promotions use of an incentive or something of value to influence a target audience to act in some manner.

Sampling sales promotion tactic that allows a consumer to try a product with no cost or obligation.

Coupon price discount or other cost reduction incentive to encourage consumer purchase or action.

Premium tangible item given to consumers in exchange for a purchase.

Promotion event held in conjunction with a sporting event that does not involve giving away a tangible item but adds value to the consumption experience.

Public relations management of communications between an organization and various audiences including customers, media, governments, local communities, employees, and stockholders.

Personal selling personal communication between a representative of a business and customers or prospects for the purpose of making a sale or building relationships.

Prospecting process of identifying potential buyers and determining their interest and ability to buy.

Direct response marketing advertising media used to deliver a message that seeks a measurable response from the target audience.

Behavioral targeting sends ads to Web surfers based on an analysis of the types of websites visited.

Discussion and Critical Thinking Exercises

1. Look through the various marketing tools available to build exposure in Figure 10.2. Suppose you are the marketing director for a minor league baseball team. If you only have the budget for two of the marketing tools, which two would you use? Why?

2. Look through the various marketing tools available to build engagement in Figure 10.3. Suppose you are the marketing director for a minor league hockey team. If you only have the budget for three of the items, which three would you choose? Why?

3. Would you agree that social media has become an effective means of building engagement between fans and sports property? Why or why not? Do you personally use social media? If so, how? If not, why not? In what way can sports brands use social media to reach you?

4. Examine the marketer-controlled communications channels listed in Figure 10.5. For your college's sports brands, rank the various channels in terms of most useful to least useful in building a strong sports brand. Does it make a difference based on the target market? Why or why not? Does it make a difference based on which sport? Why or why not?

5. Refer back to the opening vignette about minor league baseball. If you were the marketing manager for a local minor league team, how would you utilize the various media advertising channels of television, radio, newspapers, and outdoor advertising? Would they be used for exposure or engagement, or both? Justify your choices of media.

6. Pick a professional sports team (major league or minor league). Discuss how the team uses sales promotions. Does it use risk-reducing incentives or value-added incentives, or both? What are the benefits of using the sales promotions? What are the dangers? Do

you think the sports team is using about the right amount, or should they be increased or decreased? Why?

7. Refer back to the opening vignette about minor league baseball. If you were the marketing manager for a minor league team and only had the budget to hire one salesperson, how would you use that person? Describe the types of individuals or businesses you would have him/her contact. Would you use the person for just selling or also for customer relations after the sale? Justify your answer.

8. Discuss the benefits of direct response advertising. Is it being used at your college to promote the athletic program and various sports? Why or why not? Assume the university asked you to develop a direct response program. Outline which direct response tools you would use and how you would use them.

9. What is your opinion of behavioral targeting? Is it an invasion of privacy? Why or why not? Should sports properties use it to market their sports brands? Why or why not?

10. Social network platforms and online communities can be valuable tools to marketers for building brand awareness and engagement. Does the athletic department at your school utilize either? If yes, suggest how it be used by your athletic department. If no, propose one social network platform the athletic department should focus on for engaging fans.

You Make the Call
Groupon

The name Groupon blends the words "group" and "coupon." Some think it is the next big thing in social media. Groupon taps into the energy of online social networking and combines it with steep discounts on goods and services where consumers live. The discounts range from 50% to 80% off retail price. The catch, however, is that a certain number of people must sign up for the discount or the deal is off. In addition, there is a time limit, so consumers must act quickly to take advantage of the coupon.

Groupon was launched in 2008 by founder and CEO Andrew Mason. The site now has more than 20 million subscribers, serving over 500 markets in 44 countries. The original premise behind Groupon was to provide small businesses with an opportunity to grow their business and attract customers. It was to be a local shopping site. For each city, Groupon would feature one local business. It might be a restaurant, a theater, a spa, or a sports property. Coupons would be sent to subscribers informing them of the deal, how long the promotion was going to last, and how many people had to sign up for the deal.

Groupon's success is based on five key principles. First, make the interaction with subscribers simple—one deal, one day, one city. Second, create urgency by ending the deal at midnight. Third, energize the subscriber to tell others because unless enough sign up, the deal is off. Fourth, make it fun. Groupon's website tone is upbeat and enjoyable. Lastly, make it fresh, with a new deal every day.

A number of sports brands have used Groupon. For example, the San Diego Padres MLB team offered a field-level ticket, soda, hot dog, and a hat for $24, a $52 value. A total of 2,700 tickets were sold in just the one day it was up on Groupon for the July 1–4 series, and the offer went out on June 30. Of 2,700 tickets sold, 92% were redeemed.

The Round Rock Express minor league baseball team has used Groupon on three different occasions. The first package was six Thursday night tickets with six passes to the stadium club for $66. The second package was five weekday tickets and five stadium passes for $59. The last package was two box seat tickets and parking for $15. Sales for the first package totaled 151, for the second package 299, and for the third package 500. Redemption rates averaged 94%. In addition to boosting sales, Groupon furnished Round Rock Express the demographic breakdown of the

© Shout It Out Design / Shutterstock

Groupon offers consumers discounts on sporting events through unique time-sensitive promotions.

ticket purchasers. An added benefit was that all of the purchasers were added to Round Rock's database for future use in any direct response marketing effort.

Real Salt Lake, a MLS team, used Groupon to sell tickets to a slow July game. Over five hundred tickets were sold. Daytona International Speedway did a one-day blitz during the week hitting multiple markets on the same day. The offer was for a race and access pass. While the revenue generated was small, Groupon was able to draw in fans that had never been to a race before.

The downside of using Groupon is the steep discount that is offered. While sales may occur, profit will certainly be negatively impacted. Groupon keeps 50% of proceeds from every deal, plus a small credit-card handling fee. So if a package that is valued at $100 is offered through Groupon for $50, the sports property will net less than $25 per coupon.

Sports properties that use Groupon look at it a different way. Rather than think about the deal as receiving only $25 for a $100 product, the company is generating $25 for what would be an empty seat. Thus, $25 is better than nothing. In addition, the sports property may have gained a new name for their database that can be used later in a direct response marketing program.

Questions:

1. Visit Groupon's website at www.groupon.com. Evaluate the site from the perspective of a subscriber. What benefit would there be for sports fans?
2. Visit Groupon's website at www.groupon.com. Evaluate the site from the perspective of a sports property. What benefits are there for a sports property to use Groupon rather than rely on its own sales force to push ticket sales?
3. What are the advantages of using Groupon for a sports brand? What are the disadvantages?
4. Describe situations in which Groupon would be a good option for a sports brand.
5. What impact do you think the steep discounts will have long term for a sports property? Will fans come to expect such deep discounts? Why or why not?
6. Would Groupon be an effective tool for college sports? Why or why not? For which college sports would Groupon be a good option? For which college sports should Groupon not be used? Justify your responses.

Sources: Marcia Froelke Coburn, "On Groupon and Its Founder, Andrew Mason," http://www.chicagomag.com/Chicago-Magazine/August-2010/On-Groupon-and-its-founder-Andrew-Mason/, accessed October 24, 2010; Michael Machosky, "Groupon: Social-networking Expands to Site Offering Coupons," *Pittsburgh Tribune-Review*, www.pittsburghlive.com/x/pittsburghtrib/lifestyles/fooddrink.687173.html, June 22, 2010; Christopher Steiner, "Meet the Fastest Growing Company Ever," *Forbes.com*, http://www.forbes.com/forbes/2010/0830/entrepreneurs-groupon-facebook-twitter-next-web-phenom.html , August 30, 2010; John Julius Sviokla, "Designing Promotions in the Internet Age: Groupon's Five Key Lessons for All Companies," http://www.sviokla.com/branding/designing-promotions-in-the-internet-age-groupons-five-key-lessons-for-all-companies/, September 8, 2009.

References

1. Matthew Coller, (2010), "Awarding the Most Unique Minor League Promotions of 2010," August 31, accessed October 4, 2010, at http://www.bizofbaseball.com/index.php?option=com_content&view=article&id=4671:awarding-the-most-unique-minor-league-promotions-of-2010&catid=79:matthew-coller-articles-archive&Itemid=176.
2. "7 Weird Minor League Baseball Promotions," (2010), April 8, accessed October 5, 2010, at http://www.weirdworm.com/7-weird-minor-league-baseball-fan-promotions/.
3. Don Muret, (2010), "Best Buy Aims for Target Market," *Sports Business Journal*, April 5, 18.
4. Internet Advertising Bureau, (2010), "Internet Ad Revenues Reach Record Quarterly High of $6.3 Billion in Q4 '09," April 7, accessed August 10, 2010, at http://www.iab.net/about_the_iab/recent_press_releases/press_release_archive/press_release/pr-040710.
5. Subscriptions: Email – Talladega Superspeedway, accessed August 10, 2010, at http://www.talladegasuperspeedway.com/This-Is-Talladega/Email-Sign-Up.aspx.

6. Anthony Bradley, (2010), "A New Definition of Social Media," accessed August 13, 2010, at http://blogs.gartner.com/anthony_bradley/2010/01/07/a-new-definition-of-social-media/.

7. Greg Ferenstein, (2010), "How Dana White Built a UFC Empire with Social Media," accessed August 17, 2010, at http://mashable.com/2010/06/08/dana-white-ufc-social-media/.

8. "BlogPulse Stats," accessed August 17, 2010, at http://www.blogpulse.com/.

9. "Vancouver Canucks Video Podcast 2010-2011," (n.d.), accessed May 19, 2011, at http://canucks.nhl.com/podcasts/podcast1011.xml.

10. "Walking the Ticketing Tightrope," (2010), *Sports Business Journal*, March 15, 31.

11. "San Francisco, CA," (2010), accessed September 20, 2010, at http://www.stationratings.com/ratings.asp.

12. "Newspaper Circulation Volume" (2012), accessed April 20, 2012, at http://www.naa.org/Trends-and-Numbers/Circulation/Newspaper-Circulation-Volume.aspx.

13. Newspaper Association of America (2003), "2003 Circulation Facts, Figures, and Logic," accessed April 20, 2012 at http://www.naa.org/Topics-and-Tools/Audience-and-Circulation/Research/2011/~/media/NAACorp/Public%20Files/TopicsAndTools/AudienceAndCirculation/Facts-Figures-and-Logic/Circulation-FFL-2003.ashx.

14. "Public Opinion," (n.d.), accessed September 21, 2010, at http://www.oaaa.org/legislative-andregulatory/issues/publicopinion.aspx.

15. *Magazine Handbook*, (2010), accessed May 20, 2011, at http://www.magazine.org/handbook.

16. "Circulation for All ABC Magazines," (n.d.), accessed May 20, 2011, at http://www.magazine.org/ASSETS/27160E54028546CAB8EE508C1EEA2BED/2010FYALLCIRC.xls.

17. Lisa F. Wilson, (2010), "Why Advertise in Trade Magazines?" January 21, accessed September 21, 2010, at http://www.ehow.com/facts_5896329_advertise-trade-magazines.html.

18. "Volleyball Magazine 2012 Media Kit," accessed April 20, 2012, at http://www.volleyball-mag.com/files/2012 Volleyball Magazine Media Kit.pdf.

19. "Public Relations Defined," (2010), accessed September 23, 2010, at http://www.prsa.org/AboutPRSA/PublicRelationsDefined/.

20. "Thunder Community," (2010), accessed September 23, 2010, at http://www.nba.com/thunder/community/news.html.

21. Gary Armstrong and Philip Kotler, *Marketing: An Introduction*, 10th edition (Upper Saddle River, NJ: Prentice Hall, 2011).

22. Fred Dreier, (2011), "MLS Training Center Adding Classes for Ticket Sales Veterans," *Sports Business Journal*, May 2, 4.

23. Bob Stone and Ron Jacobs, *Successful Direct Marketing Methods*, 8th edition (New York: McGraw-Hill, 2008).

24. Direct Marketing Association (2009), "DMA's Power of Direct Marketing Report Finds DM Ad Expenditures Climb to Over 54% of All Advertising Expenditures," October 19, accessed September 26, 2010, at http://www.the-dma.org/cgi/dispannouncements?article=1335.

25. Allyson Kapin, (2009), "Is Direct Mail Really Headed for the Exit?" May 29, accessed September 27, 2010, at http://www.frogloop.com/directmail.

26. "Emails Reach 210 Billion per Day," (2009), January 26, accessed September 28, 2010, at http://www.techwatch.co.uk/2009/01/26/emails-reach-210-billion-per-day/.

27. "Email Open Rates Increase in Q4 2009," (2010), February 12, accessed September 28, 2010, at http://www.emarketingandcommerce.com/article/email-open-rates-increased-q4-2009/1.

28. Brian Socolow, (2010), "Using Behavioral Targeting to Reach Fans: New Laws on the Horizon," May 22, accessed September 28, 2010, at http://groupynetwork.com/tools/legal/using-behavioral-targeting-to-reach-fans/.

29. "USA to Add 80 Million New Smartphone Users by 2011," (2010), March 26, accessed September 30, 2010, at http://twittown.com/mobile/mobile-blog/usa-add-80-million-new-smartphone-users-2011.

30. Charlene Li and Josh Bernoff, *Groundswell* (Boston: Forrester Research, 2008).

31. "Planet Orange," (n.d.), accessed October 3, 2010, at http://www.nba.com/suns/fans/planet_orange.html.

11

Leveraging Sports Brands through Sponsorship-Linked Marketing

Learning Objectives:

By the end of this chapter you should be able to:

1. Discuss the methods, characteristics, and growth of sports sponsorships
2. Explain how corporate sponsors benefit from sponsorship investments
3. Describe the steps of effective sponsorship management
4. Identify reasons that sponsorships end

Bridgestone has entered into partnerships with some of the most high profile sport properties in the world, inlcuding The International Olympic Committee.

Bridgestone Rides Sports to Build Brand

Automobile tire manufacturer Bridgestone began in Japan in 1931 and has had a presence in the U.S. market since its 1988 acquisition of Firestone. Bridgestone's American division had a modest involvement with sports in its first few years, most notably returning to IndyCar racing in 1995 through its Firestone brand.[1] The association with auto racing was logical given the importance of tires to a race car, and the Bridgestone brand was involved with auto racing outside of the United States through a sponsorship in the Formula One series. The strategy for using sports as a marketing vehicle changed dramatically during the first decade of the 21st century as the Bridgestone brand became associated with several high-profile sports properties in the United States.

A bold strategy to link the Bridgestone brand with top sports properties required a sizeable financial commitment. The company's sponsorship expenditures more than doubled in a three-year period, and the increased investment in sponsorships gave Bridgestone associations with a variety of professional sports properties. An important piece of Bridgestone's sponsorship strategy has been to acquire the "official tire" designation for the properties it sponsors. The PGA Tour was Bridgestone's first category sponsorship, signed in 2006. Deals followed with the NFL (2007) and NHL (2008) to be the official tire of these leagues. Not only did Bridgestone secure the designation of official tire for these leagues, but it also became title sponsor of two premier events: the Super Bowl Halftime Show and the NHL Winter Classic.

According to Bridgestone marketing executive John Baratta, these properties were selected because the company wanted to "get away from the shotgun advertising and sponsorship

Insider Expert Terry Lefton – Sports Business Journal

Terry Lefton, a pioneer of sports business reporting, has been the editor-at-large at *Sports Business Daily* and *Sports Business Journal* since 2001. Owner of an expansive Rolodex and the confidant of hundreds of well-placed industry sources, Lefton is well known for breaking news stories across the sports marketing landscape. He built a reputation as the leading reporter in sports marketing while at *Brandweek* from 1992 through 2000, when he left the weekly trade magazine to write about marketing and sports business for *The Industry Standard*.

Lefton graduated from Temple University with a bachelor's degree in communications in 1979. He worked as a writer for the Sports Network, Gannett Newspapers, *Electronic News*, and the *New York Daily News* before joining *Brandweek* as one of its founding editors. He lives in Connecticut with his wife Denise and three children: Clara, Margaret, and Madison. Lefton is a founding board member of The National Sports Marketing Network.

Terry Lefton, Editor-at-Large for *Sports Business Daily* and *Sports Business Journal*.

approach we had been doing with the Bridgestone brand. It was spread out across a lot of different areas. We really wanted to hone it in on a more defined target audience."[2] Baratta indicated that the impact of Bridgestone's sports sponsorship portfolio has helped move Bridgestone from a reliance on push tactics to move products through distribution channels to a brand that is being pulled through channels by consumer demand.[3] The timing of Bridgestone's escalation of its sports sponsorship program was unusual. The recession that began in 2008 led many corporate sponsors to reevaluate their sports spending and in many cases discontinue sponsorships as a cost-cutting measure. Bridgestone's renewal of its NFL and NHL deals in 2010 was a signal of its confidence in sponsorship as a marketing channel to reach its target market.

For Bridgestone, selecting sponsorship partners is not merely a matter of being associated with top sports properties. The company has sought to sponsor properties whose audience demographics include concentrations of the affluent consumer Bridgestone seeks to target for performance tires. Bridgestone could have stayed with the familiar and focused its sponsorships on automobile-related properties like auto racing, but the decision to sponsor mainstream sports gave it access to a broader audience and has led to greater brand awareness.[4]

Introduction

Bridgestone's success as a partner with the PGA Tour, NFL, and NHL demonstrates the role that sponsorship can play in a brand's growth. Too often, the tactical aspects of a sponsorship such as placing signage at a sporting event or receiving exposure in a sports property's advertising inventory dominate a manager's focus. While these tangible benefits of a sponsorship are important, there is a bigger picture to consider. Managerial involvement in sponsorship planning should reach the highest levels within an organization's marketing unit. Sponsorship is more than a communication tactic; it is a strategy to reinforce brand positioning and can support a strategy to target specific customer segments. Sponsorship even has the capability to become an organizational resource that gives a brand a competitive advantage.[5] When a sponsor associates its brand with a sports property that is relevant to its target market and for which the market has affinity, it enjoys a form of customer intimacy that competitors are hard pressed to match.

In this chapter, sports sponsorship is examined from the standpoint of a business that uses sports as a marketing platform to access customers or prospects. The chapter begins with an overview of sponsorship's development in the past three decades. Next, benefits that corporate sponsors value from an association with a sports property are discussed to shed light on why companies invest in sponsorships. Sponsorship management responsibilities are presented, from defining expectations of outcomes (i.e., objectives) before a sponsorship begins and at the other end of the process, measuring a sponsorship's impact against objectives. Not all sponsorships are successful. The last section identifies reason for sponsorship failures.

Evolution of Sponsorship

Sponsorship has gone from a decision often based on a manager's personal interests to a strategic marketing tool that is a vibrant sector of the sports industry. Expenditures for sponsorships in 2009 were estimated to be $17.2 billion in North America and $46.3 billion globally.[6] Since the early 1990s, annual growth rates for sponsorship have been greater than those of media advertising and sales promotions. International Events Group (IEG), the leading authority on the sponsorship industry, defines **sponsorship** as "a cash and/or in-kind fee paid to a property in return for access to the exploitable commercial potential associated with that property."[7] Sponsorship is the primary channel used for marketing *through* sports, defined in Chapter 1 as strategic marketing efforts of companies in which they partner with a sports entity for commercial benefit.

This definition brings out two representations of sponsorships. First, a sponsorship is a product that is bought and sold. The buyer values "the exploitable commercial potential" of a sports property such as the appearance of the NFL logo on the Bridgestone website along with the designation "official tire of the NFL." The seller, of course, values the payment that a company is willing to give. Note the definition identifies two forms of payment: cash or in-kind. An in-kind payment is the exchange of a nonmonetary item that a sports property values. Examples of in-kind payments include an airline that gives a sports property a certain number of flight tickets in exchange for the designation of "official airline," or an athletic footwear company that gives a collegiate team shoes or clothing in exchange for recognition as an official sponsor.

Second, a sponsorship is a relationship that must be nurtured in order for it to be successful. Sponsorship is different from corporate philanthropy in which a donation is made with little or no expectation of leveraging the association for commercial gain. Sponsors *do* expect something in return for their investment. Otherwise, they will not continue making the investment! Thus, it is imperative that sports properties work closely with their sponsors to help them maximize the impact of their sponsorships.

Types of Sponsorships

As shown in Figure 11.1, sports properties have historically received the lion's share of attention from corporate sponsors. Sports accounts for more than two-thirds of all marketing dollars spent on sponsorships. Another category that is growing in usage by companies in many industries is cause marketing. Although it represents only 9% of total sponsorship spending, it is expected to have continued growth, as is sports sponsorship. Figure 11.2 identifies within sports a number of different ways a brand can develop sponsorship associations.

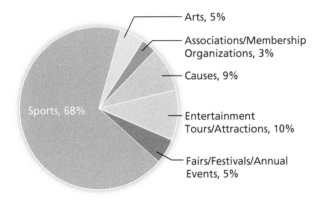

FIGURE 11.1 Sponsorship Spending by Category

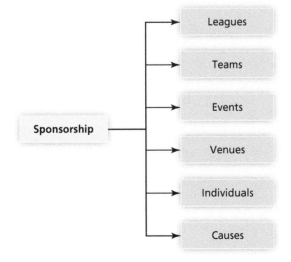

FIGURE 11.2 Types of Sponsorships

LEAGUES. Associating a brand with a particular sport is often achieved by a company connecting with a league or organization. The number of partners and scope of partner sponsorship associations vary by league. For example, Women's Professional Soccer (WPS) re-launched in 2009 and as of 2011 had only five corporate sponsors and a media partner. WPS sponsors are not designated by product category; rather they are referred to as founding partners or official partners.[8] In contrast, the National Collegiate Athletic Association has two groups of sponsors known as Corporate Champions and Corporate Partners. Sponsorships for both levels designate official sponsor status by product category. Corporate Champions are broad partnerships for top-dollar investments by sponsors. Capital One is one of only three Corporate Champions, but its rights include consumer, commercial, and small banking services, which encompasses a wide range of financial services. In contrast, The Hartford is one of the NCAA's 10 Corporate Partners and is the official partner for mutual funds, a small piece of the broader financial services category.[9]

A league must decide how narrow or broad it wishes to grant sponsorship rights. The narrower the sponsor categories, the more opportunities there are to carve out pieces of sponsorship inventory. However, if companies perceive the number of categories or the manner in which exclusive rights are granted are too restrictive, the appeal of the property as a sponsorship vehicle may be hurt.

TEAMS. While team sponsorship inventory is managed in much the same way as their league counterparts, there are three significant differences (see Figure 11.3). First, the geographic scope of team sponsorship tends to be local, focusing on the market in which a sponsored team plays. This characteristic of team sponsorship makes it a viable option for smaller regional firms. Metcalf Bank, a regional bank with a strong presence in the Kansas City area, became the official bank of the Kansas City Chiefs.[10] The geographic fit between Metcalf Bank's target market and the Kansas City Chiefs audience base made the partnership appropriate for the two parties.

FIGURE 11.3
Advantages of Team Sponsorships over League Sponsorships

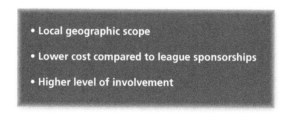

- Local geographic scope
- Lower cost compared to league sponsorships
- Higher level of involvement

Second, the cost of a team sponsorship can be a fraction of the cost of rights as an official league partner. The lower cost is related directly to the narrower geographic scope of a team sponsorship (i.e., the audience reach is less than what is offered by a league sponsorship).

Third, sponsoring a specific team allows a sponsor to be involved with a property on a large scale, even if a competitor holds exclusivity in a given product category. This situation occurs with MasterCard's involvement with the NFL. MasterCard's rival, Visa, is associated with the NFL as its official credit card. Rather than writing off an association with the NFL as unattainable due to Visa's presence, MasterCard has struck sponsorship deals with twenty-three different teams.[11] Team sponsorships give MasterCard a chance to compete against Visa for the attention of NFL fans and at the same time have leeway in deciding which markets to focus its sponsorship investments.

EVENTS. An alternative to marketing through sports at the league or team level is to associate with specific events in which leagues or teams compete. This strategy taps into affinity for a sport in general rather than specific teams or players within a sport. Three types of events that are sponsored are single-day events, multi-day events, and off-field events (see Figure 11.4).

FIGURE 11.4 Types of Sponsored Events

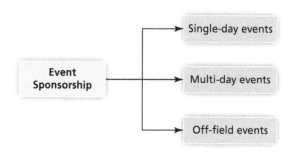

Event Sponsorship → Single-day events
Event Sponsorship → Multi-day events
Event Sponsorship → Off-field events

A single-day event is a game or contest that is a one-time event, held once or a few times annually. Title sponsorship of auto races is an illustration of single-day event sponsorships. Only two races in the 2011 NASCAR Sprint Cup Series season did not have title sponsors—the Daytona 500 and Brickyard 400—and those events are without title sponsors only because the brand equity of these prestigious races takes precedence over having a corporate name for the events. For the other thirty-four races, brands like AAA, Ford, Geico, Samsung, and Subway partnered with race promoters to sponsor single-day events. Although the duration of a single-day event is short, sponsors take advantage of the event by implementing marketing programs in the weeks leading up to the event.

A multi-day event involves games or contests for several days, which means that sponsors can reach attendees and fans over a longer period of time. Clothing retailer Aeropostale has used multi-day events in college basketball to target young males. The brand has been a past sponsor of the Madison Square Garden Holiday Festival and several conference end-of-season tournaments including the Big East Conference, Conference USA, and the Southland Conference. Because multi-day events usually cover a wider geographic area, the marketing potential of a multi-day event is often greater than a single-day event. A collegiate conference basketball tournament will attract fans from each participating team. This characteristic of a multi-day event means that the footprint of the event extends beyond the market in which it is held. Thus, while the event is held in a single city it becomes a regional, if not national, sponsorship.

A third type of event sponsorship does not involve a game or contest at all. Some off-field events that attract fan interest may be viable options as a sponsorship platform. Under Armour has tapped the year-round passion of NFL fans through sponsorship of the NFL Scouting Combine, a four-day event held prior to the NFL Draft each year in which college players take part in workouts for NFL scouts. Another type of off-field event gaining in popularity is fan conventions for professional sports teams. The Washington Capitals of the NHL is among teams offering fans this off-season connection point with their favorite team. Auto insurance company Geico signed as presenting sponsor of the second annual Capitals Convention described in Chapter 7, which attracted more than five thousand attendees.[12] Off-field events have an advantage for sponsors of having fewer (if any) sponsors with which to compete for attention of event attendees. And rights fees for an off-field event may be less than a sponsor would be asked to pay for sponsorship of single-day or multi-day sporting events.

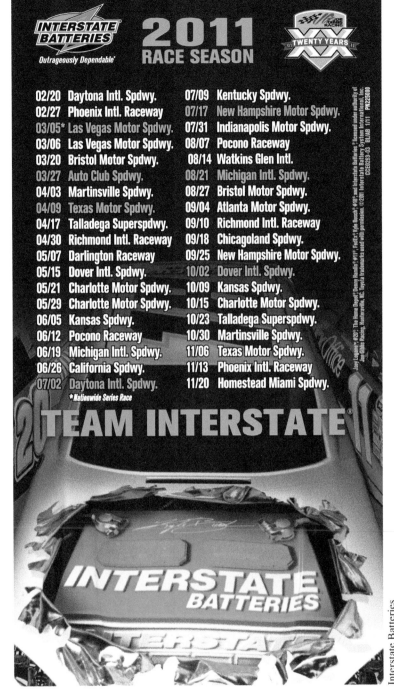

2011 RACE SEASON

02/20	Daytona Intl. Spdwy.	07/09	Kentucky Spdwy.
02/27	Phoenix Intl. Raceway	07/17	New Hampshire Motor Spdwy.
03/05*	Las Vegas Motor Spdwy.	07/31	Indianapolis Motor Spdwy.
03/06	Las Vegas Motor Spdwy.	08/07	Pocono Raceway
03/20	Bristol Motor Spdwy.	08/14	Watkins Glen Intl.
03/27	Auto Club Spdwy.	08/21	Michigan Intl. Spdwy.
04/03	Martinsville Spdwy.	08/27	Bristol Motor Spdwy.
04/09	Texas Motor Spdwy.	09/04	Atlanta Motor Spdwy.
04/17	Talladega Superspdwy.	09/10	Richmond Intl. Raceway
04/30	Richmond Intl. Raceway	09/18	Chicagoland Spdwy.
05/07	Darlington Raceway	09/25	New Hampshire Motor Spdwy.
05/15	Dover Intl. Spdwy.	10/02	Dover Intl. Spdwy.
05/21	Charlotte Motor Spdwy.	10/09	Kansas Spdwy.
05/29	Charlotte Motor Spdwy.	10/15	Charlotte Motor Spdwy.
06/05	Kansas Spdwy.	10/23	Talladega Superspdwy.
06/12	Pocono Raceway	10/30	Martinsville Spdwy.
06/19	Michigan Intl. Spdwy.	11/06	Texas Motor Spdwy.
06/26	California Spdwy.	11/13	Phoenix Intl. Raceway
07/02	Daytona Intl. Spdwy.	11/20	Homestead Miami Spdwy.

*Nationwide Series Race

TEAM INTERSTATE

Interstate Batteries sponsored seven different NASCAR races during the 2011 season.

Interstate Batteries

VENUES. Physical spaces occupied by sports properties have become fertile sources of sponsorship revenue in the past fifteen years. The most visible form of venue sponsorship is **naming rights sponsorship**, an association in which a corporate sponsor acquires the rights to have a corporate

Pittsburgh Penguins

CONSOL Energy obtained naming rights for the arena of the Pittsburgh Penguins for an estimated $100 million.

or brand name incorporated into the venue's official name. A naming rights sponsorship usually requires a long-term commitment from the corporate partner of ten years or more. One reason for this time frame is that the value of a naming rights deal is enhanced for buyer and seller when a venue's brand name remains constant. Changing names too often can create confusion. The home of the NFL's Miami Dolphins had seven different names between 1987 and 2010: Joe Robbie Stadium, Pro Player Park, Pro Player Stadium, Dolphins Stadium, Land Shark Stadium, and Sun Life Stadium.[13] This lack of continuity can decrease the value of the venue as a marketing asset to marketers each time the name changes. Also, the cost of a naming rights sponsorship can be an enormous investment for a company. Two of the most expensive deals in American professional sports are Reliant Energy's partnership with the Houston Texans (thirty years, $300 million for Reliant Stadium) and Citigroup's partnership with the New York Mets (twenty years, $400 million for Citi Field).[14]

Venue sponsorship opportunities are not limited to naming rights. Sports properties have introduced creative options for corporate sponsors to brand within a venue that are less costly than a long-term naming rights deal. This trend has developed partially out of necessity. When the new Meadowlands Stadium in New Jersey was being constructed for a 2010 opening, the U.S. economy was mired in recession. Corporate sponsors were hesitant to make long-term commitments not knowing how economic recovery would take shape, making it very difficult to attract a naming rights partner for a high-profile venue like Meadowlands Stadium. Rather than losing sponsorship revenue while waiting out the recession, the stadium's two tenants (the New York Giants and New York Jets) sold four "Cornerstone Partnerships" worth an estimated $8 million annually.[15] The four Cornerstone Partners, Bud Light, MetLife, Pepsi, and Verizon, receive high visibility in the venue at a cost that is significantly less than what they would have had to pay for venue naming rights. Eventually, MetLife escalated its partnership with the stadium by acquiring stadium naming rights in 2011. The name *MetLife Stadium* will cost the company an estimated $18 million a year for 20 years, a significant increase in commitments of rights fees (an additional $10 million per year) and time (16 years longer than the cornerstone partnership agreement).[16]

Other venue-related sponsorship options are possible, perhaps limited only by a venue's physical layout and amenities. In Chapter 7, branded spaces were discussed asBranded spaces are a tactic for enhancing attendees' experience at a sporting event through use of branded restaurants, bars, and lounge areas. Similarly, sponsorship of parking areas allows companies to reach sporting event attendees at their first and last point of contact with the venue. Automobile-related brands, such as Ford, Lexus, Toyota, and Geico, have purchased parking area sponsorships with fees that range from $700,000 to more than $1,000,000 annually.[17]

INDIVIDUALS. Sponsorship of individual athletes or coaches, active or retired, is another way to associate a brand with the affinity an audience has for sports. Some sports lend themselves to corporate sponsorship of individuals because competition is not team-based. Golf, tennis, auto racing, and the Olympics are mainstream sports in the United States in which sponsorship typically occurs at the individual performer level.

The most unique individual sponsorships involve collaboration of sponsor and athlete in business development. For instance, Shaun White, the best-known action sports athlete in the U.S., earns an estimated $7.5 million a year in endorsements. Companies such as Burton,

Target, and Oakley feature signature product lines designed by White. The image and personality of Shaun White is transferred to sponsors through his creative input in ventures such as the White Collection of apparel for Burton, a snowboard equipment and apparel company.[18]

The main drawback of sponsoring an individual is the ramifications of unacceptable behavior or scandal that can befall an athlete. Negative brand associations that develop when a celebrity endorser receives negative publicity could become a reflection on brands that sponsor the celebrity. Sponsors protect themselves against such situations by including a "morals clause" in endorsement contracts. A morals clause provides a sponsor with an exit from a contract with an endorser if that person becomes involved in a legal, ethical, or moral controversy that brings adverse publicity or even embarrassment to him or her. A corporate sponsor must protect its brand reputation when associating with an external entity like a sports brand or athlete. A highly publicized example of sponsors ending associations with an athlete for moral reasons is the situation of golfer Tiger Woods. Following revelation of extramarital affairs, Accenture, AT&T, and Gatorade ended relationships with Woods. The sponsors opted to distance their brands from Woods's personal problems.

CAUSES. Sponsorship spending by category shown in Figure 11.1 reflects that sponsorships of causes are a small portion of the industry total (9%), but in recent years it has been the sector that has experienced significant growth. Cause marketing is similar to other forms of sponsorship in that a sponsor seeks to exploit the commercial potential of being associated with a nonprofit organization or charity. With a cause promotion, a percentage of sales usually is donated to the sponsored nonprofit. Cause marketing is mutually beneficial as the nonprofit organization benefits from proceeds generated by the sponsor's promotion and receives exposure through the sponsor's marketing of the promotion. Sponsors often realize image enhancement benefits in the form of favorable brand associations such as "caring," "responsible," or "good citizen." At the same time, revenues generated by cause promotions can have a direct impact on the sponsor's profits.

Cause sponsorships take two forms in the sports industry: 1) sports properties support causes, and 2) sport properties are the beneficiary of a corporate partner's cause sponsorship. Sports organizations and their employees (e.g., coaches and players) are role models and looked up to in the community. These expectations make supporting a cause a logical marketing initiative to undertake. Investing in cause sponsorships may not lead directly to increased sales of licensed merchandise or tickets, but it can solidify a sports brand's standing among consumers and other stakeholders. In some cases, a sports property's cause sponsorship can lead to observable business impacts. The University of Denver's men's basketball program faces intense competition in the market from professional and collegiate sports teams. To increase brand relevance, the University of Denver implemented a cause sponsorship program in which the team partnered with thirty local nonprofit organizations for ticket sales fundraisers. The nonprofits marketed basketball tickets to their databases of donors and contacts, with 50% of the proceeds from tickets sold kept by the nonprofits. In the first season of the cause marketing initiative, average attendance jumped 71% to 3,487 fans per game.[19] For the University of Denver, cause marketing not only brought more revenue to the basketball program, but it attracted many new fans to attend men's basketball games.

The other role that sponsorship plays in sports is for properties to be the recipient of cause support from corporate partners. Sponsors that want to link with sports brands can use cause marketing as a strategy for becoming associated with a sports brand while benefiting a cause tied to the brand. For example, Major League Baseball supports a program called Reviving Baseball in Inner Cities (RBI). The program was founded in 1989 and serves more than 120,000 youth each year, providing resources to organize leagues and make playing baseball affordable for urban youth. MLB has an obvious self-interest in supporting RBI—future generations of baseball fans can be developed through participation as youth. In addition, MLB has enlisted a corporate partner to sponsor RBI, too. Athletic footwear brand New Balance is an RBI sponsor, benefiting the program's participants while targeting baseball players and fans to link the company's baseball footwear and other products to MLB. An added advantage for corporate sponsors to use cause marketing in this way is that the investment in rights fees required to be associated with a sports property may be lower for a cause marketing relationship than a league-wide "official sponsor" designation.

Distinguishing Characteristics of Sponsorship

As sponsorship grew to become a $46 billion global enterprise, it was sometimes classified as a form of public relations; other times it was classified as a type of sales promotion. Today, sponsorship is a distinct brand communications tactic, viewed as a tool in the IMC tool kit much like advertising, sales promotions, and other channels for reaching audiences. Two characteristics of sponsorship set it apart as a distinct brand communications tactic: 1) inseparable medium and message, and 2) influence of secondary brand associations.

In this interview of Tony Stewart by Lindsay Czarniak, Coca-Cola not only is prominently displayed, but it is a pre-race broadcast of the Coke Zero 400 race.

Application of the traditional communications process to marketing entails a marketer creating a message for a target audience and deciding on a channel to deliver the message so that it reaches the intended target. The message and medium typically are two different things. For example, if Pepsi wants to send a message to young males, it might decide to purchase commercial time on MTV. The medium and message are independent. In contrast, sponsorship is the message *and* the medium. Pepsi's sponsorship of the NFL to reach the same young male audience entails a medium (NFL as a channel for placing messages) and a message (the brand associations consumers develop for Pepsi as a result of its association with the NFL). Another aspect of the medium-as-message characteristic of sponsorship is that the interconnectivity of medium and message makes it more difficult for the target audience to ignore the message.

A sponsorship message (i.e., a brand's presence and involvement) can be woven into the property being sponsored. Title sponsorships are a prime example of how medium and message are inseparable. Most college football bowl games have title sponsors: Allstate Sugar Bowl, Chick-fil-A Bowl, Capital One Bowl, and many others. In addition to the marketing possibilities that arise from sponsoring a sports property, association as a title sponsor, category sponsor, or some other sponsorship provides access to the property's audience that other brand communication tactics cannot match.

Sponsorship differs from other IMC tools in how the consumer responds. Advertising messages are used to persuade consumers by communicating product-related cues such as features, benefits, and superiority to competing brands. Even when non-product cues are used to gain an audience's attention, such as a TV commercial that uses humor or music, product-related cues are often introduced in the message so that consumer learning about the brand is impacted.

Sponsorship relies on brand attitude being influenced by the learning of associations that are unrelated to a product's attributes. Instead, brand building occurs through development of **secondary brand associations**. This type of brand association is inferred by consumers by the linking of a brand with information already stored in memory.[20] Secondary brand associations have been formed via sponsorship with Mountain Dew's involvement in action sports. As discussed in Chapter 8, Mountain Dew has been a committed partner to action sports events over the years like the X Games, Winter X Games, and the Dew Tour as well as individual action sports athletes. Linking Mountain Dew with consumers' associations of action sports as "edgy," "extreme," and "youthful" helps create similar brand associations for the Mountain Dew brand.

Sponsorship Growth

The reasons for the consistent growth in sponsorship expenditures in the past twenty years can be attributed to three strengths inherent in sponsorship: 1) targeted audience reach, 2) connection with the affinity of sports fans, and 3) avoidance of media clutter (see Figure 11.5). While these three characteristics are not sponsorship's only strengths, they differentiate sponsorship from other brand communication tools and contribute to its effectiveness.

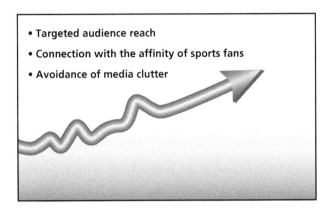

- Targeted audience reach
- Connection with the affinity of sports fans
- Avoidance of media clutter

FIGURE 11.5 Reasons for Growth in Sponsorship

TARGETED REACH. The concept of reach is important to marketers when planning brand communications. **Reach** is the total number of persons or percentage of a total population that is exposed to a brand message within a specified time period. Measures of reach include audience ratings for television and radio, circulation for newspapers and magazines, and visits to websites. Maximizing reach is desirable since more people are exposed to the brand messages. However, an important distinction exists between reaching a *large* audience and reaching the *right* audience.

The concept of targeted reach addresses the need to reach the right audience. **Targeted reach** is the number of persons or percentage of a population exposed to a brand message that is also part of the target market for the brand. It is possible for a brand message to be delivered through a channel that offers high reach but low targeted reach. Sales Genie, a business-to-business marketing services company, has aired commercials during Super Bowl telecasts. The reach was enormous—more than 100 million people tuned in to the big game. The targeted reach was poor, as most people watching the Super Bowl would never have a need for Sales Genie's services and therefore were not part of the company's target market.

Sponsorship is effective for delivering targeted reach if partners are strategically chosen. The characteristics of a brand's target market can be matched with the characteristics of an audience or fan base of a sports property. Companies that approach sponsorship in this way will likely find that many of the people reached via sponsorship are similar to their customers.

CONNECTION WITH AFFINITY FOR SPORTS. In Chapter 1, theThe affinity advantage possessed by sports was introduced as a unique characteristic of sports marketing. Sports are the envy of many companies because of the raw emotion and passion that a fan has for his or her favorite team or sport. Companies can connect with fans' affinity for sports by linking their brands to a sports property via sponsorship. The benefits of sponsorship for tapping fans' emotion-based relationships with sports are not limited to devout fans. Even casual followers of sports often throw their support behind their local teams. As author Isaac Asimov noted, "You root for your own sex, your own culture, and your own locality. . . . Whomever you root for represents you, and when he or she wins, you win!"[21] Positive brand associations can be created for a brand through sponsorship of a sports property.

FedEx is a formidable global package delivery and logistics company, but many customers' associations with FedEx are limited to associations they have with the company's capabilities to move products and packages efficiently. While such associations are important to have, particularly when they are positive, brands aspire to have richer, more extensive relationships with customers. FedEx succeeds in extending its relationships with customers beyond its core services through linking the brand with three different sports properties that evoke passions from their fans: NASCAR, NFL, and the PGA Tour. Although audience characteristics differ for these three sports properties, each one is capable of connecting deeply with committed fans.

AVOIDANCE OF MESSAGE CLUTTER. One of the strongest attractions of sponsorship is it provides an alternative to traditional media to reach an audience. The prevalence of **message clutter**, or the high volume of marketing messages placed in a communication channel that vies for an audience's attention, means that when marketers place messages in media like TV, radio, magazines, or newspapers it is possible that an advertisement will get ignored, overlooked, or lost among other messages. The combination of a high number of marketing messages in communication channels and consumers' tendencies to avoid or ignore advertisements has led marketers to seek innovative ways to cut through the clutter and gain their target audience's attention.

Sponsorship is considered a channel for avoiding message clutter because of how it differs from traditional media advertising in terms of intrusiveness. Advertisements are "timeouts" from one's enjoyment of watching a TV program or reading a magazine. Ads intrude on the consumption of the information or entertainment. In contrast, sponsorship is woven into the property being sponsored. It can become part of a sporting event, associating with elements that exist already. For example, Hardee's is a sponsor of the NHL's Nashville Predators, and as part of its sponsorship is integrated into Predators games through the "Hardee's Starting Lineup" announced before each game. It is a seamless way to provide a sponsor exposure to the fans of the game that goes beyond signage. Utilization of sponsorship as a "clutter buster" in the live event has seemingly limitless possibilities. Promotions and giveaways, pregame activities, in-game contests, and postgame events are a few ways a sporting event can be part of a sponsorship package.

Value to Sponsors

As the definition of sponsorship suggests, companies engage in sponsorships in order to access the exploitable commercial potential a property possesses. The sponsorship must provide value to the sponsor, identified in Figure 11.6.

FIGURE 11.6 Value of Sponsorship to Sponsors

Targeted Reach

Identified in the previous section as a reason for the growth of sponsorship as a marketing vehicle, targeted reach can be realized when a sponsor partners with a sports property whose audience characteristics match closely the consumer characteristics of the sponsor's target market. Peak, a performance motor oil brand, is the official motor oil of the IndyCar Series. The sponsorship allows Peak to target an audience that will likely have high involvement with automobiles, and thus, an interest in motor oil and lubricants. Targeted reach is not limited to a logical link such as a motor oil brand sponsoring auto racing. Taco Bell is the "official quick-service restaurant" of the NBA, because Taco Bell values the ability to reach the heavy concentration of young males who are fans of the NBA.

Image Transfer

Connecting with fans' affinity for sports is of value to sponsors. The payoff comes in the form of image transfer from a sponsored property to a sponsoring brand. **Image transfer** occurs in sponsorship when the meaning consumers hold for a sports property is assigned to a brand that is linked to the property. Image transfer in sponsorship is similar to how consumers respond to a celebrity endorsement of a product.[22] Secondary brand associations are formed as a result of the pairing of a sports property and sponsor. It is communication of the property–sponsor linkage that influences the creation of secondary associations and, ultimately, the effectiveness of image transfer. In other words, merely acquiring the rights to be an official sponsor of the Big 12

Conference does not create transfer of meaning for sponsors. Articulation of the sponsorship through advertising, sales promotions, and other forms of brand communications persuades the Big 12's audience that the associations they hold for the conference should be shared or transferred to an official sponsor, like Phillips 66.

Image transfer is an important benefit for sponsors, because a natural, logical association does not always exist between a company and sports property. Powerade is a brand that one would expect to find linked to sports, given that the product is used by athletes. Often, however, a sponsor must persuade the target audience that its brand should be associated with the property. The goal is to increase the likelihood that consumers' image of the sponsored property will influence their image of a sponsor. For example, Office Depot is a brand that has no apparent connection with auto racing. However, its designation as Official Office Products sponsor of NASCAR communicates to fans that Office Depot and NASCAR are partners, that they have a shared involvement. The strength of the shared association can be enhanced by brand communications that tout the NASCAR sponsorship through tactics such as advertising, in-store signage, and the website.

Exclusivity

Important to sponsors is the ability to secure category exclusivity in a sponsorship agreement. **Category exclusivity** occurs when a sponsor is the only company within its product category associated with the sponsored property.[23] Exclusivity is valued by sponsors because they do not have to be concerned with competing brands vying for the attention of a property's target audience. Ford's category exclusivity with the Professional Bull Riders (PBR) through title sponsorship of the Built Ford Tough Series means that it does not have to worry about Chevrolet, Dodge, or any other truck brand being associated with PBR. Category exclusivity can be obtained with a lesser commitment than a title sponsorship. For instance, Enterprise is the official rental car of the PBR. Enterprise is one of approximately thirty sponsors representing different categories of products and services.

Category exclusivity can be negotiated by a sports property to be broad or narrow. Broad exclusivity rights add value for a sponsor by granting exclusive rights across multiple related categories. Coca-Cola is a top-level sponsor for the NCAA (a Corporate Champion). As part of Coca-Cola's agreement with the NCAA, it has category exclusivity for soft drinks, sports drinks, and water. For the sports property, granting broad exclusivity rights can be a strategy for commanding higher rights fees from a sponsor. If a company like Coca-Cola wishes to have broad rights to multiple categories, then it must be willing to pay a price premium to lock up those categories to prevent competitors from being associated with the property.

Narrow category exclusivity limits a sponsor to rights for a specific segment or niche within a product category. A category like financial services can be narrowed into separate sponsorship categories for retail bank, credit card, and investment services. The criterion for a sports property to decide whether to market broad or narrow category exclusivity is the degree of similarity among related categories that fall under a broad category. For example, the nonalcoholic beverage category consists of soft drinks, sports drinks, energy drinks, teas, and water. But, all of these products meet a general consumer need of quenching thirst. Thus, a potential beverage sponsor might aspire to have broad rights to lock up the beverage category. On the other hand, if categories within a general category are not as related to each other, narrow sponsorship categories are appropriate.

Marketing Opportunities

As shown in Figure 11.7, three types of marketing opportunities can be linked to a brand's involvement in a sponsorship. A **branding campaign** is a strategy to communicate or promote an association with a sports property by a sponsor to its target market. One of the rights enjoyed by top-tier sponsors of the International Olympic Committee, a level known as The Olympic Programme (TOP) sponsors, is use of the Olympic rings logo in their marketing communications messages. When Dow Chemical Company became a TOP sponsor, it had rights to use the Olympic rings logo and the term "Worldwide Partner" in advertisements, on its website, on product packaging, and any other form of communication. Branding campaigns are an appropriate strategy when the objective of a sponsorship is to create brand awareness or build a desired image for the sponsoring brand.

FIGURE 11.7
Marketing Opportunities from Sponsorship

On-site marketing allows a sponsor to reach a sports property's audience at the physical location where they interact with the sports brand. Beer and soft drink marketers often compete fiercely to secure pouring rights to sell their products at sports venues through an association as an official sponsor of a team or facility. Pouring rights are valuable because not only does a sponsor receive brand exposure and usually category exclusivity, but it puts product into the hands of customers. This benefit of sponsorship can be instrumental in developing brand-loyal customers who seek the same brands they enjoy at a sporting event. On-site marketing can be used even for products that do not lend themselves to on-site sale. Best Buy's placement of its private label TVs throughout Target Field, home of the Minnesota Twins, described in Chapter 10 illustrates how product capabilities can be demonstrated through integration into the experience of attending a Twins game.

Cross-marketing opportunities involve collaboration between a sponsor, sports property, and in some cases a sponsor's marketing partners to create campaigns with the aim of benefiting all involved parties. For example, convenience store chain 7-Eleven is a sponsor of IndyCar Series driver Tony Kanaan. One way 7-Eleven leverages its association with IndyCar and Kanaan is by having permission to allow 7-Eleven product suppliers to tie in with IndyCar-themed marketing campaigns even though they are not official sponsors. This privilege, called **pass-through rights**, adds value to a sponsorship because it allows a sponsor's partners to enhance the sponsor's association with a sports property through themed promotions that can benefit consumers, such as sweepstakes or price-based promotions. In the case of 7-Eleven, a pass-through promotion developed around its IndyCar sponsorship could lead to increased store sales for the retailer as well as its vendors that participate.

Cross-marketing opportunities do not always include pass-through rights. They can simply be an arrangement between a sports property and sponsor, such as Gillette's relationship with NASCAR. Gillette is the official shaving product, and one of the primary ways it has marketed the sponsorship is through the Gillette Young Guns program. Seven of NASCAR's youthful, emerging drivers, including Kyle Busch, Carl Edwards, and Denny Hamlin, are used in advertising, retail promotions, and social media campaigns to endorse Gillette's grooming products.

Protection of Investment

As costs to sponsor sports properties have increased sharply in recent years, particularly for marquee properties like the Olympics, FIFA World Cup, and NFL, sponsors have called on their sports property partners to be proactive in protecting the value of sponsors' investments. Specifically, sponsors increasingly are seeking relief from a practice known as ambush marketing carried out by competitors. **Ambush marketing** is a planned effort by a company that is not an official sponsor to create the impression that it is associated with the property in some way. It is a serious problem for sponsors because their strategy and campaigns can be thwarted intentionally by competitors that do not pay the sponsorship fee.

One tactic often used is airing commercials during a TV or radio broadcast of a sporting event for which it is not an official sponsor. If an ambusher is able to associate itself with a sport or event in this way, it gets around having to pay rights fees for the right to call itself an official sponsor, but it may be perceived by consumers as an official sponsor by virtue of its advertisements airing on event broadcasts.

Ambush marketing also occurs through an ambusher's efforts to have a presence at or near sporting events. At the Winter Olympics in Salt Lake City, Mountain Dew hosted an entertainment area with interactive games and evening concerts just two blocks away from a similarly themed experience offered by official sponsor Coca-Cola. The Salt Lake City Organizing Committee took steps to make sure Mountain Dew's name was not mentioned in radio commercials promoting the exhibit, but many attendees may have associated Mountain Dew with the Olympics.[24]

While it cannot be eliminated totally, sports properties must take a proactive stance to minimize ambush marketing threats. If they do not, a sponsor may feel it has not received full value from its sponsorship investment and opt to end the relationship when its contract expires.

Sponsorship Management

Planning and implementation of a sponsorship mirrors the steps required for a brand communications campaign. Listed in Figure 11.8, decisions must be made about the target audience, objectives, the appropriate sports property, budget, activation, and measurement. Lack of thorough planning at any of these steps increases the chances a sponsorship will not reach its potential effectiveness.

- Define the target audience
- Set objectives
- Select the sports property
- Establish a budget
- Develop an activation plan
- Measure effectiveness

FIGURE 11.8 Steps in Managing a Sponsorship

Step One: Define the Target Audience

The target audience for a sponsorship can be a number of different stakeholder groups. For companies that sell to individual buyers, consumers are an obvious target. An implication of the importance of target audience selection is that the linkage of a brand and sports property can suggest to consumers the type of person who should use the brand. For example, Anheuser-Busch InBev has associated its Michelob Ultra brand with properties that communicate rather clearly the type of user who should consider drinking the product. Michelob Ultra was the brand Anheuser-Busch InBev featured in its sponsorship of the LPGA and FIFA Women's World Cup, two properties that give the company access to a largely female audience. In addition to those sponsorships, Michelob Ultra has been a sponsor of cyclist Lance Armstrong. Associating with an athlete well known for his physical fitness suggests that Michelob Ultra is a beer that can be enjoyed by people who follow a healthy lifestyle. Whether the characteristics of the target audience are based on demographics (e.g., women) or psychographics (e.g., healthy lifestyle), defining who is to be reached by a sponsorship is important because it will guide the decision on the type of sports property to sponsor.

Consumers are not the only potential target for a sponsorship. For business-to-business marketers, clients and prospects are often attractive targets. Clients may be targeted by a sponsorship to reward them for their business through hospitality functions hosted by a sponsor at sporting events. Similarly, prospects may be entertained in an effort to develop relationships that could lead to business opportunities. Also, sports properties with audience demographics that include high percentages of above-average income and white-collar professions are often considered possible properties that can be used to target B2B buyers.

Step Two: Set Objectives

Once the audience segment or segments to be targeted is determined, the next step is to set the objectives that a sponsorship should achieve. At a broad level, sponsorship objectives relate to the same two categories as the IMC objectives discussed in Chapter 8, communication

**FIGURE 11.9
Sponsorship
Objectives**

- Create brand awareness
- Influence brand image or personality
- Strengthen client relationships
- Stimulate product trial
- Increase sales
- Generate media exposure

Courtesy of Ken Clow

objectives and behavioral objectives. Six objectives commonly set by sponsors are identified in Figure 11.9. Creating awareness and building image are used most frequently by sponsors.

CREATE BRAND AWARENESS. Building brand awareness among an audience can be achieved through repetition of brand name or logo. Sponsorship is effective in this regard because a benefit sponsors usually receive is signage placement at event venues. Also, title sponsorships serve to create awareness as the title sponsor's brand is mentioned in references to the event (e.g., the AutoZone Liberty Bowl college football game). For new products or situations in which a sponsor is moving into a new market segment, sponsorships that build brand awareness can be an effective tactic for laying a foundation to build customer relationships. Mountain Dew used sponsorship to create awareness for its energy drink, Amp. The company launched Amp Energy Juice by investing in title sponsorship of the Amp Energy Juice 500 NASCAR Sprint Cup Series.

INFLUENCE BRAND IMAGE OR PERSONALITY. The other most frequently set objective is to shape a desired brand image or personality. Sponsors often aspire to either creating new brand associations or changing current brand perceptions so that image transfer from the sponsored sports property to the sponsor's brand occurs.

For a new product or for a brand entering a new customer market, shaping perceptions customers have for the brand is an outcome that, if achieved, could enhance the brand's competitiveness with established brands. Russian air carrier Aeroflot, a relatively unknown brand among Americans, is using sponsorship to shape its brand image as well as create awareness through a sponsorship deal with the New Jersey Nets. The partnership not only brings greater visibility to Aeroflot in the New York market, but its association with a professional sports team in the largest U.S. market can impact consumers' perceptions about the prominence of Aeroflot.

An image-oriented objective is appropriate when a brand lacks a distinctive image or wishes to change its image. Vizio is a leading brand of high-definition televisions but is a rather young brand, having been founded in 2002. The lack of a history or track record in the marketplace means that many consumers know less about Vizio than more established TV brands. In a move to raise the profile of Vizio and influence college football fans' perceptions of the brand, it signed a four-year deal to be presenting sponsor of the Rose Bowl ("Rose Bowl presented by Vizio").

STRENGTHEN CLIENT RELATIONSHIPS. For many B2B marketers, one of the greatest attractions of sponsorship as an IMC tool is the potential to engage clients and prospects extensively. Client hospitality can take the form of perks such as providing game tickets, hosting a pre-event reception or meal, providing access to a meet-and-greet session with players or coaches, and taking out-of-town trips to watch an event.

Use of hospitality can have the effect of creating a desire for reciprocation on the part of the guest. A regional director for a supermarket chain who is given an all-expenses-paid trip to the Daytona 500 NASCAR race by Coca-Cola may feel led to return the favor of Coca-Cola's hospitality by allocating more shelf space for Coke products in his stores. Although business buyers are assumed to behave more rationally than individual consumers because they are making buying decisions for an organization and not themselves, they may be inclined to do business with *people* they like and trust. Client hospitality opportunities arising from a sponsorship create an environment in which personal relationships between sellers and buyers can be built and strengthened. Not all business buyers are receptive to hospitality invitations, but for those who are it is a powerful tactic for building rapport in a relaxed environment.

STIMULATE PRODUCT TRIAL. The presence of large crowds at sporting events makes sponsorship an attractive channel for many marketers that target consumers. Having consumers use a product for the first time (product trial) is a key step toward a person becoming a customer and, eventually, loyal user. If marketers can get a product into the hands of consumers, it will often result in future consideration when purchasing that particular product. Thus, use of product sampling as a communication tactic can mean the difference between a product gaining traction in the market or failure.

Product trial through sports sponsorship can be executed directly or indirectly. Direct trial occurs when a sponsor distributes samples at sporting events. Consumer packaged goods lend themselves to direct distribution by hand-

Direct trial occurs when a sponsor distributes samples at a sport event.

ing out samples as people enter or leave an event. Indirect trial requires that consumers take an additional step to try a product. If Wendy's wanted to use its sponsorship of a minor league baseball team to encourage trial of a new sandwich, it could distribute coupons for a free sandwich to everyone in attendance. Then, it is up to the consumer to decide whether to take action on the offer.

INCREASE SALES. An association with a sports property may serve as a differentiator in a consumer's mind when evaluating competing brands. If few or no differences exist between brand choices, a consumer may be swayed to select a brand because of its linkage to a sport, team, event, or athlete that the consumer likes. If a consumer who is also a hockey fan is selecting a wireless communications provider and is considering AT&T, Sprint, and Verizon Wireless, he or she may go with Verizon because of its sponsorship of the NHL. It is doubtful that sponsorship can swing the pendulum in all buying decisions, but there are occasions in which the affinity consumers have for sports can be tapped to create brand preference and ultimately influence purchases.

Recently, Dr Pepper's Snapple Group signed on as official beverage sponsor of the NHL's Pittsburgh Penguins when the team moved into its new arena. As part of the deal, Dr Pepper Snapple Group sold thirty of its flavors in the CONSOL Energy Center.[25] The absence of competition and a captive audience during events gave Dr Pepper Snapple Group a platform for putting products in consumers' hands and hopefully influencing their choices when buying beverages in retail outlets.

The sales potential of a sponsorship can be exercised through a sports property's involvement in a sponsor's cross-marketing tactics, which can be passive or active. Passive involvement by a sports property occurs when tactics are limited to use of the sports property's name or other brand marks. If retail promotions for Dasani bottled water communicated that it is a sponsor of the NCAA men's basketball tournament, but do nothing else, then the sports property's role in marketing Dasani's sponsorship is passive. Dasani is relying on consumers recognizing the prominence of the NCAA men's basketball tournament and Dasani's sponsorship to create a favorable impact on the target audience.

In contrast, active involvement in a sponsor's cross-marketing tactics is a planned effort to influence sales for both sponsor and property. Each party hopes to cash in on its partnership by offering products with added value as a result of the cross-marketing campaign. NASCAR and some of its consumer packaged goods sponsors like Kraft, Unilever, Coca-Cola, and Procter & Gamble partnered with supermarket chain Brookshire's in the southwest U.S. to create in-store promotions that featured sponsors' products and discounted race tickets. The promotion, dubbed "Rev Up," was credited with generating sales of approximately four hundred tickets worth $30,000 in revenues for a Sprint Cup race at Texas Motor Speedway. Sponsors benefited by acquiring additional display space for their products in more than 120 supermarkets.[26] A cross-marketing campaign with active involvement from a sports property can boost revenues for sponsors and properties by tapping the shared interest consumers hold for a sports property, and, by association, its official partners.

GENERATE MEDIA EXPOSURE. Setting awareness objectives for a sponsorship focuses on an outcome of the target audience knowing the sponsor's brand exists, that it is recognized in the marketplace. Sometimes, a sponsor may wish to have an impact beyond being known and recognized by consumers. It wants a sponsorship to create an audience impact comparable to a traditional media advertising campaign. When a media exposure objective is set for a sponsorship, the aim is to achieve a certain number of impressions through the channels used to deliver sponsorship messages, such as venue signage, TV and radio broadcasts, the sponsor and property's websites, and news coverage of the event. **Impressions** are the total number of exposures of an audience to a brand message.[27] In addition to measuring the number of impressions a sponsorship creates, sponsors that set media exposure objectives usually are interested in determining the total amount of time a brand is mentioned or shown in media coverage of a sporting event. The exposure received is then assigned a dollar value that is an equivalent of what advertising in traditional media channels would have cost the sponsor.

One research firm that provides impression measurement services is Joyce Julius & Associates. Its methodology captures visual and verbal exposures a brand receives during a televised sporting event. An estimate of the dollar value of the impressions is made based on the length of exposure time and cost to buy advertising during the event. One measurement collected by Joyce Julius is the level of exposure that NASCAR drivers receive during race telecasts. In the first half of one season, Jimmie Johnson received the most exposure of any Sprint Cup Series driver in terms of a combination of on-camera impressions and verbal mentions. The value of the media exposure Johnson received was estimated to be $48 million.[28] The amount of media exposure and equivalent dollar value to traditional media of sponsorships is sometimes used to tout sponsorship as an alternative to buying advertising in traditional media. Media exposure differs from other sponsorship objectives in that it is measured by *output* in terms of impressions and their dollar value and not *impact* in terms of a customer's relationship with the sponsor's brand.

Step Three: Select the Sports Property

A crucial step in sponsorship management is selecting a sports property or properties that offer the best opportunity to reach the target audience and achieve the objectives that a sponsorship should meet. Sports properties communicate sponsorship opportunities with prospective partners through a **sponsorship proposal**, which is a document created by a sports property that gives an overview of the property, information on the property's customers or audience, and benefits of partnering via sponsorship.[29]

In deciding on a sponsorship, company managers use three primary criteria: 1) fit with brand objectives, 2) duration of sponsorship, and 3) partner relationship.[30] Criteria such as level of involvement (title sponsor, category sponsor, etc.) and exposure type (radio, television, etc.) are typically low in importance, suggesting that for many managers the delivery of sponsorship messages is secondary to the strategic considerations such as fit with brand objectives and length of sponsorship agreement (see Figure 11.10). Also, the relatively high level of importance attached to partner relationships serves as a reminder that investing in a sponsorship involves more than a product purchase; it is a relationship between sponsor and sports property that when nurtured adds value for both parties.

The process for a business and sports property coming together to form a partnership via sponsorship can occur in one of three ways. First, sports properties solicit companies they have identified as potential candidates to be a sponsor. Some companies are inundated with proposals from properties of all sizes and from a variety of sports. Other companies have a policy of not accepting sponsorship proposal solicitations directly. Many of these companies use a third party, such as Conxeo, an online sponsorship proposal submission service. Proposals are screened. Those that do not meet a company's criteria are rejected. If a proposal meets screening criteria, it is forwarded for further consideration by sponsorship decision makers in the organization.[31] Second, companies may approach a sports property to inquire about sponsorship opportunities. This scenario is more likely to occur when a company views the property as highly desirable as a prospective partner. Third, a sports marketing or advertising agency may serve as a liaison

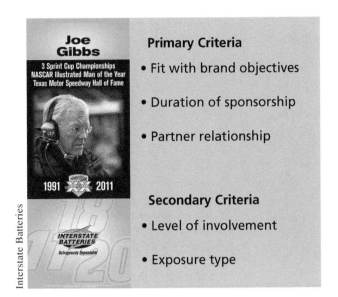

FIGURE 11.10 **Criteria Used in Selecting a Sponsorship**

between a company and sports property. The expertise and contacts an agency offers usually justifies the expense of outsourcing the sponsorship selection process.

Step Four: Establish a Budget

Planning expenditures for a sponsorship requires budgeting for two types of costs that are incurred: 1) rights fees and 2) activation costs. **Rights fees** represents the cost a company pays, either in dollars or in-kind, to be recognized as an official sponsor of a property. The amount a property charges in rights fees will depend on the factors identified in Figure 11.11.

FIGURE 11.11 **Factors in Determining Rights Fees**

- **Prestige or status of property**
- **Geographic scope**
    — Global, national, regional, or local
- **Audience reach**
- **Sponsorship level**
    — title sponsorship, presenting sponsor, category sponsor, etc.
- **Time frame of sponsorship**
    — year round, season, weekend, or one day
- **Duration of sponsorship**
    — Number of years

Rights fees can be thought of as "pay to play" for a corporate sponsor. A company must pay rights fees to receive designation as a sponsor and in order to receive benefits a sports property offers such as signage and use of brand marks in marketing materials. However, rights fees are only one part of a sponsorship budget. The other component is **activation costs**, which are monies spent on marketing activities to communicate a brand's sponsorship. The meaning and value of a brand's association with a sports property is enhanced when activation occurs. The key to achieving the desired effect among the target audience (e.g., brand image, product trial) is for sponsors to communicate their partnership with a sports property through advertising, public relations, and other marketing programs.[32] A designation of "official sponsor" may mean little to consumers, but articulating why a sponsor is partnering with a particular sports property aids in consumers understanding a brand–property linkage as well as their acceptance of the sponsor's association with the property.

A measure used by sponsorship managers to assess the proportion of sponsorship budget spent on rights fees and activation is known as a **leverage ratio**. The leverage ratio is a

Interstate Batteries

Interstate Batteries distributes a quarterly publication to its dealers that provides photos and news about NASCAR and Interstate's sponsorships.

comparison of activation dollars spent to rights fees. If a sponsor spends a total of $700,000 on activation for marketing a sponsorship on tactics such as television advertising, a sweepstakes, and public relations, and spent $400,000 on rights fees for the sponsorship, the leverage ratio would be 1.75:1. Sponsorship consulting firm IEG estimates that an average leverage ratio is approximately 1.40:1. IEG's figures on leverage ratios reveal that many sponsors are either unwilling or unprepared to spend on activation, as 24% of sponsors report spending less on activation than on rights fees. Another 44% of sponsors spend the same amount on activation as they do for rights fees.[33] Realistic expectations for a sponsorship to meet its objectives must include planning for activation.

Step Five: Develop an Activation Plan

A sponsorship deal gives a corporate partner access to a sports property's marketable assets, but the effectiveness of a sponsorship depends on how a sponsor leverages those marketable assets to communicate its association. An activation plan established prior to making a commitment to sponsor a sports property is essential for: 1) meeting sponsorship objectives and 2) developing a realistic budget that goes beyond requirements for rights fees. Activation is important to sponsorship success.

In Figure 11.12, sponsorship expert Tim Lynde gives an example of how activation by a soft drink company can be carried out with a Major League Baseball team. The items in the left column are rights received through sponsorship; items on the right are marketing tactics that could be implemented to impact the target audience. While the rights granted are attractive to potential sponsors, their impact may be minimal unless activation plans are developed that utilize the rights by connecting them with target audience segments and the sponsorship's objectives. Receiving 10,000 tickets is a significant sponsorship benefit, but if there is no strategy for distributing the tickets in terms of who should be targeted and what should result from the ticket giveaways, the benefit will not have the impact it is capable of delivering.

FIGURE 11.12
Leveraging Sponsorship Assets through Activation

Soft Drink Sponsor of a MLB Team	
Asset	**Activation**
Rotational signage for ½ inning per game	1) Advertise new flavor 2) Reminder advertising of existing flavors
Pouring rights throughout stadium	1) Products sold in concessions and in club areas; 2) "Flavor of the Month" promotion
Lunch for 10 people with General Manager	1) Entertain key retail buyers; 2) Sweepstakes to win insider experience
Sampling opportunities at up to 100 team-related events (including community events)	1) Sample new or low volume flavors; 2) Distribute coupons for select flavors or products (e.g., 12-packs)
Pool of 10,000 tickets over course of the season	1) Employee appreciation event 2) Ticket giveaway with product purchase 3) 2-for-1 ticket promotion for select games

Step Six: Measure Effectiveness

The final step in the sponsorship management process is to assess a sponsorship's performance in meeting stated objectives. Measures of performance can be classified into three primary areas: 1) awareness, 2) image, and 3) financial.

AWARENESS MEASURES. Sponsors that set awareness objectives can evaluate the effectiveness of creating brand awareness through a pre/post sponsorship comparison of awareness levels. If retail pharmacy CVS wanted to determine the impact of its sponsorship of an LPGA tournament, it could conduct brand awareness studies of consumers with an interest in the LPGA two months prior to the tournament and two months following the tournament. If brand awareness for CVS is greater following the tournament, the gain can be attributed, at least partially (if not completely), to the sponsorship.

As shown in Figure 11.13, brand awareness can be measured on three levels: 1) recognition, 2) recall, and 3) top-of-mind. The level of brand awareness that a sponsor seeks to impact will depend on the brand's standing in the market and objectives of the sponsorship.

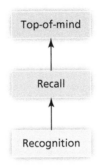

FIGURE 11.13 Levels of Brand Awareness

Brand recognition is the simplest impact to achieve with an audience. Measurement of brand recognition is straightforward. For the LPGA sponsorship example it can be as simple as asking a person, "Have you heard of CVS?" If the answer is "yes," the person has recognition awareness of the CVS brand. Increasing brand recognition via sponsorship may not be an objective for a brand like CVS that enjoys a rather high level of recognition already. However, for a newer brand or a company expanding into a new market, brand recognition may be an appropriate objective to set.

A more ambitious awareness objective would be to increase brand recall among a sponsorship's target audience. **Brand recall** occurs when a consumer can select or name a brand when given a prompt like the brand's product category. In the example of measuring awareness related to CVS's sponsorship of the LPGA, brand recall could be measured by asking consumers to "name brands of retail pharmacies." The prompt is the category of retail pharmacies; brand recall is achieved in this case if consumers include CVS in their list of brands.

Another form of recall used in sponsorship measurement is to ask consumers to identify official sponsors of a sports property. Recently, NBA fans were asked to identify the official Quick-Service Restaurant (QSR) sponsor of the NBA. Approximately 22% of NBA fans correctly recalled Taco Bell as an official sponsor. Another 19% incorrectly recalled McDonald's as the official QSR sponsor. The largest percentage of fans (33%) reported they did not know what company was the official QSR sponsor.[34] This result suggests Taco Bell faces challenges in communicating sponsorship associations to their target audiences.

The ultimate accomplishment in achieving brand awareness with consumers is to achieve **top-of-mind brand awareness**. When a brand is top-of-mind with a consumer, that brand is the first one that comes to mind for a given product category. If Shannon is asked to identify the first brand of chocolate candy that pops into her mind and responds "M&M's," it is top-of-mind with her. Does it mean that Shannon will buy M&M's the next time she is considering a purchase of chocolate candy? Not necessarily, but marketers of low-involvement products purchased frequently like chocolate candy aspire to be top-of-mind with consumers because of the importance of brand name and other information held in memory when making a buying decision. Thus, the sponsorship by M&M's of NASCAR Sprint Cup driver Kyle Busch can serve to keep the brand in front of NASCAR fans and influence their recall as their top-of-mind brand. For established brands like M&M's, increasing top-of-mind awareness would be a more ambitious advancement of the brand's standing with consumers than measuring brand recognition or recall.

IMAGE MEASURES. The image transfer capability of a sports property's associations to a sponsor can influence how consumers perceive brands associated with the property. Sponsors can do a pre/post sponsorship measurement to compare brand perceptions in order to determine the impact of sponsorship on brand image. Common methods of measuring brand image include: 1) attribute agreement, 2) semantic differential ratings, or 3) free association. Figure 11.14 shows how these different techniques could be used by a snack food brand's sponsorship of an action sports event. Attribute agreement evaluates relevant brand associations by using a rating scale with anchors of "strongly disagree" and "strongly agree." Semantic differential ratings use a series of bipolar adjectives to assess how consumers perceive a brand for attributes or associations that are considered central to a brand's image. Free association asks consumers to identify or describe associations they have for a brand. This technique invites candid feedback, positive and negative, from a target audience.

FIGURE 11.14
Examples of Brand Image Measurement

Attribute Agreement:					
Below are statements that have been made about Larry's Meat Snacks. Rate your agreement with each statement:					
	Strongly Disagree	Disagree	Neither Agree nor Disagree	Agree	Strongly Agree
A fun brand					
An exciting brand					
A youthful brand					

Semantic Differential Ratings:					
Below are words that might be used to describe Larry's Meat Snacks. Rate your perceptions by marking the point on the scale that reflects your view:					
Exciting					Boring
Young					Old
Stagnant					Energetic

Free Association:
In the space below, write down any words or thoughts about Larry's Meat Snacks that come to mind.

FINANCIAL MEASURES. Building relationships with consumers by increasing the level of brand awareness or by influencing associations that make up brand image are meaningful impacts that can be delivered by sponsorship. However, many managers are not satisfied with sponsorships merely changing how people think about their brand; they want to see results! The results sought are financial measures of how a brand benefits from a linkage with a sports property via sponsorship. While gains in sales, new customers, or revenue per customer are outcomes that any business would welcome, attributing such gains to a sponsorship can be difficult to verify. Other marketing mix variables such as product quality and price as well as other promotion tactics can sway buyers, too. Despite the realization that getting a true read on a sponsorship's financial impact is difficult, the financial measures shown in Figure 11.15 are the most frequently used indicators of sponsorship effectiveness.

FIGURE 11.15 Most Frequently Used Financial Measures for Sponsorships

Return on Investment

$

Financial Measures for Sponsorships

Sales

Media Equivalents

Media equivalents were discussed earlier in this chapter as a measure of media exposure. Some companies engage in sponsorships to gain exposure received during broadcasts and other media coverage of events that they sponsor. Media exposure differs from most other measures of sponsorship performance because it does not deal with customer impact; it focuses on media impact. The belief concerning media exposure is that the higher the dollar value of the exposure, the greater its reach or impact. Thus, if a U.S. Open Tennis Tournament sponsorship generated brand exposure equivalent to $2.5 million in paid placement, it may be viewed as effective for generating exposure if the media equivalent figure is greater than the investment in rights fees.

Measuring sales, whether done as a post-sponsorship period measure or a pre/post comparison, is an ideal metric if an objective of a sponsorship is to increase revenues. Unfortunately, establishing a cause-and-effect relationship between sponsorship activity and sales can be difficult. Other variables influence consumers' buying decisions.

One measure of sales impact is tracking on-site sales at sporting events for sponsors such as soft drink or beer companies that have pouring rights at event venues. Also, sales impact can be measured in a brand's usual distribution channels during the time period of a sponsorship to determine if there is a relationship between sponsorship involvement and sales volume. The design of activation tactics can aid in measuring the effect of a sponsorship on sales. For example, if a sponsor distributes coupon offers for its products at games or events, the number of coupons redeemed is a measure of the effectiveness of the sponsorship in stimulating product purchases.

Financial measures of sponsorship effectiveness seek to quantify a sponsor's **return on investment (ROI)**. There are increased demands of accountability on sponsorship managers to justify their decisions to spend on sports by showing how sponsorships impact sales, customer acquisition, and customer retention. Despite the growing interest in quantifying the financial impact of sponsorship, challenges to isolating sponsorship's effects on revenues and customer status remain. Thus, many sponsorship experts advocate a combination of ROI measurement with **return on objective (ROO)** measures. ROO assesses how a sponsorship performed against the objectives set prior to execution (e.g., increase brand awareness or create certain brand associations). Not only are these performances against objectives easier to measure than financial objectives that use ROI measures, but objectives assessed using ROO are vital given that they set the stage for influencing buyer behaviors that ultimately impact ROI.

Reasons Sponsorships End

For all of sponsorship's strengths as a brand communications tool and the many successes that can be used as examples of its effectiveness, sponsorships can fail to reach their stated objectives. Figure 11.16 highlights four reasons sponsorships come to an end. Any of these reasons can contribute to the demise of a sponsorship, even when it has succeeded in creating an impact.

FIGURE 11.16 Reasons Sponsorships End

Unclear Expectations

One of the strongest triggers to sponsors ending a relationship with a sports property is that they are dissatisfied with how the sponsorship has impacted their business. However, in most cases dissatisfaction is not the real problem. The issue is a lack of clear expectations on the sponsor's part. In other words, well-defined objectives were not set on the front end of the relationship. When objectives are not clearly set, it can lead to sponsorship managers feeling disappointed that a sponsorship did not "perform."

A related trigger is an undefined or unrealistic time horizon for expecting results. It is not unusual to see a sponsor discontinue a relationship after one season or year. Sponsors often cite insufficient return on investment or simply that the sponsorship did not work. Sponsorship, like other forms of brand communication, benefits from a cumulative effect of repeated exposure (i.e., frequency). A sponsor that exits a relationship after a short period of time may not have been associated with the sports property long enough for the target audience to get the message. Sports properties can help sponsors and themselves by negotiating multiyear agreements with corporate partners.

Not only does a multiyear deal lock in sponsors and revenue, but it gives a sponsor time to develop activation programs that communicate the brand's association with sports property. And properties can take other steps to minimize sponsors' disappointment with sponsorship performance. The NASCAR B2B Council introduced in Chapter 4 is an example of how a sports property can help its corporate partners form realistic expectations for their sponsorships. The B2B Council is an information resource that sponsors can tap to learn from successes of other NASCAR sponsors as well as network with fellow sponsors to explore business opportunities. Partners are more likely to continue their relationship if they see benefits of being a sponsor like those delivered by a program like NASCAR's B2B Council.

Inadequate Budget/Activation

Inadequate budget for activation or lack of a well-developed activation program can leave a sponsor feeling it should end a relationship. If a manager's view of budget allocation focuses on rights fees, it is possible that the budget for activation is not enough to communicate the sponsor's association with a property. Recall that 24% of all sponsors spend less on activation than on rights fees. This practice is alarming. When activation is not managed as a priority, a sponsor is in effect hoping that the association received from paying rights fees will reach the target audience. A high leverage ratio does not guarantee a sponsorship's success, but it does create additional brand touch points with the target audience that can be used to tout a link between a brand and sports property.

Change in Strategic Focus

Not all sponsor–property partnerships end because of poor decisions by sponsorship managers or unmet results. In some cases, even sponsorships that succeed in delivering desired impact on the target audience are discontinued. This decision is made when a sponsor believes the relationship is no longer a fit with the brand's marketing objectives or new strategic direction. Such was the case with Internet search engine Ask.com. The brand was associated with a NASCAR Sprint Cup Series team. Despite observing usage of Ask.com among NASCAR fans increase dramatically and investing $15 million in the sponsorship, Ask.com opted not to return as a sponsor the following year. Was Ask.com disappointed in the sponsorship's performance? Not at all; the reason for ending the relationship was a shift in strategic priorities to investing more marketing dollars in developing the company's website.[35]

Change in Managerial Personnel

Turnover in personnel responsible for brand management decisions can result in a company ending a sponsorship in favor of other marketing strategies or simply deciding the relationship is not a good fit for the company. A characteristic of sponsorship that should not be minimized is the importance of personal relationships between decision makers for each party (sponsor and sports property). The decision to make sizeable investments in a sponsorship is influenced by the rapport and trust managers develop through personal interactions. In some cases, when a manager responsible for sponsorship leaves his or her position, much of the "relationship equity" that has been built between a sports property and the corporate partner is gone, and the new manager may not share the same vision that the sponsorship fits into the brand's overall marketing strategy.

Chapter Summary

Sports is the largest category of sponsorship, with an estimated $16 billion spent in North America and $44 billion worldwide. Sponsorships can involve leagues, teams, events, venues, or individuals. Sponsoring teams is more attractive to local or regional companies and leagues to national or international companies because of costs and differences in coverage area.

Insider Insights Terry Lefton – Sports Business Journal

Q. From a historical viewpoint, what events or trends can you point to as significant to sponsorship's growth as a marketing vehicle?

1. Sports signage at venues dates to the early days of baseball. Gillette, desperate to reach male shavers, has been a sponsor of MLB teams, players, and the league since at least 1910. Gillette now calls itself MLB's oldest corporate sponsor. That is a debatable claim, but it has been leveraging MLB longer than any other sponsor. In some years (1930s and '40s) it bought out all ad inventories on World Series broadcasts. Imagine an advertiser doing that on a Super Bowl today, which would be the closest equivalent.

Sports Business Journal & Sports Business Daily

Terry Lefton talks about sponsorship in marketing.

2. 1984, L.A. Olympics: Peter Ueberroth's 1984 Olympics, which yielded a surplus of $230 million and allowed unprecedented use of corporate names on buildings and venues, is often thought of as the beginning of modern sports sponsorship.

3. As media clutter increased, the need for distinction did as well, as did the need for those selling sports marketing inventory to sell products with more value, and thus, a higher price tag. This started with entitlements of sport venues like the Carrier Dome (1980) and Schaefer Stadium (1971) and has progressed to an age where buildings without corporate names are the exception. Entitlements and presenting sponsorships of media-based sports properties are commonplace, like the many network NFL halftime and postgame studio shows that carry corporate monikers.

Q. What mistakes do you observe companies make when investing in sports sponsorships?

A. Neophyte sponsors often do not understand that purchase of intellectual property and media packaged in their sponsorship is only the beginning of the spending. Supporting or activating the sponsorship with team, player, venue, and additional media rights can often cost from three to five times as much as the original sponsorship expenditure. Absent definitive metrics of media activation, these budgets are always under pressure and often the first to get cut.

Also, the number of "official" designations within the realm of teams and leagues can be comical. Consider Mexican restaurant chain Rubio's dubious claim as "the official fish taco of the San Diego Padres," or Flanagan Krrrrisp, "the official sauerkraut of Lambeau Field." The key is to design a program that uses those rights and designations skillfully. "Official pudding of the New York Mets" sounds downright silly, but after Kozy Shack started sampling its desserts outside New York Mets games, it leapfrogged past rival Jell-O in New York market sales.

Q. Measurement of sponsorship effectiveness seems to be an area of weakness for many sponsors. Why is measurement such a challenge?

A. The effect on sales through association, can it be measured? It is always difficult. As the price has escalated, so has the quest for measurement, yet it remains elusive. You can research awareness of a sponsorship before and after, and you can do studies that ask whether a product or service now in the fans' consideration set was or was not before the sponsorship. Direct correlation of sponsorship to sales remains elusive, but so does the cause/effect of advertising on sales.

The Nielsen TV metric is flawed; it does not indicate anyone is watching the TV, in reality it just shows a TV was on. However, as an accepted metric it gives comfort to those spending sports marketing dollars. Thus, media budgets, while under some scrutiny, are never questioned to the degree sponsorship budgets are, especially in tougher economic times.

We are on similar paths when it comes to advertising research, and yet sponsorship is held to a higher standard of accountability. Of late, tougher questions are being asked. But it is rare to find a client demanding the same accountability from sponsorship he gets from his advertising. It all harkens back to John Wannamaker, who supplied the most famous aphorism in marketing history when he said almost a century ago, "Half the money I spend on advertising is wasted; the trouble is I don't know which half."

Sponsorships can involve a single-day event, multi-day event, or an off-field event. Venues, especially sports stadiums, have become a popular type of sponsorship. At the lowest level is sponsorship of individuals, especially in certain sports such as golf and auto racing. Sponsorship has grown recently because of three inherent strengths: targeted audience reach, connection with the affinity of sports fans, and avoidance of media clutter.

Sponsorship is of value to companies because of targeted reach, image transfer capability, exclusivity, marketing opportunities, and protection of the investment. Marketing opportunities arise from the brand's involvement in branding campaigns, on-site marketing, and cross-marketing. Because of the high cost of sponsorship, sponsors seek protection from sports properties from ambush marketing efforts by competitors. While ambush marketing cannot be eliminated, sports properties can take actions to reduce its impact on sponsors.

Managing a sponsorship involves six steps. First, the sponsor must define the target market of the sponsorship. Second, objectives need to be set. The most common objectives include creating brand awareness, influencing brand image or personality, strengthening client relationships, stimulating product trial, increasing sales, and generating media exposure. The third step is to select the sports property. Primary criteria used in the selection include fit with brand objectives, duration of sponsorship, and partner relationship. Secondary criteria would be the level of involvement and exposure type.

Step four is the establishment of a budget, which involves both rights fees and activation costs. The fifth step is development of an activation plan. Sponsorships with only rights fees or inadequate budgets for activation are likely to fail. The last step is to measure effectiveness. Three common categories of measures are awareness measures, brand image measures, and financial measures.

Not all sponsorships are a success. While some fail to meet objectives, others are discontinued for alternative reasons. The most common reasons sponsorships end are 1) unclear expectations of a sponsor, 2) inadequate budget to activate the sponsorship, 3) change in strategic focus, and 4) change in managerial personnel.

Review Questions

1. Describe the various types of sponsorships.
2. What are the distinguishing characteristics of sponsorship?
3. Identify the three strengths of sponsorship that have led to its growth.
4. What is the difference between reach and targeted reach?
5. Identify the ways that value is created for sponsors by sponsorship.
6. Explain the concept of image transfer in terms of sponsorship.
7. Explain the concept of exclusivity in sponsorship, and why exclusivity is important.
8. What three types of marketing opportunities arise from a brand's involvement with sponsorship?
9. List the six steps in managing sponsorship.
10. What objectives do sponsors frequently set for sponsorship? Which two are the most used?
11. What primary and what secondary criteria are used in selecting a sponsorship?
12. List the factors a sports property uses in determining rights fees.
13. Why is it important to develop an activation plan? What is the industry average for leverage ratio to activate sponsorship rights?
14. Describe the different levels of brand awareness.
15. Discuss how brand image can be measured.
16. What financial measures can sponsors use? What is the challenge of using a financial measure?
17. Identify the four primary reasons sponsorships end.

New Terms

Sponsorship   investment of money, products, or services by a company in exchange for the rights to be associated with a sports property and use that association in marketing activities.

Naming rights sponsorship   association in which a corporate sponsor acquires the rights to have a corporate or brand name incorporated into the venue's official name.

Secondary brand association   brand association inferred by consumers by linking a brand to information already stored in memory.

Reach   total number of persons or percentage of a total population that is exposed to a brand message within a specific time period.

Targeted reach number of persons or percentage of a population exposed to a brand message that also is part of a brand's target market.

Message clutter high volume of marketing messages placed in a particular medium that vies for an individual's attention.

Image transfer occurs when the meaning consumers hold for a sports property is assigned to a brand that is linked to that property.

Category exclusivity situation in which a sponsor is the only company within its product category associated with a sponsored property.

Branding campaign strategy to communicate or promote an association with a sports property by a sponsor to its target market.

On-site marketing opportunity to reach a sports property's audience at the physical location of the sports property.

Cross-marketing involves collaboration between a sponsor, sports property, and a sponsor's marketing partners to create campaigns with the aim of benefiting all involved parties.

Pass-through rights added value to a sponsorship through allowing a sponsor's partners to enhance the sponsor's association with the sports property through themed promotions.

Ambush marketing planned effort by a company that is not an official sponsor to create the impression that it is associated with the property or sporting event in some way.

Impressions total number of exposures of an audience to a brand message.

Sponsorship proposal document created by a sports property that gives an overview of the property, information on the property's audience, and benefits of partnering through sponsorship.

Rights fees the cost a company pays to be recognized as an official sponsor.

Activation costs monies spent on marketing activities to communicate a brand's sponsorship.

Leverage ratio activation dollars divided by rights fees.

Brand recognition ability of an individual to identify awareness of a brand sponsor.

Brand recall ability of an individual to identify a brand when prompted with the product category.

Top-of-mind brand awareness the first brand that comes to mind when consumers are given a product category.

Return on investment (ROI) financial return on a sponsorship in comparison to the monies invested in the sponsorship.

Return on objective (ROO) assessment of how well a sponsorship performed in respect to the objectives of the sponsorship.

Discussion and Critical Thinking Exercises

1. Review the opening vignette about Bridgestone. In your opinion, is it a wise strategy to become involved in different major sports, such as golf, football, and hockey? Would Bridgestone be better off concentrating on one sport? Justify your answer.
2. Approximately 68% of all sponsorship dollars are spent on sports. Why do you think sports sponsorship is so much more attractive than the other categories identified in Figure 11.1?
3. Pick one pro sports team in each of the following sports. From their websites, identify official sponsors of each team. Do you think there is a good fit between the team and the sponsors?
   a. National Football League (NFL)
   b. National Hockey League (NHL)
   c. Major League Baseball (MLB)
   d. National Basketball Association (NBA)
4. Using the Internet, identify three different sponsors of NASCAR racing events. Evaluate the fit between the sponsor and the NASCAR event being sponsored.

5. Naming stadiums for companies has become a very popular form of sponsorship. What is your personal opinion of this type of sponsorship? Is it worth the high cost? Does it impact an individual's attitude towards a brand and his or her purchase decisions?

6. Sponsoring individuals can be risky. Identify two sports personalities that you would consider low risk. What makes them low risk, and what brands do they endorse? Identify two athletes that you would consider high risk. What makes them a high risk, and what brands do they endorse or did they endorse? For a company, which can provide the highest impact in terms of brand image and sales revenue, a low-risk individual or a high-risk one? Why?

7. For each of the following brands, discuss the three types of marketing opportunities (branding campaign, on-site marketing, and cross-marketing) as they would relate to sponsoring a WNBA team. Which brands are a good fit with a WNBA team, and which are not? Why?
   a. Pepsi-Cola
   b. Taco Bell
   c. Enterprise Rent-a-Car
   d. UPS
   e. Covergirl

8. Suppose a quick-service restaurant such as Wendy's obtained a sponsorship with a minor league hockey team in your area. With the sponsorship, Wendy's receives the following assets. Describe two to three activation strategies for each asset that Wendy's could use to maximize its sponsorship.
   a. Signage in the arena on the rink boards and in the concourse
   b. Concession rights (not exclusivity, there are two other food vendors)
   c. Sponsor of two different autograph-signing events at the mall
   d. VIP party at the arena to include meeting the players and tour of locker rooms and other facilities
   e. Pool of ten tickets for front-row exclusive seats for ten games

9. Suppose your university or college wanted to measure awareness of one of your sports. Pick a sport other than football, basketball, or baseball. Describe how you would measure brand recognition, brand recall, and top-of-mind brand awareness for that sport.

You Make the Call

Distilled Spirits Sponsorships?

Sponsorship is an attractive marketing approach for a large number of companies and brands to reach new and current markets. It is also lucrative for sports properties in terms of generating additional revenue. As long as there is a logical fit, any type of company or brand is free to develop sponsorship deals with about any sports properties. Even in situations where there does not appear to be a logical fit, deals are often consummated. The one exception area has been for distilled spirits. Regulations prohibited any type of advertising or sponsorship by liquor brands.

A number of reasons have been given for this ban on liquor deals. The two most common are the influence it would have on children and teenagers under the age of 21 and the increased consumption of liquor at a sporting event that would then lead to an increase in the number of impaired drivers on the roads. While both arguments carry weight and make sense, liquor companies argue they should have the right to advertise and market their products to consumers at sporting events just as much as any other product category.

This hard rule against liquor in professional sports began to erode with the recession that began in 2008. As sponsorship dollars declined, teams and professional sports leagues looked for additional ways of boosting revenue. It was time to revisit the ban on liquor advertising and sponsorship. After all, several sports stadiums already had branded taverns, such as Diageo's Cuervo Cantina at Reliant Stadium in Houston.

When the NBA reversed its longtime ban on courtside advertising by distilled spirits brands, Bacardi immediately seized the opportunity. Bacardi was already a major sponsor of the Miami Heat and in the company's last contract had written into the agreement a deal for courtside advertising if the NBA lifted the ban. So when the ban was lifted, Bacardi exercised its option to install courtside advertising.

Although the NBA lifted the ban, the league still maintained tight control on what could and could not be done. Rules allowed for camera-visible ads, but the sign had to have social-responsibility messaging. On teams' websites, liquor ads also had to include a social-responsibility message. Brand messages were permitted, but could not encourage direct sales or have any other tag line. At the retail level in stadiums, no league intellectual property could be used and no team logos could appear on any primary or secondary packaging. Similar rules were established in Major League Baseball, the NFL, the NHL, and in NASCAR.

Major sports have lifted the ban on advertising of distilled spirits.

The PGA Tour was one of the last major sports to lift the ban on distilled spirits. Tournaments and players can now accept sponsorships from liquor companies as long as the event does not have any rounds broadcast on network television. Also, a player's image cannot be used on any liquor bottles or containers, and players cannot put the logo of a liquor brand on their clothing or bags during competition. As with the other sports, ads must have a social-responsibility message.[36]

Questions:

1. Do you think the decision to lift the ban on liquor sponsorships was a good decision? Why or why not?
2. What is your evaluation of the current rules concerning distilled spirits and what they can or cannot do in terms of sponsorship and advertising? Justify your response.
3. What about the two major arguments against sponsorships by liquor brands? Do you agree or disagree with these arguments? Why?
4. Locate an example of sponsorship or advertising by a liquor company or brand of a league, team, event, or venue. Describe how it was done and evaluate its effectiveness.
5. Some argue that there should not be any restrictions of any type on product sponsorship in sports. Would you agree or disagree? Why?

References

1. "A Global Dream," (2010), accessed October 15, 2010, at http://www.bridgestone.com/corporate/history/index.html.
2. Barry Janoff, (2010), "Even on the Road, Bridgestone Drives for Home Field Advantage," June 11, accessed October 14, 2010, at http://www.nysportsjournalism.com/bridgestone-plays-the-field-61/.
3. Terry Lefton, (2010), "Food Fight: Papa John's Gets Subway's Jared Booted from Radio Row," *Sports Business Journal*, March 1, 12.
4. Karl Greenberg, (2008), "Bridgestone Goes Beyond Comfort Zone, onto the Green," February 7, accessed October 15, 2010, at http://www.mediapost.com/publications/?fa=Articles.showArticle&art_aid=75957.
5. Donald P. Roy, "Global Sport Sponsorship: Towards a Strategic Understanding," in *Global Sport Sponsorship*, eds. John Amis and T. Bettina Cornwell (New York: Berg, 2005).
6. "Sponsorship Spending: 2010 Proves Better than Expected; Bigger Gains Set for 2011," (2011), accessed October 14, 2011, at http://www.sponsorship.com/Resources/Sponsorship-Spending.aspx.

7. "IEG Lexicon and Glossary," (n.d.), accessed October 16, 2010, at http://www.sponsor-ship.com/Resources/IEG-Lexicon-and-Glossary.aspx. IEG, LLC.

8. "Founding Partners and Official Partners," (2010), accessed October 17, 2010, at http://www.womensprosoccer.com/about/official-partners-sponsors.

9. "Coporate Champions and Partners" (2012), March 7, accessed April 26, 2012 at http://www.ncaa.com/news/ncaa/article/2011-02-25/corporate-champions-and-partners.

10. "Metcalf Bank Becomes Official Sponsor of the Kansas City Chiefs," (2009), June 23, accessed October 17, 2010, at https://www.metcalfbank.com/pages/aboutDetail.aspx?tid=2142&cid=4765&lid=1033.

11. "Making the Right Connections," (2010), accessed October 17, 2010, at http://www.mastercard.com/us/merchant/acceptance/corporate_sponsorship.html.

12. "2010 Capitals Convention," (2010), accessed October 18, 2010, at http://capitals.nhl.com/club/page.htm?id=62849.

13. "New Name for Same Stadium," (2010), January 20, accessed October 18, 2010, at http://sports.espn.go.com/nfl/news/story?id=4842320.

14. Kurt Badenhausen, (2006), "Mets Break the Bank," November 14, accessed October 18, 2010, at http://www.forbes.com/2006/11/14/baseball-mets-citigroup-biz_cz_kb_1114naming.html.

15. John Brennan, (2010), "Don't Expect Name for Meadowlands Stadium Soon, Exec Says," August 11, accessed October 18, 2010, at http://www.northjersey.com/news/081110_Dont_expect_name_for_Meadowlands_Stadium_soon_exec_says.html.

16. Mark Decambre (2011), "New Meadowlands Stadium to Become MetLife Stadium," August 19, accessed April 26, 2012 at http://www.nypost.com/p/news/business/metlife_inks_deal_with_meadowlands_PG2HRPjVKrrtaSLaklGdEN.

17. Don Muret, (2010), "Branded Parking Lots Have Room for Perks," *Sports Business Journal*, October 11, 20.

18. Tripp Mickle, (2010), "Whiteout," *Sports Business Journal*, May 31, 1.

19. Paul Pogge, (2011), "How Doing Good Worked Well for Denver Basketball," *Sports Business Journal*, May 2, 20.

20. Kevin Lane Keller, (1993), "Conceptualizing, Measuring, and Managing Customer-Based Brand Equity," *Journal of Marketing*, 57 (January), 1–22.

21. "For Love or Money? The Unrequited Passion of the Sports Fan," (2007), January 3, accessed October 20, 2010, at http://knowledge.wpcarey.asu.edu/article.cfm?articleid=1353.

22. Kevin Gwinner, (1997), "A Model of Image Creation and Image Transfer in Event Sponsorship," *International Marketing Review*, 14 (3), 145–158.

23. "IEG Lexicon and Glossary," (n.d.), accessed October 22, 2010, at http://www.sponsorship.com/Resources/IEG-Lexicon-and-Glossary.aspx.

24. Andy Bernstein, (2002), "Drawn to the Flame, Pepsi Mounts Ambush," *Sports Business Journal*, February 25, 35.

25. Tripp Mickle, (2010), "Pens Sign Dr Pepper Snapple Group for New Arena," *Sports Business Journal*, May 3, 6.

26. Michael Smith, (2010), "Promo Moves Products, Race Tickets," *Sports Business Journal*, July 12, 8.

27. Kenneth E. Clow and Donald Baack, *Integrated Advertising, Promotion, and Marketing Communications*, 4th ed. (Upper Saddle River, NJ: Prentice Hall, 2010).

28. "Jimmie Johnson Tops NASCAR Driver Exposure with $48M," (2010), *Sports Business Daily*, July 22, accessed November 2, 2010, at http://www.joycejulius.com/Press/news_July_22_10.htm.

29. Joseph Vinu, (2010), "Sponsorship Proposals: Is the Devil Really in the Details? Or Are You Missing the Forest for the Trees?" accessed November 2, 2010, at http://www.sponsorship.com/About-IEG/Sponsorship-Blogs/Vinu-Joseph/May-2010/Sponsorship-Proposals--Is-the-Devil-Really-in-the.aspx.

30. Margaret Johnston and Neil Paulsen, (2007), "The Relative Importance of Sponsorship Selection Criteria: A Choice-Based Conjoint Study Using Hierarchical Bayes Analysis," accessed November 1, 2010, at http://conferences.anzmac.org/ANZMAC2007/papers/Johnston_1.pdf.

31. "SponsorPort Standard Edition. A Comprehensive Sponsorship Management System That Works the Way You Do," (2009), accessed November 2, 2010, at http://www.sponsordirect.com/products/sponsorship/standard.aspx.

32. James Crimmins and Martin Horn, (1996), "Sponsorship: From Management Ego Trip to Marketing Success," *Journal of Advertising Research*, 36 (July–August), 11–21.

33. "IEG/Performance Research Study Highlights What Sponsors Want," (2010), accessed November 4, 2010, at http://www.sponsorship.com/Resources/IEG-Performance-Research-Study-Highlights-What-Spo.aspx.

34. "Which of the Following Is an Official Sponsor of the NBA?" (2010), *Sports Business Journal*, July 26, 15.

35. Michael Smith, (2010), "NASCAR's Back, but Ask.com Isn't," *Sports Business Journal*, February 8, 4.

36. Terry Lefton, (2009), "Clubs to Vet Liquor, Lottery Options," *Sports Business Journal*, March 30, 3; John Lombardo, (2009), "Liquor Deals Start to Flow," *Sports Business Journal*, June 15, 1; Jon Show, (2009), "Liquor Sponsors? PGF Tour Will Drink to That," *Sports Business Journal*, February 22, 5; Terry Lefton, (2009), "NBA Gives Ground Rules for Liquor Marketing," *Sports Business Journal*, March 9, 4.

12 Measuring Sports Brand Performance

Learning Objectives

By the end of this chapter you should be able to:

1. Compare and contrast variable and dynamic pricing
2. Discuss the reasons for measuring sports brand marketing performance
3. Describe the benefits and uses of six types of sports marketing performance metrics
4. Discuss the limitations of sports brand performance measurement

Dynamic pricing is used by sports teams to optimize profit margins.

Winds of Change Are Variable for Ticket Pricing

Sports properties that rely on ticket sales as a revenue source have long struggled with how to set prices that please customers and at the same time maximize revenues. For years, it seemed impossible to achieve both; either reduce ticket prices to make customers happy or raise prices to a threshold of what the market would bear to boost revenues. The pricing approach taken for sporting events was that a price for a given seat location was set for all scheduled events. This strategy assumed that the "product" was the same every time, thus justifying the same price for all events. However, not all sporting events are equal. Take the long Major League Baseball season, for example. A game against a low-quality opponent on a chilly Tuesday night in April does not have the same appeal to fans as a Saturday afternoon game against a rival in June. Yet, for years pricing was the same for these very different products. The result was often lots of empty seats for the Tuesday night game in April and a full house for the Saturday game in June. Surprisingly, in both cases a team likely misses out on revenues because of a one-size-fits-all pricing strategy.

Two alternatives for ticket pricing are now being embraced by more teams and fans: Variable pricing and dynamic pricing. Although there is a difference between these two pricing strategies, a common characteristic of variable and dynamic pricing is that factors influencing customer demand are the basis for a ticket's price. **Variable pricing** improves upon a single price for a type of seat or seat location for all events by establishing different prices based on demand. Variables that impact demand include opponent, day of week, and month of year. For instance, the NHL's Florida Panthers designated five games as premium games, setting ticket prices that were $25 above other games. These games fell during the Thanksgiving and Christmas holidays, when more visitors were expected to be in the South Florida area. Similarly, the Buffalo Sabres employed variable pricing for individual game tickets by segmenting its forty-one-game home schedule into five categories: platinum (two games), gold (eight games), silver (eighteen games), bronze (nine games), and value (four games). A ticket priced at $100 for a silver game jumped to $191 for a platinum game and dropped to $58 for a value game.[1]

Variable pricing is a win-win situation, as price-sensitive fans can be more selective about games they attend with the option to pay less for games with lower demand or pay a premium for tickets to games with greater appeal. At the same time, teams are able to capture greater revenue by lowering the price of tickets for low-demand events that might go unsold and reaping rewards from premium games that are priced higher.

An innovation in pricing that builds on the concept of variable pricing is **dynamic pricing**, which utilizes technology to continuously adjust prices based on supply and demand factors. Dynamic pricing is similar to yield management pricing used by hotels and airlines in pricing their services. The lowest prices are often available shortly after tickets go on sale. As an event approaches, ticket prices will fluctuate depending on demand for tickets, performance of teams involved, and developments that could change demand such as a star player on an opposing team being injured or traded. One team on the forefront of dynamic pricing has been MLB's San Francisco Giants. The team experimented with dynamic pricing in some sections of AT&T Park in 2009 before fully implementing in 2010.

One characteristic of dynamic pricing that distinguishes it from standard pricing is a dizzying number of prices for tickets. Prior to the 2010 season, a visit to the San Francisco Giants website revealed a whopping 1,680 different prices for the team's eighty-four-game home schedule.[2] For sports properties, dynamic pricing is more than revenue maximization; it is responding to customers' perceptions of the value of tickets. According to Mike Tomon, Cleveland Cavaliers vice president of sales, "dynamic pricing has helped us engage the fan and be relevant by offering them the right product at the right price at the right time."[3] Other teams in MLB, the NBA, the NHL, as well as racetracks owned by International Speedway Corporation have adopted dynamic pricing in their pursuit to increase revenue without across-the-board price increases.

Despite the appeal of dynamic pricing, there are concerns that many sports properties feel they must address before adopting a demand-based pricing system. Protecting the value of tickets purchased by buyers of full- and partial-season ticket plans is a high priority. The St. Louis Cardinals, one of several MLB teams to adopt dynamic pricing, added a twist to the system that insures ticket prices in sections of Busch Stadium where season ticket customers are located will not fall below the average price per game paid by season ticket buyers. Other teams have adopted a similar policy in order to demonstrate to season ticket buyers that there are benefits in making a commitment to buy more games. Russ Stanley, a Giants team executive, sums up the importance of keeping season ticket buyers happy when he said, "I simply wouldn't be doing this if it meant putting our season-ticket holders at risk."[4] Also, perceptions exist that dynamic pricing is another way teams are seeking to squeeze more money for big games. As one NHL team marketing executive put it "People's initial reaction is always 'variable pricing screws fans.' For us, it's almost a way to be smart about our discounting."[5] Sports marketers may view dynamic pricing as a win for fans, but it will be a win only if consumers are persuaded that there are benefits of demand-based pricing for them.

Introduction

The increased use of variable and dynamic pricing highlights the need for performance measurement. Like any other business, a sports organization has objectives that it seeks to meet. Performance against objectives should be assessed in order to determine to what extent marketing decisions such as prices charged contribute to business growth. Measurement is the last step in the sequence of marketing activities in the strategic marketing planning process. The best strategies cannot impact business growth if outcomes are not measured. Just as a college student would not sit through an entire course and not have his performance evaluated by exams, papers, or creative projects, a sports organization cannot go about its business of serving customers without measuring the effectiveness of marketing tactics and their impact on the organization's financial picture.

This chapter examines issues related to measuring sports brand performance. First, motivations for measuring performance are discussed. Measurement is part of the strategic marketing planning process. It brings closure to a planning cycle and charts the course for future brand strategies. Second, different performance metrics are introduced and discussed, with two general categories being marketing metrics and financial metrics. Third, challenges to measuring performance in sports organizations are identified.

Importance of Measuring Performance

Measuring marketing performance is analogous to keeping a scorecard or analyzing statistics. Performance in football is measured by points on a scoreboard, total yards of offense, and other statistics that reflect a team's performance on offense, defense, and special teams. Coaches analyze a team's performance in various statistical categories to identify strengths and weaknesses. Adjustments to strategies are made based on what a team does well and its vulnerabilities. Similarly, marketing managers in a sports organization should specify measures to be used to evaluate performance against marketing objectives and guide decisions on making adjustments to strategy. Three reasons for sports marketers to be concerned with measuring performance are shown in Figure 12.1.

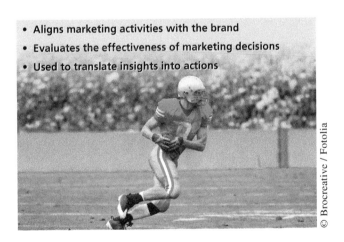

- **Aligns marketing activities with the brand**
- **Evaluates the effectiveness of marketing decisions**
- **Used to translate insights into actions**

© Brocreative / Fotolia

FIGURE 12.1 Reasons for Measuring Performance

Align Marketing Activities with the Brand

The importance of managing a brand's identity, image, and promises was established in Chapter 5. Given the prominent role of the brand in marketing, it is important that marketing activities are evaluated to determine the effectiveness of marketing tactics in brand building. Any strategy pertaining to target marketing, positioning, or the 4Ps of the marketing mix (product, price, place, and promotion) can impact perceptions people have of a brand. Measures should be established to assess the impact of marketing activities on reinforcing brand identity.

The Tampa Bay Rays use measurement in this way through a comprehensive list of brand traits. As shown in Figure 12.2, the Rays organization has identified five major traits that managers aspire to have associated with the brand: 1) baseball magic, 2) family fun, 3) Tampa Bay, 4) community pillar, and 5) sharp. Each trait includes descriptors that give guidance as to how

ENERGIZE OUR COMMUNITY THROUGH THE MAGIC OF BASEBALL				
Baseball Magic	**Family Fun**	**Tampa Bay**	**Community Pillar**	**Sharp**
• Pitchers and catchers report • Purity of the game • Hot dogs, cracker jacks • Immortals • Six months, every day • Summer, story line • Play the game right, fundamentals • Catching a foul ball • Numbers: 755, 56, 6-4-3 • Character • America, apple pie • National Anthem • History, tradition	• Multi-generational shared experience and time • Memories, emotion • Fathers and son (parents and children) • Enjoyable bonding • Playing catch • Relaxed • Silly, funny, kid-oriented • Cotton Candy • Togetherness • Non-violent, PG	• Growing • Better than the big boys • Winning attitude • Sunny, beaches, water • Upstart • Converting transplants • 1st generation building • Spots unite • Hard working • Baseball heritage	• Strong values • High involvement • Good for the region • Neighborly • Caring, kind • Service oriented • Outstanding corporate citizens • A community asset	• Smart • Edgy • Crisp • Bold • Daring • Unconventional • Intelligent risk-talking • Youthful • Glow-emitting • Professional

FIGURE 12.2 **Tampa Bay Rays Brand Traits**

the traits can be exhibited. Simply put, any planned or executed marketing tactic must be consistent with the brand traits. The evaluation method of the Tampa Bay Rays illustrates that quantitative measures are not the only means of evaluating performance. Qualitative standards like the Tampa Bay Rays brand traits can be used to compare actions with strategies.

Evaluate Marketing Decisions

Measuring performance is an essential final stage in the strategic planning cycle. Measurement provides answers to the question "How did we do?" In the marketing planning process, managers make predictions about the impact of planned strategies by examining past performance, surveying customers, and applying expertise. However, none of these views of expected performance is a substitute for determining actual outcomes. Thus, post-implementation measurement of performance is needed so at the very least, decisions that were mistakes are not repeated.

MLB, NBA, and NHL teams seeking to increase total attendance are using some type of measurement process to evaluate marketing decisions. The number of home games in these leagues (forty-one regular season games in the NBA and NHL; eighty-one in MLB) poses a challenge in how to allocate marketing dollars to maximize attendance. Some teams have adopted the strategy of focusing marketing efforts on weekend games, targeting these more attractive days of the week for ticket sellouts. Postgame concerts, fireworks shows, and giveaways are examples of marketing investments made to pull more people to these games. Measurement is needed to determine if these tactics generate more ticket sales and higher revenue. In addition to measuring overall ticket sales and total revenue, further analysis can examine other relevant metrics such as average ticket price and average expenditure per customer on food and merchandise. A manager cannot assume that marketing tactics work; a commitment to performance measurement is vital in providing a complete picture of the impact of marketing activity.

Translate Insights into Actions

The use of measurement to evaluate marketing performance is an endgame activity, done after a marketing strategy is implemented. However, measurement has a role at the front end of marketing planning, too. Information collected through primary and secondary data sources about customers, competitors, and other aspects of the external environment can reveal insights that lead managers to make informed decisions on marketing strategy. The Tampa Bay Rays have incorporated measurements to gain a better understanding of customers in order to more effectively segment the market. The Rays organization used information about its fans to identify the five customer segments identified in Figure 12.3.

FIGURE 12.3 **Five Customer Segments of Tampa Bay Rays**

These segments reflect more than labels put on groups of customers. For each segment, the team is able to describe the customers in terms of demographic characteristics like age and behavioral characteristics such as motivations for attending games. The true value of possessing this knowledge for different customer types is that the team can tailor its marketing mix to reach each segment.

The Tampa Bay Rays are one of many teams that focus marketing efforts on maximizing attendance for weekend games. Themed events were designed to reach specific audience segments. "Friday Fests" targeted young adults aged 18 to 34; Saturdays featured postgame concerts as added value events to target 25- to 54-year-olds and music lovers. Sunday games targeted families through kid-oriented advertising and involving kids in contests and running the bases after the game. Marketing managers for the Rays could not have arrived at the decisions on targeting and the mix of product, price, and communication to reach its targets without measurement of consumer characteristics and behaviors.

Measuring Marketing Performance

Marketing encompasses a wide scope of activities designed to meet the needs of customers and the organization (i.e., implementing the marketing concept). Thus, measuring marketing effectiveness should evaluate how well a firm does in adding value for customers as well as contributing to the organization's profitability. Six aspects of marketing performance shown

FIGURE 12.4
Measuring Marketing Performance

in Figure 12.4 that are priorities for sports organizations to measure are: 1) fan engagement, 2) customer satisfaction, 3) return on investment, 4) ticket sales, 5) sponsorship sales, and 6) retail services.

Fan Engagement

Measurement in traditional media channels such as TV and radio tends to focus on exposure. Ratings and audience size are primary indicators that quantify the number of viewers. Similarly, measurement in social media can be done that evaluates audience size. In addition, a more in-depth assessment of consumer engagement is possible by evaluating topics of conversation and the favorability of brand mentions online. For social networking websites like Facebook and Twitter, indicators of audience reach include the number of unique visitors to a brand's page, the number of page views during a period of time (per week or month), and the number of fans or followers for the brand.

An effort to measure the reach of social media in sports globally is performed by Coyle Media's Sports Fan Graph (http://sportsfangraph.com). Leagues, teams, and media brands representing sports from around the world are ranked based on the sum of their fans on Facebook and followers on Twitter. Rankings are updated every twelve hours, capturing the rapidly changing audiences of these social networks. A check of the Sports Fan Graph reveals that consumers' identification with sports brands in social media mirrors the popularity of those brands in the offline world. In late 2011, the top five brands on the Sports Fan Graph were:

1. National Basketball Association (25,013,679)
2. FC Barcelona (24,584,774)
3. Manchester United (22,654,026)
4. Real Madrid (15,570,843)
5. Los Angeles Lakers (12,809,090)[6]

Measures such as the Sports Fan Graph are useful for quantifying the reach of social media channels, but the strength of social networking websites like Facebook is the ability of a marketer to engage consumers in conversation and listen to what customers and others have to say about a brand. Thus, measurement of social media should go beyond the number of people reached; it must include assessment of the content of online conversations. Comments and opinions shared by people online can be analyzed and themes of conversations identified. Mining social media content in this manner can provide insight into fans' attitudes and signal potential problems that need to be addressed. If conversations on a team's Facebook page show a trend of negative comments about poor service by foodservice vendors, managers may be alerted to look into the matter. Similarly, if fans' dissatisfaction with team performance spills over onto social networking sites into conversations about not renewing season tickets, team marketers can be proactive in exploring ways to strengthen the value proposition for season ticket holders.

Customer Satisfaction

An important area of marketing operations for which measurement is not only beneficial but should be an emphasis is monitoring customer satisfaction. Collecting information from customers on their experiences is needed to identify strengths of the brand offering and uncover sources of dissatisfaction that could harm customer relationships if unaddressed. Focus groups or surveys are frequently used methods to evaluate how effectively customers' expectations are being met.

The Tennessee Titans of the NFL have conducted a fan survey at one home game each season to measure satisfaction with elements of fans' game-day experience such as parking, security, concessions, and replay board use. Survey results were tracked over time and along with comments made by fans were used to make improvements to customer service. For example, input from several fans about the number of parking spaces for handicapped fans led to the team adding more handicapped spaces in parking lots around LP Field.

Another aspect of measuring customer satisfaction in the sports industry is to monitor customer retention rates. For sports properties, recurring revenue is vital to profits, and as discussed in Chapter 4, marketing efforts aimed at retaining customers can be done at a lower cost than acquiring new customers. Two metrics pertaining to customer retention are season ticket renewal rates and sponsorship renewals. Season ticket renewal rate as a percentage is determined using the following formula:

$$\text{Renewal rate} = \frac{\text{Number of season tickets renewing for following season}}{\text{Number of season tickets}}$$

A similar formula can be used to measure sponsorship renewal rate:

$$\text{Renewal rate} = \frac{\text{Number of sponsors renewing for following season}}{\text{Number of total sponsorships}}$$

Conducting surveys of fans during a sporting event provides valuable information on customer satisfaction.

A sports brand usually benefits from the affinity that customers have for a team or event. Many season ticket renewals are driven by loyalty arising from buyers' identification as fans. However, not all buyers will renew for the next season due to reasons such as dissatisfaction, change in personal financial situation, or relocation. The challenge for marketers is to minimize the number of nonrenewals. This feat can be accomplished by studying past ticket renewal campaigns to pinpoint characteristics of lost customers. Information that might be gleaned from studying past nonrenewals is number of years as customer, price paid, and number of game tickets used. Knowledge of variables that contribute to nonrenewal can assist a ticket sales staff to identify customers who may decide not to return and intensify sales efforts to retain them.

Retention rate for season ticket customers can be used to compare retention effectiveness over time, compare to other franchises, or evaluate against a league average. For instance, the NBA had a league average of an 80% renewal rate for the 2010–2011 season, a gain of 5 percentage points over the previous year. Individual franchises can benchmark their retention rate against the previous year as well as compare with the league average. One franchise, the Charlotte Bobcats, experienced a dreadfully low 59% renewal rate that could be attributed to a combination of franchise turmoil and a weak economy. The next year, the team addressed retention by adding marketing staff and increasing budgets for game production. These enhancements, along with Michael Jordan becoming team owner, led to an astounding 84% retention rate.[7] While retention rate is a measure of past performance, it can be used to set performance goals for a ticket sales staff for the next season.

Sponsorship managers should focus on retention, too, as extending partnerships with corporate sponsors is a key recurring revenue source. Retention rate is less important in sponsorship because the number of customers is small in comparison to a sports property's ticket customer base. However, tracking retention in terms of number of sponsorships renewed or the dollar value of renewals should be done each year. Measuring sponsorship renewals not only quantifies the performance of mangers responsible for corporate partnerships, but if renewal measures decline, it can be a signal that weaknesses or threats exist which sponsorship sales personnel must identify and address.

Return on Investment

While the other types of marketing metrics discussed so far are useful for guiding marketing decisions, return on investment (ROI) is viewed by many marketers as the ultimate measure because it links marketing investments to their impact on profits. The marketing activities assessed by metrics such as brand awareness, media exposure, and customer retention rates are done in pursuit of a larger aim: profits.

The marketing concept is based on a dual focus of meeting customers' needs and meeting the organization's needs. Profitability is the primary organizational need that marketing supports. According to marketing expert James Lenskold, "every strategy and tactic should be intended to increase profits. It is completely reasonable, and highly beneficial, to expect a return on investment for each incremental marketing dollar spent."[8] Measuring ROI evaluates the effect of marketing activities on profits and creates accountability for marketers that make decisions on strategy and tactics.

Marketing ROI measures *incremental* effects of a marketing activity. Thus, data for measuring ROI should reflect incremental revenue, costs, and marketing expenses. It is important that data used in ROI calculations reflect additional revenue and marketing expenses related to the marketing investment being measured, not total revenue and expenses. When calculations isolate incremental spending and revenue, the resulting ROI percentage represents the true impact of a marketing investment. The formula for marketing ROI is:

$$\text{Return on Investment (ROI)} = \frac{(\text{Revenue} - \text{Expenses}) - \text{Marketing Investment}}{\text{Marketing Investment}}$$

It is recommended that a threshold be set for ROI, and any proposed marketing tactic should be capable of meeting the threshold. Suppose that the threshold for ROI is set at 30%; then any marketing activity (e.g., direct mail offer or telemarketing blitz targeting prospective season ticket customers) should deliver at least a 30% return on the marketing investment. Marketing ROI can be used as a post-event measurement of actual performance or a pre-event projection of profit impact that can be used in making a yes/no decision to proceed with a marketing tactic.

Assume that the Tucson Padres AAA minor league baseball team in the Pacific Coast League is planning an online advertising campaign to promote a ten-game ticket package. Assume the following information:

- Revenue per ticket package: $89
- Service costs and expenses per package: $55
- Advertising expenses: $2,000

Marketing ROI for the planned campaign could be projected at different levels of sales from forty packages to one hundred packages. Figure 12.5 shows the calculations for this situation.

FIGURE 12.5 Sample ROI Calculations

	Per package	Packages Sold			
		40	**59**	**77**	**100**
Revenue	$89.00	$3,560	$5,251	$6,853	$8,900
Service costs & expenses	$55.00	$2,200	$3,245	$4,235	$5,500
Advertising costs	$2,000.00	$2,000	$2,000	$2,000	$2,000
Total costs		$4,200	$5,245	$6,235	$7,500
Contribution margin		($640)	$6	$618	$1,400
ROI		−32.00%	0.30%	30.90%	70.00%

- Revenue per ticket package: $89
- Service Costs and expenses per package: $60
- Advertising expenses: $2,000

Using these sales projections and an ROI threshold of 30%, the campaign would break even at fifty-nine packages. The $2,000 investment in advertising is covered with a $6.00 profit. If less than fifty-nine packages are sold, then the minor league baseball team will not recover all of their $2,000 investment costs. However, to achieve the targeted 30% ROI, the team would need to sell seventy-seven ticket packages. At that point all costs have been covered and $618 in additional profit has been generated. Notice if the sales team would happen to sell one hundred special game packages, the marketing ROI would be 70%, with a profit margin of $1,400 above costs. Projections can be made by using different scenarios of sales volume, price points, costs and expenses incurred, and marketing investment levels in order to determine the optimal level of marketing investment.

Tickets

Ticket sales are the lifeblood of sports properties whose main product is live events. Revenue from ticket sales makes up at least 50% of total revenues for the four major professional sports leagues in the United States (NFL, MLB, NBA, and NHL). For some franchises, the contribution of ticket sales to total revenues approaches 80%.[9] Given the significance of ticket sales to total revenues, it is vital to maximize performance in all areas of ticket sales. The ticket category contains the five areas shown in Figure 12.6 for which financial performance should be tracked.

FIGURE 12.6 **Ticket Sales Metrics**

SEASON TICKETS. Purchasers of multiple-game ticket packages, either full season or partial season, represent a key customer segment for a sports property. They are a key segment because of their loyalty. A season ticket buyer's commitment to purchase tickets for all games demonstrates his or her loyalty to a team. That loyalty must be protected because of the long-term financial value a season ticket holder represents. The approach to pricing multiple-game ticket packages historically has been to position season ticket holders as enjoying the benefit of receiving discounted pricing off of single-game prices. The Columbus Clippers, a Class AAA minor league baseball team in the International League, offered a season ticket price for box seats for $675, or about $9 per game. This price compares with an advance purchase price of $12 per game and game-day price of $15.[10]

An alternative approach to pricing multiple-game tickets is that season ticket prices become the base, and pricing of partial-season or single-game tickets will reflect a premium compared to what the season ticket customer pays on a per game basis. Establishing season ticket price per game as the base protects the value of loyal season ticket buyers in two ways. First, the benefits of being a season ticket customer are enhanced when prices paid by this customer segment represent the best value. Second, using season ticket price as a base is important for properties using dynamic pricing. As discussed at the beginning of this chapter, many teams using dynamic pricing have established a price floor below which ticket prices cannot fluctuate. The floor is typically the price paid by season ticket customers, so that a buyer shopping for a deal on single-game tickets does not get more favorable pricing than a loyal season ticket buyer.

Another way customer loyalty of season ticket customers can be protected is offering to lock in prices in exchange for a multiyear purchase. The Toledo Mud Hens, also in the Class AAA International League, offered seats at field level for $576, an average of $8 per game. Buyers were offered the opportunity to guarantee this price for three seasons in exchange for agreeing to a three-year commitment.[11] The benefit of multiyear pricing for season tickets is creating some degree of revenue certainty by assuring some customers are booked for the current season and beyond. Also, these committed customers are ones that will not be lost. The year-to-year nature of season ticket renewals means that it is inevitable that some customers will be lost, even when customer renewal rates are high.

Important metrics for evaluating performance in season ticket sales pertain to the number of tickets sold. Obvious measures are number of full-season tickets sold and number of other multi-game plans. Team marketers have shown more creativity in selling multi-game ticket plans. The practice of selling a full-season and half-season ticket has expanded to include packages that require buyers to commit to fewer games (say, five to ten games). Another innovation in marketing multi-game ticket plans is giving buyers more flexibility in terms of the games that comprise their ticket plan rather than having a preset package of games for all buyers. The Providence Bruins of the American Hockey League offered three different partial-season ticket plans for last season: five-game, ten-game, and twenty-game. In addition, the Bruins sold "flex ticket" packages of either ten or forty tickets that could be redeemed for any game with available seats.[12]

The increased emphasis on multiple-game tickets that are smaller increments than full-season packages leads to two other ticket sales measures having greater significance. Total tickets sold is a figure that is the sum of games sold to each multi-game buyer. Figure 12.7 illustrates how this figure would be calculated. The season ticket package is for seventy two games and 1,250 were sold, which produces a total of 90,000 tickets (72 × 1,250). The same process was followed for the thirty-five-game package plan, the twenty-game package, the ten-game package, and the five-game package. When all of these package plans are added together it produces a total ticket sales of 184,510.

FIGURE 12.7 Example of Calculations of Total Tickets Sold

Game Package	Games in Package	Number Sold	Total Tickets Sold
Season Tickets	72	1,250	90,000
35 Game Plans	35	920	32,200
20 Game Plans	20	1,440	28,800
10 Game Plans	10	2,127	21,270
5 Game Plans	5	2,448	12,240
Total Game Package Tickets Sold			184,510
Ticket sales to reach average of 7,500 average attendance			540,000
Single and group ticket sales needed to reach goal			355,490

In this scenario, the total tickets sold metric gives team marketers a picture of the revenue that is booked and the level of sales needed to individual game customers and groups in order to reach sales goals. If the goal is to average 7,500 in attendance per game at the seventy-two home games, the team will need to sell a grand total of 540,000 tickets. The ticket sales booked to multi-game package buyers is 184,510, which means that 355,490 tickets will need to be sold to single-game buyers and groups to reach the attendance target.

Another metric that quantifies season ticket sales effectiveness is **full-season equivalents** (FSEs), which is the total tickets sold in multi-game packages divided by the number of games or events in a full season. In the minor league baseball team example, FSEs would be calculated as follows:

$$FSE = \frac{184,510 \text{ tickets}}{72 \text{ games}}$$

$$= 2,563$$

The FSE figure means that the team has sold the equivalent of 2,563 full-season tickets. In an economic environment in which consumers may be more reluctant to commit spending discretionary income on full-season tickets, partial-season plans take on greater importance. FSE can be calculated post-campaign to determine actual sales, and it can be used pre-campaign for renewals and new customer sales to determine the mix of full-season and partial-season packages that are needed in order for the organization to reach its unit sales goals for tickets.

PREMIUM SEATING. A category that has grown significantly in importance and revenue potential for sports properties is **premium seating**, which includes special seating areas in a sports venue such as boxes, club areas, and suites as well as seats with unique vantage points such as between the benches at an NHL arena. Premium seat customers are largely businesses that use tickets to sporting events as client hospitality opportunities or as rewards for employees. Also, customers in this category may be individuals with high incomes who value the amenities and experience of a premium seat location. In some cases, premium seating represents two commitments by a buyer: 1) rental or purchase of premium space such as a box or suite and 2) purchase of tickets for events. Alternatively, a property may set an all-inclusive price for premium seat locations and event tickets.

Premium seating appeals to certain segments of customers, but just like any other product, buyers' changing needs and desires require adapting strategies to maximize revenues in this category. Recent developments in premium seating include:

- Lower demand for club seating – Club seats typically have been located in the mid-level area of a stadium or arena. The number of customers placing high value on those locations has decreased in recent years.

- Relocation of premium seats – As mid-level locations of club seats have fallen out of favor somewhat, some sports properties have experimented with moving some high-dollar seating areas close to (or on) playing surface level. The St. Louis Rams added twenty-four seats behind each end zone on field level, just nine feet from the end line. These limited seats were offered only to suite customers for an additional $5,000 and sold out quickly.[13] These premium locations are few in number, and the scarcity of availability fuels demand and the price that can be asked.

- Resizing of suites – New venues that included suites during a construction boom in the 1990s and 2000s often featured suites seating twelve to eighteen people. A one-size-fits-all approach to marketing suites simply does not work today. Many venues have remodeled parts of their suite inventory to create smaller suites that target groups of six to ten people.

- Changing suite usage arrangements – The typical suite customer is a corporate buyer that commits to a full season or year. However, the economic recession that hit businesses forced a pullback on discretionary spending such as suite leases at sports venues. Many sports properties responded to this change in the marketing environment by allowing corporate customers to share a suite or committing to shorter contract periods.[14]

Despite changes in needs and buying patterns of premium seat customers, this category will continue to be a key to revenue growth given that the target market typically has available buying power and values the experiential benefits of premium seats.

INDIVIDUAL EVENT TICKETS. Driving revenue growth from ticket sales for individual events is a challenge that varies among sports properties. Some events are held only once or infrequently such as a college football bowl game or a college basketball conference tournament. In these situations, selling multi-game tickets is less important, or in the case of a one-time event, irrelevant, compared to maximizing sales for a single event. On the other hand, sports properties that have lengthy season schedules are challenged with selling tickets for dozens of games. In most cases, the market reality is that an NBA or NHL team cannot sell out all forty-one home games, nor can an MLB team sell out all eighty-one home games. Thus, strategies are needed to maximize sales of specific games or events in order to increase total ticket sales revenues for the season.

Maximizing sales of individual events can be managed by analysis of advance sales versus walk-up sales. **Advance sales** refer to the number of tickets sold prior to the day of a scheduled event. Customers who buy multi-game ticket packages help drive the number of advance ticket sales. Also, events for which a high level of customer interest exists can create higher demand. Buyers may be inclined to buy tickets as a response to perceived scarcity of tickets. **Walk-up sales** are tickets sold to customers on the day of the event, with walk-up referring to buyers arriving at the event venue without a ticket and seeking to buy tickets on-site.

Advance sales are vital to an organization's financial success for two reasons. First, advance sales represent revenue certainty; it is business that has been booked. Like other services, a sporting event is perishable, meaning that there is only one opportunity to sell tickets for any given event. When the event is over, it is over! Second, generating advance sales not only enhances revenues, it can reduce marketing expenses if additional advertising and promotion is not needed to move unsold ticket inventory at the last minute prior to an event. Similarly, proactively managing advance sales can minimize the number of unsold tickets as an event date

Advance ticket sales are important to sports properties.

approaches. Deep price discounts that take away from revenue potential can be avoided if advance sales are healthy.

Advance sales can be emphasized as a tactic that rewards buyer commitment. The Michigan International Speedway (MIS) has gone away from a traditional pricing model of offering price discounts for unsold tickets to late buyers in favor of offering early buyers the lowest prices. When the track hosted two NASCAR Sprint Cup Series races in June and August, general admission tickets for the races could be purchased for $10 if bought by the end of January. Price of the same ticket increased to $25 if purchased in February and $30 in March. An MIS executive remarked that "fans are appreciating the fact that we aren't dumping tickets on the market. If we have 20,000 unsold seats, so be it. We're going to try to be loyal to fans who buy early."[15] This approach to managing advance ticket sales can be positioned as a customer-focused approach to pricing as well as a strategy for maximizing ticket revenues.

GROUP TICKETS. Marketing sports to groups can be an effective strategy for selling excess ticket inventory and attracting new individual ticket buyers. The definition of the number of people that comprise a group varies among sports properties, although a minimum of twenty tickets is common as a requirement for a group to be eligible for special pricing. Prospective group clients include businesses, schools, churches, nonprofit organizations, and youth sports teams.

Groups represent an attractive customer segment because of their buying power. One sale could mean anywhere from twenty tickets to several hundred tickets. From the standpoint of ticketing operations, it is much more efficient to make a sale to a group of fifty people than to sell fifty tickets through twenty-five transactions of two tickets each. The impact groups can have on ticket revenues as well as other revenue streams like parking, food and beverage, and merchandise is significant. In the 2009–2010 season, five NBA teams (Chicago, Denver, Detroit, New Jersey, and Washington) averaged at least 3,000 group tickets per game.[16] Over the course of a forty-one-game home schedule, this level of group sales activity means that more than 120,000 customers attend games, many of whom may have attended primarily because of their relationship with a group.

Ticket sales managers may seek to maximize sales of tickets to groups, but the desire to sell to groups should have limits. One consideration is the difference in pricing offered to groups and loyal customers who purchase partial- or full-season ticket plans. A member of a group receives a discount because of the group's buying power, but an individual customer within a group may have little or no loyalty toward a team. Yet that person may buy at a price that is comparable (if not lower) than prices offered to loyal customers. Just as team marketers set price floors in dynamic pricing programs to prevent an individual buyer from enjoying lower prices than season ticket buyers, pricing for group tickets should strike a balance between discounting to reward buying power and protecting the value proposition of being a season ticket holder.

A second consideration is whether a cap is needed on the number of group tickets made available for any given event. Selling groups is a proven tactic for filling seats for events that have relatively low customer demand, whether it is due to time of year, day of week, or quality of opponent. But in other cases demand variables may work in favor of a marketer and more tickets can be sold at regular or premium prices. In these situations, selling groups could negatively impact ticket revenues, as discounted tickets sold to groups could have been sold for higher prices. Ticket sales managers can analyze historical sales data, advance ticket sales, and other variables such as team performance and appearance of star players on opposing teams when making decisions on whether a maximum number of group ticket sales should be set for a given event and what that figure should be.

SECONDARY TICKET MARKET. A fifth category of ticket revenues has emerged in recent years, one which had been nonexistent for sports properties, but had been around for many years. It is the **secondary ticket market**, or the market for selling tickets purchased from a sports property. Season ticket holders, entrepreneurs, and individuals have different motives for reselling tickets. The large number of events in the season schedule for MLB, NBA, and NHL teams makes it difficult for season ticket holders to attend every game. Thus, selling tickets is a means of recouping some of their ticket expense. For others, buying tickets to prime events and reselling in the secondary market is a for-profit endeavor. The image many people hold of ticket resellers is people standing on street corners near sports venues hawking tickets, often scalping tickets to high-demand events. Today, ticket reselling has gone high tech, as websites like StubHub, TicketsNow, and Vivid Seats connect sellers and buyers of tickets for sports, music, and theater.

As the secondary ticket market became more sophisticated with the emergence of ticket reseller websites, it became clear that one party was missing out on revenues for marquee events: the properties that sold the tickets in the first place. While a sports property profits from the sale of tickets in the primary market, tickets that change hands in the secondary market are transactions between the ticket owner and secondary buyer. This arrangement means that properties stand to receive no revenues from tickets sold for more than face value on the secondary market. That is, unless a property decides to take on a role to help facilitate transactions in the secondary market.

Some organizations have taken a proactive approach to the secondary ticket market by joining forces with their ticketing partner to create a marketplace for their customers to sell tickets on the secondary market. The most notable participant in the secondary ticket market is Ticketmaster, which has signed deals with more than fifty professional sports teams to be their official secondary ticket provider. The Ticketmaster Ticket Exchange is the secondary market service that teams encourage (and in some cases require) their season ticket holders to use for reselling tickets. Teams receive a fee from their ticket resale partner, and the reseller collects a percentage of the transaction price from the seller and buyer.[17] Rather than settle for being a bystander in the secondary ticket market, sports properties can create revenues by partnering with ticket resellers to make fan-to-fan ticket sales possible.

Another way that managers can benefit from monitoring the secondary ticket market is to observe pricing trends for tickets for their events. Ticket reseller websites are an electronic marketplace where sellers can set a dollar value on tickets and buyers are free to choose whether to meet a seller's offer, even if that offer is a price that is above the face value paid for the ticket in the primary market. This characteristic of ticket reseller websites suggests that they can be used as sources of information to assist in decisions on selling prices for event tickets. Also, a website like SeatGeek (www.seatgeek.com) that provides a centralized listing of offers by ticket resellers can be used to monitor fans' interest as measured by prices in the secondary market. For example, a review of the secondary market for NBA teams revealed average prices in a seven-day period ranged from a high of $156.21 for tickets to games involving the Los Angeles Lakers to a low of $28.77 for Utah Jazz games.[18] These data can be valuable for linking ticket prices to fan interest, particularly if a property uses a dynamic pricing model in which prices can fluctuate up or down in response to consumer demand.

Sponsorships

The contribution of revenue from sponsorships to an organization's total revenues can be analyzed through use of financial metrics. Figure 12.8 identifies sponsorship-related measures that can be quantified by sports properties.

FIGURE 12.8
Sponsorship Metrics

- Sponsorship inventory sold
- Rights fees paid by corporate partners
- Sponsorship renewals secured

One step that sponsorship managers should take is to develop an inventory of all marketable assets that are potentially of interest to current or prospective sponsors. Examples of assets that would appear on a sports property's inventory appear in Figure 12.9. When sponsorship assets are grouped in a manner like that shown, opportunities to market unsold assets can be identified. The sample inventory list identifies four categories of sponsorship assets a sports property might have. The number and marketability of assets a property possesses varies, but developing a comprehensive list of the assets that can be sold to corporate sponsors captures existing sponsorship relationships as well as identifies targets for corporate partnership personnel to pursue new business.

FIGURE 12.9 Example of a Sponsorship Asset Inventory

Facility	Business Categories	Promotions	Special Events
Facility naming rights	Community partners	Giveaways	Off-site events
Practice areas	Image partners	Promotions	Fan conventions
Parking lots	Endemic partners	Themed events	
Gates/entrances		In-game contests	
Premium dining areas			
Club seating areas			
Turnstiles			
Seating areas			
Seats/cup holders			

An asset category often overlooked is the business category. Community partners are key firms in a sports property's area that are well known and respected. **Image partners** can sponsor a particular audience that is a good match for the sports property. The American Express sponsorship of the U.S. Open tennis and the PGA Tour are good examples of image partners. **Endemic partners** are sponsored products that are associated with a sport or event because of a logical fit, such as Gatorade and the NFL.

The most evident measure pertaining to rights fees is total rights fees revenue realized from sponsorships. The length of sponsorship agreements varies from annual deals to multiyear contracts. A lower-level sponsorship may require only a one-year commitment by corporate partners. The advantage of one-year deals is the ease with which companies can enter and exit sponsorships. The disadvantage is that corporate partnership account executives may spend a great deal of time engaged in securing commitments for renewals of these short-term deals. In contrast, a property can encourage longer commitments from corporate partners by offering to lock in rights fees for the duration of the agreement. The amount sponsors pay may be a fixed amount each year for the length of the contract, or rights fees over the course of a contract can be a first-year fee with subsequent years' fees based on the initial fee plus annual escalators.

An **escalator** is a dollar or percentage increase in rights fees after the first year of an agreement. It is similar to a cost-of-living adjustment. Fixed fees or fees with escalators provide cost certainty to sponsors. They know exactly the investment required for their association with a sports property. Achieving cost certainty can be beneficial in the event that rights fees increase substantially due to a property's success, greater interest among fans, or some other development that enhances a sports property's value as a marketing vehicle.

Suppose a bank signs a five-year sponsorship agreement with a college basketball team to be "Official Financial Services Partner" that requires a first year fee of $30,000 plus a 4%

escalator in years two through five; the bank's sponsorship commitment would be calculated as shown in Figure 12.10. The second year rate is figured by multiplying the $30,000 for Year 1 by 1.04, which represents the 4% increase. Year 3's rate is Year 2 times the 1.04, and so on. This process provides for a 4% increase in the sponsorship rights fee per year.

Initial fee (Year 1)	$30,000
Year 2	$31,200
Year 3	$32,448
Year 4	$33,746
Year 5	$35,096
Total	**$162,490**

FIGURE 12.10 **Example of Rights Fees with 4% Escalator**

In this scenario, a property would increase sponsorship revenues over offering rights for a locked-in rate of $30,000 annually for the length of the contract. The property would earn a total of $162,490 instead of $150,000 without the escalator clause. The sponsor could benefit from this multiyear arrangement by knowing the exact cost of the sponsorship over the five-year period. If the value of sponsorships would increase substantially due to success of the sports property, the bank is locked in and would not have to renegotiate every year the rights fee that is requested by the sports property.

Retail Services

For sports properties that hold events or games, doing business with patrons on-site is an important contributor to an organization's financial picture. Revenue from foodservice sales represents opportunities that arise from a customer's lengthy stay at a sports venue, which can range from a couple of hours to the better part of a day. Sales of products and souvenirs at retail, whether it be on-site at sporting events, online, or through licensing agreements with manufacturers, create a revenue stream that taps the affinity fans have for their favorite teams and players. While these revenues are important to the financial success of a sports organization, measurement of merchandising revenues entails more than totaling revenues generated from foodservice, retail sales, and licensing. Managers can use metrics that allow a deeper analysis of business performance and serve to give direction on making decisions to grow merchandising revenues.

Performance measurement in foodservice and on-site retail operations has tended to focus on a single metric: per capita expenditures, better known as per cap. **Per cap revenue** is the dollar amount spent on average by attendees at a sporting event. For example, if a minor league hockey team made $62,000 in foodservice sales for one game that was attended by 6,000 people, the per cap for that game would be determined as follows:

$$Per Cap Expenditures = \$62,000 / 6,000 = \$10.33$$

In this situation, an average of $10.33 was spent by each person at the game on food and drinks. A per cap figure can be calculated separately for foodservice and retail sales, or a per cap number can be determined that reflects total consumer spending. Calculating separate per caps for foodservice and retail sales would give greater insight by showing the contribution of each area to total per cap spending. Also, if per cap revenue is tracked for each event, patterns or trends of patron spending can be uncovered and tactical responses made to grow this revenue stream. Suppose a review of per caps for a minor league baseball team reveals that Tuesdays tend to have lower per cap figures than other days. Foodservice managers may then want to consider developing promotions on Tuesdays that give incentives to customers to spend more on food and beverage.

An alternative to a focus on total revenue and per caps that is advocated by one sports foodservice company is to use what it calls "total return" as a measure of effectiveness. Centerplate, which has more than one hundred sports venue clients, views **total return** as a function of margin earned on each transaction coupled with the number of transactions, referred to by the company as **velocity**. Thus, the formula for measuring performance is:

$$Total Return = Margin \times Velocity[19]$$

Figure 12.11 illustrates a very simple calculation of total return for just eight items. The margin for each item is determined by subtracting the costs from the sales price. The velocity is the number of transactions that occurred during the game or event. The return is the product of the margin times the velocity. For soft drinks it is the margin of $2.25 times the velocity of 2,754. The total return for the eight items was $21,912

FIGURE 12.11 Example of Calculation of Total Return

Item	Sales price	Costs	Margin	Velocity	Return
Soft drink	$4.00	$1.75	$2.25	2,754	$6,196.50
Hamburger	$6.00	$3.22	$2.78	1,143	$3,177.54
Hotdog	$3.00	$1.85	$1.15	1,843	$2,119.45
Nachos	$8.50	$4.68	$3.82	924	$3,529.68
Popcorn	$7.50	$4.10	$3.40	748	$2,543.20
T-shirt	$28.00	$18.75	$9.25	83	$767.75
Cap	$22.00	$14.59	$7.41	91	$674.31
Game program	$5.00	$3.10	$1.90	1,528	$2,903.20
Total Return					**$21,911.63**

This approach to measuring the financial impact of an operation gives a relatively simple prescription for increasing performance in any of the specific areas by either: 1) increasing margins or 2) increasing velocity (number of transactions). The prescription may be simple, but the "how" behind the prescription is more challenging. The Centerplate example makes the point that marketers do not measure performance simply for the sake of creating a scorecard. Performance measures that have clearly defined inputs such as margin and velocity give direction on how marketing mix elements such as price, product offerings, and customer service impact financial results.

Challenges in Measuring Performance

Despite the importance of establishing performance measures that align marketing activities with brand strategy, determine effectiveness of marketing tactics, and guide decisions on adjusting strategies, implementing a measurement program is not necessarily a simple process. All marketing organizations are vulnerable to three limitations of performance measurement: 1) uncontrollable factors that affect marketing or financial performance, 2) selecting appropriate measures related to desired outcomes of marketing strategy, and 3) pinpointing the impact of a marketing tactic on the intended response. For sports marketers, each of these three limitations has situations or characteristics that are specific to the sports industry. Managers must recognize the limitations yet plan and carry out performance measurement to bring closure to the strategic planning cycle.

Uncontrollable Factors

An often mentioned point throughout this book has been that on-field performance is out of a marketer's control but can impact marketing and financial performance. Because this characteristic of marketing sports is significant, it must be considered. In the case of marketing a team, developments such as a star player being traded, poor performance eliminating a team from playoff contention, or a style of play that fans find unappealing are all potential contributors to decreased revenues. When a customer experiences disappointment with a product, it can lead to the decision to stop using the brand. Sports brands are not immune to this possibility despite fans' emotional connections with a team or players.

Other factors beyond the control of marketers that could impact marketing and financial performance are the quality of opponents or events, weather conditions, and economic factors. For professional sports leagues, game scheduling is done at the league level and choice of opponents usually is not an option. Teams in the NBA and NHL may have input on days of week they prefer home games scheduled and starting time, but otherwise the attractiveness of their home schedule will be determined at a league level. Weather can wreak havoc on financial performance, particularly for properties that rely on large walk-up sales, or sales that occur on the day an event is scheduled. Regardless of the size of a property's walk-up sales, revenue stands to take a hit in the form of lost sales in foodservice and merchandise if bad weather postpones games or discourages fans from attending.

Unlike the first two factors, which are largely out of a sports marketer's control, economic factors are more conducive to being addressed through marketing strategies that take into account lower consumer spending and confidence. Examples have been cited in previous chapters of how many sports properties have refined their value propositions to give customers lower-cost alternatives for products such as tickets, food and beverage, and merchandise. However, even when marketing strategy can be adapted to respond to economic shifts, a negative effect on an organization's financial picture may still be felt. Economic downturns may happen so quickly that they are not factored into an organization's profit projections, and missing profit goals can impact nonmarketing areas of operations such as monies available to invest in player personnel.

Selecting Appropriate Measures

Measurement is a mindset that must be embraced by top management and shared throughout all levels of a firm, but committing to measure is only part of the challenge. Selecting which outcomes to measure is vital to the contribution that measurement can make to an organization. Specifically, performance measurement should focus on two areas: 1) metrics directly related to financial outcomes (e.g., ticket sales, profit, foodservice revenue) and 2) metrics indirectly related to financial outcomes (e.g., radio broadcast ratings, reach of social media platforms). For these two categories, the common characteristic is that metrics used focus on *results*, not *activity*. For example, measurement of marketing activities such as number of e-mails sent to a permission marketing list, amount spent on a billboard advertising campaign, or number of sales presentations made by account executives do not relate to the two categories of metrics described above. Ultimately, metrics should focus on marketing's impact on consumers and financial health of the organization.

Even when managers select metrics that focus on customer and financial impacts, the number and mix of metrics used are important to meet measurement's goals of post-implementation evaluation and more informed strategic planning. A focus on one or few metrics could provide an incomplete picture of brand performance and health. In team sports, marketers obsess with ticket sales and attendance figures, but attendance numbers alone may not fully reflect fan

It is challenging to choose appropriate measures for events such as Coca-Cola's involvement with the Food Lion Speed Festival in Charlotte, North Carolina, during the Coca-Cola 600 NASCAR event.

interest in the brand. If a team's average attendance per game is below plan but audience ratings for radio broadcasts are ahead of the previous year and revenue per customer from concessions and merchandise (i.e., per cap) is higher, consideration of multiple measures may reveal that brand strength may be greater than the lone measure of average attendance suggests.

Similarly, utilization of multiple metrics may lead to a conclusion that a single metric may overstate long-term brand strength. If a team experiences an increase in average attendance per game, marketers may be tempted to point to the gain as evidence of enhanced brand performance. However, if a financial metric like average ticket price shows a decrease and a marketing metric such as number of Facebook fans reveals slowed growth or is below comparable sports brands, brand performance is likely not as positive as the average attendance measure suggests. In summary, managers must select appropriate outcomes to measure and employ multiple metrics in an effort to get a comprehensive view of marketing and financial performance.

Determining Impact

Perhaps the greatest challenge in measuring the effectiveness of marketing is the availability of information that enables isolation of the incremental impact of a marketing tactic. For sports properties, this dilemma surfaces frequently when attempting to measure the effect of a marketing communications tactic on customer behavior. If a bobble-head doll giveaway is held, how persuasive was the promotion in attracting buyers who bought tickets because of the giveaway? Promotion effectiveness can be assessed in terms of the number of items given away, time elapsed before the giveaway items were handed out, or change in attendance on the date of the promotion compared to average attendance. Still, none of these measures truly answer the

Insider Insights Tom Hoof – Tampa Bay Rays

Q. What is the importance of measuring marketing performance for a Major League Baseball franchise like the Tampa Bay Rays?

A. In baseball, the season is six months long. Organizations spend months analyzing and planning for the season. Strong planning based on facts enables teams to put together strategic marketing plans that will attract fans to the ballpark. Teams that know their fan base well can also react to events that occur during the season. If the season is going well, perhaps the messaging is adjusted to talk about postseason. If something special occurs like a no-hitter, a team can put together something quickly targeting a specific segment of consumers that will help get results. Teams armed with as much information as possible can make the best strategic and tactical decisions.

Q. Performance measurement often is an afterthought, with most attention focused on formulating marketing strategies and executing them. Why should sports organizations place a greater emphasis on assessing marketing effectiveness?

A. Most sports fans judge teams by the win/loss record and by the number of people attending games. For a sports marketer, brand performance is so much more than just wins and losses and attendance. The organization needs to know what is successful, what is working, what has potential, and what should be discontinued. Teams spend

Tom Hoof explains the importance of measuring performance.

a lot of money on a variety of entertainment items: concerts, giveaways, fan experience enhancements, cleaning, and merchandise just to name a few. Teams develop a variety of metrics to see if these are working for the consumer. Budgets are limited. They must be utilized as wisely as possible. Management needs to have as much information at its disposal as possible to be able to focus resources.

Q. Can you give an example of how a sports property could use measurement to set or adapt marketing strategy?

A. Let's say an organization features a special giveaway every Tuesday night. The organization spends ad dollars, promotional dollars, and manpower on its Tuesday night efforts. It sees a slight increase in attendance, but not much. The organization would see better attendance on Tuesdays than other weeknights. Through research, however, it is discovered the potential increase in attendance would be better if resources were focused on weekends. The organization switched all of its advertising and promotional efforts to weekends. It experienced dramatic increases on Fridays, Saturdays, and Sundays, and a slight decrease on Tuesdays. Plus, since Tuesday featured a two-for-one ticket, and the weekend efforts did not, it increased the revenue as well. Without measurement, without research, the team would have never had the information on hand to be able to make this decision.

question "How many customers were attracted by the promotion?" Similarly, if a postgame concert after a Seattle Mariners game targets nonfans of baseball, how can a manager determine that the event succeeded in attracting people who usually do not attend Mariners games? Consumer-targeted research in the form of surveys is about the only way to capture information that can pinpoint marketing's impact on buyer behavior.

Corporate sponsors wrestle with the issue of determining impact of their investments, too. While sponsorship managers would be thrilled to be able to demonstrate to their superiors an X-causes-Y relationship between sponsorship investment and customer impact, the reality is that a lack of direct measures makes it is rather difficult to determine sponsorship's effectiveness. Some outcomes related to sponsorship exposure are rather easy to pinpoint. For example, brand awareness measured before a sponsorship launches compared with awareness levels during or after the time period of a sponsorship leads to conclusions about a sponsorship's impact on changing brand awareness among the target market. However, higher-level sponsorship objectives such as product purchase and brand loyalty are harder to attribute to a single marketing tactic like a sponsorship. Other variables can factor into a buying decision, making it difficult to establish a direct link between sponsorship and sales. Lack of effective measures has long been cited as a limitation of using sponsorship in brand communication programs.

Chapter Summary

In an effort to increase revenues, many sports properties have looked at new models for pricing. Variable pricing involves using different price schedules based on demand issues, such as seat location, time of the game, day of the week, and date of the game. Dynamic pricing involves using technology to analyze supply and demand to yield the optimal price point to increase ticket sales.

Measuring marketing performance is important because it 1) aligns marketing activities, 2) evaluates the effectiveness of marketing decisions, and 3) lays the foundation for making adjustments to the marketing strategy. Performance can be measured after a season is over to evaluate the results and then can be used as inputs for the next marketing plan.

Types of marketing metrics that can be evaluated are brand communications, media exposure, public relations, fan engagement, customer satisfaction, and return on investment. Direct measures of brand communications do not exist. Instead marketers need to measure concepts such as awareness, image, and personality. Media exposure is primarily measured in ratings, which is the total number or percentage of audience that is exposed to programming. Public relation efforts are typically measured by the number of community and charity events with which the sports property has involvement and the number of individuals affected. Customer engagement is often measured by the size of audience on social networking sites, such as Facebook, and the types of communication. It is both a quantitative and qualitative measure. Customer satisfaction can be measured by survey research, but also by renewal rates of season ticket holders and sponsorships. Return on investment (ROI) attempts to measure the impact of a marketing-related investment.

Financial metrics include ticket sales, sponsorship numbers, and merchandise sales. Financial metrics for ticket sales incorporate season tickets, premium seating, individual game tickets, group ticket sales, and the secondary ticket market. Sports teams often calculate full-season equivalents to quantify their season ticket sales effectiveness. The concept of premium seating has changed and now involves lower demand for club seating, relocation of premium seats, resizing of suites, and changes in suite seasons or arrangements. Individual ticket sales include both advance sales and walk-up sales. Sports teams are putting more emphasis on advance sales to maximize attendance at events and games. Teams are now becoming involved in secondary ticket markets to assist their fans in selling tickets and also to control the process and pricing of secondary tickets.

For sponsorships, financial metrics include level of sponsorship inventory sold, rights fees paid by corporate sponsors, and sponsorship renewals secured. Merchandising can be evaluated using the concepts of per cap revenue and total return.

Marketing organizations are vulnerable to three limitations in terms of measuring performance. First, uncontrollable factors can affect marketing and outcomes. Second, selecting appropriate measures related to the outcomes of marketing strategies is difficult. Third, pinpointing the impact of a marketing tactic on the intended response is challenging.

Review Questions

1. Explain the difference between variable pricing and dynamic pricing.
2. What are three reasons sports marketers should be concerned with measuring performance?
3. What are the six types of marketing metrics?
4. How can a sports property measure brand communications?
5. How can customer satisfaction be measured?
6. Why should sports teams use renewal rates for season ticket holders and sponsorships as a measure of customer satisfaction?
7. Why is return on investment (ROI) viewed as the ultimate measure of performance?
8. What are the three categories of financial metrics?
9. Identify the five types of financial metrics for ticket sales.
10. What is meant by the term "full-season equivalents" and why is it important?
11. What is the difference between advance sales and walk-up sales in season ticket sales? Which is more important? Why?
12. Why have sports properties become involved in the secondary ticket market?
13. Identify three financial metrics for measuring sponsorship performance.
14. In terms of measuring merchandising, explain the difference between per cap revenue and total return.
15. What are the three limitations to measuring marketing performance?

New Terms

Variable pricing establishes different prices based on demand and variables such as opponent, day of the week, and month of the year.

Dynamic pricing utilizes technology to continuously adjust prices based on supply and demand factors.

Full-season equivalents (FSEs) total tickets sold in multi-game packages divided by the number of games or events in a full season.

Premium seating special seating areas in sports venues.

Advance sales   tickets sold prior to the day of a game or event.

Walk-up sales tickets sold on the day of the event at the sports venue.

Secondary ticket market market for selling tickets purchased from a sports property to other customers.

Image partners sponsors whose brand associations are a good fit or match with a sport or event.

Endemic partners sponsored products that are associated with or related to a sport or event.

Escalator clause in a sponsorship agreement that calls for a dollar or percentage increase in rights fees after the first year of an agreement.

Per cap revenue dollar amount spent on average by attendees at a sporting event.

Total return function of margin earned on each transaction coupled with the number of transactions.

Velocity Number of transactions by customers at a sporting event or game.

Discussion and Critical Thinking Exercises

1. What do you think about variable pricing and dynamic pricing as a sports fan? Does it affect the types and quantity of tickets you purchase?
2. Examine the traits of the Tampa Bay Rays listed in Figure 12.2. If you were asked to prioritize these traits in terms of marketing to the Tampa community, which would be at the top of your list? Why? Assume the Rays have a limited marketing budget; rank the traits from highest to lowest. Explain your rankings.
3. Calculate the renewal rate for each of the following scenarios.
   a. A total of 836 season ticket holders, 627 were renewed.

    b. A total of 1,539 season ticket holders, 1,046 were renewed.

    c. A total of 32 sponsors, 24 renewed.

    d. A total of 18 sponsors, 13 renewed.

4. A sports property is considering selling five-game ticket packages for a special price of $28.50. Service costs and expenses associated with the package are $13.75. The marketing manager has requested $900 to advertise the special package and to send some direct mailers. Create a table similar to Figure 12.5 calculating the ROI for sales of 40, 60, 80, and 100 packages. What is the ROI for each sales amount?

5. Use the following data to construct a table similar to Figure 12.7 that shows the total tickets sold through multi-game and season ticket sales. What is the total number of tickets sold through multi-game and season ticket holders?

Game Package	Games in Package	Number Sold
Season Tickets	72	843
40-Game Plans	40	1537
20-Game Plans	20	1,952
10-Game Plans	10	2,845

6. Using the data from Question 5, how many total tickets would have to be sold to reach an average attendance of 6,000 at the seventy-two home games? How many single-game tickets would have to be sold to reach the goal? What is the full-season equivalent (FSEs) for the game packages?

7. Access www.stubhub.com, www.ticketsnow.com, and www.vividseats.com. Compare these secondary ticket market websites in terms of ease of use from the perspective of the seller, and of the buyer. Which site do you prefer? Why?

8. A business has been offered two different seven-year sponsorship deals. The first has an initial fee of $90,000 the first year and an escalator of 8% each the following six years. The second has an initial fee of $100,000 with a 4% escalator clause. Calculate the amount to be paid each year for both plans and total cost of the sponsorship. From the perspective of the business, which deal is the better option? Why?

9. The table below shows the total on-site revenue and attendance for a nine-game home stand for a MLB team. Calculate the per cap revenue for each game. Calculate a per cap revenue figure for the home stand. Which games and days of the week tend to have the highest per cap revenue?

Day of the Week	Total On-Site Revenue	Attendance	Per Cap Revenue
Friday, Game 1	$643,217	32,465	
Saturday, Game 2	$991,653	40,639	
Sunday, Game 3	$988,792	44,276	
Tuesday, Game 4	$527,984	28,410	
Wednesday, Game 5	$580,539	31,863	
Thursday, Game 6	$369,421	21,328	
Friday, Game 7	$577,842	29,231	
Saturday, Game 8	$891,927	35,294	
Sunday, Game 9	$864,357	37,282	
Total for home stand	$6,435,732	300,788	

10. The table below shows prices and costs of selected menu items for a sports property's foodservice operations. The velocity for a recent game is shown in the fifth column. Calculate the margin for each item and the return for each item. Calculate the total return for all five menu items. Which menu items have the highest return? Which ones have the highest margin per unit?

Item	Sales Price	Costs	Margin	Velocity	Return
Soft drink	$3.00	$1.40		27,432	
Hamburger	$5.00	$2.70		10,252	
Hot dog	$2.00	$0.80		22,830	
Nachos	$3.00	$2.10		3,426	
Popcorn	$4.00	$1.75		2,948	
				Total Return	

You Make the Call

Jacksonville Suns

Professional baseball in Jacksonville, Florida, has a history that stretches back more than a hundred years. Jacksonville made its minor league debut in 1904 as the Jacksonville Jays competed in the South Atlantic League. During the first half of the 20th century, Jacksonville fielded teams at different times in the South Atlantic League, Florida State League, and Southeastern League under names including Scouts, Tarpons, Roses, Indians, and Tars. The Suns were a member of the Southern League in 1953 when it had one of the first African-American players in the league, a 19-year-old prospect named Hank Aaron.

In 1970, the Suns became a member of the Class AA Southern League, and the franchise holds the distinction of the longest-running affiliation with the Southern League. Sam W. Wolfson Baseball Park, which was its home from 1962 until 2002, lacked amenities that appealed to the desires of today's sports spectators. The answer to this problem was a new home; the Baseball Grounds of Jacksonville opened in 2003. The new stadium can seat 11,000 fans, an increase of nearly 3,000 over the team's former home. The Baseball Grounds incorporates the best of the past and present in its design. Retro design features include the stadium's brick façade, a grass seating area in the outfield, and a bleacher seating area. Modern amenities blended with the nostalgic features include a video scoreboard, luxury skyboxes and sky deck, in-seat concession service in certain sections, and a souvenir shop. The payoff for the new stadium was immediate; nearly 360,000 people attended Suns game in the inaugural season of the Baseball Grounds in 2003, a leap from 230,000 the previous year.

The move to a new stadium for the Jacksonville Suns led to attendance gains typical of what a team experiences when opening a new venue. Academic researchers have dubbed this phenomenon a novelty effect, which means that a new facility attracts visitors curious to check out the amenities and experience of attending a game there. Unfortunately, increases in attendance are often short-lived, as by as early as the second season in a new stadium attendance decreases are noticed. Although annual attendance in a new stadium usually is higher after the novelty fades than in the final seasons in the previous home, financial performance related to ticket, concessions, and merchandise sales is not sustained after a strong start. Over time, the Suns have found that they were not immune to the novelty effect. The move to the Baseball Grounds of Jacksonville has paid off for the team in that the Suns have led the Southern League in attendance every season since the stadium opened in 2003. Average attendance for the Suns in 2010 was nearly 1,000 per game higher than any other team in the league, a trend that has been consistent since 2003.

Despite the success of the Suns at the box office compared to the rest of the Southern League, annual attendance trends show the presence of the novelty effect. A review of attendance figures shows the peak occurred in the 2004 at 420,495. By 2010, attendance was down 12% from 2004. The decline in attendance may be surprising to some people given the team's success. The Suns won the Southern League championship in 2009 and 2010, yet average attendance per game was down by 300 from 2008. In 2011, the Suns hit a low point for the new stadium of 4,419 average attendance, which was a sharp 13% decrease from the previous year (see Figure 12.12).

The Jacksonville Suns is in an enviable position, as the team has won back-to-back Southern League championships and the Jacksonville market has very little head-to-head competition during the summer months. The Jacksonville Jaguars are the top pro team in the market, but its season has little overlap with the Suns schedule. Other competition includes collegiate baseball at the University

Year	Attendance	# Dates	Average
2011	309,310	70	4,419
2010	354,725	69	5,141
2009	354,553	69	5,138
2008	364,365	67	5,438
2007	396,012	69	5,739
2006	404,992	70	5,786
2005	359,957	67	5,372
2004	420,495	67	6,276
2003	359,979	66	5,454

FIGURE 12.12
Jacksonville Suns Attendance, 2003–2011

of North Florida, Jacksonville University, and to a lesser extent, Florida State University. Direct competition from these teams is limited to the early part of the Southern League season (April and May). The Suns can take pride in consistently being the top-drawing team in the Southern League, but the team's average attendance represents just under half of the capacity of the Baseball Grounds of Jacksonville. A goal of increasing ticket sales revenue requires analysis of pricing for individuals and groups, breakdown of dates for the team's seventy home games, and developing promotional tactics that will stir fan interest and drive attendance to Suns games.

A summary of options for purchasing tickets is given in Figure 12.13. Full-season tickets offer the greatest value on a per game basis, with that price reflecting a discount of 40% to 50% compared to the price of a single-game ticket. However, a seventy-game commitment can be difficult for customers to make, so the Suns offer four other multi-game ticket options that offer discounts to single-game prices, although not as great as price breaks full-season ticket holders enjoy. Prices for single-game tickets are the same every game; the Suns do not use variable or dynamic pricing strategies to adjust prices for individual games.

Option	# Games or Tickets	Price
Full-Season Ticket	70 games	Dugout Box = $795 Home Plate Box = $550 Reserved Seat = $450
Weekender Plan	33 (all Fri., Sat., & Sun. games plus opening night)	Dugout Box = $425 Home Plate Box = $295 Reserved Seat = $235
Fireworks Plan	14 (all Fri. games plus July 2–3 & Sept. 4)	Home Plate Box = $155 Reserved Seat = $125
Flex Plan	10 tickets (reserved seat for any available games)	$120
Tickets on Demand	100 tickets - can be used in any quantity for any game	Home Plate Box = $1,100
Single-Game Ticket	1 game	Dugout Box = $22.50 Home Plate Box = $13.50 Reserved Seat = $10.50 Bleacher/Berm = $6.50

FIGURE 12.13
Jacksonville Suns Individual Ticket Options

Another category of ticket sales critical to increasing attendance is groups. The Suns offers discounted pricing to groups of twenty-five people or more. Figure 12.14 shows discounted pricing for three tiers of groups: 25–99, 100–499, and more than 500. Typical group discounts for groups of

**FIGURE 12.14
Jacksonville Suns
Group Ticket Options**

Seating	1–24	25–99	100–499	500+
Dugout Box	$22.50	$19.50	N/A	N/A
Home Plate Box	$13.50	$11.50	$10.50	$9.50
Reserved	$10.50	$8.50	$7.50	$6.50
Bleacher Berm	$7.50	$6.50	$5.50	$4.50

25–99 people range from 9% to 19%. The $2 discount of a reserved seat ticket may not seem like a huge deal for group members, but at a nearly 20% discount it is a notable price break.

In addition to exploring revenue creation options in pricing structure for tickets, any plan for growing ticket sales should include a review of the dates on which games will be held. Each date or game can be thought of as a product; unfortunately, there is only one opportunity to sell any given date—then it is gone forever. Thus, the Suns marketing staff should examine the schedule to identify key selling opportunities and develop tactics to maximize ticket sales. A breakdown of the Suns' schedule is given in Figure 12.15, looking at home dates by month and day of week.

**FIGURE 12.15
Jacksonville Suns
Game Schedule
Analysis**

	Monday	Tuesday	Wednesday	Thursday	Friday	Saturday	Sunday	Total
Apr.	2	1	1	1	1	2	2	10
May	3	2	1	2	2	1	1	12
Jun.	1	3	3	3	2	2	2	16
Jul.	1	0	1	1	3	3	4	13
Aug.	2	3	2	2	2	2	1	14
Sept.	1	0	0	1	1	1	1	5
Total	10	9	8	10	11	11	11	70

A variable that could be a key to increasing attendance at Jacksonville Suns games is the promotions created to attract fans. With a seventy-game home schedule to sell, the Suns have a promotion scheduled for virtually every date. Ticket specials, giveaways, special events, and fireworks well known throughout minor league baseball are standard fare for the team's promotional schedule. Promotion decisions are aligned with demand. For example, fireworks are scheduled on Fridays, when more people are looking for entertainment. Similarly, giveaways and events like concerts are done with Friday or Saturday games. The promotional schedule for days with lower attendance such as Mondays and Tuesdays focuses on value-oriented deals like Fifty-Cent Family Feast Night and Kraft Singles Tuesday Night ticket promotion.

The Jacksonville Suns and its marketing department find themselves in a precarious situation. A strange statement, perhaps, given the success the team has had on the field and at the box office. However, the reality is that attendance is about a thousand per game less than the best attendance year from its peak.

Questions:

1. Review Figure 12.13. How would you evaluate the Jacksonville Suns' ticket options for individuals? Too many options? Too few options? A good mix of options? Explain.
2. Should the Suns adopt a form of variable pricing, whether it is charging higher prices for certain games, charging higher prices for walk-up purchases, or some other variable pricing structure? Support your position.
3. How would you recommend the Jacksonville Suns pursue growth in ticket revenue? Should the focus be on:
   a. increasing revenue on a per ticket basis
   b. increasing number of tickets sold by offering more price-based ticket promotions
   c. another approach
4. Review Figure 12.14. Would you propose any changes in the Suns' group ticket sales program? If yes, what changes would you propose and why? If no, why would you leave the group sales program as is?

5. The breakdown of games by month and day of week is given in Figure 12.15. In order to make decisions about scheduling investments of marketing dollars against this schedule, what data or information that is not provided in the case would be beneficial? Why?

6. Research on the Internet promotions that have been used for minor league baseball. Create a list of twelve promotions. Evaluate each one on the list and recommend seven promotions, one for each day of the week, for the Jacksonville Suns. Justify your choice of promotions.

Sources: "Baseball Grounds of Jacksonville," (2011), accessed February 26, 2011, at http://web.minorleaguebaseball.com/ballpark/page.jsp?ymd=20061206&content_id=147550&vkey=ballpark_t564&fext=.jsp&sid=t564, "Wacky Promotions Abound for Jacksonville Suns' New Season," (2010), April 8, accessed February 27, 2011, at http://jacksonville.com/entertainment/2010-04-07/story/getting-you-out-ball-games.

References

1. "2010–2011 Individual Game Tickets," (2010), accessed January 24, 2011, at http://sabres.nhl.com/club/page.htm?id=39501.
2. Don Muret, (2010), "Variable or Dynamic, Ticket Pricing Gets Fresh Look from Teams," *Sports Business Journal*, March 8, accessed January 22, 2011, at http://www.sportsbusinessdaily.com/Journal/Issues/2010/03/20100308/Facilities/Variable-Or-Dynamic-Ticket-Pricing-Gets-Fresh-Look-From-Teams.aspx.
3. Eric Fisher, (2010), "Ticketing's Changeup," *Sports Business Journal* May 31, 15–18.
4. Ibid.
5. Greg Wyshynski, (2009), "Are Hockey Fans, Scalpers Ready for 'Dynamic' Ticket Prices?" September 14, accessed April 8, 2010, at http://sports.yahoo.com/nhl/blog/puck_daddy/post/Are-hockey-fans-scalpers-ready-for-dynamic-ti?urn=nhl-189394.
6. "Sports Fan Graph," (2011), accessed October 14, 2011, at http://www.sportsfangraph.com/.
7. "Season-Ticket Revenue Ahead of '09," (2010), *Sports Business Journal*, June 14, accessed January 29, 2011, at http://www.sportsbusinessdaily.com/Journal/Issues/2010/06/20100614/This-Weeks-News/Season-Ticket-Revenue-Ahead-Of-09.aspx.
8. James D. Lenskold, *Marketing ROI* (New York: McGraw-Hill, 2003).
9. Bill King, (2010), "Always Be Closing," *Sports Business Journal*, March 15, 1, 21–22, 30.
10. "The Official Site of Minor League Baseball - Columbus Clippers Home Page," (2011), accessed February 4, 2011, at http://web.minorleaguebaseball.com/index.jsp?sid=t445.
11. "Field Level Full Season Tickets," (2011), accessed February 4, 2011, at http://web.minorleaguebaseball.com/tickets/page.jsp?ymd=20100318&content_id=8829104&vkey=tickets_t512&fext=.jsp&sid=t512.
12. "2011–2012 20-Game Season Tickets," (2011), accessed February 4, 2011, at http://www.providencebruins.com/View/Page/79.
13. Don Muret, (2010), "Field-Level Seats Get Patrons Close to the Action," *Sports Business Journal*, November 1, 19.
14. "Trends and Challenges," (2010), *Sports Business Journal*, November 1, 26–27.
15. Tripp Mickle, (2010), "Track Offers Deals for Early Birds," *Sports Business Journal*, October 18, 8.
16. "Cavs Among NBA Elite in Sales, Retention," (2010), *Sports Business Journal*, January 18, accessed February 9, 2011, at http://www.sportsbusinessdaily.com/Journal/Issues/2010/01/20100118/This-Weeks-News/Cavs-Among-NBA-Elite-In-Sales-Retention.aspx.
17. "Scalping Goes Upscale: The Secondary Ticket Market's Online Revolution," (2007), July 2, accessed February 9, 2011, at http://knowledge.wpcarey.asu.edu/article.cfm?articleid=1439.
18. "NBA Ticket Prices and Rankings," (2011), accessed February 9, 2011, at http://seatgeek.com/basketball-nba-ticket-prices/.
19. "Maximum Return," (2011), accessed February 16, 2011, at http://centerplate.com/clients/maximum-return.

13

Living the Brand Promise: Delivery of Sports Experiences

Learning Objectives

By the end of this chapter you should be able to:

1. Describe the components and management of service quality
2. Discuss the advantages and disadvantages of outsourcing marketing tasks
3. Identify marketing functions that can be outsourced

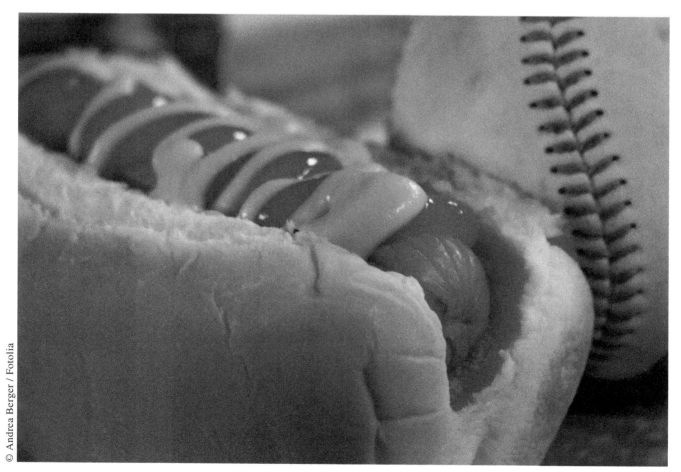

Good food service is important to the enjoyment of a sporting event.

© Andrea Berger / Fotolia

Customer Service Is Key Ingredient to Quality for Sportservice

Foodservice operations at sports venues have come a long way since 1915, the year that Delaware North Companies entered the hospitality management business. Today, its Sportservice unit is the foodservice partner for more than thirty professional sports venues across the United States. Concessions offerings at sports venues have evolved from basics such as hot dogs, popcorn, and peanuts to menus that rival quick-service restaurants in assortment and quality.

Insider Expert Jeff Gregor – Turner Broadcasting, Inc.

Jeff Gregor serves as executive vice president and chief marketing officer for TNT, TBS, TCM and General Manager of TCM. In this capacity, he leads all entertainment marketing and on-air promotions for the three networks, as well as their digital extensions. He also oversees TCM programming. Gregor is based in Atlanta and reports to Steve Koonin, president of Turner Entertainment Networks.

Jeff Gregor, VP and Chief Marketing Officer of TNT, TBS, and TCM.

Turner Broadcasting System

Gregor's duties as chief marketing officer of TNT, TBS, and TCM include oversight of three groups: the Entertainment Marketing Group, which involves all marketing strategies and campaigns to support network programming; the Brand Development/Digital Platforms/Festivals Group, covering brand management, expansion onto alternative platforms, and live events; and the Creative Group, which includes design, print, and on-air promotions.

As general manager of TCM, Gregor oversees marketing and programming. Gregor leads TCM's ongoing shift into a lifestyle brand, which includes enhancing the network's value to its affiliate partners; cultivating TCM's passionate fan base; diversifying network revenues with e-commerce initiatives; presenting special events such as the TCM Classic Film Festival; merchandising opportunities; and unique partnerships.

Gregor and his marketing team led the award winning and highly innovative launch campaign for Conan, Conan O'Brien's hit late-night series on TBS. Gregor also supervises campaigns for TNT's slate of high-profile original series, including *The Closer, Rizzoli & Isles, Dallas,*

and *Falling Skies.* For TBS, Gregor oversees marketing for the network's original sitcoms *Men At Work, Sullivan & Sons,* and Tyler Perry's *House of Payne, Meet the Browns* and *For Better or Worse.* For TCM, Gregor's team was responsible for campaigns behind the recent seven-part documentary series *Moguls & Movie Stars: A History of Hollywood* and for such annual events as *31 Days of Oscar,*® *Summer Under the Stars,* and the TCM Classic Film Festival.

Previously, Gregor served as senior vice president of sports marketing and programming for TNT and TBS. He developed campaigns for the NBA and NASCAR, and he led strategic planning and scheduling of sports programming, management of contractual agreements, and oversight of the sports units for TNT and TBS. Gregor's accomplishments included acclaimed promotional campaigns for the NBA All-Star game and its surrounding events.

Prior to joining TNT, Gregor served as director of sports asset management for the Coca-Cola Co., where he led marketing management and system utilization of key sponsorships with NASCAR, the NFL, the NBA, the NHL, and Major League Baseball. He also worked with Wunderman Cato Johnson, a Young & Rubicam marketing services agency, overseeing the Miller Brewing account group, and he held marketing sales positions with the Cleveland Indians and the Philadelphia Phillies.

Jeff is a native of East Chicago, Indiana. He holds a bachelor of arts in economics from Albion College in Michigan.

These improvements in foodservice operations can be attributed to what many sports properties have decided *not* to do: manage foodservice operations themselves. Outsourcing the foodservice business to a company like Sportservice puts responsibility for this aspect of the customer experience in the hands of experts. It also poses a challenge to foodservice operators to deliver value to sports properties and their customers in order to prove their worth and retain clients.

Sportservice is faced with satisfying two different customers: visitors that attend games and events and the teams or venues that hire the company. A key part of Sportservice's strategy to managing relationships with these two customer groups is to deliver outstanding customer service. At the heart of the company's customer service program is GuestPath, a training and development program for front-line service employees. Guest-Path outlines ten universal customer service standards that an employee should practice, including facing a guest, greeting guests as soon they approach, and maintaining an attentive posture. The 600-page GuestPath employee guide has every detail. It has identified 1,200 customer touch points, or interactions that impact the customer service experience. Sportservice's commitment to customer service has not gone unnoticed. When the Minnesota Twins evaluated foodservice companies to hire for Target Field, team executives visited several stadiums that partner with Sportservice. "GuestPath was a major part of Sportservice's pitch for our business, and it also helped differentiate their proposal from any other bidder," said Twins president Dave St. Peter.[1]

The selection of an outside foodservice firm is a decision with significant implications on customer satisfaction and profitability. Customer satisfaction with concessions has long been a weakness for many sports properties. Complaints about prices, menu variety, and customer service are aimed at the team or venue. Some foodservice vendors take an adversarial stance with their clients, seeking to avoid dealing with customer complaints out of fear that solutions might increase costs. Sportservice management views customer service and innovation as keys to improving their business, which in turn improves their clients' business. Company president Rick Abramson said, "We spend as much time focused on customer service as we do on research and development. It's really important. People need to feel special."

To meet the dual focus on customer service and innovation, Sportservice installed self-ordering kiosks in the concessions area at the St. Pete Times Forum, home of the NHL's Tampa Bay Lightning. The result was shorter wait times for customers to receive orders and a 10% sales increase at that location. The stakes for delivering high-quality service with concessions are high for sports properties. With foodservice firms paying commissions to their partners as high as 50% on some parts of their operations, teams and venues embrace outside firms that offer fresh ideas and energy to create satisfied customers and grow the foodservice business.[2]

Introduction

Much of the focus in previous chapters has been on strategic considerations for marketing of sports and marketing through sports. Understanding consumers, monitoring the external environment, and devising marketing strategies emphasize planning and preparation that must precede engaging in marketing activities. In this chapter, another aspect of effective management practices for sports marketers is discussed: execution of strategies. Objectives and strategies are meaningless unless they are supported with plans to implement the ideas that are intended to advance a sports organization's business.

Jeff Gregor of Turner likens execution to owning an automobile. Buying a shiny new car may be exciting, but without fuel it will go nowhere. Execution (or activation) is the fuel that that brings the brand promise to life. Customers do not relate to a brand's strategy; they relate to their experiences with the brand. A customer's contacts with a brand have been referred to as "moments of truth."[3] Execution of marketing strategy is all about managing those moments of truth. The best-devised plans are worthless if customer contact points are not managed so that a customer's encounter with a brand reinforces brand identity and validates the customer's decision to be a customer or fan. The importance of managing customer contact points is a reason why outside firms like Sportservice are hired by sports properties to execute marketing tasks that impact customer value.

This chapter addresses strategies for living the brand promise, with a focus on two aspects of marketing execution. First, executing delivery of brand promises through managing quality is examined. Quality has some unique elements in sports entertainment, which create quality management issues that must be addressed. Also, the relationship between quality and customer satisfaction is discussed as well as strategies sports marketers can adopt for equipping employees to deliver high-quality experiences. Second, implementing marketing strategies is examined in terms of the decision to hire to an outside firm or manage in-house. The Sportservice example illustrates that some functions can be performed more effectively by an outside firm.

Managing Quality

The notion that encounters between a person and brand are aptly described as moments of truth suggests that for the consumer great marketing is not about planning or strategy. Consumers experience great marketing when their interactions with a seller add value to the consumption choice. Individual consumers assign varying levels of importance on different aspects of their experience with a brand. Whether consumers place a premium on fast service, courtesy shown by service employees, cleanliness of the physical environment, or some other aspect of the consumption experience, quality of the customer experience is largely within the control of the sports property. Delivery of brand promises can be proactively managed so that moments of truth strengthen customer relationships.

Defining Service Quality

In order to manage quality in the delivery of sports entertainment experiences, one must be familiar with what quality is from the consumer's viewpoint. One of the most influential research studies on **service quality** defined quality as a comparison of consumers' expectations of what a marketer should deliver with actual performance.[4] Thus, this customer-based view of quality is a perceived quality that resides in the consumer's mind. Experiences and services differ from products in that quality for products is largely objective, focusing on minimizing mechanical error (e.g., zero defects). The intangible nature of services and consumer involvement in their delivery makes service quality in the service sector more subjective.

As shown in Figure 13.1, service quality is comprised of five factors: 1) intangibility, 2) reliability, 3) responsiveness, 4) assurance, and 5) empathy.[5] Although sports was not one of the contexts in which service quality factors were defined originally, their relevance in influencing sports consumers' assessment of quality is undeniable. However, unique characteristics of sports entertainment experiences mean that the implications of these five factors on customer satisfaction may differ for sports properties compared to other types of services.

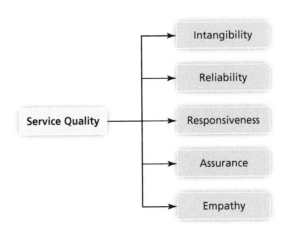

FIGURE 13.1 Service Quality Factors

INTANGIBILITY. The benefits provided by sports entertainment are largely **intangible**, meaning they cannot be observed with the physical senses prior to purchase or consumption. Thrill of competition, sense of community with other fans, and escape from the rigors of daily life are some of the benefits consumers receive from sports that cannot be physically assessed. In the absence of observable benefits, marketers of services and experiences can make certain aspects of their offerings tangible. Bringing tangibility to a service experience can influence consumers' perceptions of the quality delivered. Tangibility can be brought to services in a number of ways, as suggested by Figure 13.2.

FIGURE 13.2 Methods of Making a Sports Property Tangible

- Sports venue
- Sportscape
- Equipment
- Appearance of employees
- Mascots
- Entertainment

© BelleMedia / Shutterstock

For sports marketers, the facility or venue in which events are held is a key element for bringing tangibility to the sports consumption experience. The role of the physical environment (i.e., sportscape) in designing experiences that elicit positive emotional responses and influence satisfaction judgments was covered in Chapter 7. Aesthetics, layout, accessibility, seating comfort, electronic equipment, electronic displays, and cleanliness were identified as elements of the physical environment largely within the control of sports marketers. A widely held belief by sports properties is that these elements of the physical environment can be managed to add value to attendees' experience, regardless of the outcome on the field of play. One of the main arguments presented when a sports franchise makes a case to build a new stadium is the potential impact on customer satisfaction. The rationale is that a pleasing physical environment will influence repeat visits. In turn, the repeat visits will generate more revenue for the organization, more tax revenues for local government, and create economic impact by supporting jobs related to the team and venue.

The appearance of personnel involved in delivering a service influences evaluations of quality as well. Just as an aesthetically pleasing and clean physical environment have an impact on attendees' enjoyment and desire to return, a sports property can take an additional step of managing perceptions by setting standards for the dress and appearance of employees. It is common to see sales, marketing, and customer support employees in business attire at games or events. Even when weather conditions make wearing a suit and tie less than ideal, customer service employees often wear a more casual "uniform" that identifies them as employees while projecting a professional appearance. Consistency of employee appearance extends to all persons involved in delivering an experience: security, ushers, concession servers, and facility support all represent customer contact points. Thus, it is beneficial to manage customers' perceptions of their initial contact with these employees given the adage "you have only one chance to make a good first impression."

The elements of tangibility discussed above are applicable across many different types of services, but two additional elements unique to sports that can impact perceived quality at live events are mascots and entertainment. Discussed in Chapter 5 as a branding element that is often is derived from a brand name or logo, a mascot is usually a representation of a team's identity that becomes associated with the brand and even is a sub-brand of the team brand. Mascots have been a staple among college athletic teams for decades, but use of mascots is not limited to colleges. Among major professional sports leagues in the United States, mascots are the norm for the NBA and NHL. Of the thirty MLB teams, twenty-six have mascots, and in the NFL it is twenty-seven of thirty-two teams. Mascots impact service quality through their involvement in entertainment that is part of event production. Games, contests, or skits featuring a mascot during a timeout or intermission appeal to fans of all ages and can elicit positive emotional responses that elevate an audience's mood. Similarly, entertainment integrated into event production (pregame, in-game, or postgame) can have a positive effect on attendees' enjoyment and perceptions of quality. Cheerleaders, dancers, bands, or music artists are used to fulfill this role.

Managing the intangibility of sponsorship as a sports product can be accomplished by a focus on activation of an association between a brand and sports property. In Chapter 11, activation was described as the tactics used to communicate a brand–sports property linkage. Acquiring naming rights without activating the sponsorship would be bad practice and falls in line with the shiny car–no fuel analogy made earlier in this chapter—a sponsorship goes nowhere in terms of marketing effectiveness without activation. Activating a sponsorship can persuade a target audience why a brand and sports property fit, or go together.

A key to successful activation is a strategy of communicating a sponsorship not only in a sports environment (i.e., at stadiums or arenas) but demonstrating the brand–property link away from that environment. For example, Rouses, a Louisiana-based supermarket chain, sponsors the NBA's New Orleans Hornets. Rouses makes its association with the Hornets tangible through media advertising, on Rouses' website, with in-store signage, and a merchandising and display program with vendors that also sponsor the Hornets. The payoff for Rouses of making an intangible relationship tangible is that the Rouses–Hornets relationship has met sponsorship objectives such as creating positive feelings about Rouses among Hornets fans and increasing their shopping frequency and spending.[6]

Tangibility can be added to a service experience through entertainment by cheerleaders.

© bikeriderlondon / Shutterstock

RELIABILITY. Perceptions of quality can be influenced by enhancing tangibility of the sports consumption experience, but those efforts can be negated if a sports property fails to demonstrate reliability in service delivery. Consumers tend to assess **reliability** in very simple terms—was the service delivered accurately and dependably? Research has consistently found that reliability is the most influential factor in determining consumers' perceptions of service quality.[7]

Evaluations of reliability are based on whether promises made by the marketer are kept. Promises are either explicitly stated or implied. For sports marketers, explicit promises would include events that begin at the scheduled time, guarantee of a seat in a specific location to a ticket holder, and fulfilling signage and advertising exposure for sponsors. Other brand promises are not expressed but assumed by consumers with expectations that the promises will be met. Sporting event attendees have expectations for parking and access to the venue, cleanliness of seating area and restrooms, courtesy shown by customer service personnel, and security. While explicit promises typically are not made for these aspects of a sports fan's experience, managers responsible for service delivery understand that ineffective handling of these moments of truth can negatively affect quality judgments and, ultimately, customer satisfaction.

A tactic used to respond to failures in the area of service reliability is offering guarantees. A service guarantee is an explicit promise to compensate a customer in some manner for failing to meet service expectations. Although guarantees are common for services such as auto repair, hotels, and restaurants, it is unusual for sports brands to make explicit promises about performance. The uncontrollable nature of the outcome of team or individual performance makes it challenging for sports marketers to offer guarantees for performance on the field of play. Instead, the focus tends to be managing implied promises and recovering from any service failures that arise.

A few sports properties have offered guarantees related to team performance even though marketers have no control over wins and losses. Why? Because poor performance on the field can influence perceptions of quality, even if the aspects of service quality under the marketer's control are managed effectively. In 2008, Stanford University made an offer to new season ticket buyers called the "Gridiron Guarantee." Customers that were unhappy with the entertainment value of attending Stanford home games could request a refund for the cost of their tickets. The move to offer a guarantee was motivated by Stanford winning only two home games the previous two seasons and the need to sell tickets to support the team's new stadium.[8] Even when guarantees are not expressed, sports marketers should make allowances to compensate customers that experience service problems. Complimentary tickets to a future event, free food and beverage, or a merchandise gift such as a cap or shirt are ways fans can be compensated when service performance does not meet expectations.

RESPONSIVENESS. The **responsiveness** dimension of service quality deals with employees' willingness to help customers and offer prompt service. Willingness to serve customers is assessed by the length of time one has to wait to receive service and how well an employee's response meets a customer's needs. Speed of service is important, but providing a satisfactory solution to a need or situation must be delivered too, to enhance customer satisfaction. For live events, two areas in which managers can proactively address a sports property's responsiveness to its customers are adequate staffing of service personnel and layout of service delivery. Unfortunately, individuals have attended a sporting event and experienced long lines to buy food and drink because the concessions areas were understaffed. Or, fans observe concessions areas that are not open, yet long lines for foodservice suggest that there is a need to open additional service areas.

Layout or flow of service delivery is another influence on perceptions of responsiveness. A service operation can be broken down to the number of steps that a customer must take and what is done at each step to receive the service. This practice is known as **service blueprinting**. A blueprint is useful because it assigns responsibility for each task that must be completed. More importantly, a blueprint may call attention to weak points in the flow of delivering a service so that they can be corrected. A blueprint breaks down a service by focusing on 1) customers (who initiate the service process), 2) frontline service employees who interact with customers, 3) backroom service employees who provide support to the frontline employees, and 4) support personnel whose services enable service employees to focus on meeting customers' needs.

An example of blueprinting a service at a sporting event is the flow of how customers purchase food and drinks. Figure 13.3 depicts the series of steps each of the parties in the service experience take during the service encounter. Developing a service blueprint for foodservice requires a manager start with the end result—the customer receiving an order. Then the steps required to provide the service and length of time involved in each step are identified.

The top of the blueprint indicates customer interactions with the service provider. The next row of the blueprint is the frontline, which includes all of the customer contact points between customers and frontline service personnel. The next row is the backstage operation, which in this case is the kitchen. The bottom of the blueprint indicates support components of the service operation that must be completed to ensure quality foodservice.

It is possible to make service delivery more efficient through blueprinting the operation. Such an analysis can reveal where more employee help is needed or spur ideas for improving the layout of work areas to serve customers more effectively. For example, the counter area where customers must go to get straws, napkins, or condiments may be in a location that requires customers to cut through lines of customers waiting to be served, or the location may be difficult for support personnel to reach to replenish supplies. Using blueprints to better understand service delivery can assist managers who do not perform these tasks regularly in identifying flaws in the process that could negatively impact customers' perceptions of responsiveness.

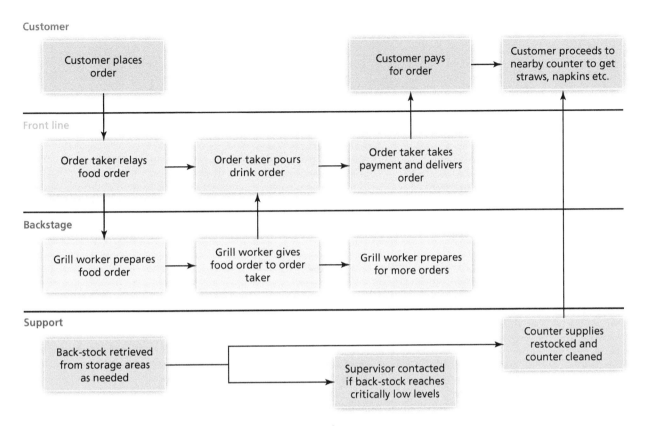

FIGURE 13.3 Blueprint for Foodservice at a Sporting Event

ASSURANCE. While responsiveness deals with the speed and reliability of service delivered, **assurance** is consumers' perceptions about the knowledge and capability of a service provider. An employee's actions can build trust and confidence in a consumer's judgment of the employee's abilities, which can have a positive impact on feelings of assurance and perceived service quality. The role of a customer service employee for a sports organization is important because that person is the "face" of the brand to a customer in terms of a business relationship, the primary point of contact between customer and organization. That point of contact can be random, as in the case of a customer service booth or roving service personnel positioned throughout a venue. The contact can also be strategically coordinated by service personnel.

Within the sales organization for sports properties, customer service responsibilities are designated to be handled by account executives as part of their duties, a dedicated account services staff that focuses solely on meeting the needs of season ticket account holders, or a hybrid of the two approaches. Regardless of the organization structure of the customer service function, the aim is to manage customers' perceptions so their needs are met. Customer satisfaction should be the number one priority. Influencing assurance judgments is particularly important at the early stages of a customer's relationship with a sports property. First-time attendees, prospective season ticket buyers, and first-year season ticket holders are key customers that are often targeted by assigning specific sales or customer service personnel to develop trust between customer and property and hopefully expand or cement the relationship.

Ticket buyers are not the only customer segment for which assurance can be a strong influence on service quality; sponsorship partners are another segment whose relationships hinge on inspiring trust and confidence. As discussed in Chapter 11, when a sponsor agrees to pay rights fees to associate with a sports property, it is only the beginning of the relationship. Sponsors have objectives tied to business growth that they seek to achieve. It is vital that sports properties be aware of those objectives and serve as a resource to help sponsors realize desired outcomes.

One benefit that many sponsors receive in their rights deals is a certain number of event tickets to be used for client or employee hospitality. Unfortunately, many sponsors do not take full advantage of this benefit. This missed opportunity could lead to the conclusion by the sponsor that the investment is not beneficial and should be discontinued. Sports properties can head

Sports properties can assist sponsors in achieving the sponsors' objectives.

off this potential outcome by monitoring ticket usage of sponsors and making suggestions for ways the tickets could be used, if necessary. This proactive approach to sponsor–property relations can signal to a sponsor that the property can be trusted because it recognizes the sponsor is not maximizing its sponsorship benefits and offers solutions to the partner.

EMPATHY. The final dimension of service quality is **empathy**, observed by customers as caring, individualized attention shown by a company or customer service personnel. Empathy can be conveyed by treating customers as individuals with unique needs and by showing customers they are important to the organization. Many examples have been shared in previous chapters on ways to enhance perceptions of empathy. Assigning a customer service representative to a customer, offering a special parking area, handwritten notes from sales personnel, and special perks or access are just a few tactics that can be used to make customers feel important. Similar efforts can be undertaken to influence empathy perceptions among corporate partners, too. Many sports properties have dedicated personnel to service the needs of sponsors, with an account services employee being the contact for a sponsor's representative. Ticket needs, support with activation efforts, and reports on sponsorship fulfillment are three methods of assistance provided to deliver a high level of service to sponsors and demonstrate concern for customers.

Service Quality and Customer Satisfaction

The terms "service quality" and "satisfaction" are sometimes used interchangeably, but they are two different concepts. **Service quality** is a determinant of customer satisfaction, but it is not the lone factor in satisfaction judgments. **Customer satisfaction** is comprised of "a person's feelings of pleasure or disappointment that result from comparing a product's perceived performance to their expectations."[9] Satisfaction judgments go beyond evaluations of service quality to include a consumer's feelings about quality and the price paid for the service. In the context of marketing sporting events, service quality and price evaluations can be managed by marketers, but assessment of total quality could include outcomes beyond the control of marketers. Specifically, a team or individual athlete's performance in terms of wins, exciting play, and effort/intensity displayed can shape a fan's perceptions about quality of the sports product. Thus, a positive service experience and a price perceived as good value can be offset by negative evaluations of the sports product quality. This characteristic of marketing sports must be recognized so that aspects of satisfaction within the marketer's control are monitored closely. As Kathleen Davis, president of Sport Management Research Institute, put it, "If you can't guarantee a win, you'd better be able to guarantee a good time."[10]

Managing Service Quality

It is understood that a high-quality service environment offers potential payoffs in the form of satisfied customers, but what is not as clear is how to create a climate within an organization that focuses on customers. One approach to implementing customer service initiatives is known as internal marketing. **Internal marketing** is a managerial focus on motivating employees within an organization, whether frontline service employees or behind-the-scenes support personnel, to understand their role in meeting customers' needs. In turn, employees are equipped and motivated to have a service orientation.[11] The foundation of internal marketing is a belief that in order to effectively serve the external market (customers) the needs of the internal market (employees) must be met. Internal marketing is a management practice founded in the services sector. Its relevance to services is significant given the importance of the employee–customer interaction during service delivery on customer judgments of satisfaction.

So, what does it take for a sports organization to adopt internal marketing? Three areas of emphasis are shown in Figure 13.4. Leadership is vital to internal marketing success. Commitment must come from the highest levels in an organization. Internal marketing cannot be treated as the latest marketing fad or "program of the month." Management must be advocates of internal marketing because part of their role is to encourage employees and provide praise to them when great customer service is observed. Managers must be involved by getting out of their offices and monitoring employees' interactions with customers.

Leadership

Internal
marketing

Training

Innovation

FIGURE 13.4 Areas of Emphasis for Internal Marketing

Training is a component that must be implemented due to the fact that employee mindset and behaviors needed to foster a customer orientation often require adaptation or change from usual customer service policies. Training requires a commitment of time and money from the sports property to educate employees. Innovation also is needed in order to support the needed changes in service processes and employee actions that make up a service orientation.

Internal marketing's embodiment of leadership, training, and innovation is supplied by what may seem an unlikely source: Mickey Mouse. Walt Disney World and other Disney properties have developed a legendary reputation for creating "magical" experiences. The superior customer experience delivered by Disney led to formation of the Disney Institute, a unit of Disney that has engaged in training companies in service sectors such as health care, retail, and education since 1986. Surprisingly, the parallel offerings of Disney theme parks and sports properties, entertainment, did not find each other until 2009. Today, Disney Institute is involved in providing training to teams, facility operators, and foodservice vendors as the sports industry seeks to tap the customer service expertise of Disney.

One of Disney Institute's sports clients is the Orlando Magic of the NBA. The team hired Disney Institute when it moved into its new arena, Amway Center. The Disney-led training initiative begins with a leadership commitment. Orlando Magic president Alex Martins acknowledged the need for a sports team to invest in developing a customer service climate when he said, "At some point for every team, there's a downturn. With a consumer product, you'll always get the same quality, but a sports team is variable. It's the other factors that will secure the longevity of our patrons."[12]

Training is at the heart of the Magic's partnership with Disney Institute. Employees of the Orlando Magic went through a multisession training program that prepared them to do their jobs better. In addition, the training equipped them with a better understanding that their service impacted customers' experiences and how Disney's customer service tactics reflect the company's attention to detail. At the first game in Amway Center, a ticket-taker was observed giving directions to a patron by using a two-fingered pointing gesture, a Disney technique that is favored over a single-finger point that can be perceived as a rude gesture.

Innovation is evident in the Magic's commitment to internal marketing, a rather unique occurrence in the sports industry. Innovation includes empowering front-line customer service personnel to address customer problems that might arise (rather than calling a supervisor) and familiarizing employees with aspects of Amway Center's operation that do not relate directly to their job duties.[13]

The Orlando Magic's commitment to service quality through its partnership with Disney Institute may seem to be rather ordinary. After all, it is not unusual for a business to emphasize customer service to its employees. What makes this example extraordinary is that the sports industry is generally considered to be far behind other service industries when it comes to instilling a customer orientation among employees. A handful of other sports properties have hired Disney, including the Arizona Cardinals, University of Tennessee, National Tennis Center (home of the U.S. Open), and organizers of the 2010 FIFA World Cup. The motivation for practicing internal marketing is significant and straightforward. More satisfied customers will lead to more revenue for an organization. Jeff James, an executive with Disney Institute, said, "We strongly believe that if you take care of the guest in the proper manner, your financial results will come."[14]

Marketing Execution

Living the brand promise not only requires strategy and plans for activation, but it also depends on clearly defined roles and responsibilities among personnel to transform ideas into actions. Sports organizations face the same decision that firms in other industries encounter. Should all tasks be performed by employees within the organization, or should the services of an outside organization be contracted to perform certain tasks? It is the classic "make or buy" question businesses face. Many functions of a sports property's operations can be outsourced and are discussed in the following section. But first an understanding is needed of the reasons why outsourcing would be considered.

Why Outsource?

Consideration of hiring an outside firm to execute one or more tasks of the marketing function may be difficult for some managers. Is it a sign of weakness that an outside company is needed to get the job done? Has this need arisen due to poor leadership in the organization? The answer to these questions can be a resounding "no." On the contrary, the decision to utilize the services of an outside marketing firm may come from a managerial strength of analyzing the organization's capabilities and determining marketing performance can be enhanced by outsourcing. The primary advantages of outsourcing are: 1) expertise, 2) objectivity, 3) resource availability, and 4) cost effectiveness (see Figure 13.5).

FIGURE 13.5
Advantages of Outsourcing

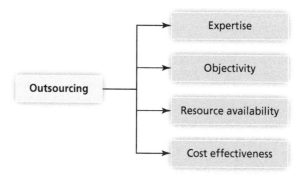

EXPERTISE. Perhaps the number one reason any business would outsource part of its operations is to take advantage of knowledge and experience that an outside firm possesses. A marketing agency's expertise can be developed through specialization in one or a few marketing functions such as advertising, consumer promotions, focusing on serving a specific industry such as sports, or by serving a wide range of clients. For example, many sports properties have online stores as a channel for their customers and fans to purchase merchandise. However, sports properties are in the sports business, not the retail or e-commerce business, and tend to lack the knowledge to integrate online retail operations into their marketing programs. One firm that specializes in this area is TeamFanShop. It can operate all aspects of a client's e-commerce business including merchandise planning, inventory management, and technology infrastructure for the e-commerce platform.[15]

Many agencies offer expertise in a particular niche or category. One way that marketing agencies develop expertise in a category is to focus on specific markets or customers. Fuse is a marketing agency with an expertise in reaching youth and teen consumers. Fuse can connect its clients' brands with young consumers through event marketing, public relations, product design, and digital media.[16] Similarly, an outside agency can be hired for its expertise in a particular sport, such as G&G Motorsports Marketing. But, within that specialization the firm offers services for drivers and race teams seeking sponsorships, companies looking to get involved with motorsports as sponsors, and Web design services for drivers and sponsors.[17]

Firms that have multiple needs to execute their sports marketing strategy may want to enlist the services of a full-service agency. A full-service agency can perform many sports marketing–related tasks, and often it has a client roster of brands from a wide range of product categories or industries. One of the largest full-service agencies is IMG, a firm that is involved in the sports, entertainment, and media sectors. In the sports category alone, it works with sponsors and properties in action sports, motorsports, tennis, Olympic Games, and college sports. IMG can assist clients in event management, sponsorship sales and consulting, brand management, media production and sales, and athlete representation.[18] The portfolio of services full-service agencies can deliver enables them to offer a one-stop shop for their clients' sports marketing needs.

OBJECTIVITY. Outside agencies offer an unbiased perspective on a client's business. An outside agency is independent, not owned or controlled by its clients. Its long-term success depends on delivering results to clients that advance their business, not saying nor doing what the client might want. When an agency works for a client, it is not going to be influenced by a sports property's organizational culture as if the work was being performed in-house.

An in-house marketing staff for a minor league hockey team may insist on having a new theme or slogan for a branding campaign each season and may engage in this practice because "that's always how we have done it." Of course, such reasoning does not necessarily lead to making the best decisions. If an outside firm was hired by the team to develop a new brand strategy, its recommendation might be to focus on building a long-term identity for the team's brand. Such a departure from the way things are always done is sometimes difficult to do, even when necessary, if the objectivity of an organization's decision makers is clouded.

RESOURCE AVAILABILITY. An outside agency may have resources the sports property does not. Hiring an agency or consultancy can bring an infusion of creativity and human resources. An outside perspective can contribute new ideas or alternative approaches to marketing operations of a sports property. For instance, interactive sports marketing agency rEvolution developed a research panel of Latino consumers to enable its clients to better understand sports consumption of the Hispanic population. NASCAR gleaned insights such as Hispanics tended to be as brand loyal as other NASCAR fans and that building community should be a focus to encourage Hispanics to watch races with friends and family.[19] Such added value might never be realized if the creative capabilities of an outside firm were not tapped for help.

Also, an agency can possess resources in the form of its network of contacts with other businesses and decision makers. This form of resource availability is particularly relevant for sponsorship sales. A sports property that is looking to sell naming rights to its venue, title sponsorship of an event, or other parts of its sponsorship inventory may benefit from enlisting the services of a sponsorship consultancy that has extensive contacts with managers whose companies engage in sponsorship. Familiarity with decision makers and opportunities to get introductions to others with whom a relationship does not exist already are advantages that a sponsorship agency can give a sports property. In contrast, approaching potential sponsors without the common ground that networking establishes would make going it alone more challenging for a sports property.

COST EFFECTIVENESS. Reasons for outsourcing marketing functions identified so far share the benefit of improving marketing effectiveness. An alternative reason for outsourcing is that in some cases it costs less to hire someone to do a job than to do it yourself. When a one-time need arises, it can be more cost effective to hire an outside firm to complete a task or project than to have an in-house staff do it. Consider a college basketball team's need to create an integrated advertising campaign for television, radio, and newspaper. Some teams' marketing departments are simply too small to assign staff to develop and manage a campaign . . . assuming there is someone on staff with the expertise to do creative work and media buying. Even among college basketball programs with larger marketing staffs, employees may have too many other duties and priorities that hinder devoting time to working on an ad campaign. In either case, hiring an advertising agency to develop the campaign would likely result in lower total cost than adding employees or having an in-house advertising department.

Staying In-House

While there are compelling arguments in favor of outsourcing marketing functions in certain situations, it is important to note that not all sports organizations will find that outsourcing is the appropriate decision for them. The strongest arguments for keeping marketing operations within an organization can be thought of as the "3 Cs"—control, consistency, and cost (see Figure 13.6).

FIGURE 13.6 Reasons for Keeping Marketing Functions In-House

- Control
- Consistency
- Costs

© Yuri Arcurs / Shutterstock

Control is a major consideration for many managers. When operations are outsourced, accountability for day-to-day execution and performance is no longer handled by someone who reports directly to a manager in the organization. When an employee has performance problems when functions are carried out in-house, he or she can be counseled or reprimanded by a manager in the organization. But if the performance problems are created by an outsourced firm it is more difficult to handle the situation, since the employee is under the control of the outsourced firm.

Consistency is highly related to the control issue. Execution that is consistent with an organization's marketing strategy as well as its policies and procedures may be challenged when tasks are being performed by an outside firm. This limitation is an issue because inconsistencies between a sports organization's brand promise and delivering on the promise to customers can hurt customer service and the brand experience. In a few cases, managing this dilemma prompted the decision to bring a function previously outsourced back in-house. The Arizona Cardinals of the NFL bucked the trend of outsourcing foodservice operations, becoming one of only three of the league's thirty-two teams to manage foodservice in-house. Its Rojo Hospitality unit immediately implemented changes such as lowering prices on concession stand favorites like hot dogs and nachos, and offering $1 refills of souvenir cup sodas and popcorn tubs. As one Cardinals executive put it, "There are things we can do to drive value and ultimately put a better product out there to the consumer."[20]

The third reason for performing marketing operations in-house pertains to costs. For sports properties with modest marketing budgets, an outlay for an agency or some other third-party service provider may be cost prohibitive. Similarly, the low revenue potential of a smaller property may discourage outside firms from pursuing them as clients. For example, a sports marketing agency that offers sponsorship sales as a service to its clients is not likely to take on properties that lack the appeal or brand equity to attract large corporate sponsors. Administrative costs and employees' salaries will require that a certain threshold be met for a client's revenue potential.

Thus, even if a property has an interest and need to outsource, there may not be a firm willing to engage with a low potential client.

Services That Can Be Outsourced

A sports property can outsource a single task or function, several functions, or its entire marketing operations. The decision to outsource all marketing activities occurs less frequently than outsourcing one or a few activities. Figure 13.7 identifies the services that can be outsourced to a marketing agency. Some services can be performed by general marketing or advertising agencies that serve clients in a variety of industries. Advertising campaigns, brand strategy, and public relations are three marketing services that an agency that does not specialize in sports can do. Other needs of a sports property are better met by the specialized expertise of agencies that focus on serving one or more areas of the sports industry. Some specialized services of sports marketing agencies are ticket sales consulting, sponsorship negotiation, and client hospitality. It is not unusual to contract with more than one firm to meet specialized needs, such as hiring an advertising agency to redesign a website and a ticket sales consultancy to increase season ticket sales revenue.

© Stephen Coburn / Shutterstock

- Ticket sales
- Sponsorship sales
- Media
- Facility operations
- Marketing communications
- Market research

FIGURE 13.7 Services That Can Be Outsourced

TICKET SALES. Ticket sales may seem like an unlikely candidate for outsourcing. Managing the transactional aspects of ticket sales such as order fulfillment and ticket distribution are relatively straightforward processes that may not require the expertise of an outside firm. In contrast, relational aspects of ticket sales including lead generation, prospecting for customers, and closing deals are more complex, with greater needs in terms of human resources and selling skills. If an organization sells tickets mainly through order taking or customer-initiated sales, the ticket sales function can usually be handled in-house. If order getting is crucial to growth in ticket sales, then the services of an outside firm can be valuable in strengthening a sports property's sales efforts.

As shown in Figure 13.8, outsourcing of ticket sales activities falls under three main categories. Many consulting firms exist that work with sports properties to develop strategies for increasing ticket sales revenues. This aspect of outsourcing ticket sales focuses on developing ideas for sports properties to increase the effectiveness of their ticket sales departments, but ultimately it is up to the client to implement the consultant's recommendations.

The Telios Group is a sports marketing agency that has offers ticket sales consulting and training for collegiate athletic departments, conferences, and professional teams. The company helps its clients develop programs for selling season tickets, group tickets, and individual event tickets.[21] Training of salespeople and sales managers is another service that can be outsourced. Turning to a ticket sales consultancy for training is beneficial for developing selling skills or exposing

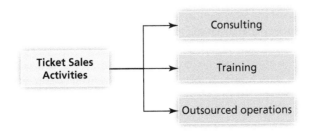

Ticket Sales Activities → Consulting

Ticket Sales Activities → Training

Ticket Sales Activities → Outsourced operations

FIGURE 13.8 Outsourcing Ticket Sales Activities

salespeople to different techniques or approaches to the selling process. Many ticket sales consultancies also offer training for salespeople and sales managers as part of their portfolio of services.

A more unusual step for outsourcing ticket sales is for a sports property to contract with an outside firm to manage its entire ticket sales operations. The decision to completely outsource the operation may be made if it is determined that revenue increases that an agency can deliver exceed the cost of hiring the agency to manage ticket sales. Thus, outsourced operations will not be an appropriate strategy for every organization. The sales potential for ticket sales may not justify the expense of hiring an agency and relinquishing control of ticket sales personnel. Also, a property with lower sales potential is less attractive to outside agencies that perform ticket sales functions. However, there are situations in which outsourcing ticket sales is a mutually profitable venture for property and agency. Georgia Tech outsourced ticket sales for football and basketball to an outside firm, The Aspire Group. In the first year of the arrangement, the agency's fifteen-person sales team assigned to Georgia Tech generated more than $1 million in new ticket revenues.[22]

SPONSORSHIP. An organization's management needs for its sponsorship business depend on whether it is a seller (property) or buyer (company) of sponsorships. Sellers are concerned with identifying prospective sponsorship partners, engaging them through the selling and negotiation processes, and managing relationships once a company signs on as a sponsor. Depending on an organization's capabilities and resources, some or all of these functions may be better performed by an outside firm that specializes in sponsorship.

Many universities lack budget resources to hire marketing personnel to serve as sponsorship specialists. Thus, bringing in a firm that specializes in sponsorship management in collegiate athletics can offer greater potential for securing sponsorship revenues and at a cost lower than maintaining an in-house sponsorship sales team. Nelligan Sports Marketing is a company that provides sponsorship services to collegiate conferences and individual institutions. Nelligan's clients included conferences such as the Colonial Athletic Association and Patriot League as well as more than twenty athletic programs.[23] Most of Nelligan's clients do not have a massive athletic department budget, which means that specialized marketing tasks such as sponsorship sales, sponsorship agreements, and sponsor fulfillment may be more effectively performed by dedicated personnel from an agency rather than handling in-house.

Sports properties are not the only ones that can benefit from outsourcing some or all sponsorship management tasks. Companies that use sponsorship as a marketing vehicle to reach customers may decide to tap a sponsorship agency or consultancy for one or more of the four reasons for outsourcing discussed earlier in the chapter. Managers might have an understanding of how sponsorship impacts an audience and brands building, but they may lack the experience or knowledge to select and manage a partnership with a sports property. An agency that is hired can add value through its familiarity with the market for rights fees, contacts and relationships with sports properties, and experience with the negotiation process for securing a sponsorship deal. Agencies can also be a resource to their clients in terms of consulting to develop activation programs that strengthen the association between sponsor and property. Even among large firms whose marketing departments handle other brand communication functions, certain sponsorships may be too complex for the in-house staff to handle.

Despite having sizeable resources of its own, JPMorgan Chase outsources part of its sponsorship management program. The global financial services firm has more than $2 trillion in assets and employs more than 200,000 people, but the company needed help evaluating a sponsorship opportunity with the Rugby World Cup. JPMorgan Chase turned to International Events Group (IEG) for an evaluation of the proposal. IEG's analysis revealed that the company would not have received adequate marketing rights from the deal to generate sufficient return on investment (ROI). As a result of IEG's work, JPMorgan Chase negotiated more favorable marketing rights that included greater category exclusivity and protection from ambush marketers and more accurately valued the property so that it did not overpay for the Rugby World Cup sponsorship.[24]

MEDIA. For some sports properties, media rights and sales is one revenue stream that can be maximized by putting it in the hands of a firm that specializes in media operations. If the scope of a team's media footprint is small, then an in-house media staff can manage operations sufficiently. The Jackson Generals, a Class AA minor league baseball team in Jackson, Tennessee, has a one-person media operations department. Play-by-play broadcasts, radio advertising sales, and media relations can be performed by a single staff member. Outsourcing is not a consideration.

At the other end of the spectrum, a trend that has developed is for sports properties with resources to invest in developing in-house media operations rather than outsource. Major league properties MLB, NBA, and NHL as well as college athletics Big Ten Conference are sports entities that are keeping the media business within their organizations. In between the extremes of small organizations that can handle their own media business and large organizations that see substantial revenue potential for a do-it-yourself approach to media operations are many properties that benefit from outsourcing media tasks.

One of the most visible aspects of media operations to sports fans that can be outsourced is television and radio broadcasts. Production of live games, coaches' TV and radio shows, and pay-per-view programming requires equipment and personnel that may be too expensive for many organizations to undertake alone. College athletics is a prime example of a sector of the sports industry in which media broadcast rights and programming are outsourced to specialized firms. IMG College is one of a number of agencies that specialize in providing marketing services to collegiate programs and conferences. More than fifty universities use IMG College, and the company provides such services as hiring on-air talent for play-by-play and color commentary, production of radio broadcasts of games, creating and distributing coaches' TV shows and call-in radio shows, sponsorship rights for media broadcasts, and advertising sales.[25]

Another media service that can be outsourced that represents a potential revenue stream is publications. Media guides, game programs, team magazines, and other print media are products for which properties may have a market but often lack the design and print production capabilities to develop the products on their own. The expertise and resources of a printer, graphic design firm, or sports marketing agency can be enlisted to oversee execution of print media.

FACILITY OPERATIONS. Putting on a sporting event requires coordination among several different functions that contribute to delivering a satisfying customer experience. Some of these functions are so specialized or removed from a marketing organization's core competencies that outsourcing parts of venue operations is preferred to managing them in-house. Figure 13.9 identifies some of the facility operations that may be outsourced.

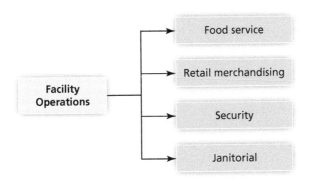

FIGURE 13.9
Outsourcing Facility Operation Functions

Foodservice operations such as concession stands, restaurants, and premium suite catering are a prime example of a part of facility operations that can be handled by an outside firm. The expertise of a foodservice company like Sportservice, introduced at the beginning of this chapter, allows a sports property to give its customers high-quality food and beverage options, relieves the property of expenses such as human resources and inventory, and creates a partnership with a firm that has a financial interest in growing the foodservice business.

Another aspect of venue operations that can be outsourced with the aim of growing revenues is retail merchandising. Similar to the rationale for outsourcing foodservice, the mission of sports properties relates to sports, not running souvenir kiosks and team stores. Thus, hiring an expert to manage inventory, staff retail outlets, or run e-commerce operations can be a profitable choice for a sports property. The NFL's Denver Broncos hired Gameday Entertainment to run the team store at Sports Authority Field and manage merchandise sales at the team's training camp. Team management felt that a specialty firm could grow Broncos merchandise sales beyond the confines of its stadium more effectively than continuing to manage retail operations in-house.[26]

Other outsourcing decisions for facility operations are driven by the prospect of reducing costs. Two non-revenue-producing areas that are outsourced often are security and janitorial services. Security service firms can perform tasks for sports clients such as parking and traffic management, fan entry/exit, and venue security. Janitorial services are similar to venue security in that they are vital to delivering the brand promise in the form of a quality service environment but fall outside a sports property's core competencies.

MARKETING COMMUNICATIONS. Outsourcing of advertising, public relations, or other forms of marketing communication is hardly unique to the sports industry. Businesses, small and large, across a wide range of industries utilize outside agencies to meet some or all of their marketing communications needs. Virtually all communication tasks can be outsourced, with some companies providing a full suite of services and others specializing in one or a few tools of brand communications.

A sports organization that is considering hiring an advertising or other marketing services agency faces a two-step decision process. First, should a generalist or specialist be hired? If an agency is hired, should that agency serve clients in different industries, or should the agency specialize in the sports industry? The second consideration is the scope of services offered by an agency. Should it be a full-service agency that offers everything or a specialty shop with a single area of expertise?

Comparing advertising agency Blue Sky to sports marketing agency Learfield Sports illustrates the differences in the marketing communications capabilities of a full-service marketing agency versus a sports marketing specialty agency. Blue Sky, an Atlanta agency led by Rob Farinella (Chapter 4 Insider Expert), has a client roster of sports properties that includes the Atlanta Braves, Bristol Motor Speedway, and Chick-fil-A Peach Bowl. Blue Sky has created billboard ads, radio and TV commercials, direct mail, and web applications for sports clients. One of Blue Sky's clients, the Atlanta Hawks, needed help in increasing the market's familiarity with the team's young players. Blue Sky used bus advertising and billboards to promote the team's young stars using the tagline "Now You Know." A full-service marketing agency like Blue Sky offers the benefit of extensive resources to serve a sports property. Creative development is only part of a client's needs. Consumer research and media planning are other aspects of an advertising campaign that may extend beyond the capabilities of many sports properties, but are standard offerings of full-service agencies.

In contrast, some specialty agencies work only with sports clients. Learfield Sports targets college athletics properties with a suite of services including sponsorship sales, media broadcast production, advertising sales, and marketing communications. One of Learfield Sport's clients is the Black Coaches & Administrators (BCA), a nonprofit organization with a mission to grow and develop ethnic minorities at all levels of sports. The agency has developed campaigns for building the BCA brand and increasing brand awareness through advertising and public relations.[27] The BCA could have hired an advertising agency to perform the same work, but a firm with industry knowledge and connections that could benefit the BCA are compelling reasons for outsourcing to a specialist agency like Learfield Sports.

Advertising agencies can provide creative skills for marketing of sports properties.

© Chris Schmidt / iStockPhoto

MARKET RESEARCH. One of the main reasons a business outsources a task or function is that it can hire someone that has the expertise and infrastructure to accomplish the task. Market research is an area that most sports properties do not have the resources or expertise to do. Specialized tasks involved in conducting market research such as conducting focus groups, designing surveys, or analyzing data may pose challenges for a marketing department that are best met by an outside firm. While most managers appreciate the value of the information and insight market research can provide, they may feel incapable of generating needed research or are too focused on other priorities such as sales and customer relationship management to conduct research projects internally. Outside research firms can offer secondary research reports or design primary research depending on the needs of a client.

Market research firms can be hired to examine any aspect of the marketing mix, such as pricing, customer satisfaction, new product or service development, or advertising effectiveness. However, two areas that receive particular emphasis from sports properties are consumer behavior and sponsorship measurement. The use of market research to better understand consumers takes the form of collecting data on-site at games or events as well as communicating with consumers off-site.

A leading market research firm serving the sports entertainment industry is Turnkey Intelligence. The company positions itself as a sport property's "marketing research department down the hall."[28] Turnkey Intelligence can manage an entire market research program by preparing an annual research plan, conducting on-site and off-site surveys, providing immediate feedback to clients, and feeding research data to other units of an organization. The primary limitation of this approach to conducting market research is cost. Many smaller sports properties would find services like those offered by Turnkey Intelligence to be cost prohibitive for their budgets.

Insider Insights Jeff Gregor – Turner Broadcasting, Inc.

Q. In your view, how do outside agencies or firms deliver value to sports properties by performing marketing functions for them?

A. To begin with, every sports property needs to have a distinct brand with an essence or promise that its product or service will deliver and be experienced by consumers. The saying "define or be defined" is relevant for any enterprise. Therefore, it is critically important to do the research to understand and stake your brand essence. This kind of work is not easily done from the inside for various reasons—preconceived notions that may exist organizationally, years of neglect, lack of expertise, etc. An important first step in addressing marketing functions and whether outside firms deliver value is to make sure that your brand is clear and distinct. If you cannot state precisely what your brand stands for, I recommend working with an outside brand marketing firm. Then, it is easier to take a holistic view to make sure all forms of communications—PR, community relations, promotions, events, stadium experiences, etc.—reinforce the brand position.

Once a brand is clearly defined, it is marketing's job to develop strategies that will reinforce the brand. For this task, I believe "yes is more." In planning stages, I want to include everything and every opinion in the mix, including marketing staff, stadium attendants, fans, players, local media, to bring out all demands, interests and concerns in order to develop insights informing strategies and plans. This can also mean working with outside agencies to help with this research. Once you feel you have gleaned the right amount of information whether though an outside vendor or internally, these insights are critical for an agency to help develop creative concepts. With any outside agency, the strategies, concepts or ideas are only as good as the information you provide them. When you provide a clear brief for an assignment, you more than likely will get back work strategically aligned with your needs.

Q. The cost to hire an outside firm to perform marketing functions compared to keeping work in-house can be a concern.

Turner Broadcasting System

Jeff Gregor talks about activation.

How do agencies overcome any resistance to their fees that a prospective client might have?

A. The approach to overcoming fear of fees is two-fold. First, determine if internal resources are capable to solve whatever need you may have. Trying to do everything in-house could have a negative impact if work is done in a less than professional manner and may detract from your brand. Consumers have so many entertainment choices; you may have only one chance to convert them. Every activity should be handled with that in mind.

Second, fear of fees can be overcome by using a performance-based fee structure. You can tie fees directly to tickets sold, attendance, level of media involvement, PR value, buzz metrics, etc. Today, more agencies are willing to provide performance based fee structures as an incentive for both you and them. Accountability has to be built into all operations, including in making decisions to use outside resources.

Q. What is the future for marketing services firms in sports entertainment – will properties trend toward more outsourcing, or will they look to perform more work in-house?

A. The future is bright for marketing services firms in sports entertainment because what is required in today's environment to recruit, connect, engage, sell, and service consumers - it is a 365 days a year job. It is an ongoing process to make sure you are always in some way willing and trying to engage consumers on some level whether through social media platforms, special events, community activities, etc. There is no "gone fishing sign" put out when a season or an event is over!

Also, I think it will become harder for any organization to be structured in such a way that everything is done in-house. The key organizationally is to understand one's capabilities and to structure for the right levels of expertise and fill in gaps where necessary. It is a balancing act. Agencies which demonstrate performance based value in meaningful ways will always find opportunities.

A more specialized area of market research in sports is sponsorship measurement. Specifically, companies that seek to determine the impact their sponsorships have with the target audience but lack the capabilities to conduct the research can hire a firm with expertise in sponsorship. One firm that performs such services is Performance Research. Services offered by Performance Research help clients determine the effects of a sponsorship on brand awareness and image, develop audience profiles of a sports property (e.g., demographic and psychographic characteristics), and assess effectiveness of activation programs. The company can collect data in a variety of ways, such as focus groups, surveys conducted on-site, online, or by telephone, and observation. These specialized skills are beyond the capabilities of many sports organizations. An understanding of how sponsorship works and being able to make recommendations for clients based on experience sets Performance Research apart from general market research firms.[29]

Chapter Summary

Great marketing is when customers interact with a service provider or sports property and leave with a great experience. These positive experiences occur because sports properties manage the quality aspect of the service, which consists of five factors: intangibility, reliability, responsiveness, assurance, and empathy. Tangibility can be brought to a sports property through design of physical spaces and facilities, equipment, and appearance of service personnel. Reliability is achieved through accurate and dependable delivery of the sports experience. Responsiveness occurs when employees are willing to help customers and provide prompt service. Customers gain assurance through employee actions that indicate employee knowledge and capability. The last dimension, empathy, happens when customers receive caring and individualized attention by service personnel.

Service quality and customer satisfaction are not the same thing. Satisfaction goes beyond evaluations of service quality and includes feelings of pleasure or disappointment with the experience. One approach to managing service quality is internal marketing, which involves meeting the needs of employees so they in turn can take care of customers. Internal marketing involves leadership from upper management, training of employees, and innovation.

A major decision that sports properties must make about marketing execution is what functions will be handled in-house and what functions will be outsourced. Advantages of outsourcing include higher level of expertise, greater objectivity, availability of additional resources, and cost-effectiveness. Advantages of keeping marketing functions in-house include control, consistency, and costs (the 3 Cs).

Functions that can be outsourced include ticket sales, sponsorship sales, media broadcasting and sales, facility operations, marketing communications, and marketing research. If outsourcing is used, sports properties must make a decision whether to use a full-service agency that can provide a wide range of services or specialty agencies that concentrate on sports marketing.

Review Questions

1. Describe the five components of service quality as each relates to sports marketing.
2. What is blueprinting, and how can it benefit a sports property?
3. What is the difference between service quality and customer satisfaction?
4. What is internal marketing?
5. What does it take for a sports organization to adopt an internal marketing culture?
6. Explain the advantages for a sports property to outsource all or part of their marketing functions.
7. In terms of outsourcing, what are the differences between a full-service agency and a specialty agency?
8. What are the reasons for keeping the marketing functions in-house?
9. What marketing functions can a sports property outsource?
10. Outsourcing of ticket sales activities falls under what three main categories?
11. What functions of facility operation can a sports property outsource? Why would these functions be outsourced?
12. Why do most sports organizations use outsourcing for marketing research?

New Terms

Service quality comparison of consumers' expectations of what a marketer should deliver with actual performance

Intangible service characteristic that cannot be observed with the physical senses prior to purchase or consumption

Reliability delivery of service accurately and dependably

Responsiveness willingness of service employees to help customers and provide prompt service

Service blueprinting diagram of a service operation that shows the number of steps that a customer must take to purchase and consume a service and what is done at each step to provide the service

Assurance perceptions of consumers about the knowledge and capability of a service provider

Empathy caring, individualized attention to customers by a company or customer service personnel

Customer satisfaction an individual's judgment of a consumption experience that compares outcomes with expectations held prior to the experience.

Internal marketing managerial focus on motivating employees within an organization to understand their role in meeting the needs of customers

Discussion and Critical Thinking Exercises

1. Quality has been defined as the difference between performance and expectations. Describe an experience with a service where you had high expectations prior to the purchase. Did the service meet your expectations? Why or why not?

2. Think about the last sporting event you attended. Go through the five components of service quality (intangibility, reliability, responsiveness, assurance, and empathy). Describe specific incidents that illustrate each component. Did each incident contribute to a positive or negative experience with the sporting event? (If you cannot think of incidents in the last event, then discuss other events that illustrate each concept.)

3. How important are tangibles to the enjoyment of a sporting event? Describe a sports facility that you believe demonstrates a positive sportscape. Describe a sports facility that demonstrates a negative sportscape. What makes the difference?

4. How do mascots add to the experience of attending a sporting event? In your view, are there any drawbacks to using mascots as part of a strategy to increase the tangibility of sports service delivery?

5. Develop a service blueprint for purchasing a ticket to a pro sports game. Be sure to include backstage and support functions that must also occur.

6. Discuss the difference between service quality and customer satisfaction. Give an example from your personal experience that illustrates the two concepts.

7. For internal marketing to be successful, leadership must support and demonstrate customer care. Why? Give examples from your personal life where leadership talks about customer care, but does not provide employee care.

8. Figure 13.5 identifies four advantages of outsourcing. If your college athletic program was going to outsource its marketing function, rank these four from most important to least important in the selection of an agency. Should the athletic department seek a full-service agency or an agency that specializes in sports marketing? Justify your answer.

9. Review the 3 Cs for keeping marketing functions in-house. Then review the list of services that can be outsourced. Suppose you were hired as the marketing director for a local minor league baseball team. Rank the six services that can be outsourced with the first being the first you would be willing to outsource to the last one you would want to outsource. Justify your ranking list.

You Make the Call

FanVision

Watching football games at home is an enjoyable experience for many football fans, for a number of reasons. Games are in high definition, and many avid sports fans now own a large HDTV. They can watch instant replays, check scores of other games, and even get commentaries on players as well as up-to-date stats. With the NFL Sunday Ticket out-of-market package, fans can watch their favorite team or almost any football team they want.

The NFL realizes they need to improve the in-stadium experience of fans if they want to fill seats and if they want to lure fans from their living rooms, dens, and local sports bars. A recent mobile technology venture by Miami Dolphins owner Stephen Ross is actively being pursued as a tool for enhancing the in-game, in-stadium experience of fans. The wireless, handheld device is called Fan-Vision. According to Ross, "The device gives you never-before-seen freedom in shaping your sports fan experience. You will be able to access live video feeds, replays, and highlights, angle cams that get you close to the action, intense audio feeds that bring you behind the scenes, and scorecards updated in real-time and much more."

FanVision has been used for NASCAR races, Formula One races, and PGA Tours. Now it is being used by NFL football teams. In addition to in-game highlights and replays, FanVision provides two out-of-town games live, real-time stat updates from all games, a customizable fantasy football roster widget, the NFL RedZone channel, audio from network and local stations, and a cheerleader camera in select stadiums.

Currently, FanVision is provided to select fans who attend football games. Each team has a different method of deciding who receives the small handheld FanVision device. For instance, the Miami Dolphins gives the device to season ticket members, including Club and Suite members. Members may keep the device as long as they maintain their season tickets.

© Neustockimages / iStockphotos

FanVision provides fans attending a sporting event with a unique in-game experience.

FanVision uses its own dedicated band of wireless spectrum. Wi-Fi and cellular networks are often clogged during heavy use, such as occurs in a football stadium with 70,000 people. FanVision, however, is working with Qualcomm to transition the current device to a mobile application such as smartphones.

The future of FanVision is still being written. In addition to football, other sports such as baseball and basketball are pursuing it as a means of enhancing the in-game experience for fans. Also, moving the application to smartphones makes it potentially accessible to every fan that attends the game.[30]

Questions:

1. Have you experienced FanVision? If so, describe your experience with the technology. If not, what are your thoughts about it?
2. Do you think FanVision enhances the in-game, in-stadium experience of fans? Why or why not?
3. How can teams capitalize on FanVision to draw more fans to games?
4. What are the advantages and disadvantages of having FanVision available on smartphones and potentially available to every fan in a stadium?
5. What other sports would be a good fit for FanVision? Why?

References

1. Don Muret, (2009), "Serving Notice," *Sports Business Journal*, June 8, 12.
2. Don Muret, (2008), "In Line for Change," Sports Business Journal, April 14, 1.
3. Jan Carlzon, *Moments of Truth* (New York: Harper & Row, 1989).
4. A. Parasuraman, Valarie A. Zeithaml, and Leonard L. Berry, (1988), "SERVQUAL: A Multiple-Item Scale for Measuring Perceptions of Service Quality," *Journal of Retailing*, 64 (1), 12–40.
5. Ibid.
6. Steve Seiferheld, (2011), "To Get Most out of Partnership, Brands Should AIM High," *Sports Business Journal*, October 3, 15.
7. Valarie A. Zeithaml, Mary Jo Bitner, and Dwayne D. Gremler, *Services Marketing*, 5th edition (Burr Ridge, IL: McGraw-Hill/Irwin, 2009).
8. Michelle Smith, (2008), "Stanford Football Banking on Bold Ticket Guarantee," August 26, accessed November 26, 2010, at http://articles.sfgate.com/2008-08-26/sports/17122435_1_tickets-stanford-coach-jim-harbaugh-stanford-football.
9. Philip Kotler and Kevin Lane Keller, *Marketing Management*, 13th ed. (Upper Saddle River, NJ: Pearson Prentice Hall, 2009).
10. "Customers-for-Hire Help Venues Sharpen Their Service," (2002), *Sports Business Journal*, April 22, 16.
11. Richard J. Varey, (1995), "A Review and Some Interdisciplinary Research Challenges," *International Journal of Service Industry Management*, 6 (1), 40–63.
12. Bruce Schoenfield, (2010), "Customer-Service Magic," *Sports Business Journal*, November 29, 1.
13. Ibid.
14. Ibid.
15. "Join the Huddle," (2010), accessed December 4, 2010, at http://www.teamfanshop.com/.
16. "Fuse," (2010), accessed December 4, 2010, at http://www.fusemarketing.com/index.php.
17. "Services," (2010), accessed December 4, 2010, at http://ggmmarketing.com/services.html.
18. "About IMG," (2010), accessed December 4, 2010, at http://www.imgworld.com/about-us.aspx.
19. Darren Marshall and David C. Tice, (2009), "Engage Hispanic Race Fans through Speed, Success, Community," *Sports Business Journal*, February 9, 14.
20. Don Muret, (2010), "Cardinals Bite into the Food Business with Rojo," *Sports Business Journal*, October 4, 9.
21. "Services" (2012), accessed May 3, 2012 at http://www.theteliosgroup.com/servicestickets.shtml.
22. Don Muret, (2010), "Colleges' Ticket Sales Efforts Go Pro," *Sports Business Journal*, August 16, 1.
23. "Nelligan Sports Marketing, Inc. Collegiate Division," (2010), accessed December 9, 2010, at http://www.nelligansports.com/collegiate.shtml.
24. "JPMorgan Chase," (2010), accessed December 9, 2010, at http://www.sponsorship.com/Case-Studies/JPMorgan-Chase.aspx.
25. "What We Do: Overview," (2010), accessed December 10, 2010, at http://www.ispsports.com/what-we-do.cfm.
26. Don Muret, (2010), "Gameday Will Run Broncos' Team Stores," *Sports Business Journal*, August 2, 27.
27. "BCA Sports Properties" (2012), accessed May 3, 2012 at http://learfieldsports.com/partners/bca-sports-properties/.
28. "Surveyor," (2010), accessed December 15, 2010, at http://www.turnkeyse.com/marketing-intelligence-surveyor.aspx.
29. "Frequently Asked Questions," (n.d.), accessed December 15, 2010, at http://www.performanceresearch.com/faq.htm#everyday.
30. Daniel Kaplan, (2010), "Three BCS Games Will Use Ross' FanVision," *Sports Business Journal*, November 22, 2010, p. 1; "FanVision" http://www.miamidolphins.com/tickets-and-stadium/guest-experience-department/fan-vision.html, accessed May 3, 2012; Eric Fisher, (2010), "Smartphones Next Target for FanVision," *Sports Business Journal*, August 30, 2010, p. 3.

14 Preparing Future Sports Marketers

Learning Objectives

By the end of this chapter you should be able to:

1. Describe job responsibilities and employee characteristics for eight types of sports marketing positions

2. Describe methods for gaining the experience necessary to launch a sports marketing career

3. Discuss the role of networking in establishing a sports marketing career

© Joe Belanger / Shutterstock

Run after your red rubber ball today, and every day it will become your future.

Finding Your Red Rubber Ball

Perhaps the question asked most often of young people is "What do you want to do when you grow up?" In American culture, one's occupation is influential in defining who we are and how others perceive us. This question is not limited to young people; many adults find themselves seeking meaning and joy in their professional lives. One of the most interesting stories about finding direction in pursuing a career is told by Kevin Carroll. His story reveals an unusual path to who he is today: an author, speaker, consultant, and advocate of social change. According to Carroll, the key to his accomplishments was what he calls the red rubber ball.

Kevin Carroll and his two brothers were abandoned by their parents when he was 3 years old and were raised by grandparents. He began to come out of a shell when he discovered the thrill of play. Sports became his escape from uncertainty and worries. Carroll says, "I played whatever sport was in season . . . soccer or football in the fall; basketball in the winter; baseball or track in the spring . . . and the red rubber ball was always there—a powerful symbol of sport." The red rubber ball represented the happiness that he experienced while playing sports. In his book *Rules of the Red Rubber Ball*, Kevin Carroll begins by saying "the red rubber ball saved my life."

Sports led him out of his grandparents' neighborhood in Philadelphia, but not directly to the success he enjoys today. Carroll enlisted in the Air Force, serving as a language specialist, and learned five languages. His passion for sports led to earning a degree in sports medicine. This path took him from athletic trainer at a high school in Philadelphia, to a similar position at a college, and ultimately to head trainer for the NBA's Philadelphia 76ers. His climb to professional sports was a significant accomplishment, but Kevin Carroll was not finished. His position with the 76ers opened the door for an opportunity at Nike. Carroll's role at Nike had little to do with his sports medicine training. Of his role at Nike, Carroll said, "It was my job to inspire . . . it was my job to push creativity to the limit. I called myself the Katalyst (the 'K' is for Kevin), because I helped spark change." The transformation into an agent of change is a role that Carroll embraces today as a consultant advocating sports as a tool for changing lives globally.

In *Rules of the Red Rubber Ball*, Carroll identifies seven guidelines for pursuing your passion, your red rubber ball:

1. *Commit to it* – A resolve to follow your passion will shape decisions about what you study, where to live and work, how you spend time, and your choice of friends.
2. *Seek out encouragers* – Find people who will be supportive of your dreams and develop relationships with those who are willing to help you.
3. *Work out your creative muscle* – Imagination will help you overcome challenges and bring opportunity.
4. *Prepare to shine* – A willingness to do tasks that are not glamorous or are behind the scenes often exceeds expectations and leads to rewards.
5. *Speak up* – Refuse to accept boundaries imposed upon you by other people.

6. *Expect the unexpected* – Embrace the possibilities of unplanned occurrences or opportunities.

7. *Maximize the day* – Live in the moment to put Rules 1–6 to work and pursue your vision of the future.

Pursuing your red rubber ball is not about finding a job or choosing a career; it is reaching a point at which you have difficulty distinguishing between work and play. Kevin Carroll says "run after your red rubber ball today, and every day it will become your future."[1]

Introduction

What is *your* red rubber ball? Have you found your passion, something that is a source of energy and enjoyment for you? Choice of a career is about more than selecting a job to earn money. It is about the pursuit of happiness—work that is fulfilling while at the same time enabling you to make a living. Landing a job in sports should be not approached from the standpoint of performing tasks that are required by an employer. Instead, begin by asking the question "How can I add value to a sports organization?" In other words, what are the skills, gifts, and talents that you possess that could be leveraged to make you a valued employee of a sports property? Such a mindset elevates a person above other candidates because the focus is on how one can benefit his or her customers and, ultimately, the organization, rather than a narrow view of completing job tasks.

This final chapter addresses questions that you may have had building as you have read this book. Sports marketing is a highly competitive field, given the immense interest that people express for working in sports compared to the number of available positions. For any given marketing position in a sports organization, it is not unusual for hundreds of applications to be submitted. Many people do not have the required training and skills to be considered; other people eliminate themselves from working in the sports industry because of the challenges faced to get the opportunity to gain experience. The long odds created by the number of job applicants discourage many aspiring sports marketers, and the low pay/no pay of many entry-level positions and internships lead others to conclude that being a sports fan is preferred over being a sports marketer.

This chapter examines three important aspects of preparing for a sports marketing career. First, an overview is given of various types of jobs available for persons interested in sports marketing. Second, positioning yourself to compete in sports marketing is discussed in terms of education, experience, and networking that can differentiate a candidate. Third, the concept of personal branding is introduced as an approach for managing your professional career. The chapter concludes with questions about career preparation and planning posed to a panel of our industry insiders by sports business students and faculty.

Career Paths in Sports Marketing

One of the greatest obstacles faced by students seeking to work in sports marketing is a lack of awareness and understanding of the types of jobs available. Without this knowledge, it is difficult to study relevant subjects in college and get valuable experience that can make the difference in one's quest to land an entry-level position. Eight different types of marketing positions found in the sports industry are shown in Figure 14.1. It is far from being a comprehensive list but identifies many of the most widely available career opportunities. For each type of position, excerpts from job announcements are provided to give a glimpse of the personal characteristics and qualifications sought by employers as well as duties performed in the position.

Ticket Sales

The primary entry-level opportunity in many sports organizations is in the area of ticket sales. For sports properties that hold live events, tickets represent a crucial revenue stream to their success. More tickets sold produces higher revenues from other purchases related to sporting event attendance such as concessions and souvenirs. An employee that has the ability to contribute to revenues by making sales can add value to an organization. Ticket sales jobs can focus on adding new season ticket customers, single-game or event sales, or selling to groups.

- Ticket sales
- Customer service
- Sponsorship
- Brand communications
- Event marketing/management
- Facility management
- Marketing operations
- Services marketing

© Pressmaster / Fotolia

FIGURE 14.1 Types of Marketing Careers

Ticket sales jobs can have a focus on order taking or order getting. **Order taking** is a selling role in which a salesperson handles inbound inquiries or orders by telephone or e-mail. This type of selling occurs when customer demand is high. The role of salespeople in this situation is completing transactions to ensure a satisfactory experience for the buyer. Unfortunately, most sports organizations do not find themselves in the position of being able to move their entire supply of tickets through inbound sales. Thus, selling that focuses on order getting is usually needed as well. **Order getting** entails ticket salespeople initiating contact with prospective or current customers in an attempt to persuade them to purchase tickets. This form of selling is also known as outbound marketing because the communication begins with the seller and goes out to the prospect. Most ticket sales outbound marketing is conducted over the telephone. Salespeople are provided with lists of **leads**, or persons who have indicated some interest with a sports brand. For example, data on customers who buy single-game tickets are captured and housed in a marketing database. These customers may become leads the next season for multi-game or season ticket plans.

A trend in ticket sales is for teams to use outbound marketing as an entry point for someone to be hired as a full-time ticket sales employee. The NHL's Nashville Predators is one of several professional sports teams with an inside sales program that serves like an audition for prospective ticket salespeople. The six-month program begins with outbound marketing training, and then salespeople make telephone sales calls to leads for full-season and partial-season ticket plans for individuals and businesses. Approximately 75% of employees completing the program have been placed in full-time ticket sales positions, either with the Predators or with NHL, MLB, NBA, or minor league teams. This type of program enables sports properties to identify high potential employees while participants get a feel for the expectations of a position as a ticket salesperson.

Figure 14.2 contains highlights from a job announcement for a ticket sales account executive. The position was advertised by the Charlotte Checkers, an American Hockey League team. Communication skills and ability to interact in social settings are important traits sought in a ticket account executive, consistent with a ticket salesperson's extensive interactions with customers and prospects.

Responsibilities	Personal Characteristics	Qualifications
Sale of multi-game ticket packages	Extroverted and social	Bachelor's degree
Participate in networking events	Comfortable interacting in social situations	Previous sports experience (internship OK)
Prospect for new leads	Well-spoken and articulate	Computer literate
Meet monthly sales goals	Solution-based	Excellent oral and written communication skills
Deliver high level of customer service	Goal-oriented	Willingness to work nights, weekends, and holidays

FIGURE 14.2 Position Description for Ticket Sales Account Executive with Charlotte Checkers

Customer Service

In contrast to ticket sales jobs that often focus heavily on customer acquisition, the role of customer service personnel is customer retention through their responsibilities for customer satisfaction. Two illustrations of customer service positions are in the areas of fan relations and account services. Fan relations personnel have responsibilities for managing the experience delivered to attendees at a game or event. They have a visible presence at fan relations or customer service booths, answering questions, responding to customers' problems or complaints, and being a resource to customers who need assistance. Also, fan relations employees can have responsibilities for fielding customer communications via telephone or e-mail.

Another customer service position with emphasis on customer satisfaction and retention is an account services representative. The organizational structure in many marketing departments separates customer acquisition and retention. Once ticket salespeople make a sale of a full- or partial-season ticket to a customer, an account services representative is assigned to the customer. That employee is responsible for making sure the customer's needs are met (e.g., receives tickets on time, has no problems with seats) and maintaining a relationship between customer and organization by being a customer's personal contact.

Figure 14.3 provides an overview of a mid-level customer service management position, director of customer service for the Tampa Bay Buccaneers of the NFL. While this position requires experiences that a new college graduate would not yet have acquired, it is a role that an early career sports marketer can set his or her sights on as a long-term career path.

FIGURE 14.3 Position Description for Director of Customer Service with Tampa Bay Buccaneers

Responsibilities	Personal Characteristics	Qualifications
Develop and implement customer service plans	Strong interpersonal skills	Bachelor's degree
Report results of Customer Service staff to upper management	Strong work ethic	10 years of premium customer service experience in sports
Recruit, hire, train, and develop service staff	Demonstrates innovation and initiative	Experience planning and executing client events
Implement customer survey program	Thrives in a deadline environment	Excellent written and verbal communication skills
Manage transition from new sale to account holder	Understands and provides superior customer service	Ability to work long and flexible hours

Sponsorship

A ticket sales job is an entryway into a sports organization that can lead to a different selling position, negotiating partnerships with corporate sponsors. Employees with proven selling abilities may desire to move into sponsorship sales. Several differences exist between the two types of sales positions. First, pricing and customer benefits for tickets are usually fixed—a price is set and that is what customers pay. Sponsorships have more flexibility in that a package of marketing rights and benefits can be customized to meet the needs of a corporate partner. The customization of the product means that price will vary among customers.

Second, the selling cycle for sponsorships is much longer than for tickets. A ticket prospect may be closed in a single sales call. Completing a partnership deal with a business can require several meetings and weeks or even months of negotiations. Third, price points between a ticket sale and sponsorship sale can be drastic. Sponsorship deals can range anywhere from a few thousand to several million dollars. Salespeople compensated on commission stand to reap a big payday when a big deal is closed, but they also assume risks of a prolonged negotiation ending in a no-sale situation.

A sponsorship sales job involves a great deal of communication, from making initial contact with prospective corporate clients, to making sales presentations, to maintaining relationships with sponsors. Figure 14.4 contains information about a sponsorship sales position with Learfield Sports, a sports marketing agency that handles corporate and media sales for many collegiate sports properties. The position is for director of corporate sales at Rupp Arena in Lexington, Kentucky, home of the University of Kentucky basketball teams. The desired qualifications and personal characteristics of applicants reflect the sales-intensive nature of marketing corporate partnerships. Successful applicants are expected to be effective communicators in terms of being able to close sales as well as maintain strong relationships with sponsors after a sale is made.

Responsibilities	Personal Characteristics	Qualifications
Prospecting and cold calling on national companies	Innovative	Bachelor's degree
Developing consultative selling approach	Energetic	Track record of results (4–6 years)
Nurturing relationships	Self-motivated	Excellent communication and organizational skills
Fulfilling advertising and sponsorship packages	Entrepreneurial spirit	Outstanding strategic selling skills
Collaborate with vendors, sponsors, and others to insure sponsorship fulfillment	Poise and ability to present himself/herself well to others	Creative solutions development

FIGURE 14.4 Position Description for Director of Corporate Sales with Learfield Sports

Brand Communications

Another category of job opportunities in sports marketing falls under the umbrella of brand communications. Careers in this area include jobs in advertising, public relations, community relations, and interactive marketing (Internet, social media, and e-mail). In some cases, sports marketing agencies or specialty agencies servicing sports properties seek to fill these positions. In other cases, sports properties manage brand communications functions in-house, recruiting and hiring employees to perform these tasks within the organization. Two types of in-house job opportunities are provided in Figures 14.5 and 14.6. Media relations, a function performed by a public relations department, is a position commonly found in the organizational charts of sport properties. Figure 14.5 provides excerpts from a job announcement for a director of media relations position with a motorsports property, Homestead Miami Speedway (HMS). Job responsibilities reflect a blend of short-term management responsibilities such as supervising media relations and access for race events as well as a long-term strategic focus on expanding interest and influence of HMS locally and nationally.

Responsibilities	Personal Characteristics	Qualifications
Build and strengthen relationships with local, regional, and national media	Self-starter	Excellent writing skills and proficiency with AP style
Raise HMS profile in local market through increased exposure of motorsports	Eager to integrate PR with marketing and ticket sales	Ability to manage volunteers and interns
Manage all aspects of media relations for race events	Ability to adjust and adapt under pressure	Knowledge of motorsports
Compile and manage media archive	Resourcefulness to tap knowledge of industry colleagues	Exceptional interpersonal and telephone skills
Establish HMS executives as motorsports experts among local and national media	Ability to brainstorm to develop "big ideas"	Ability to work non-traditional hours for events

FIGURE 14.5 Position Description for Director of Media Relations with Miami Homestead Speedway

As new communication channels have emerged with technological innovations, the need has increased to hire employees who have expertise in utilizing new media channels. E-mail marketing and Internet marketing (including website development and search engine marketing) are two areas in which many sports organizations have opted to add personnel. A job announcement for a social media director position with the NHL's Tampa Bay Lightning is highlighted in Figure 14.6. Qualifications for the position such as engagement with blogging and experience with social media are job requirements that diverge from skill sets traditionally sought in sports marketing positions. Increased opportunities to work in digital media with sports organizations are likely as use of those channels in the sports industry continues to grow.

FIGURE 14.6 Position Description for Social Media Coordinator with Tampa Bay Lightning

Responsibilities	Personal Characteristics	Qualifications
Write, edit, and update content for team-related social media sites	Self-motivated	Bachelor's degree
Plan monthly social media calendar	Deadline-oriented	1–3 years online marketing and social media experience
Track and analyze social media performance	Passion for social media	Excellent writing skills
Create and post content to mobile application	Cutting-edge attitude	Blog reader, writer, publisher
Assist in editing and updating website content		Flexibility to work nights, weekends, and holidays

Event Marketing/Management

Sports organizations that put on live events or sponsors that use events as marketing vehicles to reach a sports property's audience have needs for marketing staff to plan and execute events. Events include games or sporting contests themselves, experiential touch points with fans such as interactive games or displays at sporting events or off-site, and sponsorship activation using experiential marketing to engage fans. Regardless of the type of event, employees are needed who demonstrate creativity in developing event marketing programs and organizational skills to implement ideas. An example of a job opportunity in the area of event marketing and management appears in Figure 14.7. The employee sought by the University of California athletics department will be responsible for executing events and promotions for women's basketball and volleyball and football tailgating activities. Successful event managers are able to creatively solve problems as well as coordinate vendors, suppliers, and staff to complete necessary tasks for an event to go off as planned.

FIGURE 14.7 Position Description for Assistant Director of Game Day Experience with the University of California

Responsibilities	Qualifications
Direct game-day experience for women's basketball and volleyball	Bachelor's degree required; Graduate degree desirable
Manage tailgating and other events for football	Event management experience
Coordinate event logistics such as setting up lighting, tents, games, and displays	Customer service skills
Recruit, train, and lead student interns	Excellent communication skills (verbal and written)
Assist Director of Game Day Experience with execution of promotional plans	Basic knowledge of NCAA regulations

Facility Management

For organizations that host live events, sports marketing is more than selling tickets and using brand communications to promote games and events. It entails being a hospitality provider, too. Opening the doors to an arena is similar to inviting guests into your home, except you probably never have had several thousand visitors drop by all at once! Event management is complemented by proactive oversight of facilities. If one considers all of the touch points, or interactions a sporting event patron has in a sports venue, there are many elements that must be managed. Parking lots, entrance/exit layouts, restrooms, foodservice areas, and seating areas are major areas of responsibility for facility managers. These responsibilities may not seem glamorous or exciting, but they are vital to creating customer satisfaction with the experience of attending a sporting event.

A position that illustrates the overlap between facility management and customer service is highlighted in Figure 14.8. It is a disability services manager position with Sports & Entertainment Services in Phoenix, the company that operates U.S. Airways Arena (home to the Phoenix Suns of the NBA) and Chase Field (home to the Arizona Diamondbacks of MLB). This position focuses on meeting the needs of a specific segment of patrons: persons with disabilities. A thorough knowledge of laws and regulations that protect the rights of persons with disabilities is essential. The payoff for an organization designating an employee to carry out these responsibilities is not merely to ensure compliance with laws, but the concern shown for these customers reflects a marketing orientation within an organization.

Responsibilities	Qualifications
Administer disability services and programs to ensure compliance with Americans with Disabilities Act (ADA)	Thorough knowledge of ADA and all laws related to rights of persons with disabilities
Be the expert in organization on ADA matters at SES facilities	Ability to evaluate public access to facilities
Develop and maintain relationships with organizations representing persons with disabilities	Knowledge of construction, equipment, and work area modifications available to ensure public access to facilities
Ensure prompt resolution of complaints related to accessibility for disabled persons	Excellent written and verbal communication skills
Provide guidance and training to staff on ADA issues	Bachelor's degree and 3 years experience in managing compliance and accommodation programs

FIGURE 14.8 Position Description for Disability Services Manager with Sports & Entertainment Services

Marketing Operations

The emergence of technologies for collecting and analyzing data has created new job opportunities in the sports industry. Marketing departments in sports organizations are increasingly adding employees with skills in customer relationship management (CRM) and database marketing. Use of CRM to segment customers, identify revenue generation opportunities, and track marketing campaign performance adds to the technical sophistication needed in a marketing organization. Hiring a specialist with responsibilities for business analysis complements the efforts of a ticket sales department by generating leads that can be closed by salespeople. Figure 14.9

Responsibilities	Personal Characteristics	Qualifications
Collect and analyze data on team ticket sales, attendance, and pricing	Self-starter	Master's degree
Support marketing efforts to increase ticket sales and sponsorship revenue	Strong work ethic	3–5 years of related experience
Provide projected ticket sales data to management team	Analytical	Sports or entertainment industry experience preferred
Provide analytics on season-ticket customers	Creative problem solving abilities	Experience with CRM helpful
Use CRM to recommend leads and strategies to increase ticket sales	Ability to work independently and as part of a team	Experience with building spreadsheets and advanced analytical techniques in Excel

FIGURE 14.9 Position Description for Business Analyst with Phoenix Suns

contains information from a job announcement for a business analyst sought by the Phoenix Suns. The analyst is responsible for assisting in the development of business strategy for the NBA's Suns as well as the Phoenix Mercury of the WNBA and the teams' venue, U.S. Airways Center. Contributions made by the analyst include recommendations for ticket prices, defining target markets, measuring marketing campaign performance, and determining the financial value of sponsorships.

Services Marketing

As discussed in Chapter 13, marketing services such as foodservice management and retail operations can be either handled in-house or outsourced to a firm that specializes in providing those services. In either case, these functions provide pathways to careers in the sports industry. These hospitality-oriented functions may hold appeal to college students preparing to launch their careers if they have gained experience working in restaurants or retail stores while in school. In many ways, job responsibilities of managing foodservice and retail operations for sports properties are similar to managerial roles outside of the sports industry, including inventory management, sales force supervision, and overseeing customer relations. However, job candidates for services marketing managerial positions in sports benefit if they have had experiences specific to the industry such as familiarity with buying licensed products or knowledge of catering for special events and upscale dining.

Figure 14.10 shares highlights from a job announcement for a retail management position with Delaware North Companies, a firm contracted to manage retail and foodservice operations at Miller Park, home of MLB's Milwaukee Brewers. The ideal candidate has a retail management background that can be applied to the merchandising, supervision, and sales performance of the team's on-site retail stores.

FIGURE 14.10 Position Description for Retail Manager with Delaware North Companies

Responsibilities	Qualifications
Oversee daily in-store operations including merchandise planning, buying, and inventory management	Minimum 5 years of retail management; experience with store operations and merchandise buying
Financial responsibility for profit and loss, preparing budgets, and sales reports	Degree in retail management or equivalent experience
Act as liaison between company and client	Strong customer service orientation
Ensure proper staff management including hiring and training	Proficiency in Microsoft Office programs
Meet financial and sales goals set by company management	Retail Pro POS software experience preferred

Positioning for Success

Working in sports is a desire held by many people—youth, college students, and professionals in the workforce seeking a new career. Why the tremendous interest in positions that require long hours and, in many cases, relatively low pay for entry-level positions? The answer can be found at the beginning of this chapter—it is the pursuit of the red rubber ball. Passion for sports influences many people to pursue a career related to something for which they care deeply. But, please recognize that being a sports fan is not a requirement for a successful sports marketing career!

The question asked most often by students taking sports business courses is straightforward and gets to the point: What can I do to get a job in the sports industry? We have heard this question asked of sports marketing professionals speaking on college campuses, at professional conferences, and in the sports business press. The answer to the question is remarkably similar and can be reduced to two words: 1) experience and 2) networking. These steps are vital to differentiating your personal brand in a crowded field competing for a chance to launch a sports marketing career.

Experience

Gaining experience is about developing knowledge and skills that can be applied to benefit a sports property. As shown in Figure 14.11, there are four ways that experience can be acquired for sports marketing.

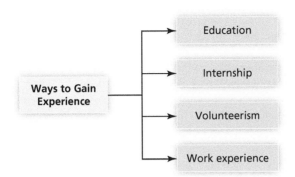

FIGURE 14.11 Ways to Gain Sports Marketing Experience

EDUCATION. Formal education lays a foundation of knowledge and represents the credentials that an individual needs. Colleges and universities have responded to the growth of the sports industry and interest in sports business careers by developing courses and programs in sport management. According to the North American Society for Sport Management, more than three hundred higher education institutions in the United States have sport management degree programs at either the undergraduate or graduate level, or both.[2] Many other institutions without sport management degree programs offer courses in sports marketing to expose students to the sports industry. Obviously, taking courses in sports business or earning a degree in sports management does not automatically qualify a person to work in the sports industry, but formal education sets the stage for gaining additional experiences that will make a job candidate more competitive in the job market.

INTERNSHIP. If a key to preparing for a sports marketing career is to get experience, then securing an internship is an important step a student can take toward breaking into the sports industry. Internships are valuable because they give students an opportunity to apply knowledge developed in their college course work in a work situation with a sports property. Most internships in sports business are unpaid for the simple reason that there is very high demand for a limited supply of intern positions. Generally, an intern is receiving college credit if he or she is not paid for work performed. Managers in the sports industry realize the benefits of developing talent by providing learning experiences to interns. For students, an internship is a chance to demonstrate capabilities in the hopes of landing a permanent position in the future. An intern who shows promise through his or her performance may not be able to get a job with the organization because of a lack of open positions, but many effective interns are recommended by their supervisors to hiring managers in other organizations that have jobs available.

The worth and appropriateness of an internship can be evaluated using the following criteria:

1. The internship provides training that is an extension of a student's college educational environment.
2. The internship provides experience that is beneficial to the intern.
3. The intern does not take the place of paid employees and works under supervision.
4. The organization offering the training does not derive immediate advantages from the work of an intern, as the focus is on training.[3]

While an internship is generally considered a positive addition to a résumé, realize that not all opportunities are the same. Unfortunately, some internships fit the negative stereotype of "making copies and coffee," with students receiving little in the way of skills development. Valid internships will give students varied experiences and help position them to compete for entry-level positions after graduation.

VOLUNTEERISM. Although internships are an ideal opportunity to gain experience and develop a network of professional contacts, not all students are in a position to do an internship. For some students, working with no compensation for a few months may not be financially possible. For other students, an internship may not be available near where they live or study. An alternative means to gain experience without having a formal internship is to volunteer to help at sporting events. Many sports properties use volunteers on the day of an event to assist in a variety of roles. Supervising attendee parking, registering participants, staffing exhibits or displays, and assisting with promotions are four tasks volunteers are enlisted to perform. Some organizations rely on volunteers because of limited resources to hire event operations employees. Nonprofit organizations and institutions with low marketing budgets such as small college athletic departments look to volunteers for staffing in order to provide a great event experience for attendees.

Volunteering to assist with individual events is a way for someone to gauge interest in working in sports by being involved in the production of a sporting event on a small scale. A large event such as the PGA Championship golf tournament relies on a legion of volunteers to make the experience positive for competitors, attendees, and sponsors. For the 2011 PGA Championship in Atlanta, volunteers were asked to work a minimum of sixteen hours in roles such as event admission, security, and merchandise sales.[4]

WORK EXPERIENCE. Gaining experience related to sports through an internship or volunteerism can differentiate a job applicant from others lacking such experience, but what if you do not have these experiences? Are your chances of working in sports marketing nonexistent? Hardly! Sports organizations are no different than firms in other industries. They seek to hire people with tangible qualifications that make them a good match and potentially contribute to the organization's success. Recall from the different job announcements that appeared in this chapter that highly desired qualifications included skills such as strong written and oral communication skills, ability to make effective presentations, and a customer service orientation. These skills can be developed and strengthened in a variety of settings and applied to sports. Students who support themselves financially while in college by working in service or retail positions may be doing more than earning a paycheck, they are often supplementing their formal education by working on the front lines serving customers. Also, a stable track record of working in a sales or service position may be perceived by employers as evidence of a desirable work ethic.

All of the experiences discussed (education, internships, volunteering, and work experience) can be used advantageously to position a student as a viable candidate for a marketing position in the sports industry. In order to effectively leverage experiences, present them as actions, not tasks, when including them in a cover letter or résumé. For example, when describing an internship experience, avoid compiling a laundry list of tasks or responsibilities such as "worked on marketing campaign for Thursday night promotions." Instead, emphasize accomplishments or results such as "helped generate an 8% increase in attendance at Thursday games." Remember that the ultimate interest an employer has is in your ability to deliver results, not that you keep busy with activities.

Networking

The other ingredient to launching a career in sports marketing may be less clear and more intimidating than gaining experience. The term networking holds different meanings and thus may not be clear to a student who is told to "build a network of contacts" or "network with others" when attending events.

Working in service and retail establishments provides valuable experience for careers in sports marketing.

© michaeljung / iStockphoto

A definition of networking can be reduced to three words: "building good relationships."[5] Whether it is done face-to-face or online, the aim of networking is to begin and build relationships with people who have shared interests for potential long-term mutual benefit. The prospect of initiating contact with someone established in an industry in which you aspire to work may seem risky. After all, you may wonder what you have to offer for that person's benefit.

A good starting point for seeking to network with a business professional is to research his or her background. Where did the person attend college? What is his hometown? Has she written any articles or books that you can read? Do you know anything about the person's hobbies or interests? The common characteristic among gathering background information is that it has nothing to do with a person's position as a sports marketer. You are learning about them as a person, and anything you share in common with someone you wish to add to your professional network is a step toward that person accepting you into his or her network. It is not an automatic path to acceptance, but sharing common interests builds trust and may remove barriers to networking with business professionals.

The description of networking as building good relationships based on shared interests illustrates what the practice of networking is *not*: It is not about acquiring as many business cards as possible, nor is it about reaching a target number of connections on LinkedIn or another social networking website. Yes, one can collect business cards like souvenirs or add people to a list of contacts on a social networking website, but those tactics are based on quantity of contacts instead of quality of contacts. The relational aspects of networking call for a focus on developing professional friendships and being a resource to help when someone in your network has a question or problem to tackle. Networking is based on interpersonal communication and therefore can be conducted in two ways: 1) face-to-face and 2) online social networking websites.

© Wavebreak Media / Alamy Stock Photo

Networking should be about building relationships with professionals.

FACE-TO-FACE NETWORKING. Opportunities for networking arise in a variety of face-to-face settings. A marketing professional visits one of your classes as a guest speaker—take a moment to approach her after class. Introduce yourself and thank her for taking time to speak to your class. If you have done your homework, bring up a conversation point that puts the two of you on common ground. When you attend career fairs, prepare to network before you go. A list of companies and organizations in attendance is usually published in advance. If you demonstrate knowledge of a company when interacting with its representatives at a career fair, you are likely to make a favorable impression. Your preparation is magnified by the fact that many career fair attendees do little or no research beforehand, making your networking efforts more noticeable. If you attend a conference or trade show, do research on the speakers and exhibitors that will be participating. The key to raising the comfort level with face-to-face networking is preparing for relationship-building opportunities that may present themselves.

SOCIAL NETWORKING WEBSITES. Technological innovations have created another channel for professional networking: the use of social networking websites. Companies and individuals use social networking sites to promote their professional brands. Facebook and Twitter, popular channels for maintaining networks of contacts with friends and acquaintances, are also used extensively by sports properties and sports business professionals. Connecting with a company on Facebook by "liking" it can aid in networking efforts by giving one access to more information about the firm.

Turnkey Sports & Entertainment, a firm that offers services in executive search and consumer research, uses its Facebook page (http://www.facebook.com/turnkeyse) to share links to case studies, media coverage of Turnkey's work and clients, articles about the company's services, and information about events in which the company participates. Connecting with Turnkey Sports & Entertainment via Facebook gives persons interested in career opportunities with Turnkey a more personable view of the company and some of its employees than can be gleaned from visiting the company's website.

Similarly, Twitter can be used to network with organizations and sports marketing professionals by following their tweets. Messages from a team's official Twitter feed or from team personnel on their individual Twitter accounts are ways to learn more background information, keep up with current events, and have a starting point for building a relationship with industry professionals. Also, Twitter's search feature, the hashtag (#), can be used to check for employment opportunities. Searches such as "#sports marketing jobs" or "#sports sales jobs" return results about job openings in these areas of the sports industry.

The social networking website that holds the greatest potential for developing and maintaining a network of contacts is LinkedIn. An often used analogy for LinkedIn is "Facebook for business." LinkedIn is used by individuals to connect with other professionals, follow companies, join groups of people with shared interests, and explore job opportunities. Do you have an interest in a specific position in sports marketing such as ticket sales or event management? Are there certain organizations or companies you have targeted for pursuing a job? Is there a city or region in which you want to work? LinkedIn enables creating connections with professionals in the sports industry to advance toward your goal for any of these situations.

A search of LinkedIn users returns more than 500,000 people with an interest in sports marketing from many different perspectives—sports property executives, team marketing personnel, agencies, sponsorship managers, and students. Networking with people with whom you have no prior relationship can be intimidating, and it must be understood that not every professional with whom you request to connect will accept your invitation. However, if you keep in mind the definition of networking (building good relationships) and principles for relationship building such as gaining trust and adding value by providing information, advice, or encouragement, building a professional network on LinkedIn is possible.

Another benefit of using LinkedIn to develop a professional network is the ability to identify people with similar interests by following companies or joining groups. By following a company on LinkedIn, information about employees who belong to the network, recent posts by employees, company developments, and job opportunities can be accessed conveniently. For example, if someone is interested in career opportunities with Octagon, a global sports and entertainment marketing agency, following Octagon on LinkedIn gives a destination for accessing profiles of more than seven hundred employees and Internet links to mentions of Octagon employees in the news media. The Groups feature of LinkedIn provides opportunities to connect with other professionals based on topic interest or industry affiliation. A search for sports marketing networking groups returns approximately three hundred fifty results. Some groups are for persons interested in sports marketing in general, while other groups are specific to a particular sport or job function (e.g., ticket sales or event marketing). Figure 14.12 gives a brief description of five of these groups, representing the types of networking groups one can join. A feature of Groups that gives newcomers to sports marketing an opportunity to establish common ground with professionals with whom they wish to network in group discussions. Members post questions asking for opinions or advice. Posting responses is a tactic that can create awareness for your personal brand and create an opening for follow-up networking with group members.

Your Personal Brand

Positioning yourself for a career in sports marketing by gaining experience and building a network of professional contacts is vital to your chances of success. However, do not lose sight of the main objective you have for adding to your experiences and network: to build a strong personal brand. Some people may feel uneasy equating themselves with a brand. After all—you are a person, not a pair of blue jeans! However, the characteristics of a brand described in Chapter 5 (identity, image, promise, and relationship) are highly relevant to how we should approach managing our careers.

FIGURE 14.12
Examples of Sports Marketing Groups on LinkedIn

Group	Description	Members
Sports Industry Network	Network of sports executives and professionals in all areas of sports industry. Its purpose is to help advance the careers of its members and create sports jobs.	77,000+
Sports Marketing and PR Pros	This group is for Sports Marketing and PR Pros to share contacts, ideas and experiences to form a mutually beneficial network.	26,000+
Baseball Industry Network	A group open to those connected to the baseball industry- from the major leagues to the minors and those seriously interested in pursuing careers in the game.	13,000+
Mentoring Future Sports Business Stars	Helping college students and young professionals make a place in the sports industry by providing career advice and ideas.	2,000+
Sports Marketing Executives Network	A sports marketing executives network to connect, interact, and innovate together with news, events, insights, and mutual help.	1,300+

Personal branding expert Dan Schawbel offers a simple definition of a personal brand: "the process by which we market ourselves to others."[6] Experience and networking used to build a personal brand can be compared to the product and promotion elements of the marketing mix. Experiences in the form of knowledge, skills, and competencies represent the "product" we have to offer to an employer. Communicating the product's availability and capabilities is accomplished through networking channels. You may not have a job in the sports industry yet, but you have tremendous responsibility already as manager of the world's most important brand: *you*!

Insider Insights Getting into the Game

The final installment of Insider Insights is a question-and-answer session with a panel of sports industry executives you have heard from throughout this book. Students and faculty in sports business courses composed questions to ask these successful professionals. The panel answering questions about career planning and management consists of:

- Kathy Carter – Soccer United Marketing
- Rob Farinella – Blue Sky Agency
- Jeff Hennion – GNC Live Well
- Tom Hoof – Tampa Bay Rays
- Terry Lefton – *Sports Business Journal*
- Tony Ponturo – Ponturo Management

Education and Experience

If someone's ultimate goal is to become a sports marketing executive, what can he or she do in college to help attain that goal?

Tom Hoof: Take business and marketing courses, plus courses in writing and some international studies. I believe the best people in marketing are the ones that are well rounded. I want people with a variety of experiences and not just sports. Show me an intellectual curiosity.

Pepper in relevant internships and leadership roles within school organizations. This will help you become more attractive to any business, including sports.

Jeff Hennion: As someone who majored in economics undergrad, has an MBA in finance, and spent fifteen years working in the financial and strategic planning fields, I think I've proven that you can become a CMO with almost any background. The key all along for me is that the undergraduate academic experience I had (at Northwestern) was what put me in a position to be successful, not what my major was.

Besides taking certain courses and completing a formal internship, what other experiences are valuable for me to obtain with an eye toward getting a sports marketing job?

Rob Farinella: Be a voracious learner—never stop educating yourself. Publications like the *Sports Business Journal* have a wealth of information about the business of sports. Participate in webinars; attend as many industry events as you can, ask for informational interviews. This is the best way to prepare for a career in sports marketing. It's not just about being a sports fan. It's about being a sports business fan.

Kathy Carter, President of
Soccer United Marketing.

Rob Farinella, founder and
owner of Blue Sky Agency.

Jeff Hennion, Executive Vice
President, Chief Marketing
Officer & E-commerce of
GNC Live Well.

Jeff Hennion: Make sure you have a well-rounded view of the world. Focusing 100% on sports marketing will help you in that field, but you need to have a really strong business sense without blinders on. Know how the rest of the world sees the marketing—finance, legal, sales—they're all good skills you need to manage any business.

Tom Hoof: First, it is not just about "completing a formal internship." It is being the best intern when you have the opportunity. What are you doing to get yourself noticed? How good and informative are your résumé and cover letter? How much do you know about my organization/industry? How well have you done any other jobs and in school overall? How involved are you in school and in your community? Getting into sports is very competitive. Look around your class; everyone in your class is a potential competitor for that rare opening. Now multiply that by all of the schools that offer sports marketing courses and all of the students in those classes. Be the one that gets noticed by being the best intern, the best student, put in the time and the effort and good things will happen.

Job Search

How can I position myself to make my résumé stand out when applying for jobs or internships in the sports industry?

Tom Hoof: You need to have a passion for marketing. You need to understand the various facets of what goes into marketing a sports entertainment entity. You should have a strong grasp of strategy and tactics. Relevant experience is important as well. Not necessarily experience with a team or even in sports, but relevant experience in marketing. I'd like to see marketing internships during the college career, then after graduation, entry level to gain more experience in marketing depending upon the opening we would have available. I want someone who can make our department better, someone we can learn from and someone who fits into our corporate culture.

Rob Farinella: Look for ways to get involved or volunteer in as many events as possible, no matter if it's sports, music, or community-related. Being around events, especially those with media coverage, is the best way to see what goes on behind the scenes. Listing that type of experience on your résumé will help it stand out.

Kathy Carter: The easiest thing to do is make your résumé look professional and make sure it does not have typos (or mistakes)! However, the real way to stand out is to *network*. A résumé can't tell the real story of who you are or what you can do . . . so find a way to make a human connection. I would try the telephone; it is a lost tool in the digital world!

Which would you recommend to someone starting out—look for a job you want or take any job you can find?

Kathy Carter: I would look for the very best boss. Find someone who will take an interest in you and in your ability to learn and experience the business. Working with, or for, someone who challenges you to be better, supports your growth, and celebrates your achievements is far more important than the logo or the title on your card.

Jeff Hennion: There has to be a balance. If you just take any job you can find, there's a good chance you'll be miserable and just be looking forward to the next thing. However, it can take quite a while to find that perfect job. My advice would be to make sure the job you can take is one about which you can be passionate and engaged. Keep in mind that what you think the perfect job is now may be very different in one to two years. Nothing can replace good experience.

Tom Hoof: I believe when you interview, you are not only interviewing for the actual opening, but also the next job that will come your way in a few years. An individual must ask himself or herself where the job I am interviewing for right now will lead me to in a few years. You must develop a plan. If you deviate too far from the plan, you may never get back on track. Identify yourself. Early in my career I was in radio and thought of myself as a radio guy who happened to be doing marketing. I evolved to thinking of myself as a marketing guy who happened to be doing radio. This thinking enabled me to change industries and become a better experienced marketing professional. It led me directly to my current position with the Rays.

Tom Hoof, Marketing and Community Relations, Tampa Bay Rays.

Terry Lefton, Editor-at-Large for *Sports Business Daily* and *Sports Business Journal.*

Tony Ponturo, Ponturo Management.

Where do you see opportunities for new jobs in the industry going forward?

Kathy Carter. The sports and entertainment business has evolved so much over the past few decades. The backbone of the industry will always be ticketing, but the diversification of the revenue business, the emergence of digital as a key component, and the continued importance of content are all areas to follow. I continue to believe there are a lot of unique opportunities in the industry.

Rob Farinella: As the channels to view and experience sports become more fragmented, understanding the various exposure touch points, the analytics involved, and how to credibly measure them will become increasingly important.

Career Management

What would you say is crucial to longevity in sports marketing?

Terry Lefton: Marketing acumen, creativity, and the ability to work long hours without tiring. A degree in sports marketing is NOT a prerequisite.

Tony Ponturo: To understand the objectives of the product that you are trying to sell to the consumer and align the right sport properties with those products. Also, understand the appeal of each sport, its consumer reach, and the best way to impact the consumer.

The sports industry is male-dominated. What advice can you offer to females wanting to work in the sports industry?

Tony Ponturo: A female or any person in the sports industry should work hard to know the sports and the objectives of the companies using the sport. Also, have extreme dedication and effort. Be collaborative and take initiative.

Kathy Carter. I have always found that being a woman in the sports business is an advantage. Clearly there are challenges when you are in a male-dominated industry, but I have chosen to look at the positives as opposed to the negatives. My advice to women as they start their careers, or as they make their way up the ranks, is to focus on substance (i.e., always be prepared and know your materials), work hard, follow up, do what you say you are going to do, and most importantly celebrate the difference we bring (as women) to every situation.

Terry Lefton: Know what you are getting into. It isn't easy, but nothing worthwhile is. Just know you will have to work at least 50% harder than your male counterparts to get to the same place.

Chapter Summary

A career in sports can be very rewarding, but it will take effort and planning to make it happen. The planning should begin with an understanding of the different career paths that can be pursued. Choices include ticket sales, customer service, sponsorship, brand communications, event marketing/management, facility management, marketing operations, and services marketing. It is important to understand the type of work performed in each career and what skills are needed to be successful.

To obtain a position in the sports industry, students will need experience and networking. Ways to gain experience include education, an internship, volunteerism, and work experience. Taking courses in sports marketing will help, but the most important is to obtain a college degree. Internships are extremely valuable. They provide real-world experience and exposure to the world of sports marketing. If internships are not possible, then volunteerism becomes more important. Volunteering to work sporting events and even in nonprofit organizations provides valuable exposure to working with people, especially crowds of people. Work is important, especially in a service or retail operation. Both types of experiences provide a rich background for dealing with people.

The old adage about getting a job is that "it doesn't matter what you know; it's who you know." Networking is important. But networking is not just collecting business cards. It is about building relationships with business professionals. It can be face-to-face or through online social networking websites. Find out about people, get to know something about them, and then approach them on some common ground.

Review Questions

1. According to Kevin Carroll and the book *Rules of the Red Rubber Ball*, what are seven guidelines for pursuing a person's passion?
2. Identify eight different career paths an individual can pursue in sports.
3. What are the four ways a student can gain experience?
4. Why is networking important?
5. What are the two different ways a student can network with sports professionals?

New Terms

Order taking selling role in which a salesperson handles inbound inquiries or orders by telephone or e-mail

Order getting ticket salespeople initiating contact with prospective or current customers in an attempt to persuade them to purchase tickets

Leads Individuals who have indicated some interest with a sports brand

Discussion and Critical Thinking Exercises

1. Reread the opening vignette. How has sports affected your life, either as a player or a spectator, or both?
2. Examine the seven guidelines presented by Kevin Carroll in the opening vignette. For each, discuss if it is a strength or weakness for you. For the ones you identified as a weakness, how can you turn it into a strength, or at least neutralize it so it is no longer a weakness for you?
3. Pick one of the marketing careers listed in Figure 14.1 that is of interest to you. Conduct library and Internet research into the position. Write a short paper about the career and the path for success.
4. Interview someone who works in sports marketing. Obtain information about their education and career path. What advice do they have for students wanting a career in sports marketing?
5. How important is an internship in sports? Discuss what you can learn from an internship and how you should approach the internship.
6. What is the benefit of volunteering at sporting events? What can you learn? How can it help you get a job?
7. Describe jobs you have held. How do they relate to a career in sports? What have you learned from your work experience that can be transferred to a career in sports?
8. Have you started networking with sports professionals? If so, describe your experience thus far. Regardless of the level of networking you have already done, outline a networking plan that will produce professional contacts that can aid in getting a job after graduation.

Online Career Resources

Job Search

General
CareerBuilder (www.careerbuilder.com)
Monster (www.monster.com)

Social Networking Websites
LinkedIn (www.linkedin.com)
Twitter (www.twitter.com)

Sports Industry
National Association of Collegiate Directors of Athletics (NACDA) – Job Center (www.nacda.com/nacdajobs/nacda-nacdajobs-center.html)
NCAA – Careers in College Athletics (http://ncaamarket.ncaa.org/jobs)
NHL Hockey Jobs (http://hockeyjobs.nhl.com)
Professional Baseball Employment Opportunities – PBEO (http://www.pbeo.com/)
TeamWork Online (http://teamworkonline.com)
Work in Sports (www.workinsports.com)

Networking and Professional Development

National Sports Marketing Network – NSME (http://www.sportsmarketingnetwork.com)
Sports Networker – (www.sportsnetworker.com)
Sport Sales Combine – (http://www.sportsalescombine.com)

References

1. Kevin Carroll, *Rules of the Red Rubber Ball* (New York: ESPN Books, 2004).
2. "Sport Management Programs: United States," (2011), accessed April 18, 2011, at http://www.nassm.com/node/96/print.
3. Susan Foster and Gil Fried, (2010), "Would Your Unpaid Internship Pass Regulatory Scrutiny?" *Sports Business Journal*, October 4, 14.
4. "PGA Championship Tickets, PGA Volunteers," (2011), accessed October 14, 2011, at https://ems.pgalinks.com/volunteers/index.cfm?event_id=21.
5. Terrance Williams, (2010), "Are You Really 'Networking'?" February 4, accessed April 21, 2011, at http://newgradlife.blogspot.com/2010/02/are-you-really-networking.html.
6. Dan Schawbel, (2009), "Personal Branding 101: How to Discover and Create Your Brand," accessed April 25, 2011, at http://mashable.com/2009/02/05/personal-branding-101/.

Name Index

Subject Index